London
2014

A SELECTION
OF RESTAURANTS
& HOTELS

The MICHELIN guide's commitments

Experienced in quality!

Whether they are in Japan, the USA, China or Europe, our inspectors apply the same criteria to judge the quality of each and every hotel and restaurant that they visit. The Michelin guide commands a worldwide reputation thanks to the commitments we make to our readers – and we reiterate these below:

→ Anonymous inspections

Our inspectors make regular and anonymous visits to hotels and restaurants to gauge the quality of products and services offered to an ordinary customer. They settle their own bill and may then introduce themselves and ask for more information about the establishment. Our readers' comments are also a valuable source of information, which we can then follow up with another visit of our own.

→ Independence

To remain totally objective for our readers, the selection is made with complete independence. Entry into the guide is free. All decisions are discussed with the Editor and our highest awards are considered at a European level.

→ Selection & choice

The guide offers a selection of the best hotels and restaurants in every category of comfort and price. This is only possible because all the inspectors rigorously apply the same methods.

→ Annual updates

All the practical information, the classifications and awards are revised and updated every single year to give the most reliable information possible.

→ Consistency

The criteria for the classifications are the same in every country covered by the MICHELIN guide. The sole intention of Michelin is to make your travels safe and enjoyable.

Dear reader,

We are delighted to present the 2014 edition of the Michelin Guide for London.

All the restaurants within this guide have been chosen first and foremost for the quality of their cooking. You'll find comprehensive information on over 570 dining establishments, ranging from gastropubs and neighbourhood brasseries to internationally renowned restaurants. The diverse and varied selection also bears testament to the rich and buoyant dining scene in London, with the city now enjoying a worldwide reputation for the quality and range of its restaurants.

You'll see that Michelin Stars are not our only awards – look out also for the Bib Gourmands. These are restaurants where the cooking is still carefully prepared but in a simpler style and, priced at under £28 for three courses, they represent excellent value for money.

To complement the selection of restaurants, our team of independent, full-time inspectors have also chosen 50 hotels. These carefully selected hotels represent the best that London has to offer, from the small and intimate to the grand and luxurious. All have been chosen for their individuality and personality.

We are committed to remaining at the forefront of the culinary world and to meeting the demands of our readers. As such, we are always very interested to hear your opinions on any of the establishments listed in our guide. Please don't hesitate to contact us as your contributions are invaluable in directing our work and improving the quality of the information we provide.

Thank you for your support and happy travelling with the 2014 edition of the Michelin Guide for London.

Consult the Michelin Guide at www.viamichelin.com
and write to us at themichelinguide-gbirl@uk.michelin.com

Contents

Commitments 2
Dear reader 3
How to use this guide 6
A culinary history of London 8
Practical London 10

Where to eat

In Central London 32

- Mayfair • Soho • St James's 36
- Strand • Covent Garden 116
- Belgravia • Victoria 132
- Regent's Park • Marylebone 154
- Bloomsbury • Hatton Garden • Holborn 182
- Bayswater • Maida Vale 198
- City of London • Clerkenwell • Finsbury • Southwark 208
- Chelsea • Earl's Court • Hyde Park • Knightsbridge • South Kensington 260
- Kensington • North Kensington • Notting Hill 296

Where to stay

In Central London 426

Index 16

Starred restaurants 18
Bib Gourmand 20
Restaurants by cuisine type 21
Restaurants with outside dining 28
Open for Breakfast 30
Open late 31

In Greater London 314

▶ North-West 318

Archway • Belsize Park • Camden Town • Church End • Crouch End • Dartmouth Park • Fortis Green • Hampstead • Kensal Green• Kentish Town • King's Cross St Pancras • Primrose Hill • Queens Park • Swiss Cottage • Willesden Green

▶ North-East 338

Barnsbury • Bow • Canonbury • Hackney • Highbury • Hoxton • Islington • Shoreditch • Wanstead

▶ South-East 360

Bethnal Green • Blackheath • Canary Wharf • East Dulwich • Greenwich • Kennington • Lewisham • Limehouse • Spitalfields • Stockwell • Wapping • Whitechapel

▶ South-West 380

Acton Green • Balham • Barnes • Battersea • Brixton • Chiswick • Clapham Common • Ealing • East Sheen • Fulham • Hammersmith • Kew • Putney • Richmond • Teddington • Shepherd's Bush • Twickenham • Wandsworth • Wimbledon

Index & Maps 484

Alphabetical list of restaurants 486
Index of maps 494
Map of London Underground 495

How to use this guide...

Restaurant classified according to comfort (particularly pleasant if in red)

- Quite comfortable
- Comfortable
- Very comfortable
- Top class comfort
- Luxury in the traditional style
- Pubs serving good food

Starred restaurants

Stars for good cooking

✿ to ✿✿✿

Cuisine type

London area or neighbourhood

Each area is colour coded:

- Central London
- Greater London

Practical information

Name, address and information about the establishment

Prices

Fixed price menu and à la carte

Restaurant symbols

- With outside dining
- Notable list of wines
- Notable list of cocktails
- Open for breakfast
- Small plates
- Vegetarian menu
- Open late
- Restaurants offering theatre menus
- Open on Sunday
- Garden
- Wheelchair access
- Air conditioning
- Private dining room
- Car park
- Garage
- Credit cards not accepted

Sample menu for starred restaurant

Birdy Nam-Nam

Fusion

South-West ▸ Plan XVIII

100 Wa…

(020)…

www.r…

Tott…

Closed 25…

Menu…

Belgravia · Victoria ▸ Plan IV

Linda House ✿✿

Seafood ▸ Plan XI

Court Road Lancaster St
SW1Y 4AN
(020) 7747 22 00
www.lindahouse.com
Leicester Square
Closed 25-26 December, 1 January, Monday and bank holidays

Menu £14/25 – Carte £20/38

Emile Lepeletier

Linda House is a handsome four storey 18th century building in the heart of Soho. To gain entry, you ring the doorbell and you'll then be ushered into one of the two dining rooms. Regulars may have their favourite but there's little to choose between them – they're both warm and welcoming, although the first floor room is slightly larger than the ground floor.

There is something about being cosseted in a characterful house that makes dining here such a pleasure and it provides the perfect antidote for those feeling bruised and buffeted by the bigger, more boisterous places.

The cooking is modern in its approach and presentation but flavours are far more vigorous and full bodied than one expects and the marriages of various ingredients bear testament to real talent. Evidence of Bob's Welsh roots pops up here and there, from the laver bread to the Welsh cheeses and his homeland provides much of the produce. Tasting and Garden menus are available for those making it an occasion.

First Course

- Ravioli of shellfish with champagne and chives
- Loin of tuna wrapped in basil with soy, avocado and a salad of radish

Main Course

- Roast sea bass with black olives, baby squid and creamed fennel
- Assiette of lamb with new season garlic, borlotti beans and rosemary

Dessert

- Lemongrass jelly with pineapple and coconut
- Vanilla yoghurt parfait with blueberries

194

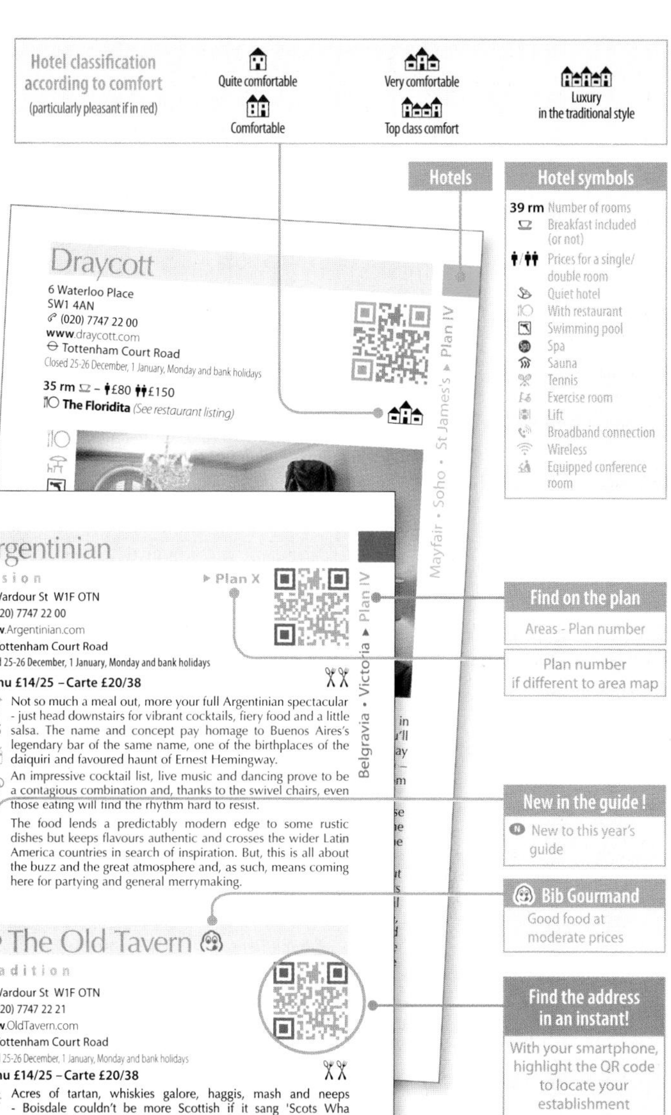

Hotel classification according to comfort
(particularly pleasant if in red)
Quite comfortable
Comfortable
Very comfortable
Top class comfort
Luxury in the traditional style
Hotels
Hotel symbols
39 rm Number of rooms
Breakfast included (or not)
Prices for a single/ double room
Quiet hotel
With restaurant
Swimming pool
Spa
Sauna
Tennis
Exercise room
Lift
Broadband connection
Wireless
Equipped conference room
Draycott
6 Waterloo Place
SW1 4AN
(020) 7747 22 00
www.draycott.com
Tottenham Court Road
Closed 25-26 December, 1 January, Monday and bank holidays
35 rm – £80 £150
The Floridita (See restaurant listing)
Mayfair • Soho • St James's ▸ Plan IV
Argentinian
Fusion
▸ Plan X
98 Wardour St W1F 0TN
(020) 7747 22 00
www.Argentinian.com
Tottenham Court Road
Closed 25-26 December, 1 January, Monday and bank holidays
Menu £14/25 – Carte £20/38
Belgravia • Victoria ▸ Plan IV
Not so much a meal out, more your full Argentinian spectacular - just head downstairs for vibrant cocktails, fiery food and a little salsa. The name and concept pay homage to Buenos Aires's legendary bar of the same name, one of the birthplaces of the daiquiri and favoured haunt of Ernest Hemingway.
An impressive cocktail list, live music and dancing prove to be a contagious combination and, thanks to the swivel chairs, even those eating will find the rhythm hard to resist.
The food lends a predictably modern edge to some rustic dishes but keeps flavours authentic and crosses the wider Latin America countries in search of inspiration. But, this is all about the buzz and the great atmosphere and, as such, means coming here for partying and general merrymaking.
Find on the plan
Areas - Plan number
Plan number if different to area map
New in the guide !
New to this year's guide
Bib Gourmand
Good food at moderate prices
The Old Tavern
Tradition
40 Wardour St W1F 0TN
(020) 7747 22 21
www.OldTavern.com
Tottenham Court Road
Closed 25-26 December, 1 January, Monday and bank holidays
Menu £14/25 – Carte £20/38
Find the address in an instant!
With your smartphone, highlight the QR code to locate your establishment on the map
Acres of tartan, whiskies galore, haggis, mash and neeps - Boisdale couldn't be more Scottish if it sang 'Scots Wha Hae' and did the Highland Fling. Owner Ranald Macdonald bought various parts of the building at different times, hence the charmingly higgledy-piggledy layout. The original Auld Restaurant is the more characterful; the Macdonald Bar has more buzz and nightly live jazz and a large cigar selection add to the masculine feel. The menu features plenty of Scottish produce, from Orkney herring to Shetland scallops, but the stand-outs are the four varieties of smoked salmon, followed by the 28-day aged Aberdeenshire cuts of beef. Ignore the lacklustre tomato and watercress garnish and just savour the quality of the meat.
195

A culinary history of London

London, influenced by worldwide produce arriving via the Thames, has always enjoyed a close association with its food, though most of the time the vast majority of its people have looked much closer to home for their sustenance.

Even as far back as the 2nd century AD, meat was on the menu: the profusion of wildlife in the woods and forests around London turned it into a carnivore's paradise, thereby setting the tone and the template. Large stoves were employed to cook everything from pork and beef to goose and deer. The Saxons added the likes of garlic, leeks, radishes and turnips to the pot, while eels became a popular staple in later years.

C. Moirenc/hemis.fr

What a lark!

By the 13th century, the taste for fish had evolved to the more exotic porpoise, lamprey and sturgeon, with saffron and spices perking up the common-or-garden meat dish. Not that medieval tastes would have been considered mundane to the average 21st century diner: Londoners of the time would think nothing about devouring roasted thrush or lark from the cook's stalls dotted around the city streets. And you'd have been unlikely to hear the cry "Eat your greens!" In the 15th century, the vegetable diet, such as it was, seemed to run mainly to herbs such as rosemary, fennel, borage and thyme.

As commercial and maritime success burgeoned in the age of the Tudors, so tables began to groan under the weight of London's penchant for feasting. No excess was spared, as oxen, sheep, boars and pigs were put to the griddle; these would have been accompanied by newly arrived yams and sweet potatoes from America and 'washed down' with rhubarb from Asia. People on the streets could 'feast-lite': by the 17th century hawkers were offering all sorts of goodies on the hoof.

Lawton/Photocuisine/Age fotostock

Full of beans

All of this eating was of course accompanied by a lot of drinking. Though much of it took place in the alehouses and taverns - which ran into the thousands - by the 18th century coffee houses had become extraordinarily popular. These were places to do business as well as being convenient 'for passing evenings socially at a very small charge'.

Perhaps the biggest revolution in eating habits came midway through the 19th century when the first cavernous dining halls and restaurants appeared. These 'freed' diners from the communal benches of the cook-house and gave them, for the first time, the chance for a bit of seclusion at separate tables. This private dining experience was an egalitarian movement: plutocrats may have had their posh hotels, but the less well-off were buttering teacakes and scones served by 'nippies' at the local Lyons Corner House.

Influenced by post World War II flavours brought in by immigrants from Asia, the Caribbean and Africa – and, most recently, from Eastern Bloc Countries – Londoners now enjoy an unparalleled cuisine alive with global flavours. Perhaps the Queen's Jubilee and the Olympics have made us more confident about waving the flag for Britain as we are also rediscovering and celebrating our own culinary heritage.

Practical London

Arrival/Departure

If you're coming to London from abroad, it's worth bearing in mind that the capital's airports are (with one exception) a long way from the city itself. Better news is that they're all well served by speedy express train services; even better news is that if you travel by Eurostar you can go by train direct from the heart of Europe to the heart of London without having to worry about luggage limits, carousels and carbon footprints...

By air

Most people coming to London from overseas arrive via Heathrow (the UK's busiest) and Gatwick airports (more on both at www.baa.com). You can catch the Heathrow Express rail service (www.heathrowexpress.com) to Paddington (just west of the centre) every 15 minutes, and that's just about how long the journey takes. Another alternative is to board the Piccadilly line tube train from Heathrow: it's cheaper, but the drawn-out travelling time can make it seem as if you've spent most of your holiday just getting into the centre. Gatwick is further out, south of London's M25 ring road, and the quickest way into the city is via the Gatwick Express rail service (www.gatwickexpress.com), which takes half an hour to reach Victoria station. There are also frequent train services run by Southern (www.southernrailway.com) between Gatwick and Victoria, and Thameslink (www.firstcapitalconnect.co.uk), which connect with a host of central London stations, including London Bridge and King's Cross. The capital has three other airports: Stansted (www.stanstedairport.com), 35 miles northeast of the city; Luton (www.london-luton.com), 30 miles to the north, and London City Airport (www.londoncityairport.com), which is nine miles to the east, and connects to the centre via the Docklands Light Railway.

By train

The days of having to fly into London from abroad are long gone. Smart travellers from the Continent now jump on the Eurostar (www.eurostar.com) from Paris, Brussels or Lille, zip along at 186mph, and step onto the platform at St Pancras International in the time it takes to devour a coffee and a croissant (a big coffee, admittedly). From there, three tube lines from the adjoining King's Cross station whisk you into town. Book Eurostar far enough in advance (which isn't very far, by any means) and you can get tickets for just £69 return.

Getting Around

By tube

First, the bad news: the tube can get hot and overcrowded; engi-

Superstock/Age fotostock

neering works can close lines at weekends and the escalators are sometimes out of action. But the good news? Generally speaking, the tube is by far the quickest way to get around town. There are 12 lines, plus the Docklands Light Railway; these cover pretty much the whole city and are all clearly shown on the free map you can pick up at any tube station or London Travel Information Centre. Trains run from 5am to just past midnight Monday-Saturday, with a reduced timetable on Sundays. For details about the line you wish to use, check the Transport for London website www.tfl.gov.uk or phone the 24-hour Travel Information Service on + 44(0) 843 222 1234.

By bus

They might move a bit slower than tubes, but when you ride on the top of a double-decker bus, you get the added bonus of an absorbing, tourist-friendly view to take in on the way. The world-famous Routemasters were all but phased out in 2005; their low-floored replacements much more accessible to wheelchair-users and passengers with buggies. The iconic Routemaster made a comeback in 2012, however, with a newly designed bus which runs between Victoria Station and Hackney – and there are more on the way. There's a handy central London bus map which you can pick up at transport information centres at larger tube stations. Or you can plan your bus trip online by checking out the useful 'Journey Planner' to be found on the Transport for London website. Most Central London routes require that you buy tickets before you board; you can get these from machines by the bus stop. The flat fare is £2.30 and this includes travel across all zones (see also 'The Pearl that is Oyster', below).

By car

The best advice is not to drive in central London, not if you want your sanity preserved anyway.

Roadworks and parking can be the stuff of nightmares, and that's before the Congestion Charge Zone, albeit now reduced in size, is even taken into consideration. This zone covers the central area and is clearly marked by the red 'C' signs painted on the road. It's in operation Monday-Friday 7am-6pm (weekends and holidays are free) and you'll need to register the car's number plate on a database (go to www.cclondon.com for details). If it all sounds a bit too much of a headache, you always have the option of hailing a black cab – just stick out your hand when you see one with its taxi light illuminated.

J. Warburton-Lee/Photononstop

By bike

A greener alternative to the taxi for short journeys is the humble bike – and those aged 14 and above can hire a so-called 'Boris Bike' from one of the many Barclays Cycle Hire docking points spread over the capital. There's no need to book ahead and they're available 24 hours a day, 7 days a week. Simply pay an access fee (£1 for 24 hours/£5 for 7 days) with a credit or debit card, either at a docking station terminal, by phone (0845 026 3630), or online (www.tfl.gov.uk). You are then charged for your usage, but the good news is that, as the scheme is designed to be used for short journeys, the first 30 minutes are free and it's only £1 for the second 30 minutes. Simply return the bike any docking station when you're done.

By boat

'Taking to the water' has become increasingly popular over the last few years: the Thames offers some little-seen views of London, and cutting through the open expanse of river can certainly lay claim to being your most relaxing travel option. Most river services operate every 20 minutes to one hour, and there are piers all over the central area where you can jump on board, from Chelsea Harbour in the west to Woolwich Arsenal in the east. For more details go to www.tfl.gov.uk

The pearl that is oyster

Londoners on the move make sure they don't leave home without their Oyster. It's an electronic smartcard and it's the fastest and easiest way to pay for single journeys around town. You don't even have to take it out of your purse or wallet: you just zap it over a yellow reader to let you through tube gates or onto a bus. Oysters are charged with a pre-paid amount of credit and can cover a set period of time or be used to pay-as-you-go. You'll always pay less for a journey than on the equivalent Day Travelcard or Bus Pass. To check out the whole deal, visit www.tfl.gov.uk/oyster

Living London Life

It almost goes without saying that visitors to the capital are spoilt for choice when it comes to having a good time. For instance, you could visit one of the city's 300 museums or galleries, many of which are free, or you could see for yourself why London's theatre scene is considered the best in the world. Come nightfall, choose from the vast number of restaurants, offering cuisines from all parts of the world, or from one of 5,000 pubs and bars. At the weekend, an interesting alternative to shopping or sports events is to browse one of the farmers' markets that have sprung up in recent years. On a Saturday, the best of the bunch can be found at Ealing, Notting Hill, Pimlico, Wimbledon and Twickenham. On Sundays, two of the favourites are in Marylebone and Blackheath, while, on the same day, the Columbia Road flower market, in the East End, is a wonderful place to spend time comparing flora while chomping on a bagel from a local café.

The more mainstream shopper might do well to steer clear of frenetic Oxford Street. Regent Street is a more alluring thoroughfare with its mid-priced fashion stores and hallowed names. If you're after a destination with a real touch of class, then nearby Jermyn Street is the place for bespoke men's clothing, but if your taste is for more outré threads, then Notting Hill or Camden are good bets. Back in the centre of town, Covent Garden is packed with speciality stores, quirky alleyways, and – if you choose the wrong time to go – an awful lot of people!

Escape can always be found in the relative quiet of a good bookshop, and London is full of them. Still in Covent Garden, Stanford's is the city's number one travel bookshop, while not far away in Charing Cross Road, the legendary Foyles has thrown over its fusty image with a stylish makeover. But for the marriage of real elegance with a good read, head to Daunt Books in Marylebone High Street, which is set in an Edwardian building with long oak galleries and skylights; the bustle of London's streets will seem a million miles away.

Stéphanie Guillaume/Fotolia.com

Where to **eat**

- Index 16
- Central London 32
- Greater London 314

Index

- Starred restaurants 18
- Bib Gourmand 20
- Restaurants by cuisine type 21
- Restaurants with outside dining 28
- Open for Breakfast 30
- Open late 31

Starred Restaurants

Within this selection, we have highlighted a number of restaurants for their particularly good cooking. When awarding one, two or three Michelin Stars there are a number of factors we consider: the quality and compatibility of the ingredients, the technical skill and flair that goes into their preparation, the clarity and combination of flavours, the value for money and, above all, the taste. Equally important is the ability to produce excellent cooking not once but time and time again. Our inspectors make as many visits as necessary, so that you can be sure of the quality and consistency.
A two or three star restaurant has to offer something very special in its cuisine; a real element of creativity, originality or personality that sets it apart from the rest. Three stars – our highest award – are given to the very best.
Cuisines in any style and of any nationality are eligible for a star. The decoration, service and comfort have no bearing on the award.
For every restaurant awarded a star we include six specialities that are typical of their cooking style.
These specific dishes may not always be available.
Let us know what you think; not just about the stars but about all the restaurants in this guide.

The awarding of a star is based solely on the quality of the cuisine.

N : highlights those establishments newly promoted to one, two or three stars.

Exceptional cuisine, worth a special journey.

One always eats here extremely well, sometimes superbly. Distinctive dishes are precisely executed, using superlative ingredients.

Restaurant	Comfort	Page
Alain Ducasse at The Dorchester	XXXXX	40
Gordon Ramsay	XXXX	283

Excellent cuisine, worth a detour.

Skilfully and carefully crafted dishes of outstanding quality.

Restaurant	Comfort	Page
Dinner by Heston Blumenthal **N**	XX	277
Le Gavroche	XXXX	67
Greenhouse **N**	XXX	70
Hélène Darroze at The Connaught	XXXX	74
Hibiscus	XXX	75
Ledbury	XXX	308
Marcus Wareing at The Berkeley	XXXX	143
Sketch (The Lecture Room and Library)	XXXX	101
Square	XXXX	104

A very good restaurant in its category.

A place offering cuisine prepared to a consistently high standard.

Restaurant	Comfort	Page
Alyn Williams at The Westbury	XXXX	42
Amaya	XXX	136
Ametsa with Arzak Instruction **N**	XXX	137
Angler **N**	XX	217
Apsleys	XXXX	138
Arbutus	X	45
L'Atelier de Joël Robuchon	XX	120
L'Autre Pied	XX	159
Benares	XXX	50
Bo London **N**	XX	54
Brasserie Chavot **N**	XX	56
Chez Bruce	XX	422
Club Gascon	XX	228
Dabbous	X	188
Galvin at Windows	XXX	68
Galvin La Chapelle	XXX	375
The Glasshouse	XX	413
Hakkasan Hanway Place	XX	191
Hakkasan Mayfair	XX	72
Harwood Arms		405
Hedone	XX	394
HKK **N**	XX	356
Kai	XXX	78
Kitchen W8	XX	306
Launceston Place	XXX	307
Lima **N**	X	166
Locanda Locatelli	XXX	167
Maze	XX	82
Medlar	XX	287
Murano	XXX	86
Nobu	XX	87
Nobu Berkeley St	XX	88
One Leicester Street	XX	90
Outlaw's at The Capital **N**	XX	289
Pétrus	XXX	148
Pied à Terre	XXX	195
Pollen Street Social	XX	93
Quilon	XXX	149
Rasoi	XX	292
River Café	XX	412
St John	X	249
Seven Park Place	XXX	99
Social Eating House **N**	X	102
Story **N**	XX	252
Tamarind	XXX	106
Texture	XX	175
Tom Aikens	XXX	294
Trishna	X	176
La Trompette	XXX	397
Umu	XX	109
Viajante	XX	366
Wild Honey	XX	112
Yauatcha	XX	114

Restaurants offering good quality cooking for less than £28 (price of a 3 course meal excluding drinks).

Restaurant		Page
Anchor and Hope	🍺	216
A. Wong **N**	X	139
Azou	X	408
Barrafina	X	48
Barrica	X	185
Bistro Union	X	398
Bocca di Lupo	X	52
Bradley's	XX	334
Brasserie Zédel	XX	55
Brawn	X	364
Cafe Spice Namaste	XX	378
Canton Arms	🍺	377
Comptoir Gascon	X	227
Copita	X	62
Corner Room	X	365
Del Mercato **N**	XX	229
Drapers Arms	🍺	350
Elliot's	X	230
Empress	🍺	345
500	X	322
Fox and Grapes	🍺	423
Gail's Kitchen **N**	X	189
Galvin Café a Vin	X	374
Grain Store **N**	X	331
Great Queen Street	X	190
Green Man and French Horn **N**	X	125
Hereford Road	X	204
Honey and Co **N**	X	190
José	X	234
Kateh	X	205
Koya	X	79
Made in Camden	X	324
Mango and Silk	X	402
Market	X	325
Medcalf	X	238
Morito	X	240
Opera Tavern	X	128
Picture **N**	X	170
Polpo Covent Garden	X	128
Polpo Smithfield **N**	X	246
Polpo Soho	X	92
Princess of Shoreditch	🍺	355
Provender	X	358
St John Bread and Wine	X	376
Salt Yard	X	196
Simply Thai	X	420
Soif	X	392
Sushi-Say	X	336
Terroirs	X	131
Trullo	X	344
Zucca	X	258

Restaurants by cuisine type

Argentinian

Casa Malevo	X	203
Zoilo	X	180

Asian

Asia de Cuba	XX	119
Bone Daddies	X	53
Cicada	X	225
E and O	XX	303
Eight over Eight	XX	276
Kopapa	X	192
Singapore Garden	XX	335
Spice Market	XX	103
Suka	XX	174
XO	XX	324

Basque

Donostia	X	163

British modern

Anchor and Hope	[pub] ☺	216
Bistro Union	X ☺	398
Bluebird	XX	268
Brown Dog	[pub]	386
Chelsea Ram	[pub]	274
Chiswell Street Dining Rooms	XX	225
Corrigan's Mayfair	XXX	62
Dean Street Townhouse Restaurant	XX	64
Dinner by Heston Blumenthal	XX ✿✿	277
Drapers Arms	[pub] ☺	350
Fox and Grapes	[pub] ☺	423
Georgina's	X	387
Great Queen Street	X ☺	190
Hampshire Hog	[pub]	410
Harwood Arms	[pub] ✿	405
Hereford Road	X ☺	204
Magdalen	XX	237
Malt House	[pub]	404
Market	X ☺	325
Narrow	[pub]	373
The National Dining Rooms	X	85
1901	XXX	242
Pantechnicon	[pub]	147
Paradise by way of Kensal Green	[pub]	328
Peasant	[pub]	245
Picture	X ☺	170
Plum + Spilt Milk	XX	331
Prince Arthur	[pub]	346
Prince of Wales	[pub]	415
Quo Vadis	XXX	95
Restaurant at St Paul's Cathedral	X	248
Rivington Grill (Greenwich)	X	371
Rivington Grill (Shoreditch)	X	357
Roast	XX	248
Sands End	[pub]	407
Tate Modern (Restaurant)	X	253
La Trompette	XXX ✿	397
Victoria	[pub]	403
Well	[pub]	257
Wells	[pub]	328

British traditional

Albion	[pub]	349
Angel and Crown	[pub]	119
Anglesea Arms	[pub]	408
Avalon	[pub]	385
Barnsbury	[pub]	350
Beagle	X	347
Bedford and Strand	X	122
Bentley's (Grill)	XXX	51
Bird of Smithfield	X	219
Bob Bob Ricard	XX	52
Boisdale of Belgravia	XX	139
Boisdale of Bishopsgate	XX	220
Boisdale of Canary Wharf	XX	367
Builders Arms	[pub]	270
Bull and Last	[pub]	327
Bumpkin (North Kensington)	X	300

Restaurant	Page
Bumpkin (South Kensington)	270
Butlers Wharf Chop House	222
Cadogan Arms	271
Canton Arms	377
Cat and Mutton	344
Dining Room	141
Foxtrot Oscar	280
Gilbert Scott	330
Grazing Goat	164
Great British	69
The Grill	71
Gun	368
HIX (Soho)	73
Hix Mayfair	76
Hix Oyster and Chop House	234
The Ivy	126
Jugged Hare	235
Lady Ottoline	193
Lamberts	386
Lots Road Pub and Dining Room	285
Medcalf	238
Morgan Arms	342
Newman Street Tavern	168
Northall	144
One Leicester Street	90
Only Running Footman	89
Paternoster Chop House	244
Pig's Ear	290
Pig and Butcher	352
Princess of Shoreditch	355
Princess Victoria	418
Quality Chop House	247
Ritz Restaurant	96
Rookery	398
Rules	129
St John	249
St John Bread and Wine	376
Savoy Grill	129
The Shed	311

Chinese

Restaurant	Page
A. Wong	139
Baozi Inn	47
Barshu	48
Ba Shan	49
Beijing Dumpling	49
China Tang	61
Good Earth	282
Grand Imperial	142
Hakkasan Hanway Place	191
Hakkasan Mayfair	72
Haozhan	71
HKK	356
Imperial China	77
Kai	78
Manchurian Legends	80
Mao Tai	406
Min Jiang	309
Mr Chow	286
Pearl Liang	206
Phoenix Palace	170
Plum Valley	92
Royal China	173
Seventeen	310
Yauatcha	114
Yipin China	352

French

Restaurant	Page
L'Absinthe	332
Alain Ducasse at The Dorchester	40
Almeida	349
Angelus	202
L'Atelier de Joël Robuchon	120
L'Aventure	158
Balcon	47
Balthazar	121
Bar Boulud	267
Bibendum	268
Bistro Aix	326
Bistrot Bruno Loubet	219
Bleeding Heart	186
Le Boudin Blanc	55
Boundary	354
Brasserie Chavot	56
Brasserie Zédel	55
Brula	421
Cellar Gascon	223
Le Cercle	273
Chabrot (City of London)	224
Chabrot (Hyde Park and Knightsbridge)	273

Chez Bruce	XX ✿	422
Cigalon	XX	226
Clos Maggiore	XX	122
Club Gascon	XX ✿	228
Colbert	XX	275
Le Colombier	XX	275
Comptoir Gascon	X ☺	227
Les Deux Salons	XX	124
The Ebury Restaurant and Wine Bar	XX	141
Galvin at Windows	XXX ✿	68
Galvin Bistrot de Luxe	XX	163
Galvin Café a Vin	X ☺	374
Galvin Demoiselle	X	280
Galvin La Chapelle	XXX ✿	375
Garnier	XX	281
Gauthier - Soho	XXX	66
Le Gavroche	XXXX ✿✿	67
Gordon Ramsay	XXXX ✿✿✿	283
Green Man and French Horn	X ☺	125
Hélène Darroze at The Connaught	XXXX ✿✿	74
Henry Root	X	282
High Road Brasserie	X	395
Koffmann's	XXX	142
Little Social	X	80
Lobster Pot	X	372
Luc's Brasserie	XX	236
Marco	XX	286
Mon Plaisir	XX	193
Morgan M	XX	240
La Petite Maison	XX	91
Pétrus	XXX ✿	148
Le Pont de la Tour	XXX	246
Provender	X ☺	358
Racine	XX	291
Rétro Bistrot	XX	419
Roux at the Landau	XXX	173
Sauterelle	XXX	250
Sketch (The Lecture Room and Library)	XXXX ✿✿	101
Soif	X ☺	392
Square	XXXX ✿✿	104
10 Cases	X	130
Terroirs	X ☺	131
Tom's Kitchen	X	295
Les Trois Garcons	XX	376
28°-50° Fetter Lane	X	254
Le Vacherin	XX	384
The Wallace	X	178

Greek

Mazi	X	309
Retsina	X	323

Indian

Amaya	XXX ✿	136
Babur	XX	373
Benares	XXX ✿	50
Bombay Brasserie	XXXX	269
Cafe Spice Namaste	XX ☺	378
Chakra	XX	301
Chutney Mary	XXX	274
The Cinnamon Club	XXX	140
Cinnamon Kitchen	XX	226
Cinnamon Soho	X	61
Dishoom	X	124
Dockmaster's House	XXX	367
Eriki	XX	335
Imli Street	X	77
Indian Zilla	XX	387
Indian Zing	XX	411
Kennington Tandoori	XX	372
Malabar	XX	305
Mango and Silk	X ☺	402
Mint Leaf	XX	84
Mint Leaf Lounge	XX	239
Moti Mahal	XX	194
Painted Heron	XX	288
Potli	XX	411
Quilon	XXX ✿	149
Rasoi	XX ✿	292
Red Fort	XXX	95
Roots at N1	XX	342
Roti Chai	X	172
Shayona	X	326
Swagat	X	417
Tamarind	XXX ✿	106
Tangawizi	X	421
Trishna	X ✿	176
Veeraswamy	XX	110
Zaika	XX	312
Zayna	XX	179

Israeli

1701	XX	250

Italian

Restaurant	Page
A Cena	420
Al Borgo	418
Al Duca	41
Alloro	41
Amaranto	43
L' Anima	353
Antico	216
Apsleys	138
Assaggi	202
Bocca di Lupo	52
Briciole	161
Brunello	300
Caffé Caldesi	161
Canonbury Kitchen	343
Cantina Del Ponte	222
Cassis	272
Cecconi's	60
Cibo	301
Cotidie	162
Daphne's	276
Del Mercato	229
Edera	303
Eleven Park Walk	278
Enoteca Turi	414
500	322
Franco's	66
Il Baretto	160
Il Convivio	140
il trillo	284
Lardo	345
Latium	165
Locanda Locatelli	167
Manicomio (City of London)	237
Manicomio (Chelsea)	285
Massimo	144
Mele e Pere	83
Metrogusto	391
Murano	86
Olivo	145
Olivocarne	145
Osteria Dell' Angolo	147
Polpo Covent Garden	128
Polpo Smithfield	246
Polpo Soho	92
Riva	388
River Café	412
Salusbury	334
Santini	150
Sartoria	98
Theo Randall	107
Tinello	151
Trullo	344
Vasco and Piero's Pavilion	110
Whitechapel Gallery Dining Room	379
Zafferano	152
Zucca	258

Japanese

Restaurant	Page
Aqua Kyoto	43
Atari-ya	400
Dinings	162
Kiku	79
Kiraku	402
Koya	79
Matsuba	416
Matsuri	81
Nobu	87
Nobu Berkeley St	88
Roka	196
Roka Canary Wharf	370
Sake No Hana	97
Shoryu	100
Sumosan	105
Sushisamba	251
Sushi-Say	336
Tonkotsu	108
Tsunami (Bloomsbury)	197
Tsunami (Clapham)	399
Umu	109
Yashin	311
Zuma	295

Korean

Restaurant	Page
Asadal	185
Bibigo	53
Hana	390

Lebanese

Restaurant	Page
Kenza	235
Levant	165
Yalla Yalla	179

Mediterranean

Restaurant	Page
Abbeville Kitchen	396

Aurelia 44
Copita 62
Dartmouth Castle 409
Dehesa 64
Dock Kitchen 302
Duke of Sussex 384
Empress 345
Gail's Kitchen 189
Garrison 231
Havelock Tavern 410
Iberica Canary Wharf 369
Light House 424
Moro 241
Nopi 89
Opera Tavern 128
The Orange 146
Ottolenghi 351
Palmerston 370
Pizarro 245
Rosita 391
Salt Yard 196
Sam's Brasserie 396
Winter Garden 178

North-African

Azou 408
Momo 85

North-American

Automat 46
Mishkin's 127
Spuntino 103

Peruvian

Ceviche 60
Coya 63
Lima 166

Spanish

Aqua Nueva 44
Barrafina 48
Barrica 185
Boqueria 392
Cambio de Tercio 271
Capote y Toros 272
Cigala 187
El Pirata De Tapas 206
Eyre Brothers 355
Fino 187
Hispania 233
Iberica Marylebone 164
José 234
Lola Rojo 390
Morito 240
Tapas Brindisa (London Bridge) 253
Tapas Brindisa (Soho) 105
Tendido Cero 293
Tendido Cuatro 407

Thai

Bangkok 267
Blue Elephant 403
Chada 389
Naamyaa Café 241
Nipa 205
Rosa's 97
Simply Thai 420
Suda 130

Turkish

Ozer 169

Vietnamese

Au Lac 347
Cây Tre 59
Viet Grill 358

Fish and seafood

Angler 217
Bentley's (Oyster Bar) 51
Bonnie Gull 160
Fish Market 231
Geales 281
J. Sheekey 126
J. Sheekey Oyster Bar 127
Kerbisher and Malt 401
Olivomare 146
One-O-One 288
Outlaw's at The Capital 289
Poissonnerie 291
Scott's 98
Smith's of Wapping 377
Wright Brothers 258
Wright Brothers Soho 113

Innovative

Restaurant	Rating	Page
Ametsa with Arzak Instruction	XXX ✿	137
Archipelago	XX	158
Bo London	XX ✿	54
Corner Room	X ☺	365
L'Etranger	XX	278
Greenhouse	XXX ✿✿	70
Hibiscus	XXX ✿✿	75
One Blenheim Terrace	XX	168
Pied à Terre	XXX ✿	195
Pollen Street Social	XX ✿	93
The Providores	XX	171
Texture	XX ✿	175
Trinity	XX	399
Vanilla Black	XX	254
Viajante	XX ✿	366

Meats and grills

Restaurant	Rating	Page
Barbecoa	XX	218
Beard to Tail	X	353
Brasserie Max	XX	186
Burger and Lobster (Mayfair)	🍺	58
Burger and Lobster (Soho)	X	57
Chicken Shop	X	329
Cut	XXX	63
Electric Diner	X	304
Goodman	XX	69
Goodman Canary Wharf	XX	368
Goodman City	XX	232
Hawksmoor (City of London)	X	232
Hawksmoor (Spitalfields)	X	374
Hawksmoor (Strand and Covent Garden)	X	125
Hawksmoor (Mayfair)	XX	73
Kew Grill	XX	414
MASH	XX	81
Maze Grill	XX	83
New St Grill	XX	242
Oblix	XX	243
Pitt Cue Co.	X	91
Redhook	XX	247
Rib Room	XXX	293
34	XXX	108
Vivat Bacchus	X	256
Vivat Bacchus London Bridge	X	256

Modern

Restaurant	Rating	Page
Admiral Codrington	🍺	266
Alyn Williams at The Westbury	XXXX ✿	42
Arbutus	X ✿	45
L'Autre Pied	XX ✿	159
Avenue	XX	46
Axis	XXX	121
Babylon	XX	299
Belvedere	XXX	299
Bingham Restaurant	XX	415
Bistrotheque	X	364
Blueprint Café	X	220
Bonds	XXX	221
The Botanist	XX	269
Bradley's	XX ☺	334
Brawn	X ☺	364
Bread Street Kitchen	XX	221
Brumus	XX	57
Le Café Anglais	XX	203
Cafe at Sotheby's	XX	58
Cannizaro House	XX	423
Le Caprice	XX	59
The Chancery	XX	224
Chapters	XX	365
Charlotte's Bistro	XX	393
Charlotte's Place	X	400
Clarke's	XX	302
Claude's Kitchen	X	404
Clerkenwell Kitchen	X	227
Clissold Arms	🍺	327
Clove Club	X	354
Crabtree	🍺	409
Crooked Well	🍺	229
Dabbous	X ✿	188
Delaunay	XXX	123
Le Deuxième	XX	123
Duck and Waffle	XX	230
Ducksoup	X	65
Dysart Arms	XX	416
Elliot's	X ☺	230
Entrée	X	389
Fellow	🍺	330
Fifteen London	X	348
Fifth Floor at Harvey Nichols	XXX	279

Five Fields	XXX	279
Giaconda Dining Rooms	X	189
The Glasshouse	XX ✿	413
Grain Store	X ☺	331
Granger and Co	X	304
The Grove	🍺	401
Harrison's	X	385
Hedone	XX ✿	394
High Timber	XX	233
House	🍺	343
Hush	XX	76
Inside	XX	371
Joe's	XX	284
John Salt	🍺	351
Kensington Place	X	305
King's Head	🍺	419
Kitchen Table at Bubbledogs	XX	192
Kitchen W8	XX ✿	306
Launceston Place	XXX ✿	307
Lawn Bistro	XX	424
Ledbury	XXX ✿✿	308
Lutyens	XXX	236
Manuka Kitchen	X	406
Marcus Wareing at The Berkeley	XXXX ✿✿	143
Market Cafe	X	346
Master and Servant	X	348
Maze	XX ✿	82
Medlar	XX ✿	287
The Mercer	XX	238
Mews of Mayfair	XX	84
Michael Nadra	XX	395
Michael Nadra Primrose Hill	XX	333
Odette's	XX	333
Orrery	XXX	169
Oxo Tower	XXX	243
Oxo Tower Brasserie	X	244
Paramount	X	194
Petersham Nurseries Café	X	417
Phoenix	🍺	290
Plateau	XX	369
Portman	🍺	171
Portobello House	🍺	310
Portrait	X	94
Prince Alfred and Formosa Dining Room	🍺	207
Quaglino's	XX	94
Refuel	XX	96
Riding House Café	X	172
Roux at Parliament Square	XXX	150
St John's Tavern	🍺	322
Seven Park Place	XXX ✿	99
Sketch (The Gallery)	XX	100
Skylon	XXX	251
Social Eating House	X ✿	102
Sonny's Kitchen	XX	388
Story	XX ✿	252
10 Greek Street	X	107
Thomas Cubitt	🍺	151
Tom Aikens	XXX ✿	294
Tramshed	X	357
28°-50° Marylebone	X	174
Upstairs	XX	393
Verru	XX	177
Village East	X	255
Vinoteca (Clerkenwell)	X	255
Vinoteca (Regent's Park and Marylebone)	X	177
Vinoteca (Soho)	X	111
Wapping Food	X	378
Waterway	🍺	207
The White Swan	XX	257
Wild Honey	XX ✿	112
The Wolseley	XXX	111
York and Albany	🍺	325

Other world kitchens

Baku	XXX	266
Baltic	XX	218
Caravan (Finsbury)	X	223
Caravan (King's Cross St Pancras)	X	329
Colchis	XX	204
Floridita	XX	65
Honey and Co	X ☺	190
Kateh	X ☺	205
Made in Camden	X ☺	324
The Modern Pantry	X	239
Shrimpy's	X	332
Tandis	X	323

Restaurants with outside dining

Abbeville Kitchen 396
Admiral Codrington 266
Albion 349
Al Borgo 418
Alloro 41
Amaranto 43
Anchor and Hope 216
Anglesea Arms 408
Avalon 385
L'Aventure 158
A. Wong 139
Barnsbury 350
Barrica 185
Beagle 347
Belvedere 299
Bentley's (Oyster Bar) 51
Bingham Restaurant 415
Bistrot Bruno Loubet 219
Bistro Union 398
Bleeding Heart 186
Blue Elephant 403
Boisdale of Belgravia 139
Boisdale of Canary Wharf 367
Le Boudin Blanc 55
Brown Dog 386
Bull and Last 327
Butlers Wharf Chop House 222
Cantina Del Ponte 222
Canton Arms 377
Caravan (King's Cross St Pancras) 329
Cecconi's 60
Chapters 365
Charlotte's Place 400
Cicada 225
Cigala 187
Cinnamon Kitchen 226
Cinnamon Soho 61
Clerkenwell Kitchen 227
Clissold Arms 327
Colchis 204
Crabtree 409
Crooked Well 229
Dartmouth Castle 409
Dean Street Townhouse Restaurant 64
Dehesa 64
Del Mercato 229
Dishoom 124
Drapers Arms 350
Duke of Sussex 384
Dysart Arms 416
Empress 345
Fish Market 231
Gail's Kitchen 189
Galvin Café a Vin 374
Galvin La Chapelle 375
Goodman Canary Wharf 368
Grain Store 331
The Grove 401
Gun 368
Hampshire Hog 410
Havelock Tavern 410
Henry Root 282
High Road Brasserie 395
High Timber 233
Hix Oyster and Chop House 234
House 343
Hush 76
Indian Zing 411
Kateh 205
King's Head 419
Kopapa 192
Lady Ottoline 193
Ledbury 308
Lola Rojo 390
Malt House 404
Manicomio (Chelsea) 285
Market Cafe 346
Master and Servant 348
Mazi 309
Medcalf 238

Restaurant		Page
Medlar	XX ✿	287
Michael Nadra Primrose Hill	XX	333
The Modern Pantry	X	239
Momo	XX	85
Morgan Arms	🍺	342
Moro	X	241
Narrow	🍺	373
New St Grill	XX	242
Odette's	XX	333
Olivomare	X	146
One Blenheim Terrace	XX	168
One Leicester Street	XX ✿	90
Orrery	XXX	169
Oxo Tower	XXX	243
Oxo Tower Brasserie	X	244
Painted Heron	XX	288
Pantechnicon	🍺	147
Paternoster Chop House	X	244
Petersham Nurseries Café	X	417
La Petite Maison	XX	91
Phoenix	🍺	290
Pig and Butcher	🍺	352
Plateau	XX	369
Polpo Smithfield	X ☺	246
Le Pont de la Tour	XXX	246
Portobello House	🍺	310
Prince of Wales	🍺	415
Princess of Shoreditch	🍺 ☺	355
Princess Victoria	🍺	418
Provender	X ☺	358
Ritz Restaurant	XXXXX	96
River Café	XX ✿	412
Rookery	X	398
Roots at N1	XX	342
St John's Tavern	🍺	322
Salusbury	🍺	334
Sands End	🍺	407
Santini	XXX	150
Shrimpy's	X	332
Singapore Garden	XX	335
Suda	X	130
Sushisamba	XX	251
La Trompette	XXX ✿	397
Victoria	🍺	403
Wapping Food	X	378
Waterway	🍺	207
Well	🍺	257
Wells	🍺	328
Wright Brothers Soho	X	113
York and Albany	🍺	325

Open for Breakfast

Restaurant	Category	Page
Al Duca	XX	41
Aurelia	XX	44
Automat	X	46
Balcon	XX	47
Balthazar	XX	121
Bird of Smithfield	X	219
Bistrot Bruno Loubet	X	219
Brasserie Chavot	XX ✿	56
Brasserie Max	XX	186
Bread Street Kitchen	XX	221
Caravan (Finsbury)	X	223
Caravan (King's Cross St Pancras)	X	329
Cecconi's	XXX	60
Chapters	XX	365
Chelsea Ram	🍺	274
The Cinnamon Club	XXX	140
Clerkenwell Kitchen	X	227
Clissold Arms	🍺	327
Colbert	XX	275
Dishoom	X	124
Duck and Waffle	XX	230
Electric Diner	X	304
Elliot's	X ☺	230
Fifteen London	X	348
Franco's	XX	66
Gail's Kitchen	X ☺	189
Garrison	🍺	231
Granger and Co	X	304
Grazing Goat	🍺	164
Great British	X	69
Hampshire Hog	🍺	410
Harrison's	X	385
Hawksmoor (City of London)	X	232
Hispania	X	233
Honey and Co	X ☺	190
Imli Street	X	77
Joe's	XX	284
Jugged Hare	🍺	235
Kopapa	X	192
Lardo	X	345
The Mercer	XX	238
The Modern Pantry	X	239
Nopi	X	89
One Leicester Street	XX ✿	90
Only Running Footman	🍺	89
The Orange	🍺	146
Ottolenghi	X	351
Ozer	XX	169
Plum + Spilt Milk	XX	331
Provender	X ☺	358
Quo Vadis	XXX	95
Riding House Café	X	172
Rivington Grill (Greenwich)	X	371
Rivington Grill (Shoreditch)	X	357
Roast	XX	248
1701	XX	250
Spice Market	XX	103
The Wolseley	XXX	111

Open late

Time of last orders in brackets.

Restaurant	Symbols	Page
Amaya *(23.30)*	XXX ✿	136
Automat *(23.45)*	X	46
Bentley's (Oyster Bar) *(23.30)*	X	51
Boisdale of Belgravia *(23.30)*	XX	139
Boqueria *(23.30)*	X	392
Brasserie Max *(23.30)*	XX	186
Brasserie Zédel *(00.00)*	XX ☺	55
Capote y Toros *(23.15)*	X	272
Le Caprice *(00.00)*	XX	59
Cecconi's *(23.15)*	XXX	60
Ceviche *(23.30)*	X	60
Chicken Shop *(00.00)*	X	329
China Tang *(23.45)*	XXXX	61
Chutney Mary *(23.30)*	XXX	274
Colbert *(23.30)*	XX	275
Daphne's *(23.30)*	XX	276
Dean Street Townhouse Restaurant *(23.45)*	XX	64
Duck and Waffle *(00.00)*	XX	230
Eleven Park Walk *(23.45)*	XXX	278
Floridita *(23.30)*	XX	65
Hakkasan Hanway Place *(00.00)*	XX ✿	191
Hakkasan Mayfair *(23.30)*	XX ✿	72
Haozhan *(02.00)*	XX	71
Imperial China *(23.30)*	XXX	77
The Ivy *(00.00)*	XXX	126
J. Sheekey *(00.00)*	XX	126
J. Sheekey Oyster Bar *(00.00)*	X	127
Malabar *(23.30)*	XX	305
Master and Servant *(23.30)*	X	348
Momo *(23.30)*	XX	85
Mr Chow *(23.30)*	XX	286
Nobu *(02.15)*	XX ✿	87
Nobu Berkeley St *(00.00)*	XX ✿	88
Paramount *(23.15)*	X	194
Plum + Spilt Milk *(23.30)*	XX	331
Plum Valley *(23.15)*	XX	92
Poissonnerie *(23.30)*	XX	291
Refuel *(00.00)*	XX	96
Roka *(23.15)*	XX	196
Roka Canary Wharf *(23.15)*	XX	370
Spuntino *(01.00)*	X	103
Tendido Cero *(23.15)*	X	293
The Wolseley *(00.00)*	XXX	111
Yauatcha *(23.30)*	XX ✿	114

Central London

- Mayfair • Soho • St James's **36**
- Strand • Covent Garden **116**
- Belgravia • Victoria **132**
- Regent's Park • Marylebone **154**
- Bloomsbury • Hatton Garden • Holborn **182**
- Bayswater • Maida Vale **198**
- City of London • Clerkenwell • Finsbury • Southwark **208**
- Chelsea • Earl's Court • Hyde Park • Knightsbridge • South Kensington **260**
- Kensington • North Kensington • Notting Hill **296**

R. Leaver/Loop Images/Age fotostock

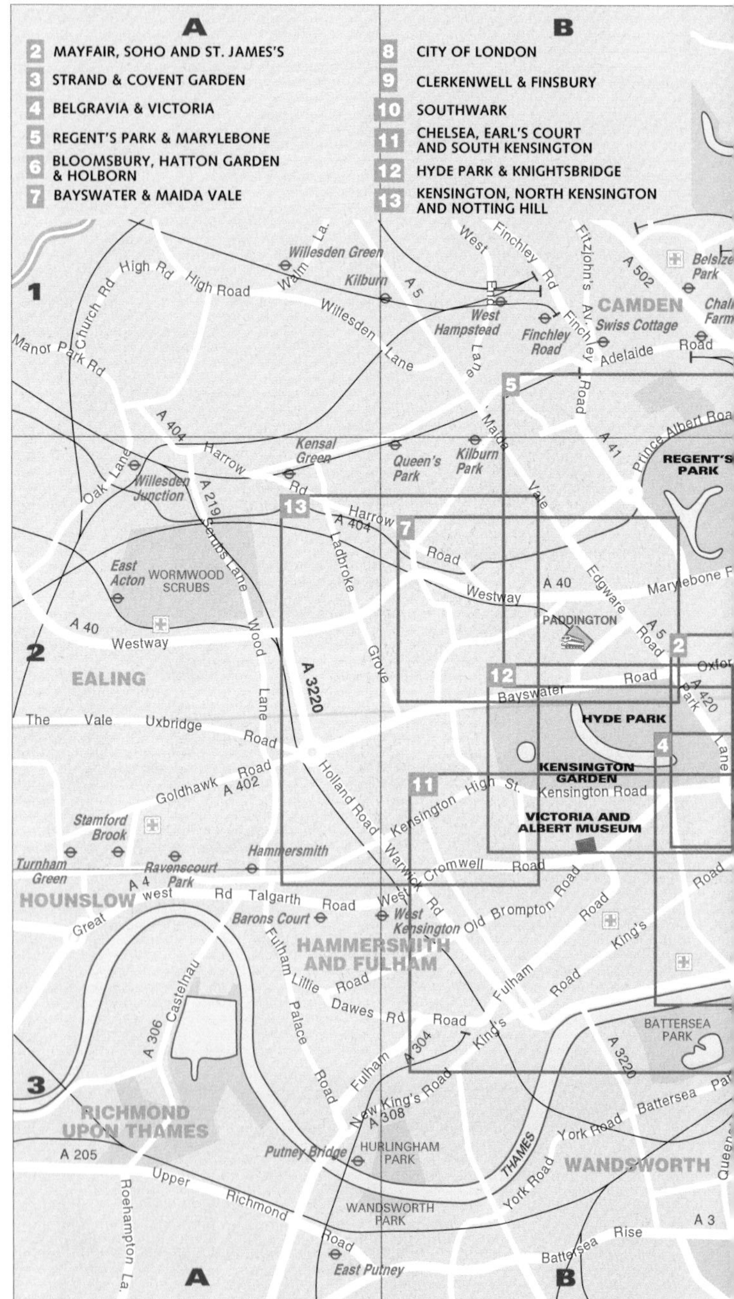
A
B
2 MAYFAIR, SOHO AND ST. JAMES'S
3 STRAND & COVENT GARDEN
4 BELGRAVIA & VICTORIA
5 REGENT'S PARK & MARYLEBONE
6 BLOOMSBURY, HATTON GARDEN & HOLBORN
7 BAYSWATER & MAIDA VALE
8 CITY OF LONDON
9 CLERKENWELL & FINSBURY
10 SOUTHWARK
11 CHELSEA, EARL'S COURT AND SOUTH KENSINGTON
12 HYDE PARK & KNIGHTSBRIDGE
13 KENSINGTON, NORTH KENSINGTON AND NOTTING HILL
1
2
3
CAMDEN
Swiss Cottage
Belsize Park
Willesden Green
Kilburn
West Hampstead
Finchley Road
Kensal Green
Queen's Park
Kilburn Park
Willesden Junction
East Acton
WORMWOOD SCRUBS
REGENT'S PARK
PADDINGTON
EALING
HYDE PARK
KENSINGTON GARDEN
VICTORIA AND ALBERT MUSEUM
Stamford Brook
Turnham Green
Ravenscourt Park
Hammersmith
HOUNSLOW
Barons Court
West Kensington
HAMMERSMITH AND FULHAM
BATTERSEA PARK
RICHMOND UPON THAMES
Putney Bridge
HURLINGHAM PARK
THAMES
WANDSWORTH
WANDSWORTH PARK
East Putney
High Rd
High Road
Willesden Lane
Church Rd
Manor Park Rd
Walm La.
A 5
West End La.
Finchley Rd
Fitzjohn's Av.
A 502
Adelaide Road
Finchley Road
A 404
Harrow Rd
Oak Lane
A 219
Scrubs Lane
Harrow Road
A 404
Ladbroke Grove
Maida Vale
A 41
Prince Albert Road
Edgware Road
A 5
A 40
Westway
Marylebone Road
A 40
Westway
Wood Lane
A 3220
Oxford
Bayswater Road
A 420
Park Lane
The Vale
Uxbridge Road
Goldhawk Road
A 402
Holland Road
Kensington High St.
Kensington Road
Warwick Rd
Cromwell Road
A 4
Great west Rd
Talgarth Road
Old Brompton Road
Road
King's Road
Fulham Road
Lillie Road
Dawes Rd
Fulham Palace Road
A 306
Castelnau
A 304
Fulham Road
New King's Road
A 308
A 3220
York Road
Battersea Park
Queens
A 205
Upper Richmond Road
Roehampton La.
York Road
Battersea Rise
A 3
A
B

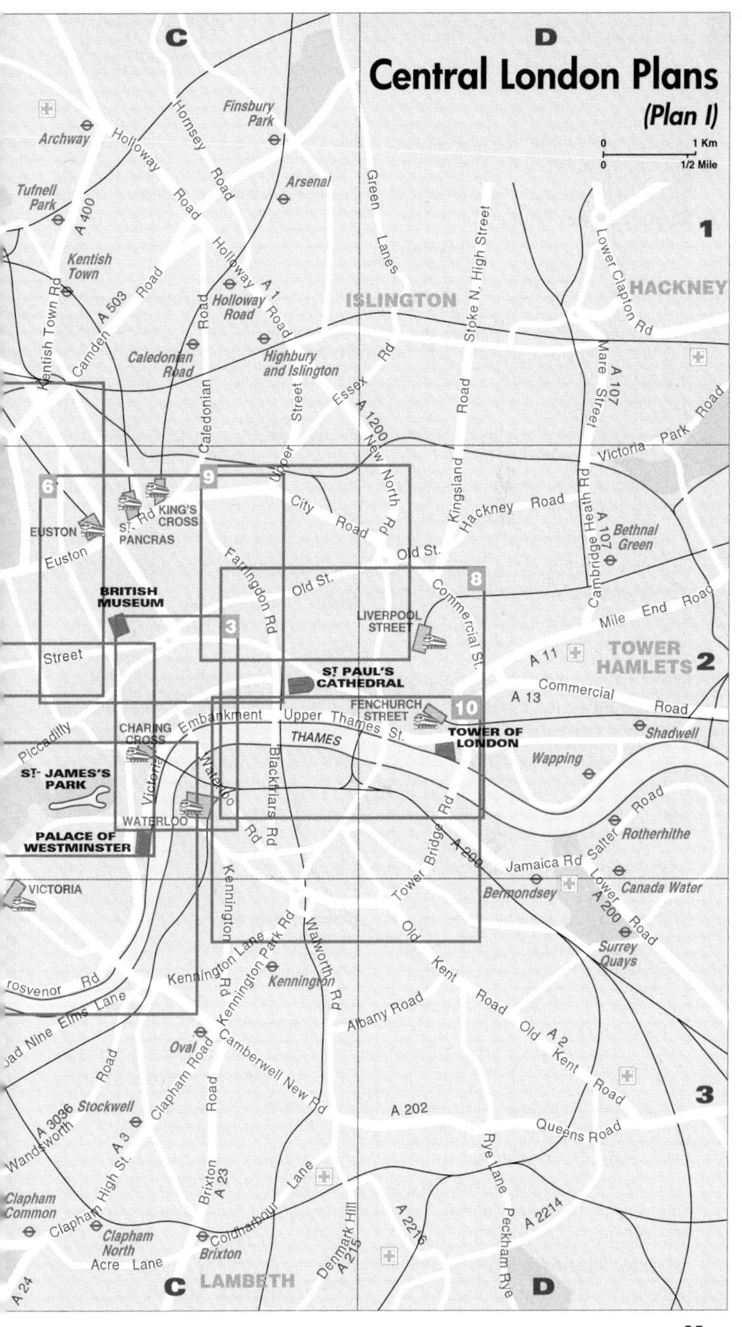
Central London Plans
(Plan I)
0 1 Km
0 1/2 Mile
C
D
1
2
3
ISLINGTON
HACKNEY
TOWER HAMLETS
LAMBETH
Archway
Finsbury Park
Arsenal
Tufnell Park
Kentish Town
Holloway Road
Caledonian Road
Highbury and Islington
Bethnal Green
Shadwell
Wapping
Rotherhithe
Canada Water
Bermondsey
Surrey Quays
Kennington
Oval
Stockwell
Clapham Common
Clapham North
Brixton
EUSTON
ST. PANCRAS
KING'S CROSS
BRITISH MUSEUM
LIVERPOOL STREET
ST PAUL'S CATHEDRAL
FENCHURCH STREET
TOWER OF LONDON
CHARING CROSS
WATERLOO
ST. JAMES'S PARK
PALACE OF WESTMINSTER
VICTORIA
THAMES
6
9
3
8
10
Holloway Road
Hornsey Road
Camden Road
Kentish Town Rd
Caledonian Road
Upper Street
Essex Rd
New North Rd
Green Lanes
Stoke N. High Street
Kingsland Road
Lower Clapton Rd
Mare Street
Victoria Park Road
Cambridge Heath Rd
Hackney Road
City Road
Old St.
Farringdon Rd
Euston Road
Commercial St.
Mile End Road
Commercial Road
Street
Piccadilly
Embankment
Upper Thames St.
Victoria
Waterloo Rd
Blackfriars Rd
Tower Bridge Rd
Jamaica Rd
Salter Road
Lower Road
Kennington Rd
Kennington Lane
Kennington Park Rd
Walworth Rd
Old Kent Road
Albany Road
Grosvenor Rd
Nine Elms Lane
Camberwell New Rd
Clapham Road
Brixton Road
Clapham High St.
Wandsworth Road
Coldharbour Lane
Acre Lane
Denmark Hill
Rye Lane
Peckham Rye
Queens Road
A 1
A 11
A 13
A 2
A 3
A 23
A 24
A 200
A 202
A 215
A 2214
A 2216
A 400
A 503
A 107
A 1200
A 3036

Mayfair · Soho · St James's

There's one elegant dividing line between Mayfair and Soho - the broad and imposing sweep of **Regent Street** - but mindsets and price tags keep them a world apart. It's usual to think of easterly Soho as the wild and sleazy half of these ill-matched twins, with Mayfair to the west the more sedate and sophisticated of the two. Sometimes, though, the natural order of things runs awry: why was rock's legendary wild man Jimi Hendrix, the embodiment of Soho decadence, living in the rarefied air of Mayfair's smart 23 Brook Street? And what induced Vivienne Westwood, punk queen and fashionista to the edgy, to settle her sewing machine in the uber-smart Conduit Street?

Mayfair has been synonymous with elegance for three and a half centuries, ever since the Berkeley and Grosvenor families bought up the local fields and turned them into posh real estate. The area is named after the annual May fair introduced in 1686, but suffice it to say that a raucous street celebration would be frowned upon big time by twenty-first century inhabitants. The grand residential boulevards can seem frosty and imposing, and even induce feelings of inadequacy to the humble passer-by but should he become the proud owner of a glistening gold card, then hey ho, doors will open wide. Claridge's is an art deco wonder, while **New Bond Street** is London's number one thoroughfare for the most chi-chi names in retailing. **Savile Row** may sound a little 'passé' these days, but it's still the place to go for the sharpest cut in town, before sashaying over to compact **Cork Street** to indulge in the purchase of a piece of art at one of its superb galleries. Science and music can also be found here, and at a relatively cheap price: the Faraday Museum in **Albemarle Street** has had a sparkling refurbishment, and the Handel House Museum in Brook Street boasts an impressive two-for-one offer: you can visit the beautifully presented home of the German composer and view his musical scores... before looking at pictures of Hendrix, his 'future' next door neighbour.

Soho challenges the City as London's most famous square mile. It may not have the money of its brash easterly rival, but it sure has the buzz. It's always been fast and loose, since the days when hunters charged through with their cries of 'So-ho!' Its narrow jumbled streets throng with humanity, from the tourist to the tipsy, the libertine to the louche. A lot of the fun is centred round the streets just south of **Soho Square,** where area legends like The Coach & Horses ('Norman's Bar'), Ronnie Scott's and Bar Italia cluster in close proximity. There's 80s favourite, the Groucho Club. The tightest t-shirts in town are found in **Old Compton Street,** where the pink pound jangles the registers in a swathe of gay-friendly bars and restaurants. To get a feel of the 'real' Soho, where old engraved signs enliven the shop fronts and the market stall cries echo back to the 1700s, a jaunt along **Berwick Street** is always

C. Barrely / MICHELIN

in vogue, taking in a pint at the eternally popular Blue Posts, an unchanging street corner stalwart that still announces 'Watney's Ales' on its stencilled windows.

Not a lot of Watney's ale was ever drunk in **St James's;** not a lot of ale of any kind for that matter. Champagne and port is more the style here, in the hushed and reverential gentlemen's clubs where discretion is the key, and change is measured in centuries rather than years. The sheer class of the area is typified by **Pall Mall's** Reform Club, where Phileas Fogg wagered that he could zip round the world in eighty days, and the adjacent **St James's Square,** which was the most fashionable address in London in the late seventeenth century, when dukes and earls aplenty got their satin shoes under the silver bedecked tables.

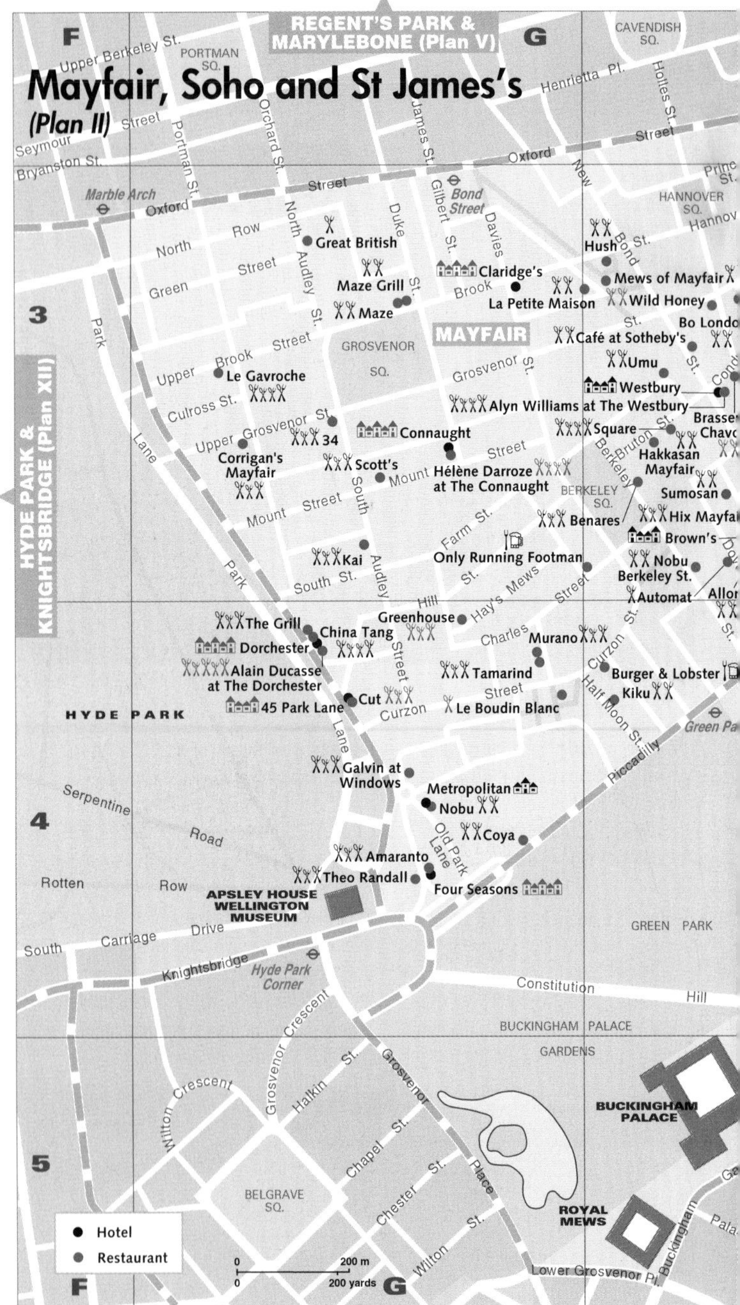

Mayfair, Soho and St James's
(Plan II)
REGENT'S PARK & MARYLEBONE (Plan V)
HYDE PARK & KNIGHTSBRIDGE (Plan XII)
F
G
3
4
5
MAYFAIR
HYDE PARK
GREEN PARK
Great British
Maze Grill
Maze
Claridge's
La Petite Maison
Hush
Mews of Mayfair
Wild Honey
Bo London
Café at Sotheby's
Umu
Westbury
Alyn Williams at The Westbury
Brasserie Chavot
Square
Hakkasan Mayfair
Sumosan
Le Gavroche
34
Connaught
Corrigan's Mayfair
Scott's
Hélène Darroze at The Connaught
Benares
Hix Mayfair
Brown's
Only Running Footman
Kai
Nobu Berkeley St.
Automat
The Grill
China Tang
Dorchester
Alain Ducasse at The Dorchester
Greenhouse
Murano
Tamarind
Burger & Lobster
Kiku
Cut
45 Park Lane
Le Boudin Blanc
Galvin at Windows
Metropolitan
Nobu
Coya
Amaranto
Theo Randall
Four Seasons
APSLEY HOUSE WELLINGTON MUSEUM
Hyde Park Corner
Marble Arch
Bond Street
Green Park
BUCKINGHAM PALACE
ROYAL MEWS
BUCKINGHAM PALACE GARDENS
BELGRAVE SQ.
GROSVENOR SQ.
BERKELEY SQ.
HANNOVER SQ.
CAVENDISH SQ.
PORTMAN SQ.
Hotel
Restaurant
0 200 m
0 200 yards

BLOOMSBURY, HATTON GARDEN & HOLBORN (Plan VI)
BELGRAVIA & VICTORIA (Plan IV)
STRAND & COVENT GARDEN (Plan III)
SOHO
PICCADILLY CIRCUS
ST JAMES'S
ST JAMES'S PARK
TRAFALGAR SQUARE
NATIONAL GALLERY
ST MARTIN-IN-THE-FIELDS
OLD ADMIRALTY
HORSE GUARDS
BANQUETING HOUSE
PALACE OF WESTMINSTER
ST MARGARET'S
WESTMINSTER ABBEY
BURLINGTON HOUSE
THEATRE ROYAL
CARLTON HOUSE TERRACE
QUEEN'S CHAPEL
ST JAMES'S PALACE
SPENCER HOUSE
LANCASTER HOUSE
CHARING CROSS
Vasco and Piero's Pavilion
Aqua Nueva
Aqua Kyoto
Copita
Red Fort
Quo Vadis
Arbutus
Hazlitt's
Soho
Imli Street
Burger & Lobster
10 Greek Street
Ducksoup
Bibigo
Social Eating House
Little Social
Yauatcha
Refuel
Barrafina
Goodman
Pitt Cue Co.
Tapas Brindisa
Floridita
Ceviche
Hibiscus
Dean Street Townhouse Restaurant
Koya
Sketch (The Gallery)
Dehesa
Vinoteca
Bone Daddies
Cây Tre
Barshu
Sketch-The Lecture Room & Library
Polpo Soho
Tonkotsu
Ba Shan
Bob Bob Ricard
Rosa's
Gauthier-Soho
Wright Brothers Soho
Nopi
Spuntino
Manchurian Legends
Haozhan
Baozi Inn
Mele e Pere
Cinnamon Soho
Bocca di Lupo
Plum Valley
Imperial China
Hix
MASH
Momo
Beijing Dumpling
Brasserie Zédel
One Leicester Street
Aurelia
Cecconi's
Veeraswamy
Hawksmoor
Spice Market
Bentley's (Grill)
Bentley's (Oyster Bar)
The National Dining Rooms
Portrait
Shoryu
Ritz Restaurant
Al Duca
Haymarket
Mint Leaf
Franco's
Brumus
The Wolseley
Balcon
Ritz
Quaglino's
Matsuri
Le Caprice
Sake No Hana
St James's Hotel and Club
Stafford
Avenue
Seven Park Place
Dukes
Oxford Circus
Tottenham Court Road
Covent Garden
Leicester Square
Piccadilly
Westminster
St James's Park
St James's Park Lake
Oxford Street
New Oxford St.
St Giles High St.
Charing Cross Rd
Shaftesbury Ave
Regent St.
Whitehall
The Mall
Birdcage Walk
Horse Guards Road
Parliament St.
Tothill St.
Victoria Street
Petty France
Buckingham Gate
Jermyn Street
Pall Mall
King St.
Haymarket
Strand
Long Acre
St Martins Lane

Alain Ducasse at The Dorchester ✿✿✿

French G4

Dorchester Hotel,
Park Ln ✉ W1K 1QA
(020) 7629 8866
www.alainducasse-dorchester.com
⊖ Hyde Park Corner
Closed 3 weeks August, first week January, 18-21 April, 26-30 December, Saturday lunch, Sunday and Monday
Menu £60/85

Alain Ducasse

Alain Ducasse is one of France's greatest post-war chefs and his London team display a confidence in their ability and maturity in their attitude that does justice to his reputation. The service is assured and the meal perfectly paced; the settled, experienced team know when to engage with guests and when to stand back. The room has a serene and luxurious feel, its tables immaculately set, but try to avoid the raised section by the windows as, although you may have a partial view of the park, you do end up feeling somewhat disengaged from the rest of the room. The kitchen team have steadily lightened the classical French dishes but they remain superbly crafted, with wonderfully complementary flavours and textures. The menu uses the best of British and French produce, from Dorset crab and Scottish lobster to Limousin veal and Anjou pigeon, and some of the dishes will remain long in the memory. The wine list is exemplary, with a particularly impressive selection of Domaine de la Romanée Conti and Château d'Yquem.

First Course

- Sauté of lobster, truffled chicken quenelles and pasta.
- Roasted foie gras, morels and Arbois wine.

Main Course

- Fillet of beef Rossini with Périgueux sauce.
- Turbot, crayfish, asparagus and Nantua sauce.

Dessert

- 'Baba like in Monte-Carlo'.
- Wild strawberry tartelette with clotted cream.

Al Duca

Italian H4

4-5 Duke of York St ✉ SW1Y 6LA
(020) 7839 3090
www.alduca-restaurant.co.uk
⊖ Piccadilly Circus
Closed Easter, 25 December, Sunday and bank holidays

Menu £17/33 XX

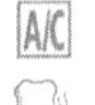

Al Duca has become as much a part of the fabric of St James's as many of the shirt makers who have made neighbouring Jermyn Street home over the years. It is also one of the those restaurants that manage the trick of appearing quiet one minute and full to the rafters the next without anyone noticing and this ensures that the atmosphere is never less than spirited. The serving team are a young, confident bunch and the manager knows who his regulars are. The menu is priced per course; there is plenty of choice and the cooking is crisp and confident, with plenty of well-priced bottles to match. The rib-eye with porcini mushrooms is a highlight. Prices are also pretty keen, especially for a restaurant in this neck of the woods.

Alloro

Italian H3

19-20 Dover St ✉ W1S 4LU
(020) 7495 4768
www.atozrestaurants.com/alloro
⊖ Green Park
Closed 25 December, Saturday lunch and Sunday – booking essential

Menu £35, £39/45

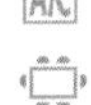

Alloro opened at the turn of the century and this comparative longevity owes much to its sensible prices, confident service and easy-to-eat Italian food. The current chef has been here for nearly half the restaurant's life; he comes from Piedmont and manages to sneak in a few specialties from his home region. The menu offers an appealing choice and nicely balanced selection, from a crisp chicory salad with bottarga to slow-cooked lamb shoulder, with all breads and pastas being made in-house. It's priced per number of courses taken; having all four represents the best value. Noise drifts in from the adjacent, boisterous baretto and so ensures that the atmosphere in the comfortable and urbane restaurant is always lively.

Alyn Williams at The Westbury 

modern

H3

Westbury Hotel,
Bond St ✉ W1S 2YF
(020) 7183 6426
www.alynwilliams.co.uk
⊖ Bond Street
Closed Saturday lunch and Sunday

Menu £25, £50/60

A/C

Alyn Williams at The Westbury

Over recent years, a small fortune has been spent putting back some of the style for which The Westbury was known when it opened back in the 1950s. But decoration is nothing without the right personnel and in 2012 the owners enticed Alyn Williams away from Marcus Wareing and put his name above the door of the restaurant. It's notoriously difficult to lend personality to hotel restaurants – and this one has the added disadvantage of being windowless – but the rosewood panelling, judicious lighting and a striking wine display more than compensate. The confident and cheery service team also ensure that the atmosphere never strays into the terminal seriousness that afflicts restaurants with ambition. In contrast to the fairly terse menu descriptions, Alyn Williams' cooking is creative and even at times quite playful—but however technically adept and elaborately constructed the dish, the combinations of flavours and textures always work. Vegetarians are well looked after; the breads are terrific and the wine list comprehensive.

First Course

- Foie gras semifreddo with liquorice and salted hazelnut caramel.
- Langoustine with mackerel, cuttlefish and watermelon.

Main Course

- Sea bass, grilled lobster, lemon gnocchi and beach vegetables.
- Wild Scottish salmon, crayfish and green tomato chutney.

Dessert

- Banana baba, rum cream and caramelised banana ice cream.
- White peach, lavender and buttermilk.

Amaranto

Italian

G4

Four Seasons Hotel,
Hamilton Pl, Park Ln ✉ W1J 7DR
✆ (020) 7499 0888
www.fourseasons.com/london/dining
⊖ Hyde Park Corner

Menu £20/26 – Carte £31/70

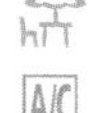

The Four Seasons hotel emerged from its huge refurbishment programme with a restaurant that's all about flexibility. Amaranto is a bar, a lounge and a dining room, and the idea is that you can have what you want, where you want it, from a largely Italian inspired menu that covers all bases. That means you can enjoy some crab cakes with your drink in the smart bar, share a plate of charcuterie with friends in the comfortable lounge or order a full 3 course meal with business clients in the handsome dining room. No expense was spared on the decoration – the space is full of the colours of the plant after which it is named and there's lots of lacquered wood. Unusually for hotels on Park Lane, there is also a fine terrace attached.

Aqua Kyoto

Japanese

H3

240 Regent St. (5th floor) (entrance on Argyll St.)
✉ W1F 7EB
✆ (020) 7478 0540
www.aqua-london.com
⊖ Oxford Circus
Closed 25 December and 1 January

Menu £20 (lunch) – Carte £26/88 s

Aqua London occupies all 17,000 square foot of the 5th floor of the former Dickins & Jones department store and boasts, along with a big bar and terrific terraces, two large restaurants. Aqua Kyoto is the more boisterous of the two, although getting to the table can be a drawn out affair, as you first give your name at the Argyll Street entrance, do so again when you get out of the lift, and only then are you handed over to the restaurant reception. However, Aqua Kyoto offers a fun night out, more so if you've come in a group – not just so you can compete with the noise, but also because the contemporary Japanese food is designed for sharing. Highlights include the eel teriyaki and the noodle dishes. Service means well but lacks direction.

Aqua Nueva

Spanish H3

240 Regent St. (5th floor) (entrance on Argyll St.)
✉ W1B 3BR
✆ (020) 7478 0540
www.aqua-london.com
⊖ Oxford Circus
Closed 25 December and 1 January

Menu £25 (lunch) – Carte £35/59

To reach the relative tranquillity of this Spanish restaurant, one first has to fight through the crowds enjoying a drink and a sense of exclusivity in Aqua Spirit, another part of this huge operation. Aqua Nueva feels more sophisticated than Aqua Kyoto with which its shares the 5th floor. It comes divided into two; the main room is more elegant and comfortable, but the tapas bar area, with its ceiling feature of 15,000 wooden beads, has more buzz and character and fills up first. The food comes in a stylised fashion that delivers the classic combinations of Spanish cuisine in original ways, although some subtle balances can get lost in the interpretation. The tapas, however, is more traditional and often features regional specialities.

Aurelia

Mediterranean H3

13-14 Cork St ✉ W1S 3NS
✆ (020) 7409 1370
www.aurelialondon.co.uk
⊖ Green Park
Closed Sunday dinner

Menu £25 – Carte £27/78

The Roman road that stretched from Rome through southern France and into Spain not only provides the inspiration for the kitchen but, it would appear, is also the favoured location for the holiday homes of many of the customers here. All dishes on this culinary journey around the Med are advertised as being ideal for sharing but this works better when it's the impressive charcuterie board in front of you rather than a plate of linguine. The dishes that everyone will expect to go around the table are those from the charcoal grill or the rotisserie, such as the tender leg of lamb with anchovies, the corn-fed baby chicken or the veal cutlet. Those in the know sit downstairs where the aromas are enticing and the atmosphere more animated.

Arbutus ✿

modern

I3

63-64 Frith St. ✉ W1D 3JW
(020) 7734 4545
www.arbutusrestaurant.co.uk
Tottenham Court Road
Closed 25-26 December and 1 January – booking advisable

Menu £18 (weekday lunch) – Carte £30/37

Arbutus

If you need reminding of what makes a great meal then look no further – Arbutus has it all: a relaxed setting, a terrific wine list that doesn't break the bank, and wonderfully flavoursome cooking. One reason why the food is so satisfying is that the kitchen has an innate understanding of the 'less is more' principle along with an appreciation of what-goes-with-what; and confident, technically assured delivery belies the apparent simplicity on the plate. Lesser cuts rarely seen, such as pig's head or lamb's tripe, vie for your attention next to Dorset crab or wild sea bass with sea purslane; a wonderful egg custard tart needs no adornment. The wine list includes greater numbers of organic wines and most of the wines are available by the carafe which allows for much experimentation and/or indulgence. As it approaches its 10th birthday, the restaurant has been freshened up a little in appearance; the black and white photos of Soho add to the feeling that this is 1 place at one with its neighbourhood.

First Course

- Squid and mackerel 'burger' with razor clams.
- Dorset crab, guacamole, peanut and lychee.

Main Course

- Elwy Valley lamb, sweet potato, Madeira braised celery.
- Roast Norfolk partridge, quinoa, grains and pear.

Dessert

- English egg custard tart, golden sultanas.
- Paris-Brest.

Automat

North-American

H3

33 Dover St. ✉ W1S 4NF

✆ (020) 7499 3033

www.automat-london.com

⊖ Green Park

Closed 25 December and 1 January

Menu £33/49 – Carte £23/47

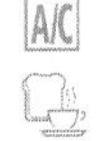

Famous restaurants abound in Mayfair but it's never been easy finding somewhere for a quick bite with friends that won't break the bank, unless all these friends are all wealthy oligarchs. Thanks then is due to the fun, noisy American brasserie that is Automat. Don't be fooled by the entrance: the place is bigger than it first seems, but make sure you ask for a table in the back room with the open kitchen as this is where the action is. You then need to head straight for what Uncle Sam does best: crab cake, a 10oz burger that uses freshly ground beef, mac 'n' cheese to set the heart pumping or USDA prime steak, followed up by an apple or pecan pie. Portions are, as one would expect, big and service is friendly.

Avenue

modern

H4

7-9 St James's St. ✉ SW1A 1EE

✆ (020) 7321 2111

www.avenue-restaurant.co.uk

⊖ Green Park

Closed Saturday lunch, Sunday dinner and bank Holidays

Menu £20 (weekday lunch) – Carte dinner £26/53

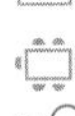

Such is The Avenue's longevity — due, in part, to an ability to subtly reinvent itself every now and again – that it risks becoming as much a part of the fabric of St James's as some of the gentlemen's clubs at which it once cocked a snook. A generous application of burgundy paint and some large canvases have left this large room looking a lot more colourful and there's greater warmth too from the service team. The menu roams predatorily around the globe looking for influences but the ingredients and particularly the main component, be it venison or salmon, come from these shores. The kitchen displays a greater degree of care and complexity than one expects, while the pre/post menus offer adequate choice and appealing prices.

Balcon

French

I4

Sofitel London St James Hotel,
8 Pall Mall. ✉ SW1Y 5NG
(020) 7968 2900
www.thebalconlondon.com
⊖ Piccadilly Circus

Menu £15 (weekdays) – Carte £26/82

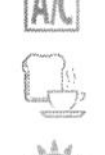

The increasingly ubiquitous Russell Sage was the designer charged with revamping this striking former banking hall and he's wrestled control of the room by installing vast chandeliers, upping the glamour and creating a balcony to house their impressive champagne 'cellar'. The room certainly has a grandeur that raises one's expectations but it needs to be near capacity to create an atmosphere. It's open from breakfast onwards and the classic brasserie menu is designed to appeal at any time of day. Dishes are rooted in French cuisine but most ingredients are British: snails are from Herefordshire, pork for the cassoulet is from Berkshire and their charcuterie, which is a feature, comes from Wales and France. A good value set menu changes weekly.

Baozi Inn

Chinese

I3

25-26 Newport Court ✉ WC2H 7JS
(020) 7287 6877
⊖ Leicester Square
Closed 24-25 December – bookings not accepted

Carte £12/14

Further proof that Chinatown is shaking off its tired, touristy image comes in the shape of Baozi Inn. Granted, there's nothing particularly noteworthy about the predictable surroundings of red lanterns and chunky tables but the friendly staff are welcoming and eager to please and the food is generously sized. It's also hard to blow your budget, which is especially significant as they only take cash. The eponymous baozi, or steamed filled buns, are a good way to start, although one is certainly enough; dishes have a fiery Sichuan slant and you'll feel the force in the noodle soup. The peanut and rolled tofu skin salad makes a perfect, calming side dish. Only Chinese beer is served but that's the ideal accompaniment anyway.

Barrafina

Spanish

I3

54 Frith St. ✉ W1D 3SL
✆ (020) 7813 8016
www.barrafina.co.uk
⊖ Tottenham Court Road
Closed 25 December and 1 January – bookings not accepted

Carte £14/33

A/C

London was once a bit iffy about restaurants that didn't take reservations but Barrafina was one of the first to show how it could be done. This is the younger sibling to the Hart brothers' Fino restaurant and its success is down to its mix of satisfyingly unfussy and authentic tapas and a buzzy atmosphere. Seafood is a speciality and the fish displays an exhilarating freshness; the Jabugo ham is also well worth trying. Four dishes per person is about par and the choice varies from razor clams a la plancha and tuna tartar to grilled chorizo and lamb sweetbreads with capers. It all centres around a counter, with seating for 20, so be prepared to talk to your neighbour - another thing that's slowly catching on in the capital. Be sure to try one of the sherries.

Barshu

Chinese

I3

28 Frith St. ✉ W1D 5LF
✆ (020) 7287 8822
www.bar-shu.co.uk
⊖ Leicester Square
Closed 24-25 December – booking advisable

Carte £22/49

A/C

Those who like their food with a kick won't be disappointed by Barshu as it features the fiery flavours of China's Sichuan Province. The menu, which looks more like a brochure, features a photo of each dish along with a chilli rating – a useful aid, as the staff can be a little reluctant to engage with customers. But it's not all mouth-numbingly hot and some of the dishes do display a more subtle balance of flavours. The legendary chillies and pepper are imported directly from China and, with the chef coming from the province too, authenticity is assured, particularly with the 'Five colour appetiser platter', which includes duck tongues and pig intestines. Lots of carved wood and lanterns decorate the place; larger groups should head downstairs.

Ba Shan

Chinese

24 Romilly St. ✉ W1D 5AH
✆ (020) 7287 3266
⊖ Leicester Square
Closed 24-25 December – booking advisable

Carte £15/30

Ba Shan is the third enterprise from the team who brought you Barshu and Baozi Inn. While this cosy place still has some Sichuan leanings, it mainly focuses on traditional styles from Northern areas and Henan province. Somewhat confusingly, there are two menus: one 'snack', the other 'home-style' - but just pick from both. Dry-wok dishes are plentiful and the guotie dumplings are their own take on a classic. Shaanxi flatbread 'sandwiches' or pork Chaoshou are a good way to start; noodles and vegetables come dressed with a provocative amount of chilli. Decoratively, it treads a fine line between cute and kitsch. There are three or four tables in each of the five rooms and service copes well with the constant influx of customers.

Beijing Dumpling

Chinese

23 Lisle St. ✉ WC2H 7BA
✆ (0207) 2876 888
⊖ Leicester Square
Closed 24-25 December

Menu £16/20 – Carte £10/40

Flashing neon or hanging roast ducks in the window appear to be the popular Chinatown method of attracting passers-by; this little restaurant catches their attention by showing its chefs hard at work preparing dumplings. It's also a lot less frenzied than many of its more excitable neighbours and a cut above the norm with its food. It serves freshly prepared dumplings of both Beijing and Shanghai styles and, although the range is not quite as comprehensive as the restaurant's name would suggest, they are still the highlight, especially varieties of the famed Siu Lung Bao. The rest of the menu has a wide base but its worth exploring the specials which include the occasional Taiwanese offering like spicy chicken.

Benares

Indian

H3

12a Berkeley Square House ✉ W1J 6BS
(020) 7629 8886
www.benaresrestaurant.com
Green Park
Closed 24-26 December and 1-2 January

Menu £35 – Carte £45/96

Benares

When Benares was re-launched a few years ago after an extended hiatus caused by a kitchen fire, it seemed that not a great deal had changed in its appearance although, apparently, much work did take place behind the scenes. One terrific addition, however, was the Chef's Table with its floor to ceiling windows looking directly into the kitchen; the Sommelier's Table doesn't quite have the same cachet. Another difference came in the subtle evolution of Atul Kochhar's cooking. His dishes appear a little simpler on the plate; the main ingredient takes centre stage, with the Indian spices adding interesting and complementary flavours but without being the dominant force. Those who want to experience as much of the cooking as they can are able to do so thanks to the Grazing menu, although those who don't care for too much modernity with their Indian food will find enough recognisable dishes to satisfy them. Much thought has also gone into the wine list and in choosing the right pairings for the food.

First Course

- Tandoori Ratan.
- Kolkata-style mackerel, crispy naan, pepper and egg.

Main Course

- Cod with coconut and curry leaf
- King prawn, scallop and squid with spiced gravy and onion parantha.

Dessert

- Rose and raspberry bhapa doi.
- Chocolate, peanut butter and jaggery cake with sugar cane ice cream.

Bentley's (Grill)

fish and seafood

H3

11-15 Swallow St. ✉ W1B 4DG
✆ (020) 7734 4756
www.bentleys.org
⊖ Piccadilly Circus
Closed 25-26 December and 1 January

Menu £26 (weekday dinner) – Carte £26/63

The green neon sign may still be outside but these days the upstairs dining room at Bentley's has a contemporary look, with leather chairs, fabric covered walls and paintings of boats and fish for those who haven't twigged that seafood is the draw here. One thing that will probably never change is the clubby feel and the preponderance of suited male customers, many of whom don't seem to mind paying the anachronistic cover charge. Much of the produce comes from St Ives and Looe in Cornwall and the freshness is palpable. Fish on the bone dissected at the table remains something of a speciality. Dover and Lemon soles feature strongly, as do oysters and soups, whilst the breads and beef remind you that owner Richard Corrigan is Irish.

Bentley's (Oyster Bar)

fish and seafood

H3

11-15 Swallow St ✉ W1B 4DG
✆ (020) 7734 4756
www.bentleys.org
⊖ Piccadilly Circus
Closed 25-26 December and 1 January

Menu £26 (lunch) – Carte £26/63

There's something about Swallow Street that always seems to get the taste buds going. Bentley's small reception area acts for both the upstairs restaurant and the ground floor Oyster Bar so be patient; dining on the ground floor means you'll be ushered through the curtain into a dimly lit bar with marbled-topped tables, banquette seating and places laid up at the counter. Oysters are naturally one of the main features, and the fish pie is a popular choice, but there are usually lots of daily specials and these often represent the most appealing option. The restaurant's illustrious past is almost tangible and the atmosphere is chummy and clubby, helped along with noise from the bar on the other side and the evening pianist.

Bob Bob Ricard

British traditional

H3

1 Upper James St ✉ W1F 9DF
✆ (020) 3145 1000
www.bobbobricard.com
⊖ Oxford Circus
Closed 25-26 December, 1 January and Sunday

Carte £29/75

A/C

Everyone needs a little glamour now and again and Bob Bob Ricard is one place that can provide it. This is a restaurant where diners still dress up a little and there's a feeling of exclusivity in the air. Start with a cocktail in their terrific basement bar then snare one of the booths in the restaurant. The room may be quite small but it clearly sees itself as a grand salon and is shiny, plush and elegant – you even get a button to push if you require more champagne. The menu is all encompassing, although the presence of caviar and vodka are clues as to the owner's nationality. For lighter eaters there are oysters, salads and grilled fish; those with heartier appetites can choose beef Wellington, a venison burger or chicken Kiev.

Bocca di Lupo

Italian

I3

12 Archer St ✉ WID 7BB
✆ (020) 7734 2223
www.boccadilupo.com
⊖ Piccadilly Circus
Closed 24 December-1 January and 25 August – booking essential

Carte £24/35

A/C

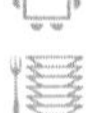

Deservedly busy from the day it opened, Bocca di Lupo is one of the best things to have arrived in Soho since the espresso bar. But be sure to sit at the marble counter in front of the chefs rather than at one of the faux-distressed tables at the back – not only is the atmosphere here more fun but the food is often better as it hasn't hung around the waiters' station waiting to be delivered. Each item has its region of origin within Italy noted on the menu and is available in a large or smaller size. The flavours don't hang back and over-ordering in all the excitement is very hard to resist. Highlights include the veal and pork agnolotti, the poussin in bread, and tripe; leave room for dessert or visit their Gelato shop opposite.

Bibigo

Korean H2

58-59 Great Marlborough St ✉ W1F 7JY
(020) 7042 5225
www.bibigouk.com
Oxford Circus

Menu £12 – Carte £16/30

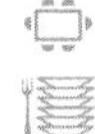

Bibigo represents the first foray into the UK market from Korea's largest food company, 'CJ'. With a little help from Psy, Korea's other famous non-electronic export, their mission is to bring healthy staples such as bibimbap – bowls of rice, vegetables, seeds and nuts finished with a hot pepper paste (gochujang) – to a wider public. Start with a soju-based cocktail then watch the kitchen behind the glass send forth dishes such as kimchi, Bossam (simmered pork belly) and hot stone galbi (chargrilled short ribs). Dishes have been adapted slightly for western tastes and the place may feel a little chainy – you can even buy the sauces at reception on the way out – but it's enthusiastically run and won't break the bank.

Bone Daddies

Asian I3

30-31 Peter St ✉ W1F OAR
(020) 7287 8581
www.bonedaddiesramen.com
Piccadilly Circus
Closed 25 December – bookings not accepted

Carte £16/21

Maybe ramen is the new rock 'n' roll. Bone Daddies' charismatic young Aussie chef-owner feels that we've only just begun to appreciate the potential of this Japanese speciality; he believes that anything can go into these warming, comforting bowls and that the combinations are endless. Along with the ramen, you'll find other dishes, such as yellowtail sashimi with ponzu and chilli, that owe their influence to the time he spent at Nobu. The staff are a confident, hospitable bunch and the shared tables add to the community spirit. You may have to queue but throughput is apparently quicker than at some of the top floor services offered close by. Those over 30, who probably don't like standing in line, at least get to recognise the music.

Ⓝ Bo London ✿

innovative

H3

4 Mill St ✉ W1S 2AX
✆ (020) 7493 3886
www.bolondonrestaurant.com
⊖ Oxford Circus
Closed 24-26 December, Saturday lunch and Sunday

Menu £27/138

Bo London

Having made his name and reputation in Hong Kong with his 'X-treme Chinese' cuisine, Alvin Leung returned to the city of his birth to open Bo London. In contrast to the bustle of Wan Chai, he chose the more sedate surroundings of Mayfair and while the restaurant may not share the intimacy of Bo Innovation it is infinitely more handsome. His cooking has always been about giving traditional Chinese flavours a modern interpretation – here in London he's gone one stage further by taking inspiration from British cuisine. So instead of the more traditional filling of pork, the wonderful Shanghainese soup dumplings Xiao Long Bao come filled with the flavours of steak and kidney. Other more playful dishes include 'Bed and Breakfast' – a jasmine-smoked quail egg wrapped in bacon and his notorious gastro-porn dessert, 'Sex on the beach'. All the dishes from this self-taught, self-styled 'demon chef' are innovative, exquisitely presented and come with interesting combinations of textures; flavours are clearly defined and will last long in the memory.

First Course

- Sichuan butter poached lobster, roasted corn and peas.
- Squid ball with kaffir lime.

Main Course

- Pigeon in an aromatic bouillon, potato and chive jiaozi.
- 'Toad in the hole'.

Dessert

- 'Beans on toast'- red beans and butter toast ice cream.
- Baijiu parfait, mandarin and liquorice caramel.

Le Boudin Blanc

French G4

5 Trebeck St ✉ W1J 7LT
✆ (020) 7499 3292
www.boudinblanc.co.uk
⊖ Green Park
Closed 24-26 December

Carte £27/56

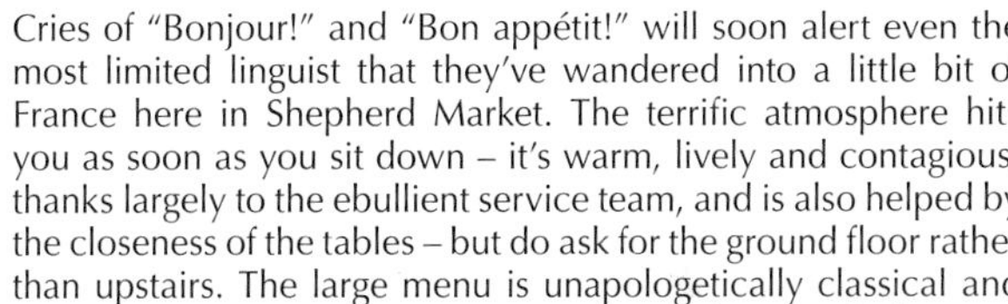

Cries of "Bonjour!" and "Bon appétit!" will soon alert even the most limited linguist that they've wandered into a little bit of France here in Shepherd Market. The terrific atmosphere hits you as soon as you sit down – it's warm, lively and contagious, thanks largely to the ebullient service team, and is also helped by the closeness of the tables – but do ask for the ground floor rather than upstairs. The large menu is unapologetically classical and very comforting; French onion soup, steak frites and of course boudin blanc are omnipresent, while daily fish or game specials are chalked up on the blackboard. Even the most nationalistic of customers will find it hard not to be swept along by the very Frenchness of it all.

Brasserie Zédel

French H3

20 Sherwood St ✉ W1F 7ED
✆ (020) 7734 4888
www.brasseriezedel.com
⊖ Piccadilly Circus
Closed 25 December – booking advisable

Menu £9/20 – Carte £14/38

After bedding in their Delaunay restaurant, Chris Corbin and Jeremy King then opened this grand French brasserie, which is far more about inclusivity and accessibility. Those mourning the old Atlantic Bar and Grill will be pleased to see this big, bustling subterranean space restored to its original art deco glory and this time it also comes with a small café, a bar and a cabaret theatre. The menu is a gloriously unapologetic roll-call of classic French dishes – from escargots to confit de canard – but what is most striking is the exceptionally fair pricing when one considers the location, the glamour, the service and the quality of the cooking. Plenty of tables are kept back for 'walk-ins' so it's always worth trying your luck.

Brasserie Chavot ✿

French

H3

41 Conduit St ✉ W1S 2YQ
(020) 7183 6425
www.brasseriechavot.com
⊖ Bond Street
Closed 25-26 December

Carte £30/45

The Westbury

The latest French chef to return to the capital is the amiable Eric Chavot and he's found a great spot in which to display his undoubted talents. The brasserie is actually part of the Westbury Hotel, but feels very much like a stand-alone operation and a smart, elegant one at that. A stunning mosaic floor, smoked mirrors, red leather seating and sparkling chandeliers add to the sophisticated look yet the buzz and bonhomie, and the unflustered service, make it all relaxed and easy. Eric's gone back to his roots and the cooking is hearteningly rustic and refreshingly unfussy: daube of beef, filet de canette with orange sauce, rum baba, profiteroles – within minutes you'll find yourself speaking French to the waiters without realising you're doing it. Yet even in relatively simple dishes like grilled poussin or île flottante, you can still see Eric's innate skill; he sees no point in 'reinterpreting' the classics, merely executing them in the best possible way. You'll leave thinking about what dish to order the next time you're here.

First Course

- Crab mayonnaise with avocado.
- Scallops with potato salad.

Main Course

- Canette à l'orange and caramelised endive.
- Pork cutlet with mustard sauce and frites.

Dessert

- Baba au rhum with crème Chantilly.
- Ile flottante.

Brumus

modern

I4

Haymarket Hotel,
1 Suffolk Pl ✉ SW1Y 4HX
✆ (020) 7470 4000
www.haymarkethotel.com
⊖ Piccadilly Circus

Menu £20 – Carte £23/49

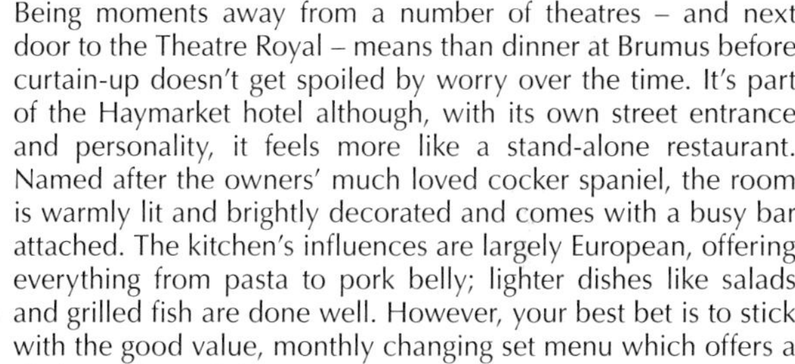

Being moments away from a number of theatres – and next door to the Theatre Royal – means than dinner at Brumus before curtain-up doesn't get spoiled by worry over the time. It's part of the Haymarket hotel although, with its own street entrance and personality, it feels more like a stand-alone restaurant. Named after the owners' much loved cocker spaniel, the room is warmly lit and brightly decorated and comes with a busy bar attached. The kitchen's influences are largely European, offering everything from pasta to pork belly; lighter dishes like salads and grilled fish are done well. However, your best bet is to stick with the good value, monthly changing set menu which offers a choice of three dishes per course.

Ⓝ Burger & Lobster

meats and grills

I3

36 Dean St ✉ W1D 4PS
✆ (020) 7432 4800
www.burgerandlobster.com
⊖ Leicester Square
Closed bank holidays

Menu £20

Virtually constant queues at the first Burger & Lobster in Mayfair meant that the opening of more branches was pretty inevitable. This one in Soho is a sizeable place, with seating for nearly 140; bookings are only taken for tables of more than six so either come as a group or be prepared to wait – the bar here is as good a place as any, or you can simply leave your phone number and they'll call you when a table becomes available. It's an ingenious concept: you simply decide whether you want a lobster roll in a brioche bun, a 1½lb Maine or Canadian lobster, or a 280g freshly minced burger made from Irish or Nebraskan beef. All are served with salad and fries and, for pudding, there's a choice of a couple of mousses.

Burger & Lobster

meats and grills H4

29 Clarges St ✉ W1J 7EF
✆ (020) 7409 1699
www.burgerandlobster.com
⊖ Green Park.
Closed Christmas and bank holidays – bookings not accepted

Menu £20

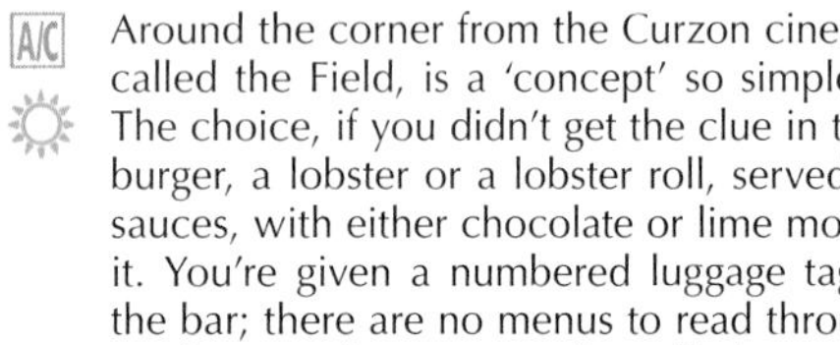

Around the corner from the Curzon cinema, in what was a pub called the Field, is a 'concept' so simple it borders on genius. The choice, if you didn't get the clue in the name, is between a burger, a lobster or a lobster roll, served with chips, salad and sauces, with either chocolate or lime mousse for dessert - that's it. You're given a numbered luggage tag if you want a tab at the bar; there are no menus to read through and no side dishes to choose. There's a small, well-chosen wine and cocktail list under headings B or L (work it out). The lobsters are Canadian; the burgers 10oz and the customers mostly men. Bookings aren't taken so get your name down on the list as soon as you arrive – it may well be a bunfight, but it's a very well organised one.

Cafe at Sotheby's

modern H3

34-35 New Bond St. ✉ W1A 2AA
✆ (020) 7293 5077
www.sothebys.com/cafe
⊖ Bond Street
Closed 3 weeks August, Christmas and New Year, Saturday, Sunday and bank holidays – booking essential – (lunch only)

Carte £26/38 s

It's usually the seasons that inform the menu of most restaurants but here at Sotheby's they change the style of the dishes according to the art being sold. For instance, experience has shown that modern and Impressionist artists attract a diet-conscious crowd who like their salads, while the Old Masters appeal to those who favour a more substantial, well-lubricated lunch which ends with a proper pudding. The lobster sandwich is a perennial feature and the wine list is brief but appealingly eclectic. Occupying a cosy space just off the lobby of the auction house, this is a little gem of a restaurant which is smarter than the 'café' moniker would suggest. Service is well-judged and the many regulars are discreetly acknowledged.

Le Caprice

modern

H4

Arlington House, Arlington St. ✉ SW1A 1RJ
✆ (020) 7629 2239
www.le-caprice.co.uk
⊖ Green Park
Closed 25-26 December

Menu £25 (dinner) – Carte £27/70

There are two types of customer at Le Caprice: those who are regulars and others who wish they were. This is one of those glamorous restaurants where the atmosphere is effortlessly sophisticated and the clientele confident and urbane; even first-timers feel in safe hands from the moment they enter. The menu offers something for everyone, whether that's a salad or pasta, their famous and very rich salmon fishcake with sorrel sauce, a burger or a more ambitious offering like well-judged game dishes or Asian spiced fish; the kitchen is well-practised and capable. Le Caprice celebrated its 30th anniversary in 2011 by having a little makeover which left it better lit and feeling a little warmer with its different sections more connected.

Cây Tre

Vietnamese

I3

42-43 Dean St ✉ W1D 4PZ
✆ (020) 7317 9118
www.caytresoho.co.uk
⊖ Tottenham Court Road
Booking advisable

Menu £23/29 – Carte £17/28

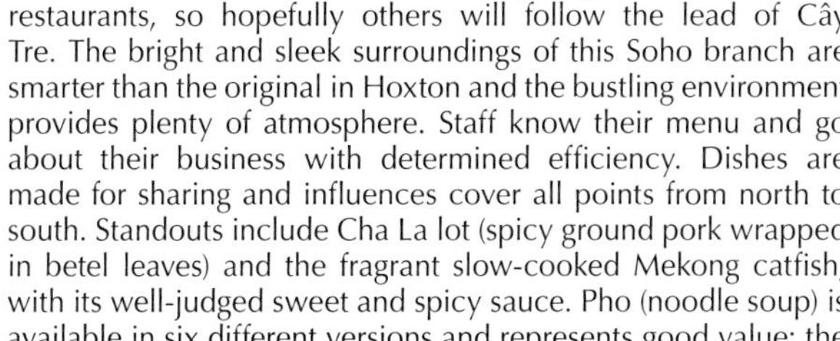

The West End could do with having plenty more Vietnamese restaurants, so hopefully others will follow the lead of Cây Tre. The bright and sleek surroundings of this Soho branch are smarter than the original in Hoxton and the bustling environment provides plenty of atmosphere. Staff know their menu and go about their business with determined efficiency. Dishes are made for sharing and influences cover all points from north to south. Standouts include Cha La lot (spicy ground pork wrapped in betel leaves) and the fragrant slow-cooked Mekong catfish, with its well-judged sweet and spicy sauce. Pho (noodle soup) is available in six different versions and represents good value; the set menu is a great starting point for neophytes.

Cecconi's

Italian

H3

5a Burlington Gdns ✉ W1S 3EP
✆ (020) 7434 1500
www.cecconis.com
⊖ Green Park
Booking essential

Carte £40/49

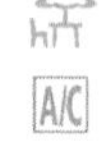

It's obviously a winning formula because Cecconi's are now popping up in various appropriately fashionable cities around the world. One can certainly see the appeal as they do feel like a private members club and even have a roped off VIP area to induce envy amongst those who find themselves insufficiently famous. The bar is the place to sit if you want to give the impression you're a regular who's often in for a quick bite; and if you are one such regular then you'll be assured of good service. The all-day menu offers a good selection of cicchetti, or small Italian tapas; prosciutto is sliced to order; the salads are popular at lunch and the classic, no-nonsense main courses are clearly prepared with care.

Ceviche

Peruvian

I3

17 Frith St ✉ W1D 4RG
✆ (020) 7292 2040
www.cevicheuk.com
⊖ Tottenham Court Road

Carte £15/28

Based on a Lima Pisco bar, Ceviche is as loud as it is fun and a great place to pop into for cocktails with a difference and some light dishes to share with friends. The long narrow room has a busy bar specialising in deliriously addictive drinks based on the Peruvian spirit Pisco, a grape brandy, and beyond it you'll find tightly packed tables, posters and photos of 1950s Peru, and waiting staff struggling to keep up. As the name suggests, ceviche, marinated in lime and chilli, is the star of the show, whether that's the sea bass or the Alianza Lima – a mix of prawns, squid and octopus. 3 per person plus perhaps an anticuchos skewer should be enough. Dishes arrive in a random order so ask if you want the ceviche before any hot dish.

China Tang

Chinese

G4

Dorchester Hotel,
Park Ln ✉ W1K 1QA
✆ (020) 7629 9988
www.chinatanglondon.co.uk
⊖ Hyde Park Corner
Closed 25 December

Menu £23 (lunch) – Carte £28/79

Sir David Tang's atmospheric, art deco inspired Chinese restaurant at The Dorchester Hotel is always a blur of activity, with noise spilling out from the large tables in the centre; regulars head for the library side, from where one can take in the whole room. In contrast to the sleek and decorative surroundings, the kitchen is a model of conservatism and rightly sticks to what it does best, namely classic Cantonese cooking. Peking duck and roasted meats are the highlights, but check out the chef's recommendations at the back of the menu too. The standard is good considering the numbers of customers and you can have dim sum in the striking bar for lunch or dinner. Apart from the set lunch menu, it isn't cheap – but it is fun.

Cinnamon Soho

Indian

H3

5 Kingly St ✉ W1B 5PF
✆ (020) 7437 1664
www.cinnamonsoho.com
⊖ Oxford Circus
Closed bank holidays – bookings not accepted

Menu £18/35 – Carte £17/28

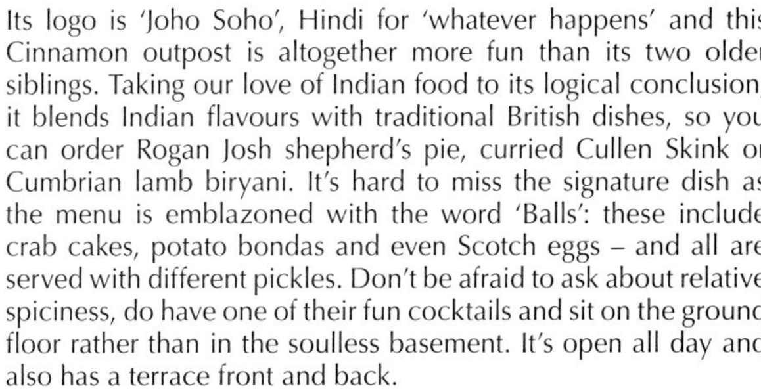

Its logo is 'Joho Soho', Hindi for 'whatever happens' and this Cinnamon outpost is altogether more fun than its two older siblings. Taking our love of Indian food to its logical conclusion, it blends Indian flavours with traditional British dishes, so you can order Rogan Josh shepherd's pie, curried Cullen Skink or Cumbrian lamb biryani. It's hard to miss the signature dish as the menu is emblazoned with the word 'Balls': these include crab cakes, potato bondas and even Scotch eggs – and all are served with different pickles. Don't be afraid to ask about relative spiciness, do have one of their fun cocktails and sit on the ground floor rather than in the soulless basement. It's open all day and also has a terrace front and back.

Copita

Mediterranean H3

27 d'Arblay St ✉ W1F 8EP
✆ (020) 7287 7797
www.copita.co.uk
⊖ Oxford Circus
Closed Sunday and bank holidays – bookings not accepted

Carte £13/20

It may not occupy a prime Soho spot but that hasn't stopped this tapas bar, a sister to Barrica, from being packed most nights. A no bookings policy means your best bet is to come before 7pm or else try your luck at lunch when there are fewer drinkers; then simply perch yourself on one of the high stools or stay standing and get stuck in. The daily menu offers a colourful array of diminutive dishes like pea and cheese croquettes, crab and spinach tart, and pumpkin and sage ravioli and you'll find it hard to stop ordering – even the delicate custard tart is delightfully moreish. Staff add to the lively atmosphere and everything on the thoughtfully compiled Spanish wine list is available by the glass or copita.

Corrigan's Mayfair

British modern G3

28 Upper Grosvenor St. ✉ W1K 7EH
✆ (020) 7499 9943
www.corrigansmayfair.com
⊖ Marble Arch
Closed 25-26 December, 1 January and Saturday lunch

Menu £25 (weekday lunch) – Carte £46/83

Richard Corrigan's flagship restaurant feels as though it has been part of the London scene for years. It's comfortable, clubby yet quite glamorous and Martin Brudnizki's design includes some playful features, such as the feather-covered lamps that give a nod to the restaurant's forte, which is game. The menu is lengthy and the food largely a celebration of British and Irish cooking. It is also fiercely seasonal, which makes having the day's special always a worthwhile choice. This relatively straightforward style of cooking still requires care and precise timing but sometimes the kitchen takes its eye off the ball. Service is smooth and well organised but the anachronistic cover charge is an unwelcome sight.

Coya

Peruvian G4

118 Piccadilly ✉ W1J 7NW
✆ (020) 7042 7118
www.coyarestaurant.com
⊖ Hyde Park Corner
Closed 25 December – booking advisable

Menu £27 (lunch) – Carte £33/53

It didn't take long for the people behind Roka and Zuma to act upon the realisation that the Next Big Thing on the London restaurant scene was Peruvian cuisine. Their loud and enthusiastically run basement restaurant on Piccadilly provides a lively spot in which to discover this fresh and zesty cuisine. Add in the live music at weekends and it also represents a great night out, especially when fuelled by the deliriously addictive Pisco Sours. Prepared in one of the three kitchens – the main room, the charcoal grill or the ceviche bar – the food is a mix of the authentic, the refined and the more contemporary; ordering a sharp, refreshing ceviche is a must and consider too the huge tiger prawns cooked in the Josper oven.

Cut

meats and grills G4

45 Park Lane Hotel,
45 Park Ln ✉ W1K 1PN
✆ (020) 7493 4545
www.45parklane.com
⊖ Hyde Park Corner
Booking essential

Menu £35 (weekday lunch) – Carte £43/124

Cut is the first European venture from Wolfgang Puck, the US-based Austrian chef whose level of celebrity makes our lot look positively anonymous. Teaming up with the Dorchester's 45 Park Lane hotel, he has created a slick, stylish and sexy room where glamorous people come to eat meat. The steaks – from Kansas, Chile, Australia and Devon— are first presented raw with a few words about their heritage and then cooked over hardwood and charcoal and finished off in a broiler. Sides are as good as the steaks, especially the fries and the macaroni cheese. Artery hardening continues with dessert which eschews the much-needed citrus in favour of lots of cream. You'll leave eminently satisfied, if slightly heavier in weight and lighter in pocket.

Dean Street Townhouse Restaurant

British modern

I3

69-71 Dean St. ✉ W1D 3SE
✆ (020) 7434 1775
www.deanstreettownhouse.com
⊖ Tottenham Court Road
Booking essential

Menu £19/28 – Carte £26/90

A restaurant for every occasion – even shouty ones, as you're hit by a cacophony of sound as soon as you open the heavy door of this attractive Georgian house. It's also a place to be seen, or perhaps not — a ban on flash photography means it's ideal for illicit trysts too. The classic brasserie aesthetic makes it look like it's been here for years and the heart-warming British comfort food fits these surroundings well. Prices for some of the fish and steak dishes can get pretty exclusive but there's plenty more proletariat fare on offer, like faggots with cabbage or mince and potatoes. The salads such as trout with truffled potato or smoked pigeon with Scotch egg are noteworthy and who can resist kipper pâté for afternoon tea?

Dehesa

Mediterranean

H3

25 Ganton St ✉ W1F 9BP
✆ (020) 7494 4170
www.dehesa.co.uk
⊖ Oxford Circus
Closed 24-25 and 31 December and 1 January

Carte £23/35

Dehesa does now take bookings, except for lunch on Saturday, so there's no longer a need to get here quite so early. It's a few streets away from its sister restaurant, Salt Yard, and repeats the format of offering delicious Spanish and Italian tapas. The menu is not an exact copy but the bestsellers all feature: the pork belly with cannellini beans; courgette flowers with Monte Enebro and honey; and the soft chocolate cake with Frangelico ice cream. They recommend 2-3 plates per person. Between 3pm and 5pm the kitchen takes a breather so the choice becomes ham on or off the bone, charcuterie and cheese. The drinks list is worthy of a visit in itself. Dehesa is a wooded area of Spain and home to Ibérico pigs who produce such great ham.

Ducksoup

modern

13

41 Dean St ✉ W1D 4PY
(020) 7287 4599
www.ducksoupsoho.co.uk
⊖ Leicester Square
Closed bank holidays and Sunday dinner

Carte £22/31

It's compact, with seating at the bar; decoratively it's knowingly underwhelming; and the menu, which includes small plates, is handwritten each day – yes, every 'on-trend' box is ticked here at Ducksoup. There's even a little retro thrown in courtesy of a turntable – for younger readers, those are 'records' being played. The chef-owner describes his food as "ambient" which translates as being as natural and seasonal as possible and the dishes, such as fried lamb chops with lemon and salt, are confidently unadorned; they do a good Brillat-Savarin cheesecake. Wines are also 'natural' and biodynamic and from small producers. There is a somewhat nebulous reservation system but this place is more about just dropping in for a quick bite.

Floridita

other world kitchens

13

100 Wardour St ✉ W1F 0TN
(020) 7314 4000
www.floriditalondon.com
⊖ Tottenham Court Road
Closed Sunday, Monday and bank holidays – (dinner only)

Menu £25/38

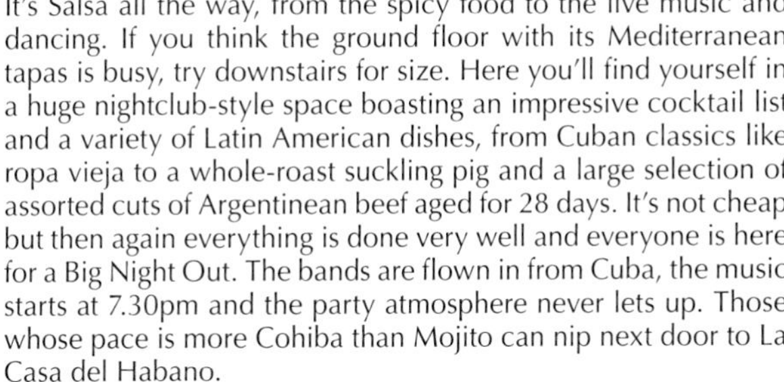

It's Salsa all the way, from the spicy food to the live music and dancing. If you think the ground floor with its Mediterranean tapas is busy, try downstairs for size. Here you'll find yourself in a huge nightclub-style space boasting an impressive cocktail list and a variety of Latin American dishes, from Cuban classics like ropa vieja to a whole-roast suckling pig and a large selection of assorted cuts of Argentinean beef aged for 28 days. It's not cheap but then again everything is done very well and everyone is here for a Big Night Out. The bands are flown in from Cuba, the music starts at 7.30pm and the party atmosphere never lets up. Those whose pace is more Cohiba than Mojito can nip next door to La Casa del Habano.

Franco's

Italian

H4

61 Jermyn St ✉ SW1Y 6LX
✆ (020) 7499 2211
www.francoslondon.com
⊖ Green Park
Closed Sunday and bank holidays – booking essential

Menu £18/22 – Carte £39/57

There can be few things more English than afternoon tea or the sound of Alan Bennett reading from The Wind in the Willows and, surprisingly enough, both can be enjoyed here at Franco's, one of London's oldest Italian restaurants that was relaunched in the mid-noughties. Open from breakfast onwards, it attracts a largely well-groomed clientele as befits its Jermyn Street address and boasts a clubby feel. Indeed, if you're not a regular visitor, you may find yourself with time to admire the service being enjoyed by other tables. The chef hails from Northern Italy but his menu covers all parts. There is a popular grill section, along with classics like Beef Rossini – ideal accompaniment for one of those big Tuscan reds on the wine list.

Gauthier - Soho

French

I3

21 Romilly St ✉ W1D 5AF
✆ (020) 7494 3111
www.gauthiersoho.co.uk
⊖ Leicester Square
Closed Monday lunch, Sunday and bank holidays except Good Friday

Menu £18/40

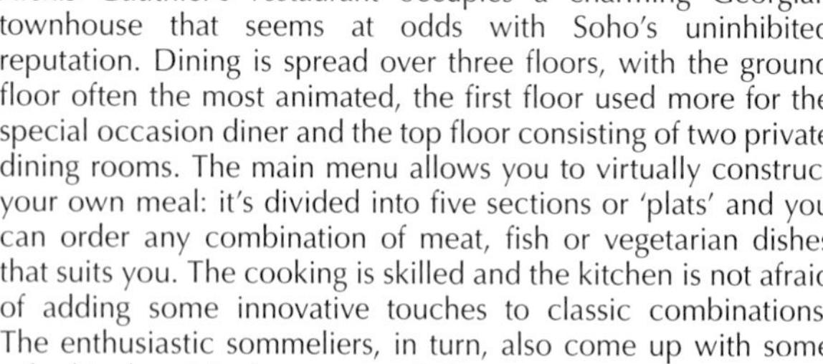

Alexis Gauthier's restaurant occupies a charming Georgian townhouse that seems at odds with Soho's uninhibited reputation. Dining is spread over three floors, with the ground floor often the most animated, the first floor used more for the special occasion diner and the top floor consisting of two private dining rooms. The main menu allows you to virtually construct your own meal: it's divided into five sections or 'plats' and you can order any combination of meat, fish or vegetarian dishes that suits you. The cooking is skilled and the kitchen is not afraid of adding some innovative touches to classic combinations. The enthusiastic sommeliers, in turn, also come up with some refreshingly original recommendations.

Le Gavroche ✿✿

French G3

43 Upper Brook St ✉ W1K 7QR
✆ (020) 7408 0881
www.le-gavroche.co.uk
⊖ Marble Arch
Closed Christmas-New Year, Saturday lunch, Sunday and bank holidays – booking essential

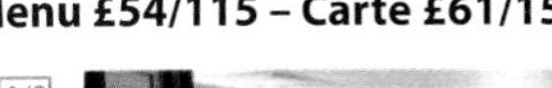

Menu £54/115 – Carte £61/156 XXXX

A/C

Le Gavroche

A little indulgence never did anyone any harm and Le Gavroche is all about indulgence. Michel Roux and head chef Rachel Humphrey's unapologetically extravagant French dishes are an exhilarating riposte to all those hectoring health-conscious calorie-counters. The menu is a roll-call of luxury ingredients, the sauces are sublime and the cooking is accompanied by one of London's best wine lists. There are oohs and aahs as trolleys are brought forward and carving knives sharpened; regulars mingle with newcomers and the atmosphere is refreshingly unstuffy, helped along by there being more of a female presence to the service these days. Anyone with an interest in Britain's post-war culinary adventures should be aware of Le Gavroche's significance, not just because of its celebration of, and dedication to, the art of French cuisine but also because of all those chefs who have benefitted from passing through its kitchen. Just avoid sitting too close to the stairs by asking for a table in the main body of this historic restaurant.

First Course

- Mousseline de homard au champagne et caviar.
- L'Assiette de crab royale.

Main Course

- Râble de lapin et galette au parmesan.
- Côte de veau aux morilles et pommes mousseline.

Dessert

- Le palet au chocolat Amer et praline croustillant.
- Millefeuille aux framboise et Gianduja.

Galvin at Windows ✿

French G4

London Hilton Hotel,
22 Park Ln (28th floor) ✉ W1K 1BE
✆ (020) 7208 4021
www.galvinatwindows.com
⊖ Hyde Park Corner
Closed Saturday lunch and Sunday dinner

Menu £29/68 XXX

Galvin at Windows

Until recently, London could claim only a handful of restaurants with great views but, as the city builds upwards as well as outwards, those who like a little vista with their venison are finding they have more and more choice. 'Windows' could provide the blueprint for these new panoramic restaurants because it has always understood the vital point that however good the views are, the food has got to match up. Choose any of the visually impressive dishes from the menu – be it classically French terrine of foie gras or more British in its influence like cured salmon with Dorset crab – and the kitchen's innate skill, technical ability and attention to detail will be evident. The team are also unafraid of adding their own touches, be it lemongrass to the lobster bisque or verjus butter to accompany the halibut. The room itself is elegant and understated, with windows on three sides; and the healthy mix of customers ensures a decent buzz, with the atmosphere flowing through from the cocktail bar next door.

First Course

- Scallops with cauliflower and mango chutney.
- Cured salmon, Dorset crab, avocado and caviar.

Main Course

- Loin of mutton, onion textures and mini shepherd's pie.
- Roast chicken, mustard cream, cos lettuce and chicken jus.

Dessert

- Banana soufflé, chocolate and caramelised peanut.
- Peanut butter parfait and popcorn ice cream.

Goodman

meats and grills

H3

✉ W1S 1QH
☎ (020) 7499 3776
www.goodmanrestaurants.com
⊖ Oxford Circus
Closed Sunday and bank holidays – booking essential

Carte £26/73

Goodman is a Russian-owned New York steakhouse in Mayfair, which sounds like a sketch from the UN's Christmas party. Wood and leather give it an authentic feel and it has captured that macho swagger that often seems to accompany the eating of red meat. Tables are usually full of guffawing men, with their jackets thrown over the back of their chairs and their sleeves rolled up. The American and Irish beef is mostly grain-fed and either dry or wet aged in-house – Australian beef is an option at lunch. It is cooked in a Josper oven using a blend of three types of charcoal and offered with a choice of four sauces. While the steaks, especially the rib-eye, are certainly worth coming for, side dishes tend to be more variable in quality.

Ⓝ Great British

British traditional

G3

14 North Audley St ✉ W1K 6WE
☎ (020) 7741 2233
www.eatbrit.com
⊖ Marble Arch
Closed 25 December, 1 January and Sunday dinner

Menu £16 (weekday dinner) – Carte £27/40

There are countless cuisines on offer in Mayfair but, for some reason, this quintessentially British part of London has never exactly been overrun with restaurants serving traditional British food. The Great British seeks to redress this balance by offering the best that Blighty has to offer, from fish pies to sherry trifles. You'll find sausages come with bubble and squeak, fish and chips with curry sauce, and apple crumble with 'proper' custard; and they haven't neglected Britain's greatest gift to the culinary world as breakfast is very popular here too. Perhaps the only gamble they've taken is in making the wine list exclusively English. The three roomed restaurant comes with photos and wood panelling and has a brooding, manly vibe.

Greenhouse ✿✿

innovative

G4

27a Hay's Mews ✉ W1J 5NY
✆ (020) 7499 3331
www.greenhouserestaurant.co.uk
⊖ Hyde Park Corner
Closed Saturday lunch, Sunday and bank holidays

Menu £29/110 – Carte £80/100

The Greenhouse

Chef Arnaud Bignon, who arrived in 2012 from Spondi restaurant in Athens, has taken the cooking at The Greenhouse to new heights. Before choosing your dishes, you have to decide on your menu and there's a plethora of them: a 6 course tasting menu, a set menu, an à la carte and a separate lunch menu, as well as a 6 course vegetable-inspired dinner menu. Whatever you go for, you'll find the food modern, innovative, technically impressive and well-balanced. The chef demonstrates his confidence and understanding of flavour combinations in dishes where coffee, morels and liquorice are matched with a veal chop, and calamansi and citrus powder are coupled with langoustines. His cooking comes with an invigorating freshness and ingredients are sourced from Europe's larder: there's Limousin veal, Dorset lamb, Cornish crab and Challans duck. The breadth of the wine list is astounding and includes vintages of Château Lafite back to 1870, Château Latour to 1900, Château Haut-Brion to 1945 and 14 vintages of La Tâche; the New World is not forgotten – there are 38 vintages of Penfolds Grange.

First Course

- Cornish crab with mint jelly, cauliflower, apple and curry.
- Scallops with ponzu, mandarin and samphire.

Main Course

- Milk-fed veal with Swiss chard, sage and galangal.
- John Dory, prawns, bomba rice, peas and satay.

Dessert

- Orange, saffron, date and filo pastry.
- Pear, lemon, ginger and coffee.

The Grill

British traditional

G4 

Dorchester Hotel,
Park Ln. ✉ W1K 1QA
✆ (020) 7629 8888
www.thedorchester.com
⊖ Hyde Park Corner

Menu £27/55 – Carte £42/64

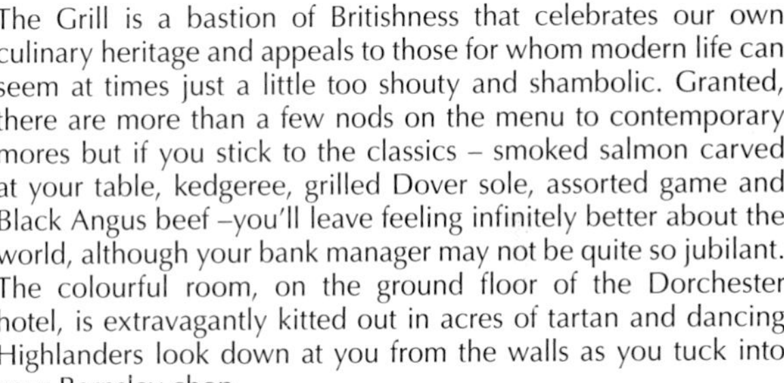

The Grill is a bastion of Britishness that celebrates our own culinary heritage and appeals to those for whom modern life can seem at times just a little too shouty and shambolic. Granted, there are more than a few nods on the menu to contemporary mores but if you stick to the classics – smoked salmon carved at your table, kedgeree, grilled Dover sole, assorted game and Black Angus beef –you'll leave feeling infinitely better about the world, although your bank manager may not be quite so jubilant. The colourful room, on the ground floor of the Dorchester hotel, is extravagantly kitted out in acres of tartan and dancing Highlanders look down at you from the walls as you tuck into your Barnsley chop.

Haozhan

Chinese

I3

8 Gerrard St ✉ W1D 5PJ
✆ (020) 7434 3838
www.haozhan.co.uk
⊖ Leicester Square
Closed 24-25 December

Menu £15/48 – Carte £20/78

A plethora of Chinatown restaurants vie for your attention by offering special deals or just brightening their neon. Haozhan adopts the more worthy policy of serving food that's a cut above the norm. Inside the somewhat garish looking menu is not the usual vast list but rather an interesting collection of dishes that owe more to a fusion style, with mostly Cantonese but other Asian influences too; head straight for the specialities, such as jasmine ribs or wasabi prawns. You'll find there's a freshness to the ingredients that also marks this restaurant out – for example, try the Tom Yum prawns in their pancake cones and leave room for the egg custard buns. Appropriately enough, the name Haozhan translates as "a good place to eat".

Hakkasan Mayfair ✿

Chinese

H3

17 Bruton St ✉ W1J 6QB
✆ (020) 7907 1888
www.hakkasan.com
⊖ Green Park
Closed 25 December – booking essential

Carte £32/74 s

Hakkasan Mayfair

This is less a copy, more a sister to the original Hakkasan; a sister who's just as fun and glamorous but simply lives in a far nicer part of town. As with many of the best addresses, it doesn't draw attention to itself – you could easily walk past the entrance without knowing, and that adds to the appeal. The biggest difference is that this Hakkasan has a funky, more casual ground floor to go with the downstairs dining room; but it's still worth booking for the lower level, as a walk down the stairs will heighten the sense of occasion and add a little mystery. The menu of Cantonese treats is an appealing tome; dim sum must surely be the only way to go at lunch, while the signature dishes, such as silver cod with champagne and honey, and Jasmine tea smoked chicken, can be saved for dinner. Desserts are unashamedly tailored towards European tastes but there's a fine range of speciality teas, as well as an impressive selection of cocktails. The staff, dressed in black – what else? – know their menu backwards, so are more than willing to help those seeking guidance.

First Course

- Crispy duck salad with pomelo, pine nut and shallot.
- Jasmine tea smoked organic pork ribs.

Main Course

- Roasted silver cod with champagne and honey.
- Short rib of beef with chanterelles.

Dessert

- Hazelnut Jivara bomb with dark chocolate sauce.
- Coconut and lime tapioca with pineapple beignet.

Hawksmoor

meats and grills

H3

5A Air St ✉ W1B 4EA
(020) 7406 3980
www.thehawksmoor.com/airstreet
Piccadilly Circus
Closed 25-26 December – booking advisable

Menu £23/26 – Carte £31/54

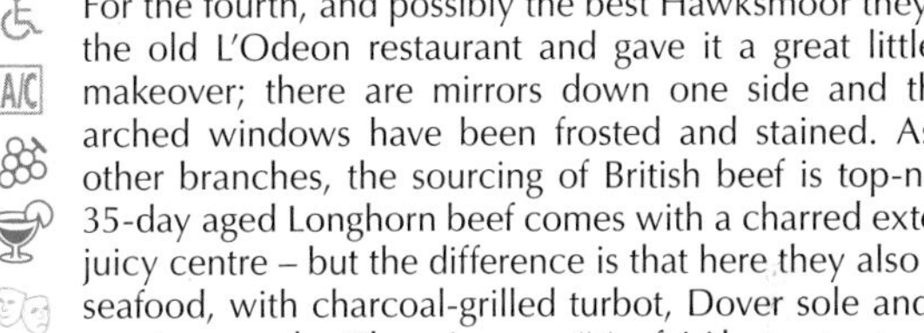

For the fourth, and possibly the best Hawksmoor they took over the old L'Odeon restaurant and gave it a great little art deco makeover; there are mirrors down one side and the famous arched windows have been frosted and stained. As with the other branches, the sourcing of British beef is top-notch – the 35-day aged Longhorn beef comes with a charred exterior and a juicy centre – but the difference is that here they also offer great seafood, with charcoal-grilled turbot, Dover sole and monkfish proving popular. The prices are 'Mayfair' but not extreme; there's an excellent Express Menu at lunch and very early evening, and staff are a delightful and well organised lot. Soak up the boisterous atmosphere by first having a cocktail in the bar.

HIX

British traditional

H3

66-70 Brewer St. ✉ WIF 9UP
(020) 7292 3518
www.hixsoho.co.uk
Piccadilly Circus
Closed 25-26 December

Menu £18 (lunch) – Carte £27/94

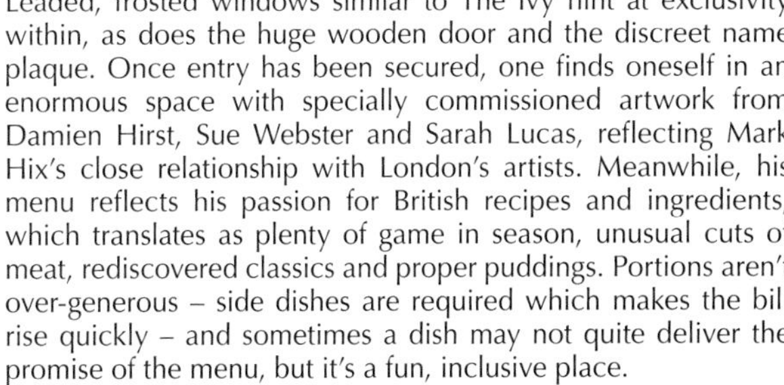

Leaded, frosted windows similar to The Ivy hint at exclusivity within, as does the huge wooden door and the discreet name plaque. Once entry has been secured, one finds oneself in an enormous space with specially commissioned artwork from Damien Hirst, Sue Webster and Sarah Lucas, reflecting Mark Hix's close relationship with London's artists. Meanwhile, his menu reflects his passion for British recipes and ingredients, which translates as plenty of game in season, unusual cuts of meat, rediscovered classics and proper puddings. Portions aren't over-generous – side dishes are required which makes the bill rise quickly – and sometimes a dish may not quite deliver the promise of the menu, but it's a fun, inclusive place.

Hélène Darroze at The Connaught ✿✿

French G3

Connaught Hotel,
Carlos Pl. ✉ W1K 2AL
✆ (020) 3147 7200
www.the-connaught.co.uk
⊖ Bond Street

Closed 2 weeks August, 2 weeks January, Sunday and Monday – booking essential

Menu £35/85

Connaught Hotel

London's diverse and vibrant dining scene has had quite an influence on Hélène Darroze and although she insists it is France and her native region of Landes that informs her cooking, she also uses interesting flavours of a more international persuasion. In essence, the dishes appear relatively simple on the plate, even though their descriptions on the menu can be quite florid. She is keen to champion the high quality produce they use, much more of which now comes from within the UK. Bayonne ham sliced on their gleaming Berkel machine heralds the start of one's meal and delightful mignardises round things off. Dishes can be surprisingly robust and the presentation is often exquisite. Service is courteous and professional and the staff also manage to inject personality into the proceedings. Meanwhile, the room itself is warm and elegant, thanks to India Mahdavi's clever softening of all that mahogany wall panelling. A small private dining room has been added adjacent to the wine cellar, two floors below.

First Course

- Duck foie gras with Yorkshire rhubarb chutney and lemon verbena jelly.
- Tagliatelle with parmesan, beurre noisette, asparagus and morels.

Main Course

- XXL scallop with tandoori spices, confit carrot and citrus mousseline.
- Duck breast glazed with maple syrup and fondant Tokyo turnip.

Dessert

- Manjari chocolate, ganache and galangal crème brûlée.
- Apple compote and sage flavoured panna cotta.

Hibiscus ✿✿

innovative

H3

29 Maddox St ✉ W1S 2PA
(020) 7629 2999
www.hibiscusrestaurant.co.uk
⊖ Oxford Circus
Closed 21 December-7 January, Monday except October-December, Sunday and bank holidays

Menu £35/88

Hibiscus

Claude Bosi is a chef who doesn't like to stand still – quite literally sometimes, because if he isn't in his kitchen he's probably off in distant lands searching for new ideas and unusual ingredients. His cooking is certainly innovative and original but where it excels is that it's always tethered to a sound base and there is rarely a redundant ingredient on the plate. Most diners submit to his skills by simply choosing the primary ingredients, deciding on the number of courses they fancy and then waiting to see what the kitchen comes up with. Those who aren't so keen on surprises should consider coming for lunch: not only is the menu appealingly priced but the culinary flights of fancy are reined in somewhat and the make-up of each dish is a little more classical. The restaurant itself has also changed; the brighter new look has not only resulted in the room feeling a little bigger but has also lead to a lightening of the atmosphere, something that has been helped too by the more confident and chattier service.

First Course

- Scallops with an apple and hazelnut crust, pork pie sauce.
- Pumpkin velouté with pickled pumpkin.

Main Course

- Sea bream filled with morels, kaffir lime, coffee and morel fricassée.
- Slow-cooked veal cheeks, chervil root, chestnut, crispy smoked eel.

Dessert

- Hibiscus tarte au chocolate, Indonesian basil ice cream.
- Iced chestnut parfait with persimmon.

Hix Mayfair

British traditional

H3

Brown's Hotel,
Albemarle St ✉ W1S 4BP
✆ (020) 7518 4004
www.roccofortecollection.com
⊖ Green Park

Menu £28/33 – Carte £31/63

Brown's is a thoroughly British hotel with a long history so it makes sense for its restaurant to celebrate Britain's own culinary traditions. Mark Hix – surely one of London's busiest restaurateurs at the moment – was the man entrusted with the task and he has put together an appealing looking menu that's big on seasonality and provenance. Good use is made of ingredients from across the UK, such as Portland crab, Morecambe Bay shrimps and Aberdeenshire beef and there's also a daily roast for lunch, served from the trolley. The traditional feel of the wood-panelled dining room is enlivened by the works from leading contemporary British artists, which ensure that the atmosphere never gets too solemn.

Hush

modern

H3

8 Lancashire Ct., Brook St. ✉ W1S 1EY
✆ (020) 7659 1500
www.hush.co.uk
⊖ Bond Street
Closed Easter, 25-26 December, 1 January and Sunday – booking essential

Menu £13 (lunch) – Carte £23/48

Any time the mercury nudges past 16° Londoners feel the need to eat outside, even if that means battling with passers-by for a few feet of pavement space. There's no such indignity at Hush as you'll find in this courtyard once used to store materials and cloth for Savile Row a large and appealing terrace. Its occupants are usually here for the long haul and it's easy to understand why: the menu is a likeable, all-purpose affair which skips merrily around Europe so that you have duck confit, a risotto or a schnitzel; if you want to stay closer to home then order one of their terrific homemade pies. You can also just pop in for cocktails and share some small plates and if you're in no hurry you can simply stay put for afternoon tea.

Imli Street

Indian

I3

167-169 Wardour St ✉ W1F 8WR
✆ (020) 7287 4243
www.imlistreet.com
⊖ Tottenham Court Road
Closed 25-26 December and 1 January – bookings not accepted

Carte approx. £16

A/C
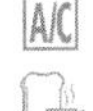
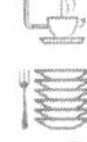

No restaurant can afford to stand still these days and Imli has responded to current trends by making a few changes. In terms of looks, the restaurant is now much brighter and that includes the once claustrophobic basement. They've also installed a horse-shoe shaped bar to satisfy the growing demand for cocktails. With the new look comes a new menu; fresh, vibrant sharing plates under the headings 'Railway Cuisine', 'Coastal Shack' and 'Food Cart' are essentially influenced by the south of India; 'Beyond Borders' dishes are more Indo-Chinese in origin. The two things that haven't changed are the service, which remains keen and attentive, and the no booking policy – but with a bar this good, waiting for a table is hardly an ordeal.

Imperial China

Chinese

I3

White Bear Yard, 25a Lisle St ✉ WC2H 7BA
✆ (020) 7734 3388
www.imperialchina-london.com
⊖ Leicester Square
Booking advisable

Menu £20 – Carte £17/70

A/C

Heave open the heavy smoked-glass double doors, cross the bamboo bridge and you'll be transported to a calm oasis that seems a world away from the bustle outside. Sharp, well-organised service and comfortable surroundings are not the only things that set this restaurant apart: the Cantonese cooking exudes freshness and vitality, whether that's the steamed dumplings or the XO minced pork with fine beans. Indeed, they pride themselves on seafood and their 'lobster feasts' are very popular - the personable staff are also more than happy to offer recommendations. There are eight private rooms of various sizes available upstairs and these are often in full swing. The owners also run Beijing Dumpling a few doors down.

Kai ✿

Chinese

G3

65 South Audley St ✉ W1K 2QU
✆ (020) 7493 8988
www.kaimayfair.co.uk
⊖ Hyde Park Corner
Closed 25-26 December and 1 January – booking essential

Menu £27 (lunch) – Carte £39/90

Kai

A warm and sincere welcome and elegant, opulent and intimate surroundings tell you immediately that Kai is a different kind of Chinese restaurant, although what the incongruously funky music is telling you is anyone's guess. Beg the indulgence of your date or dining companions by taking time to read the menu fully because the descriptions of exotically named dishes like 'A nest of imperial jewels' and 'Mermaids of the mist' will have a Pavlovian effect on your appetite, although the prices may also have the reverse effect on your wallet. The cooking uses influences from across China; some dishes are re-workings of popular classics – the Sichuan chicken cashew nuts being a sophisticated Kung Pao. The best ones are those created by chef Alex Chow such as the wasabi prawns and oriental lamb shank but do also order the superb Peking duck. The kitchen can adapt the spiciness of certain dishes but it's dangerous to say you like it hot if you don't really. Charming staff are on hand to offer friendly advice; and ask for the ground floor, not the basement.

First Course

- Braised abalone with broccolini.
- Prawns with wasabi mayonnaise, mango and basil seeds.

Main Course

- Roasted Chilean sea bass with black vinegar syrup.
- 5 hour oriental spiced pork belly with ginger, rice wine, cinnamon and soy.

Dessert

- Mango cake, palm sugar ice cream and pandan milkshake.
- Almond panna cotta with dragon fruit, strawberries and kiwi.

Kiku

Japanese H4

17 Half Moon St. ✉ W1J 7BE
✆ (020) 7499 4208
www.kikurestaurant.co.uk
⊖ Green Park
Closed 25-27 December, 1 January, Sunday and lunch on bank holidays

Menu £20/25 – Carte £21/84

A/C

It's not just the fact that it's family owned and has been here for over 35 years that makes Kiku unlike most Mayfair restaurants – this Japanese restaurant is also very sweet. There's an authentic simplicity to its decoration and a pleasing earnestness to the service; most evenings the majority of diners appear to be homesick Japanese. Virtually every style of Japanese cuisine is on offer, from shabu shabu to sukiyaki, yakitori to teriyaki and if you want to try something a little different, like sliced squid and guts or salmon zosui (rice soup), then here's your chance. The extensive à la carte menu is supplemented by a number of set menus and these are worth exploring if you want an all-round experience.

Koya

Japanese I3

49 Frith St ✉ W1D 4SG
✆ (020) 7434 4463
www.koya.co.uk
⊖ Tottenham Court Road
Closed Christmas – bookings not accepted

Carte £13/28

Authenticity is the key to Koya's success: the Japanese wheat is kneaded by foot, while the dashi base stock is freshly made every day. Do your bit by slurping unselfconsciously to get the full benefit of these delicious noodles with their wonderful chewiness or 'koshi'. They come in three styles: hot in a hot broth, cold with a hot broth or cold with a cold dipping sauce, and arrive on a bamboo mat and with a sprinkling of nori (seaweed). Be sure to order some small plates too, such as the onsen tamago, a delicate poached egg, or crisp tempura. A small selection of sake, shochu, beer and wine is also available. The decoration is modest, service is sweet and if you aren't here before the noren curtain is put out then be prepared to queue.

Little Social

French

H3

5 Pollen St ✉ W1S 1NE
✆ (020) 7870 3730
www.littlesocial.co.uk
⊖ Oxford Circus
Closed Sunday and bank holidays – booking essential

Menu £25 (lunch) – Carte £33/41

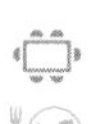

Jason Atherton wisely decided that keeping an eye on your growing restaurant empire is easier when you have two restaurants in the same street. In contrast with the more formal Pollen Street Social, Little Social is a lively French bistro with a clubby, masculine feel and an appealing, deliberately worn look. The best seats are the discreet leather booths at the back; avoid the bar as you can get crowded out by those having a pre-prandial drink. Service is bright, breezy and capable and the French food is fairly classic, with the occasional modern twist. The menu constantly evolves and the choice is enhanced by daily specials; the soups and steaks are winners but, for the more adventurous, there could be pork head terrine or ox cheeks.

Manchurian Legends

Chinese

I3

16 Lisle St ✉ WC2H 7BE
✆ (020) 7287 6606
www.manchurianlegends.com
⊖ Leicester Square
Closed Christmas

Menu £14/22 – Carte £19/31

China's cuisine is one of enormous diversity, with each region having its own style and specialities. With Manchurian Legends, Londoners now have the chance to try dishes from a less familiar part of the country: Dongbei, which means 'northeast'. As winters here are long, stews and BBQ dishes are popular and so are pickled ingredients; try the delicious Xin-Jian-style fried lamb or the juicy duck with pickled vegetables. The cooking is certainly robust of flavour yet also delivers on richness – but ignore the chilli scale next to each dish at your peril! Further warmth comes from the sweet natured service.

MASH

meats and grills

H3

77 Brewer St ✉ W1F 9ZN
✆ (020) 7734 2608
www.mashsteak.dk/restaurants/london
⊖ Piccadilly Circus
Closed 23-25 December and Sunday lunch

Menu £22/25 – Carte £35/71

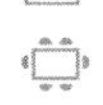

It took a brave team to take on the daunting task of raising the old Titanic restaurant from the depths of Brewer Street but that is what a group of experienced Copenhagen restaurateurs did in 2012. In restoring many of the original art deco features and combining them with contemporary fittings, they have created a striking 350-seater restaurant. Instead of showcasing Danish cuisine, they have gone for a 'Modern American Steak House'. They offer mostly Danish prime and corn-fed Nebraskan and Uruguayan beef and it's clear the kitchen knows what it's doing. Starters are equally robust and include charcuterie and foie gras. Add in a great cocktail bar, slick service and an impressive wine list and you have a seriously grown up restaurant.

Matsuri

Japanese

H4

15 Bury St. ✉ SW1Y 6AL
✆ (020) 7839 1101
www.matsuri-restaurant.com
⊖ Green Park
Closed 25 December and 1 January

Menu £39/55 – Carte £30/126

One of the capital's longest running Japanese restaurants remains refreshingly impervious to the contemporary trend towards 'reinterpretation' and instead focuses on traditional dishes and combinations. You're whisked downstairs past the drums, fans and masks by gracious and traditionally costumed ladies where you can choose between teppan-yaki or a seat at the sushi counter. You'll be assailed by a plethora of menus ranging from a chef's special to a Wagyu beef menu as well as a monthly changing list of seasonal specials such as crab marinated in rice vinegar or pork shabu-shabu. Once decided, you need do nothing except sit and appreciate a bit of knife juggling while enjoying fresh ingredients that taste of what they should.

Maze ✿

modern

G3

10-13 Grosvenor Sq ✉ W1K 6JP
✆ (020) 7107 0000
www.gordonramsay.com/maze
⊖ Bond Street

Menu £25 (lunch) – Carte £32/44

Gordon Ramsay Holdings

Standing still should never be an option for any restaurant – however successful – and at Gordon Ramsay's Maze there has been a little tinkering taking place. A cocktail 'mixologist' has arrived to draw in more customers to the bar and there is now a greater element of Asian influence to the cooking. The hallmark precision is evident in all the dishes; combinations are not overworked and flavours and textures have been intelligently thought out. There's a deceptive simplicity here and a playful element too; the Asian tones enhance rather than overpower the ingredients. Four dishes per person should be about right, and the set lunch and early evening menus are bargains. The iPad wine list is more than just a gimmick – it's a great way of running through the list, which may be light on mature vintages but has strength in depth across all regions. The David Rockwell designed room looks as good as ever and the restaurant continues to attract an appealingly mixed crowd, from the romantically inclined to the corporately minded.

First Course

- Beef fillet tataki, wakame seaweed, pickled onion and ginger.
- Duck and foie gras parfait, peaches and wine jelly.

Main Course

- Lobster, tiger prawn and salmon dumpling in a lemongrass broth.
- Rose veal loin and tongue with spring bean casserole.

Dessert

- Lemon tart with toasted meringue and crème fraîche sorbet.
- Mango mousse with yuzu ice cream.

Maze Grill

meats and grills

G3

London Marriott Hotel Grosvenor Square,
10-13 Grosvenor Sq ✉ W1K 6JP
✆ (020) 7495 2211
www.gordonramsay.com/mazegrill
⊖ Bond Street

Menu £24 (lunch and early dinner) – Carte £27/73

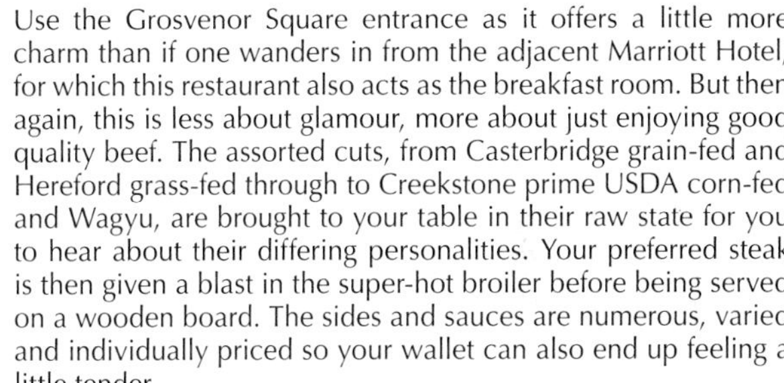

Use the Grosvenor Square entrance as it offers a little more charm than if one wanders in from the adjacent Marriott Hotel, for which this restaurant also acts as the breakfast room. But then again, this is less about glamour, more about just enjoying good quality beef. The assorted cuts, from Casterbridge grain-fed and Hereford grass-fed through to Creekstone prime USDA corn-fed and Wagyu, are brought to your table in their raw state for you to hear about their differing personalities. Your preferred steak is then given a blast in the super-hot broiler before being served on a wooden board. The sides and sauces are numerous, varied and individually priced so your wallet can also end up feeling a little tender.

Mele e Pere

Italian

I3

46 Brewer St ✉ W1F 9TF
✆ (020) 7096 2096
www.meleepere.co.uk
⊖ Piccadilly Circus
Closed 25-26 December, 1 January and Easter

Menu £18 (dinner) – Carte £23/38

Faced with a wall of Murano glass apples and pears as colourful as the street you're standing in, you'd be forgiven for thinking this is a gallery. But head downstairs – the 'apple and pears'? – and you'll find yourself in a vaulted, if somewhat hard-edged room with an appealing Vermouth bar. The owner-chef has worked in some decent London kitchens over a few years but hails from Verona so expect a selection of gutsy Italian dishes, like rabbit with olives, shoulder of lamb, and tripe with grated Parmigiano. Main courses come with a side dish that you get to choose and puds are excellent, especially the panna cotta. The weekly changing pre-theatre menu should be enough in itself for this restaurant to make its mark in Soho.

Mews of Mayfair

modern

H3

10-11 Lancashire Ct, Brook St (1st floor) ✉ W1S 1EY
✆ (020) 7518 9388
www.mewsofmayfair.com
⊖ Bond Street
Closed 25 December and Sunday dinner

Carte £20/72

Mews manages that trick of being cool and bright in summer and warm and inviting in winter. The relative serenity of the pretty restaurant is in sharp contrast to the crowds in the narrow lane and busy cocktail bar below, while the private dining room on the next floor up is a very pleasant space. The menu is very appealing and sufficiently sensitive to the changing seasons, so expect venison in winter, spring lamb and summer fruit. Simpler dishes are also pepped up, so burgers come with an optional foie gras topping and fish and chips arrive with a wasabi tartare. Flavours are sometimes compromised by an over-eagerness to make dishes look pretty but prices are generally sensible and the atmosphere thoroughly civilised.

Mint Leaf

Indian

I4

Suffolk Pl ✉ SW1Y 4HX
✆ (020) 7930 9020
www.mintleafrestaurant.com
⊖ Piccadilly Circus
Closed 25-26 December and 1 January

Menu £14 – Carte £28/42

Indian restaurants come in a variety of guises these days: Mint Leaf is from the contemporary, slick and designery school. This vast subterranean space with its moody lighting can seat over 250 but it comes divided into seven different areas so you're never rattling around. There is even an enormous bar running the length of the room for those wanting to make a night of it. The menu is also quite a lengthy affair, with many choices available in small or larger sizes. The best bet is to share a few dishes such as the soft shell crab or jumbo prawns, and then have your own curry – the kitchen's strength. The serving team are a mixed bunch: some will explain dishes enthusiastically; others seem keener upselling drinks.

Momo

North-African H3

25 Heddon St. ✉ W1B 4BH
✆ (020) 7434 4040
www.momoresto.com
⊖ Oxford Circus
Closed 25 December, 1 January and Sunday lunch

Menu £20/52 – Carte £31/47

Lanterns, rugs, trinkets and music all contribute to the authentic Moroccan atmosphere that makes Momo such a fun night out. That being said, it's even more fun if you come with friends as tables of two can get somewhat overawed. The menu is divided into three: a rather expensive set menu, traditional dishes and Momo specialities. The traditional section is the best as here you'll find the classics from pastilla to tagines; the Momo specialities are more contemporary in their make-up. Whatever you order, you'll end up with a pile of couscous and enough good food to last the week. The wine list lacks affordable bottles but there's a great bar downstairs. If it weren't for the absence of cigarette smoke, you could be in Marrakech.

The National Dining Rooms

British modern I3/4

Sainsbury Wing, The National Gallery, Trafalgar Sq
✉ WC2N 5DN
✆ (020) 7747 2525
www.peytonandbyrne.co.uk
⊖ Charing Cross
Closed 24-26 December – (lunch only and Friday dinner)

Menu £20 – Carte £30/37

There's usually a queue but don't panic – it's either those wanting the bakery section or others realising they should have booked. Oliver Peyton's restaurant on the first floor of the National Gallery's Sainsbury Wing is a bright, open affair, enriched by Paula Rego's complex mural 'Crivelli's Garden'. Ask for a table by the window, not just for the views of Trafalgar Square but also because the other half of the room is darker and under the eaves of the early Renaissance on the floor above. The menu champions British cooking and produce; fish and cheeses are the highlight – pies and puds will write-off the afternoon. The set menu represents decent value and is popular with the customers, who resemble a bridge club up from Winchester for the day.

Murano ✿

Italian

G4

20 Queen St ✉ W1J 5PP
✆ (020) 7495 1127
www.angela-hartnett.com
⊖ Green Park
Closed Christmas and Sunday

Menu £25, £30/85

XXX

A/C

Murano

Chef owner Angela Hartnett is clearly immeasurably proud of her stylish Mayfair restaurant and it's easy to understand why. The cooking exhibits an appealing lightness of touch borne out of greater confidence in her ingredients, which come from Italy and the British Isles, but also in her own abilities and those of Diego Cardoso, her head chef. Her passion for Italian food is palpable. The food uses a blend of classical techniques so that flavours are refined, defined and balanced. The fish dishes, such as sea bass with mussels, are particularly delicious and stand out for their clarity and freshness. The service has also become a little more relaxed these days which suits the place more than the somewhat overly formal style previously adopted; it helps too when you have plenty of regulars who have got to know the staff well. Named after the famous glassware from the Venetian island of Murano, the restaurant is stylish and elegant and comes with an appealing freshness and vitality.

First Course

- Pumpkin tortelli, sage butter, crushed amaretti.
- Peas, mint and duck egg.

Main Course

- Monkfish, broccoli purée, crushed almonds, chicken jus.
- Loin and belly of rabbit with Dijon mustard.

Dessert

- Rice pudding soufflé with rum and raisin ice cream.
- Apple bavarois, Granny Smith sorbet and popcorn tuille.

Nobu ✿

Japanese

G4

Metropolitan Hotel,
19 Old Park Ln ✉ W1Y 1LB
✆ (020) 7447 4747
www.noburestaurants.com
⊖ Hyde Park Corner
Booking essential

Menu £35 – Carte £29/78

Nobu

Nobu restaurants now number over twenty and are spread around the world, but this one was the first to open in Europe, back in 1997, and came not long after the original in Manhattan. The two London branches can be considered the pick of the bunch and much of the credit is down to the long-standing executive chef, Mark Edwards. He has also been responsible for introducing the Osusume menu, which is exclusive to London and is aimed at offering neophytes the opportunity to discover what makes the food – Japanese with South American influences – quite so interesting. The reason is that the flavours are unique, the combinations wholly complementary and the ingredients top-notch – it's little wonder the dishes have been plagiarised across the city. The enthusiasm of the staff is undimmed and while the restaurant is perhaps less obviously glitzy than its younger sibling, that does mean that the fashionable crowd here are a little less excitable. Those who don't have the time to visit can now simply pick up a lunch or pre-theatre bento box.

First Course

- Rock shrimp ceviche.
- Yellowtail sashimi with jalapeño.

Main Course

- Snow crab with spicy sauce.
- Tenderloin of beef with wasabi pepper sauce.

Dessert

- Chocolate bento box.
- Banana split 3000.

Nobu Berkeley St ✿

Japanese H3

15 Berkeley St. ✉ W1J 8DY
✆ (020) 7290 9222
www.noburestaurants.com
⊖ Green Park
Closed 25 December, 1 January and lunch Saturday and Sunday – booking essential

Menu £35, £33/90 – Carte £34/73

Nobu

Judging by the packs of paparazzi who jostle for space by the entrance, Nobu's appeal shows no sign of wavering, particularly amongst those who like a little glitz and glamour with their sushi and sashimi. You can expect the usual favourites, from Nobu tacos to the ubiquitous black cod with miso but it's the use of the wood oven that makes this branch of the international chain a little different from the others. It's used to prepare a number of meat dishes, from whole roast poussin to duck breast with wasabi salsa, and these are well worth ordering as the wood flavour really comes through. The South American element adds zest to the dishes and, with Peruvian food being all the rage at the moment, it means that Nobu is as on-trend as ever. The service is very well organised and staff have an impressive knowledge of the menu – do take heed of their recommendations as they can balance your meal well. Have a cocktail in the busy ground floor bar before heading up to the restaurant. And put your sunglasses on as you leave if you want your photo taken.

First Course

- Yellowtail sashimi with jalapeño dressing.
- Rock shrimp tempura.

Main Course

- Black cod with miso.
- Secreto Iberian pork with Nobu sauces.

Dessert

- Chocolate tart with sake kasu ice cream.
- Spiced rice pudding.

Nopi

Mediterranean H3

21-22 Warwick St. ✉ W1B 5NE
✆ (020) 7494 9584
www.nopi-restaurant.com
⊖ Piccadilly Circus
Closed 25-26 December, 1 January and Sunday dinner

Carte £22/50

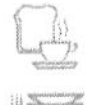

After relishing his delis and devouring his cookbooks, fans of Yotam Ottolenghi are now flocking to his first 'proper' restaurant. It's an enthusiastically run and luminous affair and is spread over two floors, all whitewashed walls, tiles, marble and brass. The communally minded can ask to share one of the two large tables downstairs which face the open kitchen and are surrounded by the chefs' supplies. Flavours take in the Mediterranean, the Middle East and various parts of Asia, and the menu is subdivided under the headings of Veg, Fish or Meat; one of each per person should suffice. The veggie dishes are best, such as burrata with coriander seeds, but the fish creations like grilled mackerel with a pea and mint salad are also refreshing.

Only Running Footman

British traditional

5 Charles St ✉ W1J 5DF
✆ (020) 7499 2988
www.therunningfootmanmayfair.com
⊖ Green Park.

Carte £24/39

Apparently the owners added 'only' to the title when they found out that theirs was the only pub in the land called 'The Running Footman'. Spread over several levels, it offers cookery demonstrations and private dinners along with its two floors of dining. Downstairs is where the action usually is, with its menu offering pub classics from steak sandwiches to fishcakes, but you can't book here and it's always packed. Upstairs is where you'll find a surprisingly formal dining room and here they do take reservations. Its menu is far more ambitious and European in its influence but the best dishes are still the simpler ones, with desserts a strength. You can't help feeling that you would be having a lot more fun below stairs, though.

One Leicester Street ✿

British traditional

I3

1 Leicester St ✉ WC2H 7BL
✆ (020) 3301 8020
www.oneleicesterstreet.com
⊖ Leicester Square
Booking advisable

Carte £20/50

One Leicester Street

There are new owners and a subtle new look for this restaurant bang in the heart of the city. The St John people had to reluctantly let it go, having spent considerable amounts of money and time converting it from the old Manzi's. It now shares the same ownership as Town Hall in Bethnal Green; they have softened the ground floor restaurant somewhat from the previous unrelentingly utilitarian look, and have also given the bedrooms a makeover. When it came to the food, they were wise enough not to make too many changes and the good news is that the kitchen team and the style of cooking have remained largely the same. The daily changing menu is not overly long and is subdivided into headings of 'shellfish/fish', 'meat/offal' and 'vegetables' and there are a few dishes to share. The food is all about seasonality and simplicity so there is no hiding place when it comes to the quality of the ingredients. Service is bright and cheerful and the staff know the menu well so can make considered recommendations.

First Course

- Crab, fennel and sea purslane.
- Salt hake and tartare sauce.

Main Course

- Smoked wild sea trout, broad beans and buttermilk.
- Ox cheek, celeriac and pickled walnuts.

Dessert

- Brown butter and honey tart.
- Rhubarb and sherry trifle.

N La Petite Maison

French H3

54 Brooks Mews ✉ W1K 4EG
✆ (020) 7495 4774
www.lpmlondon.co.uk
⊖ Bond Street
Closed Christmas-New Year – booking essential

Carte £31/62 s

A/C

A little piece of southern France and Ligurian Italy in Mayfair. The sister operation to the Nice original has a great, buzzy feel which is almost as enticing as the aromas from the kitchen. There's more than a soupçon of glamour and the staff, in their aprons and bow ties, give the impressive that nothing ever fazes them. Simply reading the menus will improve your tan: there are over 20 starters and mains and you can expect lots of healthy olive oil, artichokes, peppers, lemons and tomatoes. There's a fresh pasta of the day, seafood is popular and the whole chicken or gigot of lamb for two are worth ordering. This is a proper neighbourhood restaurant – but as that neighbourhood happens to be Mayfair, don't expect down-to-earth prices.

N Pitt Cue Co.

meats and grills H3

1 Newburgh St ✉ W1F 7RB
✆ (020) 7287 5578
www.pittcue.co.uk
⊖ Oxford Circus
Closed 25 December, 1 January and Sunday dinner – bookings not accepted

Carte £21/28

When the young owners started selling their version of American barbecue out of a van, word of (electronic) mouth spread so quickly that they soon found this more permanent spot. It's a tiny place, with a bourbon bar on the ground floor – try one of their whiskey sours – and seating for just 18 in the stark basement, so be prepared for some queuing. The menu changes daily but the three constants are house sausage, pulled pork and beef ribs; these are dry-rubbed, smoked in-house for 6 hours and then roasted. All meats come with house pickle and a side dish like bone marrow mash or excellent green chilli slaw and the food's served on enamel tin trays, which adds a little penitentiary chic to proceedings. It's loud, messy, filling and fun.

Plum Valley

Chinese I3

20 Gerrard St. ✉ W1D 6JQ
✆ (020) 7494 4366
⊖ Leicester Square
Closed 23-24 December

Menu £38 – Carte £19/37

Is Chinatown finally casting off its tourist-trap reputation? Plum Valley is the latest venture with genuine aspirations to open in Gerrard Street and its contemporary styling gives the street a much-needed boost. The striking black façade makes it easy to notice, while flattering lighting and layered walls give the interior a dash of sophistication. The chef is from Chiu Chow, a region near Guangdong, and his menu is largely based on Cantonese cooking, with occasional forays into Vietnam and Thailand as well as the odd nod towards contemporary presentation. Dim sum is his kitchen's main strength which fits nicely with the all-day opening of the restaurant. If only those doing the service could muster the same levels of enthusiasm.

Polpo Soho

Italian H3

41 Beak St. ✉ W1F 9SB
✆ (020) 7734 4479
www.polpo.co.uk
⊖ Oxford Circus
Closed dinner 24 December, 25-26 and 31 December, 1 January and Sunday dinner – (bookings not taken at dinner)

Carte £12/32

Opening a Venetian bacaro in an 18C townhouse where Canaletto once lodged does seem providential and Polpo has indeed been packing them in since day one. The stripped-down faux-industrial look is more New York's SoHo than London's Soho, as is the evening no-reservation policy which means you'll probably have to wait. But the fun atmosphere and the appealing prices of the small plates will assuage any impatience you feel in waiting your turn. Order a couple of cicheti, like arancini or prosciutto, a plate of fritto misto, ham and pea risotto or Cotechino sausage along with a vegetable dish per person and you should leave satisfied; if you do over-order, it's not going to break the bank. Venetian wines, available by the carafe, complete the picture.

Pollen Street Social ✿

innovative H3

8-10 Pollen St ✉ W1S 1NQ
✆ (020) 7290 7600
www.pollenstreetsocial.com
⊖ Oxford Circus
Closed 25-26 December, 1-2 January, Sunday and bank holidays – booking essential

Menu £30 (lunch) – Carte £51/64

Pollen Street Social

Jason Atherton may have opened another couple of places in town but there's been no dropping of standards here at his HQ, and Pollen Street Social is now firmly established, with everyone clear about the look and direction of the restaurant. There was a little tinkering done in their second year when Jason stopped with the 'small plates' thing and reverted back to the more traditional starter-main course-dessert format. It's well worth asking for a table in the main room with its 'dessert' bar and glass-fronted kitchen, because this is where the action is. What has never changed is the cooking here, which marries innovation and imagination with sound culinary techniques and an innate understanding of good ingredients. Dishes are elaborately constructed but there are never too many flavours or any discordant notes. Not only has a wine list been created that boasts impressive depth, breadth and variety, but there's also a great cocktail list, which includes their terrific version of a negroni.

First Course

- Roasted quail 'brunch' cereals, toast and tea.
- Crab salad, asparagus, citrus and radish.

Main Course

- Salt marsh lamb with Jerusalem artichoke and spiced aubergine.
- Squab, salt-baked red cabbage and beetroot stained onions.

Dessert

- Peanut parfait, cherry yuzu sorbet and nitro peanut.
- Lemon and white chocolate ganache.

Portrait

modern

I3

National Portrait Gallery (3rd floor), St Martin's Pl.
✉ WC2H 0HE
✆ (020) 7312 2490
www.searcys.co.uk
⊖ Charing Cross

Closed 24-26 December – booking essential – (lunch only and dinner Thursday-Saturday)

Menu £18/35

Portrait is on the third floor of the Ondaatje wing of the National Portrait Gallery and is run by the catering company Searcy's. You needn't ask for a window seat because the views, of recognisable rooftops and Nelson in Trafalgar Square, are just as good from any of the tables. Although open for breakfast and tea, this is principally a lunchtime operation, with dinner limited to Thursday, Friday and Saturday - the nights of the gallery's extended opening hours. The à la carte menu keeps things relatively light and the influences mostly from Europe; there is a good value set menu at weekends. This is a useful spot, not only for gallery visitors but also for those attending matinee performances at various nearby theatres.

Quaglino's

modern

H4

16 Bury St ✉ SW1Y 6AJ
✆ (020) 7930 6767
www.quaglinos-restaurant.co.uk
⊖ Green Park

Closed Christmas, Easter Monday and Sunday

Menu £15/26 – Carte £32/75

Few London restaurants are as synonymous with the early '90s as Quaglino's when, for a time, securing a table at this vast, glamorous, colourful and glitzy restaurant was the overriding ambition of many. The in-crowd may have since moved on – to other bustling, design-led restaurants which owe a debt to the trail blazed by 'Quag's' – but the old girl can still shake it on a weekend for those wanting a fun night out. The kitchen also feels invigorated and successfully delivers on the promise of the appealing, brasserie-style menu. Classics like pork belly, duck confit and chargrilled steaks are done well, along with shellfish from the 'Crustacea Counter'; look out too for the 'dish of the day'; perhaps a smoked haddock fishcake.

Quo Vadis

British modern

I3

26-29 Dean St ✉ W1D 3LL
✆ (020) 7437 9585
www.quovadissoho.co.uk
⊖ Tottenham Court Road
Closed 25-26 December, 1 January and bank holidays

Menu £18/20 – Carte £22/41

A/C

The neon sign and stained glass windows have long been familiar Dean Street landmarks and the building is inextricably linked with Soho's colourful past – it was once home to Karl Marx and opened as a restaurant in 1926. The current owners, the Hart brothers, recruited the services of Jeremy Lee in 2012 to rejuvenate the kitchen and his menu is a celebration of all things British. Start with some bites like delicious baked salsify or potted pork before enjoying excellent crab or grilled mackerel. There's a daily pie and a braised dish, and the grill dishes are flavoursome and filling. The pre-theatre menu is a steal. The room is stylish and elegant and while service is quite formally structured, it does need the occasional nudge.

Red Fort

Indian

I3

77 Dean St. ✉ W1D 3SH
✆ (020) 7437 2525
www.redfort.co.uk
⊖ Tottenham Court Road
Closed 25 December, lunch Saturday, Sunday and bank holidays – bookings advisable at dinner

Menu £15/59

Red Fort has been in Soho since 1983, although anyone who hasn't visited for a while will be surprised to see how up-to-date this Indian restaurant now is in the looks department. It's still quite a sizeable place but neatly broken up; the far end even boasts a little waterfall. Service isn't quite so memorable and staff could do with being a little more willing to engage with their customers but the menu does impress. It is not overlong and comes divided between starters, grills and main courses. Much of the produce comes from within the UK, such as Herdwick lamb, and there are also more unusual ingredients like rabbit used. Cooking is nicely balanced but the final bill can be a little high, especially when one has added breads, rice and vegetables.

Refuel

modern

I3

Soho Hotel,
4 Richmond Mews ✉ W1D 3DH
✆ (020) 7559 3007
www.sohohotel.com
⊖ Tottenham Court Road

Menu £15 – Carte £26/57

It comes as no surprise that a hotel as fashionable as The Soho has a restaurant as cool as Refuel. A large part of the room is given over to a slick cocktail bar and the lively atmosphere here tends to seep through into the restaurant through osmosis. Service in the hotel is one of its great strengths and the serving team here are a bright and enthusiastic bunch who are always ready with a smile. The menu is all about ease of eating and includes a popular section of grilled dishes, which could range from Dover sole to a burger, as well as assorted pasta dishes and salads for the image-conscious. Side dishes are needed but can leave you with a sizeable bill so it's worth considering the better value set menu.

Ritz Restaurant

British traditional

H4

Ritz Hotel,
150 Piccadilly ✉ W1J 9BR
✆ (020) 7493 8181
www.theritzlondon.com
⊖ Green Park

Menu £47/55 s – Carte £66/83 s

Dining at The Ritz is not just a mightily grand occasion but also provides a lesson in how things used to be done. The room is certainly unmatched in the sheer lavishness of its Louis XVI decoration; the table settings positively gleam thanks to all that polishing and there are probably more ranks to the serving team than in a ship's company. Little wonder they insist on jackets and ties. There's a plethora of menus: Ritz Classics could be saddle of Kentish lamb or roast sirloin; Ritz Traditions might include smoked salmon carved at your table or Dover sole filleted in front of you. For the full experience, have the six-course Sonata Menu, go at a weekend for a dinner dance and don't tell your bank manager.

Rosa's

Thai

I3

48 Dean St ✉ W1D 5BF
✆ (020) 7494 1638
www.rosaslondon.com
⊖ Leicester Square
Closed Easter and Christmas – booking advisable

Menu £20/30 – Carte £21/33

Those instinctively suspicious of anywhere too shiny and flashy will find Rosa's worn-in appearance suitably reassuring. The simple, pared down look of this authentic Thai café also adds to its intimate feel; the waitresses, in bright red T-shirts to match the colour of the façade, provide cheerful and swift service. The menu is appealing and wide-ranging and the relative heat levels of each dish are indicated. The chef may be from Chiang Mai but his cooking is influenced by all parts of the country. Signature dishes include warm minced chicken salad and a sweet pumpkin red curry; while squid, prawns, mussels and scallops all go into their seafood Pad Cha. The refreshing Tom Yam soup comes with lovely balance of sweet, sour and spice.

Sake No Hana

Japanese

H4

23 St James's St ✉ SW1A 1HA
✆ (020) 7925 8988
www.sakenohana.com
⊖ Green Park
Closed 25 December and Sunday

Menu £29/45 – Carte £18/91

It's not often one finds good food at the end of an escalator, but then not many restaurants occupy a building like this Grade II listed '60s edifice. What was once the office of The Economist is now home to this modern Japanese restaurant, where an enormous amount of cedar wood and bamboo is used to soften the surroundings. The original tatami seating has been replaced by regular tables and the corner sushi bar adds a little theatre. As with the great cocktails, the menu is best enjoyed when shared with a group; although there is plenty of sushi and sashimi on offer, it's best to stick to the more popular dishes like the snow crab tempura or one of the Iron Pot or Toban dishes like black cod rice or chicken with ginger and garlic.

Sartoria

Italian H3

20 Savile Row ✉ W1S 3PR
✆ (020) 7534 7000
www.sartoria-restaurant.co.uk
⊖ Green Park
Closed 25 December, Saturday lunch, Sunday and bank holidays

Menu £21 – Carte £31/55

If you're going to have any restaurant occupying a prime site in Savile Row then it might as well be Italian as they know one or two things about tailoring themselves. Sartoria is an elegant, smartly dressed restaurant that always seems to exude a certain poise and self-assurance, along with a little charm. There are subtle allusions to tailoring in the decoration and the sofa-style seating in the middle of the room is very appealing. The à la carte menu is an extensive number and prices can quickly add up, but the cooking, which covers all parts of the country, is undertaken with care and it's apparent that the ingredients are top-notch. Service is also not lacking in confidence and is overseen by assorted suited managers.

Scott's

fish and seafood 

20 Mount St ✉ W1K 2HE
✆ (020) 7495 7309
www.scotts-restaurant.com
⊖ Bond Street
Closed 25-26 December and 1 January

Carte £34/55

Standing in one of Mayfair's smartest streets is one of London's swankiest restaurants. Scott's is both an institution with a long, proud history and also a pretty fashionable hangout – a feat that few restaurants manage to pull off. The room has a wonderful buzz and rhythm to it and the wood panelling juxtaposed with the modern art adds to the clubby, but far from staid, atmosphere. The seafood menu is a comforting thing: there are six types of oyster, super fresh shellfish and fresh fish on the bone; meat eaters aren't forgotten and neither are veggies. Cooking is unfussy and satisfying, although all this simplicity and freshness doesn't come cheap. The service team are younger, brighter and more enthusiastic than in previous years.

Seven Park Place ✿

modern

H4

St James's Hotel and Club,
7-8 Park Pl ✉ SW1A 1LS
✆ (020) 7316 1615
www.stjameshotelandclub.com
⊖ Green Park
Closed Sunday and Monday – booking essential

Menu £26, £30/72

St James's Hotel and Club

The problem facing the owners of the St James's Hotel when they converted it from a private club, was in operating within the limited amount of space available. Accordingly, this small restaurant is somewhat concealed at the end of a bar through which one has to navigate. It's divided between two very contrasting rooms: the plush back room is the place to sit, as it holds just three large tables in its gilded setting; the outer room is not quite so intimate. The restaurant does, however, have a grown-up feel to it and the professional serving team make everyone feel suitably relaxed. The hotel has also got the right chef, cooking the right food. William Drabble made his name at Michael's Nook in Grasmere and Aubergine in Chelsea and his food has always displayed a sense of clarity, offering clean, unadulterated flavours. It is French at its base but the ingredients are decidedly British and mostly from more northerly parts, so expect lamb from the Lune Valley, game from Cumbria and shellfish from the west coast of Scotland.

First Course

- Seared scallops, braised celeriac purée and smoked bacon.
- Warm foie gras with vegetable confit.

Main Course

- Assiette of lamb.
- Grilled sea bass with artichokes, tomato and olives.

Dessert

- Milk chocolate mousse with clementine, salted caramel ice cream.
- Peach with lemon verbena, white chocolate and yoghurt cream.

Shoryu

Japanese

I3

9 Regent St. ✉ SW1Y 4LR
www.shoryuramen.com
⊖ Piccadilly Circus
Closed Christmas-New Year – bookings not accepted

Carte £11/27

The restorative powers of ramen are so great it should be prescribed on the NHS. Shoryu is owned by the Japan Centre opposite and specialises in Hakata tonkotsu ramen, which originated in Kyushu in the south and is the most popular style of ramen in Japan. At its base is a milky broth made from pork bones; to this is added springy hosomen noodles made in-house; nitamago (the boiled, marinated egg – an important element); sesame, and extra toppings of your choice; if you want a more robust flavour try a miso-based ramen. The surprisingly large menu includes other items with their roots in Chinese cooking, such as gyoza dumplings. Bookings aren't taken but waiting time is limited as customers are ready to face the world as soon as their bowl is empty.

Sketch (The Gallery)

modern

H3

9 Conduit St ✉ W1S 2XG
✆ (020) 7659 4500
www.sketch.uk.com
⊖ Oxford Circus
Closed 25-26 December – booking essential – (dinner only)

Carte £37/73

Martin Creed was the artist charged with changing the look of The Gallery restaurant on the ground floor of Sketch and he's turned it into a vibrant, witty and provocative space, where every piece of furniture and cutlery is different. The room is awash with collages of colour and is a cross between a restaurant and an art installation. The menus have also been updated and are now a blend of influences; some dishes are re-workings of brasserie classics, some are dishes with some added luxury, others are more original. So you can order steak tartare, a burger where the beef comes with foie gras, or scallops poached in a mussel jus with added galangal. The place is certainly fun, although the prices are not always particularly friendly.

Sketch (The Lecture Room & Library) ✿✿

French H3

9 Conduit St (1st floor) ✉ W1S 2XG
✆ (020) 7659 4500
www.sketch.uk.com
⊖ Oxford Circus

Closed last 2 weeks August, Saturday lunch, Sunday and Monday – booking essential

Menu £35/95 – Carte £88/126

A/C

Sketch

Stroll up Conduit Street and the only hint that something intriguing may be happening in this 18C townhouse is the presence of a bowler-hatted doorman and some flickering flames. Celebrated chef Pierre Gagnaire's glamorous London lair comes with various quirky design touches and eye-catching elements and that's even before you get to the beautifully decorated first floor Library and Lecture Room. The room is split in two, with the front section being the place to sit, although the chairs are so comfortable, sitting can easily become slumping. The menu may initially appear quite limited but the number of elements that make up each dish are certainly not. Gagnaire's style is highly individual, with the main 'plate' surrounded by its accompaniments; the quality of the produce is second to none and the kitchen's skill is evident. The wine list is impressive but with such elaborate constructions it's worth enlisting the sommelier's help to find a suitable match. The front of house team provides detailed service but does so with genuine warmth.

First Course

- 'Perfume of the Earth'.
- 'Sea Garden N° 10'.

Main Course

- Saddle of Quercy Lamb.
- Sea bass and Gillardeau oyster.

Dessert

- Pierre Gagnaire's 'Grand Dessert'.
- Vanilla soufflé, pear sorbet.

N Social Eating House ✿

modern H3

58 Poland St ✉ W1F 7NR
✆ (020) 7993 3251
www.socialeatinghouse.com
⊖ Oxford Circus
Closed Christmas, Sunday and bank holidays

Menu £21 (lunch) – Carte £29/42

Social Eating House

Jason Atherton has created a little bit of Brooklyn in one of Soho's lesser known streets – and by expanding his empire solves the problem of how to hang on to ambitious chefs. It's one of those places where the noise and bustle from the throng of customers hit you as you enter and you instantly feel you've come to the right place. It feels like it's been around for ages and the bare bricks, raw plastered walls, low ceiling and smoked glass help create what is a very sexy room – one that's bigger than you expect. One of Jason's trusty lieutenants, Paul Hood, runs the kitchen and his style of cooking, with its 'faites simple' approach, would make Escoffier proud. It's pure and nicely balanced, with a touch of originality and refinement but with the emphasis always on flavour, so that you'll find yourself wiping your plate clean. The service is great too – there's a refreshing lack of stuffiness yet the staff are always completely on the ball – and there's a terrific cocktail bar upstairs too.

First Course

- 'CLT'- crab, lettuce and tomato with roast tomato vinaigrette.
- Ravioli of wild boar bolognaise, Berkswell, peppered hearts and kidneys.

Main Course

- Lamb neck fillet, sheep's ricotta potato, garlic and parsley.
- Baked curried hake with roasted cauliflower cheese.

Dessert

- London honey almond sponge, goat's curd ice cream and orange.
- Lemon curd pie with peppered pastry crumble and sour yoghurt sorbet.

Spice Market

Asian

I3

W London Hotel,
10 Wardour St ✉ W1D 6QF
✆ (0207) 7581 000
www.wlondon.co.uk
⊖ Leicester Square

Menu £38/48 – Carte £20/45

Leicester Square might not be as hip as Manhattan's Meatpacking district but this offshoot of Jean-Georges Vongerichten's New York original may just start to change things around here. This London branch certainly learnt about service from its American cousin because staff are all very confident, keen and clued-up. The restaurant is spread over two floors, linked by a spiral staircase, with eye-catching screens of gold mesh, walls of spices and ceilings of upturned woks. The kitchen traverses various Asian countries for influences and dishes are designed for sharing; ingredients are good and curries are a highlight. 'Street food' is how they describe their cooking, although the street in question is clearly a well-to-do one.

Spuntino

North-American

I3

61 Rupert St. ✉ W1D 7PW
www.spuntino.co.uk
⊖ Piccadilly Circus
Closed dinner 24 December, 25-26, 31 December and 1 January – bookings not accepted

Carte £16/23

Despite its Italian name – meaning 'snack'– Spuntino draws its influences from Downtown New York and is so convincing you feel you could be on Clinton Street. It has the so-discreet-you-walk-straight-past-it entrance, a no-reservations policy (not even a phone number) and an interior that more than hints at a former industrial life – this was once a dairy. Just grab, or wait for, space at the counter and, from the brown paper menu, go for the more American dishes such as Mac 'n' Cheese, soft-shell crab, farmhouse cheddar grits or 'sliders', which are mini burgers. The peanut butter and jelly sandwiches for dessert will be always on your mind. The staff, who look like they could also fix your car, really add to the fun.

Square ✿✿

French

H3 

6-10 Bruton St. ✉ W1J 6PU
✆ (020) 7495 7100
www.squarerestaurant.com
⊖ Green Park
Closed 24-26 December and Sunday lunch

Menu £35/80

The Square

Fame rather than acclaim appear to drive many chefs in this age of celebrity. By contrast, and despite being much in demand and having interests in other restaurants, Philip Howard is a chef who is nearly always to be found in his own kitchen – and this is one of the reasons The Square has been one of London's leading restaurants for two decades. His sophisticated food has its roots in classic French cooking but he isn't put off by new techniques if he thinks they will improve the dish. His menu is one of those that is so appealing it's hard to choose; it changes seasonally but there are some dishes like the crab lasagne that his regulars wouldn't allow him to take off. The dishes are visually appealing and come with a lightness of touch and finesse that few can match and the tasting menu, with its matching wines, provides a memorable experience. The wine list has an Old World bias and is strong on burgundies. The room is comfortable and understated and the service discreet and detailed.

First Course

- Lasagne of crab, cappuccino of shellfish and champagne foam.
- Rillette of smoked mackerel, seawater jellies, oyster and caviar.

Main Course

- Roast leg of lamb with Jerusalem artichoke gratin.
- Loin of venison, pumpkin and potato galette.

Dessert

- Banana soufflé with milk and granola ice cream.
- Milk chocolate bar with salted peanuts, praline and banana.

Sumosan

Japanese

H3

26 Albemarle St. ✉ W1S 4HY
✆ (020) 7495 5999
www.sumosan.com
⊖ Green Park
Closed lunch Saturday-Sunday and bank holidays

Menu £25 (weekday lunch)/75 – Carte £20/101

One minute your restaurant is the hot ticket in town; the next it's celebrating its 10th birthday. In the increasingly ephemeral world of London restaurants, Sumosan's relative longevity is proof that it gets a lot of things right. The large square room in browns and creams provides a stylish backdrop to the Japanese food and the atmosphere is sufficiently strident to drown out the pretty awful muzak. The produce used in the menu is of unimpeachable quality; there's a pleasing balance between the traditional and the more innovative; and the kitchen knows how to make a dish look good. Ignore the fact that the staff lack personality and the bill adds up quicker than a calculator – and just buy yourself a little glamour.

Tapas Brindisa

Spanish

H3

46 Broadwick St. ✉ W1F 7AF
✆ (020) 7534 1690
www.brindisa.com
⊖ Oxford Circus
Closed dinner 24-27 December – (bookings not accepted at dinner)

Menu £20 (weekday lunch) – Carte £11/29

The owners didn't quite get it right when they first opened this sister to their successful operation in Borough Market, but it didn't take them long before they made the necessary changes – and the place has been packed ever since. In true tapas style, bookings are not taken – they want people to simply stroll in, have a drink and get something to eat and there are now plenty of other places in Soho doing the same thing. Look out for the specialities marked out in bold, such as Basque salt cod with spicy tomato sauce. The owners' expertise in importing Spanish produce is evident; although it's amazing how quickly the bill mounts up. Service is obliging and there's no 'push' to move you off, despite the clamour in the bar.

Tamarind 

Indian

G4

20 Queen St. ✉ W1J 5PR
(020) 7629 3561
www.tamarindrestaurant.com
⊖ Green Park
Closed 25-26 December, 1 January and Saturday lunch

Menu £20/68 – Carte £35/60

Tamarind

A constant re-laying of tables is required to keep up with the demand for Alfred Prasad's cooking and this, combined with the sometimes slightly hectic service, adds a reassuring buzz to proceedings at Tamarind. It is easy to see the appeal of the cooking: the flavours really shine through and the spicing is so deft that you can taste each component, whether that's the crushed peppercorns on the Jhinga Kalimirch tiger prawns, the green chillies with the Gilafi Reshmi kebab of ground chicken, or the cumin flavouring the side dish of seasonal green vegetables. Tamarind's dishes are mostly influenced by traditional Moghul cuisine so the tandoor oven is used to great effect – the breads and kebabs are terrific and the tandoori pineapple is a refreshing way to end the meal. Those seated closer to the kitchen get to see the chefs at work with the ovens, under Alfred's watchful eye. The basement location adds to the sense of exclusivity and the smoked mirrors and gilded columns lend a dash of Mayfair gloss.

First Course

- Scallops with star anise and smoked tomato chutney.
- Tilapia and mint chutney rolls with ginger and ajwain.

Main Course

- Hyderabadi lamb shank with turmeric, yoghurt and browned garlic.
- Supreme of chicken with ginger, garlic, green chilli and cardamom.

Dessert

- Dark chocolate mousse with cinnamon.
- Basmati rice with pistachio and stewed figs.

10 Greek Street

modern I3

10 Greek St ✉ W1D 4DH
✆ (020) 7734 4677
www.10greekstreet.com
⊖ Tottenham Court Road
Closed Christmas, Easter and Sunday

Carte £21/35

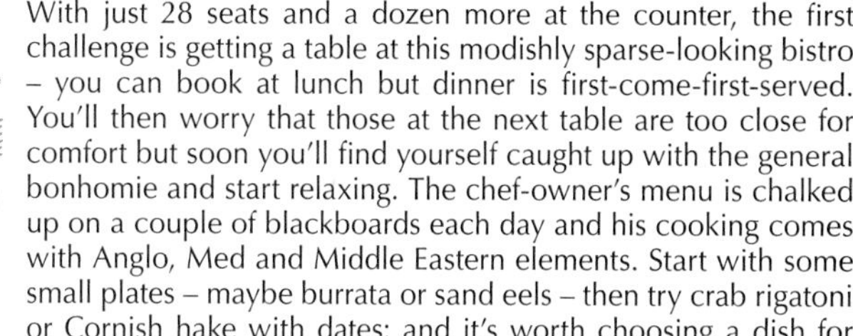

With just 28 seats and a dozen more at the counter, the first challenge is getting a table at this modishly sparse-looking bistro – you can book at lunch but dinner is first-come-first-served. You'll then worry that those at the next table are too close for comfort but soon you'll find yourself caught up with the general bonhomie and start relaxing. The chef-owner's menu is chalked up on a couple of blackboards each day and his cooking comes with Anglo, Med and Middle Eastern elements. Start with some small plates – maybe burrata or sand eels – then try crab rigatoni or Cornish hake with dates; and it's worth choosing a dish for two, like leg of lamb. Wine is the passion of the other owner and the list is constantly evolving.

Theo Randall

Italian G4

Intercontinental Hotel,
1 Hamilton Pl, Park Ln ✉ W1J 7QY
✆ (020) 7318 8747
www.theorandall.com
⊖ Hyde Park Corner
Closed 25-26 December, 1 January, Saturday lunch, Sunday and bank holidays

Menu £27/33 – Carte £45/65

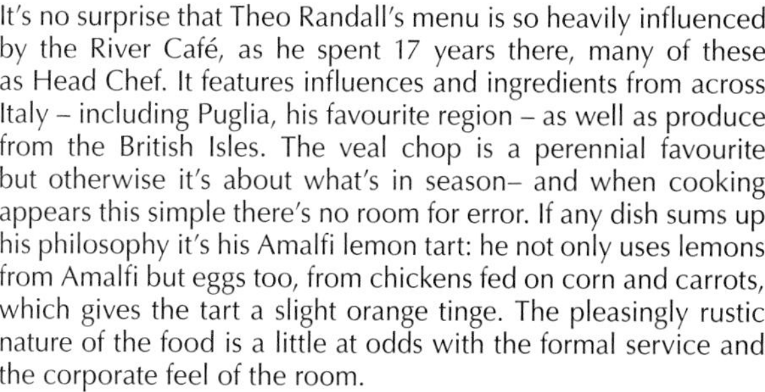

It's no surprise that Theo Randall's menu is so heavily influenced by the River Café, as he spent 17 years there, many of these as Head Chef. It features influences and ingredients from across Italy – including Puglia, his favourite region – as well as produce from the British Isles. The veal chop is a perennial favourite but otherwise it's about what's in season– and when cooking appears this simple there's no room for error. If any dish sums up his philosophy it's his Amalfi lemon tart: he not only uses lemons from Amalfi but eggs too, from chickens fed on corn and carrots, which gives the tart a slight orange tinge. The pleasingly rustic nature of the food is a little at odds with the formal service and the corporate feel of the room.

34

meats and grills G3

34 Grosvenor Sq (entrance on South Audley St)
✉ W1K 2HD
✆ (020) 3350 3434
www.34-restaurant.co.uk
⊖ Marble Arch
Closed 25-26 December

Carte £31/100

Caprice Holdings' restaurants are all about glamour and exclusivity and 34 is no exception. Both its main culinary influences and intended customer base are announced by the flying of the Union Flag and the Stars and Stripes above the door, while inside is a wonderful mix of art deco style and Edwardian warmth – it feels like a classic brasserie that's been around for years. The star is the parrilla, an Argentinian charcoal grill used for the cooking of Dover sole and brochettes as well as the meat, which is a mix of Scottish dry-aged, US prime, organic Argentinian and Australian Wagyu. Game also features, along with short ribs which are becoming more popular over here. It may not come cheap but then glitz never does.

Tonkotsu

Japanese I3

63 Dean St ✉ W1D 4QG
✆ (020) 7437 0071
www.tonkotsu.co.uk
⊖ Tottenham Court Road
Bookings not accepted

Carte £15/25

If you want to see why ramen is all the rage in various cities around the world then stand in line and wait for a table at this simple Soho stop. Good ramen is all about the base stock and here 18 hours goes into its preparation to ensure the bowls of soup and homemade wheat-based noodles reach a depth of flavour that seems to nourish one's very soul. Tonkotsu is named after the pork bone broth favoured in southern Japan; you can also try the soy based Tokyo ramen or go for a little northern Japanese influence with the miso base ramen – and when it arrives, with its seasoned egg and assorted toppings like pork belly and bamboo shoots, don't forget to slurp. While you wait for your ramen, share some of the gyoza – handmade Japanese dumplings.

Umu ✿

Japanese H3

14-16 Bruton Pl. ✉ W1J 6LX
✆ (020) 7499 8881
www.umurestaurant.com
⊖ Bond Street
Closed Saturday lunch, Sunday and bank holidays

Menu £25, £35/100 – Carte £48/122

A/C

Umu

Allowing the natural flavours of the ingredients to shine through is a fundamental element of Japanese cuisine. Accordingly, the search for the best produce is an integral part of any chef's responsibilities. Here at Umu the head chef has been working directly with select Cornish fishermen to ensure that his fish arrives at the restaurant in as fresh a state as possible and, as the quality improves, he plans to make his menus a little less westernised and a little more authentic. At the moment the menu choice is extensive, but for the best overall experience head to the one of the seasonally changing, multi-course kaiseki menus, where the dishes are both flavoursome and visually appealing. The perfect accompaniment, especially for the sashimi, is sake; not only is the list impressive in its depth and range but the sommelier also offers thoughtful advice. The mostly French wine list is equally extensive in its scope. Warm wood, natural materials and judicious lighting make the restaurant feels as discreet as ever.

First Course

- Sake-cured Scottish langoustines and tomato jelly.
- Lobster with coral sauce.

Main Course

- Wood pigeon, enoki sauce, Kabocha pumpkin puree.
- Grade 6 Wagyu beef, Hoba-Yaki, miso nut sauce.

Dessert

- Mikan cake sansho ice cream , Earl Grey tea jam and pomelo.
- 'Snow crystal' purple potato cake with root vegetable ice cream.

Vasco and Piero's Pavilion

Italian H2/3

15 Poland St ✉ W1F 8QE
(020) 7437 8774
www.vascosfood.com
Oxford Circus
Closed Saturday lunch, Sunday and bank holidays – booking essential at lunch

Carte £25/44

This Soho institution celebrated its fortieth anniversary in 2011; if you ask them for the secret of their success the reply will be, "we just do what we believe in". That means a menu that changes twice a day, ingredients and influences from Umbria and simple but effective cooking, with homemade pasta a highlight. Service can sometimes lack a little enthusiasm but it does get the job done – it is not as if they don't care, more that their customers are often regulars who know the score, so why over-egg the pudding? The owners' confidence in their operation and their honest endeavours add to the grown-up feel. The restaurant, which was originally located in Oxford Street, remains fresh and bright.

Veeraswamy

Indian H3

Victory House, 99 Regent St (entrance on Swallow St.)
✉ W1B 4RS
(020) 7734 1401
www.realindianfood.com
Piccadilly Circus

Menu £18/45 – Carte £36/64

The manager here knows not to come between a regular and their favourite table: some were first brought here by their grandparents and are now, in turn, introducing their own grandchildren to London's oldest surviving Indian restaurant, which dates from 1926. You'd be excused for thinking it might be a tad old-fashioned but Veeraswamy is anything but: it is awash with vibrant colours and always full of bustle. The Hyderabad lamb biryani may have been on the original menu but there are plenty of other dishes with a more contemporary edge. The meaty Madagascar prawns are a good way of kicking things off; slow-cooked lamb dishes are also done very well. There's a tasting menu available and desserts, prepared with a flourish, shouldn't be ignored.

Vinoteca

modern

H3

53-55 Beak St ✉ W1F 9SH
✆ (020) 3544 7411
www.vinoteca.co.uk
⊖ Oxford Circus
Closed 24-26 December and 1 January – booking advisable

Carte £18/35

London is the wine capital of the world – largely because we're not allied to any particular wine producing region – so we should have many more wine bars than we do. This is the third Vinoteca and it's easy to see their appeal. Based on the wine bars and shops of Spain and Italy, the list of wines is terrific and mixes the classic with the esoteric; prices are fair and there's plenty of choice – even under £30. There are biodynamic and organic wines but there's no bandwagon-jumping going on here – emerging markets are also covered and if anything on the shelves catches your eye they all priced for take away. The food isn't forgotten – cured meats and cheeses are a highlight and European dishes like bavette and risotto also hit the spot.

The Wolseley

modern

H4

160 Piccadilly ✉ W1J 9EB
✆ (020) 7499 6996
www.thewolseley.com
⊖ Green Park
Closed dinner 24 December – booking essential

Carte £24/64

Opened back in 2003, The Wolseley did not take long to earn iconic status, thanks to its stylish décor, celebrity following and smooth service. Its owners, Chris Corbin and Jeremy King, created a restaurant in the style of a grand European café, all pillars, arches and marble. Open from breakfast until late, the flexible menu offers everything from Austrian and French classics to British staples, so the daily special could be coq au vin or Lancashire hotpot. Pastries come from the Viennoiserie and lunch merges into afternoon tea. So, one table could be tucking into Beluga caviar or a dozen oysters while their neighbours enjoy a salt beef sandwich or eggs Benedict. The large clock reminds you that there are probably others waiting for your table.

Wild Honey ✿

modern

H3 

12 St George St. ✉ W1S 2FB
(020) 7758 9160
www.wildhoneyrestaurant.co.uk
⊖ Oxford Circus
Closed 25-26 December and 1 January

Menu £27/30 (weekdays) – Carte £35/51

Wild Honey

All the best restaurants evolve by listening to their customers and responding to the needs of their regulars. When Wild Honey first opened, it was not too different from Will Smith and Anthony Demetre's other restaurant, Arbutus, but now there's clear blue water between them – and that's not just in the prices. Geographically, Mayfair is not that far from Soho, but in demographic terms the difference is noticeable – Wild Honey's wine list, for example, is more big-shot than bourgeois. The difference is reflected in the kitchen too, which uses more expensive ingredients than its sister restaurant, so you'll find fillet rather than neck, langoustines instead of sardines, and John Dory in place of pollock. There's also a degree of extra sophistication in their preparation too, but always with an appreciation of when to leave the dish alone. The most recent decorative retouch was quite subtle – the wood panelling remains but the booths have gone and the lovely marble-topped bar has been extended – so that the relaxed, comfortable yet intimate feel of the room remains.

First Course

- Scottish crab, avocado guacamole, green mango.
- Langoustines, persimmon and sea vegetables.

Main Course

- Roast chicken 'Label Anglais', morels, potato gnocchi.
- Wild turbot, asparagus, shrimps and lemon.

Dessert

- Wild honey ice cream with honeycomb.
- Classic English custard tart.

Wright Brothers Soho

fish and seafood

H3

13 Kingly St. ✉ W1B 5PW
✆ (020) 7434 3611
www.thewrightbrothers.co.uk
⊖ Oxford Circus
Closed 24-28 December, 1-2 January, Easter Sunday and bank holidays

Menu £15 – Carte £21/55

A/C

This branch is bigger than the original Wright Brothers in Borough Market and is spread over three levels; the best seats are on the lower floor and certainly at the counter if you want to watch the expert oyster shucking. Oysters are the first choice of many as they grow their own in Cornwall; the plates of fruits de mer are also popular and you can create your own platter. The menu is divided between cold and hot starters and 'house staples' which include everything from prawn cocktail to fish pie. The specials board also has plenty on offer, from sardines on toast to a perfectly judged whole sea bream; and desserts have been improved. There's an all-day menu and the restaurant opens out into Kingly Court.

Somewhere for breakfast?
Look for the !

Yauatcha ✿

Chinese

13

15 Broadwick St ✉ W1F 0DL
✆ (020) 7494 8888
www.yauatcha.com
⊖ Tottenham Court Road
Closed 24-25 December

Menu £45 – Carte £18/49

Yauatcha

No cuisine or style of eating is immune from revolution, due largely to the changing ways we all live our lives. Go to Hong Kong and you'll see that even dim sum is evolving and has come to mean so much more than merely snacks to accompany the daytime drinking of tea. In London Yauatcha has always been at the heart of this change and its success is not hard to understand. The food is so good and the surroundings so slick and stylish that customers found it hard to be in and out in their allotted time – so now you can keep hold of your table for a couple of hours. They have also put in a bar on the ground floor which means you can wait for your table in a little more comfort. Three dim sum per person followed by some noodles or a stir-fry should be enough. Stand-out dishes are the scallop shui mai, prawn cheung fun, the wonderfully light baked venison puff and the Kung Po chicken. Those who prefer something sweet to accompany their Silver Needle white tea from Fujian can also come for cakes, tarts and pastries during the day.

First Course

- Scallop Shui Mai.
- Venison puff.

Main Course

- Dover sole with shiitake and soya.
- King crab dumplings.

Dessert

- Jasmine honey with milk chocolate, caramelised honey and almond.
- Mandarin and chocolate square.

M. Ripani/Sime/Photononstop

Strand · Covent Garden

It's fitting that Manet's world famous painting 'Bar at the Folies Bergère' should hang in the **Strand** within a champagne cork's throw of theatreland and Covent Garden. This is the area perhaps more than any other which draws in the ticket-buying tourist, eager to grab a good deal on one of the many shows on offer, or eat and drink at fabled shrines like J.Sheekey or Rules. It's here the names already up in lights shine down on their potential usurpers: celeb wannabes heading for The Ivy, West Street's perennially fashionable restaurant. It's here, too, that Nell Gwyn set up home under the patronage of Charles II, while Oscar Wilde revelled in his success by taking rooms at the Savoy.

The hub of the whole area is the piazza at **Covent Garden,** created by Inigo Jones four hundred years ago. It was given a brash new lease of life in the 1980s after its famed fruit and veg market was pulled up by the roots and re-sown in Battersea. Council bigwigs realised then that 'what we have we hold', and any further redevelopment of the area is banned. Where everyone heads is the impressive covered market, within which a colourful jumble of arts and crafts shops gels with al fresco cafés and classical performers proffering Paganini with your cappuccino. Outside, under the portico of St Paul's church, every type of street performer does a turn for the tourist trade. The best shops in Covent Garden, though, are a few streets north of the market melee, emanating out like bicycle spokes from Seven Dials.

For those after a more highbrow experience, one of London's best attractions is a hop, skip and ***grand jeté*** from the market. Around the corner in **Bow Street** is the city's famed home for opera and ballet, where fire – as well as show-stopping performances – has been known to bring the house down. The **Royal Opera House** is now in its third incarnation, and it gets more impressive with each rebuild. The handsome, glass-roofed Floral Hall is a must-see, while an interval drink at the Amphitheatre Café Bar, overlooking the piazza, is de rigeur for show goers. At the other end of the Strand the **London Coliseum** offers more opera, this time all performed in English. Down by Waterloo Bridge, art lovers are strongly advised to stop at **Somerset House** and take in one of London's most sublime collections of art at the Courtauld Gallery. This is where you can get up close and personal to Manet's barmaid, as well as an astonishing array of Impressionist masters and twentieth century greats. The icing on the cake is the compact and accessible eighteenth century building that houses the collection: real icing on a real cake can be found in a super little hidden-away café downstairs.

Of a different order altogether is the huge **National Gallery** at Trafalgar Square which houses more than two thousand Western European pieces (it started off with 38). A visit to the modern Sainsbury Wing is rewarded with some

AGE / PHOTONONSTOP

unmissable works from the Renaissance. It can get just as crowded in the capital's largest Gallery as in the square outside, so a good idea is to wander down **Villiers Street** next to Charing Cross station and breathe the Thames air along the Victoria Embankment. Behind you is the grand Savoy Hotel, which reopened in 2010 after major refurbishment; for a better view of it, you can head even further away from the crowds on a boat trip from the **Embankment,** complete with on-board entertainment. And if the glory of travel in the capital, albeit on the water, has whetted your appetite for more, then pop into the impressively renovated Transport Museum in Covent Garden piazza, where gloriously preserved tubes, buses and trains from the past put you in a positive frame of mind for the real live working version you'll very probably be tackling later in the day.

Strand & Covent Garden
(Plan III)

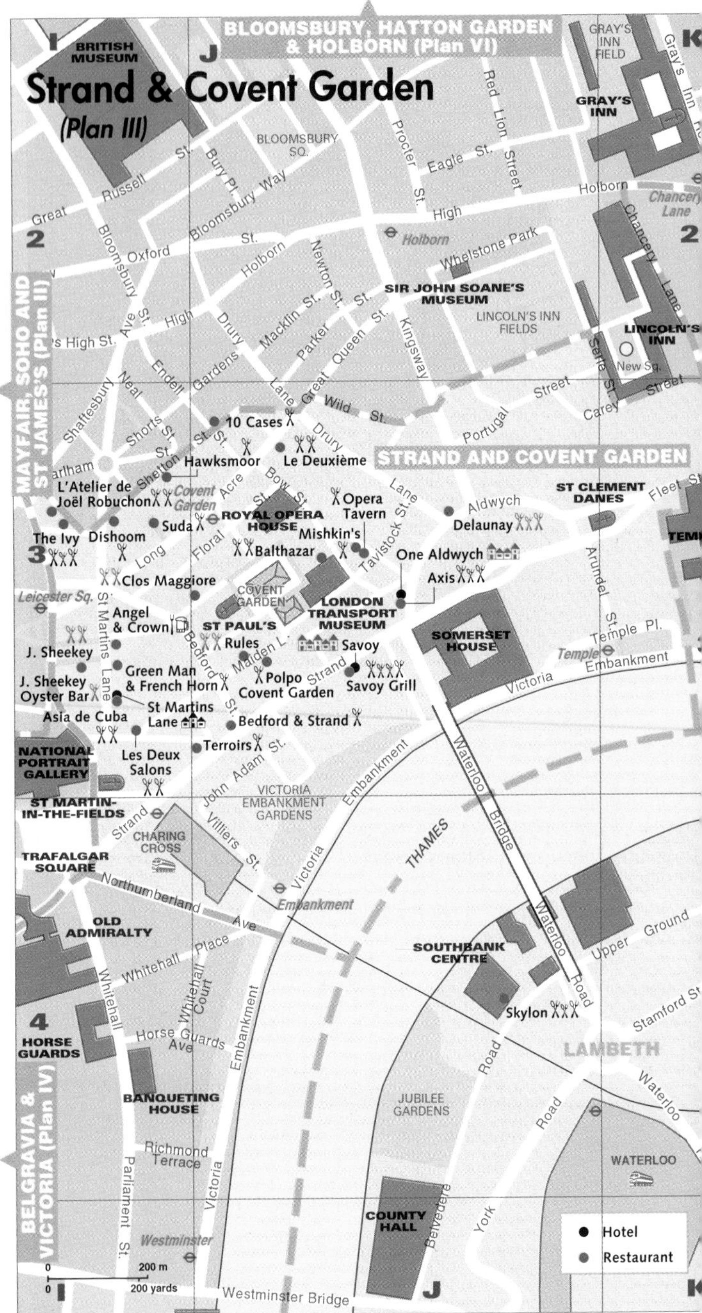

Angel & Crown

British traditional

I3

58 St Martin's Ln ✉ WC2N 4EA
✆ (020) 7748 5244
www.theangelandcrown.com
⊖ Leicester Square.
Closed 25 December

Carte £23/34

Tourist spots and good food are rarely enjoyed together and London is no exception, but fortunately the gastropub revolution is now creeping into the West End. The Angel & Crown is part of the Martin Brothers' portfolio which includes The Well and The Gun and here they've converted a handsome Victorian pub in the heart of theatre-land. The ground floor, with its pewter tankards hanging above the bar, is the sort of place you want to stand up in; most of the eating is done upstairs in the dining room. The menu wisely sticks to British dishes, with nothing to scare away the out-of-towners, and uses decent ingredients, so the pie may be venison and bone marrow and the sausages that go with the mash and onion gravy are made using wild boar.

Asia de Cuba

Asian

I3

St Martins Lane Hotel,
45 St Martin's Ln ✉ WC2N 3HX
✆ (020) 7300 5588
www.morganshotelgroup.com
⊖ Charing Cross

Menu £15/23 – Carte £35/50

Every restaurant has its core fans and this über trendy hangout attracts that most coveted demographic: the young and the hip, with cash to burn. It's on the ground floor of St Martins Lane hotel, a celebrity favourite with a fashionably louche relationship with apostrophes, and the design – pillars wrapped in books and photos and a single light bulb above each table – comes courtesy of Philippe Starck. As the name suggests, the food fuses the flavours of Asia with those of Cuba; dishes are designed for sharing and, apart from the size of the bill, there's nothing particularly eye-watering. Fish dishes such as glazed salmon or Ahi tuna with wasabi are particularly easy to enjoy. Do it properly and have cocktails first.

L'Atelier de Joël Robuchon ✿

French

13

13-15 West St. ✉ WC2H 9NE
✆ (020) 7010 8600
www.joelrobuchon.co.uk
⊖ Leicester Square
Closed 25-26 December,1 January, Sunday and August bank holiday Monday

Menu £28, £95/129 – Carte £36/99

L'Atelier de Joel Robuchon

London's L'Atelier de Joël Robuchon differs from his other 'branches' dotted around the world's culinary hotspots by being two restaurants under one roof: on the ground floor is L'Atelier itself, with an open kitchen and large counter; upstairs is the monochrome La Cuisine, a slightly more structured, sleek and more brightly-lit affair with table seating. Apart from a few wood-fired dishes upstairs, the menus are largely similar. The cooking is artistic, creative and occasionally playful; it is technically accomplished and highly labour intensive – there are over thirty chefs in the building – but it is never overworked and each dish is nicely balanced and its flavours true. French is the predominant influence, supported by other Mediterranean flavours, and ordering a number of smaller dishes is the best way to fully appreciate Robuchon's craft and vision, although your final bill can quite quickly get pretty lofty. Service is well timed and confident and sitting at the counter will give you some insight into this polished operation.

First Course

- Crab with citrus dressing and asparagus.
- Crispy langoustine fritters with pistou.

Main Course

- Halibut cooked with rosemary, baby fennel and citrus sauce.
- Pork chop with girolles and pineapple.

Dessert

- Manjari chocolate dome, crunchy almonds, cognac ice cream and caramel sauce.
- Whisky soufflé with bourbon and Baileys ice cream.

Axis

modern

J3

One Aldwych Hotel,
1 Aldwych ✉ WC2B 4RH
✆ (020) 7300 0300
www.onealdwych.com/axis
⊖ Temple

Closed 16 August-3 September, 20 December-14 January and Saturday lunch

Menu £20/24 – Carte £30/49

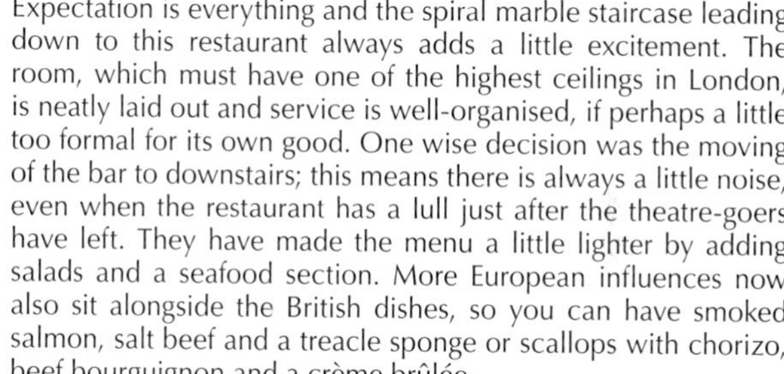

Expectation is everything and the spiral marble staircase leading down to this restaurant always adds a little excitement. The room, which must have one of the highest ceilings in London, is neatly laid out and service is well-organised, if perhaps a little too formal for its own good. One wise decision was the moving of the bar to downstairs; this means there is always a little noise, even when the restaurant has a lull just after the theatre-goers have left. They have made the menu a little lighter by adding salads and a seafood section. More European influences now also sit alongside the British dishes, so you can have smoked salmon, salt beef and a treacle sponge or scallops with chorizo, beef bourguignon and a crème brûlée.

Balthazar

French

J3

4-6 Russell St. ✉ WC2B 5HZ
✆ (020) 3301 1155
www.balthazarlondon.com
⊖ Covent Garden

Booking essential

Carte £25/56

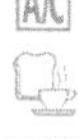

It's not just musicals and plays that transfer between London and New York – the world's two greatest cities now trade in restaurants as well. Balthazar has long been a landmark in Manhattan's SoHo district but now there's a London version occupying the old Theatre Museum in Covent Garden which, thanks to its red leather seats, mosaic floor, mirrors and flattering lighting, will seem uncannily familiar to anyone who knows the original. This being a London copy of a New York copy of a classic Parisian brasserie means that the Franglais menu plays is safe and focuses on reassuringly familiar dishes like moules frites, coq au vin and duck confit. It's open from breakfast onwards; the cocktails are great; and the atmosphere lively and excitable.

Bedford & Strand

British traditional

J3

1a Bedford St ✉ WC2E 9HH
✆ (020) 7836 3033
www.bedford-strand.com
⊖ Charing Cross
Closed 24 December-2 January, Sunday and bank holidays – booking essential

Menu £18 – Carte £20/36

However many advertising boards you place outside, it is never easy enticing passers-by down into your basement restaurant. Despite its subterranean location, Bedford & Strand deserves a wider audience, beyond hungry troglodytes and those in the know, because it's usefully placed for theatre-goers and offers an appealing, sensibly priced menu. The room's divided into two: on one side is the wine bar, with around 20 wines by the glass or carafe and an interesting selection of nibbles like smoked sprats and potted crab. The far side is the restaurant, whose menu is a pleasingly familiar mix of French and English – go for the plat du jour which could be fishcakes or onglet. There's also a very good value lunch and early evening Menu Rapide.

Clos Maggiore

French

J3

33 King St ✉ WC2E 8JD
✆ (020) 7379 9696
www.closmaggiore.com
⊖ Leicester Square
Closed 24-25 December

Menu £16/49 – Carte £32/55

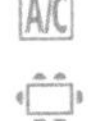
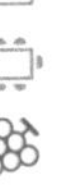

Any West End restaurateurs still half-hearted about pre and post theatre dining should come to Clos Maggiore to see how it can be done: the menu represents excellent value, the kitchen is well organised and the staff get on with the serving, which means the theatregoer doesn't have to keep checking the time. Clos Maggiore is also one of the most romantic restaurants around – just be sure to ask for the table in the enchanting conservatory at the back, with its retractable roof. The chef is from Provence and you can almost smell the lavender when reading his menu. The French dishes are sophisticated in their make while the ingredients come mostly from the British Isles. The wine list has great depth and reflects the owner's passion.

Delaunay

modern

J3

55 Aldwych ✉ WC2B 4BB
✆ (020) 7499 8558
www.thedelaunay.com
⊖ Temple
Closed dinner 24 December and 25 December – booking essential

Carte £21/47

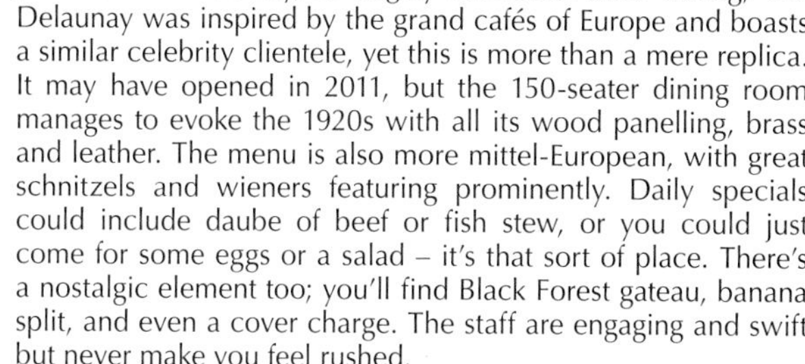

Just like The Wolseley, its hugely successful older sibling, The Delaunay was inspired by the grand cafés of Europe and boasts a similar celebrity clientele, yet this is more than a mere replica. It may have opened in 2011, but the 150-seater dining room manages to evoke the 1920s with all its wood panelling, brass and leather. The menu is also more mittel-European, with great schnitzels and wieners featuring prominently. Daily specials could include daube of beef or fish stew, or you could just come for some eggs or a salad – it's that sort of place. There's a nostalgic element too; you'll find Black Forest gateau, banana split, and even a cover charge. The staff are engaging and swift but never make you feel rushed.

Le Deuxième

modern

J3

65a Long Acre ✉ WC2E 9JH
✆ (020) 7379 0033
www.ledeuxieme.com
⊖ Covent Garden
Closed 24-25 December

Menu £15/28 – Carte £28/44

Don't think that because it's busy in the early evening before curtain-up in all the local theatres that's it's going to quieten down when all the early-diners have gone – it seemingly stays busy most of the evening, most nights. This certainly gives the room plenty of energy but it also means that this is the sort of place where, if you get the attention of the waiter or waitress, you'll want to be ready with your order so as not to waste the opportunity. The menu offers an extensive range of dishes, whose influences come largely from within Europe. In amongst the pastas and the salads are some fairly classic French dishes and this is where the kitchen's experience lies. Side dishes, though, can quickly bump up the bill.

Les Deux Salons

French

I3

40-42 William IV St ✉ WC2N 4DD
(020) 7420 2050
www.lesdeuxsalons.co.uk
⊖ Charing Cross
Closed 25-26 December and 1 January

Menu £10/20 – Carte £14/46

After the success of Arbutus and Wild Honey, Will Smith and Anthony Demetre turned their attention towards France and came up with Les Deux Salons – a Parisian brasserie so authentic in its look you half expect to see Sartre sitting in the corner. Of the two salons, the ground floor is the more atmospheric and visually impressive, with its smoked mirrors, globe lights, zinc-topped bar and striking mosaic floor. The menu makes for an appealing read; you'll find French classics like bouillabaisse, assorted meats grilled on the Josper and even the occasional interloper from this side of the Channel, like cottage pie; desserts are full-on Gallic and all the better for it. It's been busy since opening its doors; service is swift, but not pushy.

Dishoom

Indian

I3

12 Upper St Martin's Ln ✉ WC2H 9FB
(020) 7420 9320
www.dishoom.com
⊖ Leicester Square
Closed 24 December dinner, 25-26 December and 1-2 January

Menu £20/35 – Carte £10/26

Dishoom is a facsimile of a Bombay café, of the sort that populated that city in the early 20th century. They were opened by Persian immigrants and served snacks and specialities that merged the two countries, along with other dishes displaying some colonial influences; and, because they were classless and casteless, they appealed to everyone. That same inclusiveness is evident here in Covent Garden: the place is usually full of everyone from couples to business-types enjoying a table of shared dishes. It's all about ordering as little or as much as you want, whether that's a full breakfast; some baked roti rolls with chai; vada pav – Bombay's version of the chip butty; a curry; or meats cooked on the grill in the open kitchen.

Green Man & French Horn

French

I3

54 St Martin's Ln ✉ WC2N 4EA
✆ (020) 7836 2645
www.greenmanfrenchhorn.co
⊖ Leicester Square

Menu £10 – Carte £21/33

It's easy to walk past without noticing this narrow old pub – but that would be a huge mistake. The people behind Terroirs, Brawn and Soif have transformed it into a French bistro/wine bar so artfully that it feels as though it's been here for years. It's lively, fun, intimate and welcoming. It differs slightly from its siblings in that the menu and wines take their inspiration from the Loire Valley and the vast flow of the Loire River. That means there's more of a focus on fish dishes, but the cooking still delivers the same satisfying earthiness that warms you in winter and brightens you in summer. The wine list is equally appealing and has over 250 bins from the region, largely sourced from organic and biodynamic growers.

Hawksmoor

meats and grills

I3

11 Langley St ✉ WC2H 9JG
✆ (020) 7420 9390
www.thehawksmoor.com
⊖ Covent Garden
Closed 24-26 and 31 December, 1-2 January and Sunday dinner

Menu £25 (lunch) – Carte £39/62

Impressive renovation work from those clever Hawksmoor people turned this former brewery cellar into a very atmospheric restaurant whose primary function is the serving and eating of red meat – a suitably apt activity as one 18C owner of the brewery used to host a steak club. You'll get a friendly greeting at the bottom of the stairs and can either eat in the bar or in the large and bustling dining room with its ersatz industrial look. Steaks from Longhorn cattle lovingly reared in North Yorkshire and dry-aged for at least 35 days are the stars of the show. A blackboard shows availability and meat is priced per 100g. But beware as side orders and competitive over-ordering on the size of the cut can push up the final bill.

The Ivy

British traditional

I3

1-5 West St ✉ WC2H 9NQ
✆ (020) 7836 4751
www.the-ivy.co.uk
⊖ Leicester Square
Closed 25-26 December

Menu £27 – Carte £30/68

The members-only Ivy Club may have siphoned off the top tier of regulars but The Ivy restaurant continues to attract new blood. It's still the sort of place where everyone looks up from their food to see who's just arrived but nowadays that's just as likely to be a reality TV contestant as a theatrical knight. Getting a table is still a challenge; try calling on the day – if they offer the bar, accept, because you may get bumped up into the main room. But the great thing about The Ivy is that it's impossible not to find the menu appealing: perfectly gratinated shepherd's pie, plump fishcakes, eggs Benedict, nursery puddings – they're all here and all done well. Staff earn their crust by frequently but discreetly re-laying the tables.

J. Sheekey

fish and seafood

I3

28-34 St Martin's Ct. ✉ WC2 4AL
✆ (020) 7240 2565
www.j-sheekey.co.uk
⊖ Leicester Square
Closed 25-26 December – booking essential

Carte £31/69

Named after the restaurant's first chef who cooked for its then owner Lord Salisbury, J.Sheekey proves that longevity and tradition need not mean old and crusty. It is as fashionable now as it was in 1896 and remains one of the first choices for the theatrical world and those whose business is show. The wood panelling and silver on the tables add to the timeless British feel and service is as charming and efficient as ever. Fish and seafood are handled deftly: the Arbroath smokie and potted shrimps are permanent fixtures and the fish pie and lemon sole are rightly renowned. Avoiding pre and post-theatre times will shorten the odds of your getting a table; ask for 'dining room 4' which is the largest of the five rooms.

J. Sheekey Oyster Bar

fish and seafood

I3 

33-34 St Martin's Ct. ✉ WC2 4AL
✆ (020) 7240 2565
www.j-sheekey.co.uk
⊖ Leicester Square
Closed 25-26 December

Carte £31/65

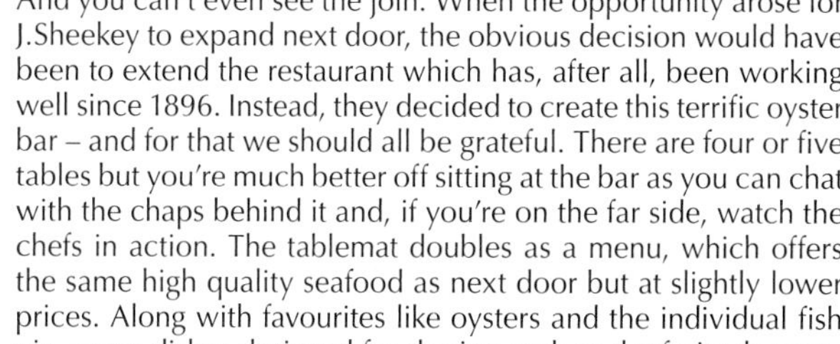

And you can't even see the join. When the opportunity arose for J.Sheekey to expand next door, the obvious decision would have been to extend the restaurant which has, after all, been working well since 1896. Instead, they decided to create this terrific oyster bar – and for that we should all be grateful. There are four or five tables but you're much better off sitting at the bar as you can chat with the chaps behind it and, if you're on the far side, watch the chefs in action. The tablemat doubles as a menu, which offers the same high quality seafood as next door but at slightly lower prices. Along with favourites like oysters and the individual fish pie, come dishes designed for sharing such as the fruits de mer.

Mishkin's

North-American

25 Catherine St ✉ WC2B 5JS
✆ (020) 7240 2078
www.mishkins.co.uk
⊖ Covent Garden
Closed 24-26 December and 1-2 January

Carte £18/27

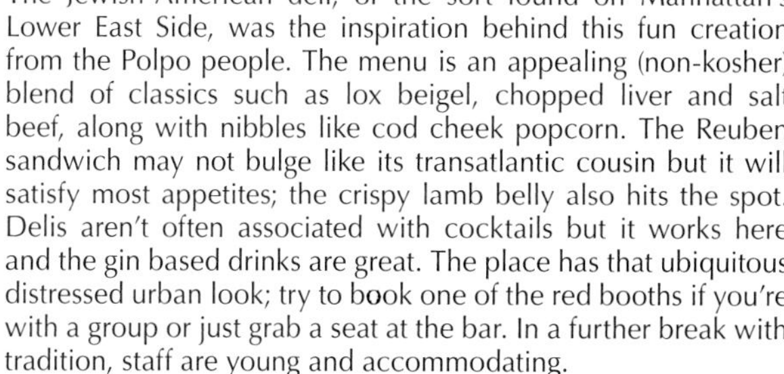

The Jewish-American deli, of the sort found on Manhattan's Lower East Side, was the inspiration behind this fun creation from the Polpo people. The menu is an appealing (non-kosher) blend of classics such as lox beigel, chopped liver and salt beef, along with nibbles like cod cheek popcorn. The Reuben sandwich may not bulge like its transatlantic cousin but it will satisfy most appetites; the crispy lamb belly also hits the spot. Delis aren't often associated with cocktails but it works here and the gin based drinks are great. The place has that ubiquitous distressed urban look; try to book one of the red booths if you're with a group or just grab a seat at the bar. In a further break with tradition, staff are young and accommodating.

Opera Tavern ☺

Mediterranean

J3

23 Catherine St. ✉ WC2B 5JS
✆ (020) 7836 3680
www.operatavern.co.uk
⊖ Covent Garden
Closed 24-26 and 31 December, 1-2 January and Sunday dinner

Menu £35/45 – Carte approx. £26

A/C

That many of its more touristy areas now boast some decent restaurants is testament to London's maturing dining scene. Opera Tavern comes from the people who brought you Salt Yard and Dehesa, so they know what they're doing, but this time they're doing it in a converted old boozer dating from 1879, albeit one that's had a complete makeover. If you haven't booked a table in the upstairs dining room then try your luck on the lively ground floor; order 2 or 3 dishes per person and be prepared to share – stand-outs are the Ibérico ham, chorizo with piquillo pepper and crispy squid. The wine list also swings between Spain and Italy and includes some rare and ancient grape varieties. The staff are all reassuringly confident and clued up.

Polpo Covent Garden ☺

Italian

J3

6 Maiden Ln. ✉ WC2E 7NA
✆ (020) 7836 8448
www.polpo.co.uk
⊖ Leicester Square
Closed 24-26 December – (bookings not taken at dinner)

Carte £12/32

A/C

After sewing up Soho with their first three restaurants, this clever little group then turned its attention to neighbouring Covent Garden to open this Venetian bacaro. Behind the delicately embroidered linen screens is another shrewdly designed spot, with a tin ceiling imported from New York and church pews contrasting with the ersatz industrial look. It covers two floors – the ground floor is best. Over-ordering is easy, as the small plates are surprisingly filling, with delights such as the wonderfully fresh flavours of pizzette of white anchovy vying with fennel and almond salad, fritto misto competing with spaghettini and meatballs. A no-bookings policy after 5.30pm means that there will be queues but turnover is naturally quick.

Rules

British traditional

J3

35 Maiden Ln ✉ WC2E 7LB
(020) 7836 5314
www.rules.co.uk
⊖ Leicester Square
Closed 25-26 December – booking essential

Carte £34/60

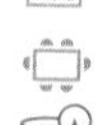

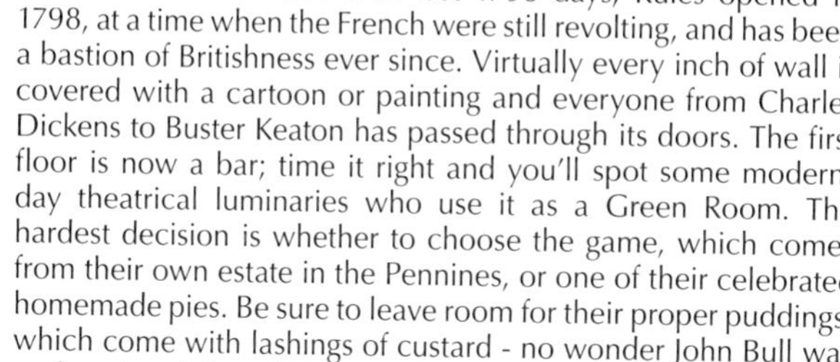

Some restaurants don't even last 1798 days; Rules opened in 1798, at a time when the French were still revolting, and has been a bastion of Britishness ever since. Virtually every inch of wall is covered with a cartoon or painting and everyone from Charles Dickens to Buster Keaton has passed through its doors. The first floor is now a bar; time it right and you'll spot some modern-day theatrical luminaries who use it as a Green Room. The hardest decision is whether to choose the game, which comes from their own estate in the Pennines, or one of their celebrated homemade pies. Be sure to leave room for their proper puddings, which come with lashings of custard - no wonder John Bull was such a stout fellow. It makes you proud.

Savoy Grill

British traditional

J3

Savoy Hotel,
Strand ✉ WC2R 0EU
(020) 7592 1600
www.gordonramsay.com/thesavoygrill
⊖ Charing Cross

Menu £26 (weekday lunch) – Carte £33/79

The Savoy Grill prepared for the future by going back to its roots. Archives were explored, designers briefed and much money spent, with the result that The Savoy Grill has returned to the traditions that made it famous. As befits the name, it is the charcoal grilling of meats that takes centre stage. Beef from the Lake District and Essex is dry-aged for a minimum of 35 days and offered in an impressive selection of cuts. There's also a daily trolley – it could be beef Wellington one day, leg of lamb the next – and an enticing section entitled 'Roasts, Braises and Pies'. The shiny art deco inspired interior evokes the 1930s, photos of past guests adorn the walls and even the table layout and numbering remains true to the original.

Suda

Thai

I3

23 Slingsby Pl, St Martin's Courtyard ✉ WC2E 9AB
✆ (020) 7240 8010
www.suda-thai.com
⊖ Covent Garden
Closed 25 January

Carte £17/26

This shiny Thai restaurant in the new St Martin's Courtyard development looks remarkably like a branded chain that's about to be rolled out and, as Oscar Wilde said, "It is only shallow people who do not judge by appearances". However, the quality of its food and the care taken in its preparation far exceeds one's expectations. OK, so the 'street' food may have had a wash and brush up and heat warnings on certain dishes are overplayed but the kitchen still delivers enough familiar flavours on a cold January night to transport you back to Sukhumvit Road. Som tam spicy salads are a speciality, as are creamy curries and there's plenty for veggies. Come in a group, sit upstairs and order cocktails and plenty of dishes to share.

10 Cases

French

J3

16 Endell St ✉ WC2H 9BD
✆ (020) 7836 6801
www.the10cases.co.uk
⊖ Covent Garden
Closed Easter, Christmas-New Year and bank holidays – booking essential

Carte £25/37

It's a simple but effective idea: serve an unpretentious daily changing menu with a choice of 3 starters, 3 main courses and 3 desserts accompanied by a wine list of 10 reds and 10 whites, all available by the glass, carafe or bottle; 10 cases of each wine are bought – hence the name – and when they're finished the wine is changed. The cooking is straightforward and honest and the menu is supplemented by nibbles such as potted crab or roasted garlic. The food suits the cosy bistrot feel of the place and though the portions may be rather small, so too are the prices. The wines are well chosen and the mark-ups limited, so most bottles are priced between £19 and £35; the 50cl carafes are particularly good value.

Terroirs

French

J3

5 William IV St ✉ WC2N 4DW
(020) 7036 0660
www.terroirswinebar.com
Charing Cross
Closed 25-26 December, 1 January, Sunday and bank holidays

Carte £24/35

The ground floor is as busy and as fun as ever but you can also eat 'Downstairs at Terroirs', where the menu is slightly different and there's a greater variety of cooking methods used; there are also dishes for two such as the roast Landaise chicken. Tables down here are a little bigger which makes sharing easier and, despite being two floors down, it is more atmospheric. If you recognise the banquette seating it's because it comes from Mirabelle. Meanwhile, both levels share the same respect for flavoursome and satisfying French cooking, with added Italian and Spanish influences. The wine list is interesting, varied and well-priced. Service remains a mixed bag and can be of the headless chicken variety.

Remember, stars (✿✿✿...✿) are awarded for cuisine only! Elements such as service and décor are not a factor.

Belgravia · Victoria

The well-worn cliché 'an area of contrasts' certainly applies to these ill-matched neighbours. To the west, Belgravia equates to fashionable status and elegant, residential calm; to the east, Victoria is a chaotic jumble of backpackers, milling commuters and cheap-and-not-always-so-cheerful hotels. At first sight, you might think there's little to no common ground, but the umbilical cord that unites them is, strange to say, diplomacy and politics. Belgravia's embassies are dotted all around the environs of **Belgrave Square,** while at the furthest end of bustling Victoria Street stands **Parliament Square.**

Belgravia – named after 'beautiful grove' in French - was developed during the nineteenth century by Richard Grosvenor, the second Marquess of Westminster, who employed top architect Thomas Cubitt to come up with something rather fetching for the upper echelons of society. The grandeur of the classical designs has survived for the best part of two centuries, evident in the broad streets and elegant squares, where the rich rub shoulders with the uber-rich beneath the stylish balconies of a consulate or outside a high-end antiques emporium. You can still sample an atmosphere of the village it once was, as long as your idea of a village includes exclusive designer boutiques and even more exclusive mews cottages.

By any stretch of the imagination you'd have trouble thinking of **Victoria** as a village. Its local railway station is one of London's major hubs and its bus station brings in visitors from not only all corners of Britain, but Europe too. Its main 'church', concealed behind office blocks, could hardly be described as humble, either: **Westminster Cathedral** is a grand concoction based on Istanbul's Hagia Sophia, with a view from the top of the bell tower which is breathtaking. From there you can pick out other hidden charms of the area: the dramatic headquarters of Channel 4 TV, the revolving sign famously leading into New Scotland Yard, and the neat little Christchurch Gardens, burial site of Colonel Blood, last man to try and steal the Crown Jewels. Slightly easier for the eye to locate are the grand designs of **Westminster Abbey,** crowning glory and resting place of most of England's kings and queens, and the neo-gothic pile of the **Houses of Parliament.** Victoria may be an eclectic mix of people and architectural styles, but its handy position as a kind of epicentre of the Westminster Village makes it a great place for political chit-chat. And the place to go for that is The Speaker, a pub in Great Peter Street, named after the Commons' centuries-old peacekeeper and 'referee'. It's a backstreet gem, where it's not unknown for a big cheese from the House to be filmed over a pint.

Winston Churchill is someone who would have been quite at home holding forth at The Speaker, and half a mile away in King Charles Street, based within the **Cabinet War Rooms** – the secret underground HQ of the war effort - is

visitlondon.com

the Churchill Museum, stuffed full of all things Churchillian. However, if your passion is more the easel and the brush, then head down to the river where another great institution of the area, **Tate Britain,** gazes out over the Thames. Standing where the grizzly Millbank Penitentiary once festered, it offers, after the National Gallery, the best collection of historical art in London. There's loads of space for the likes of Turner and Constable, while Hogarth, Gainsborough and Blake are well represented, too. Artists from the modern era are also here, with Freud and Hockney on show, and there are regular installations showcasing upwardly mobile British talent. All of which may give you the taste for a trip east along the river to Tate Modern. This can be done every twenty minutes courtesy of the Tate-to-Tate boat service, which handily stops en-route at the London Eye, and, even more handily, sports eye-catching Damien Hirst décor and a cool, shiny bar.

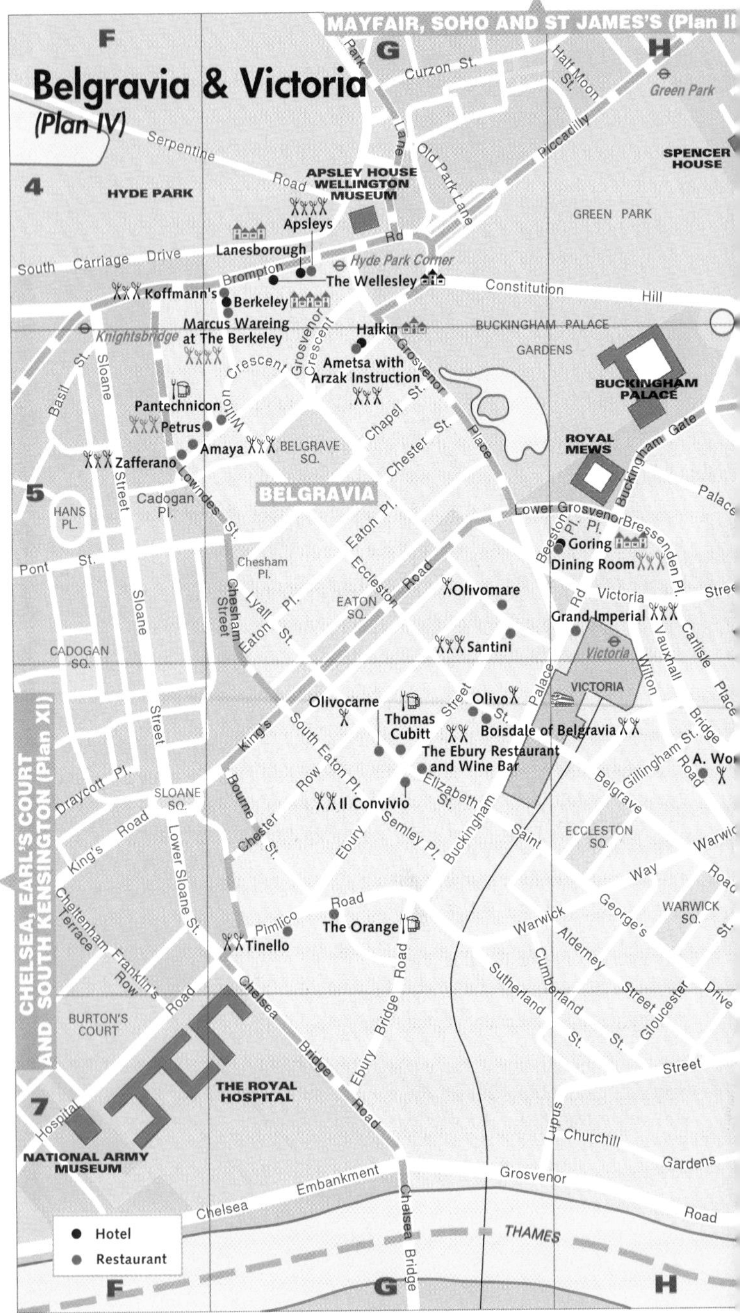
Belgravia & Victoria
(Plan IV)
MAYFAIR, SOHO AND ST JAMES'S (Plan II
CHELSEA, EARL'S COURT AND SOUTH KENSINGTON (Plan XI)
F
G
H
4
5
7
HYDE PARK
APSLEY HOUSE WELLINGTON MUSEUM
Apsleys
Lanesborough
The Wellesley
Hyde Park Corner
Koffmann's
Berkeley
Marcus Wareing at The Berkeley
Halkin
Ametsa with Arzak Instruction
Pantechnicon
Petrus
Amaya
Zafferano
BELGRAVE SQ.
BELGRAVIA
Green Park
SPENCER HOUSE
GREEN PARK
BUCKINGHAM PALACE GARDENS
BUCKINGHAM PALACE
ROYAL MEWS
Goring
Dining Room
Olivomare
Grand Imperial
Santini
Victoria
VICTORIA
Olivocarne
Thomas Cubitt
Olivo
Boisdale of Belgravia
The Ebury Restaurant and Wine Bar
A. Wo
Il Convivio
The Orange
Tinello
HANS PL.
CADOGAN SQ.
SLOANE SQ.
EATON SQ.
ECCLESTON SQ.
WARWICK SQ.
BURTON'S COURT
THE ROYAL HOSPITAL
NATIONAL ARMY MUSEUM
THAMES
Knightsbridge
Serpentine Road
South Carriage Drive
Brompton Rd
Constitution Hill
Curzon St.
Half Moon St.
Piccadilly
Park Lane
Old Park Lane
Grosvenor Crescent
Grosvenor Place
Wilton Crescent
Chapel St.
Chester St.
Lowndes St.
Sloane St.
Basil St.
Cadogan Pl.
Pont St.
Chesham Pl.
Chesham Street
Eaton Pl.
Eccleston Road
Lyall St.
Eaton Pl.
Lower Grosvenor Pl.
Beeston Pl.
Bressenden Pl.
Buckingham Gate
Palace Street
Victoria Street
Carlisle Place
Vauxhall Bridge Road
Wilton Rd
Gillingham St.
Belgrave Road
Warwick Way
King's Road
South Eaton Pl.
Elizabeth St.
Semley Pl.
Buckingham Palace Road
Bourne St.
Chester Row
Ebury St.
Draycott Pl.
Lower Sloane St.
Cheltenham Terrace
Franklin's Row
Pimlico Road
Ebury Bridge Road
Chelsea Bridge Road
Saint George's Drive
Alderney Street
Cumberland St.
Sutherland St.
Gloucester Street
Lupus St.
Churchill Gardens
Hospital Road
Royal Hospital Road
Chelsea Embankment
Grosvenor Road
Chelsea Bridge
Hotel
Restaurant

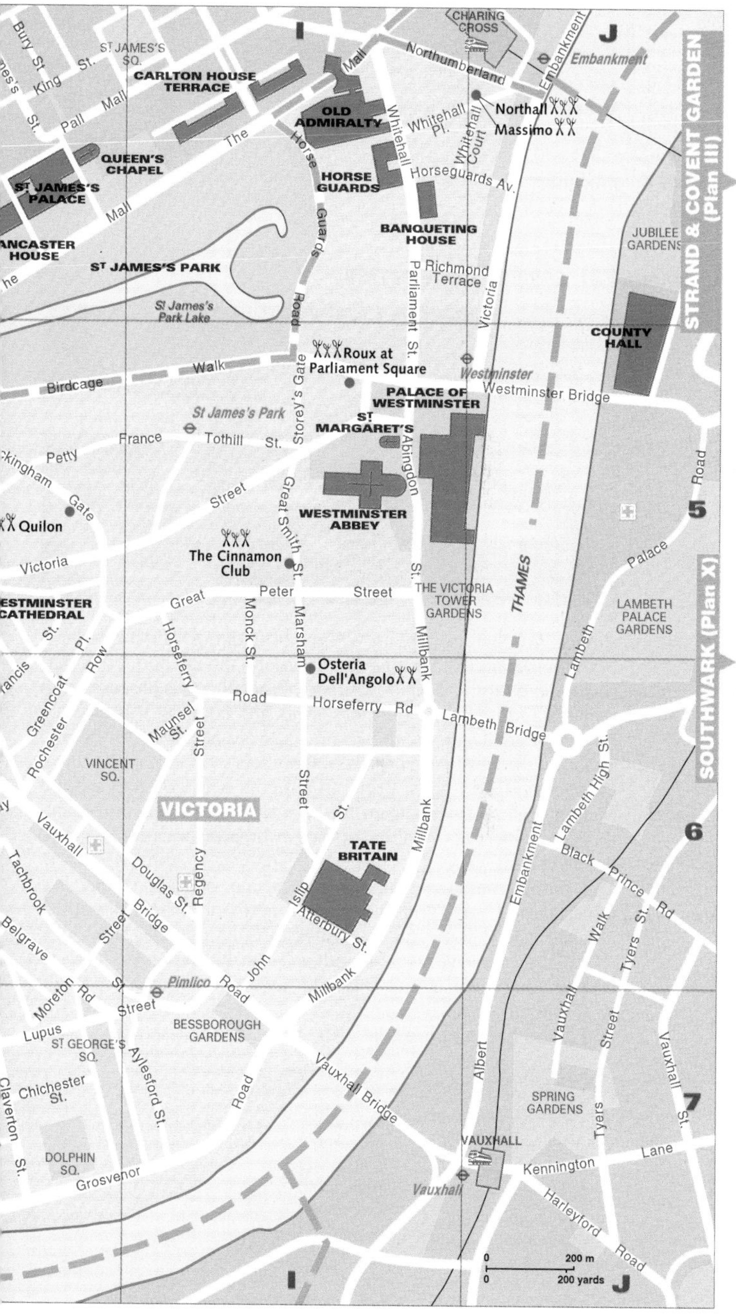
CHARING CROSS
Northumberland
Embankment
Northall
Massimo
CARLTON HOUSE TERRACE
OLD ADMIRALTY
QUEEN'S CHAPEL
ST JAMES'S PALACE
HORSE GUARDS
BANQUETING HOUSE
ST JAMES'S PARK
St James's Park Lake
Horseguards Av.
Whitehall
Whitehall Pl.
Whitehall Court
Richmond Terrace
Parliament St.
Victoria
JUBILEE GARDENS
COUNTY HALL
Roux at Parliament Square
Birdcage Walk
Westminster
Westminster Bridge
PALACE OF WESTMINSTER
St James's Park
ST MARGARET'S
WESTMINSTER ABBEY
Tothill St.
Petty France
Quilon
The Cinnamon Club
Great Peter Street
THE VICTORIA TOWER GARDENS
THAMES
LAMBETH PALACE GARDENS
Palace Road
WESTMINSTER CATHEDRAL
Osteria Dell'Angolo
Horseferry Rd
Lambeth Bridge
Lambeth High St.
VINCENT SQ.
VICTORIA
TATE BRITAIN
Atterbury St.
Millbank
Black Prince Rd
Pimlico
BESSBOROUGH GARDENS
ST GEORGE'S SQ.
Vauxhall Bridge
SPRING GARDENS
VAUXHALL
Kennington Lane
Harleyford Road
DOLPHIN SQ.
Grosvenor Road
Vauxhall
STRAND & COVENT GARDEN (Plan III)
SOUTHWARK (Plan X)
200 m
200 yards

Amaya ✿

Indian

F5

Halkin Arcade, 19 Motcomb St ✉ SW1X 8JT
✆ (020) 7823 1166
www.realindianfood.com
⊖ Knightsbridge
Closed dinner 25 December

Menu £21, £55/80 – Carte £37/59

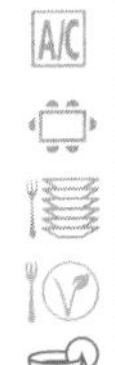

Amaya

Amaya loosely translates as 'without boundaries' and this reflects both the Indian restaurant's open layout – the kitchen forms part of the main room – and its desire to attract all types of diner, from families and friends to business-types and couples. It is this mix of customer that lends the room its lively atmosphere, helped along by the noise and aroma of the chefs working on the tawa, tandoor and Sigri grills. Bring an appetite with you and order a couple of small plates from the first two sections of the menu then a main course each and some breads; and don't ignore the excellent vegetable dishes like calabrese and sweetcorn. The menu changes regularly but certain popular dishes like grilled lamb chops, griddled scallops and tandoori black pepper chicken rarely come off it. Dishes taste as good as they look – and they look very good indeed. The kitchen takes care to ensure your meal is nicely paced and vegetarians are equally well looked after. The waiting staff are helpful and enthusiastic and if you haven't booked, try the long, communal table.

First Course

- Minced chicken parcels with coconut and lime dressing.
- Rock oysters with coconut and ginger moilee sauce.

Main Course

- Slow-roasted leg of lamb with royal cumin and garam masala.
- Tandoori prawns with tomato and ginger.

Dessert

- Blood orange brûlée.
- Rasmalai chocolate terrine with saffron milk.

Ⓝ Ametsa with Arzak Instruction ✿

innovative

G5

Halkin Hotel,
5 Halkin St ✉ SW1X 7DJ
✆ (020) 7333 1234
www.comohotels.com/thehalkin
⊖ Hyde Park Corner
Closed lunch Sunday and Monday

Menu £52/105 – Carte £53/69

A/C

The Halkin

The clever people behind the Halkin hotel always seem to sense when their restaurant has run its course and it's time for a change. The room on the ground floor of the hotel has been an Italian and a Thai, and now it's Spanish – but not just any Spanish restaurant because it's the Arzak father and daughter team who are bringing the Basque country to Belgravia. Despite the rather clumsy name, this isn't a direct copy or a clone of their iconic restaurant in San Sebastián, rather a restaurant specifically for London. The ingredients are largely from the UK yet the flavour combinations are typically Basque, even when dishes are playful or idiosyncratic. The menus are concise and its descriptions fairly economical, so help from the staff will be needed. The dishes are certainly appealing to the eye, without seeming to be overworked, and are often served with a finishing flourish of sauce-pouring at the table. The restaurant is much brighter and the thousands of test tubes filled with spices hanging from the ceiling are its most eye-catching element.

First Course
- King prawns with sweetcorn.
- Red skin sardines.

Main Course
- Lamb with macchiato.
- Ox cheeks with vanilla.

Dessert
- 'Moon Rocks'.
- Basque toast.

Apsleys ✿

Italian

G4

Lanesborough Hotel,
Hyde Park Corner ✉ SW1X 7TA
✆ (020) 7333 7254
www.apsleysrestaurant.com
⊖ Hyde Park Corner

Menu £25 (lunch) – Carte £60/113

The Lanesborough

Apsleys is the London outpost of Heinz Beck, the German-born chef who runs La Pergola restaurant in Rome. The kitchen here at the Lanesborough hotel works under his guidance and the food is sophisticated and refined, and proves that Italian food need not always be of the rustic variety. The dishes demonstrate a deft touch without slipping into fussiness and there are subtle hints of innovation, such as in the signature dish carbonara fagottelli. Meat, fish and shellfish are sourced from the British Isles but the rest of the ingredients come directly from Italy. Designed by the ubiquitous Adam Tihany, the room is elegant and undeniably opulent, but its grandeur never intimidates. If sitting in such a comfortable, well-dressed restaurant isn't enough, you can always ask for a table on the raised section if you really want to feel superior. The assured service team are adept at putting their guests at ease – they're also well-versed in the menu and offer fuller explanations, which is just as well as the menu descriptions are understated to say the least.

First Course

- Fish crudo.
- Tuna tartare with white tomato mousse.

Main Course

- Carbonara fagottelli.
- Dover sole with ratatouille.

Dessert

- Chocolate soufflé with vanilla and raspberry.
- Orange jelly with bergamot ice cream.

N A. Wong

Chinese H6

70 Wilton Rd ✉ SW1V 1DE
✆ (020) 7828 8931
www.awong.co.uk
⊖ Victoria
Closed 23-27 December, 1-2 January, Sunday and Monday lunch – booking essential

Menu £13/39 – Carte £15/24

Andrew Wong may have transformed what was formerly Kym's into a relaxed, modern and lively Chinese restaurant but you won't find him disparaging the previous owner, as she was his mother. He's taken classics from across China and, while there's the odd twist here and there, he keeps the original combinations intact, with dishes such as razor clams with sea cucumber and sausage. His food tastes light and fresh and flavours are nicely balanced. Start with snacks like peanuts in vinegar or egg with shredded filo; then, if it's lunch, try their excellent dim sum; otherwise, the 'Taste of China' 8 course menu offers a good summation of his style. Service is keen, as are the prices. Sit at the counter if you want to see the woks in action.

Boisdale of Belgravia

British traditional G6

15 Eccleston St ✉ SW1W 9LX
✆ (020) 7730 6922
www.boisdale.co.uk
⊖ Victoria
Closed 25 December, Saturday lunch, Sunday and bank holidays

Menu £20 – Carte £27/78

Acres of tartan, whiskies galore, haggis, mash and neeps - Boisdale couldn't be more Scottish if it sang 'Scots Wha Hae' and did the Highland Fling. Owner Ranald Macdonald bought various parts of the building at different times, hence the charmingly higgledy-piggledy layout. The original Auld Restaurant is the more characterful; the Macdonald Bar has more buzz and nightly live jazz and a large cigar selection add to the masculine feel. The menu features plenty of Scottish produce, from Orkney herring to Shetland scallops, but the stand-outs are the four varieties of smoked salmon, followed by the 28-day aged Aberdeenshire cuts of beef. Ignore the lacklustre tomato and watercress garnish and just savour the quality of the meat.

The Cinnamon Club

Indian

I5

30-32 Great Smith St ✉ SW1P 3BU
✆ (020) 7222 2555
www.cinnamonclub.com
⊖ St James's Park
Closed bank holidays and Sunday

Menu £24/75 – Carte £31/60

It may still look like a library, albeit a smart one with lovely parquet flooring, original wood panelling and a gallery of bookcases, but this Grade II listed building is actually home to some pretty ambitious modern Indian cooking. You can come for breakfast – eschew the fry-up and try the spiced scrambled eggs or rice cakes instead; lunch sees a good value set menu, while at dinner the main menu is supplemented by a monthly changing themed menu resolving around perhaps game of Indo-Malaysian fish but this plethora of menus can put the kitchen under some pressure. Presentation is quite arty and tandoori dishes stand out. The atmosphere is buzzy and the basement bar is funky; service is well organised but perhaps a little over-formal.

Il Convivio

Italian

G6

143 Ebury St ✉ SW1W 9QN
✆ (020) 7730 4099
www.ilconvivio.co.uk
⊖ Sloane Square
Closed Christmas-New Year, Easter, Sunday and bank holidays

Menu £18/24 – Carte £24/51

If passing by, you'll find yourself being drawn in by the appealing façade of this handsome Georgian townhouse – and there's usually an eager welcome to boot, whether you're a regular or first-timer. Inside is equally pleasant, with Dante's poetry embossed on the wall to remind you you're in an Italian restaurant and a retractable roof at the back, under which sit the best tables. All pasta is made on the top floor of the house; the squid ink spaghetti with lobster is a menu staple. Dishes are artfully presented but not so showy as to compromise the flavours. Artisanal cheeses are carefully selected and looked after, while service is confident and able. Using the private dining room allows you to imagine being the owner of the house.

Dining Room

British traditional

H5

Goring Hotel,
15 Beeston Pl ✉ SW1W 0JW
✆ (020) 7396 9000
www.thegoring.com
⊖ Victoria
Closed Saturday lunch

Menu £38/50

A/C

Like the hotel in which it is found, The Goring Dining Room is a paean to all things British and is perfect for those who still like things done 'properly'. Designed by Viscount Linley, the room is as urbane as it is serene; its staff are supremely proficient and service is not without a little theatre. The chef tours the country looking for the best ingredients for his unambiguously British menu; his beef comes from the Castle of Mey estate, his lobsters are Scottish and his butter from Gloucestershire. On the menu you'll find potted game and jugged hare, beef Wellington, poached salmon, and eggs Drumkibo, which was a favourite dish of the late Queen Mother. Lunch – here still called luncheon—features a daily special from the trolley.

The Ebury Restaurant & Wine Bar

French

G6

139 Ebury St. ✉ SW1W 9QU
✆ (020) 7730 5447
www.eburyrestaurant.co.uk
⊖ Victoria
Closed Christmas-New Year

Menu £19 – Carte £28/41

A/C

There are probably many reasons why The Ebury Wine Bar has been going strong for over 50 years but likeability and adaptability must surely be two. It has an endearing honesty that is largely down to the eagerness of the longstanding staff, and changing habits have meant that the focus is now more on the food than the wine; even the bar offers a decent snack menu. Go through to the dining room, with its trompe l'oeil, and you'll find a kitchen that brings imaginative international influences to some dishes but is equally happy doing the classics such as lamb cutlets or liver and bacon. The set menu includes a glass of champagne; there are separate dairy and gluten free menus and the wine list is thoughtfully compiled and keenly priced.

Grand Imperial

Chinese

H5

Grosvenor Hotel,
101 Buckingham Palace Rd ✉ SW1W 0SJ
✆ (020) 7821 8898
www.grandimperiallondon.com
⊖ Victoria

Menu £16/75 – Carte £22/192

Grand it most certainly is, as this elegant Chinese restaurant is to be found in the impressive surroundings of The Grosvenor hotel's former ballroom. In fact, in between the pillars and the ornate ceiling, the only indication that this is a Chinese restaurant is the calligraphy on the walls. The Grand Imperial is a collaboration between the hotel owners and a Malaysian restaurant company and specialises in Cantonese cuisine, particularly the version found in Hong Kong. Techniques of steaming and frying are used to great effect with such signature dishes as diced beef steak with black pepper sauce and steamed lobster with Chinese wine and egg white. There is no fusion food here; just authentic flavours and quality ingredients.

Koffmann's

French

G4

Berkeley Hotel,
Wilton Pl ✉ SW1X 7RL
✆ (020) 7235 1010
www.the-berkeley.co.uk
⊖ Knightsbridge

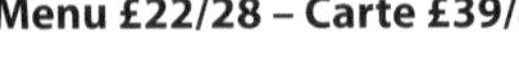

Menu £22/28 – Carte £39/84

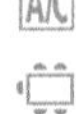

There are several talented chefs in the UK who owe much of their success to the time they spent working with Pierre Koffmann. The next generation now have the opportunity to learn from this celebrated chef, here at his eponymous restaurant in The Berkeley hotel where he cooks gutsy, flavoursome dishes close to his heart from the Gascony region of France. Those with fond memories of his former restaurant, La Tante Claire, will recognise some of his signature dishes – scallops with squid ink, and stuffed pig's trotter – but try too his newer creations such as squid bolognaise. Service is smooth and confident, sommeliers are clued up and the dining room comfortable and discreet. Be sure to ask for a table in the main body of the room.

Marcus Wareing at The Berkeley ✿✿

modern

G4

Berkeley Hotel,
Wilton Pl ✉ SW1X 7RL
✆ (020) 7235 1200
www.marcus-wareing.com
⊖ Knightsbridge
Closed 1 January and Sunday

Menu £30 (weekday lunch), £60/115

A/C

Marcus Wareing at The Berkeley

Marcus Wareing's media profile may have risen over the last few years but it hasn't been at the detriment of his eponymous restaurant at The Berkeley hotel, where standards remain high. His cooking is still underpinned by sound techniques but these days it is less classically French and now has a lighter, more modern element to it. What hasn't changed is the care and attention shown in each dish or the complimenting flavours and textures. Three menus are offered: the à la carte and two tasting menus; the latter two offering the best gastronomic tour of his culinary style. The restaurant itself remains elegant and very comfortable. If you like to see how it's all done, then consider booking the Chef's Table which is one of London's best and a great option for small groups. The front of house team is young and sometimes a little over-confident but a meal here will always be a special event. The predominantly French wine list is an impressive and weighty tome and the tasting menus' wine pairings have been thoughtfully considered.

First Course

- Mackerel, scallop, pine nut and yuzu.
- Portland crab with radish and cucumber.

Main Course

- Suckling lamb with beans, oregano and Flower Marie.
- Grouse with celeriac and blackberries.

Dessert

- Horlicks, honey and whisky.
- Coffee, marsala and mascarpone.

Massimo

Italian

J4

Corinthia Hotel,
10 Northumberland Ave. ✉ WC2N 5AE
✆ (020) 7321 3156
www.corinthia.com/london
⊖ Embankment
Closed Sunday

Menu £28/30 – Carte £21/54

David Collins has been responsible for designing some of London's most striking restaurants but few can match the grandeur of Massimo. This huge room is dominated by vast, striped Corinthian columns; beautiful mosaics and plenty of marble augment the feeling of unrelenting luxury, while leather-covered booths add some warmth and comfort to proceedings. Taking up the challenge provided by these surroundings is a kitchen specialising in seafood and while the menu may be written in Italian, the cooking could be considered largely Mediterranean. Dishes are kept fairly classical in influence and relatively simple in make-up, and although the food may not always live up to the splendour of the room, the prices do.

Northall

British traditional

J4

Corinthia Hotel,
Whitehall Pl. ✉ WC2N 5AE
✆ (020) 7321 3100
www.thenorthall.co.uk
⊖ Embankment

Menu £28/30 – Carte £29/61

The Corinthia Hotel's British restaurant not only celebrates our indigenous food but also champions its producers by acknowledging them all on the menu. It is certainly an appealing document with the likes of potted shrimps, Dover sole meunière and roast venison with swede alongside a grilled section using Cumbrian shorthorn cattle aged for 28 days. The kitchen is also not averse to looking across the Channel for the occasional influence. The restaurant occupies two rooms; the most appealing is the more modern room with its bar counter and booths while the other section is more formally arranged and better suited for a business lunch. An attractive 'market place' set up with cheese and meat displays links the two rooms.

Olivo

Italian G6

21 Eccleston St ✉ SW1W 9LX
✆ (020) 7730 2505
www.olivorestaurants.com
⊖ Victoria
Closed lunch Saturday-Sunday and bank holidays – booking essential

Menu £24 (lunch) – Carte £28/41

A/C

The cooking at Olivo has always been highly capable and reassuringly reliable, which does tend to make up for the service which is never quite as engaging as you hope it will be. Nevertheless this is a popular, pleasant and relaxed little neighbourhood Italian, with vivid blues and yellows, rough wooden floorboards and intimate lighting. The menu showcases the robust flavours of Sardinia and changes fortnightly, although some dishes, such as spaghetti bottarga and linguine with crab, remain permanent features. There are normally a few daily specials – particularly for the regulars – dishes are clearly prepared with care and desserts continue the regional theme; try sebada, a traditional Sardinian cheese fritter.

Olivocarne

Italian G6

61 Elizabeth St ✉ SW1W 9PP
✆ (020) 7730 7997
www.olivorestaurants.com
⊖ Sloane Square

Menu £27 (lunch) – Carte £28/49

A/C

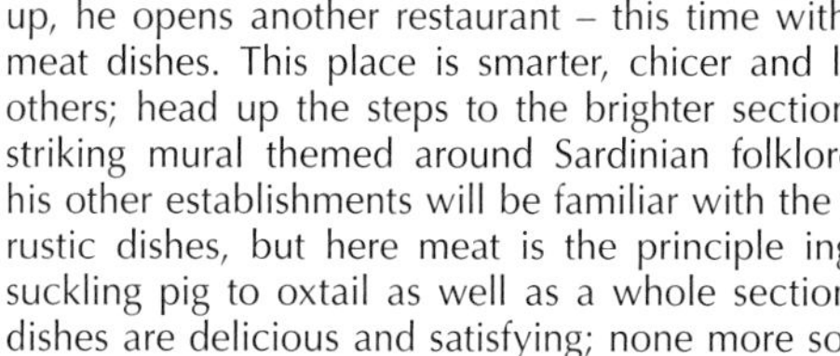

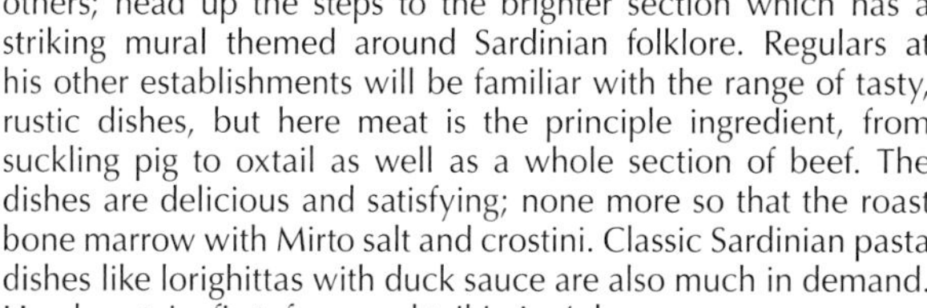

Just when you thought Mauro Sanno had this part of town sewn up, he opens another restaurant – this time with the focus on meat dishes. This place is smarter, chicer and larger than his others; head up the steps to the brighter section which has a striking mural themed around Sardinian folklore. Regulars at his other establishments will be familiar with the range of tasty, rustic dishes, but here meat is the principle ingredient, from suckling pig to oxtail as well as a whole section of beef. The dishes are delicious and satisfying; none more so that the roast bone marrow with Mirto salt and crostini. Classic Sardinian pasta dishes like lorighittas with duck sauce are also much in demand. Head upstairs first, for a cocktail in Joe's bar.

Olivomare

fish and seafood

G5

10 Lower Belgrave St ✉ SW1W 0LJ
(020) 7730 9022
www.olivorestaurants.com
⊖ Victoria
Closed bank holidays

Carte £34/48

Italian seafood, particularly Sardinian seafood, is celebrated here at Olivomare, a bright and lively restaurant whose design owes as much to Barbarella as it does M.C. Escher. Bottarga naturally features and not just with spaghetti – it also comes with Sardinian artichokes and even burrata. The stews are terrific as are the couscous soups; the octopus, whether in a salad, a stew or just roasted is always worth ordering. For pud the 'gelato allo yoghurt' is good and is just one of the items that can also be bought from their well-stocked deli next door. The wine list is a little limited by the glass but otherwise this is a very warmly run and understandably popular local, where freshness and simplicity combine to great effect.

The Orange

Mediterranean

G6

37 Pimlico Rd ✉ SW1W 8NE
(020) 7881 9844
www.theorange.co.uk
⊖ Sloane Square.

Carte £22/40

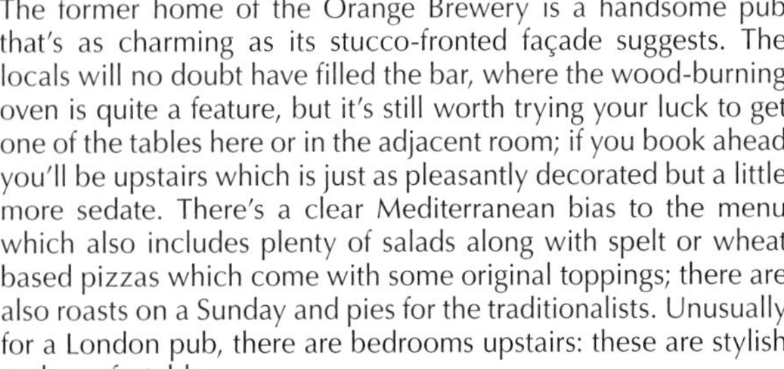

The former home of the Orange Brewery is a handsome pub that's as charming as its stucco-fronted façade suggests. The locals will no doubt have filled the bar, where the wood-burning oven is quite a feature, but it's still worth trying your luck to get one of the tables here or in the adjacent room; if you book ahead you'll be upstairs which is just as pleasantly decorated but a little more sedate. There's a clear Mediterranean bias to the menu which also includes plenty of salads along with spelt or wheat based pizzas which come with some original toppings; there are also roasts on a Sunday and pies for the traditionalists. Unusually for a London pub, there are bedrooms upstairs: these are stylish and comfortable.

Osteria Dell' Angolo

Italian

I6

47 Marsham St ✉ SW1P 3DR
✆ (020) 3268 1077
www.osteriadellangolo.co.uk
⊖ St James's Park
Closed Easter, 17-31 August, 23-27 December, 1-7 January, Saturday lunch, Sunday and bank holidays – booking essential

Menu £17/28 – Carte £30/45

The name may suggest a simple little neighbourhood trattoria but this is, in fact, a rather smart, conscientiously run Italian restaurant offering some authentic, carefully prepared Italian food. As it's opposite the Home Office, lunch is quite a busy time and regulars, who include the odd MP, tend to get the tables on the raised section at the back rather than the less comfortable area by the bar where the Johnny-come-latelys get seated. The kitchen team, visible behind the glass, offer a fairly comprehensive culinary tour of the country's regions and their dishes deliver reassuringly emphatic flavours. There's also a decent selection of wines by the glass for anyone who fears the ignominy of having their expense claims examined.

Pantechnicon

British modern

G5

10 Motcomb St ✉ SW1X 8LA
✆ (020) 7730 6074
www.thepantechnicon.com
⊖ Knightsbridge.
Closed 25 December – booking advisable

Carte £27/63

It may be the very antithesis of the spit 'n' sawdust pub, but The Pantechnicon is still a very welcoming and busy local. The brightly run ground floor is crammed with tables and works on a first-come-first-served basis; upstairs you'll find a far more formal, Georgian style dining room and there's even a top floor cocktail bar – this is Belgravia after all. Wisely, the same menu is served throughout – an appealing mix of the refined and the comforting. Castle of Mey 28-day aged steaks and salt and chilli squid are the two most popular choices; home-smoked salmon, burgers and fish pie are also done well. The name comes from the horse-drawn wagons that once transported the belongings of locals to and from a repository on Motcomb Street.

Pétrus ✿

French

G5

1 Kinnerton St ✉ SW1X 8EA
✆ (020) 7592 1609
www.gordonramsay.com/petrus
⊖ Knightsbridge
Closed Christmas and Sunday

Menu £35/75

Gordon Ramsay Holdings

Gordon Ramsay's smart Belgravia restaurant is an unapologetically sophisticated and discreet affair, geared to an urbane and international clientele. It is attractively decorated in understated tones of silver, oyster and – to add warmth to the room and as a nod to the name – claret. Tables are immaculately dressed and service is under the watchful eye of an experienced and courteous team who never let proceedings get too reverential. Downstairs is the 'show' kitchen with its horseshoe-shaped chef's table, for those whose enjoyment of a meal is sharpened by watching a large brigade of chefs – in this case around 14 – beavering away in front of them. The uninitiated should initially try lunch, when they'll find a set menu that won't break the bank; there are also vegetarian and chef's menus alongside the appealing à la carte of French-based dishes. The restaurant's name is not just reflected in the décor – the superb wine list includes over 20 vintages of Château Pétrus going back to 1924.

First Course

- Scallops with cauliflower, anchovy and capers.
- Langoustines, crispy chicken wing, leeks, artichokes and bisque.

Main Course

- Fillet of beef, roast onion, braised shin, bone marrow and barolo jus.
- Loin of venison, red cabbage, macaroni and stilton.

Dessert

- Chocolate sphere with milk ice cream and honeycomb.
- Banana millefeuille, caramel crème and peanut butter ice cream.

Quilon ✿

Indian

St James' Court Hotel,
41 Buckingham Gate ✉ SW1E 6AF
✆ (020) 7821 1899
www.quilon.co.uk
⊖ St James's Park
Closed 25 December

Menu £24/58 – Carte £30/53

Quilon

An extensive 2012 makeover left this longstanding Indian restaurant looking slick and contemporary. A stylish bar was added, along with a striking private dining room which comes with its own kitchen. These elegant surroundings provide the ideal backdrop to chef Sriram Aylur's accomplished cooking, which focuses on India's southwest coast. 'Progression' is one of his watchwords and he has overseen a transformation in the food which is now considerably lighter than much Indian cuisine. There's a high degree of originality in some of the dishes, such as his own version of black cod and his imaginative dishes involving game, but traditionalists will still find much to savour, whether that's masala dosa or a fish curry with coconut. The crab cakes are a delight and the colourful and crisp okra is very moreish. The serving team are charming and helpful; the wine list has been thoughtfully compiled to complement the food and there's an interesting selection of beers too. The re-launch of Quilon is something to be celebrated by all lovers of Indian food.

First Course

- Fisherman's catch.
- Cauliflower chilli fry.

Main Course

- Braised lamb shank.
- Venison with coconut and spices.

Dessert

- Spiced chocolate with lentil cappuccino.
- Caramelised banana pudding with rum and raisin ice cream.

Roux at Parliament Square

modern I5

Royal Institution of Chartered Surveyors, Parliament Sq.
✉ SW1P 3AD ✆ (020) 7334 3737
www.rouxatparliamentsquare.co.uk
⊖ Westminster
Closed 23 December-4 January, Saturday, Sunday and bank holidays – bookings advisable at lunch

Menu £35/65 – Carte £42/65

XXX

The offices of the Royal Institute of Chartered Surveyors play host to this attractive Westminster restaurant. It's really a Compass-run operation, in conjunction with Michel Roux of Le Gavroche fame. However, instead of the classical French cuisine for which M. Roux is known, here the food is more contemporary in style and adopts some modern techniques. Dishes are still carefully crafted but occasionally you can expect some interesting combinations of flavours. The decoration is cool and comfortable, with plenty of natural light flooding through the Georgian windows. Service, from a well-trained team, comes with personality and there is a particularly attractive private dining room in the library.

Santini

Italian G5

29 Ebury St ✉ SW1W 0NZ
✆ (020) 7730 4094
www.santinirestaurant.com
⊖ Victoria
Closed 23-26 December, 1 January and Easter

Carte £30/80

XXX

Despite the high prices within, and the economic meltdown without, Santini 's loyal and immaculately coiffured customers continue to eschew cheaper alternatives and instead turn up here with impressive regularity. Indeed, it is by looking after its regulars so well for nearly 30 years that the restaurant has managed to remain largely unruffled by the winds of recession. The menu of classic Italian dishes broadly Venetian in style is supplemented by daily specials; the cooking is reliable and confident, while pasta dishes and desserts remain the standout courses. If you are one of the regulars, you'll find yourself not only charmed by the flattery you'll receive, but you'll also be offered their excellent Carasau bread.

Thomas Cubitt

modern

G6

44 Elizabeth St ✉ SW1W 9PA
(020) 7730 6060
www.thethomascubitt.co.uk
⊖ Sloane Square.
Booking essential

Carte £28/40

The Thomas Cubitt is a pub of two halves: on the ground floor it's perennially busy and you can't book which means that if you haven't arrived by 7pm then you're too late to get a table. However, you can reserve a table upstairs, in a dining room that's a model of civility and tranquillity. Here, service comes courtesy of a young team where the girls are chatty and the men unafraid of corduroy. Downstairs you get fish and chips; here you get pan-fried fillet of brill with oyster beignet and truffled chips. The cooking is certainly skilled, quite elaborate in its construction and prettily presented. So, take your pick: upstairs can get a little pricey but is ideal for entertaining the in-laws; if out with friends then crowd in downstairs.

Tinello

Italian

G6

87 Pimlico Rd ✉ SW1W 8PH
(020) 7730 3663
www.tinello.co.uk
⊖ Sloane Square
Closed Sunday – booking essential at dinner

Carte £29/51

Italian restaurants have always thrived in this neighbourhood but it's no bad thing for a newcomer to shake things up and that's exactly what Tinello is doing. It is run by two Italian brothers, Max and Federico, who previously worked as sommelier and head chef respectively at Locanda Locatelli. The majority of the menu leans on their native Tuscany for inspiration and this is especially evident in the tempting antipasti or 'small eats' section. Pasta is exemplary and main courses ooze confidence. Service is undertaken with a refreshing earnestness and the sleek restaurant is spread over two floors; the ground floor is more fun, but if you are downstairs you do get to see the kitchen in action through the glass windows.

Zafferano

Italian

15 Lowndes St ✉ SW1X 9EY
✆ (020) 7235 5800
www.zafferanorestaurant.co.uk
⊖ Knightsbridge
Booking essential

F5

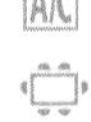

Carte £33/60

Zafferano may be a senior member of London's Italian restaurant fraternity but for the gilded few who live in Belgravia's grand terraces and white stucco houses, it is more like their local canteen –and the restaurant is sensible enough to realise that looking after these guests is their primary concern. The menu is written for those who like their Italian food to be reassuringly familiar and, as everyone has their favourite dishes, the kitchen has settled into something of a routine. Unfortunately this has led to a little complacency, with some of the sparkle going out of the cooking. But the place does still deliver on the bustle and bonhomie, especially if you are sitting in the main room rather than in the extension.

The sun is out – let's eat alfresco! Look for 🏖.

Regent's Park · Marylebone

The neighbourhood north of chaotic Oxford Street is actually a rather refined place where shoppers like to venture for the smart boutiques, and where idlers like to saunter for the graceful parkland acres full of rose gardens and quiet corners. In fact, Marylebone and Regent's Park go rather well together, a moneyed village with a wonderful park for its back garden.

Marylebone may now exude a fashionable status, but its history tells a very different tale. Thousands used to come here to watch executions at Tyburn gallows, a six hundred year spectacle that stopped in the late eighteenth century. Tyburn stream was covered over, and the area's modern name came into being as a contraction of St Mary by the Bourne, the parish church. Nowadays the people who flock here come to gaze at less ghoulish sights, though some of the inhabitants of the eternally popular Madame Tussauds deserved no better fate than the gallows. South across the busy Marylebone Road, the preponderance of swish restaurants and snazzy specialist shops announces your arrival at **Marylebone High Street.** There are patisseries, chocolatiers, cheese shops and butchers at every turn, nestling alongside smart places to eat and drink. At St Marylebone Church, each Saturday heralds a posh market called Cabbages & Frocks, where artisan food meets designer clothing in a charming garden. Further down, the century old Daunt Books has been described as London's most beautiful bookshop: it has long oak galleries beneath graceful conservatory skylights. Close by, the quaintly winding Marylebone Lane boasts some truly unique shops like tiny emporium The Button Queen, which sells original Art Deco, Victorian and Edwardian buttons. In complete contrast, just down the road from here is the mighty **Wigmore Hall,** an art nouveau gem with great acoustics and an unerringly top-notch classical agenda that can be appreciated at rock-bottom prices. Meanwhile, art lovers can indulge an eclectic fix at the **Wallace Collection** in **Manchester Square,** where paintings by the likes of Titian and Velazquez rub shoulders with Sevres porcelain and grand Louis XIV furniture.

Regent's Park – an idyllic Georgian oasis stretching off into London's northern suburbs - celebrated its two hundredth birthday in 2011. Before architect John Nash and his sponsor The Prince Regent gave it its much-loved geometric makeover, it had been farming land, and prior to that, one of Henry VIII's hunting grounds. His spirit lives on, in the sense that various activities are catered for, from tennis courts to a running track. And there are animals too, albeit not roaming free, at **London Zoo,** in the park's northerly section. Most people, though, come here to while away an hour or two around the boating lake or amble the Inner Circle which

C. Eymenier / MICHELIN

contains **Queen Mary's Gardens** and their enchanting bowers of fragrant roses. Others come for a summer sojourn to the Open Air Theatre where taking in a performance of 'A Midsummer Night's Dream' is very much ***de rigueur***. The Regent's Canal provides another fascinating element to the park. You can follow its peaceful waters along a splendid walk from the **Little Venice** houseboats in the west, past the golden dome of the **London Central Mosque,** and on into the north-west confines of Regent's Park as it snakes through London Zoo, before it heads off towards Camden Lock. On the other side of Prince Albert Road, across from the zoo, the scenic glory takes on another dimension with a climb up Primrose Hill. Named after the grassy promontory that sets it apart from its surrounds, to visitors this is a hill with one of the best panoramas in the whole of London; to locals (ie, actors, pop stars, media darlings and the city set) it's an ultra fashionable place to live with pretty Victorian terraces and accordingly sky-high prices. Either way you look at it (or from it), it's a great place to be on a sunny day with the breeze in your hair.

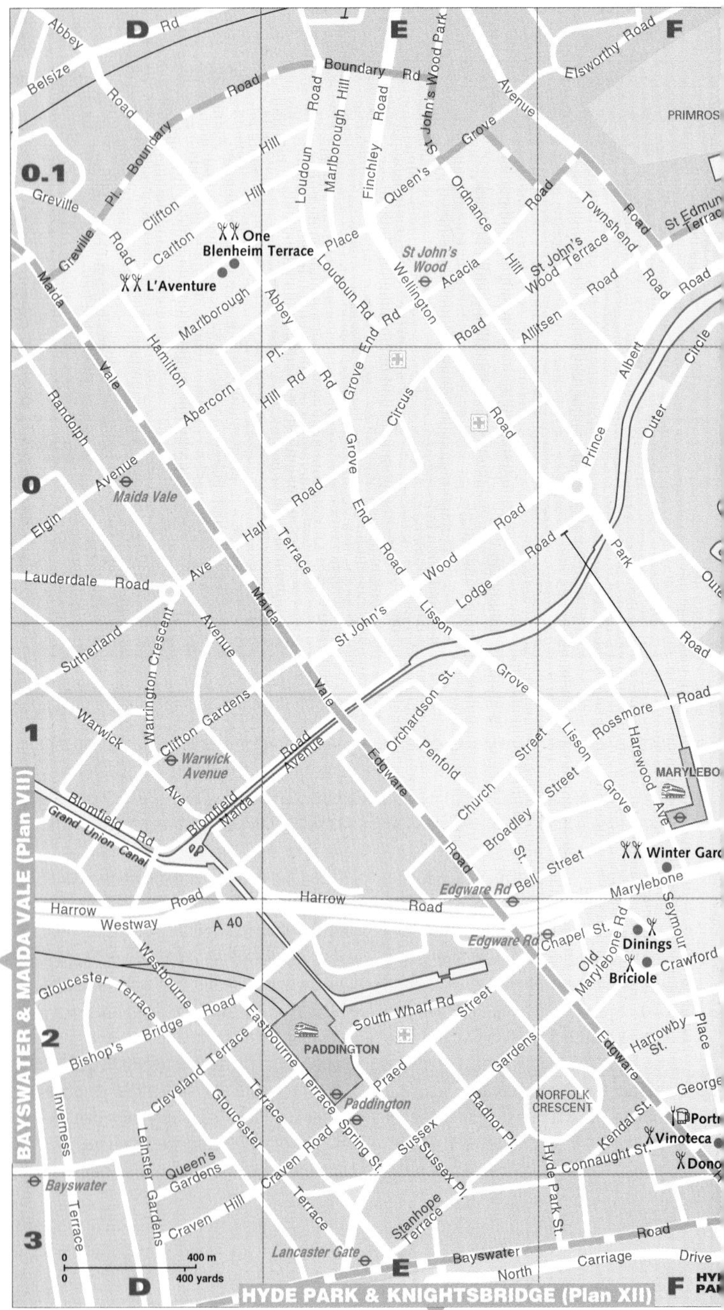

BAYSWATER & MAIDA VALE (Plan VIII)
HYDE PARK & KNIGHTSBRIDGE (Plan XII)
One Blenheim Terrace
L'Aventure
Winter Garden
Dinings
Briciole
Vinoteca
St John's Wood
Maida Vale
Warwick Avenue
Edgware Rd
Paddington
Bayswater
Lancaster Gate
PADDINGTON
MARYLEBONE
NORFOLK CRESCENT
PRIMROSE
0 400 m
0 400 yards

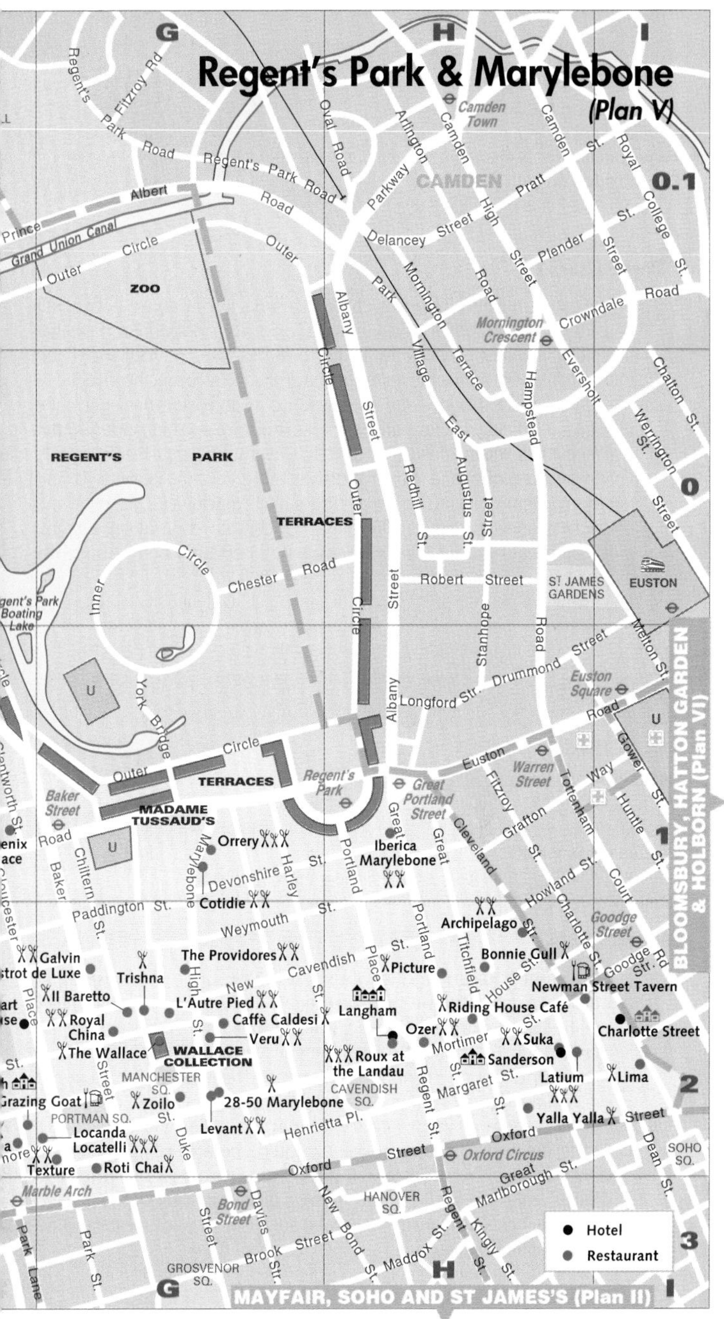
Regent's Park & Marylebone
(Plan V)
REGENT'S PARK
ZOO
TERRACES
CAMDEN
Camden Town
Mornington Crescent
EUSTON
Euston Square
Warren Street
Great Portland Street
Regent's Park
Baker Street
MADAME TUSSAUD'S
WALLACE COLLECTION
ST JAMES GARDENS
Orrery
Iberica Marylebone
Cotidie
Archipelago
Bonnie Gull
Galvin Bistrot de Luxe
Trishna
The Providores
Picture
Newman Street Tavern
Il Baretto
L'Autre Pied
Langham
Riding House Café
Royal China
Caffè Caldesi
Charlotte Street
The Wallace
Veru
Ozer
Suka
Roux at the Landau
Sanderson
Latium
Lima
Grazing Goat
Zoilo
28-50 Marylebone
Yalla Yalla
Locanda Locatelli
Levant
Texture
Roti Chai
Oxford Circus
Marble Arch
Bond Street
Hotel
Restaurant
BLOOMSBURY, HATTON GARDEN & HOLBORN (Plan VI)
MAYFAIR, SOHO AND ST JAMES'S (Plan II)

Archipelago

innovative H2

53 Cleveland St ✉ W1T 4JJ
(020) 7383 3346
www.archipelago-restaurant.co.uk
⊖ Goodge Street
Closed 24-28 December, Saturday lunch, Sunday and bank holidays

Carte £28/37

Bored with beef? Tired of chicken? How about some zebra? Or a little crocodile? Not only is the gloriously oddball Archipelago unlike any other restaurant in London but tales of your meal can also be used to frighten small children. 'Exploring the exotic' is their slogan although 'eating the exotic' would be more exact: the menu reads like an inventory at an omnivore's safari park and the place itself resembles an eccentric Oriental bazaar that's rapidly running out of space. Several dishes are given an Asian twist and side dishes include the 'love-bug salad' made with locusts and crickets. Apart from a somewhat laborious reservation system, it's all great fun and the experience will certainly be memorable.

L'Aventure

French DO.1

3 Blenheim Terr ✉ NW8 0EH
(020) 7624 6232
www.laventure.co.uk
⊖ St John's Wood
Closed 2 weeks August, first week January, Saturday lunch, Sunday and bank holidays

Menu £22/43

Tailor-made for anyone with a sound grasp of French wishing to impress a date - the menu is written entirely in French so politely decline the waiter's offer of a quick translation and wait for the admiring looks. What's more, if it's a warm day, you'll be sitting in the enchanting front terrace where the shrubs are covered in twinkly lights. This is a charming neighbourhood restaurant with a cosy and warm interior, owned and run by the delightful Catherine who'll make you feel you're being unfaithful if you don't return. The set menu is good value at lunch but pricier at dinner when the well-heeled locals come out. Expect the French bourgeois classics, from artichoke salad to rack of lamb and an ile flottante to finish.

L'Autre Pied ✿

modern

G2

5-7 Blandford St. ✉ W1U 3DB
✆ (020) 7486 9696
www.lautrepied.co.uk
⊖ Bond Street
Closed 4 days Christmas, 1 January and Sunday dinner

Menu £26, £62/70 – Carte £50/62

L'Autre Pied

Head Chef Andy McFadden's food is marked out by a refreshing lack of showiness on the plate. He and his team present their dishes in a fairly natural way so that, despite some of the constructions being quite elaborate, the final result never looks too fiddly or overworked. The kitchen gets in whole animals – venison is a particular strength here – and creates robust yet easy to eat dishes which also provide very pleasing contrasts in textures. The chef's greater confidence and the restaurant's growing reputation have resulted in the presence of more luxury ingredients on the à la carte but prices are not stratospheric when one considers the levels of skill involved; the albeit simpler set lunch menu represents very good value indeed. The restaurant remains very different in style from its older sibling, Pied à Terre; it's very much part of the local 'village' and has a more casual, buoyant atmosphere. Ask for a table by the window as the middle section can be something of a thoroughfare.

First Course

- Scallop ceviche with black quinoa, radishes, fennel and dill.
- Foie gras with Brazil nuts, endive, apricots and nutmeg.

Main Course

- Roe deer, cocoa, juniper with black pudding, beetroot and watercress.
- Megrim sole with gem lettuce, broad beans, peas and mint.

Dessert

- Chocolate pavé, honeycomb, pistachio and tonka bean ice cream.
- Stem ginger mousse, mandarin and cherries.

Il Baretto

Italian G2

43 Blandford St. ✉ W1U 7HF
✆ (020) 7486 7340
www.ilbaretto.co.uk
⊖ Baker Street
Closed 25-26 December, lunch 31 December and 1 January

Menu £45/75 – Carte £25/54

The discreet entrance and small ground floor bar of this Italian restaurant don't give much away, but downstairs you'll find a large room with a degree of character and quite a lively atmosphere. The menu covers all bases so eating here can be as pricey or an inexpensive as you want: come along for a pizza and a beer and you'll do fine; push the boat out with a three course meal and you could find yourself with a surprisingly large bill. The cooking, though, is reliable and the star of the show is the robata grill – it delivers some very succulent lamb chops; pasta is done well and desserts show some ambition. Service can be a little more hit and miss: some staff members are very confident while others seem a little disinterested.

Bonnie Gull

fish and seafood H2

21a Foley St ✉ W1W 6DS
✆ (020) 7436 0921
www.bonniegull.com
⊖ Goodge Street
Booking essential

Carte £21/39

The very sweet Bonnie Gull calls itself a 'seafood shack' – a reference perhaps to its modest beginnings as a pop-up before it docked permanently here in the West End. It's kitted out in a pretty fishing-village kind of way and the tables are packed into the small room in an appropriately sardine-like manner. There's a decent raw bar to kick things off, offering oysters and cockles, winkles and whelks. The main menu is a mix of traditional favourites and more ambitious dishes, although the kitchen appears to be more adept at the former. Many go for the fish and chips but you can also get a decent Cullen Skink and a huge Devon cock crab; it's also worth getting a side order of chunky chips cooked in beef dripping.

Briciole

Italian

F2 

20 Homer St ✉ W1H 4NA
✆ (020) 7723 0040
www.briciole.co.uk
⊖ Edgware Road
Closed 25-26 December

Carte £13/25

Maurizio Morelli opened this fun, all-day Italian as a less expensive and more relaxed alternative to his Latium restaurant. Its credentials as a local neighbourhood spot lie in its accessible menu, faux-rustic surroundings and admirable prices. Service from the young team is also fairly laid back, although at times their unhurried approach makes it hard to figure out who are the customers and who are the staff. The menu is neatly divided into sections offering everything from hams and salamis to smoked fish and barbecue; worth exploring are the meatballs and sausages, which are homemade and suitably filling, along with the range of salads. Locals can also take advantage of the entire menu being available to take away.

Caffé Caldesi

Italian

G2 

118 Marylebone Ln. (1st floor) ✉ W1U 2QF
✆ (020) 7487 0754
www.caldesi.com
⊖ Bond Street

Menu £15/20 – Carte £21/46

This former pub is the hub of the Caldesi family business, which takes in restaurants, cookbooks and cookery schools, and it fits perfectly into the fabric of local Marylebone life. Upstairs is simply but warmly decorated and is enthusiastically run by a young team of Italians – the owners maintain they have staff from all of Italy's 20 regions. The atmosphere is never less than cheery, thanks in no small part to the seasonal menu, which offers up classics from across Italy that have one thing in common – they are generously proportioned and really deliver on flavour; the pasta dishes are particularly satisfying. On the ground floor you'll find a less structured operation with a slightly abridged but more accessibly priced menu.

Cotidie

Italian

G1

50 Marylebone High St ✉ W1U 5HN
✆ (020) 7258 9878
www.cotidierestaurant.com
⊖ Baker Street
Closed Christmas

Menu £27 (lunch) – Carte £37/65

'Cotidie' means 'everyday' in Italian which, in this instance, refers to the regularly changing menu rather than the style of the food. Bruno Barbieri may no longer be involved but the restaurant continues to serve food that is sophisticated, imaginative and far from 'everyday'. Inspiration comes from all parts of Italy and the elaborately constructed dishes show this to be a kitchen with ambition. Prices, though, are undeniably high and this means that, unlike many establishments around these rather charming parts, this is not so much a drop-in joint but more a destination for that special occasion. With that in mind it provides elegant and comfortable surroundings, well-made drinks and service that is organised and eager.

Dinings

Japanese

F2

22 Harcourt St. ✉ W1H 4HH
✆ (020) 7723 0666
www.dinings.co.uk
⊖ Edgware Road
Closed Christmas and Sunday – booking essential

Carte £19/59

In Tokyo the hanging sign outside would be considered positively flamboyant but in London it's the very definition of discretion, making this sweet little place easy to miss. There are half a dozen seats at the counter on the ground floor and a few tables downstairs in the somewhat claustrophobic basement; but wherever you sit, it's hard not to be charmed by it all. The menu is an extensive document, supplemented by blackboard specials, and takes many of its influences from the style of Japanese food found at Nobu, the owner's alma mater: accordingly, highlights are the more creative dishes like the 'sashimi four ways'. The temptation is to order plenty to share but beware because the prices can make this an expensive activity.

Donostia

Basque F2

10 Seymour Pl ✉ W1H 7ND
✆ (020) 3620 1845
www.donostia.co.uk
⊖ Marble Arch
Closed Monday lunch

Carte £14/32

As London's love affair with tapas continues, many diners are now keen on learning more about Spain's regional specialties. The bright and lively Donostia, which is the Basque name for San Sebastiàn, was opened by two young owners inspired by this coastal municipality. Anyone who has visited the area, known for the quality of its restaurants and its terrific pintxos, will recognise classic Basque dishes like cod with pil-pil sauce, chorizo from the native pig Kintoa and tender, slow-cooked pig's cheeks. Add in a thoughtful wine list along with the traditional drinks of cider and Txakoli and you have a winning recipe. You can book a table but it's worth trying for one of the 10 seats at the marble counter in front of the kitchen.

Galvin Bistrot de Luxe

French G2

66 Baker St. ✉ W1U 7DJ
✆ (020) 7935 4007
www.galvinrestaurants.com
⊖ Baker Street

Closed dinner 24 December, 25-26 December and 1 January

Menu £20/30 – Carte £31/54

Despite the enormous success of Galvin La Chapelle in The City, brothers Chris and Jeff Galvin have never taken their eyes off the ball here at their eponymous 'bistrot de luxe' in Baker Street. Regulars still flock here for the clubby, relaxed atmosphere and the traditional French food, which may look simple on the plate but is carefully constructed behind the scenes. The emphasis is very much on flavour; the kitchen's understanding and appreciation of ingredients, and the classic combinations in which they are used, really come through. The menu has enough variety to satisfy those happy to indulge but those with one eye on the cost should come for lunch or before 7pm if they want to take advantage of a good value fixed menu.

Grazing Goat

British traditional

F2 

6 New Quebec St ✉ W1H 7RQ
(020) 7724 7243
www.thegrazinggoat.co.uk
⊖ Marble Arch.
Booking essential at dinner

Carte £28/44

The Portman Estate, owners of some serious real estate in these parts and keen to raise the profile of its investment, encouraged an experienced pub operator more at home in Chelsea and Belgravia to venture a little further north and take over the old Bricklayers Arms. Renamed in homage to a past Lady Portman (who grazed goats in a field where the pub now stands as she was allergic to cows' milk), it is now a smart city facsimile of a country pub. It's first-come-first-served in the bar but you can book in the upstairs dining room. Pub classics are the order of the day, such as pies or Castle of Mey steaks, and Suffolk chicken is cooked on the rotisserie. The eight bedrooms are nicely furnished, with their bathrooms resembling Nordic saunas.

Iberica Marylebone

Spanish

H1 

195 Great Portland St ✉ W1W 5PS
(020) 7636 8650
www.ibericalondon.co.uk
⊖ Great Portland Street
Closed 24-26 December, Sunday dinner and bank holidays

Menu £10 (weekday lunch) – Carte £18/46

In 2012, after successfully launching a second branch in Canary Wharf, the original Iberica here at the top end of Great Portland Street was given a fresh new look. It's a sizeable space spread over two floors and comes divided into assorted areas so instead of taking the table you're offered, politely ask if you can wander around first – some prefer the intimacy of upstairs, others the bustle of the ground floor with its bar and deli. Along with an impressive array of Iberico hams, cured meats and cheeses are plenty of tapas style dishes to share. Highlights include the more filling dishes such as glossy black rice with cuttlefish and prawns, and a slowly braised beef cheek. Charming young staff are on hand to offer advice.

Latium

Italian H2

21 Berners St. ✉ W1T 3LP
✆ (020) 7323 9123
www.latiumrestaurant.com
⊖ Oxford Circus
Closed 25-26 December, 1 January, Saturday lunch, Sunday and bank holidays

Menu £17/36

The last revamp made it brighter and more contemporary but such is the loyalty of its followers that a simple lick of paint would have been enough. There's now a window into the kitchen for those who like to know where their food comes from, and a chef's table for those who want to watch them at it. Tables by the entrance are given away first but it's worth asking to be seated further in; you'll almost certainly be accommodated as staff are a friendly and considerate bunch. The chef-owner is from Lazio, hence the name, so expect cooking that is free from over-elaboration. Recipes from across Italy also feature and many use British ingredients. The good value lunch menu changes weekly and homemade ravioli is the speciality.

Levant

Lebanese G2

Jason Ct., 76 Wigmore St. ✉ W1U 2SJ
✆ (020) 7224 1111
www.levant.co.uk
⊖ Bond Street
Closed 25-26 December

Menu £10/50 – Carte £23/71

Levant shows how a basement location can be turned into a positive. As you walk down the stairs past the lanterns and the rose petals, with the scent of joss sticks and hookah pipes in the air, your expectations start to rise and your pulse begins to quicken – especially if it sounds as though the belly dancing has already started. As with anywhere with a little spice, this is a restaurant best enjoyed in a group: not only because of the principle of safety in numbers but because Lebanese and Middle Eastern food is there to be shared. The best thing to do is order one of the Feast menus as you get a balanced, all-round selection which includes plenty of mezze. And don't come for lunch – it's like arriving at a party on the wrong day.

Lima ✿

Peruvian I2

31 Rathbone Pl ✉ W1T 1JH
✆ (020) 3002 2640
www.limalondon.com
⊖ Goodge Street
Closed 23 December-3 January and Sunday

Menu £20 (lunch and early dinner) – Carte £29/46

A/C

Michelin

Lima is one of those restaurants that just makes you feel good about life – and that's even without the Pisco Sours which, to be honest, will get you in the mood for anything. Peruvian food is the ideal antidote to our recessionary times: it's full of punchy, invigorating flavours and fantastically vivid colours. Virgilio Martinez, who runs the acclaimed 'Central' restaurant in Lima, has created somewhere intimate, informal and fun in which to enjoy his refreshing and exciting cuisine. The menu may be awash with unfamiliar ingredients like tiger's milk and sacha inchi oil but the staff are more than willing to offer help. Most ingredients are from the UK but some are from small suppliers in Peru such as 'huayro potatoes 4000 metres' (a reference to the altitude rather than the depth at which these tubers are grown). Tiradito and its cousin ceviche are popular starters (the former being a slightly punchier version) and there is plenty of originality throughout the menu along with some playfulness, but there's also great skill.

First Course

- Sea bream ceviche, tiger's milk, pepper and cancha corn.
- Scallops tiradito with aji emulsion and casava.

Main Course

- Lamb shoulder 'seco', dried potato and pisco mosto verde.
- Halibut, Andean herbs, cancha corn parfait and mirasol aioli.

Dessert

- Lucuma fruit ice cream, chocolate powder, annatto and chancaca cream.
- Andean kiwicha with sheep's milk.

Locanda Locatelli ✿

Italian

G2

8 Seymour St. ✉ W1H 7JZ
✆ (020) 7935 9088
www.locandalocatelli.com
⊖ Marble Arch
Closed 25-26 December and 1 January

Carte £29/61

Locanda Locatelli

When your clientele is made up of lots of buffed and shiny people then it is important that you're looking pretty good yourself. So every year the cherry wood is given a fresh coat of varnish and the tan leather seating gets a good clean and this keeps the room looking dapper and slick. Despite the vicissitudes of fashion, Locanda Locatelli has remained an ever popular choice for the cognoscenti, thanks largely to the excellence of the cooking. The large serving team in their black shirts and white ties may look like they've just come from a Sicilian wedding, but they get the job done with alacrity and efficiency. The menu offers around ten dishes per section so there is enough choice for everyone, even those with food allergies. Pasta is a perennial highlight, especially the risotto and gnocchi, and desserts, which always include the toothsome tiramisu and tart of the day, are expertly rendered with flair and care. Thinly sliced calf's head makes an interesting start, while unfussy presentation allows the quality of fish to really shine.

First Course

- Scallops, celeriac purée and saffron vinaigrette.
- Chargrilled quail with liver crostino and apple balsamic.

Main Course

- Wild sea bass baked in salt and herb crust, escarole, sultanas and pine kernels.
- Breast of duck, spelt, broccoli with garlic and chilli.

Dessert

- Tasting of Amedei chocolate.
- Amalfi lemon 'Eton Mess'.

Ⓝ Newman Street Tavern

British traditional H2

48 Newman St ✉ W1T 1QQ
✆ (020) 3667 1445
www.newmanstreettavern.co.uk
⊖ Goodge Street
Closed bank holidays

Carte £23/39 

Provided it isn't preceded by "ye" and "olde", there's something very comforting about the word "tavern". The experienced foursome behind Newman Street Tavern chose the word deliberately as they wanted to create a genuinely warm and welcoming place for customers to come and celebrate British food – and they got it spot on. The menu has been thoughtfully compiled and, with its soused Cornish anchovies, Blackface lamb, game tea, and Banbury cakes, is instantly appealing. There are no short cuts in the kitchen: they do their own butchery, smoke their own fish, work closely with their suppliers and take issues of sustainability seriously. You can eat in the bustle of the bar or the charming and more sedate first floor dining room.

One Blenheim Terrace

innovative  D0.1

1 Blenheim Terrace ✉ NW8 0EH
✆ (020) 7372 1722
www.oneblenheimterrace.co.uk
⊖ St John's Wood
Closed Monday

Carte £16/51 

For his first solo venture the young chef has taken on premises that proved unsuccessful for the two previous incumbents, so support from St John's Wood locals is going to be vital. He hopes to draw them in by doing something a little different: some of his dishes are re-interpretations of '60s and '70s classics like crepe Suzette and beef Wellington. However, this is less about nostalgia and more about modern cooking techniques as the updated dishes bear little relation to the original – which may actually be no bad thing in some cases. It is not as gimmicky as it sounds and clearly there is talent in the kitchen. The restaurant itself comes into its own in the summer, thanks to the large terrace and glazed front section.

Orrery

modern

G1

55 Marylebone High St ✉ W1U 5RB
✆ (020) 7616 8000
www.orrery-restaurant.co.uk
⊖ Regent's Park
Booking essential

Menu £26 (weekday lunch)/60

Enthusiastic post-prandial shopping can be a perilously expensive pastime – the danger is doubled here as Orrery is perched temptingly above a Conran shop. These are actually converted stables from the 19C but, such is the elegance and style of the building, you'd never know. What is sure is the long, narrow restaurant looks its best when the daylight floods in; on warm days make time to have a drink on the terrific rooftop terrace. To complement these charming surroundings you'll be offered a bewildering array of menus, all of which feature quite elaborate, modern European cooking. Dishes are strong on presentation and there is the occasional twist but it's usually done with some meaning rather than merely straining for effect.

Ozer

Turkish

H2

5 Langham Pl., Regent St. ✉ W1B 3DG
✆ (020) 7323 0505
www.ozer.co.uk
⊖ Oxford Circus

Menu £12/25 – Carte £18/44

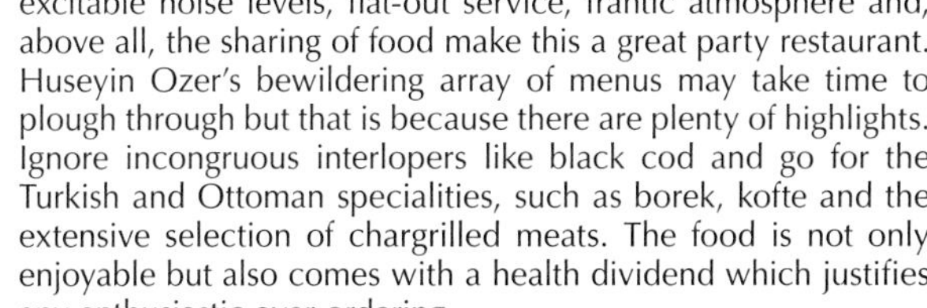

There are plenty of London restaurants ideal for a romantic dinner; Ozer is not one of them. Come here with a group of friends, though, and you'll have a fun time because its large bar, excitable noise levels, flat-out service, frantic atmosphere and, above all, the sharing of food make this a great party restaurant. Huseyin Ozer's bewildering array of menus may take time to plough through but that is because there are plenty of highlights. Ignore incongruous interlopers like black cod and go for the Turkish and Ottoman specialities, such as borek, kofte and the extensive selection of chargrilled meats. The food is not only enjoyable but also comes with a health dividend which justifies any enthusiastic over-ordering.

Phoenix Palace

Chinese F1

5 Glentworth St. ✉ NW1 5PG
✆ (020) 7486 3515
www.phoenixpalace.co.uk
⊖ Baker Street
Closed 25 December – bookings advisable at dinner

Menu £33 – Carte £24/65

Phoenix Palace may be around the corner from Baker Street but is the sort of vast restaurant that could just as easily be found off Stanley Street in Hong Kong. Come in a large group and there'll be a table big enough to accommodate you; order plenty of dishes to share and they'll be delivered swiftly by the well-drilled staff. The menu may be disconcertingly long but the dishes to go for are the Cantonese specialities like the soups, the roast meats and the king prawn dishes, along with the 'chef's specials' like fish maw with conpoy and winter melon. Dim sum is served until 5pm and is very popular with business types and locals. Ask for a table on the raised section which gives you a good view of this well-oiled machine.

Picture

British modern H2

110 Great Portland St. ✉ W1W 6PQ
✆ (020) 7637 7892
www.picturerestaurant.co.uk
⊖ Oxford Circus
Closed 25 December and Sunday

Carte £18/26

Two chefs and a manager, who all made their reputations at Arbutus and Wild Honey, set out on their own in 2013 and opened this terrific place in an under-developed part of Central London. The look may be a little stark – there's a large counter at the front fashioned out of recycled flooring and tables at the back beneath a skylight – but the service team add enormous warmth to the place and their enthusiasm is palpable. What was saved on the decoration was clearly spent on the shiny new kitchen downstairs, and it's paying dividends for these very skilful chefs. The small plates are vibrant, fresh and colourful; the flavours are assured and the contrasting textures a delight. And at these prices, Picture deserves success.

Portman

modern

F2 

51 Upper Berkeley St ✉ W1H 7QW
(020) 7723 8996
www.theportmanmarylebone.com
⊖ Marble Arch.

Menu £30/38 – Carte £21/35 

When it went by the name of The Masons Arms this pub was widely known for its gruesome history. It was here that the condemned, on their way to Tyburn Tree gallows, would take their last drink, which purportedly led to the phrase "one for the road". Reincarnated as The Portman, the pub these days boasts a less disreputable clientele who are more attracted by the quality of the cooking. Food is served all day and you can choose to eat in the busy ground floor bar or in the unexpectedly formal upstairs dining room, all thick-pile carpet and starched tablecloths. Fortunately, the style of food remains thoroughly down-to-earth and satisfying and is accompanied by a well-organised wine list and an interesting selection of cocktails.

The Providores

innovative

G2 

109 Marylebone High St. ✉ W1U 4RX
(020) 7935 6175
www.theprovidores.co.uk
⊖ Bond Street
Closed 25-26 December

Menu £25 (weekday lunch) – Carte £35/48 

'Marylebone Village' offers so many restaurants and cafés that it's becoming a destination in itself. Included in the roll call is this fusion restaurant within a former Edwardian pub. The warmth of the staff and the general buzz hit you immediately in the ground floor Tapa Room, where tables and tapas are shared. Upstairs is a slightly more sedate room but the staff are equally charming. Here all dishes come in starter size to "minimise food envy" and allow for sharing; three courses plus a dessert should suffice. There is no doubting the quality of the ingredients, although sometimes there's a flavour or two too many on the plate. The wine list champions New Zealand. Bookings are needed upstairs; downstairs, it's first-come-first-served.

Riding House Café

modern H2

43-51 Great Titchfield St ✉ W1W 7PQ
✆ (020) 7927 0840
www.ridinghousecafe.co.uk
⊖ Oxford Circus
Closed 25-26 December

Carte £22/41 

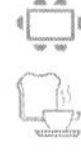

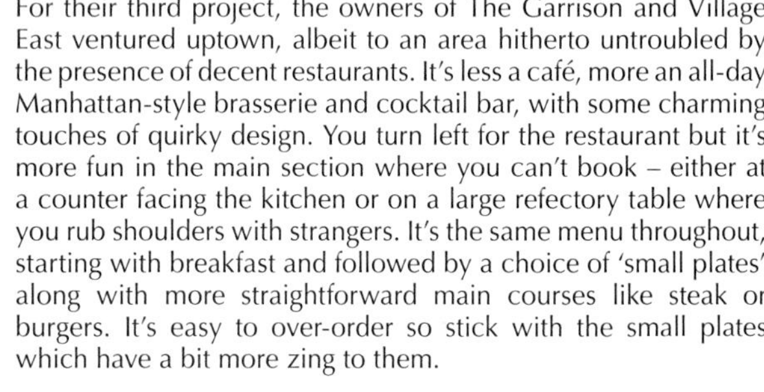

For their third project, the owners of The Garrison and Village East ventured uptown, albeit to an area hitherto untroubled by the presence of decent restaurants. It's less a café, more an all-day Manhattan-style brasserie and cocktail bar, with some charming touches of quirky design. You turn left for the restaurant but it's more fun in the main section where you can't book – either at a counter facing the kitchen or on a large refectory table where you rub shoulders with strangers. It's the same menu throughout, starting with breakfast and followed by a choice of 'small plates' along with more straightforward main courses like steak or burgers. It's easy to over-order so stick with the small plates which have a bit more zing to them.

Roti Chai

Indian 

3 Portman Mews South ✉ W1H 6HS
✆ (020) 7408 0101
www.rotichai.com
⊖ Marble Arch
Closed 25 December

Carte £15/31 

The very colourful Roti Chai represents the new wave of modern yet informal Indian restaurants and also shows what can be done to a huge concrete shell with a little imagination. It's divided in two: the ground floor is about quick and easy pan-Indian street food, from Dhokla chickpea cake to 'Railway' lamb curry, and no bookings are taken; the downstairs 'dining room', with its faux-industrial aesthetic, is somewhat swankier and more expensive but bookable. Here the separate kitchen offers a contemporary update of Indian home cooking, in such dishes as crisp Chennai-style chicken and plump and tasty Bengali crab cakes. It's fun, enthusiastically run and a little different, from the spirited T-shirted waiting team to the Indian cocktails.

Roux at The Landau

French

H2

Langham Hotel,
1c Portland Pl., Regent St. ✉ W1B 1JA
✆ (020) 7636 1000
www.langhamhotels.com
⊖ Oxford Circus
Closed Saturday lunch and Sunday

Menu £35/60 – Carte £35/59

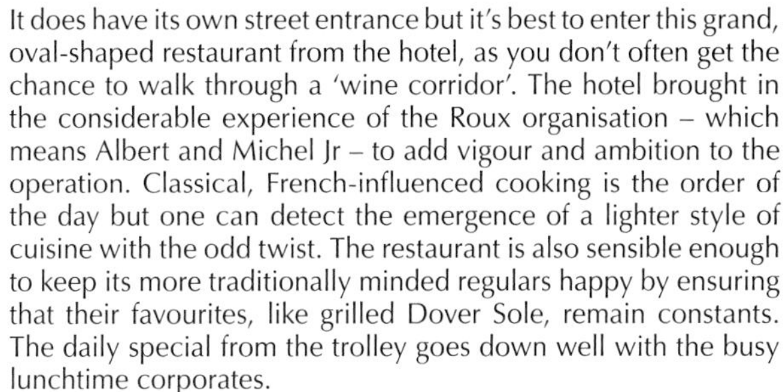

It does have its own street entrance but it's best to enter this grand, oval-shaped restaurant from the hotel, as you don't often get the chance to walk through a 'wine corridor'. The hotel brought in the considerable experience of the Roux organisation – which means Albert and Michel Jr – to add vigour and ambition to the operation. Classical, French-influenced cooking is the order of the day but one can detect the emergence of a lighter style of cuisine with the odd twist. The restaurant is also sensible enough to keep its more traditionally minded regulars happy by ensuring that their favourites, like grilled Dover Sole, remain constants. The daily special from the trolley goes down well with the busy lunchtime corporates.

Royal China

Chinese

24-26 Baker St ✉ W1U 7AB
✆ (020) 7487 4688
www.royalchinagroup.co.uk
⊖ Baker Street

Carte £22/53

It could be just as at home in Hong Kong's Wanchai or Central districts but, as it is, Royal China sits very comfortably in Baker Street. The large kitchen is staffed exclusively by Chinese chefs, including the early rising dim sum chef, who is responsible for the specialities served between midday and 5pm each day. The Cantonese dishes are strong on aroma and colour and, while the restaurant does not sell a great deal of seafood due to a lack of tank space, the lobster dishes remain one of the more popular choices. However, it is the barbecued meats, assorted soups, stir-fries and the choice of over 40 different types of dim sum that draw the large groups and ensure that this branch of the Royal China group remains as bustling as ever.

Suka

Asian H2

Sanderson Hotel,
50 Berners St ✉ W1T 3NG
(020) 7300 5588
www.morganshotelgroup.com
⊖ Oxford Circus

Menu £21 – Carte approx. £29 

The Long Bar is one of the busiest parts of the Sanderson hotel so be prepared to fight your way through to get to Suka, the hotel's Malaysian restaurant. The place has an easy-going charm and a menu designed to be shared between friends; just choose between the high stools on one side and the more traditional seating parallel to the open kitchen. The menu offers an appealing précis of the multicultural nature of Malaysian cuisine and features street food alongside more sophisticated dishes. Nasi Lemak, the closest thing to a national dish, is a good place to start and comes with a choice of assorted curries and braised meats. Laksa is suitably creamy and filling, and fruits with which to finish are in abundance.

28°-50° Marylebone

modern G2

15-17 Marylebone Ln. ✉ W1U 2NE
(020) 7486 7922
www.2850.co.uk
⊖ Bond Street
Closed 25-26 December

Carte £25/36 

If only wine bars had looked like this in the '80s. The second 28°-50° from the people behind Texture restaurant follows the successful formula adopted in their first branch in The City. That means a well-priced wine list where everything is offered in sizes ranging from a mouthful or a glass to a carafe or a bottle, and a supplementary Collectors' List with an impressive roll-call of largely Old World classics. On the food-front, grilled meats from their coal burning oven are the highlight of the menu, while salads, soups and starters all come in a choice of size. You can also simply pop in for a plate of charcuterie, salmon or cheese to share with your wine. Service is as bright as the room which is dominated by the central counter bar.

Texture ✿

innovative G2

34 Portman St. ✉ W1H 7BY
✆ (020) 7224 0028
www.texture-restaurant.co.uk
⊖ Marble Arch
Closed 1-14 August, 1 week Easter, Christmas, New Year, Sunday and Monday

Menu £27/79 – Carte £52/77

Texture

Chef-owner Agnar Sverrisson and his business partner Xavier Rousset, who trained as a sommelier, have steadily gone about creating an exceedingly good restaurant. The Champagne bar at the front has become a destination in itself and is separated from the restaurant by a large cabinet so you never feel too detached from it. The high ceilings add a little grandeur and the service is very pleasant, with staff all ready with a smile. Agnar's cooking is a little less showy than when Texture opened in 2007 and is all the better for that; you feel he's now cooking the food he wants to cook rather than the food he thought he should be cooking. Iceland is his country of birth so it is no surprise to find lamb, cod (whose crisp skin is served with drinks), langoustine and skyr, the dairy product that nourished the Vikings. There's considerable technical skill and depth to the cooking but dishes still appear light and refreshing and, since the use of cream and butter is largely restricted to the desserts, you even feel they're doing you good.

First Course

- Norwegian king crab, garlic, ginger and wasabi.
- Asparagus, parmesan, hazelnuts and olives.

Main Course

- Milk-fed veal, artichokes and Tio Pepe sauce.
- Suckling pig, celeriac choucroute and quince.

Dessert

- Valrhona white chocolate mousse and ice cream with dill cucumber.
- Skyr, vanilla ice cream, rye breadcrumbs and blueberries.

Trishna ✿

Indian

G2 

15-17 Blandford St. ✉ W1U 3DG
(020) 7935 5624
www.trishnalondon.com
⊖ Baker Street
Closed 24-28 December and 1-6 January

Menu £20 (lunch), £40/55 – Carte £26/41

Trishna

The coast of southwest India provides many of the influences at this crisply decorated, double fronted modern Indian restaurant. The menu is full of appealing dishes, ranging from the playful – try their own mini version of 'fish and chips' as a starter – to the original; the succulent guinea fowl comes with lentils, fennel seed and star anise. However, the undoubted star of the show is a version of the dish made famous by the original Trishna in Mumbai: brown crab, in this case from Dorset, comes with lots of butter and a little kick of wild garlic; it is so wondrously rich no man alone can finish a bowl, and you'll be licking your lips for days afterwards. All the dishes are as fresh tasting as they are colourful and there is even a recommended wine to go with each one. Doing things a little differently also extends to the cocktail list, although the mango chutney martini is perhaps one brave step too far. Ignore the slightly dodgy acoustics or the occasional need to prompt the staff and just enjoy some wonderfully satisfying Indian food.

First Course

- Hariyali bream with green chilli, coriander, tomato and cucumber.
- Crispy squid, fennel, chilli and lime.

Main Course

- Guinea fowl tikka.
- Dorset brown crab.

Dessert

- Cardamom kheer with fig, raisin and pistachio.
- Coconut and jaggery pudding.

Verru

modern

G2

69 Marylebone Ln ✉ W1U 2PH
✆ (020) 7935 0858
www.verru.co.uk
⊖ Bond Street

Menu £15/18 – Carte £33/41

The great thing about this part of town is that you can still come across tiny, tucked away restaurants doing something a little different. This is a warm, genially run and smartly dressed little place but it's not just the look that's appealing on a winter's night: Verru's chef-owner is Estonian and accordingly his cooking not only displays a Baltic boldness of flavour but also uses influences from the more northerly parts of Europe. Despite the occasional tendency to gild the lily, the kitchen produces dishes that have an appealing frankness to them but they are also underpinned by some sound classical techniques – and you certainly won't leave hungry. Sit at the front for more atmosphere; at the back for greater intimacy.

Vinoteca

modern

F2

15 Seymour Pl. ✉ W1H 5BD
✆ (020) 7724 7288
www.vinoteca.co.uk
⊖ Marble Arch

Closed 24-26, 31 December, 1 January, bank holiday Mondays and Sunday dinner – booking advisable

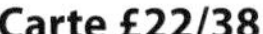

Carte £22/38

They've transferred the winning formula from their Clerkenwell original, so expect a great selection of wines, gutsy and wholesome cooking, young and enthusiastic staff and almost certainly a wait for a table. One side of the room is given over to shelves of wine; not only is the selection immeasurably appealing but the staff display both a knowledge and, more importantly, enormous enthusiasm when giving advice. The daily changing menu takes its cue from the sunnier parts of Europe and includes thoughtfully compiled salads and good charcuterie. There are also some firmly British dishes too, like mutton and oyster pie, and each one comes with its own wine pairing recommendation. It's great fun, basic in comfort and always very busy.

The Wallace

French

G2

Hertford House, Manchester Sq ✉ W1U 3BN
✆ (020) 7563 9505
www.thewallacerestaurant.com
⊖ Bond Street
Closed 24-26 December – (lunch only and dinner Friday-Saturday)

Menu £27 (lunch) – Carte £32/43

The Wallace Collection of 18 and 19C decorative art is one of London's finest, if lesser known museums and is found within Sir Richard and Lady Wallace's former home, Hertford House. Go through the French windows in what was once the dining room of this imposing mansion and you'll find yourself in a vast, glass-roofed courtyard. The restaurant occupies one half, a café the other, and, while there are often large groups in for lunch, there is room for everyone. The menu is heavily influenced by France but the kitchen keeps things relatively light. The à la carte is wide-ranging and includes plenty of terrines along with fruits de mer, but the menu du jour represents much better value and usually offers a nicely balanced selection of dishes.

Winter Garden

Mediterranean

F1

The Landmark London Hotel,
222 Marylebone Rd ✉ NW1 6JQ
✆ (020) 7631 8000
www.landmarklondon.co.uk
⊖ Edgware Road

Menu £34 (lunch) – Carte £33/57

Dining options tend to get more limited once you find yourself north of Marylebone Road, so the Winter Garden at the Landmark Hotel is a useful place to have up your sleeve, particularly if that sleeve is covered with a business suit. The kitchen displays a pleasing lightness of touch and the best dishes are those of a Mediterranean persuasion. At lunchtime the set menu is nicely balanced and served promptly, which is one of the reasons it's a good spot for meetings – Marylebone Station around the corner being the other reason. Dinner is more leisurely paced and more popular with hotel guests, with assorted grilled dishes adding to the choice. A pianist gallantly tries to help fill the enormous atrium in which the restaurant sits.

Yalla Yalla

Lebanese H2

12 Winsley St. ✉ W1W 8HQ
☏ (020) 7637 4748
www.yalla-yalla.co.uk
⊖ Oxford Circus
Closed 25-26 December, 1 January and Sunday

Carte £19/29

Close to the clamour of Oxford Street is this fun, good value restaurant whose Beirut street food is much tastier than anything you'll find along the Edgware Road. The name means "Hurry up!" which is a message no doubt endorsed by those waiting for a table as bookings are only taken for larger parties. The crowds come for the broad selection of mezze, which ranges from fattoush and sawda djej (chicken livers) to soujoc (spicy sausages). For the main course, succulent charcoal-grilled lamb dishes stand out, while desserts come from the enticing pastry corner. They also do a brisk takeaway trade in flatbreads, pastries and wraps. Wines from the Bekaa Valley are available alongside the juices and teas. The tiny, original branch is in Soho.

Zayna

Indian 

25 New Quebec St. ✉ W1H 7SF
☏ (020) 7723 2229
www.zaynarestaurant.co.uk
⊖ Marble Arch

Carte £20/33 

When a restaurant is named after the owner's daughter you know there's going to be a lot of love around. Zayna reflects the personality of Riz Dar who spent his formative years around Kashmir and Punjab and whose first job was in his father's restaurant in Pakistan. It's no surprise then to find a menu of North Indian and Pakistani delicacies. It comes divided according to cooking method, from the pan, grill, tawa or oven; but look out for the refined street food using offal. He is passionate about produce: spices are roasted and ground in house and only halal meat and free-range chicken are used. Dishes come packed with flavour, although the final bill can quickly mount up. The ground floor is the more elegant of the two rooms.

Zoilo

Argentinian

G2

9 Duke St. ✉ W1U 3EG
(020) 7486 9699
www.zoilo.co.uk
⊖ Bond Street

Carte £12/33

A/C

London's current crush on all things South American shows no sign of waning. Zoilo comes from the same people behind Casa Malevo but whereas that restaurant focuses on meat and Malbec this venture introduces us to Argentina's regional specialities. It's also all about sharing so plonk yourself down at the counter and order away. Highlights include a wonderfully chewy melted provoleta cheese, a great beetroot salad with goat's curd and garrapiñada (candied nuts with a soft centre: a Buenos Aires street snack) and an expert mackerel escabeche. The beef is naturally good but why not try grilled sweetbreads with lemon instead? The ground floor is livelier but if you want to know how it's all done then sit downstairs in front of the kitchen.

Bib Gourmand indicates our inspectors' favourites for good value.

SuperStock/Age Fotostock

Bloomsbury · Hatton Garden · Holborn

A real sense of history pervades this central chunk of London. From the great collection of antiquities in the British Museum to the barristers who swarm around the Royal Courts of Justice and Lincoln's Inn; from the haunts of Charles Dickens to the oldest Catholic church in Britain, the streets here are dotted with rich reminders of the past. Hatton Garden's fame as the city's diamond and jewellery centre goes back to Elizabethan times while, of a more recent vintage, Bloomsbury was home to the notorious Group (or Set) who, championed by Virginia Woolf, took on the world of art and literature in the 1920s.

A full-on encounter with **Holborn** is, initially, a shock to the system. Coming up from the tube, you'll find this is where main traffic arteries collide and a rugby scrum regularly ensues. Fear not, though; the relative calm of London's largest square, part-flanked by two quirky and intriguing museums, is just round the corner. The square is **Lincoln's Inn Fields,** which boasts a canopy of characterful oak trees and a set of tennis courts. On its north side is **Sir John Soane's Museum,** a gloriously eccentric place with twenty thousand exhibits where the walls open out like cabinets to reveal paintings by Turner and Canaletto. On its south side, the Hunterian Museum, refitted a few years ago, is a fascinating repository of medical bits and pieces. Visitors with a Damien Hirst take on life will revel in the likes of animal digestive systems in formaldehyde, or perhaps the sight of half of mathematician Charles Babbage's brain. Others not so fascinated by the gory might flee to the haunting silence of **St Etheldreda's church** in Ely Place, the only surviving example of thirteenth-century Gothic architecture in London. It survived the Great Fire of 1666, and Latin is still the language of choice.

Contemplation of a different kind takes centre stage in the adjacent **Hatton Garden.** This involves eager-eyed couples gazing at the glittering displays of rings and jewellery that have been lighting up the shop fronts here for many generations, ever since the leafy lane and its smart garden environs took the fancy of Sir Christopher Hatton, a favourite of Elizabeth I. After gawping at the baubles, there's liquid refreshment on hand at one of London's most atmospheric old pubs, the tiny Ye Old Mitre hidden down a narrow passageway. The preserved trunk of a cherry tree stands in the front bar, and, by all accounts, Elizabeth I danced the maypole round it (a legend that always seems more believable after the second pint).

Bloomsbury has intellectual connotations, and not just because of the writers and artists who frequented its townhouses in the twenties. This is where the University of London has its headquarters, and it's also home to the **British Museum,** the vast treasure

C. Eymenier / MICHELIN

trove of international artefacts that attracts visitors in even vaster numbers. As if the exhibits themselves weren't lure enough, there's also the fantastic glass-roofed Great Court, opened to much fanfare at the start of the Millennium, which lays claim to being the largest covered public square in Europe. To the north of here by the Euston Road is the **British Library,** a rather stark red brick building that holds over 150 million items and is one of the greatest centres of knowledge in the world. Meanwhile, Dickens fans should make for the north east corner of Bloomsbury for the great man's museum in **Doughty Street:** this is one of many London houses in which he lived, but it's the only one still standing. He lived here for three years, and it proved a fruitful base, resulting in Nicholas Nickleby and Oliver Twist. The museum holds manuscripts, letters and Dickens' writing desk. If your appetite for the written word has been truly whetted, then a good tip is to head back west half a mile to immerse yourself in the bookshops of Great Russell Street.

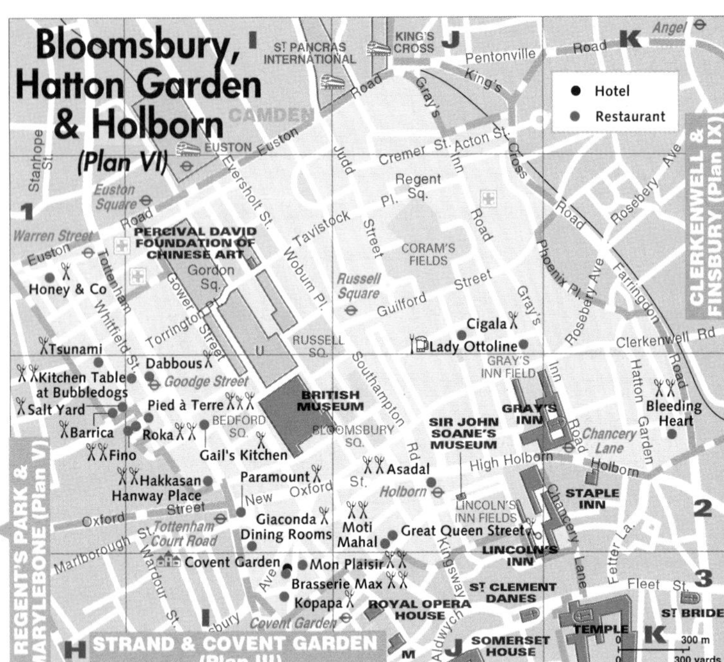
Bloomsbury, Hatton Garden & Holborn
(Plan VI)
Hotel
Restaurant
Honey & Co
Tsunami
Kitchen Table at Bubbledogs
Salt Yard
Barrica
Fino
Hakkasan Hanway Place
Dabbous
Pied à Terre
Roka
Gail's Kitchen
Paramount
Giaconda Dining Rooms
Covent Garden
Mon Plaisir
Brasserie Max
Kopapa
Moti Mahal
Great Queen Street
Asadal
Cigala
Lady Ottoline
Bleeding Heart
BRITISH MUSEUM
PERCIVAL DAVID FOUNDATION OF CHINESE ART
SIR JOHN SOANE'S MUSEUM
GRAY'S INN
STAPLE INN
LINCOLN'S INN
ST CLEMENT DANES
ROYAL OPERA HOUSE
SOMERSET HOUSE
TEMPLE
ST BRIDE
CLERKENWELL & FINSBURY (Plan IX)
REGENT'S PARK & MARYLEBONE (Plan V)
STRAND & COVENT GARDEN (Plan III)
300 m
300 yards

Asadal

Korean

J2

227 High Holborn ✉ WC1V 7DA
✆ (020) 7430 9006
www.asadal.co.uk
⊖ Holborn
Closed 25-26 December, 1 January and Sunday lunch

Carte £20/30 

If it was any nearer Holborn Tube station you'd need an Oyster card to get in. But head down the stairs and you'll soon be oblivious to what's going on at street level, thanks to a comfortable room which is divided up and kitted out with lots of wood. Those unfamiliar with Korean food will find that, by and large, the menu explains itself, since many of the dishes have had their photo taken. One thing to note is that the more there are in your party the better, as sharing is the key. Kimchi provides the perfect starter; there's plenty of seafood but the stars of the show are the hotpots, the delicate dumplings and the barbecues where meats are cooked on the hot-plate on the table. The young staff cope well with the early evening rush.

Barrica

Spanish

H2

62 Goodge St ✉ W1T 4NE
✆ (020) 7436 9448
www.barrica.co.uk
⊖ Goodge Street
Closed 25-26 December, 1 January, Sunday and bank holidays – booking essential

Carte £12/26 

Staff at this lively little tapas bar all appear to be Spanish so perhaps it's national pride that makes them run it with a passion lacking in many of their competitors. They make a concerted effort to look after their diners, of whom there are always many, so it's worth booking ahead unless you're okay squeezing onto a seat at the counter. When it comes to the food, authenticity is high on the agenda and it's hard to avoid temptation. Lamb chop with romesco sauce, and smoked duck breast with cherry butter, are a couple of standouts and it's worth ordering another savoury dish or one of their Spanish cheeses in place of dessert. They also offer an interesting selection of around 20 sherries and assorted Spanish wines – try one from the blackboard.

Bleeding Heart

French K2

Bleeding Heart Yard (off Greville St.) ✉ EC1N 8SJ
✆ (020) 7242 2056
www.bleedingheart.co.uk
⊖ Farringdon
Closed 24 December-1 January, Saturday, Sunday and bank holidays – booking essential

Menu £25/45 s – Carte £28/52 s

Dickensian tales of murder and intrigue still haunt the wonderfully evocative Bleeding Heart Yard, while contented bankers and modern day industrialists sit in its candlelit and atmospheric restaurant, feasting on classic French cuisine. Weekly changing set menus sit alongside the fairly pricey à la carte, which comes written in French and English, and well-drilled French staff exhibit a fair degree of personality. The kitchen can sometimes overcomplicate dishes so you're better off going for the more traditional choices with their relative simplicity. The wine list is a splendid affair and the owners have their own estate in New Zealand. If you want something altogether less formal then cross the yard for the Bistro.

Brasserie Max

meats and grills I3

Covent Garden Hotel,
10 Monmouth St. ✉ WC2H 9HB
✆ (020) 7806 1007
www.firmdalehotels.com
⊖ Covent Garden
Booking essential

Menu £24 – Carte £33/69

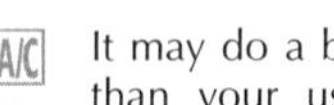

It may do a brisk trade in afternoon tea but this is much more than your usual hotel restaurant. For a start, the room is refreshingly free from chintz and has its own identity. The menu is appealingly accessible and will always have something on it that fits the bill, whether you're grabbing a bite before the theatre or making an evening of it. There's also an interesting cocktail list, as one end of the room is dominated by a large zinc-topped bar. Expect Asian and Mediterranean influences, carefully compiled salads and plenty of grilled meats; they also do a 'dish of the day' which could be fish pie or surf 'n' turf, but be aware of getting too enthusiastic about side dishes otherwise your final bill will be bigger than expected.

Cigala

Spanish J1

54 Lamb's Conduit St. ✉ WC1N 3LW
✆ (020) 7405 1717
www.cigala.co.uk
⊖ Russell Square
Closed Christmas – booking essential

Menu £18 (lunch) – Carte £24/36 

Tapas and small plates may be all the rage these days but Cigala has been going about its business in the part-pedestrianised Lamb's Conduit Street for a few years now. It's not just local medics, lawyers and advertising execs who flock here in their droves – the combination of hassle-free surroundings, sensible prices and an accessible menu means it appeals to a wide audience, with the result that staff can sometimes be a little overwhelmed. Highlights include grilled black pudding, hams from the open kitchen counter, homemade chorizo and squid with mojo sauce. Those in no great hurry should order one of the filling paellas. The entirely Spanish wine list includes some interesting sherries and cocktails.

Fino

Spanish I2

33 Charlotte St (entrance on Rathbone St.) ✉ W1T 1RR
✆ (020) 7813 8010
www.finorestaurant.com
⊖ Goodge Street
Closed Saturday lunch, Sunday and bank holidays

Menu £18/45 – Carte £18/31 

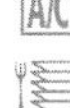

Fino's basement location and discreet entrance engender in its clientele that warm, satisfyingly smug feeling of being 'in the know'. While it is more formally structured than most restaurants that serve tapas, the atmosphere is always lively and the crowd, particularly at night, is pleasingly mixed. Start with a sherry and some croquetas while you scour the sensibly laid out menu. The young staff all know what's on offer and the more effort you put in with them the more they'll be inclined to offer guidance. Then order a bottle of Albariño and dig in; seafood is a delight, especially the squid from the plancha. Dishes are easy to share and, as in life, the more people in your party, the greater will be your enjoyment.

Dabbous ✿

modern

I2

39 Whitfield St ✉ W1T 2SF
✆ (020) 7323 1544
www.dabbous.co.uk
⊖ Goodge Street
Closed 21 December-14 January, 18-22 April, three weeks August, Sunday and Monday – booking essential

Menu £28/59 – Carte £22/38

A/C

Dabbous

There are many London restaurants that are hard to get into but, more often than not, that's because they appeal to those whose business is show. A table at Dabbous remains one of the hottest tickets in town but that owes more to the fact that Ollie Dabbous is an extremely talented chef and his cooking is something special. An advocate of the 'less is more' approach, his food comes with elegantly restrained finesse and a bewitching purity. His cooking is also influenced by his two primary alma maters – Le Manoir aux Quat' Saisons and Texture – with the result that some dishes owe more to classical theories while others are guided by modern techniques and ideas. Most tables go for the 7-course Tasting menu which showcases his stimulating and sublime combinations of ingredients and things kick off straight away with the arrival of a wonderful warm seeded loaf (in a paper bag) with homemade butter. The room is ersatz industrial, with ubiquitous exposed ducting and pendant lighting, although there is a simple elegance to the place, with its 14 wooden tables.

First Course

- Avocado, pistachio and lemon balm in a chilled osmanthus infusion.
- Speckled endive with gingerbread, bergamot and mint.

Main Course

- Grilled mackerel, iodized sour cream, samphire and lovage.
- Rare grain-fed beef, Avruga, horseradish buttermilk.

Dessert

- Fresh milk curds, birch sap, winter fruit and vegetables.
- Warm buckwheat waffle, smoked fudge sauce and sour cream.

Gail's Kitchen

Mediterranean

I2 

11-13 Bayley St ✉ WC1B 3HD
✆ (020) 7323 9694
www.gailskitchen.co.uk
⊖ Goodge Street
Closed 25 December

Carte £17/27

Everyone would like a Gail's bakery shop in their local high street and now the people behind them have opened a restaurant. It occupies a rather small space within the Myhotel: the downside being that when it's busy you might find yourself eating adjacent to the reception desk. There are plenty of upsides though: the small plates of enticing Mediterranean dishes are carefully prepared and the kitchen understands the importance of temperature in enhancing flavour. Start with great snacks like polenta chips with warm gorgonzola, then from the wood oven try pizza bianca with artichoke and Parma ham or a terrific leek vinaigrette with maple and mustard croutons. Naturally you should try the bread, and leave room for the ice cream sandwich.

Giaconda Dining Rooms

modern

I2 

9 Denmark St. ✉ WC2H 8LS
✆ (020) 7240 3334
www.giacondadining.com
⊖ Tottenham Court Road
Closed 2 weeks August, Saturday lunch and Sunday

Menu £19 – Carte £18/31

The observant will notice the subtle name change: they've added an 's' to 'room'. That may not seem much but it was actually a huge change as they now have two dining rooms and the place has doubled in size. The new room, with a skylight and some greenery, makes you feel you're outside, which is the effect the affable Aussie owner-chef was hoping to achieve. The menu has always changed daily and represents value for money, even before you consider the portion sizes. Dishes like roast field mushrooms with garlic purée sum up his philosophy: good seasonal ingredients prepared with little fuss and lots of flavour. Steak tartare and duck confit remain favourites and how many chefs have the courage to put 'today's staff meal' on their menu?

Great Queen Street

British modern J2

32 Great Queen St ✉ WC2B 5AA
✆ (020) 7242 0622
⊖ Holborn
Closed Christmas-New Year, Sunday dinner and bank holidays – booking essential

Carte £20/33

This is one of those restaurants that is perfect on a cold winter's night, with its candlelight, burgundy coloured walls, busy atmosphere and, most importantly, its heartwarming food. Its popularity does mean that service can sometimes need a prompt but there is no doubting the staff's enthusiasm for the food they serve. The menu descriptions are unapologetically concise but then dishes come equally unembellished. There's little difference between what constitutes a starter or main course and there's always a daily special or two. Highlights are the shared dishes such as the roast chicken crown or the shoulder of lamb, but offal is also done very well. Wine is served in tumblers and the list is thoughtfully put together.

Honey & Co

other world kitchens H1

25a Warren St ✉ W1T 5LZ
✆ (020) 7388 6175
www.honeyandco.co.uk
⊖ Warren Street
Closed first week January, last week August, Christmas, Monday dinner, Sunday and bank holidays – booking essential

Menu £27 (dinner) – Carte £20/29

When Itamar and Sarit decided to open their own place they did so knowing that they didn't have to worry too much about the kitchen – they'd both been head chefs at Ottolenghi restaurants. The philosophy at their sweet little café is to offer the same sort of food and hospitality you'd get if you were guests in their home. The friendly girls certainly provide charming, chatty and tactile service and the cooking is full of freshness and colour. The influences stretch beyond Israel to the wider Middle East; start by sharing some mezze, follow with roasted baby chicken or delicious lamb shawarma. Breads are great, cakes are hard to resist and the prices are commendable – which is another reason why the place is packed most evenings.

Hakkasan Hanway Place ✿

Chinese

I2

8 Hanway Pl. ✉ W1T 1HD
✆ (020) 7927 7000
www.hakkasan.com
⊖ Tottenham Court Road
Closed 24-25 December

Menu £29, £60/118 – Carte £33/82

Hakkasan

The original, subterranean Hakkasan remains as cool and seductive as ever and, despite the opening of another branch in Mayfair, its popularity shows no sign of slowing. Despite the size and general bustle, it is actually possible to have quite an intimate experience here, thanks to the clever lighting and good acoustics. However, service can be a little hit and miss and depends largely on who your waiter is and their level of enthusiasm. Lunchtime dim sum is a real highlight, although they sometimes appear curiously reluctant to offer you that particular menu. There are 20 chefs in the kitchen, many of whom are, like the head chef, from Singapore. The extensive menu is laid out clearly and logically, although there can be a marked difference in price between similar sounding dishes. Cantonese remains the starting point but the kitchen adds its own signature of inventiveness to give the dishes zip and the flavours depth. One thing the waiting staff do get right is telling you when you've unwittingly but understandably succumbed to over-ordering.

First Course

- Crispy duck salad with pomelo, pine nut and shallot.
- Jasmine tea-smoked organic pork ribs

Main Course

- Stir-fry black pepper rib eye beef with merlot.
- Spicy prawns with lily bulb and almonds.

Dessert

- Hazelnut Jivara bomb with dark chocolate sauce.
- Jalousie with caramel sauce.

Kitchen Table at Bubbledogs

modern I2

70 Charlotte St ✉ W1T 4QG
(020) 7637 7770
www.kitchentablelondon.co.uk
Goodge Street
Closed 1-14 January, 18-25 April, 19 August-2 September, 23-30 December, Sunday and Monday – booking essential – (dinner only) – (set menu only)

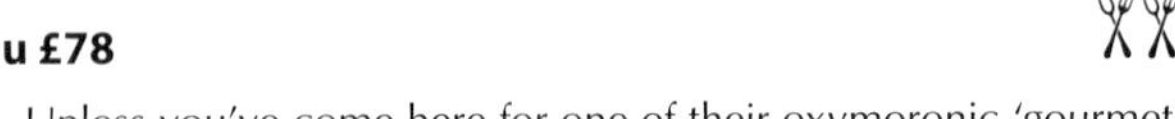

Menu £78

A/C

Unless you've come here for one of their oxymoronic 'gourmet' hot dogs – which come accompanied by glasses of grower champagne – just skip jauntily past the queue of skinny-jeaners to the back of the restaurant where you'll be escorted to the inner sanctum downstairs. Here you take your seat at a horseshoe-shaped counter and watch as the experienced chef-owner James Knappett and his young team cook, and then introduce in some detail, around 12 courses. The cooking is modern, produce has been carefully sourced, preparation is meticulous without being overly elaborate and enthusiastic amateurs will enjoy the interaction with the chefs. There are two sittings: 6pm and 7.30pm and the counter seats a maximum of 19.

Kopapa

Asian I3

32-34 Monmouth St ✉ WC2H 9HA
(020) 7240 6076
www.kopapa.co.uk
Covent Garden
Closed 25 December – booking advisable

Menu £18/39 – Carte £27/59

A/C

Stroll past in the early evening and it looks like another tourist trap but Peter Gordon's cleverly disguised restaurant is a more than useful spot for those in search of some West End refuelling. There are broadly two parts to the menu: the left side offers fairly predictable fare like Caesar salad, burgers and charcuterie boards; but head to the right and you'll find small or large plates of Peter Gordon's signature style of cooking: dishes that use plenty of ingredients and fuse all sorts of influences from around the world. These could be Asian, Mediterranean or Middle Eastern and, while the combinations may appear ambitious, they're well-judged and so stimulating so that you almost forget about the disorganised service.

Lady Ottoline

British traditional J1

11a Northington St ✉ WC1N 2JF
✆ (020) 7831 0008
www.theladyottoline.com
⊖ Chancery Lane.
Closed 24 December-2 January and bank holidays

Carte £22/38

Apart from some repair work on the cornicing and the tiled floor, this substantial red-brick Victorian pub is largely unchanged from when it was called The Kings Arms. The menus in the packed and slightly chaotic ground floor bar and the Queen Anne style upstairs dining room are not hugely different: cold winter nights see dishes like braised pig cheeks with lentils or venison haunch with squash purée. The kitchen takes more care with its cooking than one expects and dishes deliver on flavour. There's also a large selection of wine by the glass. This is the second pub for this husband and wife team and a sister to Princess of Shoreditch. It is named after the society hostess who was a friend to the Bloomsbury set.

Mon Plaisir

French I3

19-21 Monmouth St. ✉ WC2H 9DD
✆ (020) 7836 7243
www.monplaisir.co.uk
⊖ Covent Garden
Closed Christmas-New Year, Sunday and bank holidays

Menu £15/25 – Carte £30/47

Mon Plaisir couldn't be more French if it wore a beret and whistled La Marseillaise; but because this institution has been around since the 1940s, and under the current ownership since the '70s, it can also give one an unexpected but palpable sense of old London. It's divided into four rooms, all of which have slightly different personalities but share the Gallic theme; even the bar was reportedly salvaged from a Lyonnais brothel. Service may lack some of the exuberance of the past but that's just down to the relative lack of experience of the current serving team. All the classics are on offer, from snails to terrines, duck to coq; the set menu represents good value while the à la carte can be a little pricey.

Moti Mahal

Indian J2

45 Great Queen St. ✉ WC2B 5AA
✆ (020) 7240 9329
www.motimahal-uk.com
⊖ Holborn
Closed 25 December, Saturday lunch, Sunday and bank holidays

Menu £15/25 – Carte £25/47

A/C

These days we expect a little more personality and authenticity from our Indian restaurants and, in this, Moti Mahal certainly delivers. Its menu follows the path of the Grand Trunk Road which was built in the 16C and stretches 2500km from Bengal through northern India to the mountains of the northwest frontier. Each dish comes with a little story and several use ingredients one rarely sees in Indian restaurants, such as lamb's brains or rabbit. There are also specialities from 'off the trunk road' which include more robustly spiced dishes from Mumbai; try too the Hyderabad dish of lamb chops cooked in a clamp grill. The tandoor features quite heavily – murghi nazarat is a trio of chicken tikka dishes served in copper pots.

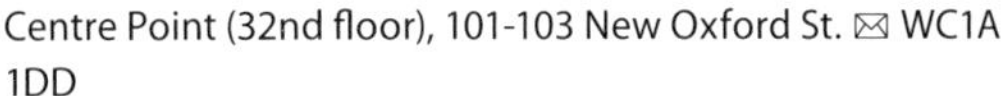

Paramount

modern I2

Centre Point (32nd floor), 101-103 New Oxford St. ✉ WC1A 1DD
✆ (020) 7420 2900
www.paramount.uk.net
⊖ Tottenham Court Road
Closed 25 December

Menu £29 (lunch) – Carte £32/54

It may not be everyone's idea of an architectural gem but the iconic Grade II listed Centre Point building certainly delivers breathtaking 360 degree views of London from its upper floors. Fortunately, Paramount, which is owned by experienced restaurateur Pierre Condou, occupies the 32nd floor, with its Viewing Gallery bar one floor above that, so diners have great westerly views. The menu sticks with the tried-and-tested: salads, steaks, terrines, slow-cooked lamb – nothing that's too stressful for the kitchen and the type of food that's popular with larger parties. Indeed, the restaurant is often so busy with after-work groups that it can resemble an animated office canteen, although staff generally cope well.

Pied à Terre ꕥ

innovative

I2

34 Charlotte St ✉ W1T 2NH
✆ (020) 7636 1178
www.pied-a-terre.co.uk
⊖ Goodge Street
Closed last week December-5 January, Saturday lunch, Sunday and bank holidays – booking essential

Menu £38/75

XXX

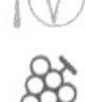

Pied a Terre

Hard to believe that when David Moore opened Pied à Terre back in 1991 some questioned whether a quality restaurant could ever survive on Charlotte Street – these days this busy street is one of the most sought-after spots in town, with restaurateurs virtually queuing up to get their hands on a lease. Marcus Eaves is the fourth chef to have led the kitchen since the restaurant's inception and his cooking is confident and bold, both in flavour and presentation. His menus are a good read – nicely balanced and with plenty of choice on offer – and while his dishes are quite elaborate in their make-up, they never feel overcrowded and the contrasts in textures make them very easy to eat. Wine remains a very strong element here: the two weighty tomes list over 700 bins, with considerable depth and quality across all major regions. Each year a different artist is commissioned to decorate the room which, despite its relatively small size, is cleverly designed so that no single table can dominate proceedings.

First Course

- Marinated scallops with avocado cream.
- Langoustine with Jerusalem artichokes, black olives and Meyer lemon.

Main Course

- Roast breast and crispy leg of quail, Wye Valley asparagus and foie gras.
- Suckling pig with choucroute.

Dessert

- Hazelnut praline mousse with rum and raisin ice cream.
- Pear and cinnamon millefeuille.

Roka

Japanese I2

37 Charlotte St ✉ W1T 1RR
✆ (020) 7580 6464
www.rokarestaurant.com
⊖ Goodge Street
Closed 25 December

Carte £18/89

Roka has one of those appealingly perceptible pulses that only really busy, well-run restaurants enjoy. It attracts a handsome crowd although they don't just come to glory in their mutual attractiveness but to share food that's original, easy to eat and just as pretty as they are. The kitchen takes the flavours, delicacy and strong presentation standards of Japanese food and adds its own contemporary touches. The menu can appear bewildering but just skip the set menus and order an assortment from the various headings; ensure you have one of the specialities from the on-view Robata grill. Sometimes too many dishes can arrive at once but the serving team are a friendly and capable bunch and they'll ease up on the delivery if you ask.

Salt Yard

Mediterranean H2

54 Goodge St. ✉ W1T 4NA
✆ (020) 7637 0657
www.saltyard.co.uk
⊖ Goodge Street
Closed 10 days Christmas, Sunday and bank holidays

Carte £14/24

The ground floor is the more boisterous and you'll feel like you're in the middle of a fun party; downstairs is better if you don't know your dining companion that well, although it too is full of life. This is all about tapas, although not just about Spanish tapas. One side of the menu has bar snacks, charcuterie and cheese but after ordering some olives or boquerones, turn over and you'll find three headings: Fish, Meat and Vegetable – one plate of each per person should do it. Unusual dishes, like braised gurnard with smoked Jersey Royals, sit alongside more traditional pairings like duck breast with parsnip purée. Prices are excellent; sharing is encouraged and service, young and sincere. Spain and Italy dominate the wine list.

Tsunami

Japanese

H2

93 Charlotte St. ✉ W1T 4PY
✆ (020) 7637 0050
www.tsunamirestaurant.co.uk
⊖ Goodge Street
Closed Saturday lunch and Sunday

Menu £37 – Carte £20/48 s

A/C

You'll never find anyone from Clapham in Nobu or Roka because they always insist they have their own cheaper version in Tsunami. Now we all have the opportunity of seeing what they mean, thanks to their second branch here in the West End. Appropriately enough, it is at the less showy end of Charlotte Street but is prettily decorated with lacquered walls and a floral motif, with colour changing lights and lounge music. Staff have good intentions but do tend to go missing at crucial moments. The contemporary Japanese food is carefully prepared and the menu covers all points and includes plenty of originality. Seafood, whether grilled, as tempura or as sashimi salad, is a highlight and much can be shared without breaking the bank.

Good food without spending a fortune? Look for the Bib Gourmand ☺.

Bayswater · Maida Vale

There may not appear to be an obvious link between Maida Vale and Italy, but the name of this smart area to the west of central London is derived from a battle fought over two hundred years ago in Southern Italy, and the most appealing visitor attraction in the neighbourhood is the charming canalside **Little Venice.** To stroll around here on a summer's day brings to mind promenading in a more distant European clime; it's hard to believe that the ear-shattering roar of the Westway is just a short walk away. South of this iconic elevated roadway – a snaking route out from Marylebone to the western suburbs – is Bayswater, a busy area of imposing nineteenth century buildings that's the epicentre of London's Middle Eastern community.

During its Victorian heyday, **Bayswater** was a grand and glamorous address for affluent and elegant types who wanted a giant green space (Hyde Park) on their doorstep. The whole area had been laid out in the mid 1800s, when grand squares and cream stuccoed terraces started to fill the acres between Brunel's curvy Paddington station and the park. But during the twentieth century Bayswater's cachet nose-dived, stigmatised as 'the wrong side of the park' by the arrivistes of Knightsbridge and Kensington. Today it's still a backpacker's paradise: home to a bewildering number of shabby tourist hotels, bedsits and B&Bs, converted from the grand houses. But this tells only a fraction of the modern story, because the area is undergoing a massive facelift that will transform it forever. The hub of this makeover is the **Paddington Basin,** a gigantic reclamation of the old Grand Union Canal basin in the shadow of the rail terminus. From a ramshackle wasteground, it's now a shimmering zone of metal, steel and glass, a phantasmagoria of blue chip HQs, homes, shops and leisure facilities. Even the barges have been turned into permanently moored 'retail opportunities'. Tree-lined towpaths along the perimeter complete the picture of a totally modern waterscape.

Lovers of the old Bayswater can still relish what made it famous in the first place: radiating out from **Lancaster Gate,** away from Hyde Park, is a web of streets with handsome squares and tucked-away mews, and it still retains pockets of close-knit communities, such as Porchester Square, west of Paddington station. Meanwhile, the 'cathedral' of the area, Whiteleys shopping centre in **Queensway**, remains a pivotal landmark, as it has been for more than a century. Just beyond Whiteleys heading away from central London, **Westbourne Grove** is still reassuringly expensive, or at least the bit that heads determinedly towards Notting Hill. But the wind of change has rustled other parts of the neighbourhood: Connaught

S. Ollivier / MICHELIN

Street has evolved into a villagey quarter of boutiques, galleries and restaurants, while, further west, Craven Hill Gardens is the height of chic.

Little Venice pretty much acts as a dividing line between Bayswater and Maida Vale. Technically, it's the point where the Paddington arm of the Grand Union Canal meets the **Regent's Canal,** but the name, coined by poet Robert Browning who lived close by, has come to encompass the whole area just to the north of the soaring Westway. Narrow boat moorings vie for attention alongside the cafés and pubs that mercifully lack the frantic high street buzz so typical of their kind away from the water's edge. The permanently moored boats were here a long time before those upstarts at Paddington Basin. This is where you can find old-time favourites including a floating art gallery and a puppet theatre barge, and all overseen by the Warwick Castle pub, a stalwart of the area that's a minute's walk from the canal. Suitably refreshed, a wander round the residential streets of Maida Vale is very pleasant, dominated by the impressive Edwardian blocks of flats that conjure up a distinctive well-to-do scene.

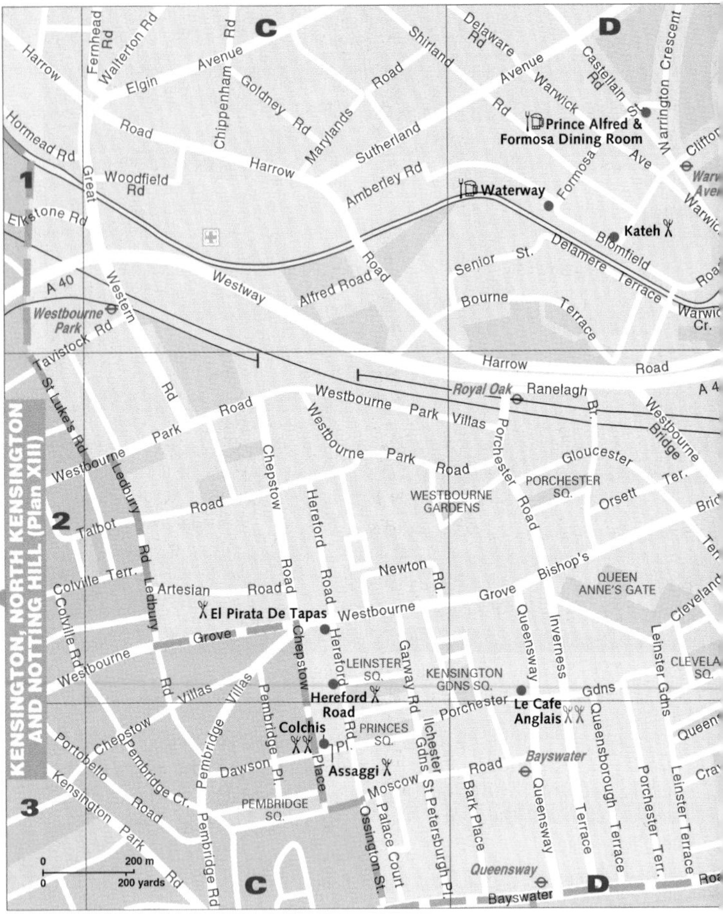

KENSINGTON, NORTH KENSINGTON AND NOTTING HILL (Plan XIII)

Prince Alfred & Formosa Dining Room

Waterway

Kateh

El Pirata De Tapas

Hereford Road

Le Cafe Anglais

Colchis

Assaggi

0 200 m
0 200 yards

Bayswater & Maida Vale
(Plan VII)
E
F
1
2
3
Hotel
Restaurant
Pearl Liang
Angelus
Nipa
Casa Malevo
PADDINGTON
MARYLEBONE
Edgware Road
Paddington
Lancaster Gate
NORFOLK CRESCENT
GLOUCESTER SQ.
HYDE PARK SQ.
CONNAUGHT SQ.
SUSSEX SQ.
HYDE PARK GARDENS
BRYANSTON SQ.
HYDE PARK
FOUNTAIN GARDEN
REGENT'S PARK & MARYLEBONE (Plan V)
HYDE PARK & KNIGHTSBRIDGE (Plan XII)

Angelus

French

E3

4 Bathurst St ✉ W2 2SD
✆ (020) 7402 0083
www.angelusrestaurant.co.uk
⊖ Lancaster Gate
Closed 24 December-2 January

Menu £20 (lunch) – Carte £40/57

Angelus has a delightfully warm and inclusive feel and much of the credit for that goes to its amiable and truly hospitable owner, Thierry Tomasin – if you're not already one of his regulars, you soon will be. The restaurant occupies what was formerly the Archer Tavern and the building dates from the 1850s. It has been charmingly decorated with art nouveau mirrors and prints and the bell that his mother would ring to call him in for meals when he was a boy growing up in the south of France takes pride of place in the bar. The cooking is French in its base but English in its ingredients; game will always be a highlight here but the kitchen is equally adept at lightly grilling some halibut or whipping up a soufflé.

Assaggi

Italian

C3

39 Chepstow Pl, (1st Floor) ✉ W2 4TS
✆ (020) 7792 5501
⊖ Bayswater
Closed 2 weeks Christmas, Sunday and bank holidays – booking essential

Carte £39/56

A/C

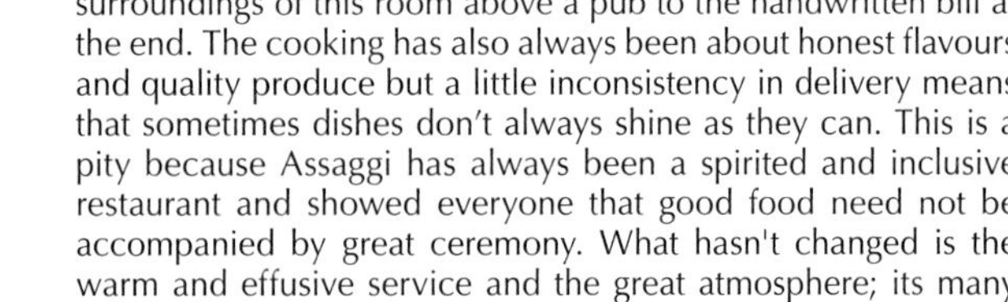

Assaggi has always been about simplicity, from the pared-down surroundings of this room above a pub to the handwritten bill at the end. The cooking has also always been about honest flavours and quality produce but a little inconsistency in delivery means that sometimes dishes don't always shine as they can. This is a pity because Assaggi has always been a spirited and inclusive restaurant and showed everyone that good food need not be accompanied by great ceremony. What hasn't changed is the warm and effusive service and the great atmosphere; its many regulars, who are kissed on the way in and the way out, treat the place like their local trattoria. However, for most of us, the prices represent a special night out.

Le Café Anglais

modern

D2

8 Porchester Gdns ✉ W2 4BD
✆ (020) 7221 1415
www.lecafeanglais.co.uk
⊖ Bayswater
Closed 25-26 December and 1 January

Menu £20/35 – Carte £19/53

The terminal blandness of Queensway received a boost when Rowley Leigh, formerly of Kensington Place, opened this vast brasserie within Whiteley's, the Grade II listed shopping centre. His place shares the same conviviality and culinary accessibility as 'KP' but on a bigger scale and with better acoustics. The art deco styling, leather banquettes and big windows may reflect Whiteley's 1911 roots but it's still best to take the lift up from the side entrance. The menu offers a huge range of brasserie classics, from rabbit rillettes and the wonderful parmesan custard to the daily specials and meats turning slowly on the rotisserie. The wine list is resolutely Old World. You can always just pop in and sit at the oyster bar.

Casa Malevo

Argentinian

F2

23 Connaught St ✉ W2 2AY
✆ (020) 7402 1988
www.casamalevo.com
⊖ Marble Arch
Closed 22-28 December

Carte £22/42

Carnivores are in clover these days due to the high number of places specialising in the cooking of red meat. Adding to the choice is this local Argentinian restaurant, with its bare brick walls and intimate lighting. Kick off by sharing the 'picada de campo': a board of grilled peppers, focaccia, pork cheek terrine and chicken matambre; then select from the grill, a piece of beef imported from Argentina – rib-eye, sirloin or fillet. The accompaniments may not quite come up to the mark but when you've got a steak and a bottle of Malbec from their exclusively Argentinian wine list, what else do you need? Those who have brought their own defibrillator can share the 'parrillada' containing rib-eye, fillet, chicken, lamb, chorizo and morcilla.

Colchis

other world kitchens C3

39 Chepstow Pl ✉ W2 4TS
✆ (020) 7221 7620
www.colchisrestaurant.co.uk
⊖ Bayswater
Closed Christmas-New Year – (dinner only and lunch Saturday-Sunday)

Carte £24/45 XX

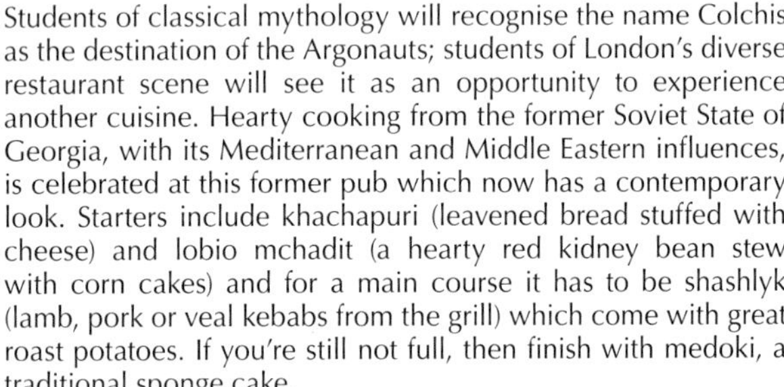

Students of classical mythology will recognise the name Colchis as the destination of the Argonauts; students of London's diverse restaurant scene will see it as an opportunity to experience another cuisine. Hearty cooking from the former Soviet State of Georgia, with its Mediterranean and Middle Eastern influences, is celebrated at this former pub which now has a contemporary look. Starters include khachapuri (leavened bread stuffed with cheese) and lobio mchadit (a hearty red kidney bean stew with corn cakes) and for a main course it has to be shashlyk (lamb, pork or veal kebabs from the grill) which come with great roast potatoes. If you're still not full, then finish with medoki, a traditional sponge cake.

Hereford Road

British modern C2

3 Hereford Rd ✉ W2 4AB
✆ (020) 7727 1144
www.herefordroad.org
⊖ Bayswater
Closed 24 December-3 January and 27-29 August – booking essential

Menu £10 (weekday lunch)/16 – Carte £20/30 X

Hereford Road is, first and foremost, a local restaurant. Lunch is usually a relaxed affair, with the room brightened by the large domed skylight, while dinner is the livelier feast, where everyone gives the impression that they live near enough to have walked here. The delightful owner-chef Tom Pemberton is often the first person you see, as the open kitchen is by the entrance – this was once a butcher's shop. He is an acolyte of St John and his cooking shares the same principles but not the same prices. So expect seasonal, British ingredients in very tasty dishes devoid of frippery. Offal is handled with aplomb and dishes designed for two, such as the shoulder of lamb or the whole oxtail, are so good you won't actually want to share them.

Kateh

other world kitchens D1

5 Warwick Pl ✉ W9 2PX
✆ (020) 7289 3393
www.kateh.net
⊖ Warwick Avenue
Booking essential – (dinner only and lunch Friday-Sunday)

Carte £19/35

Booking is imperative if you want to join those locals who have already discovered what a little jewel they have here in the form of this buzzy, busy Persian restaurant. Kateh is a type of rice from the Gilan Province in Iran; the fishermen there cook it to a sticky consistency and mix it with their daily catch. It features as a traditional accompaniment here, along with herbs and fruits. The baby calamari is delicious, the stews are very satisfying and the grilling is expertly done over charcoal. Warm sesame-coated flatbreads are moreish and be sure to finish with an authentic dessert like 'kolouche' (date and walnut pastries) along with tea made with cardamom. There's a delightful decked terrace at the back.

Nipa

Thai E3

Lancaster London Hotel,
Lancaster Terr ✉ W2 2TY
✆ (020) 7551 6039
www.niparestaurant.co.uk
⊖ Lancaster Gate
Closed Christmas-NewYear and lunch Saturday-Monday

Menu £10/38 – Carte £27/45

You'll find Nipa to be a little oasis of calm and hospitality, once you've made it up to the first floor of the Royal Lancaster and sidestepped the businessmen on their laptops in the adjacent lounge. Its teak panelling and ornaments are all imported from Thailand and they've done a convincing job of replicating the original Nipa in Bangkok's Landmark Hotel – if anything, it's even a little smarter. The menu is comprehensive, with a mix of the recognisable blended with more regional specialities. Dishes are marked 1-3 in chillies for their respective heat, come in decent sizes and the harmonious blend of flavours and textures successfully delivers what the aromas promise. Set menus are at the back and provide a convenient all-round experience.

Pearl Liang

Chinese

E2

8 Sheldon Sq, Paddington Central ✉ W2 6EZ
✆ (020) 7289 7000
www.pearlliang.co.uk
⊖ Paddington
Closed 24 and 25 December

Menu £11/25 – Carte £13/65

Chain restaurants tend to dominate corporate developments like 'Paddington Central' therefore thanks should be extended to Pearl Liang for flying the flag of independence. The weighty menu dedicates each page to a different main ingredient, be it poultry, fish, prawns or duck. There is the occasional interloper from other Asian cuisines but it's best to stick to the Chinese specialities. Prices allow for enthusiastic ordering and the prawn and pork dishes score highly, especially the king prawn with chilli. It's a big place whose large tables are more likely to be occupied by business types than families but the fast and furious service gives it an authentic edge. The surrounding offices make use of the takeaway lunch menu.

El Pirata De Tapas

Spanish

C2

115 Westbourne Grove ✉ W2 4UP
✆ (020) 7727 5000
www.elpiratadetapas.co.uk
⊖ Bayswater
Closed 26-27 August, 24-26 December and 1 January

Menu £9/25 – Carte £19/38

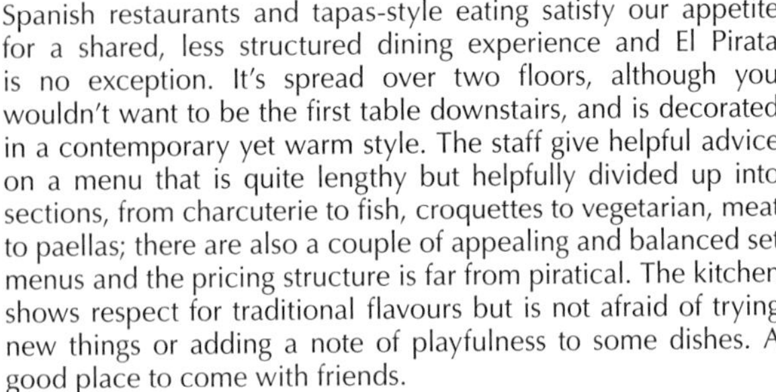

Spanish restaurants and tapas-style eating satisfy our appetite for a shared, less structured dining experience and El Pirata is no exception. It's spread over two floors, although you wouldn't want to be the first table downstairs, and is decorated in a contemporary yet warm style. The staff give helpful advice on a menu that is quite lengthy but helpfully divided up into sections, from charcuterie to fish, croquettes to vegetarian, meat to paellas; there are also a couple of appealing and balanced set menus and the pricing structure is far from piratical. The kitchen shows respect for traditional flavours but is not afraid of trying new things or adding a note of playfulness to some dishes. A good place to come with friends.

Prince Alfred & Formosa Dining Room

modern

D1

5A Formosa St ✉ W9 1EE
✆ (020) 7286 3287
www.theprincealfred.com
⊖ Warwick Avenue.

Menu £12 (weekdays) – Carte £24/36

The Prince Alfred is a wonderful example of a classic Victorian pub and its period features include ornate tiles, plate glass, panels and snugs. Unfortunately, the eating is done in the Formosa Dining Room extension on the side but at least it's a lively room and the open kitchen adds to the general bonhomie. There's more than a rustic edge to the appealing menu which will please all traditionalists; the mature steaks, pork belly and sticky toffee pudding are perennials but there are also dishes geared to those whose tastes are a tad more continental, such as sea bream with couscous and peppers. The service team could perhaps try revealing a little more personality but prices are kept realistic and the place still feels like a local.

Waterway

modern

D1

54 Formosa St ✉ W9 2JU
✆ (020) 7266 3557
www.thewaterway.co.uk
⊖ Warwick Avenue.

Carte £23/39

It sits by the canal offering refreshment to passing narrowboaters, its large terrace gets besieged by drinkers and there's live music on a Thursday night – it sounds like a pub, it has the warmth and bustle of a pub, but it's all surprisingly smart. A bar occupies one side of the room and a restaurant the other – and there's no evidence anywhere of any spit or sawdust. The menu and cooking also sit somewhere between a restaurant and an urban gastropub, with dishes like rump of lamb with couscous sitting alongside more delicate offerings, such as scallops with pea purée, which reveal the kitchen's lighter touch. Desserts keep up the standard and prices are kept sensible. Service is youthful, bubbly and capable.

City of London · Clerkenwell Finsbury · Southwark

Say what you like about London, **The City** is the place where it all started. The Romans developed this small area – this square mile – nearly two thousand years ago, and today it stands as the economic heartbeat of not only the capital, but the country as a whole. Each morning it's besieged with an army of bankers, lawyers and traders, and each evening it's abandoned to an eerie ghost-like fate. Of course, this mass exodus is offset by the two perennial crowd-pullers, **St Paul's** and the **Tower of London**, but these are both on the periphery of the area, away from the frenetic commercial zone within. The casual visitor tends to steer clear of the City, but for those willing to mix it with the daytime swarm of office workers, there are many historical nuggets hidden away, waiting to be mined. You can find here, amongst the skyscrapers, a tempting array of Roman ruins, medieval landmarks and brooding churches designed by Wren and Hawksmoor. One of the best ways of encapsulating everything that's happened here down the centuries is to visit the Museum of London, on London Wall, which tells the story of the city from the very start, and the very start means 300,000 BC.

For those seeking the hip corners of this part of London, the best advice is to head slightly north-west, using the brutalist space of the **Barbican Arts Centre** as your marker. You're now entering **Clerkenwell**. Sliding north/south through here is the bustling and buzzy **St John Street,** home to some of the funkiest eating establishments in London, their proximity to **Smithfield** meat market giving a clue as to much of their menus' provenance. Clerkenwell's revivalist vibe has seen the steady reclamation of old factory space: during the Industrial Revolution, the area boomed with the introduction of breweries, print works and the manufacture of clocks and watches. After World War II, decline set in, but these days city professionals and loft-dwellers are drawn to the area's zeitgeist-leading galleries and clubs, not to mention the wonderful floor-to-ceiling delicatessens. Clerkenwell is home to The Eagle, one of the city's pioneering gastropubs and still a local favourite, which even has its own art gallery upstairs. Meanwhile, the nearby **Exmouth Market** teems with trendy bars and restaurants, popular with those on their way to the perennially excellent dance concerts at Sadler's Wells Theatre.

The area was once a religious centre, frequented by monks and nuns; its name derives from the parish clerks who performed Biblical mystery plays around the Clerk's Well set in a nunnery wall. This can be found in **Farringdon Lane** complete with an exhibition explaining all. Close by in St John's Lane is the 16C gatehouse which is home to the Museum of the Order of St John (famous today for its

C. Eymenier / MICHELIN

ambulance services), and chock full of fascinating objects related to the Order's medieval history.

Not too long ago, a trip over London Bridge to **Southwark** was for locals only, its trademark grimness ensuring it was well off the tourist map. These days, visitors treat it as a place of pilgrimage as three of London's modern success stories reside here in the shadow of The Shard. **Tate Modern** has become the city's most visited attraction, a huge former power station that generates a blistering show of modern art from 1900 to the present day, its massive turbine hall a must-see feature in itself. Practically next door but a million miles away architecturally is Shakespeare's **Globe,** a wonderful evocation of medieval showtime. Half a mile east is the best food market in London: **Borough Market.** Foodies can't resist the organic, feel-good nature of the place, with, its mind-boggling number of stalls selling produce ranging from every kind of fruit and veg to rare-breed meats, oils, preserves, chocolates and breads. And that's just for hors-d'œuvres…

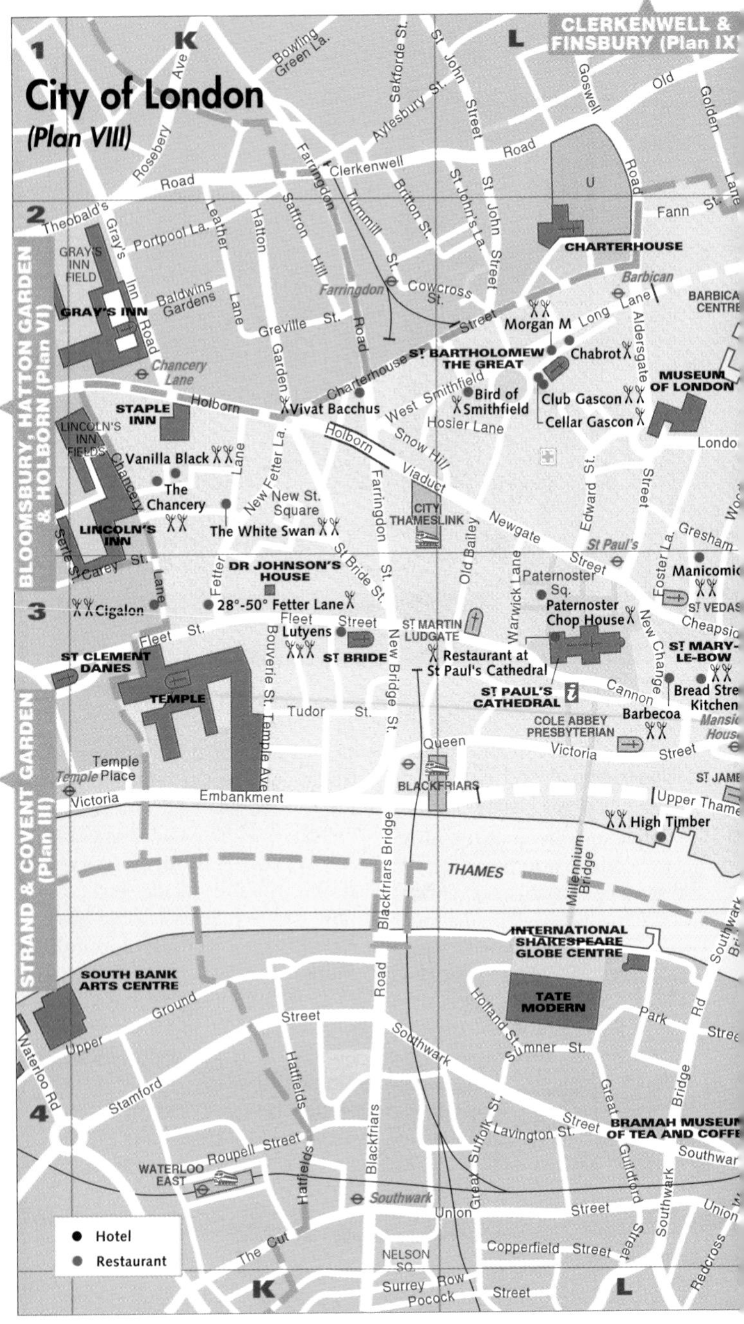
City of London
(Plan VIII)
CLERKENWELL & FINSBURY (Plan IX)
BLOOMSBURY, HATTON GARDEN & HOLBORN (Plan VI)
STRAND & COVENT GARDEN (Plan III)
CHARTERHOUSE
GRAY'S INN
GRAY'S INN FIELD
STAPLE INN
LINCOLN'S INN FIELDS
LINCOLN'S INN
ST BARTHOLOMEW THE GREAT
MUSEUM OF LONDON
BARBICAN CENTRE
CITY THAMESLINK
DR JOHNSON'S HOUSE
ST MARTIN LUDGATE
ST BRIDE
ST CLEMENT DANES
TEMPLE
ST PAUL'S CATHEDRAL
COLE ABBEY PRESBYTERIAN
ST VEDAST
ST MARY-LE-BOW
BLACKFRIARS
INTERNATIONAL SHAKESPEARE GLOBE CENTRE
TATE MODERN
SOUTH BANK ARTS CENTRE
BRAMAH MUSEUM OF TEA AND COFFEE
WATERLOO EAST
NELSON SQ.
THAMES
Morgan M
Chabrot
Bird of Smithfield
Club Gascon
Cellar Gascon
Vivat Bacchus
Vanilla Black
The Chancery
The White Swan
Cigalon
28°-50° Fetter Lane
Lutyens
Restaurant at St Paul's Cathedral
Paternoster Chop House
Manicomio
Bread Street Kitchen
Barbecoa
High Timber
Hotel
Restaurant

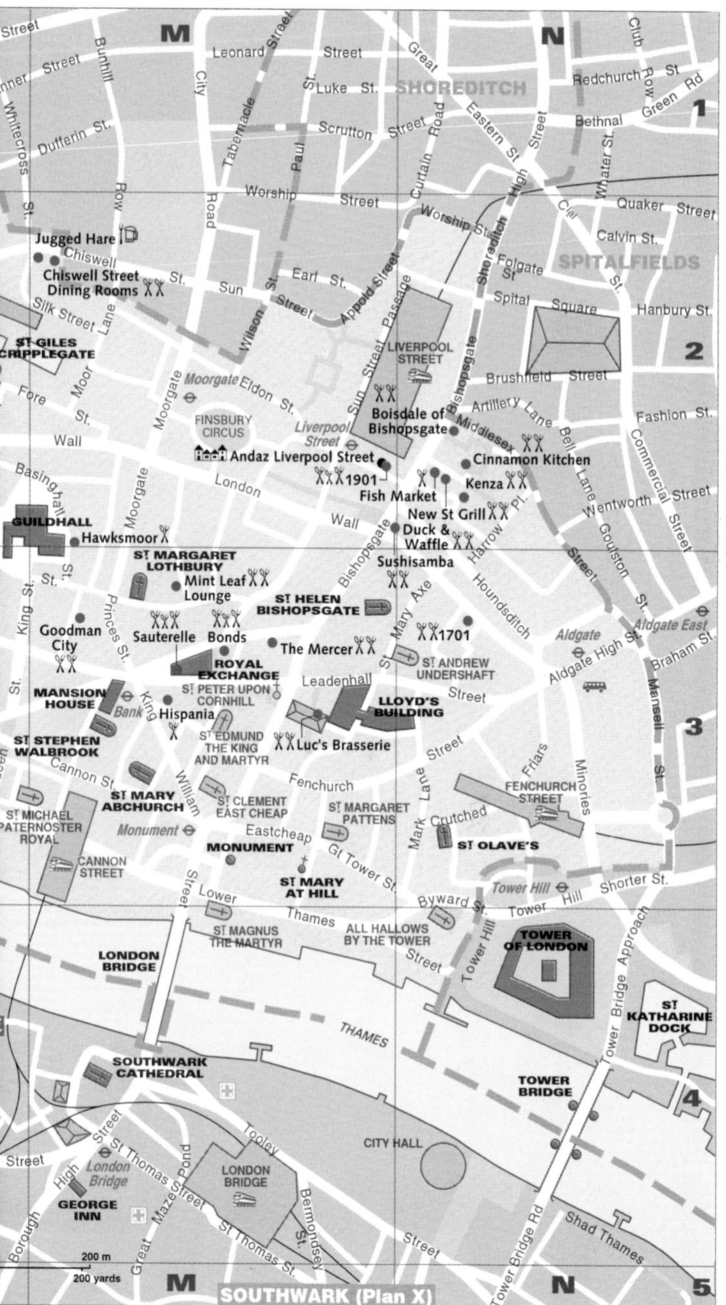

M
N
SHOREDITCH
SPITALFIELDS
Jugged Hare
Chiswell Street Dining Rooms
ST GILES CRIPPLEGATE
LIVERPOOL STREET
Boisdale of Bishopsgate
FINSBURY CIRCUS
Andaz Liverpool Street
1901
Fish Market
Cinnamon Kitchen
Kenza
New St Grill
Duck & Waffle
Sushisamba
GUILDHALL
Hawksmoor
ST MARGARET LOTHBURY
Mint Leaf Lounge
ST HELEN BISHOPSGATE
Goodman City
Sauterelle
Bonds
The Mercer
1701
ROYAL EXCHANGE
ST ANDREW UNDERSHAFT
MANSION HOUSE
ST PETER UPON CORNHILL
LLOYD'S BUILDING
Hispania
ST STEPHEN WALBROOK
ST EDMUND THE KING AND MARTYR
Luc's Brasserie
ST MARY ABCHURCH
ST CLEMENT EAST CHEAP
ST MARGARET PATTENS
FENCHURCH STREET
ST MICHAEL PATERNOSTER ROYAL
Monument
MONUMENT
ST OLAVE'S
CANNON STREET
ST MARY AT HILL
Tower Hill
ST MAGNUS THE MARTYR
ALL HALLOWS BY THE TOWER
TOWER OF LONDON
LONDON BRIDGE
THAMES
ST KATHARINE DOCK
SOUTHWARK CATHEDRAL
TOWER BRIDGE
CITY HALL
London Bridge
LONDON BRIDGE
GEORGE INN
200 m
200 yards
SOUTHWARK (Plan X)
1
2
3
4
5

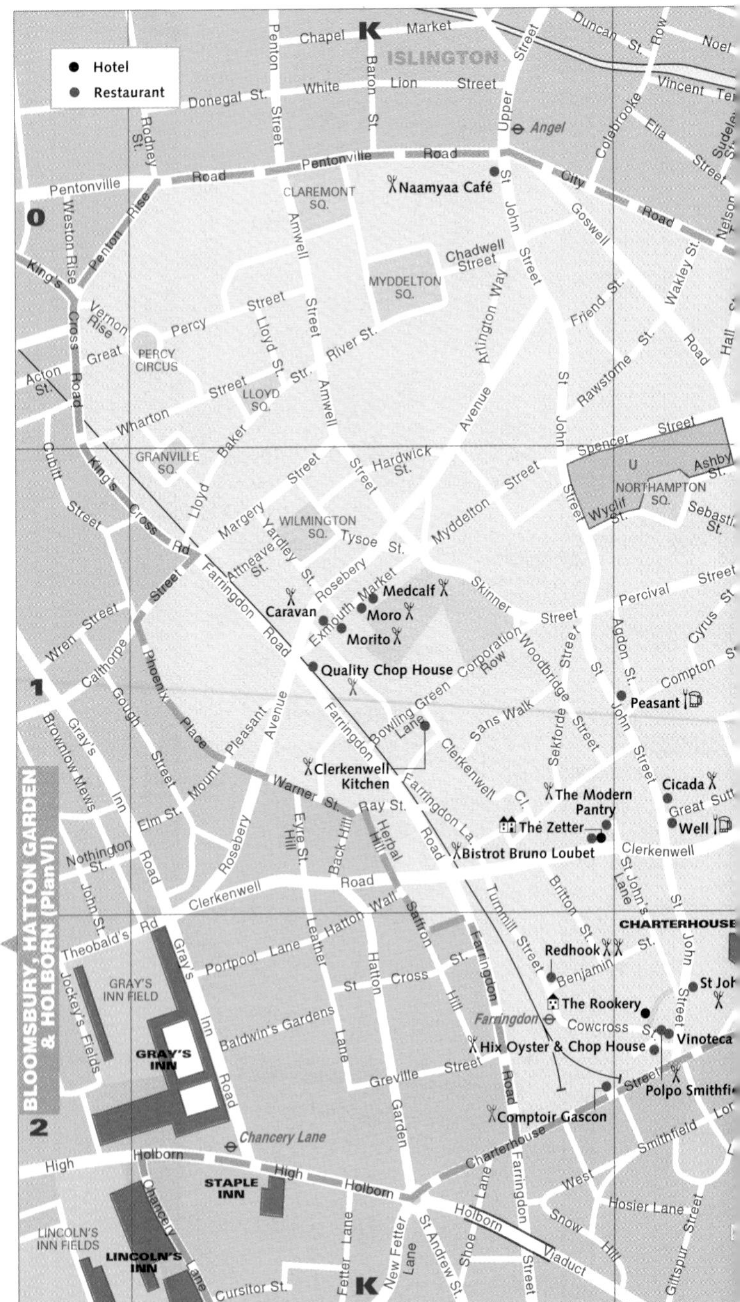
Hotel
Restaurant
ISLINGTON
K
0
1
2
BLOOMSBURY, HATTON GARDEN & HOLBORN (Plan VI)
Angel
Naamyaa Café
CLAREMONT SQ.
MYDDELTON SQ.
PERCY CIRCUS
LLOYD SQ.
GRANVILLE SQ.
WILMINGTON SQ.
NORTHAMPTON SQ.
Medcalf
Caravan
Moro
Morito
Quality Chop House
Peasant
Clerkenwell Kitchen
The Modern Pantry
Cicada
The Zetter
Well
Bistrot Bruno Loubet
CHARTERHOUSE
Redhook
St John
The Rookery
Farringdon
Vinoteca
Hix Oyster & Chop House
Polpo Smithfield
Comptoir Gascon
GRAY'S INN FIELD
GRAY'S INN
Chancery Lane
STAPLE INN
LINCOLN'S INN FIELDS
LINCOLN'S INN
Chapel Market
White Lion Street
Donegal St.
Pentonville Road
Penton Street
Baron St.
Rodney St.
Upper Street
Duncan St.
Noel
Vincent Ter.
Colebrooke Row
Elia Street
City Road
Goswell Road
St John Street
Chadwell Street
Arlington Way
Amwell Street
Weston Rise
Penton Rise
King's Cross Road
Vernon Rise
Great Percy Street
Lloyd St.
River St.
Wharton Street
Acton St.
Friend St.
Wakley St.
Rawstorne St.
Spencer Street
Ashby St.
Wyclif St.
Sebastian St.
Cubitt Street
Lloyd Baker Street
Hardwick St.
Myddelton Street
Margery Street
Yardley St.
Tysoe St.
Attneave St.
Rosebery Avenue
Exmouth Market
Skinner Street
Percival Street
Farringdon Road
Wren Street
Calthorpe St.
Phoenix Place
Gough Street
Corporation Row
Woodbridge Street
Agdon St.
Cyrus St.
Compton St.
Bowling Green Lane
Sans Walk
Sekforde Street
Brownlow Mews
Gray's Inn Road
Mount Pleasant
Warner St.
Ray St.
Clerkenwell Cl.
Elm St.
Nothington St.
John St.
Eyre St. Hill
Back Hill
Herbal Hill
Farringdon Lane
Great Sutton St.
Clerkenwell Road
Britton St.
St John's Lane
Theobald's Rd
Portpool Lane
Leather Lane
Hatton Wall
Saffron Hill
Farringdon Road
Turnmill Street
Jockey's Fields
Hatton Garden
Cross St.
Benjamin St.
Baldwin's Gardens
Cowcross St.
Greville Street
Charterhouse Street
Smithfield
High Holborn
Holborn
Chancery Lane
West Smithfield
Hosier Lane
Snow Hill
Holborn Viaduct
Fetter Lane
New Fetter Lane
St Andrew St.
Shoe Lane
Farringdon Street
Giltspur Street
Cursitor St.

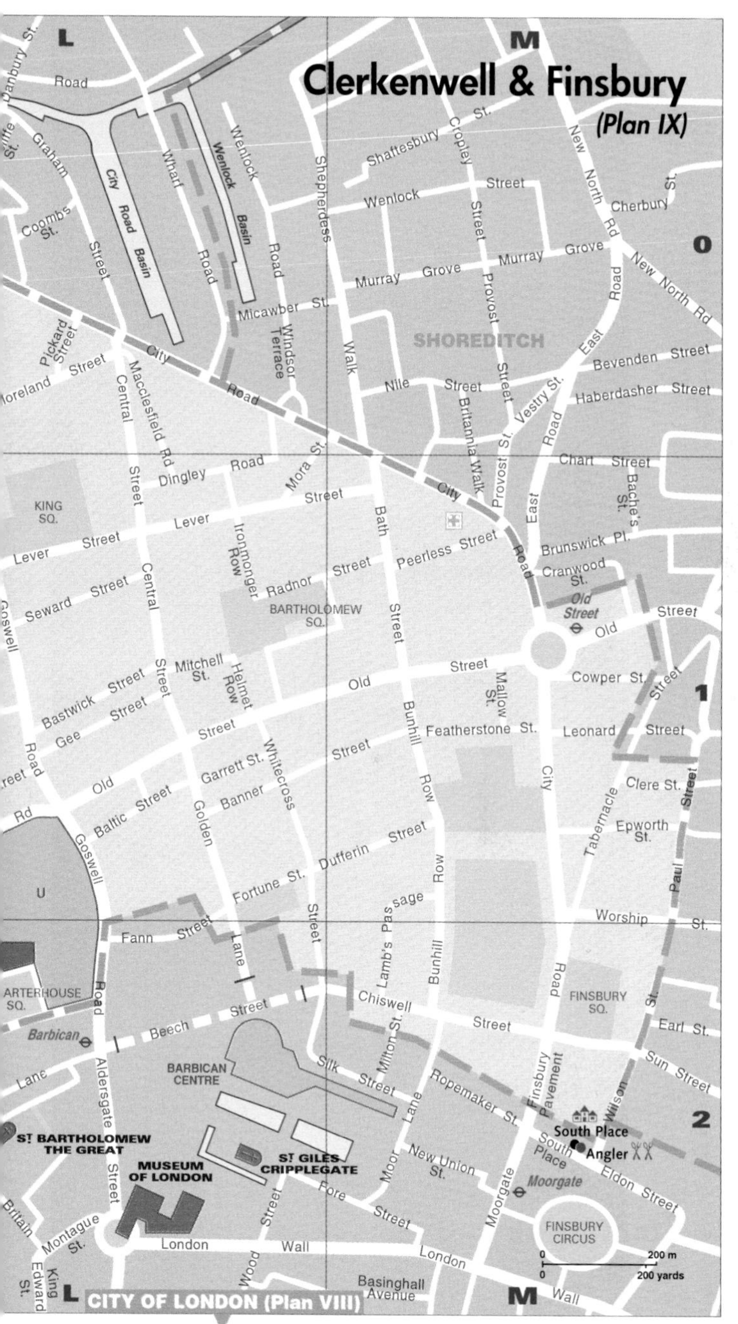
Clerkenwell & Finsbury
(Plan IX)
SHOREDITCH
KING SQ.
BARTHOLOMEW SQ.
FINSBURY SQ.
FINSBURY CIRCUS
BARBICAN CENTRE
ST BARTHOLOMEW THE GREAT
MUSEUM OF LONDON
ST GILES CRIPPLEGATE
South Place
Angler
Barbican
Moorgate
Old Street
CITY OF LONDON (Plan VIII)
200 m
200 yards

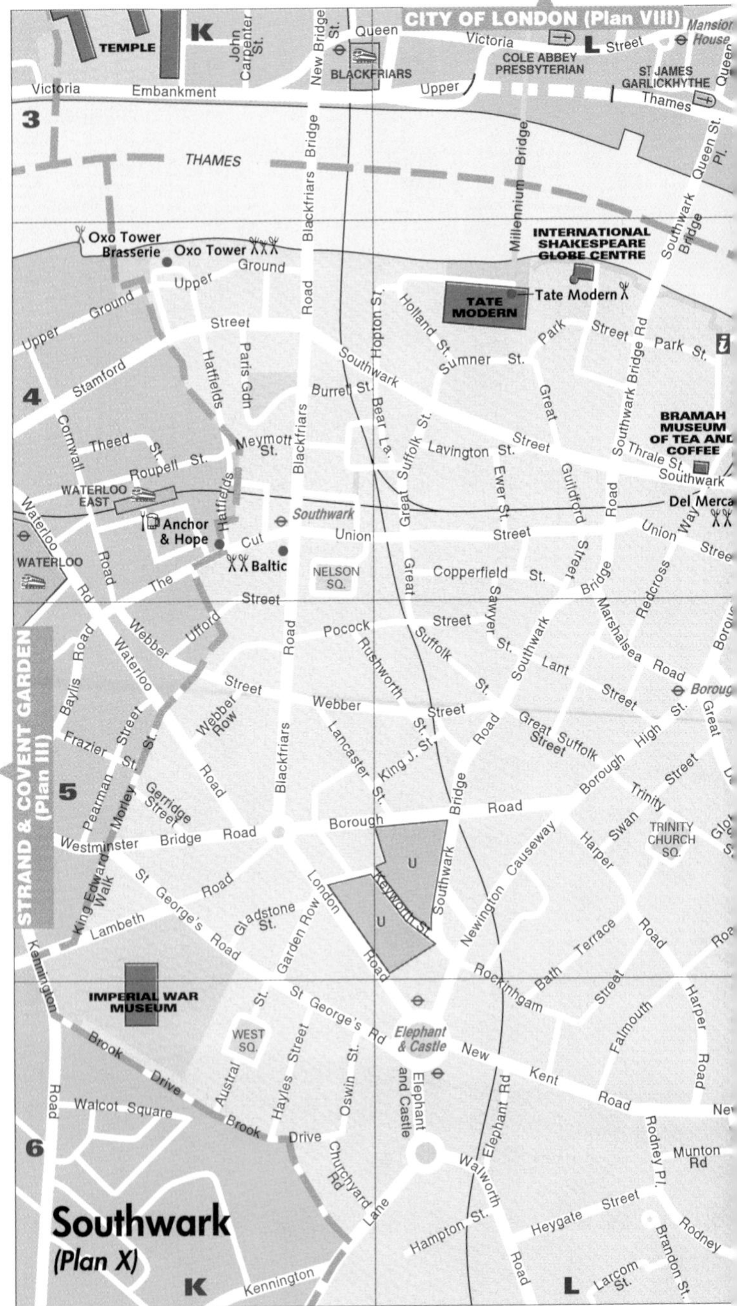

CITY OF LONDON (Plan VIII)
TEMPLE
K
L
3
4
5
6
BLACKFRIARS
COLE ABBEY PRESBYTERIAN
ST JAMES GARLICKHYTHE
Mansion House
THAMES
Oxo Tower Brasserie
Oxo Tower
INTERNATIONAL SHAKESPEARE GLOBE CENTRE
TATE MODERN
Tate Modern
BRAMAH MUSEUM OF TEA AND COFFEE
WATERLOO EAST
WATERLOO
Anchor & Hope
Baltic
Southwark
NELSON SQ.
Del Merca
Borough
TRINITY CHURCH SQ.
STRAND & COVENT GARDEN (Plan III)
IMPERIAL WAR MUSEUM
WEST SQ.
Elephant & Castle
Southwark
(Plan X)

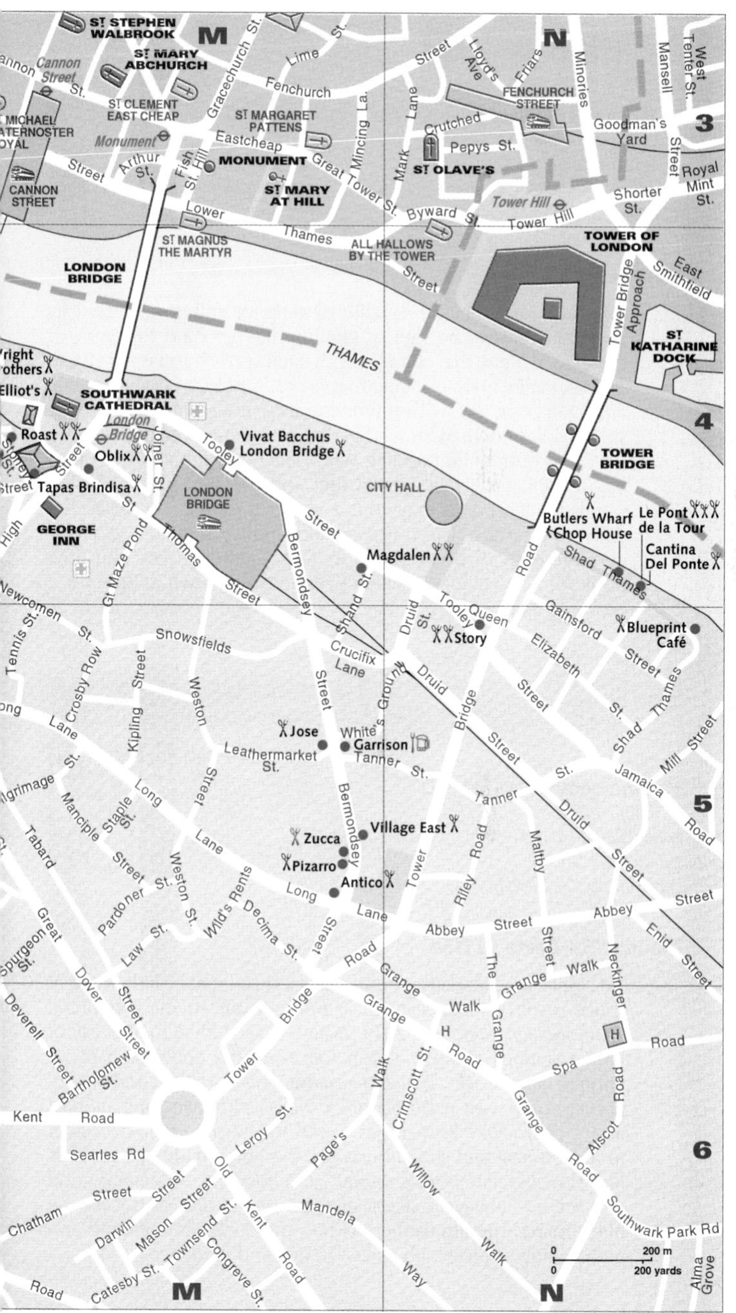

ST STEPHEN WALBROOK
ST MARY ABCHURCH
ST CLEMENT EAST CHEAP
ST MARGARET PATTENS
MONUMENT
ST MARY AT HILL
ST OLAVE'S
FENCHURCH STREET
CANNON STREET
ST MAGNUS THE MARTYR
ALL HALLOWS BY THE TOWER
TOWER OF LONDON
LONDON BRIDGE
THAMES
ST KATHARINE DOCK
SOUTHWARK CATHEDRAL
TOWER BRIDGE
Roast
Oblix
Tapas Brindisa
GEORGE INN
Vivat Bacchus London Bridge
CITY HALL
Butlers Wharf Chop House
Le Pont de la Tour
Cantina Del Ponte
Magdalen
Story
Blueprint Café
Jose
Garrison
Village East
Zucca
Pizarro
Antico
M
N
3
4
5
6
200 m
200 yards

Anchor & Hope

British modern Plan X – K4

36 The Cut ✉ SE1 8LP
✆ (020) 7928 9898
⊖ Southwark.
Closed Christmas-New Year, Sunday dinner, Monday lunch and bank holidays – bookings not accepted

Carte £26/37

The Anchor & Hope is still running at full steam and its popularity shows no sign of abating. It's not hard to see why: combine a menu that changes with each service and is a paragon of seasonality, with cooking that is gutsy, bold and wholesome, and you end up with immeasurably rewarding dishes like suckling kid chops with wild garlic, succulent roast pigeon with lentils or buttermilk pudding with poached rhubarb. The place has a contagiously congenial feel and the staff all pull in the same direction; you may spot a waiter trimming veg or a chef delivering dishes. The no-reservation policy remains, so either get here early or be prepared to wait – although you can now book for Sunday lunch, when everyone sits down at 2pm for a veritable feast.

Antico

Italian Plan X – M5

214 Bermondsey St ✉ SE1 3TQ
✆ (020) 7407 4682
www.antico-london.co.uk
⊖ London Bridge
Closed Sunday dinner and Monday

Menu £15 – Carte £21/54

Art galleries, markets, pubs, bars, restaurants, independent shops, even a local festival...if only all our streets resembled Bermondsey Street. In 2012 Antico was added to the list of dining options along the strip following the conversion of an antique warehouse – hence the name. This is a bright and breezy corner spot, with exposed brick walls acknowledging its past and a downstairs lounge bar a nod to the present. The Italian food is honest and straightforward; the homemade pasta dishes like slow-roasted pork shoulder tortelloni are especially good and there is always a seasonal ragu, risotto and sorbet on the blackboard. The atmosphere is fun, the cocktails are good and the clientele is pleasingly mixed in age and affluence.

Angler ✿

fish and seafood Plan IX – M2

South Place Hotel,
3 South Pl ✉ EC2M 2AF
✆ (020) 3215 1260
www.anglerrestaurant.com
⊖ Moorgate
Closed Saturday lunch and Sunday – booking advisable

Menu £25 – Carte £33/61

Angler

The rooftop restaurant of D&D's South Place hotel is a bright, light and supremely comfortable space; its adjoining bar and terrace the perfect place for a pre-prandial cocktail. Sloping floor to ceiling windows allow the light to flood in and the contemporary styling represents something of an antidote to all those clubby, masculine rooms that have recently opened. Service is smooth and detailed and gets the balance between formality and friendliness just right. The menu champions the best of British seafood: there are oysters from Mersea, langoustines from Orkney and crab and cod from Cornwall. The cooking is confidently executed and the freshness of the ingredients really shines through; cheeses are British and puddings hit the spot.

The glass-fronted wine cabinets are more than just a feature at one end of the restaurant – they have also been thoughtfully stocked. The ever-changing selection by the glass is first-rate and the Enomatic machine keeps the wines fresh and at the perfect temperature.

First Course

- Langoustine minestrone with dressed crab on toast.
- Shellfish ravioli with buttered leeks and lobster sauce.

Main Course

- Turbot with red wine braised squid, fennel purée and sea purslane.
- Cod with cockles and squid, basil emulsion.

Dessert

- Hazelnut cake, salted caramel, lime and vanilla sorbet.
- Lemon tart.

Baltic

other world kitchens Plan X – K4

74 Blackfriars Rd ✉ SE1 8HA
✆ (020) 7928 1111
www.balticrestaurant.co.uk
⊖ Southwark
Closed 24-27 December and 1 January – bookings advisable at dinner

Menu £27/37 – Carte £24/36

There's nothing like a nondescript façade to lower expectations and Baltic's dull exterior goes even further by giving few clues as to what lies within: a large, bright restaurant housed in what was once an 18C coach builder's works. The menu is an appealing read and specialises in dishes from various countries out east – Poland, Russia, Bulgaria, even Siberia. Expect two types of beetroot soup, Barszcz and Chlodnik; assorted dumplings including pierogi and spaetzle, which are done well; lots of meat dishes such as pork schnitzel and lamb shashlik – and great vodkas. The cooking is executed with more subtlety that you expect and the largely Polish staff are clearly proud and pleased to be serving food with which they are familiar.

Barbecoa

meats and grills Plan VIII – L3

20 New Change Passage ✉ EC4M 9AG
✆ (020) 3005 8555
www.barbecoa.com
⊖ St Paul's
Closed 24-26 December and 1 January – booking essential

Carte £30/55

There are many things that us Brits lead the world in, but barbecuing ain't one of them. So we owe thanks to the Good Ole US of A - and to our very own Jamie Oliver who help set up this restaurant to show us how it should be done. For starters, that means the kitchen has all the right kit to ensure the prime meats are cooked to perfection, whether that's rib-eye or half a chicken. But to really see the standard to aim for when next entertaining in your garden, order the pulled pork shoulder with BBQ sauce and cornbread. If you haven't quite got the appetite for crispy pig cheeks, then try one of the interesting salads; by dessert you may be willing to share so go for Chocolate Nemesis, Jamie's homage to his alma mater.

Bird of Smithfield

British traditional Plan VIII – L2

26 Smithfield St ✉ EC1A 9LB
✆ (020) 7559 5100
www.birdofsmithfield.com
⊖ Farringdon
Closed Christmas, New Year, Sunday dinner and bank holidays – booking essential

Menu £24 (lunch) – Carte £22/51

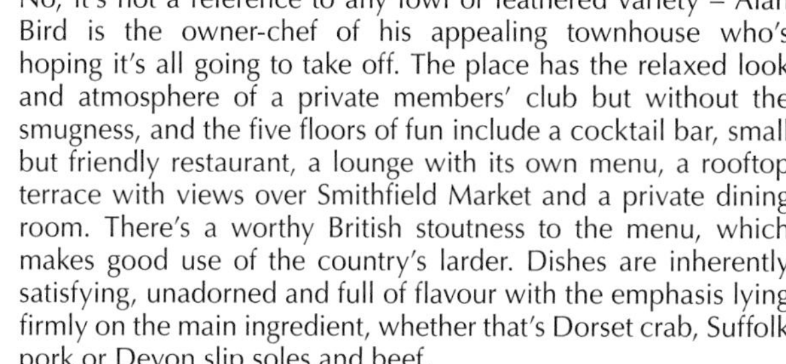

No, it's not a reference to any fowl or feathered variety – Alan Bird is the owner-chef of his appealing townhouse who's hoping it's all going to take off. The place has the relaxed look and atmosphere of a private members' club but without the smugness, and the five floors of fun include a cocktail bar, small but friendly restaurant, a lounge with its own menu, a rooftop terrace with views over Smithfield Market and a private dining room. There's a worthy British stoutness to the menu, which makes good use of the country's larder. Dishes are inherently satisfying, unadorned and full of flavour with the emphasis lying firmly on the main ingredient, whether that's Dorset crab, Suffolk pork or Devon slip soles and beef.

Bistrot Bruno Loubet

French Plan IX – K1

Zetter Hotel,
St John's Sq., 86-88 Clerkenwell Rd. ✉ EC1M 5RJ
✆ (020) 7324 4444
www.bistrotbrunoloubet.com
⊖ Farringdon
Closed 24-26 December to non-residents – booking advisable

Carte £29/36

Bruno Loubet may have surprised a few people by pitching up in Clerkenwell after his sojourn in Australia, but the trendy Zetter hotel is actually a very good fit for his satisfying and rustic cooking. The restaurant has been busy from day one, and it is clear that he's attracting plenty of new followers because not everyone here is old enough to remember 1994 when he made his name in Soho. The menu is largely influenced by bistro classics but the dishes here come with a greater degree of depth and sophistication than one expects; and neither are they exclusively French, as the occasional touch of Asian spicing finds its way in. The closely set tables ensure the room has plenty of buzz and staff provide informed, unhurried service.

Blueprint Café

modern — Plan X – N5

Design Museum, Shad Thames, Butlers Wharf ✉ SE1 2YD
✆ (020) 7378 7031
www.blueprintcafe.co.uk
⊖ London Bridge
Closed 26-27 December, 1-4 January and Sunday dinner

Menu £15/30 – Carte £27/41

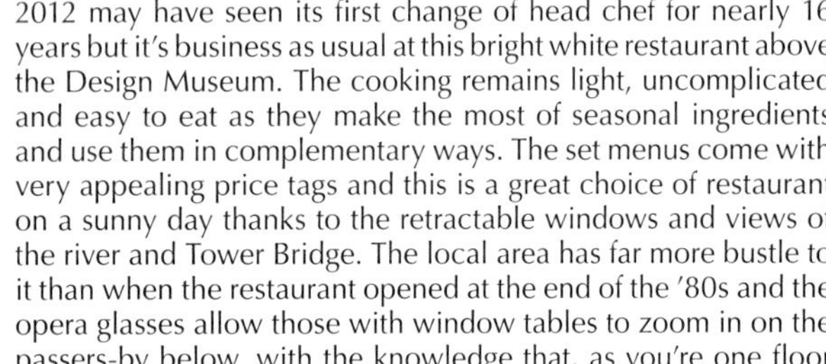

2012 may have seen its first change of head chef for nearly 16 years but it's business as usual at this bright white restaurant above the Design Museum. The cooking remains light, uncomplicated and easy to eat as they make the most of seasonal ingredients and use them in complementary ways. The set menus come with very appealing price tags and this is a great choice of restaurant on a sunny day thanks to the retractable windows and views of the river and Tower Bridge. The local area has far more bustle to it than when the restaurant opened at the end of the '80s and the opera glasses allow those with window tables to zoom in on the passers-by below, with the knowledge that, as you're one floor up, they won't notice you doing so.

Boisdale of Bishopsgate

British traditional — Plan VIII – N2

Swedeland Crt, 202 Bishopsgate ✉ EC2M 4NR
✆ (020) 7283 1763
www.boisdale.co.uk
⊖ Liverpool Street
Closed Saturday, Sunday and bank holidays

Menu £20 – Carte £28/61

A narrow alley littered with drinkers and smokers is perhaps an unlikely place in which to find old-fashioned Scottish hospitality. The ground floor is given over to the guiltless consumption of champagne and oysters but the main event happens in the vaulted cellar below, with its long bar and green leather seating – ask for one of the three booths or table 13 which comes with its own alcove. The menu is varied but it's best to stick to the Scottish staples: smoked salmon, roast haggis with mash and neeps and, in particular, the 28 day dry-aged cuts of beef. The wine list is strong on top end producers from the Auld Alliance partner; cigars and whiskies are also in abundance, while live jazz accompanies all this revelry.

Bonds

modern

Plan VIII – M3

Threadneedles Hotel,
5 Threadneedle St. ✉ EC2R 8AY
✆ (020) 7657 8088
www.bonds-restaurant.com
⊖ Bank
Closed Saturday, Sunday and bank holidays

Menu £24/28 – Carte £28/44

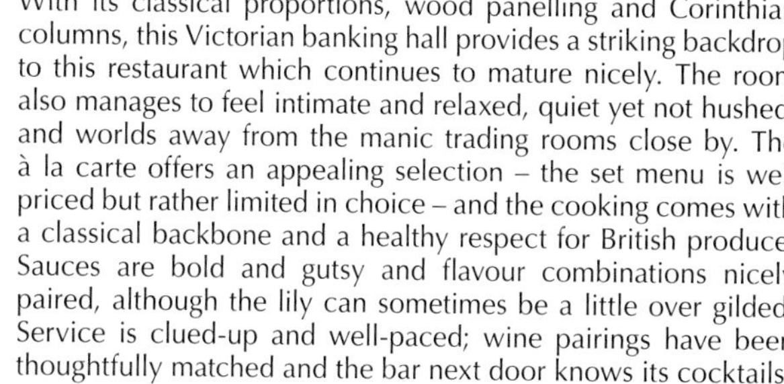

With its classical proportions, wood panelling and Corinthian columns, this Victorian banking hall provides a striking backdrop to this restaurant which continues to mature nicely. The room also manages to feel intimate and relaxed, quiet yet not hushed, and worlds away from the manic trading rooms close by. The à la carte offers an appealing selection – the set menu is well priced but rather limited in choice – and the cooking comes with a classical backbone and a healthy respect for British produce. Sauces are bold and gutsy and flavour combinations nicely paired, although the lily can sometimes be a little over gilded. Service is clued-up and well-paced; wine pairings have been thoughtfully matched and the bar next door knows its cocktails.

Bread Street Kitchen

modern

Plan VIII – L3

10 Bread St ✉ EC4M 9AJ
✆ (020) 3030 4050
www.breadstreetkitchen.com
⊖ St Paul's
Closed 25 December – booking advisable

Carte £28/72

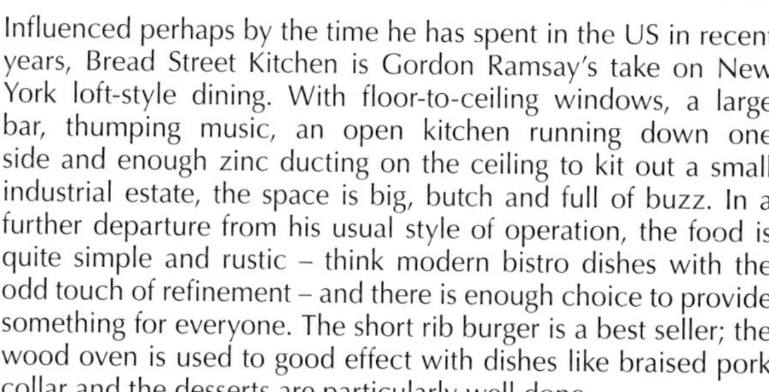

Influenced perhaps by the time he has spent in the US in recent years, Bread Street Kitchen is Gordon Ramsay's take on New York loft-style dining. With floor-to-ceiling windows, a large bar, thumping music, an open kitchen running down one side and enough zinc ducting on the ceiling to kit out a small industrial estate, the space is big, butch and full of buzz. In a further departure from his usual style of operation, the food is quite simple and rustic – think modern bistro dishes with the odd touch of refinement – and there is enough choice to provide something for everyone. The short rib burger is a best seller; the wood oven is used to good effect with dishes like braised pork collar and the desserts are particularly well done.

Butlers Wharf Chop House

British traditional **Plan X – N4**

36e Shad Thames, Butlers Wharf ✉ SE1 2YE
✆ (020) 7403 3403
www.chophouse-restaurant.co.uk
⊖ London Bridge

Carte £24/51

A chophouse means meat and, where there is meat, there are usually men. You'll see plenty of them here, their suit jackets slung over their seats as they get stuck into a charcoal-grilled rib-eye or prepare to wrestle with a game bird. The menu is a paean to all things British so other choices such as steak and kidney pudding or lamb with haggis are equally sturdy; finish off with sticky toffee puddings and you'll wonder if you'll ever be hungry again. The large room comes with light wood panelling that'll prompt cricketers to think of linseed oil and the bar at the entrance end offers a simpler and cheaper menu. Come in the summer for a table on the fantastic terrace – few restaurants can match the stunning views.

Cantina Del Ponte

Italian **Plan X – N4**

36c Shad Thames, Butlers Wharf ✉ SE1 2YE
✆ (020) 7403 5403
www.cantina.co.uk
⊖ London Bridge
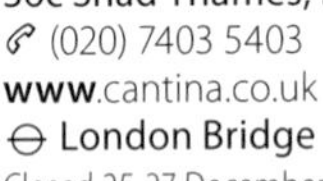
Closed 25-27 December

Menu £13/35 – Carte £28/43

A refurbishment a few years back revitalised this Italian stalwart. They kept the large mural on one wall and created a pleasantly relaxing, faux-rustic environment. The menu was also tweaked: it was out with the pizzas and in with a greater degree of authenticity. The focus is on appealing and flavoursome dishes and the set menu represents decent value. There's a good selection on offer, with the focus very much on recognisable standards and old favourites; flavours are well-defined and portions are bigger than expected. The wine list covers all of Italy and there's ample choice by the glass. The first tables to go on a summer's day are naturally those on the riverside terrace under the awning.

Caravan

other world kitchens Plan IX – K1

11-13 Exmouth Market ✉ EC1R 4QD
✆ (020) 7833 8115
www.caravanonexmouth.co.uk
⊖ Farringdon
Closed Christmas-New Year and Sunday dinner – booking advisable

Carte £22/33

A discernible Antipodean vibe pervades this casual eatery, from the laid-back, easy-going charm of the serving team to the kitchen's confident combining of unusual flavours; even in the excellent flat-whites served by the barista. There's an ersatz industrial feel to the room and a randomness to the decorative touches that belies the seriousness of the ambition. The 100% Arabica beans are roasted daily in the basement, the wine list features an unusual selection of producers and plenty of organic wines, and the owners' travels (hence the name) inform the innovative and inventive cooking. There's something for everyone, from breakfast to small plates to share, or even main courses for two – this really is a caravan of love.

Cellar Gascon

French Plan VIII – L2

59 West Smithfield ✉ EC1A 9DS
✆ (020) 7600 7561
www.cellargascon.com
⊖ Barbican
Closed Christmas-New Year, Saturday, Sunday and bank holidays – booking essential at lunch

Menu £11 (lunch) – Carte approx. £19

Tucked into the side of Club Gascon is their narrow cellar, which began life as a wine bar with a few nibbles thrown in but now, with the whole 'small plates' thing being all the rage, the food enjoys more of a starring role. It's not unlike a smart tapas bar and the monthly changing menu has plenty of treats: pâtés, rillettes, farmhouse hams, cheeses and even some salads for the virtuous, but the Toulouse sausages and the Gascony pie of duck and mushrooms really stand out. The terrific value 'express' lunch, which includes a dish of the day, is hard to beat and understandably popular. The wine list is a shorter version of next door's and focuses on France's south west; they also hold monthly wine tasting evenings.

 Chabrot

French

62-63 Long Ln ✉ EC1A 9EJ
✆ (020) 7796 4550
www.chabrot.com
⊖ Barbican
Closed Christmas, Saturday lunch and Sunday

Menu £20 – Carte £24/51

If you're yearning to relive that romantic weekend in Paris then a meal at this classic French bistrot could help, although its location opposite Smithfield meat market may reduce some of your ardour. This is the second Chabrot, following the success of the original branch in Knightsbridge, and it shares the same reassuringly familiar Gallic look and lively, inclusive atmosphere. If you're looking for value head for the keenly priced set menu, otherwise enjoy the rustic delights of the main menu, where gutsy classics like tête de veau, confit de canard and boudin noir are there in all their glory. If you're still not sated after that, then finish with some French farmhouse cheeses or a classic crème brûlée.

The Chancery

modern

Plan VIII – K2

9 Cursitor St ✉ EC4A 1LL
✆ (020) 7831 4000
www.thechancery.co.uk
⊖ Chancery Lane
Closed 23-30 December,1 January, Saturday lunch, Sunday and bank holidays

Menu £35/49

The Chancery is an elegant, discreet restaurant that's so close to the law courts you'll assume your fellow diners are barristers, jurors, or the recently acquitted. The ground floor, with its contemporary artwork and smartly laid tables, is more comfortable than the basement, although there are plans afoot to expand into next door. The menu is appealing concise and understated and most of the dishes have a reassuringly classical backbone, whether that's the mackerel escabeche or the saddle of rabbit. The kitchen clearly knows what it is doing – flavours are bold and sauces are a particular highlight. The service team can seem a little withdrawn at first – maybe it's dealing with all those formal legal types – but they do get the job done.

Chiswell Street Dining Rooms

British modern — Plan VIII – M2

Montcalm London City at The Brewery Hotel,
56 Chiswell St ✉ EC1Y 4SA
✆ (020) 7614 0177
www.chiswellstreetdining.com
⊖ Barbican

Menu £25 (weekdays) – Carte £27/47

The Martin brothers used their successful Botanist restaurant as the model for their corner spot at the former Whitbread brewery. It may double as a dining room for the Montcalm Hotel, but the place really comes alive in the evening, thanks in no small part to its lively cocktail bar. There's a pleasing Britishness to the menu and the kitchen makes good use of nearby Billingsgate, with classics like whole Cornish lemon sole, and poached langoustines. Those who prefer more muscular cooking can head for the Hereford snail and smoked bacon pie or Aberdeen Angus rib-eye; and who cannot fail to smile when they see 'Knickerbocker Glory' on a menu? The smartly kitted-out staff cope very well with the constant buzzy atmosphere.

Cicada

Asian — Plan IX – L1

132-134 St John St ✉ EC1V 4JT
✆ (020) 7608 1550
www.rickerrestaurants.com
⊖ Farringdon
Closed 25 December and 1 January

Carte £19/45

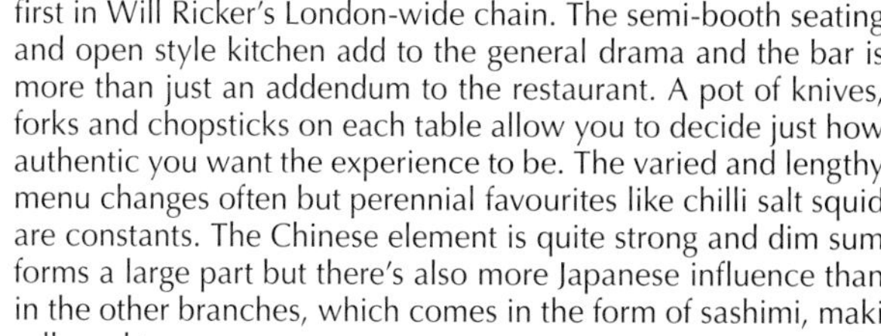

You'll need to book ahead to guarantee a table at this busy, noisy and infectiously entertaining Pan-Asian restaurant, which was the first in Will Ricker's London-wide chain. The semi-booth seating and open style kitchen add to the general drama and the bar is more than just an addendum to the restaurant. A pot of knives, forks and chopsticks on each table allow you to decide just how authentic you want the experience to be. The varied and lengthy menu changes often but perennial favourites like chilli salt squid are constants. The Chinese element is quite strong and dim sum forms a large part but there's also more Japanese influence than in the other branches, which comes in the form of sashimi, maki rolls and tempura.

Cigalon

French Plan VIII – K3

115 Chancery Ln ✉ WC2A 1PP
✆ (020) 7242 8373
www.cigalon.co.uk
⊖ Chancery Lane
Closed Christmas and New Year, Saturday, Sunday and bank holidays

Menu £13/25 – Carte £23/41

A huge skylight bathes the room in light while the kitchen pays homage to the food of Provence – this is a restaurant that really comes into its own in the summer. A former auction house for law books, the space is stylishly laid out, with the booths in the centre being the prized seats – ask for No.9 if you want to watch the chefs in action. Along with the traditional dishes such as soupe au pistou, bouillabaisse, salade niçoise and pieds et paquets are popular grilled dishes such as venison, and there's even the occasional detour to Corsica. Equal thought went into the name: it refers to both a 1935 Marcel Pagnol film about a haughty chef and the local name for the summer cicada. There's also a busy bar downstairs in the cellar.

Cinnamon Kitchen

Indian Plan VIII – N2

9 Devonshire Sq ✉ EC2M 4YL
✆ (020) 7626 5000
www.cinnamonclub.com
⊖ Liverpool Street
Closed Saturday lunch, Sunday and bank holidays

Menu £19/60 – Carte £24/63

Having successfully established Westminster's Cinnamon Club and made it a popular choice with those who run the country, the team behind it opened a second branch here in The City, to appeal to those who own, or thought they owned, the country. This is all about contemporary Indian dining: the cooking is creative and original, the surroundings light and unobtrusive and the service keen and sprightly. The menu bears little resemblance to the usual Indian fare and includes ingredients like quinoa, red deer and scallops. The arresting presentation doesn't come at the expense of the punchy flavours. The grill section is worth exploring and enthusiastic amateur cooks should position themselves at the Tandoor Bar to watch all the action.

Clerkenwell Kitchen

modern Plan IX – K1

27-31 Clerkenwell Cl ✉ EC1R 0AT
✆ (020) 7101 9959
www.theclerkenwellkitchen.co.uk
⊖ Farringdon
Closed Christmas-New Year, Saturday, Sunday and bank holidays – booking advisable – (lunch only)

Carte £17/25

Time spent working in Dorset with Hugh Fearnley-Whittingstall has clearly influenced Emma, the owner of this busy, tucked away eatery: she sources her ingredients from small producers who use traditional methods and is committed to sustainability, recycling and the reduction of food miles. But this is more than just a worthy enterprise – the food is rather good too. Local office workers flock in for breakfast and takeaway sandwiches but it is well worth booking for the appealing daily changing lunch menu. Two of the six main courses will be vegetarian and offer, along with dishes like venison and pancetta pie, plenty of freshness and flavour. Even the juices are seasonal and the tarts, pies and cakes are all made daily.

Comptoir Gascon

French Plan IX – K2

61-63 Charterhouse St. ✉ EC1M 6HJ
✆ (020) 7608 0851
www.comptoirgascon.com
⊖ Farringdon
Closed Christmas-New Year, Sunday, Monday and bank holidays – booking essential

Menu £15 (weekday lunch) – Carte £16/30

This buzzy restaurant should be subsidised by the French Tourist Board as it does more to illustrate one component of Gascony's famed 'douceur de vivre' – sweetness of life – than any glossy brochure. The wines, breads, foie gras, duck and cheeses all celebrate SW France's reputation for earthy, proper man-food. The menu is divided into 'mer', 'vegetal' and 'terre'; be sure to order duck, whether as rillettes, confit or in a salade Landaise. After these big flavours, it'll come as a relief to see that the desserts, displayed in a cabinet, are delicate little things. The prices are also commendable; even the region's wine comes direct from the producers to avoid the extra mark-up. There's further booty on the surrounding shelves.

Club Gascon ✿

French

Plan VIII – L2

57 West Smithfield ✉ EC1A 9DS
✆ (020) 7600 6144
www.clubgascon.com
⊖ Barbican
Closed Christmas-New Year, Saturday lunch, Sunday and bank holidays – booking essential

Menu £25/90 – Carte £35/48

A/C

Club Gascon

Those living in Gascony enjoy a diet with the highest fat content in France yet they tend to live longer than their compatriots. Leaving aside the magical powers of Armagnac, this 'Gascony paradox' is surely reason enough to explore further this most indulgent of cuisines. Chef-owner Pascal Aussignac is passionate about all things south-western: get him started on the quality of the produce and he'll talk the hind legs off an âne. Whilst familiar ingredients appear on the menu, the cooking is surprisingly contemporary and often quite original; the ambition may not always be matched by the execution but the dishes will certainly grab your attention. Lunch is a slightly pared down version of the evening menu but the tasting menu remains the benchmark and comes with some intelligent and well considered wine matches. Service is appropriately and unapologetically Gallic, while marble pillars, panelling and huge floral displays add grandeur to the high-ceilinged room, which was once a Lyons Corner House.

First Course

- Royale of marrow bone, Aquitaine caviar and geraniums.
- Razor clams, crackling and white asparagus.

Main Course

- Crackled capon wings, scallop ballotine and lovage.
- New season lamb, olive pearls, pop and corn sauce.

Dessert

- Black olive and chocolate millionaire, lemon gel and thyme ice cream.
- Pineapple mikado, crispy rum baba, lime and ginger.

Crooked Well

modern

Plan XVII – O2

16 Grove Ln ✉ SE5 8SY
✆ (020) 7252 7798
www.thecrookedwell.com
Closed Monday lunch

Carte £20/34

Three friends scoured the south of England before finding this old boozer in Camberwell. They've done it up very cleverly because it manages to look both new and lived-in at the same time and also feels like a proper 'local'. There's a strong emphasis on beers, great cocktails and an interesting wine list with plenty available by the glass and pichet, but the pub's growing reputation is mostly down to its food. The kitchen mixes things up by offering stout, traditional classics like rabbit and bacon pie alongside more playful dishes such as a deconstructed Peach Melba. There are lots of things 'on toast' at lunchtime, while dishes like Scotch egg with Heinz tomato soup are designed to evoke memories of childhood.

 Del Mercato 

Italian

Plan X – L4

Park St ✉ SE1 9AD
✆ (020) 7407 3651
www.delmercato.co.uk
⊖ London Bridge

Menu £20/30 – Carte £18/29

Just when you think every wharf and warehouse in this part of town has been converted into something new and shiny, along comes Del Mercato, which is owned by the Vinopolis people. It occupies 3,000 sq ft of space under railway arches and has been divided up into a bakery, a little espresso bar that's open for breakfast, a trattoria that does a brisk trade in pizzas and homemade pastas, and upstairs, a more formal restaurant. This room is bright and contemporary yet still manages to evoke something of its past. The on-view kitchen is an accomplished one: the à la carte is extensive and traverses Italy, offering Sicilian caponata to Caprese cake to Venetian mackerel 'in saor'; there is also a competitively priced set menu run alongside it.

Duck & Waffle

modern — Plan VIII – M2

Heron Tower (40th floor), 110 Bishopsgate ✉ EC2N 4AY
✆ (020) 3640 7310
www.duckandwaffle.com
⊖ Liverpool Street
Booking essential

Menu £65 – Carte £28/60

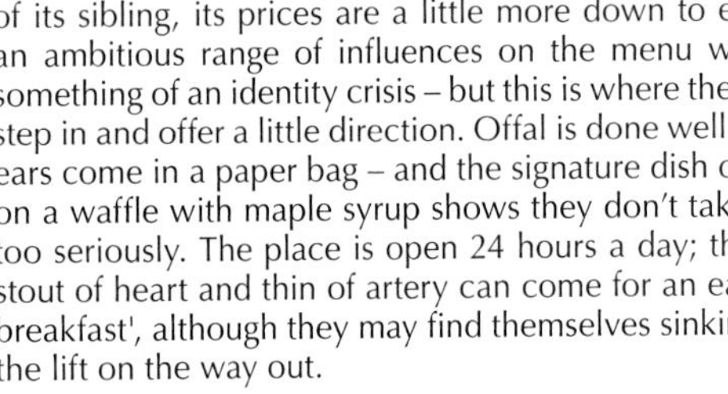

The UK's highest restaurant sits one floor up from Sushisamba in the Heron Tower and, while it lacks the shouty, blingy showiness of its sibling, its prices are a little more down to earth. There's an ambitious range of influences on the menu which gives it something of an identity crisis – but this is where the friendly staff step in and offer a little direction. Offal is done well – crispy pig's ears come in a paper bag – and the signature dish of duck confit on a waffle with maple syrup shows they don't take themselves too seriously. The place is open 24 hours a day; those who are stout of heart and thin of artery can come for an early 'foie gras breakfast', although they may find themselves sinking faster than the lift on the way out.

Elliot's

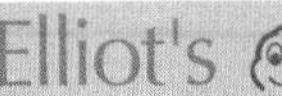

modern — Plan X – M4

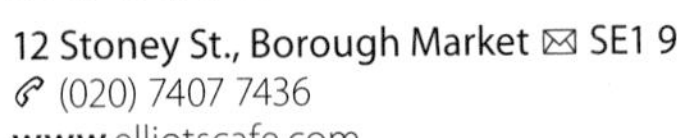

12 Stoney St., Borough Market ✉ SE1 9AD
✆ (020) 7407 7436
www.elliotscafe.com
⊖ London Bridge
Closed Sunday and bank holidays – booking advisable

Carte £21/54

If you want to satisfy the powerful Pavlovian pangs induced by the bounty on display in Borough Market then head for Elliot's Café. This unpretentious spot sources its ingredients directly from the market and has a kitchen that's wise enough not to muck about with them too much. It's open from breakfast time onwards and the menu is concise, regularly changing and instantly appealing. Earthy and uncomplicated dishes like squid with aioli and dukkah, and beef cheek with market-fresh winter vegetables, will leave anyone feeling sated and satisfied; many just pop in for their burger which has quickly established its own fan-base. The appeal of Elliot's Café lies in the fact that it does the simple things well.

Fish Market

fish and seafood Plan VIII – N2

16B New St ✉ EC2M 4TR
✆ (020) 3503 0790
www.fishmarket-restaurant.co.uk
⊖ Liverpool Street
Closed 20 December-6 January, Saturday lunch, Sunday and bank holidays – booking advisable

Menu £17 – Carte £23/58

An antidote to the plethora of steakhouses comes in the form of this traditional seafood restaurant, courtesy of the D&D group. Housed within a former warehouse of the East India Company, it has an appealing ersatz industrial look, with cast-iron pillars, rough-hewn walls and limed oak; the chef shucking oysters behind the full-length marble-topped bar adds to the feeling that you've stepped from Liverpool Street straight into St Ives. From its lengthy menu of classics, the kitchen concentrates on delivering familiar flavours and, by using Cornish crab, oysters from Colchester and West Mersea, day-boat plaice, line-caught cod and farmed bass from Greece, demonstrates it has the appropriate sustainability credentials.

Garrison

Mediterranean Plan X – M5

99-101 Bermondsey St ✉ SE1 3XB
✆ (020) 7089 9355
www.thegarrison.co.uk
⊖ London Bridge.
Closed 25-26 December – booking essential at dinner

Carte £23/37

You'd be hard pressed to find a more charming pub than The Garrison. With its appealing vintage look, warm atmosphere and delightful staff, it's the perfect antidote to those hard-edged boozers that we've all accidentally found ourselves in at some point. Open from 8am for smoothies and breakfast, it gets busier as the day goes on – and don't bother coming for dinner if you haven't booked. Booth numbers 4 and 5, opposite the open kitchen, are the most popular while number 2 at the back is the cosiest. Daily specials on the blackboard supplement the nicely balanced menu and the cooking is perky and bright, with a subtle Mediterranean slant. Salads are done well and there's a daily steak, while puds are of a more traditional bent.

Goodman City

meats and grills Plan VIII – M3

11 Old Jewry ✉ EC2R 8DU
(020) 7600 8220
www.goodmanrestaurants.com
⊖ Bank
Closed Saturday, Sunday and bank holidays

Menu £22 (lunch) – Carte £30/61

The Mayfair branch proved such a success that the opening of a second steakhouse was inevitable. For it, they chose the more appropriate setting of a semi-industrial looking space in The City, perfect for this incontestably macho style of food. Steaks are obviously the stars of the show: the corn-fed USDA beef is imported a tonne at a time and wet-matured for 60 days; the Scottish and Irish beef is grass-fed. Competitive eating from suited City types mean that steaks weighing an impressive 700g are the most popular; the meats are cut to order in the kitchen using a band saw. Commendably – and perhaps unusually for a steakhouse – equal care goes into the other dishes, whether that's calamari to start, or a sorbet at the end.

Hawksmoor

meats and grills Plan VIII – M2

10-12 Basinghall St ✉ EC2V 5BQ
(020) 7397 8120
www.thehawksmoor.com
⊖ Bank
Closed 20 December-4 January, Saturday, Sunday and bank holidays – booking essential

Menu £26 (dinner) – Carte £39/62

Fast and furious, busy and boisterous, the third Hawksmoor provides another testosterone filled celebration of the serious business of beef eating– this is about red meat, red wine and red faced City types in duels to see who can order the biggest steak. It's a handsome room, with its low ceiling, leather seating and wood panelling, which was once used in specimen cupboards at the Natural History Museum. It comes with a great cocktail list and an impressive wine list offering plenty of Mouton Rothschild for when bonuses are handed out. The Longhorn steaks are nicely aged, particularly the D-Rump, and well-rested before coming to the table. With notice you can order 'meat feasts' which take you on a 7-course 'tour of a cow'.

High Timber

modern Plan VIII – L3

8 High Timber St. ✉ EC4V 3PA
✆ (020) 7248 1777
www.hightimber.com
⊖ Mansion House
Closed 23-30 December, 1 January, Saturday dinner, Sunday and bank holidays

Menu £17 (lunch) – Carte £26/53 XX

Surprisingly few restaurants in London overlook the river, especially on the north side, so High Timber is already off to a good start. Add an impressive wine cellar with over 900 bins, including much from the owners' homeland of South Africa, and you've virtually guaranteed a good night out. Heavy wood tables and slate floors lend a slightly rustic look to what is the ground floor of a purpose-built office block; but the room has a fluid feel, as diners are encouraged to visit the cellar or indeed the cheese room to make their choice. The highlight of the concise, seasonal menu is the beef from the grill; they use 28-day matured Cumbrian beef, cut to order from the bone. Dishes have a muscular vigour and come served on slate or chopping boards.

Hispania

Spanish Plan VIII – M3

72-74 Lombard St ✉ EC3V 9AY
✆ (020) 7621 0338
www.hispanialondon.com
⊖ Bank
Closed Saturday, Sunday and bank holidays

Carte £23/34

In the current economic climate, there may be some irony in a Spanish restaurant opening in a former Lloyds banking hall in The City, but the important thing is that Hispania, the Roman name for the Iberian Peninsula, gives Londoners the chance to continue their love affair with Spanish gastronomy. Some 9,000 square feet are given over to its enjoyment, with the ground floor offering authentic tapas ideal for sharing (the upstairs à la carte restaurant was due to open as we went to print). The Spanish staff all know their menu well and are keen to recommend dishes, which come from all regions of the country and are satisfying and full of flavour. There's even a shop if you want to take some Spanish produce home.

Hix Oyster and Chop House

British traditional Plan IX – L2

36-37 Greenhill Rents ✉ EC1M 6BN
✆ (020) 7017 1930
www.hixoysterandchophouse.co.uk
⊖ Farringdon
Closed 25-29 December, Saturday lunch, Sunday dinner and bank holidays

Menu £18 (lunch and early dinner) – Carte £27/59

Utilitarian surroundings, seasonal British ingredients, plenty of offal and prissy-free cooking: this may sound like a description of St John but was in fact Mark Hix's first solo venture and the start of his rapidly expanding restaurant empire. Smithfield Market seems an appropriate location for a restaurant that not only celebrates Britain's culinary heritage with old classics like rabbit brawn, nettle soup and beef and oyster pie but also reminds us of our own natural bounty, from sand eels and asparagus, whiting to laver bread. It's also called an Oyster and Chop House for a reason, with four types of oyster on offer as well as plenty of meat, including Aberdeen beef aged for 28 days and served on the bone.

José

Spanish Plan X – M5

104 Bermondsey St ✉ SE1 3UB
✆ (020) 7403 4902
www.josepizarro.com
⊖ London Bridge
Closed Christmas and Sunday dinner – bookings not accepted

Carte approx. £25

Included on any list of 'things to be enjoyed while standing up' must surely be the eating of tapas. Here at this snug Bermondsey tapas bar they don't take bookings, but fear not – just turn up and you'll get in because they pack 'em in like boquerones and that adds to the charm. The eponymous José was formerly with Brindisa in Borough Market, so he knows what he's doing and is usually found at the counter carving the wonderful acorn-fed Iberico ham. Five plates per person should be more than enough but it's hard to stop ordering when you see what the person next to you has got. The food is dictated by the markets; you'll find the daily fishy dishes on the blackboard. There's a great list of sherries and all wines are available by the glass.

Jugged Hare

British traditional Plan VIII – M3

42 Chiswell St ✉ EC1Y 4SA
(020) 7614 0134
www.thejuggedhare.com
⊖ Barbican.
Booking advisable

Menu £27/48 – Carte £26/61

The famous 18C recipe created by Hannah Glasse, the UK's first domestic goddess, provided the inspiration for the renaming of this Grade II listed pub, previously known as The King's Head. It's an apt name because committed vegetarians may feel ill at ease – and not just because of the collection of glass cabinets in the bar which showcase the art of taxidermy. The atmospheric and appealingly noisy dining room, which has a large open kitchen running down one side, specialises in stout British dishes, with Denham Estate venison, Yorkshire guinea fowl and Cumbrian Longhorn steaks from the rotisserie and the grill being the highlights. If the main course doesn't fill you, puddings like treacle tart or bread and butter pudding will.

Kenza

Lebanese Plan VIII – N2

10 Devonshire Sq. ✉ EC2M 4YP
(020) 7929 5533
www.kenza-restaurant.com
⊖ Liverpool Street
Closed Saturday lunch, Sunday and bank holidays

Menu £33/50 – Carte £29/43

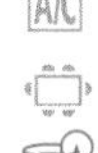

Proving that a party atmosphere and good food are not mutually exclusive, Kenza's Middle Eastern exotica instantly transports you away from the city institutions above. It's not easy to find which adds a frisson of expectation, as does descending the staircase into a room full of Moroccan tiles, beaded lamps, lanterns, silk cushions, mosharabi screens and thumping lounge music. Most of the menu is Lebanese but with Moroccan influences; meze is varied and satisfying and the best main courses are slow-cooked lamb shoulder, chargrilled chicken and marinated swordfish; all meat is Halal. Larger parties need not waste time choosing and can order the 'feasting' menus thus allowing more time to appreciate the skills of the belly dancers.

Luc's Brasserie

French — Plan VIII – M3

17-22 Leadenhall Mkt ✉ EC3V 1LR
✆ (020) 7621 0666
www.lucsbrasserie.com
⊖ Bank
Closed Christmas, New Year, Saturday, Sunday and bank holidays – booking essential at lunch – (lunch only and dinner Tuesday-Thursday)

Menu £20 – Carte £24/45

Go into Leadenhall Market and look up – that's Luc's Brasserie, a restaurant which first appeared in the late 1890s and was reinvigorated and re-launched in 2006. The top floor is fairly sedate but the main room - from where you can admire the Victorian splendour of the market – is where the action is. The menu is an unapologetic paean to all things French, from snails to steak tartare, confit of duck to crème brûlée. The kitchen wisely sticks to conventional and classic recipes and it's easy to see why ties are quickly loosened. Staff do their bit by getting on with things but do so with a smile. As one would expect, the mood relaxes somewhat on the three nights they open for dinner, when a fixed price menu is also available.

Lutyens

modern — Plan VIII – K3

85 Fleet St. ✉ EC4Y 1AE
✆ (020) 7583 8385
www.lutyens-restaurant.com
⊖ Blackfriars
Closed 1 week Christmas-New Year, Saturday, Sunday and bank holidays

Menu £22 – Carte £28/61

This impressive building, designed by Sir Edwin Lutyens and previously Reuters' HQ, is now the ideal backdrop to Sir Terence Conran's elegant and understated restaurant. Evidence that this is a smoothly run operation comes in the fact that they can often serve over 130 at lunch in about 1½ hours; dinner is a more languid affair. The menu closely follows the seasons and is an appealing blend of the classic, like Dover sole, and the more contemporary, such as squid with ink sauce or smoked venison carpaccio. The cooking is crisp and confident, game is handled well and the kitchen avoids any lily-gilding. Over 30 wines are offered by the glass; from the young and exciting to the fine and rare, and in a super range of measures.

Magdalen

British modern Plan X – M4

152 Tooley St. ✉ SE1 2TU
✆ (020) 7403 1342
www.magdalenrestaurant.co.uk
⊖ London Bridge
Closed Sunday, Saturday lunch and bank holidays

Menu £16 (weekday lunch) – Carte £26/43 XX

A/C The Magdalen's kitchen is a clever one: super sourcing and direct contact with farmers take care of the ingredients; the cooking demonstrates a solid, unshowy technique and the influences are kept largely from within the British Isles. Shoulder of Middle White pork with fennel and lemon is a highlight and the rabbit leg with broad beans leaves you wondering why this meat isn't sold in every supermarket. French toast with apricots and vanilla ice cream provides a suitably comforting finale. The lunch menu is a steal, the wine list has been thoughtfully put together by someone who knows the menu well and staff are an eager, genial bunch. The restaurant is divided between two floors; it's more fun on the ground floor.

Manicomio

Italian Plan VIII – L3

6 Gutter Ln ✉ EC2V 8AS
✆ (020) 7726 5010
www.manicomio.co.uk
⊖ St Paul's
Closed 1 week Christmas, Saturday, Sunday and bank holidays

Carte £27/49 XX

A/C You'll find this sibling to the King's Road branch on the first floor of a Norman Foster designed building. On the ground floor is the deli/café while the bar is kept separately on the top floor and is away from the restaurant, which makes a nice change in this part of town. The owners' other business is importing Italian produce so they know their cipollas. There's also plenty of British meat, game and fish but prepared in an Italian way, with top notch Italian accompaniments. The cooking covers many regions, with daily specials; one or two side dishes are needed for the main course and these, together with the bread, may bump the final bill up somewhat. The room has a bright, fresh feel and all the furniture is imported from Italy.

Medcalf

British traditional Plan IX – K1

40 Exmouth Mkt. ✉ EC1R 4QE
✆ (020) 7833 3533
www.medcalfbar.co.uk
⊖ Farringdon
Closed 31 December-3 January, Sunday dinner and bank holidays – booking essential

Menu £17 (dinner) – Carte £24/30

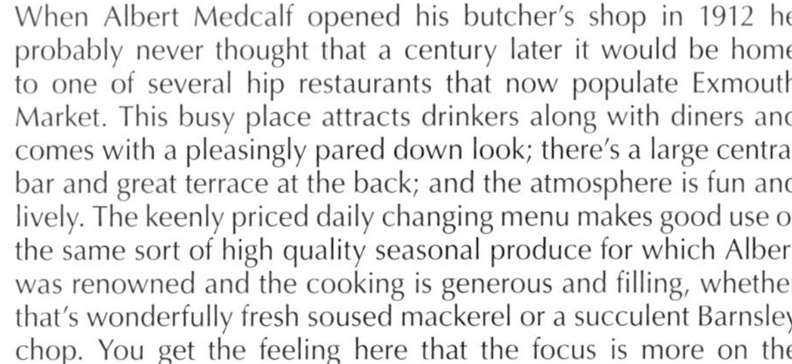

When Albert Medcalf opened his butcher's shop in 1912 he probably never thought that a century later it would be home to one of several hip restaurants that now populate Exmouth Market. This busy place attracts drinkers along with diners and comes with a pleasingly pared down look; there's a large central bar and great terrace at the back; and the atmosphere is fun and lively. The keenly priced daily changing menu makes good use of the same sort of high quality seasonal produce for which Albert was renowned and the cooking is generous and filling, whether that's wonderfully fresh soused mackerel or a succulent Barnsley chop. You get the feeling here that the focus is more on the customer and less on the bottom line.

The Mercer

modern Plan VIII – M3

34 Threadneedle St ✉ EC2R 8AY
✆ (020) 7628 0001
www.themercer.co.uk
⊖ Bank
Closed 25-26 December, Saturday, Sunday and bank holidays

Carte £27/60

The credit crunch means it's even less likely that a restaurant will ever be converted into a bank so, at the moment, the trend remains from bank to restaurant; here at The Mercer you can even see where the tellers used to sit. The high ceilings and windows let in plenty of light and the place has a pleasingly animated brasserie feel, with service that is slick and well paced. Open from breakfast, the kitchen concentrates on familiar flavours and comforting classics. While the cooking may not always live up to the promise of the menu, it is nonetheless satisfying. Scottish beef features in the Grill section and there are daily specials which could be corned beef hash or a fish pie. There's a huge choice of wines by the glass or carafe.

Mint Leaf Lounge

Indian Plan VIII – M3

12 Angel Ct, Lothbury ✉ EC2R 7HB
✆ (020) 7600 0992
www.mintleaflounge.com
⊖ Bank
Closed 25-26 December, 1 January, Saturday, Sunday and bank holidays

Menu £14 – Carte £28/46

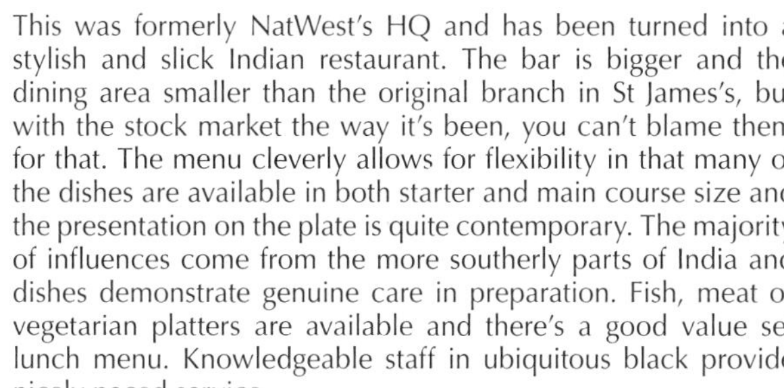

This was formerly NatWest's HQ and has been turned into a stylish and slick Indian restaurant. The bar is bigger and the dining area smaller than the original branch in St James's, but with the stock market the way it's been, you can't blame them for that. The menu cleverly allows for flexibility in that many of the dishes are available in both starter and main course size and the presentation on the plate is quite contemporary. The majority of influences come from the more southerly parts of India and dishes demonstrate genuine care in preparation. Fish, meat or vegetarian platters are available and there's a good value set lunch menu. Knowledgeable staff in ubiquitous black provide nicely paced service.

The Modern Pantry

other world kitchens Plan IX – K1

47-48 St John's Sq. ✉ EC1V 4JJ
✆ (020) 7553 9210
www.themodernpantry.co.uk
⊖ Farringdon
Closed 25 August and 25-26 December – booking advisable

Menu £22 (weekday lunch)/27 – Carte £25/39

This Georgian building has been everything from a foundry to a carpentry workshop but these days plays host to New Zealander Anna Hansen's fusion restaurant. The smart glass doors lead into a simple, crisp space; there's an upstairs too, split between two rooms, which offers a little more intimacy but lacks the buzz of downstairs. The kitchen's peregrinations are reflected in a menu that has few boundaries. You'll probably need to ask for an explanation of at least one ingredient but the staff are clued up, which is no mean feat since menus change daily as ingredients come in. Despite all that's happening on the plate, flavours are well-judged and complementary. Most dishes also come with thoughtfully suggested wine matches.

Morgan M

French Plan VIII – L2

50 Long Ln ✉ EC1A 9EJ
✆ (020) 7609 3560
www.morganm.com
⊖ Barbican
Closed 22-30 December, Saturday lunch and Sunday

Menu £22/52 – Carte £39/55

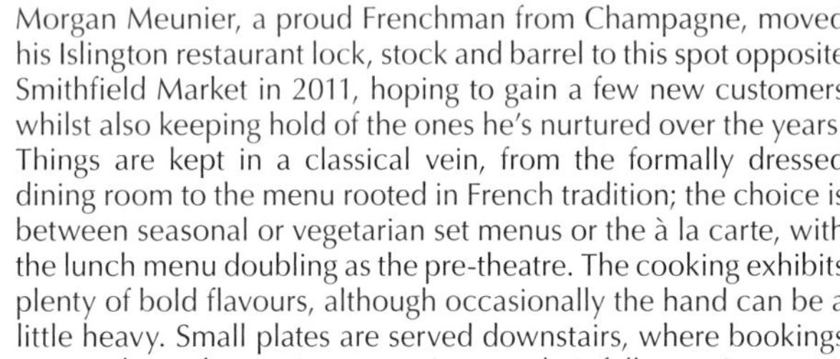

Morgan Meunier, a proud Frenchman from Champagne, moved his Islington restaurant lock, stock and barrel to this spot opposite Smithfield Market in 2011, hoping to gain a few new customers whilst also keeping hold of the ones he's nurtured over the years. Things are kept in a classical vein, from the formally dressed dining room to the menu rooted in French tradition; the choice is between seasonal or vegetarian set menus or the à la carte, with the lunch menu doubling as the pre-theatre. The cooking exhibits plenty of bold flavours, although occasionally the hand can be a little heavy. Small plates are served downstairs, where bookings aren't taken. The serving team give you their full attention.

Morito

Spanish Plan IX – K1

32 Exmouth Mkt ✉ EC1R 4QE
✆ (020) 7278 7007
www.morito.co.uk
⊖ Farringdon
Closed 24 December-3 January and bank holidays – bookings not accepted

Carte £12/19

Morito may not seduce you with its looks but once you start eating you'll find it hard to tear yourself away. This authentic tapas bar comes courtesy of the owners of next door Moro and shares their passion for Moorish cuisine. It's modestly kitted out but endearingly so, with a two-tone formica counter and half a dozen small tables; just turn up and if they haven't got space they'll take your number and you can have a drink in Exmouth Market while you wait. Seven or eight dishes between two should be enough but at these prices you can never overspend. Highlights of the immensely appealing menu include jamon and chicken croquetas and succulent lamb chops with cumin and paprika, all served in authentic earthenware dishes.

Moro

Mediterranean Plan IX – K1

34-36 Exmouth Mkt ✉ EC1R 4QE
✆ (020) 7833 8336
www.moro.co.uk
⊖ Farringdon
Closed 23 December-3 January, Sunday dinner and bank holidays – booking essential

Carte £30/39

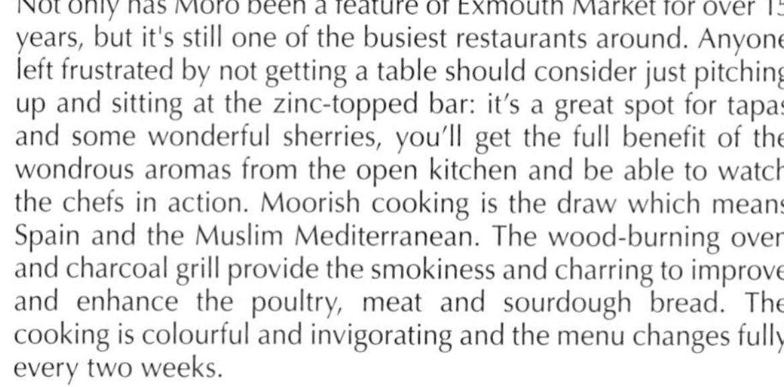

Not only has Moro been a feature of Exmouth Market for over 15 years, but it's still one of the busiest restaurants around. Anyone left frustrated by not getting a table should consider just pitching up and sitting at the zinc-topped bar: it's a great spot for tapas and some wonderful sherries, you'll get the full benefit of the wondrous aromas from the open kitchen and be able to watch the chefs in action. Moorish cooking is the draw which means Spain and the Muslim Mediterranean. The wood-burning oven and charcoal grill provide the smokiness and charring to improve and enhance the poultry, meat and sourdough bread. The cooking is colourful and invigorating and the menu changes fully every two weeks.

Naamyaa Café

Thai Plan IX – K0

407 St John St ✉ EC1V 4AB
✆ (020) 3122 0988
www.naamyaa.com
⊖ Angel
Closed 25 December – bookings not accepted

Carte £18/28

From restaurateur supreme Alan Yau comes his version of the all-day Thai café; although, with its sleek look and impressive design details – like the golden Buddhas on the brickwork – it's actually a world away from the places on Bangkok's Khaosan Road. The menu does have thumbnails of each dish as they do in Thailand and is great value, whether that's the chicken satay with its authentic street food flavour, a nicely balanced curry with the kanom jeen noodles especially flown in or one of their zesty, fresh salads; a few western dishes show they don't take themselves too seriously. The drinks list has also been thoughtfully compiled; try the Krating Daeng, as drunk by tuk tuk drivers. This is a great concept, with more branches to follow.

New St Grill

meats and grills Plan VIII – N2

16A New St ✉ EC2M 4TR
(020) 3503 0785
www.newstreetgrill.com
⊖ Liverpool Street
Closed 23 December-7 January except dinner 31 December, Saturday lunch and Sunday dinner

Carte £28/66

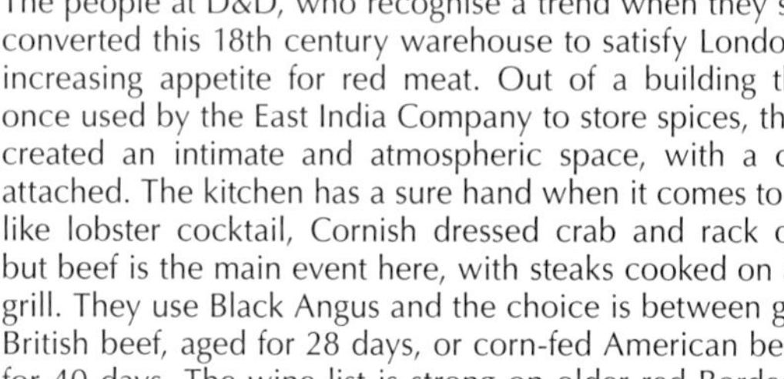

The people at D&D, who recognise a trend when they see one, converted this 18th century warehouse to satisfy London's ever increasing appetite for red meat. Out of a building that was once used by the East India Company to store spices, they have created an intimate and atmospheric space, with a chic bar attached. The kitchen has a sure hand when it comes to classics like lobster cocktail, Cornish dressed crab and rack of lamb, but beef is the main event here, with steaks cooked on a Josper grill. They use Black Angus and the choice is between grass-fed British beef, aged for 28 days, or corn-fed American beef, aged for 40 days. The wine list is strong on older red Bordeaux and mixes the classic with the more esoteric.

1901

British modern Plan VIII – M2

Andaz Liverpool Street Hotel,
Liverpool St. ✉ EC2M 7QN
(020) 7618 7000
www.andaz.com
⊖ Liverpool Street
Closed Christmas, Saturday lunch, Sunday and bank holidays

Menu £30 – Carte £36/53

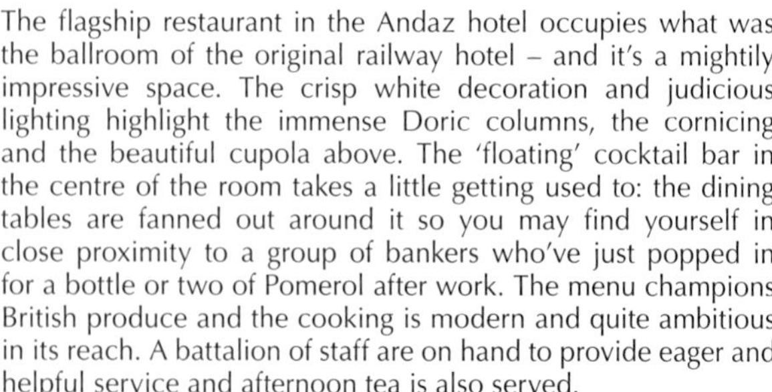

The flagship restaurant in the Andaz hotel occupies what was the ballroom of the original railway hotel – and it's a mightily impressive space. The crisp white decoration and judicious lighting highlight the immense Doric columns, the cornicing and the beautiful cupola above. The 'floating' cocktail bar in the centre of the room takes a little getting used to: the dining tables are fanned out around it so you may find yourself in close proximity to a group of bankers who've just popped in for a bottle or two of Pomerol after work. The menu champions British produce and the cooking is modern and quite ambitious in its reach. A battalion of staff are on hand to provide eager and helpful service and afternoon tea is also served.

Oblix

meats and grills — Plan X - M4

Level 32, The Shard, St Thomas St. ✉ SE1 9RY
✆ (020) 7268 6700
www.oblixrestaurant.com
⊖ London Bridge

Carte £34/61 — XX

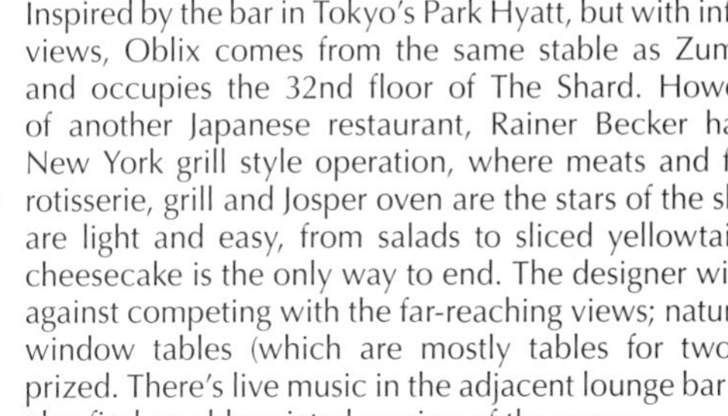

Inspired by the bar in Tokyo's Park Hyatt, but with infinitely better views, Oblix comes from the same stable as Zuma and Roka and occupies the 32nd floor of The Shard. However, instead of another Japanese restaurant, Rainer Becker has created a New York grill style operation, where meats and fish from the rotisserie, grill and Josper oven are the stars of the show. Starters are light and easy, from salads to sliced yellowtail, and a NY cheesecake is the only way to end. The designer wisely decided against competing with the far-reaching views; naturally enough, window tables (which are mostly tables for two) are highly prized. There's live music in the adjacent lounge bar where you'll also find an abbreviated version of the menu.

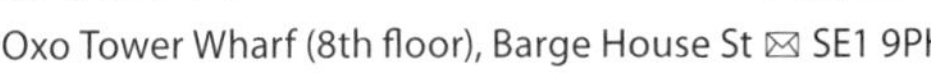

Oxo Tower

modern — Plan X - K4

Oxo Tower Wharf (8th floor), Barge House St ✉ SE1 9PH
✆ (020) 7803 3888
www.harveynichols.com
⊖ Southwark
Closed 25 December, dinner 24 December and lunch 26 December

Menu £35/50 – Carte £44/75 — XXX

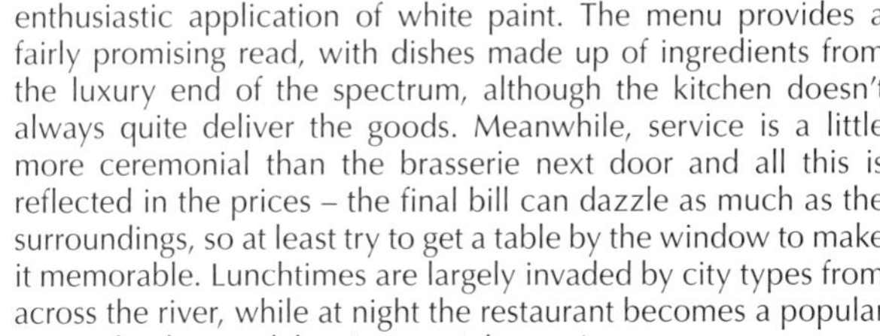

There can be few brighter restaurants than this one on the 8th floor of the Oxo Tower, thanks to its huge windows and enthusiastic application of white paint. The menu provides a fairly promising read, with dishes made up of ingredients from the luxury end of the spectrum, although the kitchen doesn't always quite deliver the goods. Meanwhile, service is a little more ceremonial than the brasserie next door and all this is reflected in the prices – the final bill can dazzle as much as the surroundings, so at least try to get a table by the window to make it memorable. Lunchtimes are largely invaded by city types from across the river, while at night the restaurant becomes a popular setting for those celebrating special occasions.

Oxo Tower Brasserie

modern Plan X – K4

Oxo Tower Wharf (8th floor), Barge House St ✉ SE1 9PH
✆ (020) 7803 3888
www.harveynichols.com
⊖ Southwark
Closed 24 December dinner and 25 December

Menu £25/60 – Carte £34/58

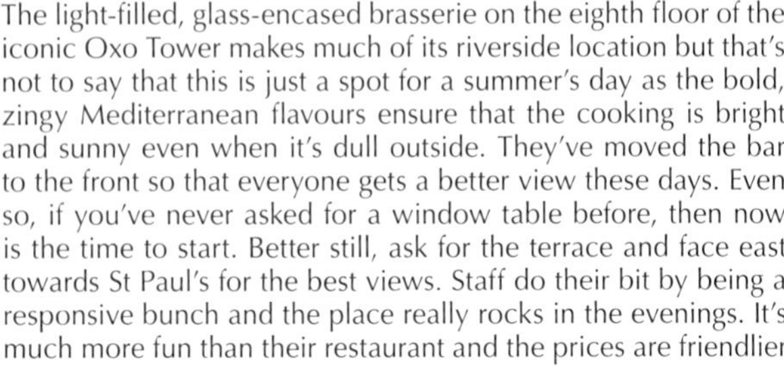

The light-filled, glass-encased brasserie on the eighth floor of the iconic Oxo Tower makes much of its riverside location but that's not to say that this is just a spot for a summer's day as the bold, zingy Mediterranean flavours ensure that the cooking is bright and sunny even when it's dull outside. They've moved the bar to the front so that everyone gets a better view these days. Even so, if you've never asked for a window table before, then now is the time to start. Better still, ask for the terrace and face east towards St Paul's for the best views. Staff do their bit by being a responsive bunch and the place really rocks in the evenings. It's much more fun than their restaurant and the prices are friendlier too.

Paternoster Chop House

British traditional Plan VIII – L3

Warwick Ct., Paternoster Sq. ✉ EC4M 7DX
✆ (020) 7029 9400
www.paternosterchophouse.co.uk
⊖ St Paul's
Closed Christmas, Sunday dinner, Saturday and bank holidays

Menu £24 – Carte £29/49

If you could make just one restaurant legally obliged to serve British food then it would probably be the one that lies in the shadow of St Paul's Cathedral, one of Britain's most symbolic landmarks. Fortunately, Paternoster Chop House negates the need for a bye-law by offering classics from all parts of these isles. The first thing you see on the neatly laid-out menu is the comfortingly patriotic sight of a 'Beer of the Day'. Their livestock comes from small farms, their fish from day boats in the southwest and all the old favourites are present and correct: native oysters, cottage pie, potted hough, liver and bacon, and apple crumble. The dining room is large and open; you might have to fight your way through the busy bar.

Peasant

British modern 
Plan IX – L1

240 St John St ✉ EC1V 4PH
✆ (020) 7336 7726
www.thepeasant.co.uk
⊖ Farringdon.
Closed 25 December-1 January and bank holidays except Good Friday – booking essential

Menu £24 – Carte £22/28

From the outside it may be starting to look its age, but this senior member of the gastropub movement still pulls in plenty of punters. Come evening, you have two choices: stay in the bar and compete for a spare table with the city boys having a post-work pint, or book a table in the sanctuary of the sedate upstairs dining room with its circus-themed prints and posters. Downstairs comes with an easy, eat-on-the-hoof type of menu: squid tempura and sharing boards such a cheese or meze stand out and are ideal accompaniments to a pint. In the restaurant dishes such as sea bream with capers and brown shrimps, and honey-roast duck with celeriac purée, come with a greater degree of sophistication but still deliver on flavour.

Pizarro

Mediterranean
Plan X – M5

171-173 Bermondsey St ✉ SE1 3UW
✆ (020) 7378 9455
www.josepizarro.com
⊖ Borough
Closed 24-28 December – (bookings not taken at dinner and weekend lunch)

Menu £17 (weekday lunch) – Carte £22/31

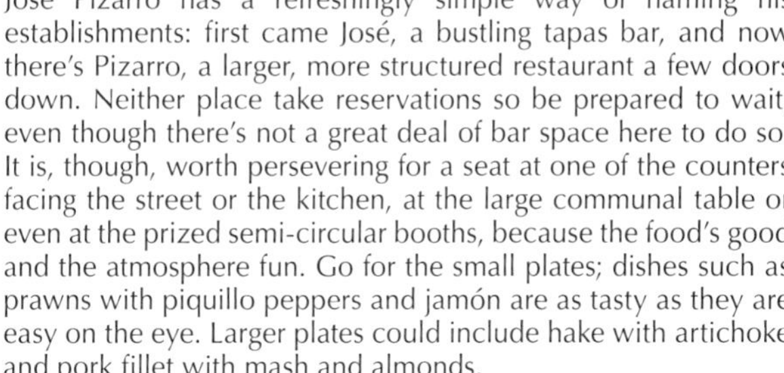

José Pizarro has a refreshingly simple way of naming his establishments: first came José, a bustling tapas bar, and now there's Pizarro, a larger, more structured restaurant a few doors down. Neither place take reservations so be prepared to wait, even though there's not a great deal of bar space here to do so. It is, though, worth persevering for a seat at one of the counters facing the street or the kitchen, at the large communal table or even at the prized semi-circular booths, because the food's good and the atmosphere fun. Go for the small plates; dishes such as prawns with piquillo peppers and jamón are as tasty as they are easy on the eye. Larger plates could include hake with artichoke and pork fillet with mash and almonds.

Polpo Smithfield

Italian

Plan IX – L2

3 Cowcross St ✉ EC1M 6DR
(020) 7250 0034
www.polpo.co.uk
⊖ Farringdon.
Closed Christmas, New Year and Sunday dinner

Carte £14/29

If you've been to a Polpo, or even if you've just bought the cookbook, then you'll know what to expect here – refreshingly uncomplicated and inherently satisfying dishes designed for sharing. For his third Venetian-style bacaro, Russell Norman converted a former meat market storage facility and the place has a charming, elegantly battered feel. Head first to the Negroni bar downstairs, with its appealingly wicked atmosphere, and order the eponymous cocktail. Afterwards, you'll find yourself eagerly over-ordering such delights as crisp pizzette or hearty meatballs. The Venetian and North Italian wines come by the glass, carafe and bottle; staff are cool and calm and the atmosphere terrific. Bookings are only taken up to 5.30pm.

Le Pont de la Tour

French

Plan X – N4

36d Shad Thames, Butlers Wharf ✉ SE1 2YE
(020) 7403 8403
www.lepontdelatour.co.uk
⊖ London Bridge
Closed 26 December and 1 January

Menu £25/30 – Carte £37/67

For over 20 years, Le Pont de la Tour has been the flagship restaurant of the Butlers Wharf development. Decoratively, it may not look quite as striking as it did in 1991 but there is no doubting the glory of its location, especially in summer when you can sit on the terrace and look out over the river and Tower Bridge. During the week the place is largely populated by noisier corporate types but at weekends the room takes on a more romantic air. The set price menu, which includes a few dishes which carry supplements, is not dissimilar to that found in a bistro moderne, but if you want even more rustic choices such as pork rillettes or coq au vin then sit in the livelier cocktail bar and grill, with its evening pianist.

Quality Chop House

British traditional Plan IX – K1

92-94 Farringdon Rd ✉ EC1R 3EA
✆ (020) 7278 1452
www.thequalitychophouse.com
⊖ Farringdon
Closed Sunday and bank holidays – booking advisable

Menu £35 – Carte £21/32

Back in the hands of owners who respect its history and heritage, the Quality Chop House is once again championing gusty British grub: ox tongue, brown crab, Middle White pork, Ayrshire veal and Cornish pollack – they're all here, in refreshingly unadorned, tasty dishes. You're unlikely to find a better example of how to put together a concise wine list – there are gems aplenty, prices are generous and, for something special, check out the Collector's list at the back. The Grade II listed room, with its trademark booths, has an almost Orwellian feel and has been an eating house since 1869; its etched windows proclaim 'Progressive working class caterer' and 'London's noted cup of tea'. The adjoining 'wine bar' has an all-day menu.

Redhook

meats and grills Plan IX – K2

89 Turnmill St ✉ EC1M 5QU
✆ (020) 7065 6800
www.redhooklondon.com
⊖ Farringdon
Closed 25 December, Sunday, lunch Saturday and Monday bank holidays – bookings advisable at dinner

Carte £19/59

Brooklyn comes to Clerkenwell in the shape of Redhook, an appealingly designed American-style restaurant whose refreshingly unambiguous menu specialises in seafood and steaks. There's assorted fish and some pasta on the menu but most diners will be busy chowing down on the Canadian lobster or the assorted cuts of beef which come from Scotland, Ireland and the US; even that '70s symbol of culinary excess, 'surf & turf', makes a comeback here. The kitchen handles the ingredients with care and desserts are not as sweet as those served in the US. Staff contribute to the pleasant atmosphere; California dominates the wine list and the bare brick walls, booths and a faux industrial aesthetic add to the New York feel.

Restaurant at St Paul's Cathedral

British modern Plan VIII – L3

St Paul's Churchyard ✉ EC4M 8AD
(020) 7248 2469
www.restaurantatstpauls.co.uk
⊖ St Paul's
Closed Good Friday and 26 December – booking advisable – (lunch only)

Menu £15/26

Tired tourists and weary worshippers in search of sustenance are ably served by this earnest little restaurant, which is tucked away in a corner of the crypt of Sir Christopher Wren's 17C masterpiece. The kitchen prepares everything from scratch and, appropriately enough, promotes and celebrates all things British, and that includes the drinks menu – refresh yourself by ordering 'Britain in a glass'. The monthly changing menu is reassuringly concise and follows the seasons; try soused mackerel, Scottish pollock or free range chicken with black pudding, followed by some cheeses from Neal's Yard or a rice pudding with Bramley apple compote. Service is well meaning and if you linger long enough, they'll start serving afternoon tea.

Roast

British modern Plan X – M4

The Floral Hall, Borough Mkt ✉ SE1 1TL
(0845) 0347 300
www.roast-restaurant.com
⊖ London Bridge
Closed 25 December and 1 January – booking essential

Menu £30 (weekdays)/35 – Carte £31/57

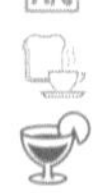

These days every restaurant seemingly name-checks its suppliers – but Roast was one of the first and has always been known for promoting British producers, whether they rear pigs or make cider. Mind you, could they do anything else considering their location – bang in the heart of Borough Market? There's a new energy to the kitchen these days and greater care shown in the preparation of the dishes. The highlight is often the 'dish of the day' which could be rare breed suckling pig with apple sauce; prices can be a little high though, as most main courses need side dishes. Service is also more personable and the bar, which hosts live music at night, is becoming a destination in its own right. Ask for a window table on the market side.

St John ꕥ

British traditional Plan IX – L2

26 St John St ✉ EC1M 4AY
✆ (020) 7251 0848
www.stjohnrestaurant.com
⊖ Farringdon

Closed Christmas-New Year, Saturday lunch, Sunday dinner and bank holidays, – booking essential

Carte £25/57

St John

There's no standing on ceremony here at St John; indeed, very little ceremony at all, and that makes eating here such a joyful experience as one's focus is directed entirely at the food. There's little distraction from the surroundings either, which come in a shade of detention centre white. You can play it safe and go for some crab and then roast beef but this is the place to try new flavours, whether that's cuttlefish or ox tongue. Game is a real favourite and the only gravy will be the blood of the bird – this is natural, 'proper' food. Seasonality is at its core – the menu is rewritten for each service – and nothing sums up the philosophy more than the potatoes and greens: they are always on the menu but the varieties and types change regularly. The waiters wear chef's jackets and spend time in the kitchen so they know what they're talking about and are worth listening to. There are dishes for two as well as magnums of wine for real trenchermen – and be sure to order a dozen warm madeleines to take home.

First Course

- Roast bone marrow and parsley salad.
- Veal breast terrine.

Main Course

- Roast grouse, bread sauce and watercress.
- Rabbit saddle, turnips and aioli.

Dessert

- Eccles cake with Lancashire cheese.
- Honey mousse with blackberries.

Sauterelle

French

Plan VIII – M3

The Royal Exchange ✉ EC3V 3LR
✆ (020) 7618 2483
www.royalexchange-grandcafe.co.uk
⊖ Bank
Closed Saturday, Sunday and bank holidays

Menu £20/45 – Carte £34/55

Sauterelle enjoys a hugely impressive setting on the mezzanine floor of The Royal Exchange and looks down over the Grand Café below which was the original trading floor. This City landmark was rebuilt in 1844, but its layout remains largely true to Sir Thomas Gresham's 1565 original. The striking ceiling and ornate arches add to the already comfortable feel of the restaurant. The menu is largely French, but more contemporary than classic which means the addition of the occasional Italian note. The kitchen certainly doesn't skimp on luxury ingredients: foie gras, turbot, Anjou pigeon and Pyrenean lamb make regular appearances and are appreciated by big spending customers for whom the credit crunch is but a distant memory.

1701

Israeli

Plan VIII – N3

Bevis Marks Synagogue, Bevis Marks ✉ EC3A 5DQ
✆ (020) 7621 1701
www.restaurant1701.co.uk
⊖ Aldgate
Closed Christmas, New Year, Saturday, Sunday and Jewish bank holidays – booking advisable

Menu £32 (lunch) – Carte £35/51

1701 is the year Bevis Marks Synagogue was built, making it the oldest in Britain and one of the oldest in Europe. 1701 is also the name of this kosher restaurant in a modern extension on its side; the room is fairly understated, with a glass roof giving it an airy feel. Service is excellent – the smart staff are keen and engaging, have a good knowledge of the dishes and are keen to offer recommendations. The menu is an impressive document too, not only because of the explanations offered to those unfamiliar with Jewish cuisine, but also in the way dishes have been bought up to date. This is a talented kitchen with a deft touch; try golden chicken soup, elevated to a new level, or short ribs, which are smoked in hay for extra depth.

Skylon

modern Plan III – J4

1 Southbank Centre, Belvedere Rd ✉ SE1 8XX
✆ (020) 7654 7800
www.skylon-restaurant.co.uk
⊖ Waterloo
Closed 25 December and Sunday dinner

Menu £25/43

The original Skylon was a steel structure built for the Festival of Britain in 1951 to promote better quality design. Its name now lives on as the restaurant within the Royal Festival Hall, which was built just yards from where this 'vertical feature' once stood. The South Bank is now a much appreciated area of London and the restaurant offers wonderful river views. It's a large space, with a busy central cocktail bar, a formally laid out restaurant on one side and a simpler grill-style operation on the other. The latter serves fishcakes, burgers, steaks and the like; the restaurant uses more expensive ingredients and puts a modern spin on classic combinations. Be sure to ask for a window table.

Ⓝ Sushisamba

Japanese Plan VIII – M2

Heron Tower (38th and 39th Floor), 110 Bishopsgate
✉ EC2N 4AY
✆ (020) 3640 7330
www.sushisamba.com
⊖ Liverpool Street
Booking essential

Carte £28/79

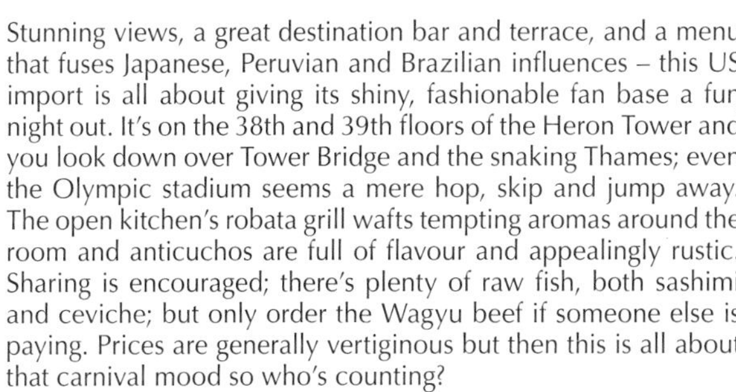

Stunning views, a great destination bar and terrace, and a menu that fuses Japanese, Peruvian and Brazilian influences – this US import is all about giving its shiny, fashionable fan base a fun night out. It's on the 38th and 39th floors of the Heron Tower and you look down over Tower Bridge and the snaking Thames; even the Olympic stadium seems a mere hop, skip and jump away. The open kitchen's robata grill wafts tempting aromas around the room and anticuchos are full of flavour and appealingly rustic. Sharing is encouraged; there's plenty of raw fish, both sashimi and ceviche; but only order the Wagyu beef if someone else is paying. Prices are generally vertiginous but then this is all about that carnival mood so who's counting?

N Story ✿

modern Plan X – N5

201 Tooley St. ✉ SE1 2UE
✆ (020) 7183 2117
www.restaurantstory.co.uk
⊖ London Bridge
Closed 2 weeks Christmas-New Year, Sunday and Monday – booking essential

Menu £45/65 XX

Story

It's amazing what you can create out of an old public toilet on a traffic island in Bermondsey. Tom Sellers is the young chef who's not only making waves with his cooking but also helped design this purpose-built restaurant. From a distance the wooden structure resembles some sort of Nordic eco-lodge; from the inside, the huge picture window allows the light to flood in, and at night the wood burning stove adds warmth to the room. But the real story is the food – and the food is very good. There are two set menus (presented in old Charles Dickens books – he lived on Tooley Street) of 6 or 10 courses; go for the 10, as 6 is too few. Whilst one can see the obvious influences of Tom's alma maters such as Noma in the food and in the style of service (the chefs occasionally bring the dishes to the table), there is also much originality, not least in the candle made from beef dripping that melts when lit. The food is governed by the seasons; it's earthy yet always delicate, playful but also easy to eat. With just 13 tables, getting in is another story.

First Course

- Burnt onion, apple gin and thyme.
- Mackerel with roots.

Main Course

- Pigeon, summer truffle and pine.
- Heritage potato, asparagus and barley grass.

Dessert

- Almond and dill.
- Lemon ice cream, curd and 'snow'.

Tapas Brindisa

Spanish Plan X – M4

18-20 Southwark St, Borough Market ✉ SE1 1TJ
✆ (020) 7357 8880
www.tapasbrindisa.com
⊖ London Bridge
Bookings not accepted

Carte £12/31

The owners spent years importing Spanish produce so it was no surprise that their restaurant on the edge of Borough Market took off immediately. It not only provided the blueprint for many of the tapas bars that subsequently sprung up over London but was also one of the first restaurants not to take bookings— a less welcome but still understandable policy that has also become more widespread. The place has an infectious energy and vitality and the young staff are as efficient as they are unflappable. Start with a glass of Fino and crisp parcels of morcilla, then share a selection of hand-carved Ibérico hams and robust, generously sized dishes such as Galician style hake, black rice with squid and braised ox cheeks.

Tate Modern (Restaurant)

British modern Plan X – L4

Tate Modern (6th floor), Bankside ✉ SE1 9TG
✆ (020) 7887 8888
www.tate.org.uk
⊖ Southwark
Closed 24-26 December – (lunch only and dinner Friday-Saturday)

Carte £26/40

The first thing you'll notice when you get up to Tate Modern's restaurant on Level 6 is the view of St Paul's – and that's about the time you wish you'd asked for a window table. The huge, bright restaurant can seat nearly 150 people so getting a table should never be a problem and there's usually no shortage of atmosphere; black and white is the chosen canvas and tables are surprisingly well spaced. The menu is very seasonal and dishes are largely British; the kitchen keeps things relatively light, even with wintry dishes like venison with red cabbage – so lunch need never impinge on plans for post-prandial art appreciation. Each dish comes with a suggested wine pairing and plenty of thought has gone into creating the drinks selection.

28°-50° Fetter Lane

French — Plan VIII – K3

140 Fetter Ln ✉ EC4A 1BT
✆ (020) 7242 8877
www.2850.co.uk
⊖ Temple
Closed Saturday, Sunday and bank holidays

Menu £16 (lunch) – Carte £22/32

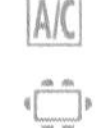

All things vinous are celebrated at this cellar restaurant and wine bar, which is named after the latitudes between which most wine-making grapes are grown. Owned by the people behind Texture restaurant, it offers a good choice of grilled meats, charcuterie, cheese and assorted European dishes – and all the dishes come with a pleasing, underlying simplicity which allows the wine star billing. Oenophiles will appreciate the carefully compiled wine list which consists of 17 reds and 17 whites, all available by the glass, carafe and bottle; sherries and dessert wines are not forgotten either. The Collector's List offers some real gems; the cross section of regions is spot on and the wines are served at their perfect temperatures.

Vanilla Black

innovative — Plan VIII – K2

17-18 Tooks Ct. ✉ EC4A 1LB
✆ (020) 7242 2622
www.vanillablack.co.uk
⊖ Chancery Lane
Closed 2 weeks Christmas and bank holidays

Menu £24/38

The City may not necessarily be the first place one would look for modern and creative vegetarian food but Vanilla Black does things a little bit differently and in the process proves that the Square Mile is not all about red meat and testosterone. The cooking here is inventive and very ambitious and the kitchen uses plenty of modern techniques; it pushes a few boundaries and, while not all the innovative elements gel, it's a fairly exhilarating ride. Along with some usual flavour combinations they also use some unexpected produce which includes foraged ingredients – and there's not a nut cutlet in sight. With its polite and professional service, smart racing green façade and understated interior, it dispels a few other clichés too.

Village East

modern

Plan X – M5

171-173 Bermondsey St ✉ SE1 3UW
✆ (0207) 3576 082
www.villageeast.co.uk
⊖ London Bridge
Closed 25-26 December

Menu £14 (weekday lunch) – Carte £24/60

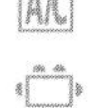

Clever name - sounds a bit downtown Manhattan; but while Bermondsey may not be London's East Village, what Village East does is give this part of town a bit more 'neighbour' and a little less 'hood'. It's tricky to find so look for the glass façade and you'll find yourself in one of the bars, still wondering if you've come to the right place. Once, though, you've seen the open kitchen you know the dining area's not far away. Wood, brick, vents and large circular lamps give it that warehouse aesthetic. The menu is laid out a little confusingly but what you get is ample portions of familiar bistro-style food, as well as some interesting combinations. The separately priced side dishes are not really needed and can push the bill up.

Vinoteca

modern

Plan IX – L2

7 St John St. ✉ EC1M 4AA
✆ (020) 7253 8786
www.vinoteca.co.uk
⊖ Farringdon
Closed 25-26 December, 1 January, Sunday and bank holidays

Carte £23/34

Vinoteca, a self-styled 'bar and wine shop', comes divided into two tiny rooms and is always so busy that you'll almost certainly have to wait for a table. But what makes this frenetic place so special is the young and very passionate team who run it so well. The wine list is thrilling: it is constantly evolving and covers all regions, including less familiar territories along with the organic and the biodynamic. In circumstances such as these, the food can often be an afterthought but here it isn't. Alongside the cheeses and the cured meats that are available all day are classic dishes like pear, chicory and Roquefort salad; potted shrimps; bavette steak and panna cotta; all fresh tasting, well-timed and enjoyable.

Vivat Bacchus

meats and grills Plan VIII – K2

47 Farringdon St ✉ EC4A 4LL
(020) 7353 2648
www.vivatbacchus.co.uk
⊖ Farringdon
Closed Christmas and New Year, Saturday, Sunday and bank holidays

Carte £20/44 

Both the name and the Paul Cluver barriques outside offer clues about the make-up of this bustling City spot: it revolves around wine and the owner is South African. From four cellars come a hugely impressive 500 labels and 15,000 bottles, not only paying homage to major players like Château Latour, d'Yquem, Lafite and Romanée Conti, but also featuring South African jewels like Meerlust Rubicon – if you can button-hole owner Gerrie, he'll give you a tour. The restaurant attracts an ebullient City crowd and the menu complements the wine: steaks and charcuterie dominate and the sharing platters are perfect with a glass or three. Ostrich and kangaroo also feature and you can choose your perfectly ripened cheese from the cheese room.

Vivat Bacchus London Bridge

meats and grills Plan X – M4

4 Hays Ln ✉ SE1 2HB
(020) 7234 0891
www.vivatbacchus.co.uk
⊖ London Bridge
Closed Christmas and New Year, Saturday lunch, Sunday and bank holidays

Carte £20/44 

Here at Vivat Bacchus, wine is regarded as the starting point rather than a supplement. Friends sharing a bottle or two after work make up a healthy part of the business and the menu looks as though it was devised to complement the wine rather than vice versa. As the owners are South African, wines from that country feature heavily, many of which have the necessary muscle for the meat-based menu which includes everything from kangaroo steaks to biltong. Avoid the more ambitious dishes and choose one of the many sharing boards which are largely themed around different countries, perhaps a platter of Italian hams or South African BBQ. It's also worth visiting their cheese room to make your own selection.

Well

British modern

Plan IX – L1

180 St John St ✉ EC1V 4JY
✆ (020) 7251 9363
www.downthewell.com
⊖ Farringdon
Closed 25-26 December

Carte £23/37

One of the smallest pubs in the Martin Brothers' portfolio is also one of the easiest to find, thanks to its wide expanse of blue canopy. This well-supported neighbourhood pub comes with the sort of food that is reassuringly familiar yet still done well, and service that instills confidence in the customer – just be sure eat on the ground floor, rather than in the less welcoming basement. Whether it's asparagus soup or veal Holstein, dishes are cooked with care and deliver on flavour. A side dish between two is needed – the macaroni cheese is worth ordering even if it doesn't necessarily match up to what you're eating – and who isn't reassured by the presence of a crumble on a menu? The only let-down is a lack of draught beers.

The White Swan

modern

Plan VIII – K2

108 Fetter Ln (1st floor) ✉ EC4A 1ES
✆ (020) 7242 9696
www.thewhiteswanlondon.com
⊖ Chancery Lane
Closed 25-26 December, Saturday, Sunday and bank holidays

Menu £27/31 – Carte £26/42

A brunoise here, a glossy sauce there – the evidence of a classical culinary education is insurmountable. There's obvious care and refinement to the cooking as well as an innate understanding of exactly what goes with what. The British provenance of the ingredients is unimpeachable but if the kitchen thinks some Mediterranean flavours will suit a dish better then that is exactly what it gets. The wine list is unapologetically Old World and even comes in a heavy leather binder and the clubby surroundings also fit the bill: the walls are half-panelled and the copper top bar has been enthusiastically polished. To reach this haven of serenity and propriety one first has to fight through the hordes of drinkers in the ground floor bar.

Wright Brothers

fish and seafood Plan X – M4

11 Stoney St., Borough Market ✉ SE1 9AD
✆ (020) 7403 9554
www.thewrightbrothers.co.uk
⊖ London Bridge
Closed dinner 24 December-dinner 28 December, 1-2 January, Easter Sunday and bank holiday Mondays – booking advisable

Carte £29/39

If you want to take a breather from the hordes at Borough Market then nip into Wright Brothers, but do it early as it quickly fills. Their motto is 'not just oysters' but then they do excel in them – hardly surprising when you consider that this small place started as an oyster wholesaler. Grab a table and enjoy them raw or cooked, by candlelight, along with the perfect accompaniment – a glass of porter – or else share a bench or the counter and opt for a platter of fruits de mer and a bottle of chilled Muscadet. If the bivalve is not your thing, then there are daily specials such as skate knobs, as well as pies and, for dessert, either chocolate truffles or crème brûlée. An air of contentment reigns.

Zucca

Italian Plan X – M5

184 Bermondsey St ✉ SE1 3TQ
✆ (020) 7378 6809
www.zuccalondon.com
⊖ Borough
Closed 24 December-7 January, Easter, Sunday dinner and Monday – booking essential at dinner

Carte £22/33

The suitably fresh faced young chef-owner seems to have got it all pretty spot-on: the simple but informed Italian cooking is driven by the ingredients, the prices are more than generous, the room is bright and crisp and the service, sweet and responsive. The antipasti forms the largest part of the weekly changing menu and the hard part – especially if you're sharing – is knowing when to stop ordering; but do always include the zucca fritti – the pumpkin speciality. The kitchen team are an unflustered group, largely because they don't fiddle with the food and know that less equals more. The freshly baked breads come with Planeta olive oil; there are usually two pasta dishes and the aromas that fill the room make it hard to leave.

Eurasia Press/Photononstop

Chelsea · Earl's Court · Hyde Park · Knightsbridge · South Kensington

Though its days of unbridled hedonism are long gone - and its 'alternative' tag is more closely aligned to property prices than counterculture - there's still a hip feel to **Chelsea.** The place that put the Swinging into London has grown grey, distinguished and rather placid over the years, but tourists still throng to the **King's Road,** albeit to shop at the chain stores which have steadily muscled out SW3's chi-chi boutiques. It's not so easy now to imagine the heady mix of clans that used to sashay along here, from Sixties mods and models to Seventies punks, but for practically a quarter of a century, from the moment in 1955 when Mary Quant opened her trend-setting Bazaar, this was the pavement to parade down.

Chelsea's most cutting-edge destination these days is probably the gallery of modern art that bears the name of Margaret Thatcher's former favourite, Charles Saatchi. Which isn't the only irony, as Saatchi's outlandishly modish exhibits are housed in a one-time military barracks, the Duke of York's headquarters. Nearby, the traffic careers round **Sloane Square,** but it's almost possible to distance yourself from the fumes by sitting amongst the shady bowers in the centre of the square, or watching the world go by from a prime position in one of many cafés. Having said that, *the* place to get away from it all, and yet still be within striking distance of the King's Road, is the delightful **Physic Garden,** down by the river. Famous for its healing herbs for over 300 years, it's England's second oldest botanic garden.

Mind you, if the size of a green space is more important to you than its medicinal qualities, then you need to head up to **Hyde Park,** the city's biggest. Expansive enough to accommodate trotting horses on Rotten Row, swimmers and rowers in the Serpentine, up-to-the-minute art exhibitions at the Serpentine Gallery, and ranting individualists at Speakers' Corner, the park has also held within its borders thousands of rock fans for concerts by the likes of the Rolling Stones, Simon and Garfunkel and Pink Floyd.

Just across from its southern border stands one of London's most imperious sights, The **Royal Albert Hall,** gateway to the cultural hotspot that is South Kensington. Given its wings after the 1851 Great Exhibition, the area round **Cromwell Road** invested heavily in culture and learning, in the shape of three world famous museums and three heavyweight colleges. But one of its most intriguing museums is little known to visitors, even though it's only a few metres east of the Albert Hall: the Sikorski is, by turns, a moving

C. Eymenier/MICHELIN

and spectacular showpiece for all things Polish.

No one would claim to be moved by the exhibits on show in nearby **Knightsbridge,** but there are certainly spectacular credit card transactions made here. The twin retail shrines of Harvey Nichols and Harrods are the proverbial honey-pots to the tourist bee, where a 'credit crunch' means you've accidentally trodden on your visa. Between them, in **Sloane Street,** the world's most famous retail names line up like an A-lister's who's who. At the western end of Knightsbridge is the rich person's Catholic church of choice, the Brompton Oratory, an unerringly lavish concoction in a baroque Italianate style. Behind it is the enchanting Ennismore Gardens Mews, a lovely thoroughfare that dovetails rather well with the Oratory.

Further west along Old Brompton Road is **Earl's Court,** an area of grand old houses turned into bedsits and spartan hotels. An oddly bewitching contrast sits side by side here, the old resting alongside the new. The old in this case is Brompton Cemetery, an enchanting wilderness of monuments wherein lie the likes of Samuel Cunard and Emmeline Pankhurst. At its southwest corner, incongruously, sits the new, insomuch as it's the home of a regular influx of newcomers from abroad, who are young, gifted and possessed of vast incomes: the players of Chelsea FC.

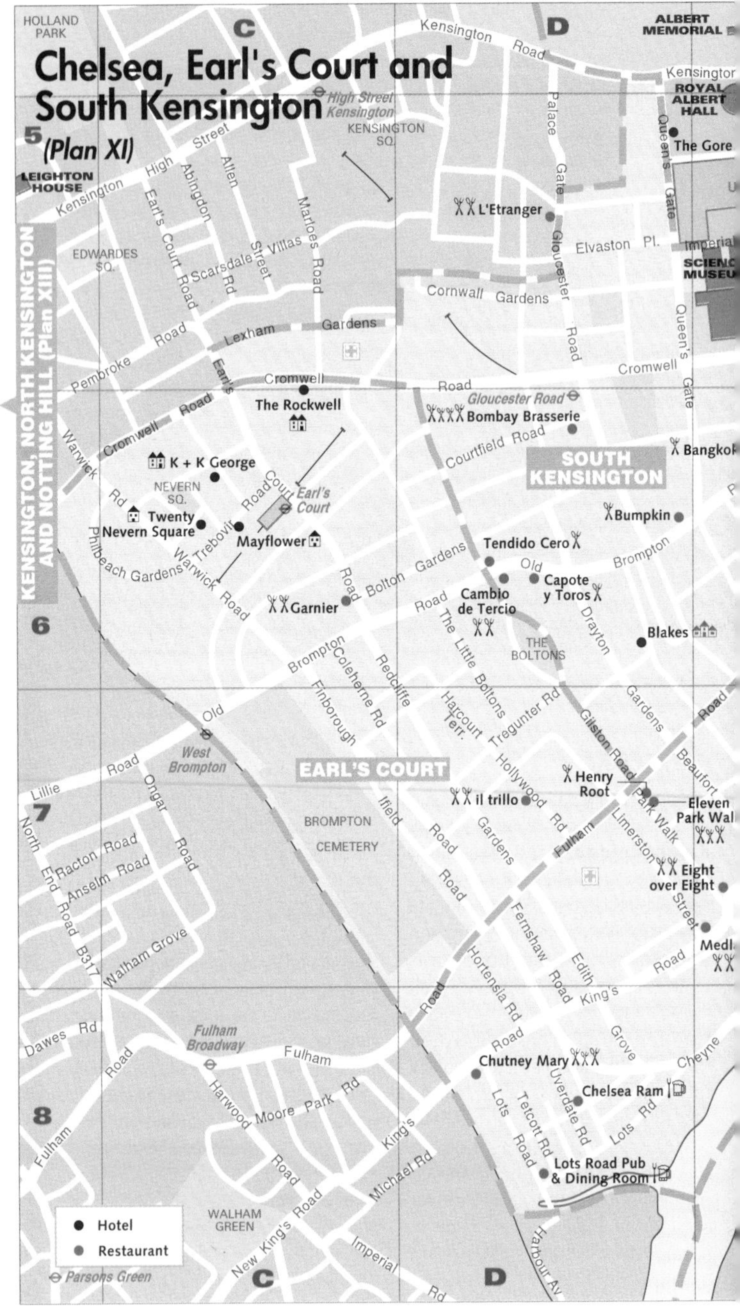
Chelsea, Earl's Court and South Kensington
(Plan XI)
Hotel
Restaurant
The Rockwell
K + K George
Twenty Nevern Square
Mayflower
Blakes
The Gore
L'Etranger
Bombay Brasserie
Bangkok
Bumpkin
Tendido Cero
Cambio de Tercio
Capote y Toros
Garnier
Henry Root
Eleven Park Walk
Eight over Eight
il trillo
Chutney Mary
Chelsea Ram
Lots Road Pub & Dining Room
SOUTH KENSINGTON
EARL'S COURT
KENSINGTON, NORTH KENSINGTON AND NOTTING HILL (Plan XIII)

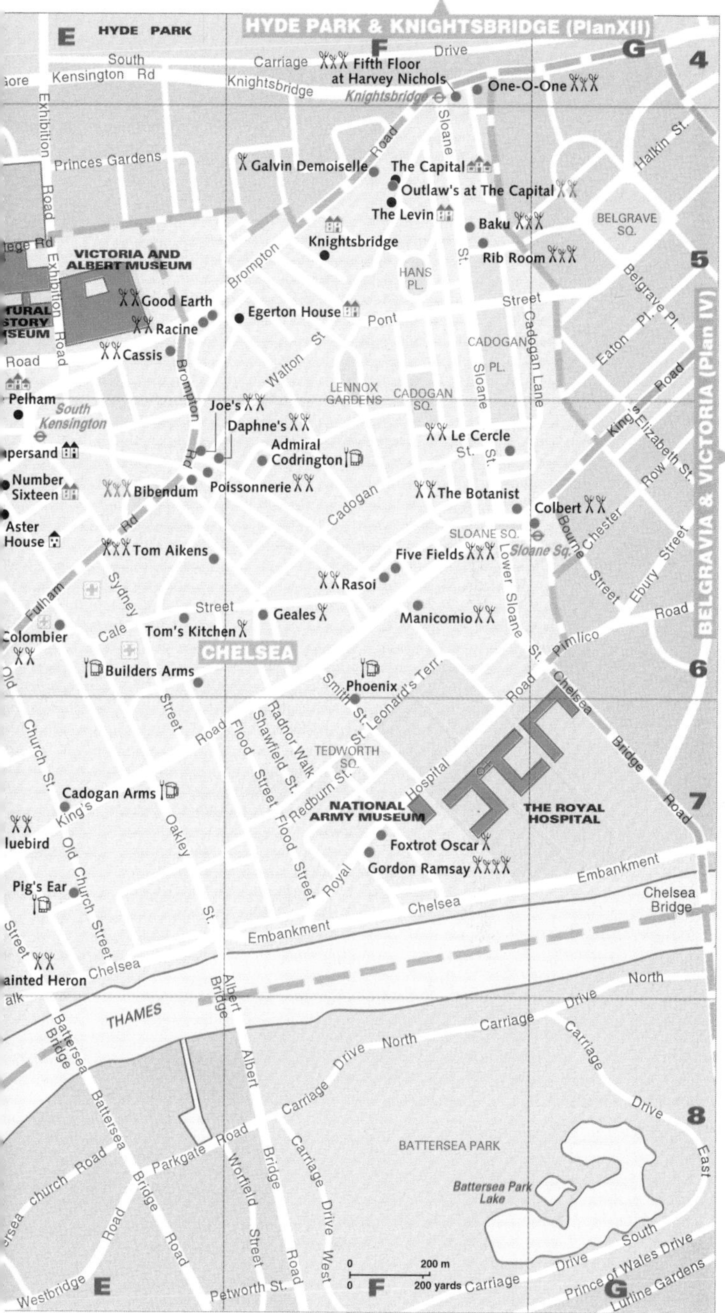
HYDE PARK & KNIGHTSBRIDGE (PlanXII)
HYDE PARK
Fifth Floor at Harvey Nichols
One-O-One
Galvin Demoiselle
The Capital
Outlaw's at The Capital
The Levin
Baku
Knightsbridge
Rib Room
VICTORIA AND ALBERT MUSEUM
Good Earth
Egerton House
Racine
Cassis
Pelham
South Kensington
Joe's
Daphne's
Admiral Codrington
Le Cercle
Number Sixteen
Bibendum
Poissonnerie
The Botanist
Colbert
Aster House
Tom Aikens
Five Fields
Rasoi
Geales
Manicomio
Colombier
Tom's Kitchen
CHELSEA
Builders Arms
Phoenix
BELGRAVIA & VICTORIA (Plan IV)
NATIONAL ARMY MUSEUM
THE ROYAL HOSPITAL
Cadogan Arms
Foxtrot Oscar
Gordon Ramsay
Pig's Ear
THAMES
BATTERSEA PARK
Battersea Park Lake
200 m
200 yards

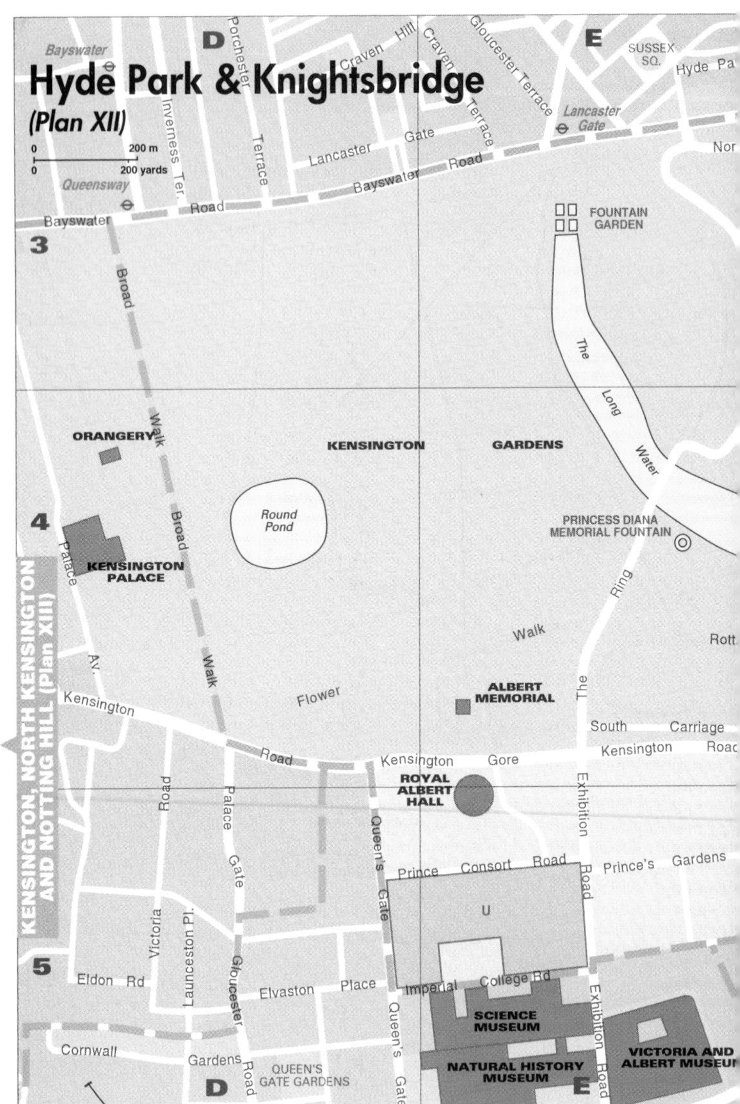
Hyde Park & Knightsbridge
(Plan XII)
0 200 m
0 200 yards
Bayswater
Queensway
Porchester
Inverness Ter.
Terrace
Lancaster Gate
Craven Hill
Craven
Gloucester Terrace
Terrace
Lancaster Gate
SUSSEX SQ.
Hyde Pa
Nor
Bayswater Road
FOUNTAIN GARDEN
Broad Walk
The Long Water
ORANGERY
KENSINGTON GARDENS
Round Pond
PRINCESS DIANA MEMORIAL FOUNTAIN
KENSINGTON PALACE
Palace Av.
Ring
Walk
Flower
The
Rott.
ALBERT MEMORIAL
Kensington Road
South Carriage Road
Kensington Gore
ROYAL ALBERT HALL
Exhibition Road
Palace Gate
Queen's Gate
Prince Consort Road
Prince's Gardens
U
Imperial College Rd
SCIENCE MUSEUM
NATURAL HISTORY MUSEUM
VICTORIA AND ALBERT MUSEU
Victoria Road
Launceston Pl.
Gloucester Road
Eldon Rd
Elvaston Place
Cornwall Gardens
QUEEN'S GATE GARDENS
KENSINGTON, NORTH KENSINGTON AND NOTTING HILL (Plan XIII)
D
E
3
4
5

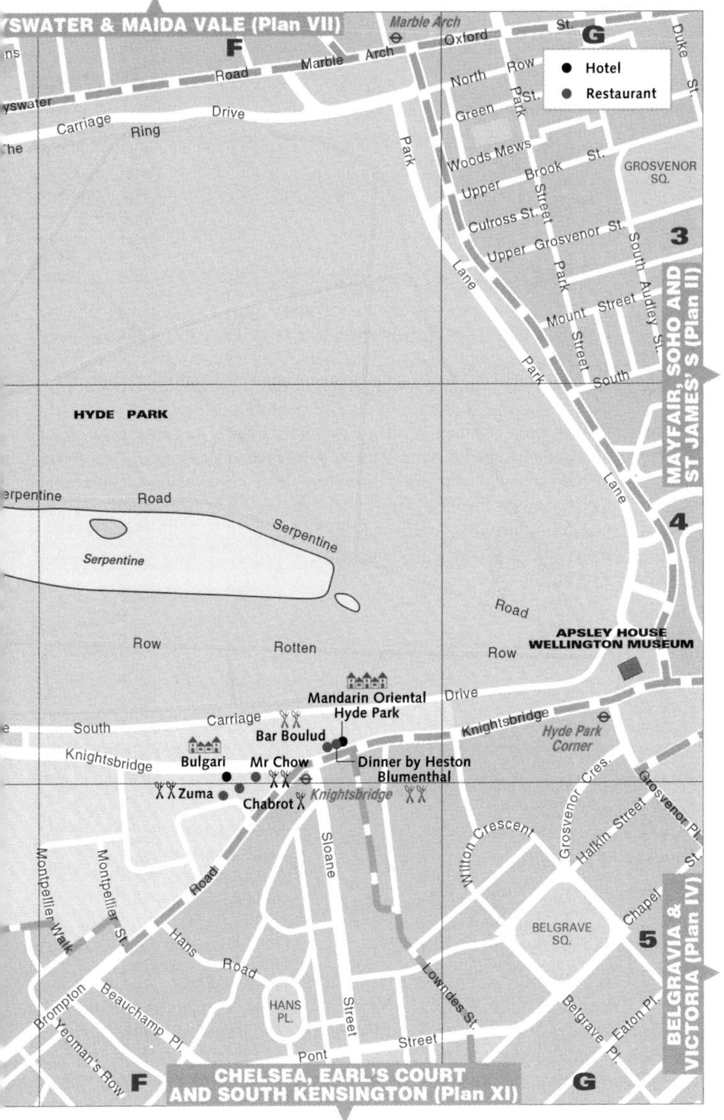

SWATER & MAIDA VALE (Plan VII)
Hotel
Restaurant
HYDE PARK
Serpentine
GROSVENOR SQ.
MAYFAIR, SOHO AND ST JAMES'S (Plan II)
APSLEY HOUSE WELLINGTON MUSEUM
Mandarin Oriental Hyde Park
Bar Boulud
Dinner by Heston Blumenthal
Bulgari
Mr Chow
Zuma
Chabrot
Knightsbridge
Hyde Park Corner
BELGRAVE SQ.
HANS PL.
BELGRAVIA & VICTORIA (Plan IV)
CHELSEA, EARL'S COURT AND SOUTH KENSINGTON (Plan XI)

Admiral Codrington

modern **Plan XI – F6**

17 Mossop St ✉ SW3 2LY
✆ (020) 7581 0005
www.theadmiralcodrington.com
⊖ South Kensington.
Closed 24-25 December

Carte £21/66

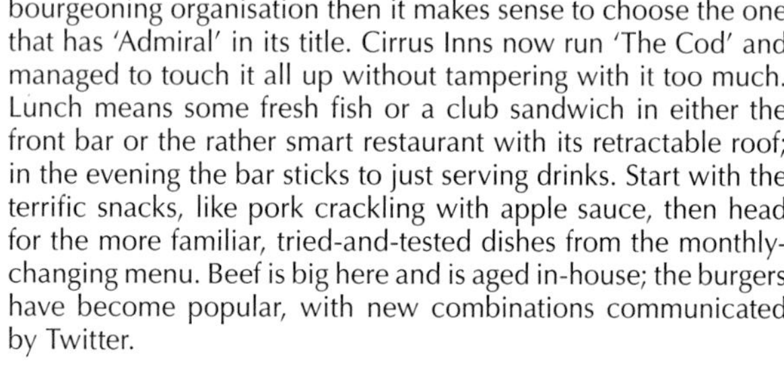

If you're going to make one of your pubs the flagship of your bourgeoning organisation then it makes sense to choose the one that has 'Admiral' in its title. Cirrus Inns now run 'The Cod' and managed to touch it all up without tampering with it too much. Lunch means some fresh fish or a club sandwich in either the front bar or the rather smart restaurant with its retractable roof; in the evening the bar sticks to just serving drinks. Start with the terrific snacks, like pork crackling with apple sauce, then head for the more familiar, tried-and-tested dishes from the monthly-changing menu. Beef is big here and is aged in-house; the burgers have become popular, with new combinations communicated by Twitter.

Baku

other world kitchens **Plan XI – F5**

164 Sloane St (1st Floor) ✉ SW1X 9QB
✆ (020) 7235 5399
www.bakulondon.com
⊖ Knightsbridge

Menu £18/75 – Carte £28/62

If evidence is needed that London is the culinary centre of the universe then simply look at the different cuisines on offer. In 2012 Azerbaijan was added to the list thanks to Baku, named after the capital and offering diners a fairly opulent, firmly run restaurant along with a far more characterful bar. Start with a fresh fruit sherbet and then traditional arishta soup. Sturgeon from the Caspian Sea features, both from the tandir and as one of the popular kebabs; and its caviar is there for the big spenders. Try a saj, a choice of meat cooked with peppers and onions on a dome shaped pan, along with plov – saffron rice. Spicing is quite subtle and, as some dishes have been lightened a little, it's worth ordering quite a few dishes.

Bangkok

Thai Plan XI – E6

9 Bute St ✉ SW7 3EY
✆ (020) 7584 8529
www.bangkokrestaurant.co.uk
⊖ South Kensington
Closed 24 December-2 January and Sunday

Carte £23/33

A/C You don't survive for over 40 years in London's capricious restaurant scene without doing something right. Bangkok opened at a time when few knew what a wok was and was the first restaurant to introduce us to fresh and zesty soups, delicate fishcakes, rich curries and moreish noodles. Over the years, Thai restaurants have sprung up throughout the UK, many of them smart and sophisticated, but Bangkok remains resolutely traditional in both its cooking and its uncomplicated surroundings and for that we should be grateful. The laminated menu lists about 20 dishes and the cooking is so fresh and satisfying and, with such down-to-earth prices, that you feel the restaurant should be sponsored by Thailand's Tourist Board.

Bar Boulud

French Plan XII – F4

Mandarin Oriental Hyde Park Hotel,
66 Knightsbridge ✉ SW1X 7LA
✆ (020) 7201 3899
www.barboulud.com
⊖ Knightsbridge

Menu £23 – Carte £22/55

Lyon-born Daniel Boulud built his considerable reputation in New York and these two cities now inform the menu here at his London outpost. Order a plate of excellent charcuterie while you look at the menu; sausages are a highlight and there are plenty of classic French dishes, from fruits de mer to coq au vin, but it's the burgers that steal the show. Designed by Adam Tihany, the restaurant makes the best of its basement location which was previously used by the Mandarin Oriental Hotel as a storeroom. Don't think you'll be in exile if they lead you to a table around the corner: it's a good spot and you'll be facing the open kitchen. Service is fast and furious; prices are sensible and the place is noisy, fashionable and fun.

Bibendum

French Plan XI – E6

Michelin House, 81 Fulham Rd. ✉ SW3 6RD
✆ (020) 7581 5817
www.bibendum.co.uk
⊖ South Kensington
Closed dinner 24 December, 25-26 December and 1 January

Menu £27 (weekday lunch)/33 – Carte £37/69

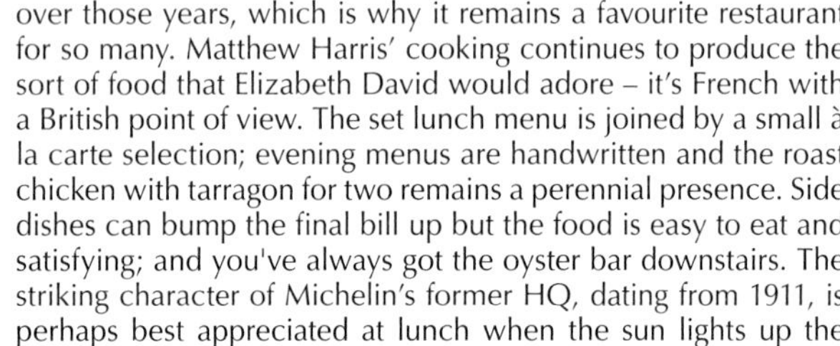

Bibendum is now well into its twenties but very little has changed over those years, which is why it remains a favourite restaurant for so many. Matthew Harris' cooking continues to produce the sort of food that Elizabeth David would adore – it's French with a British point of view. The set lunch menu is joined by a small à la carte selection; evening menus are handwritten and the roast chicken with tarragon for two remains a perennial presence. Side dishes can bump the final bill up but the food is easy to eat and satisfying; and you've always got the oyster bar downstairs. The striking character of Michelin's former HQ, dating from 1911, is perhaps best appreciated at lunch when the sun lights up the glass Bibendum - the Michelin Man.

Bluebird

British modern Plan XI – E7

350 King's Rd. ✉ SW3 5UU
✆ (020) 7559 1000
www.bluebird-restaurant.co.uk
⊖ South Kensington

Menu £20 – Carte £22/57

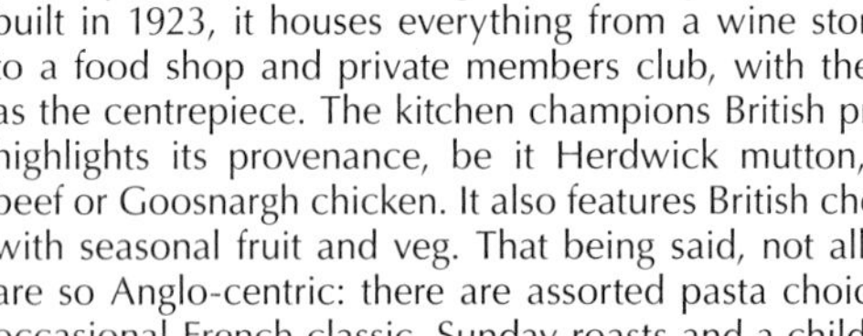

The last refurbishment may have softened the huge space a little but Bluebird still delivers the atmosphere and excitement one expects from such a large industrial space. A former garage built in 1923, it houses everything from a wine store and café to a food shop and private members club, with the restaurant as the centrepiece. The kitchen champions British produce and highlights its provenance, be it Herdwick mutton, Cumbrian beef or Goosnargh chicken. It also features British cheeses along with seasonal fruit and veg. That being said, not all the dishes are so Anglo-centric: there are assorted pasta choices and the occasional French classic. Sunday roasts and a children's menu ensure that all bases are covered.

Bombay Brasserie

Indian Plan XI - D6

Courtfield Rd. ✉ SW7 4QH
✆ (020) 7370 4040
www.bombaybrasserielondon.com
⊖ Gloucester Road
Closed 25 December – bookings advisable at dinner

Menu £24 (weekday lunch) – Carte £30/42

Going strong since 1982, The Bombay Brasserie has always been one of the smartest Indian restaurants around, but a few years ago it emerged with a brand new look which revitalised the whole place. Plushness abounds, from the deep carpet and huge chandeliers of the large main room to the show kitchen of the conservatory and the very smart bar. The staff also got a new look with their burgundy waistcoats, but they continue to offer charming and professional service. The menu wasn't forgotten either and was overhauled by Hemant Oberoi. They replaced the predictable with the more creative, while at the same time respecting traditional philosophies; influences are a combination of Bori, Parsi, Maharashtrian and Goan cuisine.

The Botanist

modern Plan XI - F6

7 Sloane Sq ✉ SW1W 8EE
✆ (020) 7730 0077
www.thebotanistonsloanesquare.com
⊖ Sloane Square
Closed 25-26 December

Carte £29/80

Unlike say New Yorkers, Londoners seemingly prefer their bars separate from their restaurants, which is a shame as The Botanist demonstrates how well the two can coexist. You enter first into the bar and, by osmosis, its general bustle adds to the convivial atmosphere of the adjoining bright and warm restaurant. The place always appears full of people who 'get' what a restaurant should feel and sound like. The menu mixes cheffy descriptions like 'escabeche' with more prosaic words like 'pie' so expect a choice that includes terrines, fish from Billingsgate or more ambitious numbers like pigeon with Puy lentils. Dishes are unfussy in appearance – always a sign of a confident kitchen – and deliver on flavour.

Builders Arms

British traditional Plan XI – E6

13 Britten St ✉ SW3 3TY
✆ (020) 7349 9040
www.geronimo-inns.co.uk
⊖ South Kensington
Bookings not accepted

Carte £20/40

The Builders Arms is very much like a packed village local – the only difference being that, in this instance, the village is Chelsea and the villagers are all young and prosperous. The inside delivers on the promise of the smart exterior but don't expect it to be quiet as drinkers are welcomed just as much as diners. In fact, bookings are only taken for larger parties but just tell the staff that you're here to eat and they'll sort you out. The cooking reveals the effort that has gone into the sourcing of some decent ingredients; the rib of beef for two is a perennial favourite. Dishes are robust and satisfying and are not without some flair in presentation. Wine is also taken seriously and their list has been thoughtfully put together.

Bumpkin

British traditional Plan XI – D6

102 Old Brompton Rd ✉ SW7 3RD
✆ (020) 7341 0802
www.bumpkinuk.com
⊖ Gloucester Road

Carte £30/37

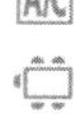

Their slogan is "for city folk who like a little country living", which is exactly the reason why many of the moneyed in this prosperous neighbourhood bought weekend retreats. This Bumpkin follows the success of the Notting Hill branch and they've largely repeated the formula by creating a restaurant with a pub-like informality that champions British produce. The rear room, with its large open-plan kitchen, is the more fun of the two and service is spirited and friendly. Quarterly printed menus double as placemats, with additional daily specials on the board. Expect lots of pies, burgers using Welsh Black beef and hotpots, with the simpler dishes often being the best ones. Weekend brunches and Sunday roasts are very popular.

Cadogan Arms

British traditional Plan XI - E7

298 King's Rd ✉ SW3 5UG
✆ (020) 7352 6500
www.thecadoganarmschelsea.com
⊖ South Kensington
Closed 25-26 December – bookings advisable at dinner

Carte £20/40 

Look no further if you like pubs to feel the way they used to. Instead of turning this Victorian corner pub into a gastropub cliché, the Martin brothers – who also own the trendy Botanist at the smart end of the King's Road – respected its heritage and kept it a 'proper' pub, albeit one with decent food. Stuffed animals, antlers on the wall, original tiling and oak panelling give it a warm, unaffected feel. The best things on the menu are those that are filling, blokey and meaty, whether that's mutton with haggis, faggots or large steaks for two – and there's no let up with puds like treacle tart. In the billiard room upstairs you'll find three American 8-ball pool tables available to hire by the hour; snacks can be had up there too.

Cambio de Tercio

Spanish Plan XI - D6

163 Old Brompton Rd. ✉ SW5 0LJ
✆ (020) 7244 8970
www.cambiodetercio.co.uk
⊖ Gloucester Road
Closed 25 December

Carte £32/40 s 

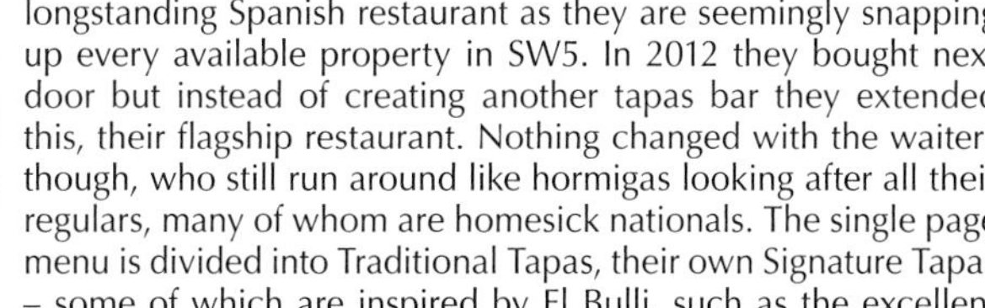

There has been no laurel resting from the owners of this longstanding Spanish restaurant as they are seemingly snapping up every available property in SW5. In 2012 they bought next door but instead of creating another tapas bar they extended this, their flagship restaurant. Nothing changed with the waiters though, who still run around like hormigas looking after all their regulars, many of whom are homesick nationals. The single page menu is divided into Traditional Tapas, their own Signature Tapas – some of which are inspired by El Bulli, such as the excellent omelette – and main courses like the popular Pluma Iberica pork. They also offer a superb selection of sherries and a wine list that proves there is life beyond Rioja.

Capote y Toros

Spanish Plan XI – D6

157 Old Brompton Road ✉ SW5 0LJ
✆ (020) 7373 0567
www.cambiodetercio.co.uk
⊖ Gloucester Road
Closed Christmas, Sunday and Monday – (dinner only)

Carte £14/39

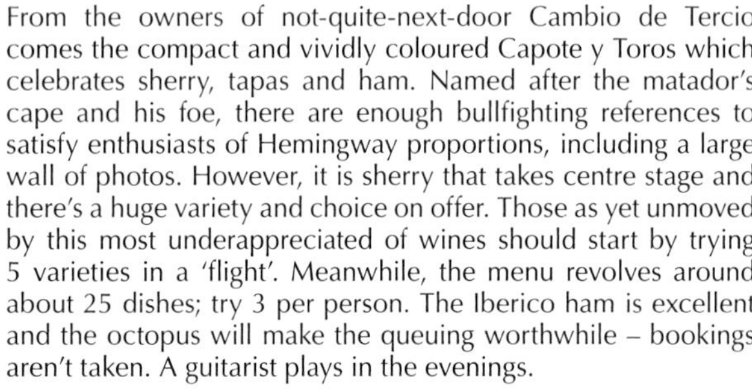

From the owners of not-quite-next-door Cambio de Tercio comes the compact and vividly coloured Capote y Toros which celebrates sherry, tapas and ham. Named after the matador's cape and his foe, there are enough bullfighting references to satisfy enthusiasts of Hemingway proportions, including a large wall of photos. However, it is sherry that takes centre stage and there's a huge variety and choice on offer. Those as yet unmoved by this most underappreciated of wines should start by trying 5 varieties in a 'flight'. Meanwhile, the menu revolves around about 25 dishes; try 3 per person. The Iberico ham is excellent and the octopus will make the queuing worthwhile – bookings aren't taken. A guitarist plays in the evenings.

Cassis

Italian Plan XI – E5

232-236 Brompton Rd. ✉ SW3 2BB
✆ (020) 7581 1101
www.cassisbistro.co.uk
⊖ South Kensington
Closed 25 December

Menu £18/35 – Carte £25/49

Marlon Abela's Cassis began life as a paean to all things Provençal and brought colour and vitality to this corner of South Kensington. Pop art and prints give character and style of the contemporary room, while pots of thyme on each table add aromatic hints of the Garrigue. The style of cooking, however, has recently been moving in a south-easterly direction and is becoming more Italian by the day –the restaurant's name may well change to reflect this. What hasn't changed is the quality of the ingredients or the kitchen's obvious care and ability. The wine list is outstanding – it features over 700 bins and includes top growers and great vintages. Service is smooth and occasionally punctuated by a little flamboyance.

Le Cercle

French

Plan XI – F6

1 Wilbraham Pl. ✉ SW1X 9AE
✆ (020) 7901 9999
www.lecercle.co.uk
⊖ Sloane Square
Closed Christmas and New Year, Sunday, Monday and bank holidays

Menu £20/60 – Carte £23/33

Knowing this is owned by the same team as Club Gascon may lead to the raising of false hopes, as this is an altogether different operation. Le Cercle positions itself as a fashionable stop on the celebrity circuit and has the unsmiling receptionist and the managers with Secret Service ear pieces to prove it. Lunch sees a bewildering mix of business types and senior local ladies but what is certain is that it all comes alive at dinner; and its drapes and high ceiling do give it a fairly striking look. Where it does follow the same theme as its City sister is in the menu format, whereby you order three or four small dishes per person from the various sections. Dishes are nicely balanced and the French flavours pronounced.

Chabrot

French

Plan XII – F5

9 Knightsbridge Grn ✉ SW1X 7QL
✆ (020) 7225 2238
www.chabrot.co.uk
⊖ Knightsbridge
Closed 25 December and 1 January

Carte £28/50

In 2011 Thierry Laborde, formerly of Le Gavroche, got together with three friends – a sommelier, a restaurant manager and a florist – to open Chabrot, a bistro that couldn't be more French if it wore a beret and sang 'La Mer'. The kitchen looks to the SW of France and the Basque country for most of its inspiration. Sharing a board of Basque charcuterie is a good way to start and there are plenty of hearty offerings like roast foie gras as a main course, along with snails, octopus skewers and veal-stuffed cabbage. Add a few daily specials and a plat du jour and there should be something for everyone. If you really can't decide on what to order, the tables are so close you can simply take a peek at what your neighbour has chosen.

Chelsea Ram

British modern

Plan XI – D8

32 Burnaby St ✉ SW10 0PL
✆ (020) 7351 4008
www.geronimo-inns.co.uk/thechelsearam
⊖ Fulham Broadway.
Closed 25 December

Carte £21/35

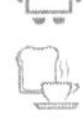

The Chelsea Ram stands out from the crowd because it's got heart and soul – this is a pub that just feels right as soon as you walk in. It has always been a proper local and comes with a palpable sense of community, but not to the extent that interlopers are given the evil eye by the regulars at the bar. Thursday is steak night and Friday, fish night; you can come for brunch at weekends and can even join the Geronimo Club for regular cheese and wine tastings. Dining tables wind themselves around the bar, with quieter ones nestling at the back under a glass roof. Blackboard specials supplement the menu of sturdy pub classics and seasonal dishes. Alternatively, you can stand at the bar for a pint and a little pork pie.

Chutney Mary

Indian

Plan XI – D8

535 King's Rd. ✉ SW10 0SZ
✆ (020) 7351 3113
www.realindianfood.com
⊖ Fulham Broadway
Closed dinner 25 December – (dinner only and lunch Saturday-Sunday)

Menu £21/45 – Carte £32/53

When Chutney Mary opened in 1990 it signalled the arrival of a new-wave of cosmopolitan Indian restaurants. Instead of the basic beer and curry house aesthetic we got smart surroundings, regional specialities, cocktails and even suggested wine pairings for the meal – and it's a combination that is still working successfully today. The place is deceptively large and comes with framed silks, mirrors, candles and prints; if you're a couple then ask for a table in the slightly less hectic conservatory. Dishes come from all across India and range in style from luxurious fish dishes from the south to redefined street food. The kitchen uses plenty of British produce and employs chefs from the different Indian regions to ensure authenticity.

Colbert

French Plan XI – G6

50-52 Sloane Sq ✉ SW1W 8AX
✆ (020) 7730 2804
www.colbertchelsea.com
⊖ Sloane Square
Closed 25 December and dinner 24 December – booking advisable

Carte £18/56

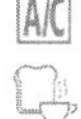

With its posters, chessboard tiles and red leather seats, Colbert bears more than a passing resemblance to a Parisian pavement café and there can't be a better spot for one than here on Sloane Square, next to the Royal Court. This is the old Oriel café and it was transformed by seasoned restaurateurs Chris Corbin and Jeremy King. It's an all-day, every day operation and the menu lists all the French classics; you can pop in for a croque monsieur, linger over a steak Diane or come for breakfast at any time of day. The best dishes are the simpler ones and if you haven't booked, try the bar. Despite the somewhat dispiriting sight of an anachronistic cover charge, this place feels set to become part of the local fabric for some time.

Le Colombier

French Plan XI – E6

145 Dovehouse St. ✉ SW3 6LB
✆ (020) 7351 1155
www.le-colombier-restaurant.co.uk
⊖ South Kensington

Menu £20 (lunch) – Carte £33/58

Le Colombier is as warm and welcoming as it is honest and reliable and thereby offers proof that being a good neighbourhood restaurant takes more than just being in a good neighbourhood. French influences abound, from the accents of the staff and the menu content to the inordinate amount of double cheek kissing that occurs – most of the customers appear to know one another or feel they should like to know one another. In summer, when the full-length windows fold back, the terrace is the place to sit although the under-floor heating ensures the place is equally welcoming in winter. Oysters, game in season, veal in various forms and regional cheeses are the highlights, as are the classic desserts from crêpe Suzette to crème brûlée.

Daphne's

Italian Plan XI – E6

112 Draycott Ave. ✉ SW3 3AE
✆ (020) 7589 4257
www.daphnes-restaurant.co.uk
⊖ South Kensington
Closed 25-26 December – booking essential

Carte £20/55 XX

One wonders if theatrical agent Daphne Rye opened her eponymous restaurant as a means of keeping her resting actors busy. Forty years on and Daphne's is a chic Chelsea institution; there's even a branch in Barbados for those who can't live without their vongole on holiday. The narrow room is Tuscan in its look and the best seats are those at the front by the large windows. The many regulars clearly like the reassurance of familiarity so the kitchen sticks largely to a tried and tested assortment of Italian classics but prepared with greater care than one usually expects in an Italian restaurant with a 'celebrity' following. The lunch menu is good value and the occasional new dish, like salt-baked sea bass, gets in under the radar.

Eight over Eight

Asian Plan XI – E7

392 King's Rd ✉ SW3 5UZ
✆ (020) 7349 9934
www.rickerrestaurants.com
⊖ South Kensington
Closed 24-27 December

Menu £14 (weekday lunch)/17 – Carte £19/47

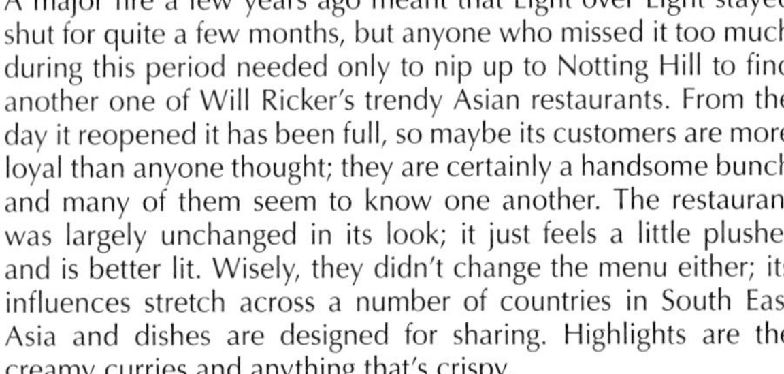

A major fire a few years ago meant that Eight over Eight stayed shut for quite a few months, but anyone who missed it too much during this period needed only to nip up to Notting Hill to find another one of Will Ricker's trendy Asian restaurants. From the day it reopened it has been full, so maybe its customers are more loyal than anyone thought; they are certainly a handsome bunch and many of them seem to know one another. The restaurant was largely unchanged in its look; it just feels a little plusher and is better lit. Wisely, they didn't change the menu either; its influences stretch across a number of countries in South East Asia and dishes are designed for sharing. Highlights are the creamy curries and anything that's crispy.

Dinner by Heston Blumenthal ✿✿

British modern Plan XII – F4

Mandarin Oriental Hyde Park Hotel,
66 Knightsbridge ✉ SW1X 7LA
✆ (020) 7201 3833
www.dinnerbyheston.com
⊖ Knightsbridge
Closed 2 days Christmas

Menu £36 (weekday lunch) – Carte £50/67

Mandarin Oriental Hyde Park

For a country with a less than stellar reputation for the quality of its food, we need reminding sometimes about the glories of our own culinary heritage. So hats off then to Heston Blumenthal because his mischievously named restaurant at the Mandarin Oriental Hyde Park should stir feelings of pride in all of us regarding our native cuisine. Don't come expecting 'molecular' alchemy; the menu reads like a record of historic kitchen triumphs, with the date of origin attached to each dish and a fashionably terse list of its parts; on the reverse you can read more. A kitchen brigade of 45 works with calm efficiency, meticulous attention to detail and intelligence to produce food that looks deceptively 'simple' but tastes sublime. The large, light room has quirky touches, like wall sconces shaped as jelly moulds, but the main focus is on the open kitchen, with its oversized watch mechanics powering the spit to roast the pineapple that goes with the Tipsy Cake (c.1810).

First Course

- Octopus, smoked sea broth, pickled dulse and lovage.
- Mandarin meat fruit.

Main Course

- Short rib, smoked anchovy and onion, ox tongue and red wine.
- Spiced pigeon, ale and artichokes.

Dessert

- Brown bread ice cream, salted butter caramel, pear and malted yeast syrup.
- Quaking pudding.

Eleven Park Walk

Italian Plan XI – D7

11 Park Walk ✉ SW10 0AJ
✆ (020) 7352 3449
www.11parkwalk.co.uk
⊖ South Kensington
Closed 25 December

Carte £25/96

It was obvious to most that Aubergine was a restaurant that had clearly run out of gas; although its place in London's culinary history is assured. Walls were knocked down, tiles imported and lighting improved to create its far more handsome replacement, Eleven Park Walk. A smart, more mature Chelsea set quickly latched on to this sophisticated Italian and the effusive Roberto has been quick to identify regulars; his team of servers go about their business with equal vigour. The menu traverses Italy and dishes are generous in both size and flavour, but the kitchen appears to handle the Sardinian specialities with added care. The menu can get quite pricey but is balanced by a wine list that offers plenty of choice for under £25.

L'Etranger

innovative Plan XI – D5

36 Gloucester Rd. ✉ SW7 4QT
✆ (020) 7584 1118
www.etranger.co.uk
⊖ Gloucester Road
Booking essential

Menu £22 (lunch) – Carte £37/94

Messing around with classic French cooking is considered sacrilegious in certain parts of France but L'Etranger has escaped the tyranny of tradition by locating itself in South Kensington, London's own little Gallic ward. It offers an eclectic mix off French dishes that are heavily influenced by Japan, so a veal chop will come with wasabi sauce and salmon is poached in sake. Not every dish has a Nipponese constituent but it certainly makes for an original experience. The room is dark and moody and better suited to evenings, while service is a little more formal than it need be. The clientele is a mix of well-heeled locals and homesick French and Japanese émigrés, who also appreciate the depth and breadth of the impressive wine list.

Fifth Floor at Harvey Nichols

modern Plan XI – F4

109-125 Knightsbridge ✉ SW1X 7RJ
✆ (020) 7235 5250
www.harveynichols.com
⊖ Knightsbridge
Closed Christmas, Easter and Sunday dinner

Menu £25 – Carte £26/42

Pressure is now on the restaurant to hold its own against the alluring look of the revamped and well stocked food hall, here on the fifth floor of Harvey 'Nics'. It certainly seems to have got its appearance right by not being too stuffy and it handles the contrasting nature of lunch and dinner with aplomb: for the former it's mostly shoppers and at night is far more intimate. Dishes are bright, light and unfussy and some of the starters and mains are now available as tasting plates, which either catches the zeitgeist by providing greater flexibility or is a tacit acknowledgment that its clientele could never be accused of overeating. What the staff may lack in wit they more than make up for in the looks department.

Five Fields

modern Plan XI – F6

8-9 Blacklands Terr ✉ SW3 2SP
✆ (020) 7838 1082
www.fivefieldsrestaurant.com
⊖ Sloane Square
Closed first 2 weeks January, first 2 weeks August, Sunday and Monday – (dinner only)

Menu £45

It was almost two years in the making but Five Fields – the name that the 18C cartographer John Rocque gave this part of town – now sits happily alongside its smart Chelsea neighbours. The restaurant may be comparatively small but it comes with a warm, intimate and chic feel. Staffing has the formality and hierarchical structure of a formal restaurant but fortunately here they realise the importance of injecting a little personality into their work. The cooking is very much in a modern idiom, with some of the ingredients coming from their own garden in East Sussex. Come expecting some rather daring combinations on the plate, along with fairly bold flavours; desserts have a unique identity all of their own.

Foxtrot Oscar

British traditional Plan XI – F7

79 Royal Hospital Rd. ✉ SW3 4HN
✆ (020) 7352 4448
www.gordonramsay.com/foxtrotoscar
⊖ Sloane Square
Closed 25 December – booking essential

Menu £25 – Carte £27/79

There are always plenty of locals in Foxtrot Oscar, which is not something you can say about many of Gordon Ramsay's restaurants. The fact that this is probably his least known is perhaps a factor. The burgundy walls and black and white photos give it an almost '80s bistro feel and there's also a downstairs, which is actually quite a nice spot and not merely an overflow. The lunch menu is appealing priced; the dinner à la carte is more mixed. Your best bet is to skip the starters and head for something braised or slow-cooked which should satisfy anyone's hunger. Another good choice is the Foxtrot burger, which arrives on a board, accompanied by tomato relish and some enormous chips. Regulars are well looked after.

Galvin Demoiselle

French Plan XI – F5

Ground Floor Food Hall, Harrods, 87-135 Brompton Rd
✉ SW1X 7XL
✆ (020) 7730 1234
www.galvinrestaurants.com
⊖ Knightsbridge
Closed 25 December and Sunday dinner – bookings not accepted

Menu £20 – Carte £24/43

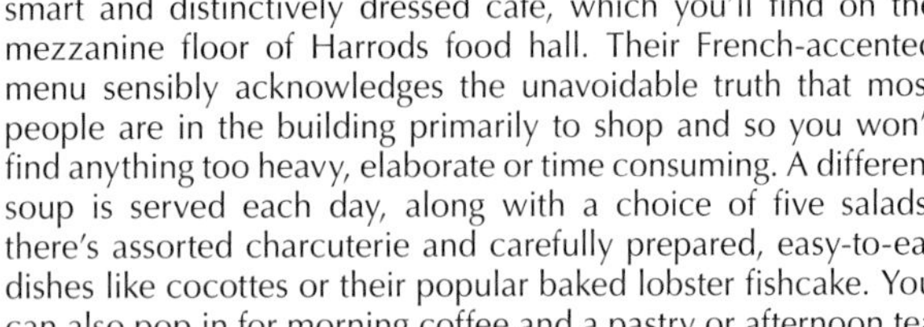

The Galvin brothers' bourgeoning company now includes this smart and distinctively dressed café, which you'll find on the mezzanine floor of Harrods food hall. Their French-accented menu sensibly acknowledges the unavoidable truth that most people are in the building primarily to shop and so you won't find anything too heavy, elaborate or time consuming. A different soup is served each day, along with a choice of five salads; there's assorted charcuterie and carefully prepared, easy-to-eat dishes like cocottes or their popular baked lobster fishcake. You can also pop in for morning coffee and a pastry or afternoon tea and a French Fancy and, although it's not inexpensive, they have got the tone and style of the service just right.

Garnier

French

Plan XI – C6

314 Earl's Court Rd ✉ SW5 9QB
✆ (020) 7370 4536
www.garnier-restaurant-london.co.uk
⊖ Earl's Court

Menu £19 – Carte £27/53

Earl's Court has never been overburdened by decent restaurants so local residents must have considered getting out the bunting when the experienced Garnier brothers decided to open a brasserie on their doorstep. Sandwiched by nondescript shops, it has an authentic traditional Gallic feel, thanks to a wall of mirrors and rows of simply dressed tables. But the decoration is not the point – it's all about the comforting food here. London was once full of French restaurants but these days finding escargots, pigeon rôti and crêpes Suzette all on the same menu is not so easy, and the extensive menu of reassuring classics is such a good read, you'll find it hard to choose. The wine list has good representation from Burgundy and Bordeaux.

Geales

fish and seafood

Plan XI – F6

1 Cale St ✉ SW3 3QT
✆ (020) 7965 0555
www.geales.com
⊖ South Kensington
Closed 24-27 and 31 December, 1-2 January and Monday

Carte £23/37

Good fish and chips shouldn't just be the preserve of visiting tourists who are hoping to catch up on new episodes of the Benny Hill Show while they're here - we all need reminding of their appeal sometimes and, for this, there is Geales. Don't be fooled by the "Established 1939" sign outside, as this branch opened in 2010. It occupies the site of Tom Aikens' short-lived chippy but the extraction system has clearly improved as there has been no uprising by locals worried about frying fumes permeating their Colefax and Fowler. The place is charmingly decorated, cosy and warmly run and the menu successfully mixes the classics with the more modern, so there's fried haddock along with soft shell crab tempura. Puds are wholesome and homemade.

Good Earth

Chinese Plan XI – E5

233 Brompton Rd. ✉ SW3 2EP
✆ (020) 7584 3658
www.goodearthgroup.co.uk
⊖ Knightsbridge
Closed 23-31 December

Menu £12/39 – Carte £27/75

The Brompton Road branch of this small chain has been a reliable constant for many a year and is suitably authentic on all levels: the service is brisk, the menu lengthy, cooking is dependable and desserts are not worth bothering with. There is no particular bias, save for a few Sichuan dishes, but they do use plenty of higher-end ingredients like scallops and Dover sole. Included among the set menus is the Lobster Dinner, a reminder of the restaurant's location and target market. More unusual dishes are often introduced but it's the old favourites and classic combinations that sell. Unlike most restaurants spread over two floors, here the basement level is actually the busier and more popular choice than the ground floor.

Henry Root

French Plan XI – D7

9 Park Walk ✉ SW10 0AJ
✆ (020) 7352 7040
www.thehenryroot.com
⊖ South Kensington
Closed 25-27 December – booking advisable

Carte £21/32

It was from his flat in Park Walk that satirist William Donaldson skewered many of the good and the great of his day through the letters of his eccentric alter ego, Henry Root. Now this little restaurant in the same street has adopted his name, which is surely a far better tribute than any blue plaque. The decoration is an appropriately curious mix of styles so expect everything from Jimi Hendrix photos to a stuffed salmon. The menu is appealingly divided into nibbles, salads, small plates, main courses and charcuterie. Terrines and ballotines are done well, as are traditional offerings like coq au vin or sea bass with cucumber and beetroot. Puddings often include a couple delivered from the nursery end of dessert-making.

Gordon Ramsay ✿✿✿

French

Plan XI – F7

68-69 Royal Hospital Rd. ✉ SW3 4HP
✆ (020) 7352 4441
www.gordonramsay.com
⊖ Sloane Square
Closed 23-27 December, Saturday and Sunday – booking essential

Menu £55/95

Gordon Ramsay

It's not just the kitchen at Gordon Ramsay's flagship restaurant that has evolved – the room itself has also had a makeover to keep it fresh and it is now a lot brighter, with light wood panels all fashioned from the same tree. Reassuringly, the ever-reliable Jean-Claude is ever-present, as he has been since the day the restaurant opened. He has instilled in his team the same care and passion for the art of service as he has demonstrated over the years; they are not only effortlessly composed but also undertake their work without the slightest arrogance or aloofness. The result is that an air of calm pervades the room. In the kitchen, head chef Clare Smyth continues to reveal more of her own personality through her cooking, with the menu being a little more daring and the combinations more original. The Menu Prestige offers the complete experience, with G. Ramsay classics alongside Clare's newer creations, but her passion is most evident in the exquisite dishes from the Seasonal Inspiration dinner menu.

First Course

- Coeur de boeuf and tomato tartare with buffalo milk curd and black olives.
- Ravioli of lobster, langoustine and salmon, lemongrass and chervil velouté.

Main Course

- Halibut with Atlantic king crab, cauliflower couscous, finger lime and ras el hanout infused broth.
- Suckling pig, chou farci, ham, crushed potatoes and spring onions.

Dessert

- Smoked chocolate cigar with blood orange and cardamom ice cream.
- Lemonade parfait, honey, bergamot and yoghurt sorbet.

il trillo

Italian — Plan XI – D7

4 Hollywood Rd ✉ SW10 9HY
✆ (020) 3602 1759
www.iltrillo.net
⊖ Earl's Court
Closed 2 weeks August and 2 weeks Christmas – (dinner only and lunch Saturday-Sunday)

Carte £26/49

A/C

The Bertuccelli family have been making wine and running a restaurant in the Tuscan Hills for over 30 years. Two of the brothers are now in London, running this smart neighbourhood restaurant which showcases the produce and wine from their region. A third brother, who's an architect, designed the room and nearly everything was brought over from Italy, from the marble to the tables and chairs. Most of the ingredients are shipped over weekly too, either from their own farm or suppliers they've known for years. The cooking is gutsy and the breads and homemade pasta stand out, as does the signature dish of stuffed onions cooked in Vermentino. The courtyard has been transformed into a pleasant decked garden, complete with lemon trees.

Joe's

modern — Plan XI – E6

126 Draycott Ave ✉ SW3 3AH
✆ (020) 7225 2217
www.joseph.co.uk
⊖ South Kensington
Closed 25 December and dinner Sunday-Monday

Menu £25/45 – Carte £23/43

A/C

Most restaurants rely on a certain amount of passing business to keep the credit side of their ledgers looking positive. Joe's faces a challenge here because its narrow entrance makes it resemble a bar more than a restaurant and this is a shame because this is a place that deserves to do well. For one thing, it understands the importance of giving its glamorous customers what they want, which means an appealing mix of Mediterranean influenced favourites and various light, healthy choices. Dishes may be quite simple but the kitchen does things with care and flavours are clearly defined. The attractive room is framed by bookcases full of wine and magazines. Service hits the spot too, as the good-looking staff really do seem to care.

Lots Road Pub & Dining Room

British traditional Plan XI – D8

114 Lots Rd ✉ SW10 0RJ
✆ (020) 7352 6645
www.lotsroadpub.com
⊖ Fulham Broadway

Carte £20/33

At lunch expect to be joined by those from the nearby Design Centre; at dinner the place is colonised by good-looking locals and at weekends it's full of folk who've been busy buying antiques. The pub may be looking a little worn around the edges but when a kitchen occupies half the bar you just know they take their food seriously. The menu may be short and at first glance rather safe but they use good produce and cook it with care and respect. Blackboards offer 'season's eatings' and there's a daily recipe too. Look out too for the weekly 'wicked wines' selection where you can pick up a bargain. Steak is still a speciality and it's worth coming on Sunday for a roast and a Bloody Mary. They also have a great customer loyalty scheme.

Manicomio

Italian Plan XI – F6

85 Duke of York Sq, King's Rd ✉ SW3 4LY
✆ (020) 7730 3366
www.manicomio.co.uk
⊖ Sloane Square
Closed 25 December- 1 January

Menu £25 (weekday lunch) – Carte £33/45

If anywhere encapsulates King's Road's journey from counterculture hub to retail playground it is Duke of York Square and its outlets. Among these is Manicomio, a glossy Italian restaurant which doesn't need to rely solely on weary shoppers as it also draws visitors from the Saatchi Gallery next door, a fact that shows just what an inspired location this was. Its success is also helped by an accessible menu, offering a greatest hits of easy-to-eat Italian food. Cooking is undertaken with care and the simplest dishes are the best ones, although prices do reflect the Chelsea postcode. Service remains sufficiently perky for one to forgive occasional moments of forgetfulness. The terrific front terrace fills quickly in nearly all seasons.

Marco

French Plan XVIII – T2

Stamford Bridge, Fulham Rd. ✉ SW6 1HS
✆ (020) 7915 2929
www.marcorestaurant.org
⊖ Fulham Broadway
Closed Christmas, Easter, Sunday and Monday – booking advisable – (dinner only)

Carte £32/52

A/C A section of Manchester United fans was once derided as being prawn sandwich eaters; London expectations being what they are, at Chelsea's ground you get a brasserie from Marco Pierre White. Some will inevitably cry foul and shed a tear for football's working class roots; others will cheer for this evidence of our growing culinary maturity. Both sides, though, should applaud the menu, which offers classics galore such as grilled Dover sole, assorted roasts and Scottish steaks. This being a polyglot club means other nationalities are also represented, in this case a bit of Italy and France, and more sophisticated fare such as foie gras terrine or duck confit is available. Puddings are a particular highlight.

Mr Chow

Chinese Plan XII – F4

151 Knightsbridge ✉ SW1X 7PA
✆ (020) 7589 7347
www.mrchow.com
⊖ Knightsbridge
Closed 1 January, 24-26 December, Easter Monday dinner and Monday lunch

Menu £26/50 – Carte £39/63

A/C

Chinese food, Italian waiters, swish surroundings, steep prices and immaculately coiffured regulars: it's an unusual mix that clearly works because Mr Chow has already celebrated its fortieth birthday. Even if you're not recognisable, you'll get a friendly welcome and the champagne chariot will be wheeled towards you. The laminated menu is long but clearly divided between sections entitled 'from the sea', 'from the land' and 'from the sky'; chickens will be pleased to find themselves in this last category. The cooking is far better than you expect, with genuine care shown. The desserts are thoroughly European and come on a trolley, with tarts the speciality. Your final bill won't be clearly itemised but this doesn't seem to bother anyone.

Medlar ✿

modern

Plan XI – E7

438 King's Rd ✉ SW10 0LJ
✆ (020) 7349 1900
www.medlarrestaurant.co.uk
⊖ South Kensington

Menu £26 (weekday lunch), £30/42

Medlar

Being a customer should be the easiest thing in the world so it can sometimes be a little dispiriting to have to sit through yet another explanation of a restaurant's 'concept'. Medlar proved to be a success from day one precisely because it wasn't trying to be different or original – the two young owners just wanted to have a really great neighbourhood restaurant and that is exactly what they have created here. Both are alumnae of Chez Bruce which proved to be a pretty good blueprint for what they had in mind. David and his front of house team get the tone of the service just right – it's warm, knowledgeable and reassuring but never intrusive, while Joe, in the kitchen, concentrates on producing carefully executed dishes using a mix of French techniques and British ingredients, where the component flavours marry perfectly. A year spent in Sydney added a lighter tone to his cooking so having all three courses is the natural choice – especially when paired with a bottle from their impressive list of burgundies and clarets.

First Course

- Crab raviolo with samphire, fondue of leeks and bisque sauce.
- Confit of lamb with salsa verde, artichokes, green beans and frisée.

Main Course

- Under blade fillet with Café de Paris snails, salad, triple-cooked chips and béarnaise.
- Rack of lamb with braised shoulder and tongue, Jersey Royals.

Dessert

- Cannelé with Camp coffee ice cream and molten Congolese chocolate.
- Treacle tart, orange syrup and clotted cream.

One-O-One

fish and seafood

Plan XI – F4

Park Tower Knightsbridge Hotel,
101 Knightsbridge ✉ SW1X 7RN
✆ (020) 7290 7101
www.oneoonerestaurant.com
⊖ Knightsbridge

Menu £17/59 – Carte £49/98

Walking past the Sheraton Park Tower hotel, one of London's less majestic buildings, you'd never know there was a restaurant behind those heavy net curtains, and a rather good one to boot. Granted, the room size and shape mean an animated atmosphere remains elusive and staff, pleasant though they are, have little presence. But the food is good and that food is mostly fish. They've found a balance between offering a traditional à la carte menu and a list of 'petits plats', 6 of which, taken together, will satisfy the fiercest of appetites. Much of the produce comes from Brittany and Norway; the latter gives us the King crab legs which are the stars of the show. The kitchen is not afraid of adding a little playfulness to its classical base.

Painted Heron

Indian

Plan XI – E7

112 Cheyne Walk ✉ SW10 0DJ
✆ (020) 7351 5232
www.thepaintedheron.com
⊖ Gloucester Road
Closed Monday

Menu £20/65 – Carte £26/37

A/C

They call their style "modern Indian" which, in essence, means the kitchen's influences come from across the land; from Kashmir and Rajasthan to Kerala and Goa. Fish, largely from Hastings, is handled dextrously and seasonal game often features on the menu, whether that's the tandoor pigeon breasts, the partridge with red chilli paste or grouse in a southern stew. Flavours tend to be well-defined and balanced. The room is bigger than you think and has quite a formal feel, thanks largely to the style of service from the young team, but it's broken up into nooks and crannies and hence quite intimate. The open courtyard is an attractive feature and, despite its tiny entrance and tucked away location, the restaurant always appears to be busy.

Outlaw's at The Capital ✿

fish and seafood

Plan XI – F5

The Capital Hotel,
22-24 Basil St. ✉ SW3 1AT
✆ (020) 7591 1202
www.capitalhotel.co.uk
⊖ Knightsbridge
Closed Sunday – booking essential

Menu £25/70 – Carte £48/60

The Capital

In an effort to reinvent this cosy dining room at The Capital hotel, Nathan Outlaw was persuaded to bring his award-winning formula from Cornwall to Chelsea. Nathan not only has the greatest name in Chefland but probably knows more about cooking fish than anyone else in the country. He's installed one of his trusted lieutenants in the kitchen and dishes very much reflect his distinct style. Essentially, it's all about the quality of the fish, which comes up daily from Cornwall and includes wreckfish, found in deep waters around shipwrecks. The cooking may appear effortless but the combination of flavours on the plate harmonises perfectly and any elements of originality are there to enhance rather than hoodwink. The room has also been given a new look, the main feature being views into the kitchen through the large picture window. Service is a little less starchy and stiff than in the restaurant's previous incarnations and is all the better for it. The well-structured wine list features the ever popular Levin Sauvignon Blanc from the owner's own estate in the Loire.

First Course

- Crab meat, celeriac and apple salad.
- Lemon sole, crispy oyster, oyster sauce and cucumber.

Main Course

- Cod with scampi, rosemary butter and crispy courgettes.
- Wreckfish, red wine tartare, anchovy and potato.

Dessert

- Treacle tart, orange syrup and clotted cream.
- Chocolate mousse, pear, honeycomb and caramel ice cream.

Phoenix

modern **Plan XI – F6**

23 Smith St ✉ SW3 4EE
✆ (020) 7730 9182
www.geronimo-inns.co.uk/thepheonix
⊖ Sloane Square.
Closed 25 December

Carte £21/38

The same menu is served throughout and, while the bar has plenty of seating and a civilised feel, head to the warm and comfortable dining room at the back if you want a more structured meal or you're impressing a date. Blackboard specials supplement the menu which keeps things traditional: fish on a Friday, a pasta of the day and the likes of fishcakes or sausage and mash with red onion jam. For lunch, you'll find some favourites for late-risers, like eggs Benedict and, in winter, expect the heartening sight of crumbles or plum pudding. Wines are organised by their character, with nearly 30 varieties offered by the glass. The side dishes can bump up the final bill but The Phoenix remains a friendly and conscientiously run Chelsea local.

Pig's Ear

British traditional **Plan XI – E7**

35 Old Church St ✉ SW3 5BS
✆ (020) 7352 2908
www.thepigsear.info
⊖ South Kensington.

Carte £21/50

This Chelsea pub may not look much like a foodie spot from the outside, or indeed from the inside, but it does have a refreshing honesty to it. Lunch is in the rough-and-ready ground floor bar, decorated with everything from 'Tintin' pictures to covers of 'Sounds' newspaper. There's a decent choice of 5-6 main courses and a wine list on a blackboard. With its wood panelling and dressed tables, the upstairs dining room provides quite a contrast, but the atmosphere is still far from starchy. Here the menu displays a little more ambition but cooking remains similarly earthy and the wine list has plenty of bottles under £30. The kitchen knows its way around an animal: slow-cooked dishes such as pork cheeks are done particularly well.

Poissonnerie

fish and seafood

Plan XI – E6

82 Sloane Ave. ✉ SW3 3DZ
✆ (020) 7589 2457
www.poissonnerie-chelsea.co.uk
⊖ South Kensington
Closed Easter and 25-26 December

Menu £22 (lunch) – Carte £34/48

XX

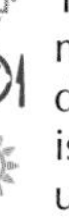

There is something heartening about dining in a restaurant that is older than its waiters. Poissonnerie de l'Avenue began life in 1946 but the owner is still to be found greeting his customers – many of whom look as though they've been coming since the doors first opened – as old friends, as indeed many are. This is a restaurant all about traditional hospitality and it's easy to understand its longevity. The wood-panelled room has an air of luxury; service is well-organised and the cooking is done 'properly'. The menu is a large affair: expect about 18 starters with everything from oysters to smoked salmon and the same number of seafood and fish main courses. The well-groomed clientele hardly blink when handed the inevitably large bill.

Racine

French

Plan XI – E5

239 Brompton Rd ✉ SW3 2EP
✆ (020) 7584 4477
www.racine-restaurant.com
⊖ South Kensington
Closed 25 December

Menu £16/20 – Carte £30/53

XX

Racine is as authentic a French brasserie as you can get at this end of the tunnel. The accents are thick; the baguettes are fresh and the room's wood and leather have that reassuring lived-in look. Some of the clientele, who are a mature and confident bunch, give the impression that they come here on a weekly basis and it's easy to understand why: along with the authentically prepared classics, such as steak tartare, tête de veau or fruits de mer, are plenty of other dishes that hit the spot, along with well priced lunch and early evening menus. Try to avoid the tables in the middle of the room because, on windier days, you'll find yourself assailed by the occasional gust of wind, whenever somebody opens the front door.

Rasoi ✿

Indian Plan XI – F6

10 Lincoln St ✉ SW3 2TS
✆ (020) 7225 1881
www.rasoirestaurant.co.uk
⊖ Sloane Square
Closed 25-26 December, 1-3 January and Saturday lunch

Menu £22, £50/89

Rasoi

With his outposts in Geneva, Mauritius and Dubai, Vineet Bhatia proves that Indian food is as open to innovation and interpretation as any other cuisine. Fortunately for fans of his original branch here in Chelsea, he has a team of loyal lieutenants who are more than capable of ensuring that things remain consistently good. What really comes across in his modern Indian food is the delicate balance of flavours and the superb quality of the ingredients. For a rounded experience of his unique style, go for the 7-course 'Prestige' menu. On the à la carte, the 'street food' chaats are almost a meal in themselves; the vegetarian dishes are as colourful as they are delicious and the desserts, such as 'Chocolate Cravings' come with more of a Western personality. Be sure to ask for a table in the larger room at the back of the house which has more personality than the one at the front, especially when filled with the sweet aroma of the smoke rising from the racks of lamb. Alternatively, come with friends and book one of the richly decorated private rooms on the first floor.

First Course

- Scallop and prawn brochette with spring onion risotto.
- Grilled lamb chop, kheem-matter timbale, goat's cheese and cashew nut samosa.

Main Course

- Grilled duck, peppercorn jus, sesame duck confit tikki and curry leaf foam.
- Maharashtrian Goda sea bass, lemon and peanut rice, Amti lentils, and coconut chutney.

Dessert

- Madras coffee cheese cake, Amaretto gel and caramelised banana roll.
- Coconut millefeuille with pink peppercorn and white chocolate kulfi.

Rib Room

meats and grills Plan XI – F5

Jumeirah Carlton Tower Hotel,
Cadogan Pl ✉ SW1X 9PY
✆ (020) 7858 7250
www.theribroom.co.uk
⊖ Knightsbridge

Menu £29/58 – Carte £48/97

The Rib Room is something of a London institution and a restaurant designed for those who didn't get where they are today by wasting time looking at prices. The menu would delight the most traditional of British trenchermen: one can start with smoked salmon or half a dozen Angel oysters then move on to Dover sole, a steak or, more appropriately, rib of Aberdeen Angus. The kitchen does things properly and wisely avoids trying to be too clever. The last designer successfully managed to add a little elegance to the room while also maintaining the overriding sense of masculinity that's often associated with this style of dining. The bar is an integral part of the set up and lends the place a pleasant buzz.

Tendido Cero

Spanish Plan XI – D6

174 Old Brompton Rd. ✉ SW5 0LJ
✆ (020) 7370 3685
www.cambiodetercio.co.uk
⊖ Gloucester Road
Closed last two weeks December

Menu £30 (dinner) – Carte £17/28

Abel Lusa has got things pretty sewn up at this end of Old Brompton Road: on one side of the road he owns Cambio de Tercio and Capote y Toros and opposite he has Tendido Cero, a warmly decorated tapas bar adorned with paintings of matadors. On offer is an appealing mix of familiar hot and cold tapas, from padron peppers and Pata Negra ham to boquerones and assorted croquetas, but there are also a few unusual choices, like a mini 'hamburger' made with sardines. Further highlights include Galician octopus, white bean stew with chorizo and pork cheeks with potato purée. Lunchtimes are relatively quiet affairs; it is at night when the place comes alive and the pace hots up. Service is more about efficiency than personality.

Tom Aikens ✿

modern — **Plan XI – E6**

43 Elystan St. ✉ SW3 3NT
✆ (020) 7584 2003
www.tomaikens.co.uk
⊖ South Kensington
Closed Christmas, Saturday lunch, Sunday and bank holidays

Menu £28/95 – Carte £56/73

Tom Aikens

Re-launched with new business partners, Tom Aikens' eponymous restaurant now has an edgier look and a subtly different style of cooking. The room resembles one of Lars von Trier's more minimalistic film sets, with oak tables, atmospheric lighting and assorted food–related aphorisms stencilled on the walls. Service remains a little overformal for the surroundings but the intentions are good. The menu layout appears somewhat baffling at first but stick to the 6 or 8 course menus and you won't go wrong. The kitchen follows the culinary zeitgeist by appearing to be influenced by all things Scandinavian; each dish focused around one main ingredient and presented on a variety of plates and bowls. There are plenty of modern techniques on show, including the occasional powdered ingredient, but there is no doubting the innate skill and the pleasing contrasts in textures. All the 'extras' are pretty good too: the terrific breads come in warm hessian bags, the canapés are excellent and the friandises are presented in an old Oxo tin.

First Course

- Homemade ricotta, green olive juice, honey jelly and pine nuts.
- Baked scallop, yeasted potatoes, osso bucco and toasted bread soup.

Main Course

- Piglet with aubergine and smoked apple.
- Pyrenean lamb shoulder, salsify, thyme curd and artichoke.

Dessert

- Candied beetroot, yoghurt parfait, sweetened beets and port syrup.
- Coconut parfait, mango mousse and coconut sorbet.

Tom's Kitchen

French

Plan XI – E6

27 Cale St. ✉ SW3 3QP
☎ (020) 7349 0202
www.tomskitchen.co.uk
⊖ South Kensington
Closed 25 December

Carte £27/42

The locals may not have taken to his fish and chip shop but they do seem to like his kitchen. This is a restaurant with a thoroughly sound plan: it's open from early in the morning until late at night and offers satisfying comfort food in relaxed surroundings. The tiled walls and open kitchen work well and there's an upstairs room for the overspill. With its shepherd's pie, sausage and mash, and belly of pork, the menu wouldn't look out of place in a pub; although, as the eponymous Tom is Tom Aikens, a few luxury ingredients like foie gras do sneak in. Bread, olives and side dishes can push up the final bill but it's a friendly place with a stress-free atmosphere. There's a less convincing second branch in Somerset House.

Zuma

Japanese

Plan XII – F5

5 Raphael St ✉ SW7 1DL
☎ (020) 7584 1010
www.zumarestaurant.com
⊖ Knightsbridge
Closed 25 December

Carte £20/96

Zuma may have become a global brand, with branches stretching from Istanbul to Hong Kong, but this is the original and it's still giving its fashionable band of fans – which includes a high quotient of celebrities and enough footballers to make up a whole team – exactly what they want. Glamorous surroundings with an open kitchen, a great cocktail bar, intelligent service and easy-to-share modern Japanese food mean that the large, stylish space is rarely less than bursting, especially at night. The menu covers all bases but instead of sushi, sashimi or tempura your best bet is to head straight for the delicately presented, modern constructions as well as those dishes cooked on the robata grill, which range from beef to sea bass.

Kensington · North Kensington · Notting Hill

It was the choking air of 17C London that helped put **Kensington** on the map: the little village lying to the west of the city became the favoured retreat of the asthmatic King William III who had Sir Christopher Wren build **Kensington Palace** for him. Where the king leads, the titled follow, and the area soon became a fashionable location for the rich. For over 300 years, it's had no problem holding onto its cachet, though a stroll down Kensington High Street is these days a more egalitarian odyssey than some more upmarket residents might approve of.

The shops here mix the everyday with the flamboyant, but for a real taste of the exotic you have to take the lift to the top of the Art Deco Barkers building and arrive at the Kensington Roof Gardens, which are open to all as long as they're not in use for a corporate bash. The gardens are now over seventy years old, yet still remain a 'charming secret'. Those who do make it up to the sixth floor discover a delightful woodland garden and gurgling stream, complete with pools, bridges and trees. There are flamingos, too, adding a dash of vibrant colour.

Back down on earth, Kensington boasts another hidden attraction in **Leighton House** on its western boundaries. The Victorian redbrick façade looks a bit forbidding as you make your approach, but step inside and things take a dramatic turn, courtesy of the extraordinary Arab Hall, with its oriental mosaics and tinkling fountain creating a scene like something from *The Arabian Knights.* Elsewhere in the building, the Pre-Raphaelite paintings of Lord Leighton, Burne-Jones and Alma-Tadema are much to the fore. Mind you, famous names have always had a hankering for W8, with a particular preponderance to dally in enchanting **Kensington Square,** where there are almost as many blue plaques as buildings upon which to secure them. William Thackeray, John Stuart Mill and Edward Burne-Jones were all residents.

One of the London's most enjoyable green retreats is **Holland Park,** just north of the High Street. It boasts the 400 year-old Holland House, which is a fashionable focal point for summer-time al fresco theatre and opera. Holland Walk runs along the eastern fringe of the park, and provides a lovely sojourn down to the shops; at the Kyoto Garden, koi carp reach hungrily for the surface of their pool, while elsewhere peacocks strut around as if they own the place.

Another world beckons just north of here – the seedy-cum-glitzy environs of **Notting Hill.** The main drag itself, Notting Hill Gate, is little more than a one-dimensional thoroughfare only enlivened by second hand record shops, but to its south are charming cottages with pastel shades in leafy streets,

S. Ollivier / MICHELIN

while to the north the appealing **Pembridge Road** evolves into the boutiques of Westbourne Grove. Most people heading in this direction are making for the legendary Portobello Road market – particularly on Saturdays, which are manic. The market stretches on for more than a mile, with a chameleon-like ability to change colour and character on the way: there are antiques at the Notting Hill end, followed further up by food stalls, and then designer and vintage clothes as you reach the Westway. Those who don't fancy the madding crowds of the market can nip into the Electric Cinema and watch a movie in supreme comfort: it boasts two-seater sofas and leather armchairs. Nearby there are another two film-houses putting the hip into the Hill – the Gate, and the Coronet, widely recognised as one of London's most charming 'locals'.

Hidden in a mews just north of **Westbourne Grove** is a fascinating destination: the Museum of Brands, Packaging and Advertising, which does pretty much what it says on the label. It's both nostalgic and evocative, featuring thousands of items like childhood toys, teenage magazines…and HP sauce bottles.

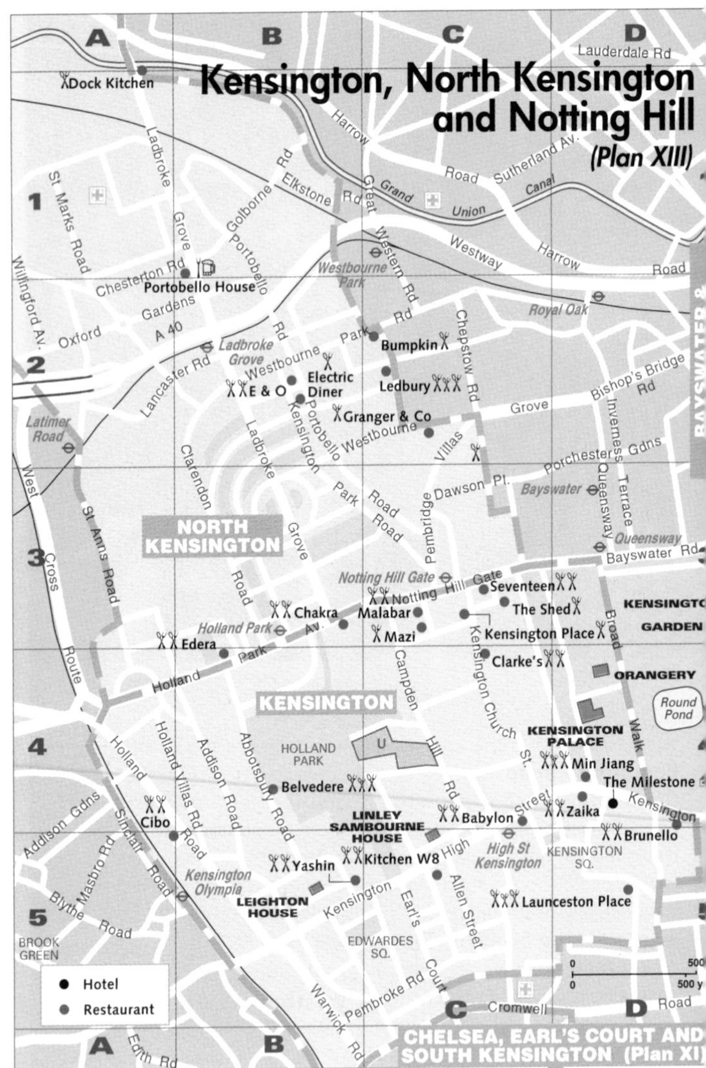
Kensington, North Kensington and Notting Hill
(Plan XIII)
Dock Kitchen
Portobello House
Bumpkin
Electric Diner
E & O
Ledbury
Granger & Co
NORTH KENSINGTON
Seventeen
The Shed
Notting Malabar
Chakra
Mazi
Kensington Place
Edera
Clarke's
KENSINGTON
ORANGERY
KENSINGTON PALACE
Round Pond
HOLLAND PARK
Min Jiang
The Milestone
Belvedere
Cibo
Babylon
Zaika
LINLEY SAMBOURNE HOUSE
Brunello
Yashin
Kitchen W8
KENSINGTON SQ.
LEIGHTON HOUSE
Launceston Place
EDWARDES SQ.
BROOK GREEN
Hotel
Restaurant
CHELSEA, EARL'S COURT AND SOUTH KENSINGTON (Plan XI)

Babylon

modern

C4

The Roof Gardens, 99 Kensington High St
(entrance on Derry St) ✉ W8 5SA
✆ (020) 7368 3993
www.roofgardens.virgin.com
⊖ High Street Kensington
Closed 24-30 December, 1-2 January and Sunday dinner

Menu £22/47 – Carte £38/75

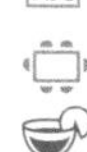

Take the lift on Derry Street up to the 7th floor and you'll find yourself staring at trees, shrubs and possibly even a flamingo in an amazing 1½ acre rooftop garden. The restaurant's terrace must surely be one of the city's best spots for a cocktail and a view, with the easterly skyline visible through the oak and fruit trees. However, be aware that private parties often have exclusive access. The food can't always compete with this bucolic scene and presentation can sometimes be at the expense of flavour but the menu does offer plenty of choice. Dishes are not too heavy, which is a plus for later as dinner at weekends entitles you to access to The Club. You could also consider coming on a Tuesday as that's jazz night.

Belvedere

modern

B4

Holland House, off Abbotsbury Rd. ✉ W8 6LU
✆ (020) 7602 1238
www.belvedererestaurant.co.uk
⊖ Holland Park
Closed 26 December and Sunday dinner

Menu £17 (weekdays)/28 – Carte £32/46

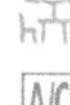

Built in the 17C as the summer ballroom to the Jacobean Holland House, The Belvedere sits in a stunning position in Holland Park. It's hard to believe you're still in London but check the location first as signposts within the park are a little elusive. The ground floor is the more glittery, with mirrors, glass balls and a small bar area. Upstairs is more traditional in style and leads out onto the charming terrace, which is well worth booking in summer. Service remains decidedly formal. The menu covers all bases from eggs Benedict to even the occasional Thai offering, but it's worth sticking to the more classical, French influenced dishes as these are kitchen's strength. Produce is well-sourced and dishes nicely balanced. France dominates the wine list.

Brunello

Italian

D4

Baglioni Hotel,
60 Hyde Park Gate ✉ SW7 5BB
✆ (020) 7368 5900
www.baglionihotels.com
⊖ High Street Kensington

Menu £23/29 – Carte £39/64

It takes time for some restaurants to find the chef that suits them best. Brunello, the Italian restaurant on the ground floor of the Baglioni hotel, has tried a couple in the last few years but now seems to have sensibly settled on a brigade that is less about showiness and more about delivering recognisable Italian classics. This works because there's frankly more than enough drama in the exuberant decoration – with all that velvet, glass, black and gold, you need something reassuringly familiar to stop you thinking you've wandered onto the stage in the middle of a performance of Turandot. Many ingredients come from Italy and there are dishes from all regions. Service is friendly and endearingly proud.

Bumpkin

British traditional

C2

209 Westbourne Park Rd ✉ W11 1EA
✆ (020) 7243 9818
www.bumpkinuk.com
⊖ Westbourne Park
Closed August bank holiday

Carte £23/39

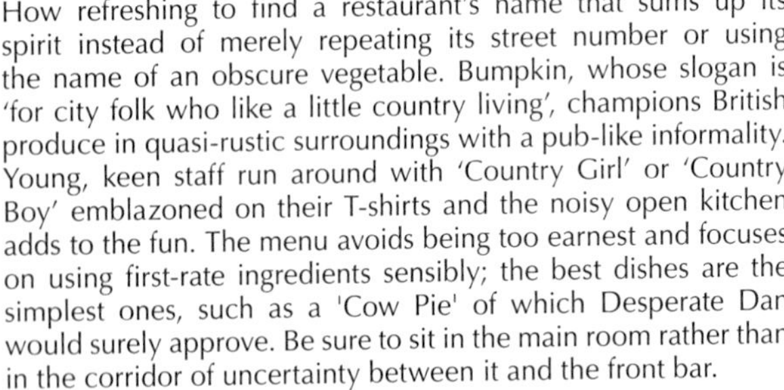

How refreshing to find a restaurant's name that sums up its spirit instead of merely repeating its street number or using the name of an obscure vegetable. Bumpkin, whose slogan is 'for city folk who like a little country living', champions British produce in quasi-rustic surroundings with a pub-like informality. Young, keen staff run around with 'Country Girl' or 'Country Boy' emblazoned on their T-shirts and the noisy open kitchen adds to the fun. The menu avoids being too earnest and focuses on using first-rate ingredients sensibly; the best dishes are the simplest ones, such as a 'Cow Pie' of which Desperate Dan would surely approve. Be sure to sit in the main room rather than in the corridor of uncertainty between it and the front bar.

Chakra

Indian

B3

157-159 Notting Hill Gate ✉ W11 3LF
✆ (020) 7229 2115
www.chakralondon.com
⊖ Notting Hill Gate
Closed 25-26 December, 1 January and Easter Monday – booking advisable

Menu £17/20 – Carte £20/42

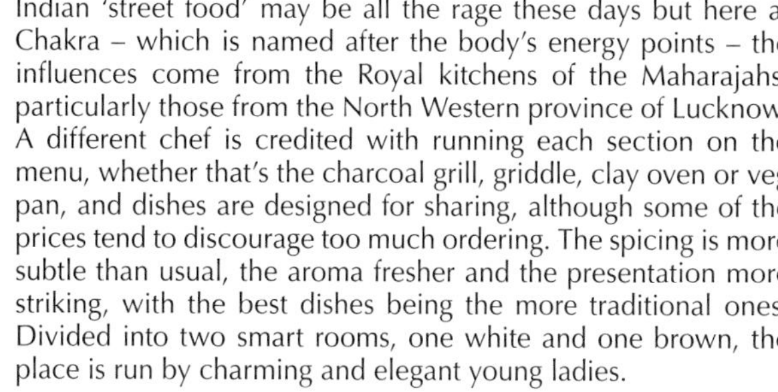

Indian 'street food' may be all the rage these days but here at Chakra – which is named after the body's energy points – the influences come from the Royal kitchens of the Maharajahs, particularly those from the North Western province of Lucknow. A different chef is credited with running each section on the menu, whether that's the charcoal grill, griddle, clay oven or veg pan, and dishes are designed for sharing, although some of the prices tend to discourage too much ordering. The spicing is more subtle than usual, the aroma fresher and the presentation more striking, with the best dishes being the more traditional ones. Divided into two smart rooms, one white and one brown, the place is run by charming and elegant young ladies.

Cibo

Italian

A4/5

3 Russell Gdns ✉ W14 8EZ
✆ (020) 7371 6271
www.ciborestaurant.net
⊖ Kensington Olympia
Closed 1 week Christmas, Easter and bank holidays

Menu £20 (dinner) – Carte £25/42

Some of the sparkle may have dimmed since Cibo opened in 1989 but its band of local followers remain committed in their enthusiasm for this friendly Italian restaurant. The interior looks a tad weary these days but the quirky pictures celebrating the naked female form are still there and the imported hand-painted crockery is a nice touch. The ever-popular platter of grilled seafood dictates that the menu pretty much changes on a daily basis, although certain dishes can never be changed; some regulars can even guess who's in the kitchen that day by the degree of spicing. Service is friendly if a touch chaotic at times and while the opening front façade is a boon in summer, it can be draughty in winter, so ask for a table at the back.

Clarke's

modern C4

124 Kensington Church St ✉ W8 4BH
✆ (020) 7221 9225
www.sallyclarke.com
⊖ Notting Hill Gate
Closed Christmas-New Year, Sunday dinner and bank holidays – booking advisable

Menu £25 (dinner) – Carte £35/44 XX

A/C

By constantly searching for the next big thing, many diners miss out on London's more dependable and worthy restaurants such as Clarke's, which has been a reassuring presence on Kensington Church Street since 1984. Regulars, of whom there are many, prefer the ground floor, although the tables downstairs benefit from the delicious aromas arising from the surprisingly serene open kitchen. The cooking remains true to Sally Clarke's founding principles of excellent ingredients and simple preparation and owes much to the influence of Alice Waters at Chez Panisse in San Francisco. There is a small, weekly changing à la carte plus 'Sally's Dinner Menu', a nicely balanced set price menu. The wine list has also been thoughtfully compiled.

Dock Kitchen

Mediterranean A0

Portobello Dock, 342-344 Ladbroke Grove ✉ W10 5BU
✆ (020) 8962 1610
www.dockkitchen.co.uk
⊖ Ladbroke Grove
Closed 24 December-5 January and Sunday dinner

Menu £25/55 – Carte £28/41 X

What started as a pop-up restaurant became a permanent feature in this former Victorian goods yard and the space is shared with designer Tom Dixon, some of whose furniture and lighting is showcased here. The open kitchen dominates one end of the room where steel girders and exposed brick add to the industrial aesthetic. The similarities to Moro, River Café and Petersham Nurseries are palpable, not just in the refreshing lack of ceremony and the fashionable crowds that flock here, but also in the cooking, where quality ingredients are a given and natural flavours speak for themselves. The chef's peregrinations also inform his cooking; look out for his themed set menus which could be Sardinian one week, Moroccan the next.

E&O

Asian

B2

14 Blenheim Cres. ✉ W11 1NN
✆ (020) 7229 5454
www.rickerrestaurants.com
⊖ Ladbroke Grove
Closed 25 December

Menu £20/59 – Carte £22/55

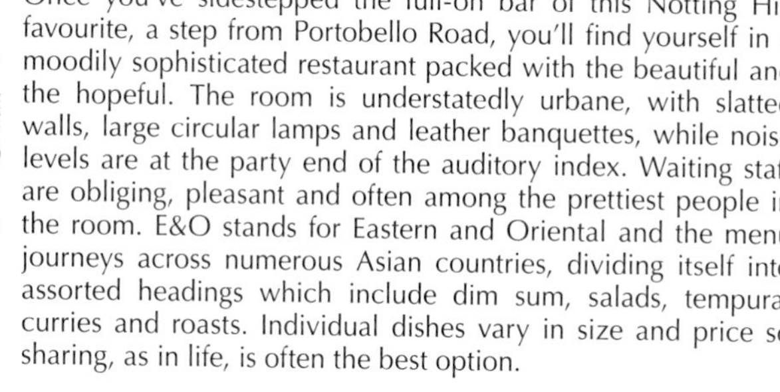

Once you've sidestepped the full-on bar of this Notting Hill favourite, a step from Portobello Road, you'll find yourself in a moodily sophisticated restaurant packed with the beautiful and the hopeful. The room is understatedly urbane, with slatted walls, large circular lamps and leather banquettes, while noise levels are at the party end of the auditory index. Waiting staff are obliging, pleasant and often among the prettiest people in the room. E&O stands for Eastern and Oriental and the menu journeys across numerous Asian countries, dividing itself into assorted headings which include dim sum, salads, tempura, curries and roasts. Individual dishes vary in size and price so sharing, as in life, is often the best option.

Edera

Italian

B4

148 Holland Park Ave. ✉ W11 4UE
✆ (020) 7221 6090
www.edera.co.uk
⊖ Holland Park

Carte £33/52

The last makeover made Edera warmer and more comfortable and, while it actually holds up to 75 people, it still manages to feel quite intimate. On a typical night it seems as though the vast majority of customers have been before, that they know one another and probably walked here. In comparison, the staff are a youthful bunch, but they are well-marshalled and quietly efficient. The menu is quite broad and portions are on the generous side so if you're having a pasta dish you may struggle with a fourth course. The list of daily specials is wisely printed so you don't have to try to memorise the waiter's recital; there is a Sardinian element to the cooking, with bottarga omnipresent, and the ingredients are first-rate.

Ⓝ Electric Diner

meats and grills

B2

191 Portobello Rd ✉ W11 2ED
✆ (0207) 7908 9696
www.electricdiner.com
⊖ Ladbroke Grove
Bookings not accepted

Carte £22/35

Any cinema that's over 100 years old deserves to be shown respect, so treat your visit to the Electric Cinema as a special occasion and start, or finish, with a meal next door at the Electric Diner. It's a loud, fun and brash all-day operation with a simple but all-encompassing menu that changes daily. The long counter, red leather booths and low ceiling certainly create the mood and look of the classic American diner – even the music comes from a reel-to-reel. Au Cheval diner in Chicago has supplied most of the influences so be prepared for big portions that are heavy on flavour. The room fills with smoke from the grill; the steak and pork chops could easily feed two and the lemon meringue pie is of Desperate Dan dimensions.

Granger & Co

modern

C2

175 Westbourne Grove ✉ W11 2SB
✆ (020) 7229 9111
www.grangerandco.com
⊖ Bayswater
Closed August bank holiday weekend and 25-26 December – bookings not accepted

Carte £20/44

Having relocated from the sun of Sydney to the cool of Notting Hill, Bill Granger decided to open a local restaurant. He's brought with him that disarmingly charming 'matey' service that only Australians can do, his breakfast sweetcorn fritters and ricotta hotcakes and a zesty menu that features everything from pasta to pork chops. At dinner a BBQ section is added along with a daily fish dish, while various puds replace the cakes offered during the day. The room is bright and open, prices are reasonable and the Asian accents lend many of the dishes an easy-to-eat quality which makes you feel healthier than when you arrived and allows you to forget that you probably had to queue for a table.

Kensington Place

modern

C3

201-209 Kensington Church St. ✉ W8 7LX
✆ (020) 7727 3184
www.kensingtonplace-restaurant.co.uk
⊖ Notting Hill Gate
Closed Sunday dinner, Monday lunch and bank holidays

Menu £17 (weekday lunch) – Carte £24/40

It must have been quite difficult for the D&D group to re-establish Kensington Place, especially as Rowley Leigh, its well-known former chef, now operates in nearby Bayswater. One thing they have got right is the menu; they dispensed with an à la carte and in its place introduced a competitively priced set menu which offers plenty of choice. There are some supplements for the few dishes using pricier ingredients but these can be easily avoided. The cooking is modern and quite dainty at times and desserts are done well. Service is still speedy and copes easily with the numbers when it needs to. The addition of cushions has succeeded in softening the acoustics so it's also easier to have a conversation these days.

Malabar

Indian

C3

27 Uxbridge St. ✉ W8 7TQ
✆ (020) 7727 8800
www.malabar-restaurant.co.uk
⊖ Notting Hill Gate
Closed 1 week Christmas – (buffet lunch Sunday)

Menu £18/25 s – Carte £14/31 s

One of the reasons why Malabar has been going strong since 1983 is that it keeps on top of its appearance, as, it seems, do most of its Notting Hill customers. These days the front has a sleek, understated look; the interior is a fashionable grey and the staff do their bit by dressing in black. What doesn't change is the quality of the food, from the breads to the piping hot thalis. The favourites remain but the seafood section has been beefed up with the addition of a monkfish curry and a whole gilt-head bream; and just because the tandoori dishes sit beside the starters on the menu, don't assume they come in starter sizes. The excellent value Sunday buffet lunch, when children under 12 eat for free, still packs them in.

Kitchen W8 ✿

modern

C5

11-13 Abingdon Rd ✉ W8 6AH
(020) 7937 0120
www.kitchenw8.com
⊖ High Street Kensington
Closed 25-26 December and bank holidays

Menu £25 (lunch and early dinner) – Carte £36/52

Kitchen W8

Over the years Abingdon Road has played host to a decent collection of restaurants but the general standard was raised considerably when Kitchen W8 arrived. This joint venture between Rebecca Mascarenhas, one of London's most experienced restaurateurs, and Philip Howard, luminary chef of The Square, has quickly established itself on the scene and it is easy to see why. For a start, their talented head chef has a crisp and confident style, which never lets presentation or construction compromise the clarity of the flavours. He also appreciates that diners don't come here to eat something they could knock up easily at home so his dishes have depth and a degree of originality. Furthermore, when one considers the quality of ingredients used and the manpower in the kitchen, prices are refreshingly restrained – and the weekly changing lunch menu is a steal. The place itself is quite big but comes divided into three smaller sections; the youthful looking staff ensure that the atmosphere remains light and relaxed, as befits a neighbourhood restaurant.

First Course

- Smoked eel with Cornish mackerel, beetroot and sweet mustard.
- Tartare of veal with smoked anchovies, pickled mooli and capers.

Main Course

- Loin and raviolo of Pata Negra pork with ruby grapefruit, charred lettuce.
- Cod poached in seaweed butter with smoked roe, cauliflower and squid.

Dessert

- Hazelnut parfait with salted caramel ice cream.
- Passion fruit tart with lime ice cream and pineapple.

Launceston Place ✿

modern D5

1a Launceston Pl ✉ W8 5RL
✆ (020) 7937 6912
www.launcestonplace-restaurant.co.uk
⊖ Gloucester Road

Closed 23-29 December, Monday lunch and dinner bank holiday Mondays – bookings advisable at dinner

Menu £25 (weekday lunch), £30/65

Launceston Place

Keeping your regulars happy is half the battle for all neighbourhood restaurants and one way of ensuring they keep returning is to give them the sort of food they want to eat as well as the sort of food that complements the surroundings. Yorkshire-born Timothy Allen joined this longstanding Kensington landmark as head chef in 2012 and his cooking appears to be a very good fit. He worked for chefs John Burton Race and Martin Burge for over ten years and their influences are evident in his own style of cooking which is refined without being dainty and, like most of the customers, sophisticated without being showy. Despite Launceston Place being part of the D&D group, the chef sources his own produce and works without interference. The restaurant comes divided into various areas and everyone has their favourite spot. The striking chocolate coloured walls and modern artwork add to the intimate and grown up feel. Service can sometimes feel a little overformal but its heart is in the right place.

First Course

- Cold-smoked and grilled mackerel, variations of cucumber and iced horseradish.
- Veal sweetbreads, Pata Negra lardo, Amalfi lemon leaf caramel.

Main Course

- Iberico pork, heritage tomatoes, broad beans and dried figs.
- John Dory with Jersey Royals, asparagus and crab cannelloni.

Dessert

- 70% Cru Virunga chocolate mousse.
- Baked English custard, pineapple roasted in Pedro Ximenez and pineapple ice cream.

Ledbury ✿✿

modern

C2

127 Ledbury Rd. ✉ W11 2AQ
(020) 7792 9090
www.theledbury.com
Notting Hill Gate
Closed 25-26 December, August bank holiday and Monday lunch

Menu £35, £50/105 – Carte approx. £59

Ledbury

As his restaurant matures, so Brett Graham's cooking becomes simpler and more confident. By working closely with his suppliers, he ensures that the main ingredient of each dish is not only the star of the show but also of the highest quality. Meats are cooked on the bone and flavours are robust and rewarding, whether that's the Galloway Belt beef or the Montjuic – Brett's a keen shot in his spare time. Careful husbandry of their resources and produce means that you'll sometimes find some rather unexpected ingredients like turbot on the good value lunch set menu that other establishments would only consider putting on their à la carte and charging a premium for. The service also comes with less showiness these days and the staff manage to be efficient, knowledgeable and friendly without being mechanical, prescriptive or intrusive. The restaurant has a reassuringly urbane buzz and does feel very much part of the local neighbourhood – this is the sort of place you can come to for a grand celebration or a casual supper.

First Course

- Buffalo milk curd with Saint-Nectaire and truffle toast.
- Risotto of celeriac and new potatoes with smoked eel and parsley.

Main Course

- Breast and confit legs of grouse with foie gras and cherries.
- Sea bass with peas, mousserons and asparagus.

Dessert

- Parfait of dried flowers, wild strawberries and vanilla tapioca.
- Brown sugar tart with poached grapes and stem ginger ice cream.

Mazi

Greek

C3

12-14 Hillgate St ✉ W8 7SR
✆ (020) 7229 3794
www.mazi.co.uk
⊖ Notting Hill Gate
Closed 24-26 December and 1-2 January

Menu £13/18 – Carte £26/46

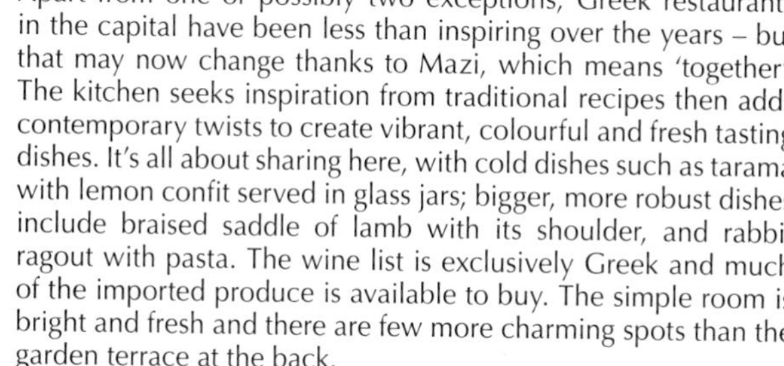

Apart from one or possibly two exceptions, Greek restaurants in the capital have been less than inspiring over the years – but that may now change thanks to Mazi, which means 'together'. The kitchen seeks inspiration from traditional recipes then adds contemporary twists to create vibrant, colourful and fresh tasting dishes. It's all about sharing here, with cold dishes such as tarama with lemon confit served in glass jars; bigger, more robust dishes include braised saddle of lamb with its shoulder, and rabbit ragout with pasta. The wine list is exclusively Greek and much of the imported produce is available to buy. The simple room is bright and fresh and there are few more charming spots than the garden terrace at the back.

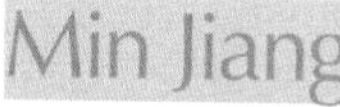

Min Jiang

Chinese

D4

Royal Garden Hotel,
2-24 Kensington High St (10th Floor) ✉ W8 4PT
✆ (020) 7361 1988
www.minjiang.co.uk
⊖ High Street Kensington

Menu £50/70 – Carte £25/97

It's got great views of Kensington Palace and Gardens below (ask for tables 11 or 16) but because of its own good looks and its collection of vases influenced by the Ming Dynasty, this stylish Chinese restaurant on the 10th floor of the Royal Garden hotel can more than hold its own. The speciality is wood-fired Beijing duck in two servings; its glistening meat is carved at the table and one then has the difficult task of choosing one of the four options offered for the second serving. The cuisine covers all provinces, although Cantonese and Sichuan are the most dominant. The dim sum is good and the signature dishes include sea bass with shredded chicken, sautéed Gong Bao chicken and spicy pork belly with leeks.

Portobello House

modern

B1

225 Ladbroke Grove ✉ W10 6HQ
(020) 3181 0920
www.portobellohouse.com
Ladbroke Grove

Menu £15 (weekday lunch) – Carte £19/32

Whether this is a pub, bistro or hotel – or even all three – may be up for discussion but what is indisputable is that Portobello House is a great addition to this end of Ladbroke Grove. It was formerly the Earl Percy and once hosted The Clash (as, seemingly, did every boozer in these parts) but has been given a complete makeover and now has 12 smart and contemporary bedrooms. Downstairs, the bar takes up most of the space and, in a reflection of the changing local demographic, offers beers and cocktails. There are plenty of sofas to relax on; grab the one by the open fire. The menu is a combination of British stoutness and Italian flair and the cooking is bold yet comforting; it is also decently priced, especially at weekday lunches.

Seventeen

Chinese

C3

17 Notting Hill Gate ✉ W11 3JQ
(020) 7985 0006
www.seventeen-london.com
Notting Hill Gate

Menu £29 – Carte £15/45

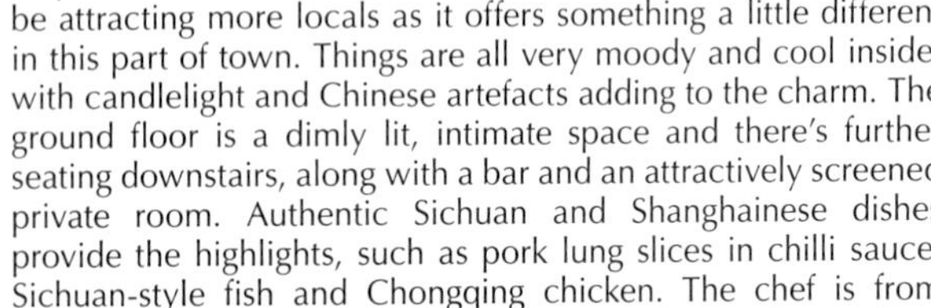

Burdening itself with an instantly forgettable name may not have helped its cause but still, this stylish Chinese restaurant should be attracting more locals as it offers something a little different in this part of town. Things are all very moody and cool inside, with candlelight and Chinese artefacts adding to the charm. The ground floor is a dimly lit, intimate space and there's further seating downstairs, along with a bar and an attractively screened private room. Authentic Sichuan and Shanghainese dishes provide the highlights, such as pork lung slices in chilli sauce, Sichuan-style fish and Chongqing chicken. The chef is from Mainland China and also offers delicacies from other regions, such as Dung Po pork, a Hangzhou speciality.

The Shed

British traditional

C3

122 Palace Gardens Terr. ✉ W8 4RT
✆ (020) 7229 4024
www.theshed-restaurant.com
⊖ Notting Hill Gate
Closed Sunday dinner and Monday

Menu £35 – Carte £12/24

Names add to expectations, so if you call your place the Grand Palace it really doesn't give you anywhere to hide. The Gladwin brothers behind The Shed instead opted for understatement and it works a treat. This is the old Ark restaurant and is obviously more than just a shed, even though it comes with a healthy dose of the outdoors. There are farming tools around, upturned barrels for tables and even an old tractor engine, all adding to its higgledy-piggledy charm. One brother cooks, one manages and the third runs the farm in West Sussex from where much of the produce comes. The cooking is appropriately British, earthy and satisfying, with the small plates divided into 'slow' or 'fast': a reference to the cooking process.

Yashin

Japanese

B5

1A Argyll Rd. ✉ W8 7DB
✆ (020) 7938 1536
www.yashinsushi.com
⊖ High Street Kensington
Closed first Monday in every month and Christmas – booking essential

Menu £45/50 – Carte £25/80

Two experienced sushi chefs joined forces to create this contemporary restaurant with its crisp, appealing black and white theme. Their worthy ambition to wean diners off fermented soya bean is reflected in their grammatically challenging but charmingly equitable slogan: "without soy sauce...but if you want to". There are three omakase choices offering 8, 11 or 15 pieces of sushi selected by the chefs and served together. The quality of the fish is clear and originality comes in the form of minuscule garnishes adorning each piece and the odd bit of searing. Service is knowledgeable and endearing but be sure to ask for a counter seat as one of the joys of sushi comes from watching the dextrous knife skills and the deft handling of the fish.

Zaika

Indian

D4

1 Kensington High St. ✉ W8 5NP
☎ (020) 7795 6533
www.zaika-restaurant.co.uk
⊖ High Street Kensington
Closed 25-26 December, 1 January and Monday lunch

Menu £18/55 – Carte £29/69

The people behind Tamarind restaurant in Mayfair have taken over Zaika; but regulars – and Zaika has many regulars – will be relieved to know that little has actually changed at their favourite Indian restaurant. It's no surprise that this wood-panelled room was once a bank – only a financial institution could create something quite so grand, but assorted Indian artefacts and judicious lighting have been used to make it seem a little less imposing. Whereas the cooking at Tamarind is traditional, here the cuisine is contemporary and the kitchen is encouraged to be original. Presentation is strong and dishes are quite elaborate. It's worth coming in the early evening to take advantage of their competitively priced pre-theatre menu.

Do not confuse ✕ with ✿ ! ✕ defines comfort, while ✿ are awarded for the best cuisine. Stars are awarded across all categories of comfort.

C. S. Pereyra / Age fotostock

Greater London

- North-West 318
- North-East 338
- South-East 360
- South-West 380

M. Jones/Age fotostock

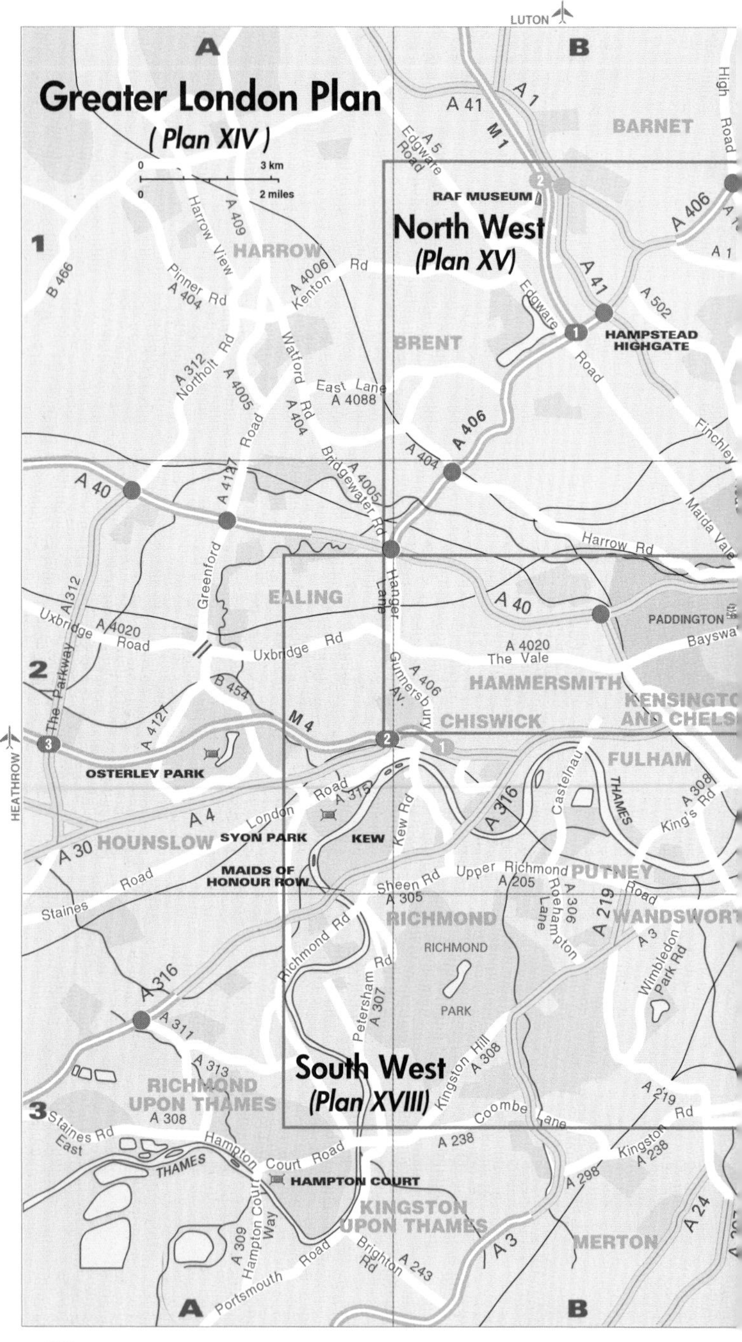
Greater London Plan
(Plan XIV)
North West
(Plan XV)
South West
(Plan XVIII)
LUTON
HEATHROW
HARROW
BARNET
BRENT
HAMPSTEAD
HIGHGATE
RAF MUSEUM
EALING
PADDINGTON
HAMMERSMITH
CHISWICK
FULHAM
OSTERLEY PARK
HOUNSLOW
SYON PARK
KEW
MAIDS OF
HONOUR ROW
PUTNEY
RICHMOND
RICHMOND
PARK
RICHMOND
UPON THAMES
HAMPTON COURT
KINGSTON
UPON THAMES
MERTON

STANSTED
North East
(Plan XVI)
Central London
(Plan I -XIII)
South East
(Plan XVII)
HARINGEY
HACKNEY
ISLINGTON
CAMDEN
WALTHAM FOREST
NEWHAM
TOWER HAMLETS
CANARY WHARF
LONDON CITY AIRPORT
THE O2
THAMES BARRIER
ISLE OF DOGS
ST KATHARINE'S DOCK
WATERLOO
LIVERPOOL STREET
EUSTON
KING'S CROSS
BATTERSEA
SOUTHWARK
LAMBETH
GREENWICH
LEWISHAM
BROMLEY
CROYDON
GATWICK

North-West London

Heading north from London Zoo and Regent's Park, the green baton is passed to two of the city's most popular and well-known locations: Hampstead Heath and Highgate Wood. In close proximity, they offer a favoured pair of lungs to travellers emerging from the murky depths of the Northern Line. Two centuries ago, they would have been just another part of the area's undeveloped high ground and pastureland, but since the building boom of the nineteenth century, both have become prized assets in this part of the metropolis.

People came to seek shelter in **Hampstead** in times of plague, and it's retained its bucolic air to this day. Famous names have always enjoyed its charms: Constable and Keats rested their brush and pen here, while the sculptors Henry Moore and Barbara Hepworth were residents in more recent times. Many are drawn to such delightful places as Church Row, which boasts a lovely Georgian Terrace. You know you're up high because the thoroughfares bear names like Holly Mount and Mount Vernon. The Heath is full of rolling woodlands and meadows; it's a great place for rambling, particularly to the crest of **Parliament Hill** and its superb city views. There are three bathing ponds here, one mixed, and one each for male and female swimmers, while up on the Heath's northern fringes, **Kenwood House,** along with its famous al fresco summer concerts, also boasts great art by the likes of Vermeer and Rembrandt. And besides all that, there's an ivy tunnel leading to a terrace with idyllic pond views.

Highgate Wood is an ancient woodland and conservation area, containing a leafy walk that meanders enchantingly along a former railway line to **Crouch End,** home to a band of thespians. Down the road at Highgate Cemetery, the likes of Karl Marx, George Eliot, Christina Rossetti and Michael Faraday rest in a great entanglement of breathtaking Victorian over-decoration. The cemetery is still in use – most recent notable to be buried here is Alexander Litvinenko, the Russian dissident.

Next door you'll find **Waterlow Park,** another fine green space, which, apart from its super views, also includes decorative ponds on three levels. Lauderdale House is here, too, a 16C pile which is now an arts centre; more famously, Charles II handed over its keys to Nell Gwynn for her to use as her North London residence. Head back south from here, and **Primrose Hill** continues the theme of glorious green space: its surrounding terraces are populated by media darlings, while its vertiginous mass is another to boast a famously enviable vista.

Of a different hue altogether is **Camden Town** with its buzzy edge, courtesy of a renowned indie music scene, goths, punks, and six earthy markets selling everything from tat to exotica. Charles Dickens grew up here, and he was none too complimentary; the area

S. Ollivier/ MICHELIN

still relishes its seamy underside. A scenic route out is the **Regent's Canal,** which cuts its way through the market and ambles to the east and west of the city. Up the road, the legendary Roundhouse re-opened its arty front doors in 2006, expanding further the wide range of Camden's alt scene.

One of the music world's most legendary destinations, the **Abbey Road** studios, is also in this area and, yes, it's possible to join other tourists making their way over that zebra crossing. Not far away, in Maresfield Gardens, stands a very different kind of attraction. The Freud Museum is one of the very few buildings in London to have two blue plaques. It was home to Sigmund during the last year of his life and it's where he lived with his daughter Anna (her plaque commemorates her work in child psychiatry). Inside, there's a fabulous library and his working desk. But the pivotal part of the whole house is in another corner of the study – the psychiatrist's couch!

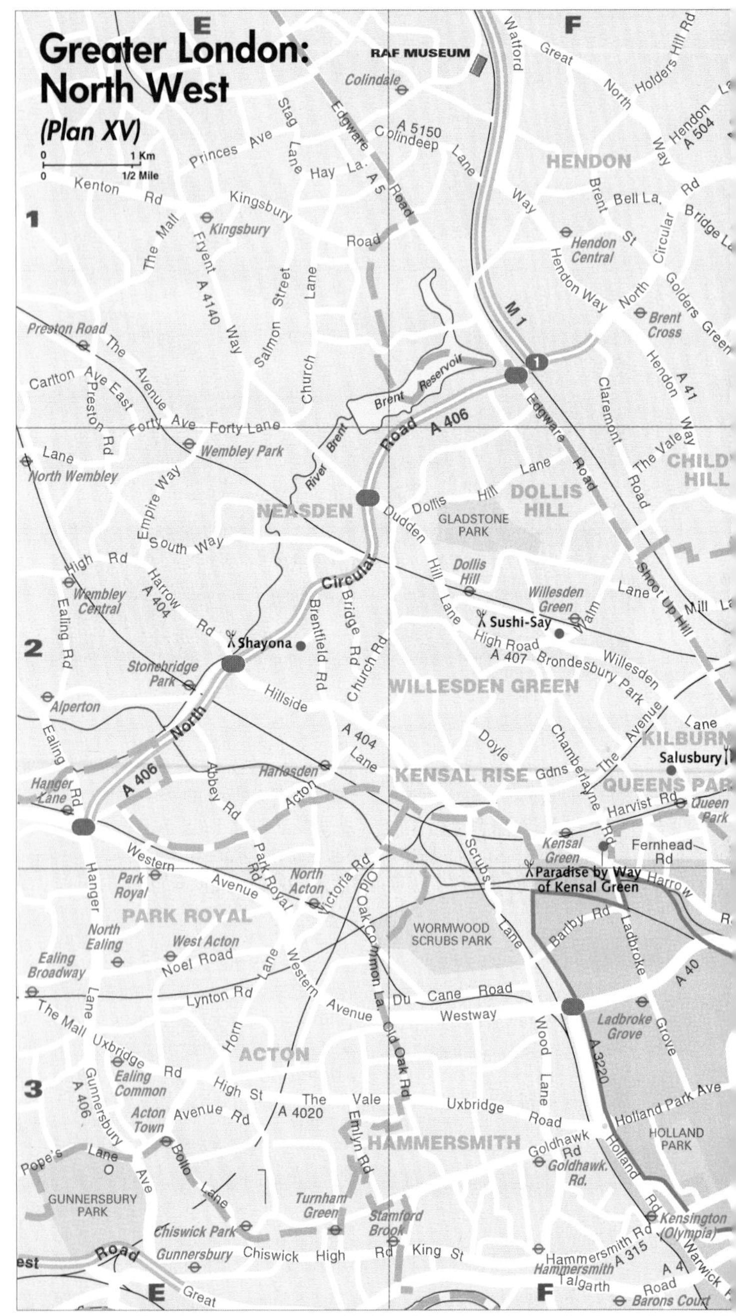
Greater London: North West
(Plan XV)
0 1 Km
0 1/2 Mile
E
F
1
2
3
RAF MUSEUM
Colindale
HENDON
Hendon Central
Brent Cross
Kingsbury
Preston Road
Wembley Park
North Wembley
NEASDEN
DOLLIS HILL
GLADSTONE PARK
Dollis Hill
Willesden Green
Sushi-Say
Shayona
Wembley Central
Stonebridge Park
Alperton
WILLESDEN GREEN
KILBURN
Salusbury
KENSAL RISE
QUEENS PARK
Queen Park
Harlesden
Hanger Lane
Kensal Green
Paradise by Way of Kensal Green
Park Royal
PARK ROYAL
North Acton
North Ealing
West Acton
Ealing Broadway
WORMWOOD SCRUBS PARK
Ladbroke Grove
ACTON
Ealing Common
Acton Town
HAMMERSMITH
HOLLAND PARK
Goldhawk Rd.
GUNNERSBURY PARK
Chiswick Park
Turnham Green
Stamford Brook
Gunnersbury
Kensington (Olympia)
Hammersmith
Barons Court
M 1
A 406
A 5
A 5150
A 41
A 504
A 4140
A 404
A 407
A 4020
A 3220
A 40
A 315
A 4
North Circular Road
Edgware Road
Brent Reservoir
River Brent

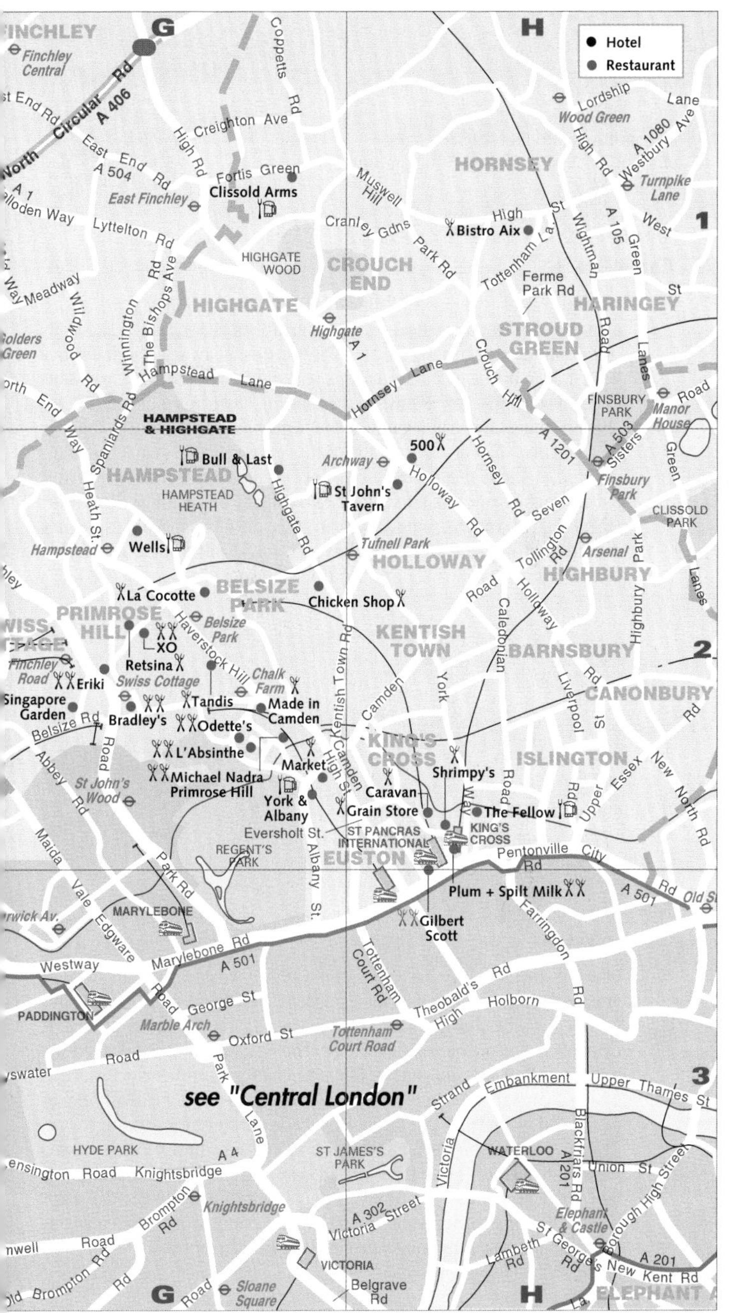

Hotel
Restaurant
Clissold Arms
Bistro Aix
500
Bull & Last
St John's Tavern
Wells
La Cocotte
Chicken Shop
XO
Retsina
Eriki
Singapore Garden
Bradley's
Tandis
Odette's
Made in Camden
L'Absinthe
Michael Nadra Primrose Hill
Market
York & Albany
Caravan
Grain Store
Shrimpy's
The Fellow
Plum + Spilt Milk
Gilbert Scott
see "Central London"

500

Italian

Archway

H2

782 Holloway Rd ✉ N19 3JH

(020) 7272 3406 – **www**.500restaurant.co.uk

⊖ Archway

Closed 2 weeks summer and 2 weeks Christmas-New Year – booking essential – (dinner only and lunch Friday-Sunday)

Carte £24/32

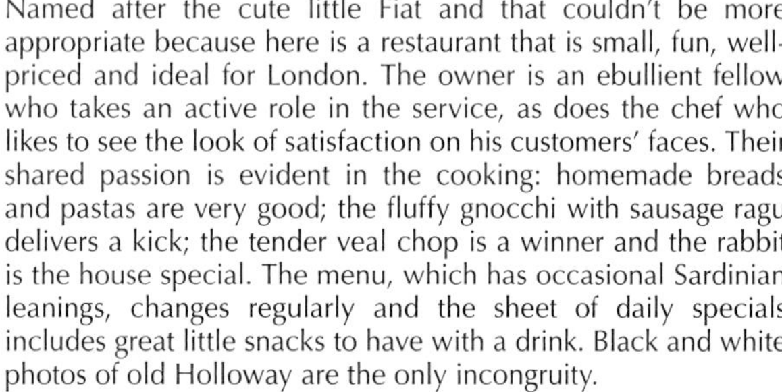

Named after the cute little Fiat and that couldn't be more appropriate because here is a restaurant that is small, fun, well-priced and ideal for London. The owner is an ebullient fellow who takes an active role in the service, as does the chef who likes to see the look of satisfaction on his customers' faces. Their shared passion is evident in the cooking: homemade breads and pastas are very good; the fluffy gnocchi with sausage ragu delivers a kick; the tender veal chop is a winner and the rabbit is the house special. The menu, which has occasional Sardinian leanings, changes regularly and the sheet of daily specials includes great little snacks to have with a drink. Black and white photos of old Holloway are the only incongruity.

St John's Tavern

modern

Archway

91 Junction Rd ✉ N19 5QU

(020) 7272 1587 – **www**.stjohnstavern.com

⊖ Archway.

Closed 25-26 December and 1 January – booking advisable – (dinner only and lunch Friday-Sunday)

Carte £21/34

Having undergone an English Heritage restoration in recent years, St John's Tavern now stands as a beacon of hope on the stubbornly unchanging thoroughfare that is Junction Road. It doesn't disappoint inside either: the laid-back front bar does an appealing line in snacks like salt cod croquettes and mutton pasties, and there are few more warming spots in North London on a cold night than the large, boldly decorated rear dining room. The chefs list the provenance of their ingredients on a board next to the open kitchen, with Devon and Dorset seemingly the favoured counties. The daily menu is largely hardy and British but with nods to the Med; heartening terrines are a highlight, as is the delicious sourdough which is baked in-house.

Retsina

Greek

G2

Belsize Park

48-50 Belsize Ln ✉ NW3 5AR
✆ (020) 7431 5855
www.retsina-london.com
⊖ Belsize Park
Closed 25-26 December, 1 January, Monday lunch and bank holidays

Menu £19 (lunch) – Carte £21/45

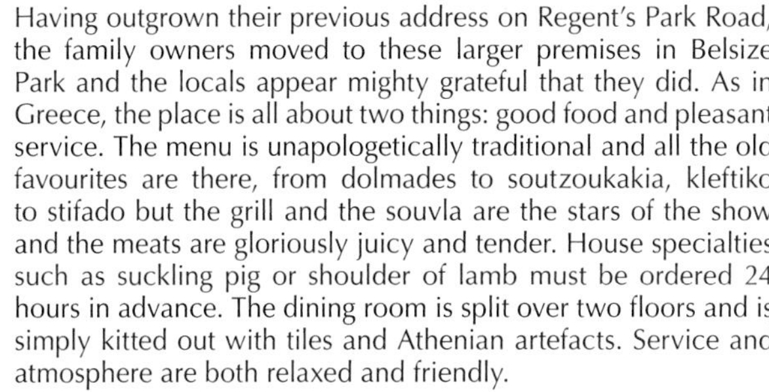

Having outgrown their previous address on Regent's Park Road, the family owners moved to these larger premises in Belsize Park and the locals appear mighty grateful that they did. As in Greece, the place is all about two things: good food and pleasant service. The menu is unapologetically traditional and all the old favourites are there, from dolmades to soutzoukakia, kleftiko to stifado but the grill and the souvla are the stars of the show and the meats are gloriously juicy and tender. House specialties such as suckling pig or shoulder of lamb must be ordered 24 hours in advance. The dining room is split over two floors and is simply kitted out with tiles and Athenian artefacts. Service and atmosphere are both relaxed and friendly.

Tandis

other world kitchens

G2

Belsize Park

73 Haverstock Hill ✉ NW3 4SL
✆ (020) 7586 8079
www.tandisrestaurant.com
⊖ Chalk Farm
Closed 25 December

Carte £17/24

Haverstock Hill's maturing restaurant scene has now acquired a little exoticism thanks to Tandis and its enticing Iranian cooking. The appeal of this contemporary looking restaurant stretches way beyond the Iranian diaspora – plenty of locals also appear to have been seduced as soon as they tasted the traditional flat bread baked in a clay oven. A varied selection of invigorating 'koresht' stews and succulent 'kababs' form the mainstay of the menu but other specialities such as 'sabzi polo' and the rich and complex flavours of 'kashke bademjaan' are well worth exploring. Finish with some of their fine teas and a 'faloodeh', where rose water sorbet is matched with a sour cherry syrup. The best seats are to be found at the back.

XO

Asian G2

Belsize Park

29 Belsize Ln. ✉ NW3 5AS
(020) 7433 0888
www.rickerrestaurants.com/xo
⊖ Belsize Park
Closed 25-26 December, 1 January and bank holidays

Menu £18 (lunch) – Carte £20/39

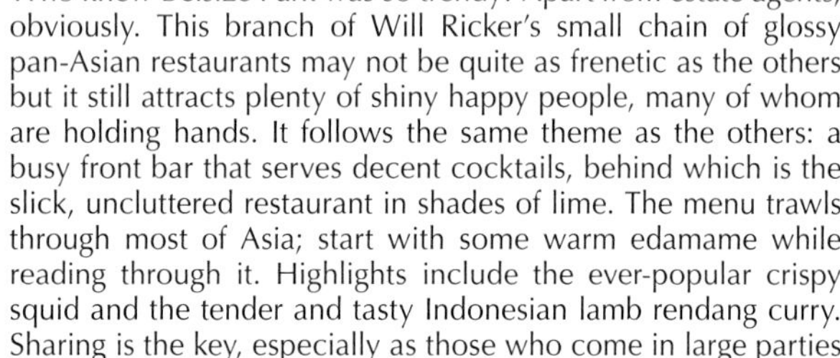

Who knew Belsize Park was so trendy? Apart from estate agents, obviously. This branch of Will Ricker's small chain of glossy pan-Asian restaurants may not be quite as frenetic as the others but it still attracts plenty of shiny happy people, many of whom are holding hands. It follows the same theme as the others: a busy front bar that serves decent cocktails, behind which is the slick, uncluttered restaurant in shades of lime. The menu trawls through most of Asia; start with some warm edamame while reading through it. Highlights include the ever-popular crispy squid and the tender and tasty Indonesian lamb rendang curry. Sharing is the key, especially as those who come in large parties get the booths.

Made in Camden 

other world kitchens G2

Camden Town

Roundhouse, Chalk Farm Rd ✉ NW1 8EH
(020) 7424 8495
www.madeincamden.com
⊖ Chalk Farm
Closed 25 December, 1-2 January, Sunday dinner and Monday

Menu £12 (weekday lunch) – Carte £23/32 

You'll find this large and relaxed bar and dining room attached to the side of the rejuvenated Roundhouse, which means it's at its most fun when it's jumping with people just before or after a show. The room's assorted posters will instil either a sense of curiosity or nostalgia, depending on your age, and the booths around the bar are a great spot for drinks. What really elevates the place, however, is the cooking; there is irony in the name because the kitchen has a global reach, from the Med to Asia. Serving small plates may be nothing new these days but here it's the combination of ingredients and flavours that sets it apart, whether that's fennel with feta and salted caramel or crispy chicken with black vinegar glaze.

Market

British modern

G2

Camden Town

43 Parkway ✉ NW1 7PN
✆ (020) 7267 9700 – **www**.marketrestaurant.co.uk
⊖ Camden Town
Closed 25 December-3 January, Sunday dinner and bank holidays – booking essential

Menu £10/18 – Carte £25/35

The name is spot on because this is all about market fresh produce, seasonality and cooking that is refreshingly matter of fact, with big, bold flavour and John Bull Britishness. Dishes come as advertised, with no pointless ornamentation, and you can expect to find the likes of brawn, ox tongue fritters and devilled kidneys alongside stews and shepherd's pie in winter, followed by proper puddings, not desserts. But be sure to have lamb or beef dripping on toast as a pre-starter – it'll leave you licking your lips for the next few hours. The exposed brick walls, zinc-topped tables and old school chairs work very well and the atmosphere is fun without ever becoming too excitable. The terrific prices entice in plenty of passers-by.

York & Albany

modern

G2

Camden Town

127-129 Parkway ✉ NW1 7PS
✆ (020) 7388 3344
www.gordonramsay.com/yorkandalbany
⊖ Camden Town
Booking essential

Menu £22 (weekday lunch) – Carte £28/50

These days things are more egalitarian down at the York & Albany, a handsome 1820s John Nash coaching inn rescued by Gordon Ramsay after lying virtually derelict for years. Gone is the separation of bar and restaurant dining – you are now offered the same menu wherever you want to sit, whether that's in the bar, the back restaurant or downstairs next to the open kitchen. The menu has also been made a little more inclusive and now includes wood-fired pizzas and pasta dishes alongside more adventurous choices like lamb shoulder with braised celery and duck with hispi cabbage. It works well because the kitchen treats a burger with the same respect as they do a rib-eye steak, although service can still wobble at times. The bedrooms have character.

Shayona

Indian

E2

Church End

54-62 Meadow Garth ✉ NW10 8HD

✆ (020) 8965 3365

www.shayonarestaurants.com

⊖ Stonebridge Park

Closed 1 November and 25 December

Menu £8 (weekday lunch) – Carte approx. £17

Shayona sits in the shadow of Neasden's remarkable Shri Swaminarayan Mandir and is actually owned by the temple. In contrast to the splendour of this Hindu gem, the restaurant is housed within a building that looks, from the outside, a little like a supermarket and indeed somewhat resembles one from the inside too — but head past the sweet counter and you'll find yourself in a comfortable and vibrantly decorated room. The fresh, balanced cooking here is sattvic which means it is vegetarian and 'pure' and so avoids certain foods like onion or garlic. The large and varied menu covers all parts of India and includes curries from the north, dosas from the south and street snacks from Mumbai. There is no alcohol available so choose a refreshing lassi instead.

Bistro Aix

French

H1

Crouch End

54 Topsfield Par, Tottenham Ln ✉ N8 8PT

✆ (020) 8340 6346

www.bistroaix.co.uk

Closed 1 January

Menu £12/15 – Carte £24/45

Bistro Aix has enough local followers that it doesn't need to entice passers-by, which is just as well as there aren't usually too many boulevardiers wandering Tottenham Lane in search of duck confit. It's easy to see why Crouch Enders have taken the bistro to their hearts: the French food is unfussy and dependable, the surroundings are rustic and relaxed, the wine list is competitively priced and the atmosphere welcoming. The menu offers bags of choice, with around 20 starters and just as many main courses, and the kitchen does the classics, like snails, onion soup, rabbit with mustard, and tart Tatin, particularly well. There is the added attraction of a very appealingly priced set menu on Tuesday to Thursday and Sunday evenings.

Bull & Last

British traditional

Dartmouth Park

G2

168 Highgate Rd ✉ NW5 1QS
✆ (020) 7267 3641
www.thebullandlast.co.uk
⊖ Tufnell Park
Closed 24-25 December – booking essential

Carte £22/44

Dartmouth Park locals know a good thing when they see it and The Bull and Last, always full of character and life, is most certainly a good thing. If you haven't booked, it's still worth trying your luck as they keep the odd table back – mind you, with enticing bar snacks like pig's trotter wontons and soft shell crab tempura, you may simply find happiness at the bar ordering some of these to go with your pint. The cooking is gloriously robust and generous and the menu mainly British with some pasta dishes thrown in. The kitchen knows its way around an animal too – the charcuterie boards are very popular. Puds are traditional; cheese is in good order and the homemade ice creams are good. And where else can you get marrowbone for your dog?

Clissold Arms

modern

Fortis Green

G1

105 Fortis Green ✉ N2 9HR
✆ (020) 8444 4224
www.clissoldarms.co.uk
⊖ East Finchley

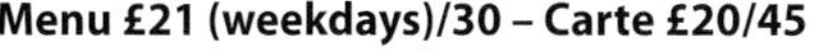

Menu £21 (weekdays)/30 – Carte £20/45

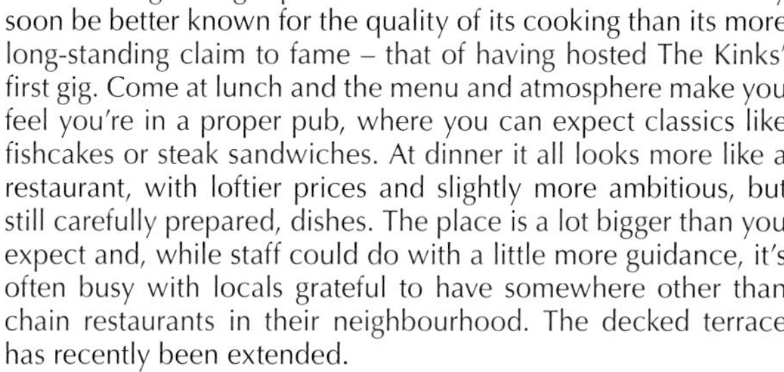

Such is the growing reputation of The Clissold Arms that it may soon be better known for the quality of its cooking than its more long-standing claim to fame – that of having hosted The Kinks' first gig. Come at lunch and the menu and atmosphere make you feel you're in a proper pub, where you can expect classics like fishcakes or steak sandwiches. At dinner it all looks more like a restaurant, with loftier prices and slightly more ambitious, but still carefully prepared, dishes. The place is a lot bigger than you expect and, while staff could do with a little more guidance, it's often busy with locals grateful to have somewhere other than chain restaurants in their neighbourhood. The decked terrace has recently been extended.

Wells

British modern G2

Hampstead
30 Well Walk ✉ NW3 1BX
✆ (020) 7794 3785
www.thewellshampstead.co.uk
⊖ Hampstead

Carte £22/40

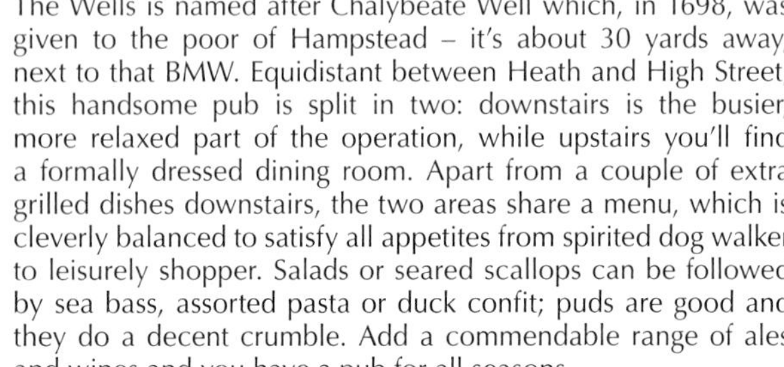

The Wells is named after Chalybeate Well which, in 1698, was given to the poor of Hampstead – it's about 30 yards away, next to that BMW. Equidistant between Heath and High Street, this handsome pub is split in two: downstairs is the busier, more relaxed part of the operation, while upstairs you'll find a formally dressed dining room. Apart from a couple of extra grilled dishes downstairs, the two areas share a menu, which is cleverly balanced to satisfy all appetites from spirited dog walker to leisurely shopper. Salads or seared scallops can be followed by sea bass, assorted pasta or duck confit; puds are good and they do a decent crumble. Add a commendable range of ales and wines and you have a pub for all seasons.

Paradise by way of Kensal Green

British modern F2

Kensal Green
19 Kilburn Ln ✉ W10 4AE
✆ (020) 8969 0098
www.theparadise.co.uk
⊖ Kensal Green
(dinner only and lunch Saturday and Sunday)

Carte £26/31

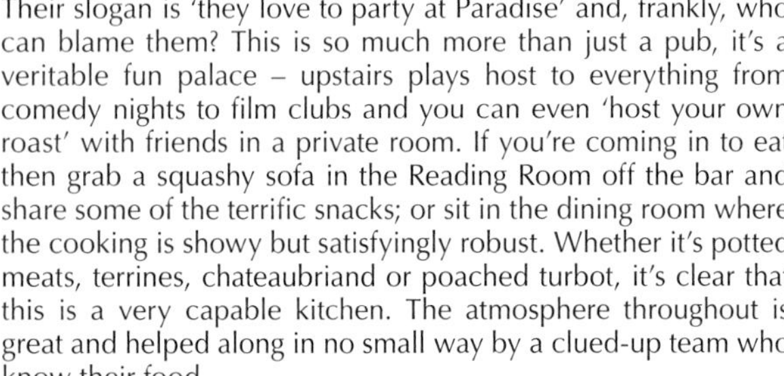

Their slogan is 'they love to party at Paradise' and, frankly, who can blame them? This is so much more than just a pub, it's a veritable fun palace – upstairs plays host to everything from comedy nights to film clubs and you can even 'host your own roast' with friends in a private room. If you're coming in to eat then grab a squashy sofa in the Reading Room off the bar and share some of the terrific snacks; or sit in the dining room where the cooking is showy but satisfyingly robust. Whether it's potted meats, terrines, chateaubriand or poached turbot, it's clear that this is a very capable kitchen. The atmosphere throughout is great and helped along in no small way by a clued-up team who know their food.

Chicken Shop

meats and grills

G2

Kentish Town

79 Highgate Rd ✉ NW5 1TL

✆ (020) 3310 2020 – **www**.chickenshop.com

⊖ Kentish Town

Closed Sunday – bookings not accepted – (dinner only and lunch Saturday-Sunday)

Carte £16/21

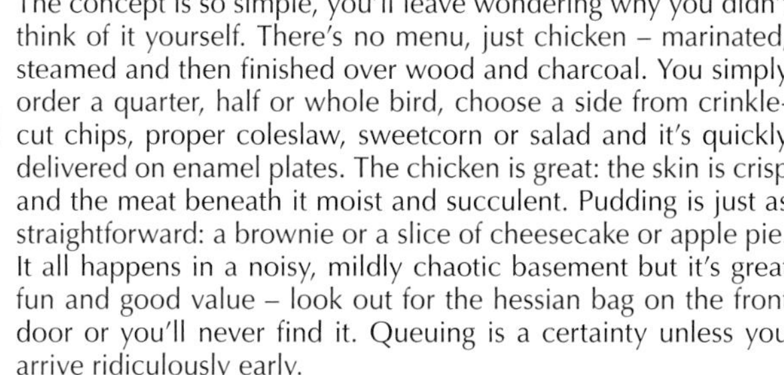

The concept is so simple, you'll leave wondering why you didn't think of it yourself. There's no menu, just chicken – marinated, steamed and then finished over wood and charcoal. You simply order a quarter, half or whole bird, choose a side from crinkle-cut chips, proper coleslaw, sweetcorn or salad and it's quickly delivered on enamel plates. The chicken is great: the skin is crisp and the meat beneath it moist and succulent. Pudding is just as straightforward: a brownie or a slice of cheesecake or apple pie. It all happens in a noisy, mildly chaotic basement but it's great fun and good value – look out for the hessian bag on the front door or you'll never find it. Queuing is a certainty unless you arrive ridiculously early.

Caravan

other world kitchens

H2

King's Cross St Pancras

The Granary Building, 1 Granary Sq. ✉ N1C 4AA

✆ (020) 7101 7661

www.caravankingscross.co.uk

⊖ King's Cross St Pancras

Closed Christmas-New Year – booking essential

Carte £23/31

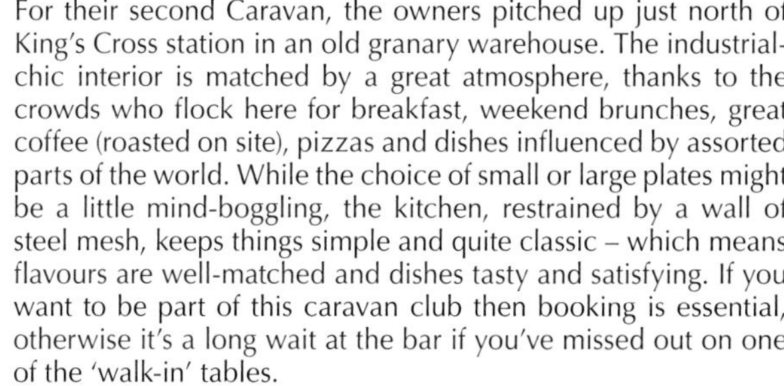

For their second Caravan, the owners pitched up just north of King's Cross station in an old granary warehouse. The industrial-chic interior is matched by a great atmosphere, thanks to the crowds who flock here for breakfast, weekend brunches, great coffee (roasted on site), pizzas and dishes influenced by assorted parts of the world. While the choice of small or large plates might be a little mind-boggling, the kitchen, restrained by a wall of steel mesh, keeps things simple and quite classic – which means flavours are well-matched and dishes tasty and satisfying. If you want to be part of this caravan club then booking is essential, otherwise it's a long wait at the bar if you've missed out on one of the 'walk-in' tables.

Fellow

modern

H2

King's Cross St Pancras

24 York Way ✉ N1 9AA

✆ (020) 7833 4395

www.thefellow.co.uk

⊖ King's Cross St Pancras

Carte £19/34

It was just a matter of time before a few decent pubs opened around the rapidly developing area of King's Cross. The Fellow is one of the busiest, attracting a youthful and local clientele; it also manages to give the impression it's been here for years. Eating happens on the dark and atmospheric ground floor, with drinkers heading upstairs to the even more boisterous cocktail bar. The menu is quite a sophisticated little number but the kitchen is up to the task. Start with ham hock terrine or potted crab, followed by roast rump of lamb or grilled haddock with champ. Desserts such as apple tart display a lightness of touch. The serving team are a bright, capable bunch. There is an outdoor terrace but you'll be surrounded by smokers.

Gilbert Scott

British traditional

H2/3

King's Cross St Pancras

St Pancras Renaissance Hotel,
Euston Rd ✉ NW1 2AR

✆ (020) 7278 3888

www.thegilbertscott.co.uk

⊖ King's Cross St Pancras

Menu £21 (weekdays), £27/27 – Carte £26/58

Britain's less than stellar reputation for the quality of its food won't change until more people come and see what's cooking in our kitchens, so snaring those tourists as soon as they step off the Eurostar is no bad thing. Run under the aegis of Marcus Wareing and named after the architect who designed this Gothic masterpiece of a hotel in 1873, the restaurant has the splendour of a Grand Salon but the buzz of a busy brasserie. More significantly, the kitchen celebrates our culinary heritage by trumpeting both our native produce and regional specialities. In amongst the Eccles cakes, Manchester tart, Cullen skink and Glamorgan sausages are also dishes like 'soles in coffins' and 'Tweed kettle' that prove someone's done some research.

Grain Store

modern

King's Cross St Pancras

H2

Granary Sq, 1-3 Stable St ✉ N1C 4AB
✆ (020) 7324 4466
www.grainstore.com
⊖ King's Cross St Pancras
Closed 24-25 December, 1 January and Sunday dinner

Menu £35 (dinner) – Carte £24/29

The redevelopment of King's Cross may be far from finished, yet already train travellers and locals have a wealth of eating places close by. Grain Store is a big, buzzing 'canteen' from Bruno Loubet and the people behind the Zetter hotel, so you know it's going to be run properly. However, don't come expecting the same style of cooking – here it's about bringing together Bruno's experiences from around the world. On offer is an exciting array of eclectic, well-priced dishes that show thought, imagination and intelligence; they're packed with interesting tastes and textures, and vegetables often take the principle role. Sustainability and seasonality are more than mere buzz words here and the large kitchen rightly takes centre stage.

Plum + Spilt Milk

British modern

King's Cross St Pancras

H2

Great Northern Hotel London,
Pancras Rd ✉ N1C 4TB
✆ (020) 3388 0818
www.plumandspiltmilk.com
⊖ Kings Cross St Pancras

Carte £25/40

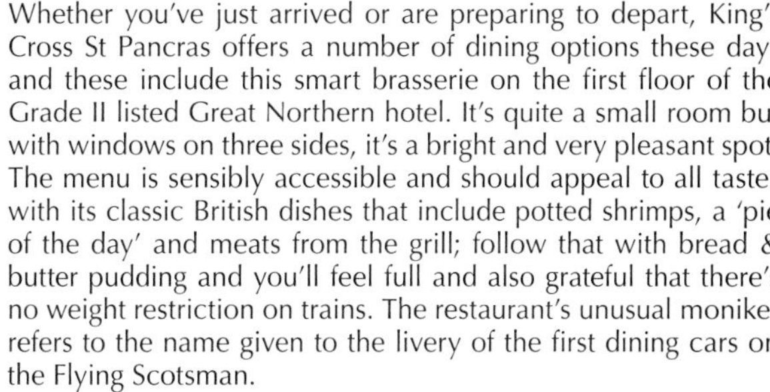

Whether you've just arrived or are preparing to depart, King's Cross St Pancras offers a number of dining options these days and these include this smart brasserie on the first floor of the Grade II listed Great Northern hotel. It's quite a small room but with windows on three sides, it's a bright and very pleasant spot. The menu is sensibly accessible and should appeal to all tastes with its classic British dishes that include potted shrimps, a 'pie of the day' and meats from the grill; follow that with bread & butter pudding and you'll feel full and also grateful that there's no weight restriction on trains. The restaurant's unusual moniker refers to the name given to the livery of the first dining cars on the Flying Scotsman.

Shrimpy's

other world kitchens H2

King's Cross St Pancras

The King's Cross Filling Station, Goods Way ✉ N1C 4UR
✆ (020) 8880 6111
www.shrimpys.co.uk
⊖ King's Cross St. Pancras
Closed Christmas – booking essential

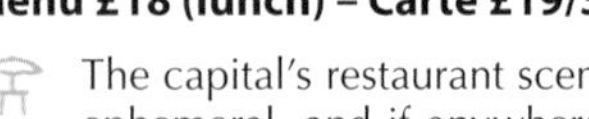

Menu £18 (lunch) – Carte £19/35

The capital's restaurant scene is fast moving, thrilling, witty and ephemeral, and if anywhere represents the zeitgeist it must be this old petrol station in the huge regeneration project behind St Pancras and King's Cross stations. The site is shrouded in a fibreglass hoarding, there are no signs and in a couple of years it will have turned into flats. Until then, the old garage shop has 14 tables squeezed into it; they are clad, ironically, in linen and staff wear crisp white jackets. The menu is California meets Latin America; chipotle, chicharrón, chimichurri and ceviche all feature and there's plenty of deep frying going on. The soft shell crab burger is the speciality; the cocktails are terrific and the whole thing is enormous fun.

L'Absinthe

French 

Primrose Hill

40 Chalcot Rd ✉ NW1 8LS
✆ (020) 7483 4848
www.labsinthe.co.uk
⊖ Chalk Farm
Closed August and Christmas

Menu £9/20 – Carte £20/37

L'Absinthe has succeeded on a site where so many tried and failed because it gives the locals exactly what they have clearly always wanted: a classic French bistro run with integrity and enthusiasm. It offers the sort of food that really hits the spot at the end of a working day: beef bourguignon, duck confit, steak frites or some fresh skate, with a crème brûlée to follow. The place has an authentic Gallic air too, with its Belle Époque posters and staff who are either French or can at least do a convincing accent. Don't be put off if they give you a table downstairs – even if you are the first down there, it'll soon fill up with regulars. The other great strength is the wine list: the owner merely charges corkage on the retail price.

Ⓝ Michael Nadra Primrose Hill

modern

G2

Primrose Hill

42 Gloucester Ave ✉ NW1 8JD

☎ (020) 7722 2800

www.restaurant-michaelnadra.co.uk/primrose

⊖ Camden Town

Closed 24-28 December and 1 January

Menu £15 – Carte £32/47

When you have a successful restaurant in Chiswick, opening a second branch in Primrose Hill would suggest that not only have you recognised similarities between the two neighbourhoods but also that you know a pretty decent shortcut to get you across town. Michael Nadra took over the old Sardo Canale premises in 2012; it's a modern space which comes with lots of glass, judicious lighting, a pleasant terrace and comfortable bar which offers a selection of over 20 martinis. His menu closely resembles the one in Chiswick, which means that flavours from the Mediterranean feature widely but he's not averse to introducing the occasional Asian accent and his cooking shows a careful hand when balancing flavours.

Odette's

modern

G2

Primrose Hill

130 Regent's Park Rd. ✉ NW1 8XL

☎ (020) 7586 8569

www.odettesprimrosehill.com

⊖ Chalk Farm

Closed 25-27 December and 1 January

Menu £15 (weekday lunch)/20 – Carte £28/37

It's amazing what a window can do: they installed a big one at the front of the restaurant and it opened the whole place up and made it feel far more welcoming. Locals used to regard Odette's as being a little bit standoffish but service is now a lot chattier and the atmosphere more relaxed, which in turn makes it feel more a part of the community. The cooking is also a little less complicated than it was and is all the better for it, although there is still depth to the dishes. Flavours are robust and braised dishes a highlight; the chef-owner also displays a passion for his Welsh roots. The lunch and early evening menus are a steal and change every fortnight; there are also tasting and vegetarian menus alongside the à la carte.

Salusbury

Italian

F2

Queens Park

50-52 Salusbury Rd ✉ NW6 6NN

✆ (020) 7328 3286

www.thesalusbury.co.uk

⊖ Queen's Park

Closed 25 December – booking essential

Menu £25/40 – Carte £19/35

When your local pub is owned by someone with a passion for Italian food and reggae then you know it's going to be somewhere a little different. The central bar is the demarcation point: the louche turn left for loud music and a dimly lit bar; the hungry head for the incongruously demure looking dining room on the right. There's an impressive degree of authenticity to the Italian cooking; try one of the tasty salads like black radish with pomegranate and pecorino then go for their classic pappardelle with duck ragu. There are more fish dishes on the menu these days but what hasn't changed is portion size – you'll never reach dessert. If, however, you think you may be hungry again one day then call in at their well-stocked foodstore next door.

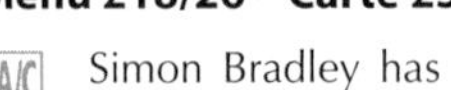

Bradley's

modern

G2

Swiss Cottage

25 Winchester Rd. ✉ NW3 3NR

✆ (020) 7722 3457

www.bradleysnw3.co.uk

⊖ Swiss Cottage

Closed Sunday dinner

Menu £18/26 – Carte £32/40

Simon Bradley has been steadily going about his business for nigh on 20 years and has engendered such loyalty in his regulars that many of them wouldn't countenance a visit to a competitor until it had been going for at least a couple of years. Whilst there is an appealing and nicely balanced à la carte, the real draw here are the very well priced set menus. This affordability is achieved by proper 'cheffing' such as braising beef and buying less fashionable and underused fish like ling to create dishes with clear, complementary flavours. Simon is also a proper neighbourhood restaurateur: he can often be found at the local farmers' market and is now also responsible for the catering at the splendid Hampstead Theatre around the corner.

Eriki

Indian

Swiss Cottage

G2

4-6 Northways Par, Finchley Rd ✉ NW3 5EN
✆ (020) 7722 0606
www.eriki.co.uk
⊖ Swiss Cottage

Menu £8/30 – Carte approx. £25

Eriki eschews tired old standards and instead offers a diverse and contrasting gastronomic tour around all parts of India, from Goan curries to Punjabi-style prawns, Hariyali scallops to Lucknowi lamb. The cooking is fresh and invigorating; vegetarians will be in clover and the breads are good. The cutlery is imported from Rajasthan and the carved tables and heavy chairs add a sense of permanence. The staff are a pleasant bunch, although this vibrantly coloured restaurant can go from quiet to full in a matter of moments so get your order in quickly. Eriki is so much more than your typical neighbourhood Indian restaurant, a fact not lost on its many regulars. The only negative is the less than inspiring view of drab old Finchley Road.

Singapore Garden

Asian

Swiss Cottage

G2

83 Fairfax Rd. ✉ NW6 4DY
✆ (020) 7328 5314
www.singaporegarden.co.uk
⊖ Swiss Cottage
Closed 24-28 December

Menu £30 (dinner) – Carte £21/52

Avoid the more generic dishes on the menu at this long-standing Swiss Cottage favourite and head instead to the back page of Singaporean and Malaysian specialities or to the separate list of seasonal dishes such as the 'grandma pork belly'. Squid blachan with sugar snap peas and plenty of chilli is a fresh and fiery number; Chiew Yim soft shell crab is full of flavour and Daging curry of tender beef and coconut is satisfying and filling. The staff are a happy and helpful lot; its female members wear traditional costumes, their male counterparts, bow ties. The room is comfortable and the clientele are a smart and mature bunch. The moped-riders keeping warm outside testify to its popularity in the local home delivery market too.

Sushi-Say

Japanese F2

Willesden Green

33B Walm Ln. ✉ NW2 5SH

✆ (020) 8459 2971

⊖ Willesden Green

Closed, 25-26 December, Wednesday after bank holidays, Monday and Tuesday – (dinner only and lunch Saturday-Sunday)

Menu £29/48 – Carte £18/58

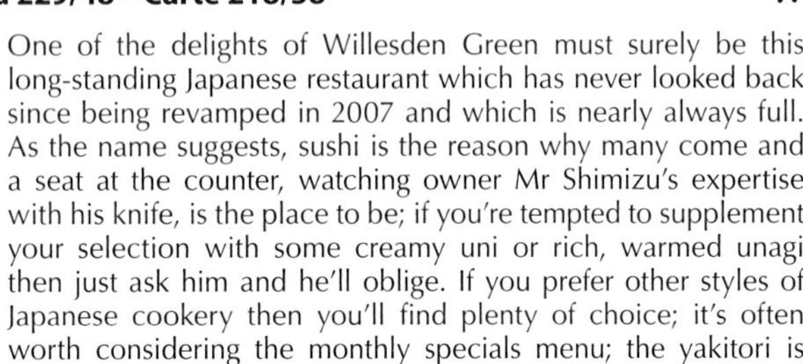

One of the delights of Willesden Green must surely be this long-standing Japanese restaurant which has never looked back since being revamped in 2007 and which is nearly always full. As the name suggests, sushi is the reason why many come and a seat at the counter, watching owner Mr Shimizu's expertise with his knife, is the place to be; if you're tempted to supplement your selection with some creamy uni or rich, warmed unagi then just ask him and he'll oblige. If you prefer other styles of Japanese cookery then you'll find plenty of choice; it's often worth considering the monthly specials menu; the yakitori is particularly good and there's a well-priced selection of sake and shochu. Mrs Shimizu leads her team with alacrity and efficiency.

Look out for **red** symbols, indicating a particularly pleasant ambiance.

SuperStock/Age Fotostock

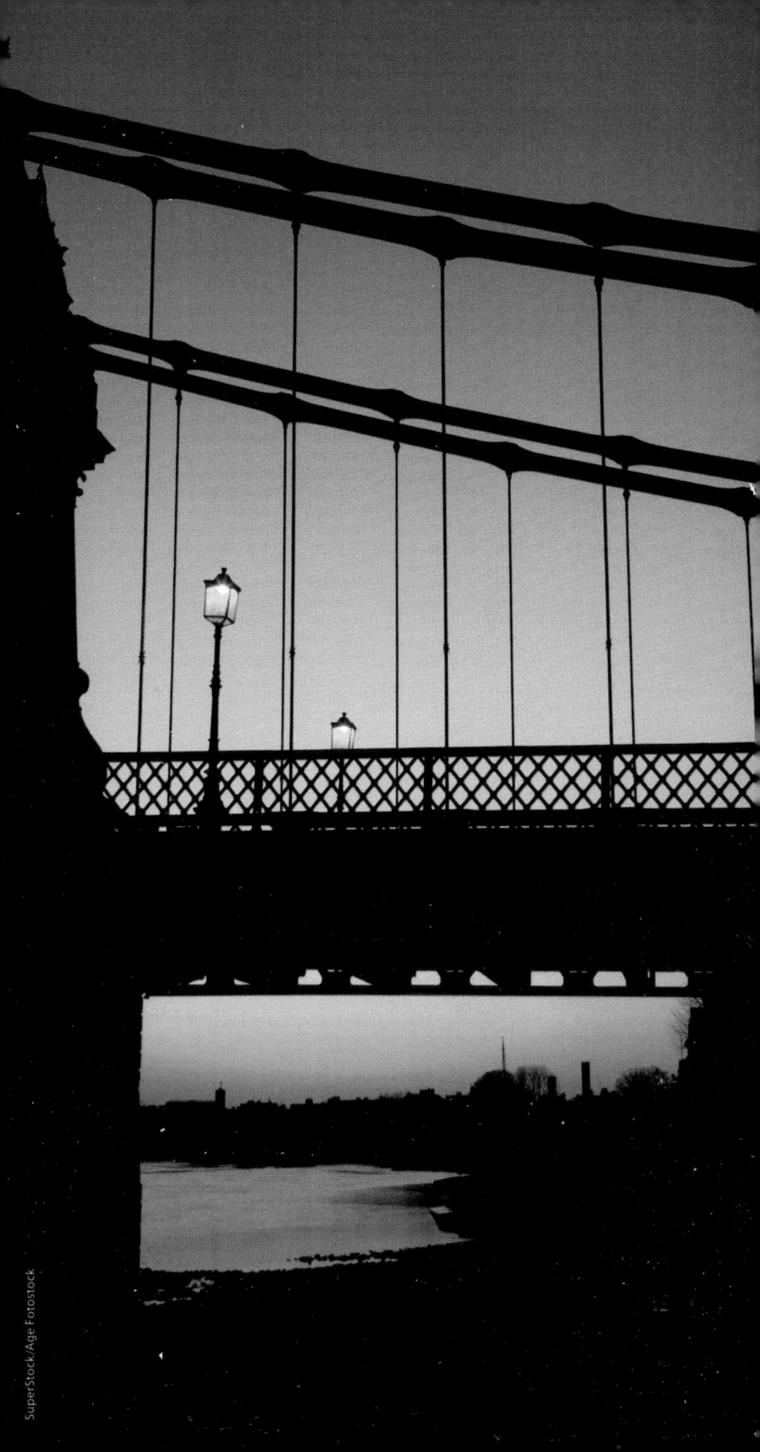

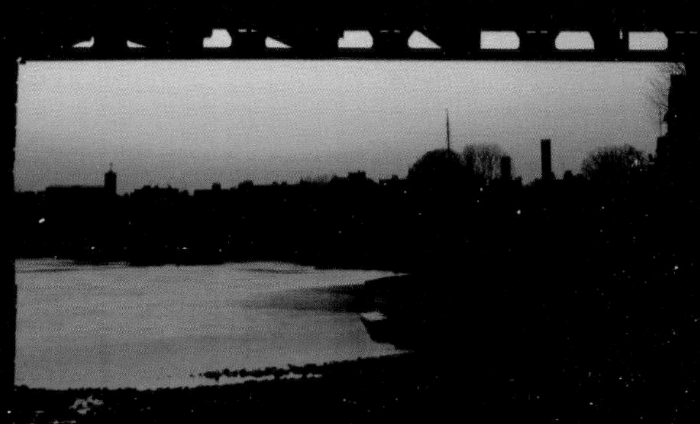

North-East London

If northwest London is renowned for its leafy acres, then the area to its immediate east has a more urban, brick-built appeal. Which has meant, over the last decade or so, a wholesale rebranding exercise for some of its traditionally shady localities. A generation ago it would have been beyond the remit of even the most inventive estate agent to sell the charms of Islington, Hackney or Bethnal Green. But then along came Damien Hirst, Tracey Emin et al, and before you could say 'cow in formaldehyde' the area's cachet had rocketed.

Shoreditch and **Hoxton** are the pivotal points of the region's hip makeover. Their cobbled brick streets and shabby industrial remnants were like heavenly manna to the artists and designers who started to colonise the old warehouses twenty years ago. A fashionable crowd soon followed in their footsteps, and nowadays the area around **Hoxton Square** positively teems with clubs, bars and galleries. Latest must-see space is Rivington Place, a terrific gallery that highlights visual arts from around the world. Nearby are Deluxe (digital installations), and Hales (galleries).

Before the area was ever trendy, there was the Geffrye Museum. A short stroll up Hoxton's **Kingsland Road,** it's a jewel of a place, set in elegant 18C almshouses, and depicting English middle-class interiors from 1600 to the present day. Right behind it is St. Mary's Secret Garden, a little oasis that manages to include much diversity including a separate woodland and herb area, all in less than an acre. At the southern end of the area, in Folgate Street, Dennis Severs' House is an original Huguenot home that recreates 18 and 19C life in an original way – cooking smells linger, hearth and candles burn, giving you the impression the owners have only just left the place. Upstairs the beds remain unmade: did a certain local artist pick up any ideas here?

When the Regent's Canal was built in the early 19C, **Islington's** fortunes nose-dived, for it was accompanied by the arrival of slums and over-crowding. But the once-idyllic village managed to hold onto its Georgian squares and handsome Victorian terraces through the rough times, and when these were gentrified a few years ago, the area ushered in a revival. **Camden Passage** has long been famed for its quirky antique emporiums, while the slinky Business Design Centre is a flagship of the modern Islington. Cultural icons established themselves around the Upper Street area and these have gone from strength to strength. The **Almeida** Theatre has a habit of hitting the production jackpot with its history of world premieres, while the King's Head has earned itself a reputation for raucous scene-stealing; set up in the seventies, it's also London's very first theatre-pub. Nearby, the Screen on the Green boasts a wonderful old-fashioned neon billboard.

C. Eymenier / MICHELIN

Even in the 'bad old days', Islington drew in famous names, and at Regency smart **Canonbury Square** are the one-time homes of Evelyn Waugh (no.17A) and George Orwell (no.27). These days it houses the Estorick Collection of Modern Italian Art; come here to see fine futuristic paintings in a Georgian villa. To put the history of the area in a proper context, head to St. John Street, south of the City Road, where the Islington Museum's shiny new headquarters tells the story of a colourful and multi-layered past.

Further up the A10, you come to **Dalston,** a bit like the Islington of old but with the buzzy Ridley Road market and a vibrant all-night scene including the blistering Vortex Jazz Club just off Kingsland Road. A little further north is **Stoke Newington,** referred to, a bit unkindly, as the poor man's Islington. Its pride and joy is Church Street, which not only features some characterful bookshops and eye-catching boutiques, but also lays claim to Abney Park Cemetery, an enchanting old place with a wildlife-rich nature reserve.

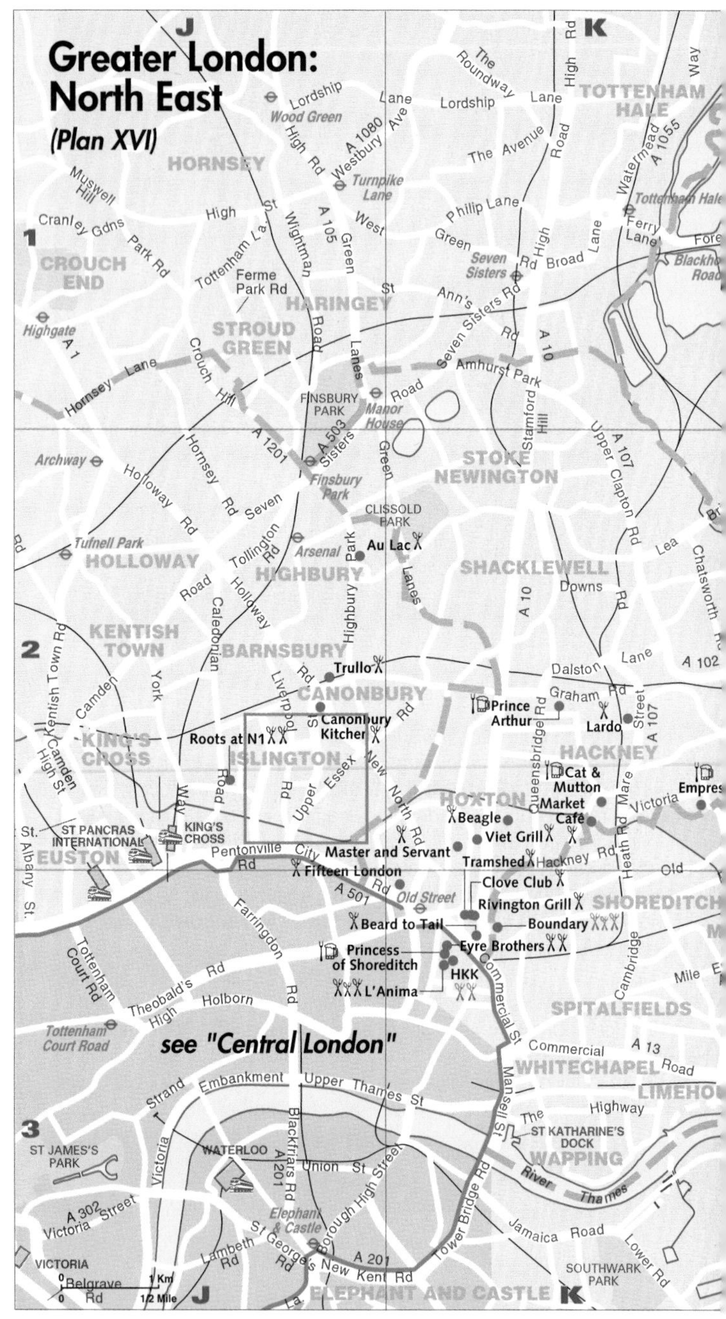
Greater London: North East
(Plan XVI)
J
K
1
2
3
HORNSEY
CROUCH END
Highgate
Wood Green
Turnpike Lane
TOTTENHAM HALE
Tottenham Hale
HARINGEY
STROUD GREEN
Seven Sisters
FINSBURY PARK
Manor House
Archway
Finsbury Park
STOKE NEWINGTON
CLISSOLD PARK
Tufnell Park
HOLLOWAY
Arsenal
HIGHBURY
SHACKLEWELL
KENTISH TOWN
BARNSBURY
CANONBURY
KING'S CROSS
ISLINGTON
HACKNEY
HOXTON
ST PANCRAS INTERNATIONAL
KING'S CROSS
EUSTON
Old Street
SHOREDITCH
SPITALFIELDS
Tottenham Court Road
WHITECHAPEL
LIMEHOUSE
ST KATHARINE'S DOCK
WAPPING
ST JAMES'S PARK
WATERLOO
Elephant & Castle
VICTORIA
SOUTHWARK PARK
ELEPHANT AND CASTLE
River Thames
Au Lac
Trullo
Prince Arthur
Lardo
Canonbury Kitchen
Roots at N1
Cat & Mutton
Market Café
Empress
Beagle
Viet Grill
Master and Servant
Tramshed
Fifteen London
Clove Club
Rivington Grill
Boundary
Beard to Tail
Eyre Brothers
Princess of Shoreditch
HKK
L'Anima
see "Central London"
0 1 Km
0 1/2 Mile

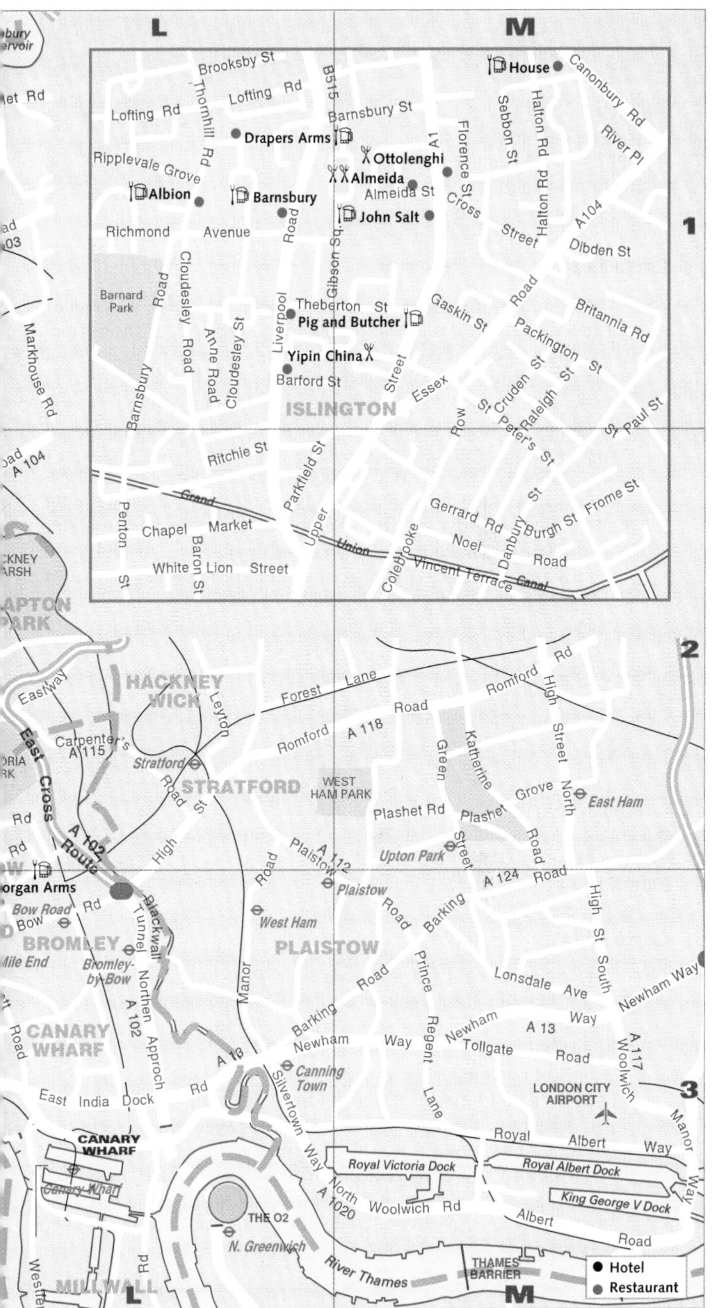
L
M
House
Drapers Arms
Ottolenghi
Almeida
Albion
Barnsbury
John Salt
Pig and Butcher
Yipin China
ISLINGTON
Barnard Park
Brooksby St
Lofting Rd
Thornhill Rd
Barnsbury St
Ripplevale Grove
Richmond Avenue
Almeida St
Canonbury Rd
River Pl
Sebbon St
Halton Rd
Florence St
Cross Street
Dibden St
Gaskin St
Britannia Rd
Packington St
Theberton St
Barford St
Liverpool Road
Gibson Sq.
B515
A1
A104
Cloudesley Road
Anne Road
Cloudesley St
Barnsbury Road
Essex Road
Ritchie St
Parkfield St
Penton St
Chapel Market
White Lion Street
Baron St
Upper Street
Grand Union Canal
Colebrooke Row
Vincent Terrace
Noel Road
Gerrard Rd
Danbury St
Burgh St
Frome St
St Peter's St
Cruden St
Raleigh St
St Paul St
Markhouse Rd
A 104
1
2
3
HACKNEY WICK
STRATFORD
WEST HAM PARK
PLAISTOW
BROMLEY
CANARY WHARF
MILLWALL
Eastway
East Cross Route
A 102
Carpenter's
A 115
Stratford
Leyton Road
Forest Lane
Romford Road
A 118
Romford Rd
High Street North
Green Street
Katherine Road
Plashet Rd
Plashet Grove
East Ham
Upton Park
Plaistow Road
A 112
Plaistow
West Ham
A 124
Barking Road
High St South
Lonsdale Ave
Newham Way
A 13
Prince Regent Lane
Tollgate Road
Manor Road
Blackwall Tunnel Northern Approch
A 102
Bow Road
Bow
Bromley-by-Bow
Mile End
Morgan Arms
East India Dock Rd
Canning Town
Silvertown Way
North Woolwich Rd
A 1020
LONDON CITY AIRPORT
A 117
Woolwich
Royal Albert Way
Manor Way
Royal Victoria Dock
Royal Albert Dock
King George V Dock
Albert Road
THE O2
N. Greenwich
River Thames
THAMES BARRIER
Canary Wharf
Hotel
Restaurant

Roots at N1

Indian

J2

Barnsbury

115 Hemingford Rd ✉ N1 1BZ

✆ (020) 7697 4488 – **www**.rootsatn1.com

⊖ Caledonian Road

Closed 25-26 December, 1 January and Monday – booking essential – (dinner only and Sunday lunch)

Carte £22/34

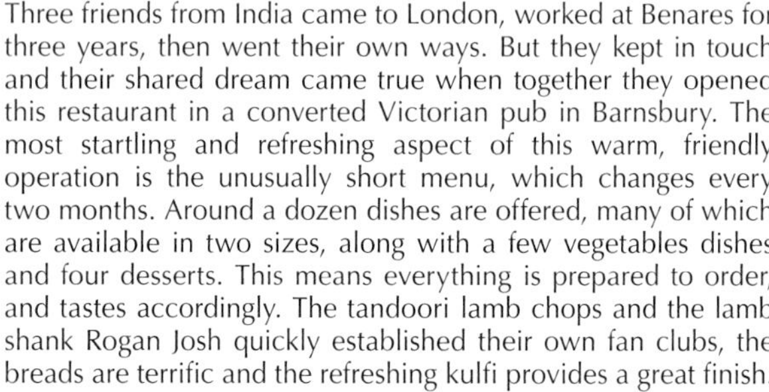

Three friends from India came to London, worked at Benares for three years, then went their own ways. But they kept in touch and their shared dream came true when together they opened this restaurant in a converted Victorian pub in Barnsbury. The most startling and refreshing aspect of this warm, friendly operation is the unusually short menu, which changes every two months. Around a dozen dishes are offered, many of which are available in two sizes, along with a few vegetables dishes and four desserts. This means everything is prepared to order, and tastes accordingly. The tandoori lamb chops and the lamb shank Rogan Josh quickly established their own fan clubs, the breads are terrific and the refreshing kulfi provides a great finish.

Morgan Arms

British traditional

L3

Bow

43 Morgan St ✉ E3 5AA

✆ (020) 8980 6389

www.capitalpubcompany.com/The-Morgan-Arms

⊖ Bow Road

Closed 25 December

Carte £21/32

This former boozer's clever makeover respects its heritage while simultaneously bringing it up to date. The bar's always busy while the dining area is more subdued. You'll find the kitchen keeps its influences mostly within Europe but also understands just what sort of food works well in a pub. The daily changing menu usually features pasta in some form and staples like whitebait - which come devilled in this instance - assorted tarts and the perennial favourite, fishcakes accompanied by a poached egg. What's more, prices are kept at realistic levels which makes this pub appealing to those who live nearby and who like a little spontaneity in their lives. Look out for the occasional themed evening and charity auction.

Canonbury Kitchen

Italian

J2 

Canonbury

19 Canonbury Ln ✉ N1 2AS
✆ (0207) 2269 791
www.canonburykitchen.com
⊖ Highbury & Islington
Closed Sunday dinner – (dinner only and lunch Saturday-Sunday)

Menu £12 – Carte £24/35 

Inserting the word 'kitchen' into the name of one's restaurant is becoming more and more common as it instantly evokes images of simple food and unpretentious dining. That certainly applies to Canonbury Kitchen, which comes with an appropriately light, fresh look, thanks to its exposed brick walls, high ceiling and painted floorboards. With seating for just forty it also feels like the very epitome of a neighbourhood restaurant. Owner Max and his team provide gently reassuring service and the kitchen – on-view at the far end – sensibly keeps things simple. That includes an ever-popular fritto misto made with cuttlefish and octopus, pan-fried hake with herbs, and a lemon tiramisu with limoncello replacing the marsala.

House

modern

M1 

Canonbury

63-69 Canonbury Rd ✉ N1 2DG
✆ (020) 7704 7410
www.thehouse.islington.com
⊖ Highbury & Islington
Closed Monday except bank holidays

Menu £30 (weekdays)/38 – Carte £23/35

A couple of tables on the pavement does not a terrace make – if you want to see the Real McCoy then come to The House with its umbrellas, marble-topped tables, hedges and heaters. Inside it pretty nice too, with one side given over to the drinkers, the other laid out in a bistro-style. An intimate atmosphere married with a laid back, friendly vibe adds to the appeal. Pubs classics and more contemporary creations jostle for supremacy but are done equally well; their spelt pizzas are proving very popular – aimed at children but largely hijacked by adults. Breakfast and brunch are offered at weekends but the pub also hosts wedding receptions for those who've got hitched at the Town Hall down the road, so check first.

Trullo

Italian J2

Canonbury

300-302 St Paul's Rd ✉ N1 2LH

(020) 7226 2733

www.trullorestaurant.com

Highbury & Islington

Closed Christmas-New year and Sunday dinner – booking essential

Carte £26/34

The owners' CVs read like a checklist of eateries known for their relaxed atmospheres and uncomplicated cooking, including Moro, St John, and the River Café, so it is no surprise to find delicious Italian cooking here in this friendly restaurant, filled every day with noisily contented diners. The menu, small in size and content, changes daily so don't be surprised when something runs out. Expect great antipasti, such as pumpkin and chilli fritti, as well as flavoursome dishes cooked on the charcoal grill – and all at terrific prices. Trullo is named after the conical-shaped buildings of southern Italy, used primarily by farm workers for meeting and eating, which seems most appropriate for somewhere exuding such contentment.

Cat & Mutton

British traditional K2

Hackney

76 Broadway Mkt ✉ E8 4QJ

(020) 7254 5599

www.catandmutton.co.uk

Bethnal Green

Closed 25-26 December

Carte £20/32

The Cat & Mutton has been a fixture here since the 1700s, when it was a drovers' inn quenching the thirst of farm workers bringing their livestock down from East Anglia. The streets round here might still frighten out-of-towners and the pub may now look a little frayed around the edges but step inside, look past the rough and ready character, and the young staff will make you feel reassuringly welcome. The open kitchen adds a little theatre to proceedings and the relatively concise menu changes often. The cooking is straightforward but is also undertaken with more care than you expect. Their beef is organic and in the evening steaks stand out amongst the more elaborate dishes. It's upstairs for quiz nights and art classes.

Empress

Mediterranean

K2

Hackney

130 Lauriston Rd., Victoria Park ✉ E9 7LH
✆ (020) 8533 5123
www.empresse9.co.uk
⊖ Mile End.

Closed 25 December and Monday lunch except bank holidays

Menu £10 (weekdays) – Carte £23/28

The name of this 1850s pub was changed from the Empress of India as some customers arrived expecting chicken tikka – information which will dishearten history teachers everywhere. Queen Victoria has been demoted to the Empress of E9 but then everything is about being 'local' these days and that includes this re-launched pub. Sourdough comes from the baker down the road and their butcher and fishmonger are within walking distance; the menu is pleasingly seasonal and the cooking is several notches above usual pub fare. Dishes like risotto made with pearl barley and feta, or lamb's liver with lentils demonstrate that this is a kitchen with confidence and ability. Prices are kept in check and Sunday lunch is a very languid affair.

Lardo

Italian

K2

Hackney

197-205 Richmond Rd ✉ E8 3NJ
✆ (020) 8985 2683
www.lardo.co.uk

Carte £16/60

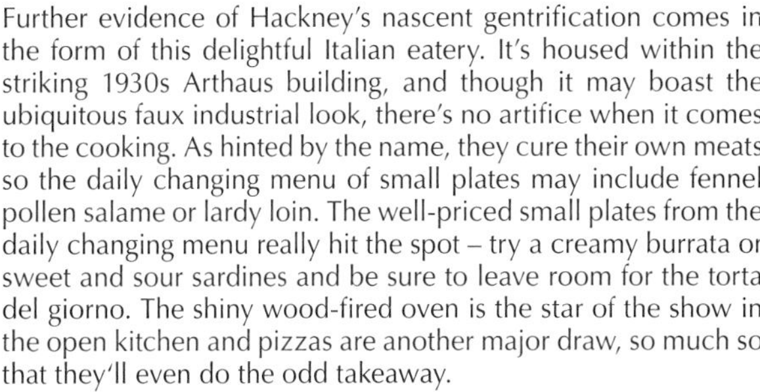

Further evidence of Hackney's nascent gentrification comes in the form of this delightful Italian eatery. It's housed within the striking 1930s Arthaus building, and though it may boast the ubiquitous faux industrial look, there's no artifice when it comes to the cooking. As hinted by the name, they cure their own meats so the daily changing menu of small plates may include fennel pollen salame or lardy loin. The well-priced small plates from the daily changing menu really hit the spot – try a creamy burrata or sweet and sour sardines and be sure to leave room for the torta del giorno. The shiny wood-fired oven is the star of the show in the open kitchen and pizzas are another major draw, so much so that they'll even do the odd takeaway.

Market Cafe

modern

K2

Hackney

2 Broadway Mkt ✉ E8 4QG
(020) 7249 9070
www.market-cafe.co.uk
⊖ Bethnal Green

Closed 25-26 December and 1 January

Carte £22/30

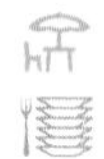

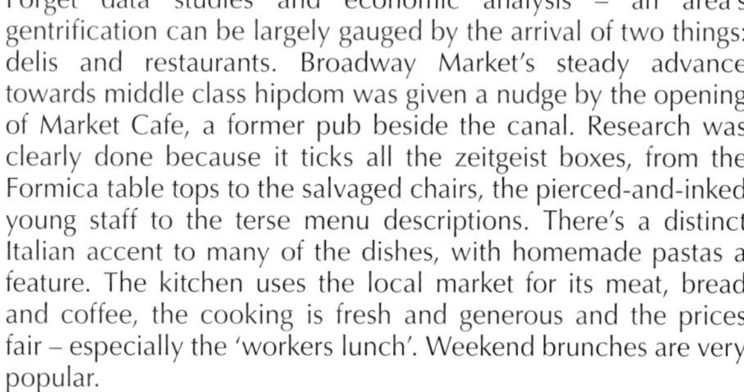

Forget data studies and economic analysis – an area's gentrification can be largely gauged by the arrival of two things: delis and restaurants. Broadway Market's steady advance towards middle class hipdom was given a nudge by the opening of Market Cafe, a former pub beside the canal. Research was clearly done because it ticks all the zeitgeist boxes, from the Formica table tops to the salvaged chairs, the pierced-and-inked young staff to the terse menu descriptions. There's a distinct Italian accent to many of the dishes, with homemade pastas a feature. The kitchen uses the local market for its meat, bread and coffee, the cooking is fresh and generous and the prices fair – especially the 'workers lunch'. Weekend brunches are very popular.

Prince Arthur

British modern

K2

Hackney

95 Forest Rd ✉ E8 3BH
(020) 7249 9996
www.theprincearthurlondonfields.com
⊖ Bethnal Green.

Closed 25 December – (dinner only and lunch Saturday-Sunday)

Carte £25/39

Those who judge by first impressions will probably walk on by as this slightly scruffy corner pub would struggle to entice anyone on looks alone. To be honest, the inside isn't much keener on the eye, apart from the stuffed animals and the postcard collection, but then this isn't about appearances, more about good food and convivial company. Sit anywhere in the U-shaped room and the amiable staff will be quick to come over. The menu reads appealingly: smoked salmon, terrines, fish and chips, sausage and mash – but the cooking is done with unexpected care and more than a little skill; fish from Billingsgate is handled particularly deftly. Just thinking about the deep-fried jam or cherry sandwich for dessert will be enough to seal an artery.

Au Lac

Vietnamese

J2 

Highbury

82 Highbury Park ✉ N5 2XE
✆ (020) 7704 9187 – **www**.aulac.co.uk
⊖ Arsenal

Closed 24-26 December, 1-2 January and 1 week early August – (dinner only and lunch Thursday-Friday)

Carte £11/25 

It's unlikely to ever attract passers-by on its looks alone but fortunately enough people know about this longstanding Vietnamese restaurant, run by two brothers, to ensure that its phone rings red hot most nights. The comforts inside may also be fairly unremarkable but that just allows everyone to focus their attention on the lengthy menu, to which new dishes are added regularly. The pho noodle soup is a favourite but along with the traditional dishes there are plenty of more contemporary creations, all exhibiting the same freshness and lively flavours. The prices are kept honest, especially as the generous portion sizes mean that you don't have to order too many dishes to feel satisfied. They also do a roaring trade in takeaways.

Beagle

British traditional

K2 

Hoxton

397-400 Geffrye St ✉ E2 8HZ
✆ (020) 7613 2967
www.beaglelondon.co.uk
⊖ Hoxton

Closed lunch Monday-Tuesday – booking essential

Carte £23/35

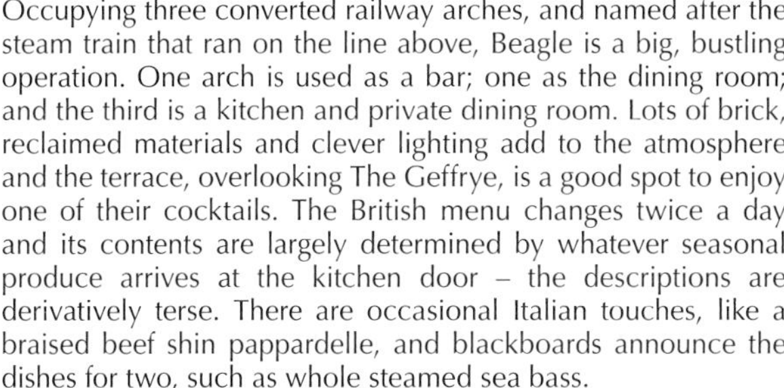

Occupying three converted railway arches, and named after the steam train that ran on the line above, Beagle is a big, bustling operation. One arch is used as a bar; one as the dining room; and the third is a kitchen and private dining room. Lots of brick, reclaimed materials and clever lighting add to the atmosphere and the terrace, overlooking The Geffrye, is a good spot to enjoy one of their cocktails. The British menu changes twice a day and its contents are largely determined by whatever seasonal produce arrives at the kitchen door – the descriptions are derivatively terse. There are occasional Italian touches, like a braised beef shin pappardelle, and blackboards announce the dishes for two, such as whole steamed sea bass.

Fifteen London

modern

K3

Hoxton

15 Westland Pl ✉ N1 7LP

✆ (020) 3375 1515

www.fifteen.net

⊖ Old Street

Closed 25 December – booking essential

Menu £24 (lunch) – Carte £30/46

When it reached its 10th anniversary in 2012, Jamie Oliver's Fifteen got itself a new look and a new style of food – but what didn't change were the principles behind its creation, namely the training and development of youngsters who've faced difficulties in their lives. The focus is now on seasonal British food rather than Italian and the menu is mostly made up of small tasting plates. The cooking certainly has personality and the wood-fired oven is used to good effect, delivering some great flavours. Service is keen and eager; the same menu is offered in both the ground floor restaurant and the livelier, noisier cellar below; and the bar is a great place to come for a cocktail. Fifteen may not come cheap but it's a very worthy cause.

Ⓝ Master & Servant

modern

K2

Hoxton

8-9 Hoxton Sq ✉ N1 6NU

✆ (020) 7729 4626

www.masterandservant.co.uk

⊖ Old Street

Closed 25-27 December and Sunday dinner

Carte £22/34

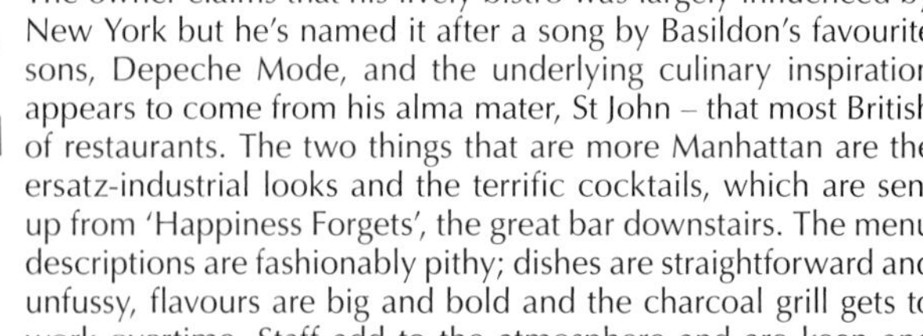

The owner claims that his lively bistro was largely influenced by New York but he's named it after a song by Basildon's favourite sons, Depeche Mode, and the underlying culinary inspiration appears to come from his alma mater, St John – that most British of restaurants. The two things that are more Manhattan are the ersatz-industrial looks and the terrific cocktails, which are sent up from 'Happiness Forgets', the great bar downstairs. The menu descriptions are fashionably pithy; dishes are straightforward and unfussy, flavours are big and bold and the charcoal grill gets to work overtime. Staff add to the atmosphere and are keen and chummy; order half a crab and your waiter may well advise you to "go in hard, like Bear Grylls".

Albion

British traditional

L1

Islington

10 Thornhill Rd ✉ N1 1HW

✆ (020) 7607 7450

www.the-albion.co.uk

⊖ Highbury & Islington

Closed 1 January

Carte £22/38

This Georgian jewel couldn't be better named and it's not just the wisteria-covered façade or the comfortingly worn-in look with its sofas and log fire that bring a patriotic tear to the eye. The menu also has a distinctive British feel with grills and rare breeds taking centre stage; Dexter, Belted Galloway and Longhorn beef all feature, along with Tamworth pork and Romney Salt Marsh lamb. For Sunday lunch expect a whole host of roast meats, and if you have 9 friends and the ability to plan ahead then consider pre-ordering the whole suckling pig. You can eat or drink anywhere – the bar has slightly more buzz than the restaurant. In summer everyone moves out into the walled garden at the back and barbeques become a regular feature.

Almeida

French

M1

Islington

30 Almeida St. ✉ N1 1AD

✆ (020) 7354 4777

www.almeida-restaurant.com

⊖ Angel

Closed 25 December, 1 January, Sunday dinner and Monday lunch

Menu £17 (weekdays)/34 – Carte £33/42

If you're not here for a pre-theatre bite before going to the Almeida theatre opposite then try not to arrive around 7-7.30pm as you'll find yourself in the midst of an almighty exodus which leaves the restaurant in a degree of disarray and the waiters looking shell-shocked. They then dim the lights and take a deep breath but it's usually a while before the atmosphere builds again. Prices at this crisply decorated restaurant are more realistic these days, especially at lunch when the room really benefits from the two large windows. The menu's French influence is a little less pronounced but dishes still use intelligent combinations, like venison with pumpkin and lamb with artichoke. Look out for some interesting regional French wines.

Barnsbury

British traditional K2

Islington
209-211 Liverpool Rd ✉ N1 1LX
✆ (020) 7607 5519
www.thebarnsbury.co.uk
⊖ Highbury & Islington
Closed lunch Monday-Wednesday

Carte £13/22

Apart from a tiresome tendency to change hands every now and again, the Barnsbury still manages to remain a reliable and welcoming local pub. The emphasis here may be more on the bar – beer drinking is given due deference and a blackboard lists the guest beers – but that doesn't stop the pub turning out gutsy and satisfying food for its many regulars. The menu is fairly concise, which allows the kitchen to fully master their repertoire, so there's a reassuring consistency and confidence to the preparation of dishes like pig's cheeks with mustard mash, salmon fishcakes with dill, and apple and rhubarb crumble. Sit at the front in among the drinkers – this is a livelier spot than the small dining area at the back.

Drapers Arms

British modern L1

Islington
44 Barnsbury St ✉ N1 1ER
✆ (020) 7619 0348
www.thedrapersarms.com
⊖ Highbury & Islington
Bookings advisable at dinner

Carte £22/34

Celebrating British cuisine means more than just putting a few old favourites on the menu; it's about making great use of indigenous ingredients and introducing them to a wider audience. At The Drapers Arms those unfamiliar with our own bounteous larder can see humble produce like lamb's tongues, smoked eels, blade steak and rabbit used to create dishes that are satisfying, gutsy and affordable. Locals, or those who find themselves in Islington at midday for whatever reason, can take advantage of their steal of a lunch menu. Just ignore the fact that the staff can be a little too cool for school and simply enjoy the good food, unpretentious atmosphere and shabby chic interior of this busy Georgian pub, with its handsome façade.

John Salt

modern

Islington

131 Upper St. ✉ N1 1QP

✆ (020) 7704 8955

www.john-salt.com

⊖ Angel

Closed 25-26 December and Monday lunch – booking essential

Carte £20/29

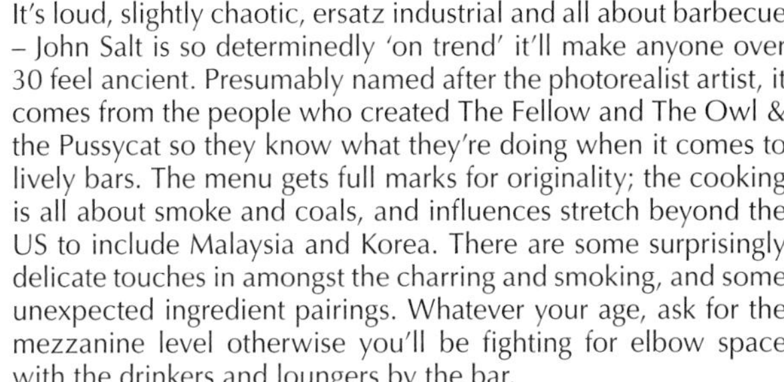

It's loud, slightly chaotic, ersatz industrial and all about barbecue – John Salt is so determinedly 'on trend' it'll make anyone over 30 feel ancient. Presumably named after the photorealist artist, it comes from the people who created The Fellow and The Owl & the Pussycat so they know what they're doing when it comes to lively bars. The menu gets full marks for originality; the cooking is all about smoke and coals, and influences stretch beyond the US to include Malaysia and Korea. There are some surprisingly delicate touches in amongst the charring and smoking, and some unexpected ingredient pairings. Whatever your age, ask for the mezzanine level otherwise you'll be fighting for elbow space with the drinkers and loungers by the bar.

Ottolenghi

Mediterranean

M1

Islington

287 Upper St. ✉ N1 2TZ

✆ (020) 7288 1454 – www.ottolenghi.co.uk

⊖ Highbury & Islington

Closed 25-26 December, dinner Sunday and bank holidays – booking essential

Carte approx. £26

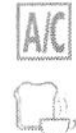

The few people in the country yet to buy one of Yotam Ottolenghi's cookbooks will find that a single visit to his crisp and coolly decorated spot on Upper Street will send them scurrying off to the nearest bookshop. If you haven't booked one of the tables for two, just sit at one of the two large communal tables and check out what everyone else is ordering. Whether you choose a dish from the kitchen or the counter, the freshness and vitality of the food is palpable and you'll never think of salad again in the same way; vegetarians will sob with gratitude. There are vibrant flavours from the Med, North Africa, the Middle East, and even the occasional Asian note. Service is well-paced and the delightful staff all know their stuff.

Pig and Butcher

British traditional L1

Islington

80 Liverpool Rd ✉ N1 OQD

(020) 7226 8304 – **www**.thepigandbutcher.co.uk

Angel

Closed 25-27 December and Monday-Wednesday lunch – booking advisable

Carte £25/42

Formerly The Islington Tap, this corner pub dates from the mid-19C when cattle drovers taking their livestock to Smithfield Market would stop for a swift one. Now sympathetically restored, it enjoys the same ownership as Lady Ottoline and Princess of Shoreditch. The busy bar offers an impressive number of bottled beers, while the dining room is secreted behind shelves of bric-a-brac. There's a strong British element to the daily menu and that's not just because they use words like 'Beeton' and 'Mrs'. Meat comes straight from the farm and is butchered and smoked in-house; fish comes from day boats off the south coast. Roasts take centre stage on Sundays; 'just like your mother's' they claim, which presumably means something different to us all.

Yipin China

Chinese L1

Islington

70-72 Liverpool Rd ✉ N1 0QD

(020) 7354 3388

www.yipinchina.co.uk

Angel

Closed 25 December

Carte £19/42

Don't be put off by the flashing fairy lights or the pink and cream colour scheme, otherwise you'll miss out on some very appealing cooking. The menu at this modest little spot features Hunanese, Cantonese and Sichuanese specialities, but it is the spicy, chilli-based dishes from Hunan province that use techniques like smoking and curing that really stand out. Dry-wok dishes are a speciality here, as are the spicy pig's intestines and offal slices. Chairman Mao red-braised pork (he came from Hunan) is a fragrant, glossy stew and the sea bass which comes with an enormous number of salted chillies is exhilaratingly fresh tasting. The staff may seem a little shy at first but will make recommendations if prompted.

L' Anima

Italian

Shoreditch

K3

1 Snowden St. ✉ EC2A 2DQ
✆ (0207) 4227 000 – **www**.lanima.co.uk
⊖ Liverpool Street

Closed 25 December, Saturday lunch, Sunday and bank holidays – booking essential

Menu £23 (weekday lunch)/35 – Carte £35/75

You know you've got a successful restaurant on your hands when the live music in the bar is barely audible above the noise being made by your contented diners. With its limestone walls, impeccably laid tables, white leather chairs and clever lighting, L'Anima is an extremely handsome restaurant, and one that looks as though it should be located somewhere slightly more glamorous than the edge of The City. The chef comes from Calabria but his team hail from all parts of Italy. The à la carte menu offers a mix of the classic and the more unusual – look out for the lesser known varieties of pasta or an occasional Moorish influence – there's also a good value midweek menu. Ask for a window table or one on the raised section at the back.

Beard to Tail

meats and grills

Shoreditch

K3

77 Curtain Rd ✉ EC2A 3BS
✆ (0207) 729 2966
www.beardtotail.co.uk
⊖ Old Street

Closed 25-26 December, Easter Sunday and bank holiday Mondays

Carte £23/37

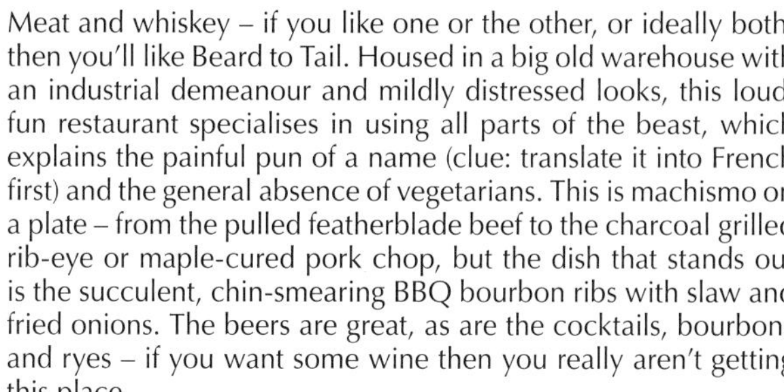

Meat and whiskey – if you like one or the other, or ideally both, then you'll like Beard to Tail. Housed in a big old warehouse with an industrial demeanour and mildly distressed looks, this loud, fun restaurant specialises in using all parts of the beast, which explains the painful pun of a name (clue: translate it into French first) and the general absence of vegetarians. This is machismo on a plate – from the pulled featherblade beef to the charcoal grilled rib-eye or maple-cured pork chop, but the dish that stands out is the succulent, chin-smearing BBQ bourbon ribs with slaw and fried onions. The beers are great, as are the cocktails, bourbons and ryes – if you want some wine then you really aren't getting this place.

Boundary

French

K3

Shoreditch

2-4 Boundary St ✉ E2 7DD

✆ (020) 7729 1051

www.theboundary.co.uk

⊖ Old Street

Menu £20 (lunch and early dinner) – Carte £33/65

When the management team took over his restaurant group, many thought Sir Terence Conran's days of opening restaurants were over. Not a bit of it, because he was soon back with a bang with Boundary. As is his way, he has taken an interesting building, in this case a large warehouse and former printworks, and turned it into a veritable house of fun. From the top, you have a roof terrace with an open fire; Albion is a ground floor 'caff' alongside a shop and bakery, and Boundary is the French-inspired 'main' restaurant below. The room is stylish, good-looking and works well, while the kitchen serves up reassuringly familiar cross-Channel treats, including fruits de mer. The fourth part of the equation are the comfy, individually designed bedrooms.

N Clove Club

modern

K3

Shoreditch

380 Old St ✉ EC1V 9LT

✆ (020) 7729 6496 – www.thecloveclub.com

⊖ Old Street

Closed 2 weeks Christmas-New Year, August bank holiday, Monday lunch and Sunday – bookings advisable at dinner

Menu £47 – Carte £19/41

The blogosphere went into overdrive when the three friends who'd made their names in 'pop-ups' decided to open something more permanent. The trio set up here at the Grade II-listed Shoreditch Town Hall. It's an unrelentingly sparse room so bang on trend, although the high ceiling and tall windows do add a little grandeur. Local hipsters pack out the bar while in the restaurant an open kitchen and simple bentwood chairs give the impression a science class is about to begin. There are no decisions to be made – it's a tasting menu in here. The British food displays a little Nordic influence, a fair degree of originality and certainly some ambition. Some dishes are more crowd than palate-pleasers but overall the food is well-executed and flavourful.

Eyre Brothers

Spanish

K3

Shoreditch

70 Leonard St ✉ EC2A 4QX

✆ (020) 7613 5346 – **www**.eyrebrothers.co.uk

⊖ Old Street

Closed 24 December-4 January, Saturday lunch, Sunday and bank holidays

Menu £18 (lunch) – Carte £23/47

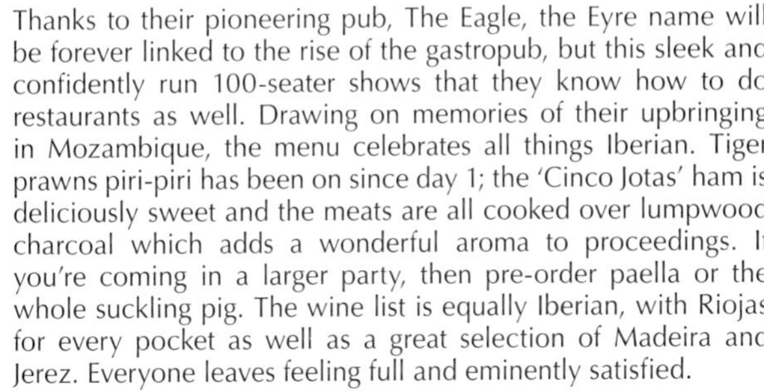

Thanks to their pioneering pub, The Eagle, the Eyre name will be forever linked to the rise of the gastropub, but this sleek and confidently run 100-seater shows that they know how to do restaurants as well. Drawing on memories of their upbringing in Mozambique, the menu celebrates all things Iberian. Tiger prawns piri-piri has been on since day 1; the 'Cinco Jotas' ham is deliciously sweet and the meats are all cooked over lumpwood charcoal which adds a wonderful aroma to proceedings. If you're coming in a larger party, then pre-order paella or the whole suckling pig. The wine list is equally Iberian, with Riojas for every pocket as well as a great selection of Madeira and Jerez. Everyone leaves feeling full and eminently satisfied.

Princess of Shoreditch

British traditional

K3

Shoreditch

76-78 Paul St ✉ EC2A 4NE

✆ (020) 7729 9270

www.theprincessofshoreditch.com

⊖ Old Street

Closed 24-27 December – booking essential

Carte £23/30

Apparently there has been a pub on this corner site since 1742 but it is doubtful many of the previous incarnations were as busy or as pleasant as the Princess is today. The owners have always been very hands-on and their welcoming attitude has rubbed off on their friendly staff; the pub comes with an appealing buzz and, to cap it all off, the prices are more than fair. It's set over two floors and the same menu is served throughout – although you can book upstairs. The menu changes daily, and sometimes between services; the food appears quite simple but the best dishes are those that come with a satisfying rustic edge, whether that's the buttery goose rillettes, the chicken pie with terrific mash or the tender pulled pork.

HKK ✿

Chinese

Shoreditch

Broadgate West, 88 Worship St ✉ EC2A 2BE
✆ (020) 3535 1888
www.hkklondon.com
⊖ Liverpool Street
Closed 24 December-6 January, Saturday lunch and Sunday

K3

Menu £42/95 – Carte lunch £32/62

A/C

HKK

From the people behind Hakkasan comes this most sophisticated of Cantonese restaurants. The room is understated, elegant and graceful; the service smooth, assured and unobtrusive. As time is money in this part of town, the lunch menu has been designed with consideration towards those who have to return to work – to really experience what HKK is all about, come for dinner when you're presented with their expertly paced 16 course menu, which evolves on a monthly basis. Cantonese has always been considered the finest of the Chinese cuisines and here at HKK it is given an extra degree of refinement. One can still expect the classic combinations of flavours but just delivered in a more modern way, whether that's abalone in truffle rice wine sauce or osmanthus flower with crispy taro milk cake. One highlight is the duck: roasted to order in a cherry-wood fired oven, it is expertly carved and served in three different ways. The presentation of all of the dishes is sublime and they come with well-considered wine pairings.

First Course

- Cherry wood roasted Peking duck.
- Poulet de Bresse with ginseng, soup and silken bean curd.

Main Course

- Gai lan, shimeji mushroom and lily bulb in XO sauce.
- Scottish sea bass with pickled chilli sauce.

Dessert

- Pineapple fritter, salted lime jelly and vanilla ice cream.
- Mandarin jelly with pandan sorbet and jasmine meringue.

Rivington Grill

British modern

Shoreditch

28-30 Rivington St ✉ EC2A 3DZ
✆ (020) 7729 7053
www.rivingtonshoreditch.co.uk
⊖ Old Street
Closed 25-26 December

K3

Carte £22/54

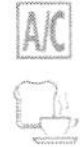

A converted warehouse surrounded by design studios, galleries and printing premises means not only that this place is popular with artistically inclined types but that it also shows work itself, including a Tracey Emin neon "Life without you, never". However, it is also close to The City so head left when you enter as larger groups tend to occupy the tables on the right. The British menu will fill you with patriotic fervour – if this was what John Major had meant when he referred to 'back-to-basics' there wouldn't have been such derision. There's a section 'on toast' and oysters are a speciality; there are pies, chops and faggots, even fish fingers and bubble and squeak. There are also plenty of bottles under £30 and special offers for weekend lunches.

Tramshed

modern

Shoreditch

32 Rivington St ✉ EC2A 3LX
✆ (020) 7749 0478
www.chickenandsteak.co.uk
⊖ Old Street
Closed 24-26 December

K3

Carte £20/44

A striking Grade II warehouse, designed by Vincent Harris in 1905 to house the generators for the trams, is the setting for this stunning brasserie from Mark Hix. The vast industrial room is dominated by a piece of work from his mate Damien Hirst and this tank with a Hereford cow and a cockerel in formaldehyde reflects what's on the menu. The choice of main course is simply chicken or beef: a whole Woolley Park Farm free-range chicken (they come head down on a spike, claws and all) or marbled sirloin steak by the 250g, dry aged in the Himalayan salt chamber and ionised for extra sweetness. Come with two friends as starters, which include chicken livers in a Yorkshire pud, come in sets of three and one chicken feeds three.

Ⓝ Viet Grill

Vietnamese K2

Shoreditch

58 Kingsland Rd ✉ E2 8DP

✆ (020) 7739 6686

www.vietnamesekitchen.co.uk

⊖ Old Street

Menu £10/24 – Carte £16/34

Vietnamese restaurants are proving very popular in this part of town, so perhaps it's about time that Hackney was twinned with Hanoi. The reason Viet Grill attracts so many customers is not down to its bright neon lighting, but because it is owned by the same team behind Cây Tre, which means that service is charming and helpful and the food is fresh and authentic. From the slurpable pho noodle soups to Devon crab (most ingredients are sourced within the UK) and La Vong monkfish for two, you'll find dishes packed with flavour and vibrancy; meats grilled on the robata also stand out. Those who don't plan ahead can take advantage of their takeaway menu; those who do can order one of their 'feast' menus, which require 48 hours' notice.

Provender

French Off-plan

Wanstead

17 High St ✉ E11 2AA

✆ (020) 8530 3050

www.provenderlondon.co.uk

⊖ Snaresbrook

Closed 26 December and Sunday dinner

Menu £15 (weekdays) – Carte £18/39

Wanstead High Street may not necessarily be the first place one would expect to find great French bourgeois cooking but the locals must be mightily glad that Max Renzland decided to pitch up in their arrondissement. Max's reputation for creating terrific French restaurants was forged in the suburbs, albeit at the opposite end of town, and Provender has his stamp all over it. That means you can expect authentic and satisfying food; plenty of choice; and prices, for the menus and the exclusively French wine list, that are very competitive. The fish is good here, as are the charcuterie boards, and there are dishes to share and even a separate menu for 'les enfants'. It's no wonder the split-level room hums with the sound of contentment.

R. Herrett /Loop Images/Age fotostock

South-East London

Once considered not only the wrong side of the tracks, but also most definitely the wrong side of the river, London's southeastern chunk has thrived in recent times courtesy of the Docklands Effect. As the gleaming glass peninsula of **Canary Wharf** (ironically, just north of the Thames) sprouted a personality of its own – with bars, restaurants, slinky bridges and an enviable view, not to mention moneyed residents actually putting down roots – the city's bottom right hand zone began to achieve destination status on a par with other parts of London. You only have to stroll around the glossy and quite vast **Limehouse Basin** – a slick marina that was once a hard-grafting East End dock – to really see what's happened here.

Not that the area hasn't always boasted some true gems in the capital's treasure chest. **Greenwich,** with fabulous views across the water to the docklands from its delightfully sloping park, has long been a favourite of kings and queens: Henry VIII and Elizabeth I resided here. The village itself bustles along with its market and plush picturehouse, but most visitors make their way to the stand-out attractions, of which there are many. The **Royal Observatory** and the Meridian Line draw star-gazers and hemisphere striders in equal number, while the palatial Old Royal Naval College is a star turn for lovers of Wren, who designed it as London's answer to Versailles. On the northern edge of Greenwich Park, the **National Maritime Museum** has three floors of sea-faring wonders; down by the pier, the real thing exists in the shape of the **Cutty Sark**. Up on the peninsula, the O2 Arena's distinctive shape has become an unmistakable landmark, but if you fancy a contrast to all things watery, the Fan Museum on Crooms Hill has more hand-held fans (over 3,000 of them) than anywhere else on earth. Strolling south from Greenwich park you reach **Blackheath,** an alluring suburban village, whose most striking feature is the towering All Saints' Church, standing proud away from the chic shops and restaurants.

Of slightly less spectacular charms, but a real crowd-pleaser nevertheless, is **Dulwich Village,** hidden deeper in the southeastern enclaves. It's a leafy oasis in this part of the world, with a delightful park that boasts at its western end, next to the original buildings of the old public school, the Dulwich Picture Gallery. This was designed in 1811, and its pedigree is evident in works by the likes of Rembrandt, Rubens, Van Dyck and Canaletto. Half an hour's walk away across the park is the brilliant Horniman Museum, full of natural history and world culture delights – as well as a massive aquarium that seems to take up much of southeast London.

C. Eymenier / MICHELIN

A bit further east along the South Circular, there's the unexpected gem of Eltham Palace, originally the childhood home of Henry VIII with a magnificent (and still visible) Great Hall. What makes it unique is the adjacent Art Deco mansion built for millionaires in the 1930s in Ocean Liner style. It's the closest you'll ever get to a setting fit for hog roast and champagne. Heading back towards London, a lifestyle of bubbly and banquets has never really been **Peckham**'s thing, but it boasts a couple of corkers in the shape of the South London Gallery with its zeitgeist-setting art shows, and the Peckham Library, a giant inverted 'L' that after a decade still looks like a lot of fun to go into.

Back in the luxury flat-lands of the **Docklands, Wapping** has become an interesting port of call, its new-build architecture mixing in with a still Dickensian feel, in the shape of glowering Victorian warehouses and Wapping New Stairs, where the bodies of pirates were hanged from a gibbet until seven tides had showered their limp bodies. You can catch a fascinating history of the whole area in the nearby Museum in Docklands.

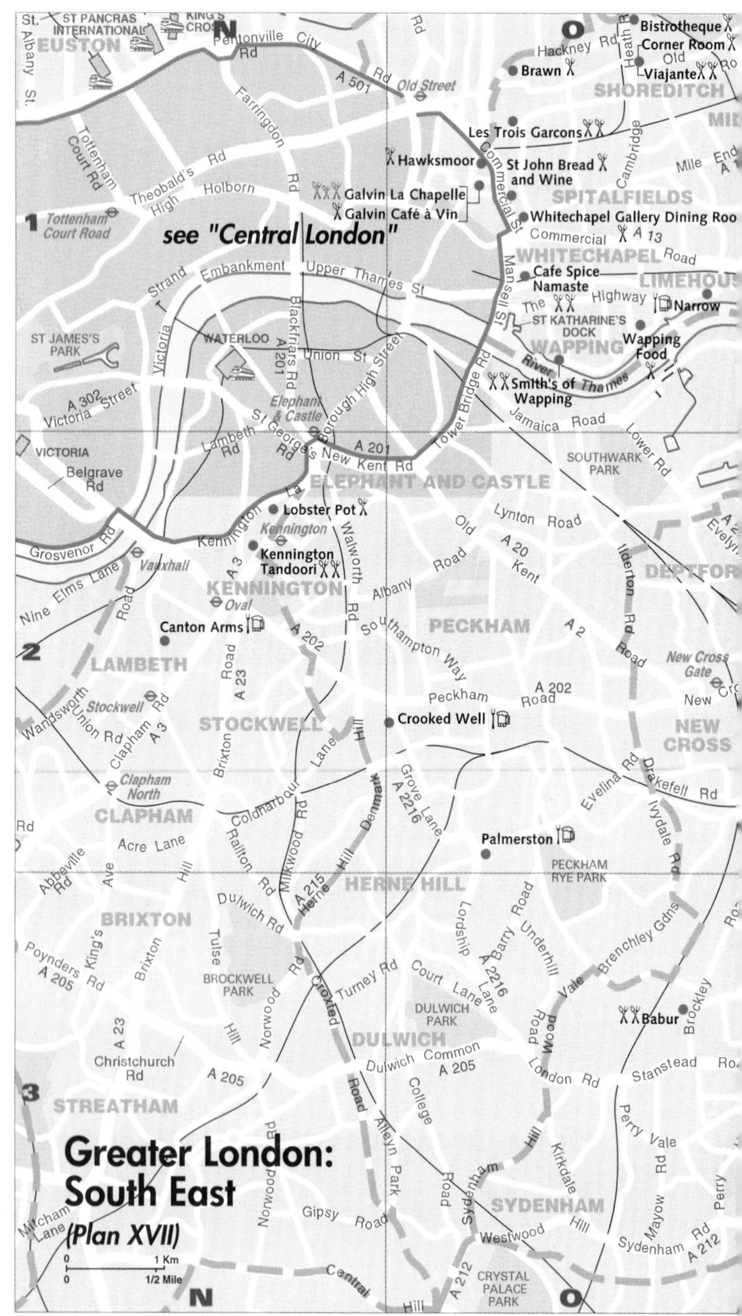

Greater London: South East
(Plan XVII)
see "Central London"
Bistrotheque
Corner Room
Viajante
Brawn
Les Trois Garcons
Hawksmoor
St John Bread and Wine
Galvin La Chapelle
Galvin Café à Vin
Whitechapel Gallery Dining Room
Cafe Spice Namaste
Narrow
Wapping Food
Smith's of Wapping
Lobster Pot
Kennington Tandoori
Canton Arms
Crooked Well
Palmerston
Babur
EUSTON
SHOREDITCH
SPITALFIELDS
WHITECHAPEL
WAPPING
ELEPHANT AND CASTLE
KENNINGTON
PECKHAM
LAMBETH
STOCKWELL
CLAPHAM
NEW CROSS
HERNE HILL
BRIXTON
DULWICH
STREATHAM
SYDENHAM
ST PANCRAS INTERNATIONAL
KING'S CROSS
WATERLOO
VICTORIA
ST JAMES'S PARK
ST KATHARINE'S DOCK
SOUTHWARK PARK
PECKHAM RYE PARK
BROCKWELL PARK
DULWICH PARK
CRYSTAL PALACE PARK
Tottenham Court Road
Old Street
Elephant & Castle
Kennington
Vauxhall
Oval
Stockwell
Clapham North
New Cross Gate
0 1 Km
0 1/2 Mile

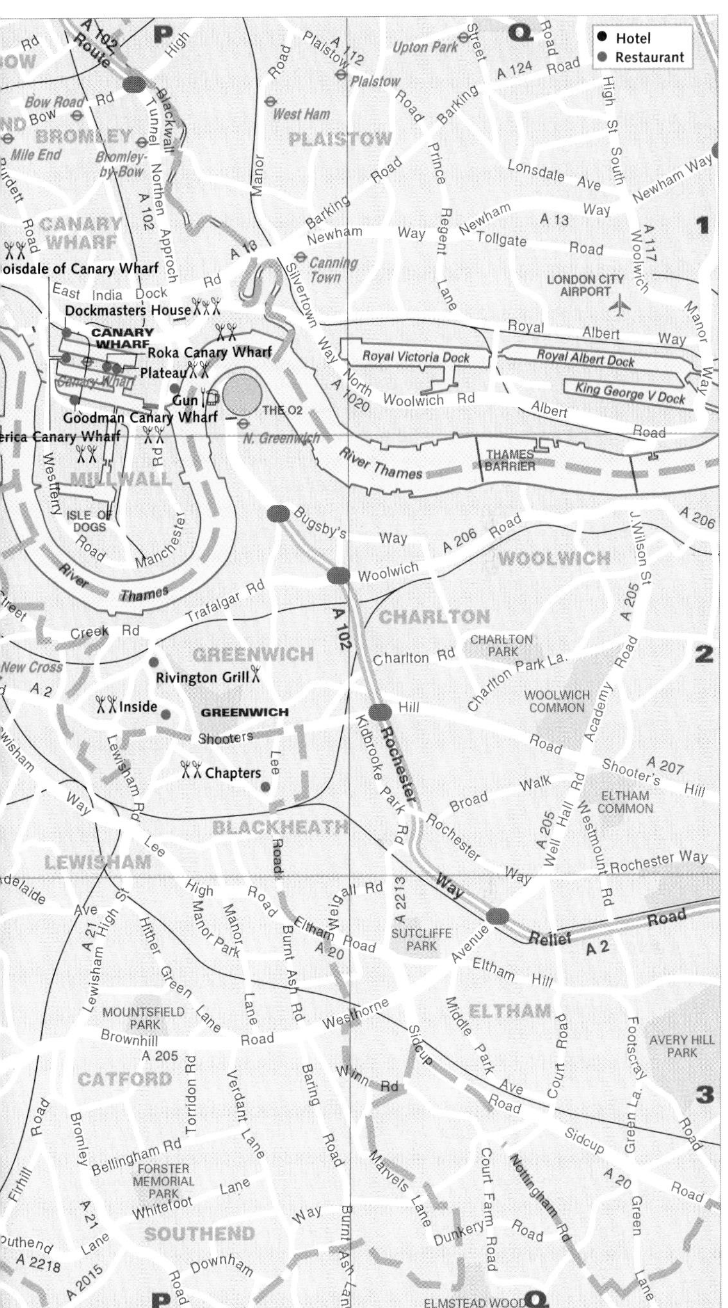
Hotel
Restaurant
CANARY WHARF
BROMLEY
PLAISTOW
MILLWALL
ISLE OF DOGS
GREENWICH
BLACKHEATH
LEWISHAM
CATFORD
SOUTHEND
CHARLTON
WOOLWICH
ELTHAM
LONDON CITY AIRPORT
Royal Victoria Dock
Royal Albert Dock
King George V Dock
THAMES BARRIER
River Thames
THE O2
Dockmasters House
Roka Canary Wharf
Plateau
Gun
Goodman Canary Wharf
Rivington Grill
Inside
Chapters
CHARLTON PARK
WOOLWICH COMMON
ELTHAM COMMON
SUTCLIFFE PARK
MOUNTSFIELD PARK
FORSTER MEMORIAL PARK
AVERY HILL PARK
ELMSTEAD WOOD

Bistrotheque

modern 01

Bethnal Green

23-27 Wadeson St ✉ E2 9DR

✆ (020) 8983 7900 – **www**.bistrotheque.com

⊖ Bethnal Green

Closed 24 and 26 December – booking advisable – (dinner only and brunch Saturday and Sunday)

Menu £18 (dinner) – Carte £23/34 

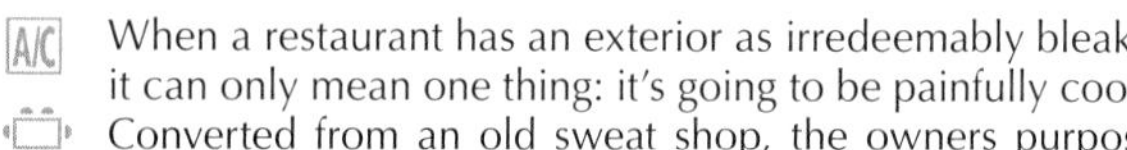

When a restaurant has an exterior as irredeemably bleak as this, it can only mean one thing: it's going to be painfully cool inside. Converted from an old sweat shop, the owners purposely left the exterior bereft of any sign of gastronomic life – just head past the anguished graffiti and take the stairs in the courtyard up to the 1st floor. Here you'll find a warmly run, wonderfully bustling industrial-looking space, with beams and girders, ducting and concrete. It's all great fun, especially as the restaurant rubs shoulders with the cabaret. The menu is predominantly French bistro in style with some British classics thrown in. A good value set menu is offered early and late in the evening and weekend brunch comes with live music.

Brawn

modern 01

Bethnal Green

49 Columbia Rd. ✉ E2 7RG

✆ (020) 7729 5692 – **www**.brawn.co

⊖ Bethnal Green

Closed Christmas and New Year, Sunday dinner, Monday lunch and bank holidays

Carte £19/34

After the success of Terroirs, the owners wisely decided against trying to duplicate it and instead created this terrific neighbourhood restaurant in a Victorian former furniture warehouse, away from the West End. It's simply kitted out, with Formica tables and white brick walls with local artists' work. The name really captures the essence of the cooking perfectly: it is rustic, muscular and makes particularly good use of pig. Order about three dishes per person, such as prosciutto or rillettes; mussels or prawns; something raw like Tuscan beef; and something slow-cooked like duck confit. It's all immeasurably satisfying and the polite young staff appear genuinely proud of the menu and happily proffer advice.

Corner Room

innovative

O1

Bethnal Green

Town Hall Hotel,
Patriot Sq ✉ E2 9NF
✆ (020) 7871 0461 – www.cornerroom.co.uk
⊖ Bethnal Green
(bookings not accepted at dinner)

Menu £19/23 – Carte approx. £28

Corner Room is Nuno Mendes' more accessible addendum to his Viajante restaurant and is secreted upstairs in the old town hall. You'll find cooking that is equally innovative and undertaken with the same care, but by using slightly lesser cuts and fewer luxury ingredients, the prices are far more down to earth. Dishes such as sea bass ceviche with edamame, Iberico pork with Portuguese bread pudding or dark chocolate with peanut butter ice cream are as tasty as they are attractive. It's open all day so just pitch up and, if they haven't got a table, simply give them your name and wander down to the bar. A backdrop of hanging lamps adds character to the simply furnished and quite small room, which has just 13 tables.

Chapters

modern

P2

Blackheath

43-45 Montpelier Vale ✉ SE3 0TJ
✆ (020) 8333 2666
www.chaptersrestaurants.com
Closed 2-3 January

Menu £15/18 – Carte £19/43

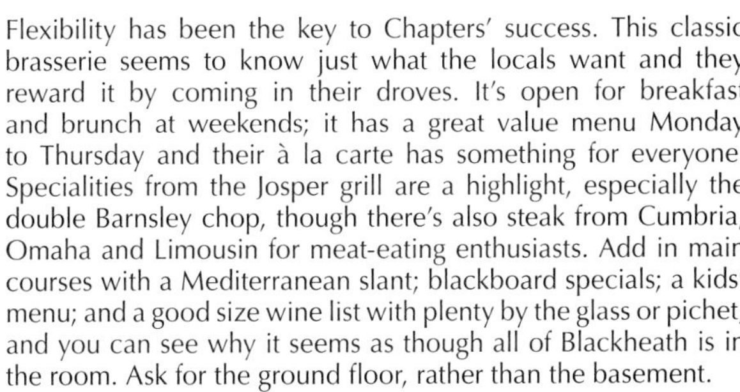

Flexibility has been the key to Chapters' success. This classic brasserie seems to know just what the locals want and they reward it by coming in their droves. It's open for breakfast and brunch at weekends; it has a great value menu Monday to Thursday and their à la carte has something for everyone. Specialities from the Josper grill are a highlight, especially the double Barnsley chop, though there's also steak from Cumbria, Omaha and Limousin for meat-eating enthusiasts. Add in main courses with a Mediterranean slant; blackboard specials; a kids' menu; and a good size wine list with plenty by the glass or pichet, and you can see why it seems as though all of Blackheath is in the room. Ask for the ground floor, rather than the basement.

Viajante ✿

innovative

01

Bethnal Green

Town Hall Hotel,
Patriot Sq. (entrance on Cambridge Heath Rd) ✉ E2 9NF
✆ (020) 7871 0461 – **www.**viajante.co.uk
⊖ Bethnal Green

Closed Monday, Tuesday and bank holidays – booking essential – (dinner only and lunch Friday-Sunday)

Menu £35, £70/95

Viajante

Portuguese chef Nuno Mendes finds the inspiration for his innovative cuisine from his travels, so it is fitting that he opened his restaurant in Bethnal Green, one of London's most culturally diverse districts. You'll find this two-roomed restaurant inside the old town hall, where a subtle scent of civic functionality still permeates. The open kitchen is an integral part of the set-up but don't arrive expecting blasts of heat and drama – this is a sleek, controlled environment that's more about sous-vide than stockpots. Choose 6, 9 or, if pre-booked, 12 courses, which is not as daunting a prospect as it sounds: even though considerable work has gone into the dishes, they are perfectly balanced and the combinations of flavours and textures have been thoroughly considered. Delicate, diminutive dishes like scallops with carrots or lobster with duck egg provide pleasingly familiar flavours, while other dishes such as pickled and raw cucumber with milk sorbet or beetroot with dark chocolate offer more challenging yet still highly enjoyable combinations.

First Course

- Scallops, liquorice and parsley.
- Crab with egg yolk and rhubarb.

Main Course

- Dehesa lamb with black quinoa.
- Turbot with spring vegetables and mussels.

Dessert

- Frozen pear, cider and pecans.
- Jerusalem artichokes with chocolate 'soil' and orange.

Boisdale of Canary Wharf

British traditional P1

Canary Wharf
Cabot Pl ✉ E14 4QT
✆ (020) 7715 5818
www.boisdale.co.uk
⊖ Canary Wharf
Closed bank holidays – booking advisable

Menu £20 – Carte £32/75

This is two operations under one roof: get out of the lift on the 1st floor for the art deco inspired Oyster bar: a richly decorated, tartan room centred around a marble topped bar. Here it's about relaxed dining, with an impressive selection of crustacea along with burgers and steaks. It has a lovely terrace overlooking Cabot Square and a walk-in humidor with an impressive selection of Cuban cigars. Climb out on the 2nd floor and three things hit you: the fabulous bay window, a stage and a remarkable wall of whiskies. Things here are grander and more comfortable and there's live jazz for which a charge in made. In amongst the caviar, steaks and assorted dishes of Scottish persuasion is the more moderately priced Jacobite menu.

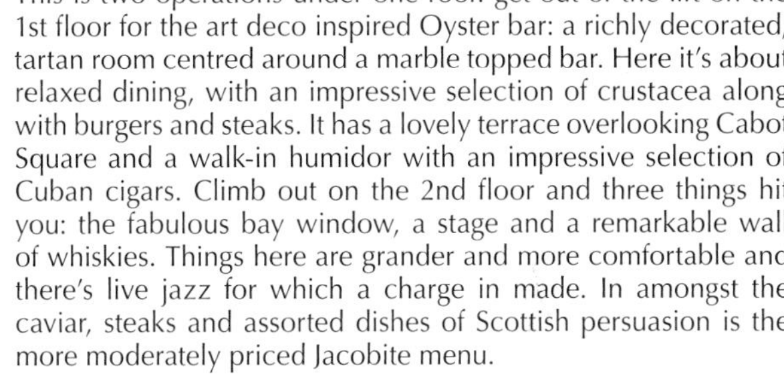

Dockmaster's House

Indian P1

Canary Wharf
1 Hertsmere Rd ✉ E14 8JJ
✆ (020) 7345 0345 – **www.**dockmastershouse.com
⊖ Canary Wharf
Closed 25 December-1 January, bank holidays, Saturday lunch and Sunday – booking advisable

Menu £20/55 – Carte £24/49

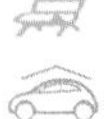

On the edge of Canary Wharf and in the shadow of its skyscrapers sits this striking three-storey Georgian house which has been given a contemporary overhaul. There are two contrasting dining rooms: one in the original part of the house with all the period features; the other more modern and shiny and encased in a glass extension. There's a funky basement bar, plus rooms upstairs and a garden for private parties. The Indian food adds modern twists to its conventional foundations. The menu is more seasonally based than many but it is also more expensive. The saffron prawns are good, the grilled section is worth exploring and there are interesting teas; but a little less pretentiousness all round wouldn't be a bad thing.

Goodman Canary Wharf

meats and grills P1

Canary Wharf

Discovery Dock East, 3 South Quay ✉ E14 9RU
(020) 7531 0300 – www.goodmanrestaurants.com
⊖ South Quay (DLR)

Closed 25-26 December, 1 January, Saturday lunch, Sunday and bank holidays – booking advisable

Menu £22 (lunch) – Carte £26/75

No one likes their meat more than those who business is business, so Canary Wharf was the logical next location for this growing group. Whether you're thinking corn or grass fed Scottish fillet, rib on the bone or US strip loin, the delightful staff will show you what's on offer and explain the maturation process. It can be wet and vac-packed from the US or dry hung from Scotland and Ireland; even the Aussies get in on the act with their Wagyu. You then decide on the cut and the weight, which depends on the relative sizes of your appetite and wallet. The quality of the beef is excellent, as are the side dishes like truffle chips. The lively brasserie style room, with semi-private booths, offers great waterfront views.

Gun

British traditional P1

Canary Wharf

27 Coldharbour ✉ E14 9NS
(020) 7515 5222
www.thegundocklands.com
⊖ Blackwall (DLR)

Closed 25-26 December

Carte £25/50

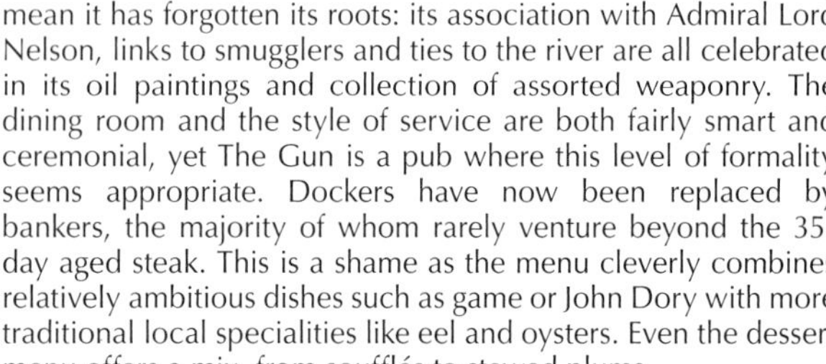

The 18C Gun may have had a 21C makeover but that doesn't mean it has forgotten its roots: its association with Admiral Lord Nelson, links to smugglers and ties to the river are all celebrated in its oil paintings and collection of assorted weaponry. The dining room and the style of service are both fairly smart and ceremonial, yet The Gun is a pub where this level of formality seems appropriate. Dockers have now been replaced by bankers, the majority of whom rarely venture beyond the 35-day aged steak. This is a shame as the menu cleverly combines relatively ambitious dishes such as game or John Dory with more traditional local specialities like eel and oysters. Even the dessert menu offers a mix, from soufflés to stewed plums.

Iberica Canary Wharf

Mediterranean P1

Canary Wharf

Cabot Sq ✉ E14 4QQ

✆ (020) 7636 8650 – **www**.ibericalondon.co.uk

⊖ Canary Wharf

Closed 24-25 December, 1 January and dinner on Sunday and bank holidays

Menu £10 (weekday lunch) – Carte £18/46 XX

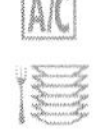

The second branch of this lively, modern Spanish restaurant opened in an attractive arcade just outside the labyrinthine Cabot Square shopping mall, its narrow shop front belying its vast interior. Walk past the appealing display of hams and the long bar and you'll find yourself in a bustling ground floor, with an open kitchen at one end. This is where to sit, unless you're on a date – in which case go up to the less frenzied mezzanine level. The menu follows the same pattern as the original in Great Portland Street by offering a mix of traditional and more contemporary tapas to share. Must tries are asparagus on toast with Manchego, grilled prawns with chilli and garlic, and the scrambled eggs with caramelised onions.

Plateau

modern P1

Canary Wharf

Canada Place (4th floor), Canada Square ✉ E14 5ER

✆ (020) 7715 7100

www.plateaurestaurant.co.uk

⊖ Canary Wharf

Closed 25 December, 1 January and Sunday

Menu £22 – Carte £28/54 XX

In a building that wouldn't look out of place in Manhattan is a restaurant that harks back to a time when bankers ruled the world. This striking room, with its subtle 1950s design influences, is an impressive open-plan space and its dramatic glass walls and ceilings make the surrounding monolithic office blocks seem strangely appealing, for some reason. There are two choices: the Grill where, as the name suggests, the choice is from rotisserie meats and classic grilled dishes, or the formal restaurant beyond it, which comes with more comfortable surroundings. Here, the range is more eclectic and dishes are constructed with more global influences. They also come in ample sizes, though, so ignore the enthusiastic selling of the side dishes.

Roka Canary Wharf

Japanese P1

Canary Wharf

4 Park Pavilion (1st Floor) ✉ E14 5FW

✆ (020) 7636 5228

www.rokarestaurant.com

⊖ Canary Wharf

Closed 25 December – booking essential

Carte £20/89 XX

London's second Roka restaurant sits in the shadow of Canary Wharf Tower, now the UK's second tallest building, and the first thing to hit you, once you've actually found the entrance, is a wall of sound. This is a big, open and perennially busy affair, with tightly packed tables which are usually occupied by large groups of City folk – and is not somewhere for a quiet dinner à deux. The menu follows the format of the Charlotte Street branch by offering a wide selection of mostly contemporary Japanese dishes. The easiest option is to head straight for one of the tasting menus which offer a balanced picture of what the food is all about. The robata grill is the centrepiece of the kitchen's operation – the lamb chops are particularly good.

Palmerston

Mediterranean O2

East Dulwich

91 Lordship Ln ✉ SE22 8EP

✆ (020) 8693 1629

www.thepalmerston.net

⊖ East Dulwich (Rail)

Menu £14 (weekday lunch) – Carte £27/64

The Palmerston has long realised that success for any pub lies in being at the heart of the local community. Since it's makeover a few years ago, this Victorian pub has been popular with families – just look at all those highchairs – and local artists work decorates the walls. It has a comfortable, lived-in feel, along with a snug, wood-panelled rear dining room with an original and quite beautiful mosaic floor. The menu is as reassuring as the service and the cooking has a satisfying, gutsy edge. There's plenty of choice, from chowders and soups to well-judged fish but it's the meat dishes that stand out, like the mature steaks or lamb chops – and if they have grouse on the menu, then forsake all others and get in quick.

Inside

modern

P2

Greenwich

19 Greenwich South St ✉ SE10 8NW
✆ (020) 8265 5060
www.insiderestaurant.co.uk
⊖ Greenwich (DLR)

Closed 24-28 December, Sunday dinner and Monday

Menu £18/25 – Carte £26/37

A/C

The advantage of having an unremarkable façade is that it dampens unrealistic expectations. Indeed, 'Inside' was so named because the chef and his fellow owners had very little money when they opened, so wisely concentrated on the interior. With seating for just under forty, the room is tidy, comfortable and uncluttered, although it does take a few diners to generate an atmosphere. On offer is an appealingly priced set menu, elements of which change every fortnight. Dishes are attractively presented, relatively elaborate in their makeup and clearly prepared with care; most of the influences come from within Europe but staples do include the chicken and coriander spring rolls. There's also a decent choice of wine for under £25.

Rivington Grill

British modern

P2

Greenwich

178 Greenwich High Rd ✉ SE10 8NN
✆ (020) 8293 9270
www.rivingtongreenwich.co.uk
⊖ Greenwich (DLR)

Closed 25-26 December and lunch Monday-Wednesday

Menu £15 (weekday lunch) – Carte £21/44

A/C

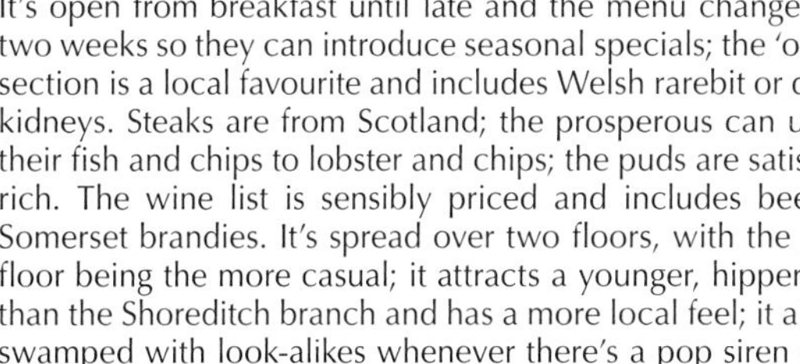

It's open from breakfast until late and the menu changes every two weeks so they can introduce seasonal specials; the 'on toast' section is a local favourite and includes Welsh rarebit or devilled kidneys. Steaks are from Scotland; the prosperous can upgrade their fish and chips to lobster and chips; the puds are satisfyingly rich. The wine list is sensibly priced and includes beers and Somerset brandies. It's spread over two floors, with the ground floor being the more casual; it attracts a younger, hipper crowd than the Shoreditch branch and has a more local feel; it also gets swamped with look-alikes whenever there's a pop siren playing the O2 arena. Tables of up to four people can get a discount at the next door cinema.

Kennington Tandoori

Indian

N2

Kennington

313 Kennington Rd ✉ SE11 4QE

✆ (020) 7735 9247

www.kenningtontandoori.com

⊖ Kennington

Closed 25 December – booking advisable

Menu £25/28 – Carte £18/31

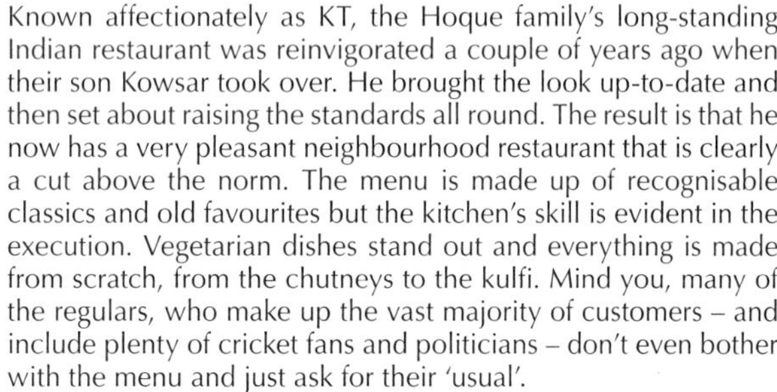

Known affectionately as KT, the Hoque family's long-standing Indian restaurant was reinvigorated a couple of years ago when their son Kowsar took over. He brought the look up-to-date and then set about raising the standards all round. The result is that he now has a very pleasant neighbourhood restaurant that is clearly a cut above the norm. The menu is made up of recognisable classics and old favourites but the kitchen's skill is evident in the execution. Vegetarian dishes stand out and everything is made from scratch, from the chutneys to the kulfi. Mind you, many of the regulars, who make up the vast majority of customers – and include plenty of cricket fans and politicians – don't even bother with the menu and just ask for their 'usual'.

Lobster Pot

French

N2

Kennington

3 Kennington Ln. ✉ SE11 4RG

✆ (020) 7582 5556

www.lobsterpotrestaurant.co.uk

⊖ Kennington

Closed 1 week Christmas-New Year, Sunday and Monday

Carte £39/65

Ignore the fairly shabby exterior, dive straight in and you'll think you've stumbled onto a French film set. Fish tanks, portholes, the cries of seagulls and the hoots of ferries...the place has the lot and it's hard to avoid getting caught up in the exuberance of it all. It's no surprise that it's also all about fish. The chef-owner, from Vannes in Brittany, goes to Billingsgate each morning and he knows what he's doing: his menu is classical and appetising, with fruits de mer, plenty of oysters, a lobster section and daily specials on the blackboard. Be sure to make room for the crêpes, which are great. It's not cheap but it is an experience. Underlining the family nature of the business, the son has opened a brasserie next door.

Babur

Indian

03

Lewisham

119 Brockley Rise ✉ SE23 1JP

✆ (020) 8291 2400

www.babur.info

Closed dinner 25 December-lunch 27 December

Carte £24/32

It's not just its good looks and innovative cooking that set Babur apart – this long-standing Indian restaurant is also run with great passion and enthusiasm. Regular customers are invited to tastings and can even have an input on the quarterly changing menus – and the makeup of each dish is fully explained when dishes are presented at the table. The south and north west of India feature most predominantly on the menu but there are also Western-influenced dishes available, like crab claws with asparagus and saffron. Seafood is certainly a highlight, so look out for the periods of the year when the separate 'Treasures of the Sea' menu appears. You'll find suggested wine pairings for each dish, along with some inventive cocktails.

Narrow

British modern

01

Limehouse

44 Narrow St ✉ E14 8DP

✆ (020) 7592 7950

www.gordonramsay.com

⊖ Limehouse (DLR)

Closed 25 December – booking essential

Menu £22 – Carte £26/50

There can't be many London pubs with better views than The Narrow and Gordon Ramsay's group have made the most of the Thames-side location by wrapping a conservatory around this Grade II listed former dockmaster's house. The place has a real buzz, thanks largely to the many regulars at the bar, the occasional live music and the large number of diners which include plenty of tourists. The menu gives them an opportunity to discover our more traditional dishes such as Scotch egg, cottage pie, toad in the hole and the ubiquitous fish and chips. Dishes on the whole hit the mark although the kitchen can be a little heavy-handed at times. Look out for the good value set menu, available at all times except after 7pm on Fridays and Saturdays.

Galvin Café a Vin

French

01

Spitalfields

35 Spital Sq (entrance on Bishops Sq) ✉ E1 6DY

(020) 7299 0404

www.galvinrestaurants.com

⊖ Liverpool Street

Closed dinner 24 December, 25-26 December and 1 January

Menu £16 (lunch and early dinner)/19 – Carte £23/32

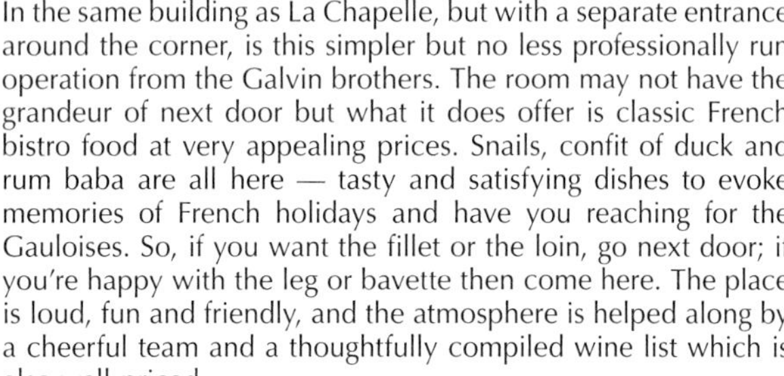

In the same building as La Chapelle, but with a separate entrance around the corner, is this simpler but no less professionally run operation from the Galvin brothers. The room may not have the grandeur of next door but what it does offer is classic French bistro food at very appealing prices. Snails, confit of duck and rum baba are all here — tasty and satisfying dishes to evoke memories of French holidays and have you reaching for the Gauloises. So, if you want the fillet or the loin, go next door; if you're happy with the leg or bavette then come here. The place is loud, fun and friendly, and the atmosphere is helped along by a cheerful team and a thoughtfully compiled wine list which is also well-priced.

Hawksmoor

meats and grills

01

Spitalfields

157 Commercial St ✉ E1 6BJ

(020) 7426 4850

www.thehawksmoor.com

⊖ Shoreditch

Closed 24-27 December, 1 January and Sunday dinner – booking essential

Menu £26 (lunch and early dinner) – Carte £39/62

Hawksmoor was a 17C architect and student of Sir Christopher Wren so you could expect this steakhouse to be found in a building of note rather than in this modern edifice of little aesthetic value. Inside is equally unremarkable but no matter because this place is all about beef and, more specifically, British beef which has been hung for 35 days. It comes from Longhorn cattle raised by the Ginger Pig Co in the heart of the North Yorkshire Moors and the quality and depth of flavour is exceptional. Just choose your preferred weight – go for 400g if you're hungry. Starters and puds don't come close in quality but again, no matter, because when you've got some fantastic red meat in front of you, all you need is a mate and a bottle of red wine.

Galvin La Chapelle ✿

French

01 

Spitalfields

35 Spital Sq ✉ E1 6DY

✆ (020) 7299 0400

www.galvinrestaurants.com

⊖ Liverpool Street

Closed dinner 24-26 December and 1 January

Menu £30 (lunch and early dinner) – Carte £43/63

Galvin La Chapelle

These days, it is rare to walk into a restaurant in London and be taken back with the grandeur and sheer scale of a room. However, this venture from the Galvin Brothers, who have already proved themselves expert restaurateurs, is one that will dazzle the most jaded of diner. The Victorian splendour of St Botolph's Hall, with its vaulted ceiling, arched windows and marble pillars, lends itself effortlessly to its role as a glamorous restaurant. There are tables in booths, in the wings or in the middle of the action and those who like some comfort with their food will not be disappointed. It is also a fitting backdrop to the cooking, which is, in essence, bourgeois French but with a sophisticated edge, which means it is immensely satisfying. There are no unnecessary fripperies, just three courses of reassuringly familiar combinations with the emphasis on bold, clear flavours. Add in a service team who are a well-drilled, well-versed outfit and you have somewhere that will be part of the restaurant landscape for years to come.

First Course

- Lasagne of Dorset crab, sweetcorn and lemongrass velouté.
- Salad of heritage tomatoes, goat's cheese and basil.

Main Course

- Tagine of Bresse pigeon with couscous, aubergine and harissa.
- Calf's liver, lyonnaise onions, bacon and pommes mousseline.

Dessert

- Chilled Valrhona chocolate fondant with banana and yoghurt ice cream.
- Raspberry soufflé with milk ice cream.

St John Bread and Wine

British traditional

O1

Spitalfields

94-96 Commercial St ✉ E1 6LZ

(020) 7251 0848

www.stjohnbreadandwine.com

Shoreditch

Closed Christmas and New Year

Carte £23/30

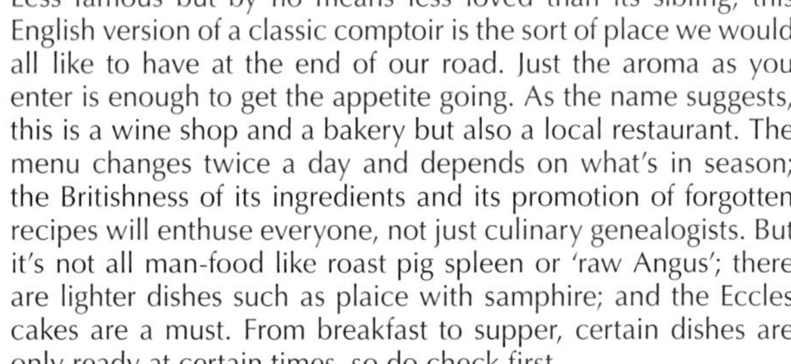

Less famous but by no means less loved than its sibling, this English version of a classic comptoir is the sort of place we would all like to have at the end of our road. Just the aroma as you enter is enough to get the appetite going. As the name suggests, this is a wine shop and a bakery but also a local restaurant. The menu changes twice a day and depends on what's in season; the Britishness of its ingredients and its promotion of forgotten recipes will enthuse everyone, not just culinary genealogists. But it's not all man-food like roast pig spleen or 'raw Angus'; there are lighter dishes such as plaice with samphire; and the Eccles cakes are a must. From breakfast to supper, certain dishes are only ready at certain times, so do check first.

Les Trois Garcons

French

O1

Spitalfields

1 Club Row ✉ E1 6JX

(020) 7613 1924 – www.lestroisgarcons.com

Shoreditch

Closed 23 December-3 January, Sunday dinner and bank holidays – (dinner only and lunch Thursday-Friday)

Menu £22 (weekday lunch) – Carte £29/59

The surrounding streets may be a little drab but the three friends (hence the name) who own this former pub happen to also be antique dealers – which is probably why the eccentric and exuberant decoration gives the impression you've stumbled into a theatrical props department. There are stuffed animals, beads, hanging handbags, assorted objets d'art and heavy velvet curtains; the lighting is dim and atmospheric. In contrast, the food is largely traditional. The kitchen uses fairly classical French cooking techniques and flavour combinations, although the majority of ingredients are British. Menus change seasonally and presentation is neat and appetising. Service can occasionally veer from the efficient to the over-confident.

Canton Arms

British traditional N2

Stockwell

177 South Lambeth Rd ✉ SW8 1XP

✆ (020) 7582 8710 – **www**.cantonarms.com

⊖ Stockwell

Closed Christmas-New Year, Monday lunch, Sunday dinner and bank holidays – bookings not accepted

Carte £19/31

Its appreciative audience prove that the demand for fresh, honest, seasonal food is not just limited to smart squares in Chelsea or Islington. The oval-shaped bar dominates the room, with the front half busy with drinkers and the back laid up for diners, although it's all very relaxed and you can eat where you want. The kitchen's experience in places like the Anchor & Hope and Great Queen Street is obvious on their menu which features rustic, earthy British food, of the sort that suits this environment so well. Lunch could be a kipper or tripe and chips; even a reinvented toasted sandwich. Dinner sees a short, no-nonsense menu offering perhaps braised venison or grilled haddock, with daily specials like steak and kidney pie for two.

Smith's of Wapping

fish and seafood O1

Wapping

22 Wapping High St ✉ E1W 1NJ

✆ (020) 7488 3456 – **www**.smithsrestaurants.com

⊖ Wapping

Closed 25-26 December, 1 January and Sunday dinner – booking advisable

Menu £20 (weekdays) – Carte £29/58

Having been providing seafood to the burghers of Essex for over 50 years, the Smith family have finally got around to opening a second branch. In 2011 they joined forces with a local restaurateur to open this large, contemporary brasserie looking out over the bobbing houseboats on the river and providing great views of Tower Bridge. The menu is a lengthy but appealing read and the kitchen is unapologetically traditional in its approach. Subsequently the best dishes are old favourites like deep-fried calamari from Cornwall, whole dressed Scottish crab or Dover sole meunière, served on or off the bone. Lobster thermidor is proving equally popular and they'll cook your fish however you wish. They also do a decent pudding.

Wapping Food

modern

01

Wapping

Wapping Wall ✉ E1W 3SG
✆ (020) 7680 2080
www.thewappingproject.com
⊖ Wapping
Closed 23 December-3 January, Sunday dinner and bank holidays

Carte £28/45

What does a former theatre director with a passion for food do when looking for a change? She buys a disused Victorian former hydraulic power station, spends two years doing it up and then opens it as the Wapping Project, a bringing together of a restaurant and an art gallery. The two functions marry perfectly: you sit among the old turbines and enjoy robust dishes fashioned from what suppliers have brought in that day. This could be mackerel with fennel, a ham hock terrine, Brecon lamb shank or panna cotta; all served by an enthusiastic team who know their onions. To make the most of your visit, be sure to take in the artwork before or after your meal; it could take the form of an installation, an exhibition or a performance.

Cafe Spice Namaste

Indian

01

Whitechapel

16 Prescot St. ✉ E1 8AZ
✆ (020) 7488 9242
www.cafespice.co.uk
⊖ Tower Hill
Closed Saturday lunch, Sunday and bank holidays

Menu £35 – Carte £25/36

A/C

Cyrus Todiwala's contribution to Indian cuisine and the hospitality industry was recognised in 2010 when he was appointed an OBE. Café Spice Namaste opened back in 1995 and was where the dining public first became aware of his ability. The bright decoration of this former magistrate's court may not be quite so effervescent these days but the food remains just as fresh and vibrant. Many of the ingredients used are from within the British Isles and the cooking influences are spread across India; the Parsee specialities are particularly memorable. There's a plethora of menus to look through but don't hesitate to ask Cyrus' wife Pervin for guidance; she's a charming hostess who runs a tight ship and keeps an eye on everything.

Whitechapel Gallery Dining Room

Italian 01

Whitechapel

77-82 Whitechapel High st. ✉ E1 7QX
✆ (020) 7522 7896
www.whitechapelgallery.org/dining-room
⊖ Aldgate East

Closed Christmas-New Year, Monday and dinner Sunday and Tuesday – booking advisable

Menu £28 (dinner) – Carte £23/34

Angela Hartnett oversees things here in her role as a consultant chef and she's made some positive changes. Out went the set menu and in came greater flexibility that is far more appropriate to an informal gallery setting. The menu is divided into 'nibbles', 'small plates' and 'bigger plates' and most of the dishes are of European provenance, with the Med supplying plenty of influences, in dishes like rump of lamb with Niçoise salad. The Whitechapel Gallery was founded in 1901 and is best known for exhibiting Picasso's 'Guernica'. It underwent a major refit in 2009, when it expanded into the former library next door and created this very sweet restaurant. It's a bright, well-lit room, with tightly packed tables.

Good food without spending a fortune? Look for the Bib Gourmand ☺.

South-West London

Meandering like a silver snake, **The Thames** coils serenely through south-west London, adding definition to the area's much-heralded middle-class enclaves and leafy suburbs. It's the focal point to the annual **university boat race** from **Putney** to **Mortlake,** and it serves as the giant glass pond attractively backing countless bank-side pubs. This area has long been regarded as the cosy bourgeois side of town, though within its postcode prowls the lively and eclectic **Brixton,** whose buzzing street markets and lauded music venues add an urban lustre and vibrant edge.

In most people's minds, though, south-west London finds its true colours in the beautiful terrace view from the top of **Richmond Hill,** as the river bends majestically through the meadows below. Or in the smart **Wimbledon Village,** its independent boutiques ranged prettily along its own hill, with the open spaces of the Common for a back garden. Or, again, in the Italianate architecture that makes **Chiswick House** and grounds a little corner of the Mediterranean close to the Great West Road.

Green space is almost as prolific in this zone as the streets of Victorian and Edwardian villas. **Richmond Park** is the largest royal park in the whole of London and teems with kite flyers, cyclists and deer – though not necessarily in that order. From here, round a southerly bend in the river, delightful grounds surround **Ham House,** which celebrated its 400th birthday in 2010, although not so excessively as during the seventeenth century when it was home to Restoration court life. Head slightly north to **Kew Gardens** and its world famous 300 acres can now be viewed from above – the treetop walkway, takes you 60 feet up to offer some breath-taking views. Just across the river from here is another from the historical hit-list: **Syon Park,** which boasts water meadows still grazed by cattle, giving it a distinctly rural aspect. Syon House is considered one of architect Robert Adam's finest works; it certainly appealed to Queen Victoria, who spent much of her young life here. Up the road in bourgeoning Brentford, two unique museums bring in hordes of the curious: the Musical Museum includes a huge Wurlitzer theatre organ (get lucky and watch it being played), while almost next door, the Kew Bridge Steam Museum shows off all things steamy on a grand scale, including massive beam engines which pumped London's water for over a century.

Hammersmith may be known for its bustling Broadway and flyover, but five minutes' walk from here is the Upper Mall, which has iconic riverside pubs and Kelmscott House, the last home of artistic visionary William Morris: down in the basement and coach house are impressive memorabilia related to his life plus changing exhibitions of designs and drawings. From here, it's just a quick jaunt across **Hammersmith Bridge** and down the arrow-straight Castelnau to the

D. Chapuis / MICHELIN

Wetland Centre in Barnes, which for ten years has lured wildlife to within screeching distance of the West End. **Barnes** has always revelled in its village-like identity – it juts up like an isolated peninsula into the Thames and boasts yummy boutiques and well-known restaurants. The Bulls Head pub in Lonsdale Road has featured some of the best jazz in London for half a century.

In a more easterly direction, the urbanised areas of **Clapham** and **Battersea** have re-established themselves as desirable places to live over the last decade. **Clapham Common** is considered prime southwest London turf, to the extent that its summer music festivals are highly prized. It's ringed by good pubs and restaurants, too. Battersea used to be famous for its funfair, but now the peace pagoda in the park lends it a more serene light. And if you're after serenity on a hot day, then a cool dip in the wondrous **Tooting** Lido is just the thing.

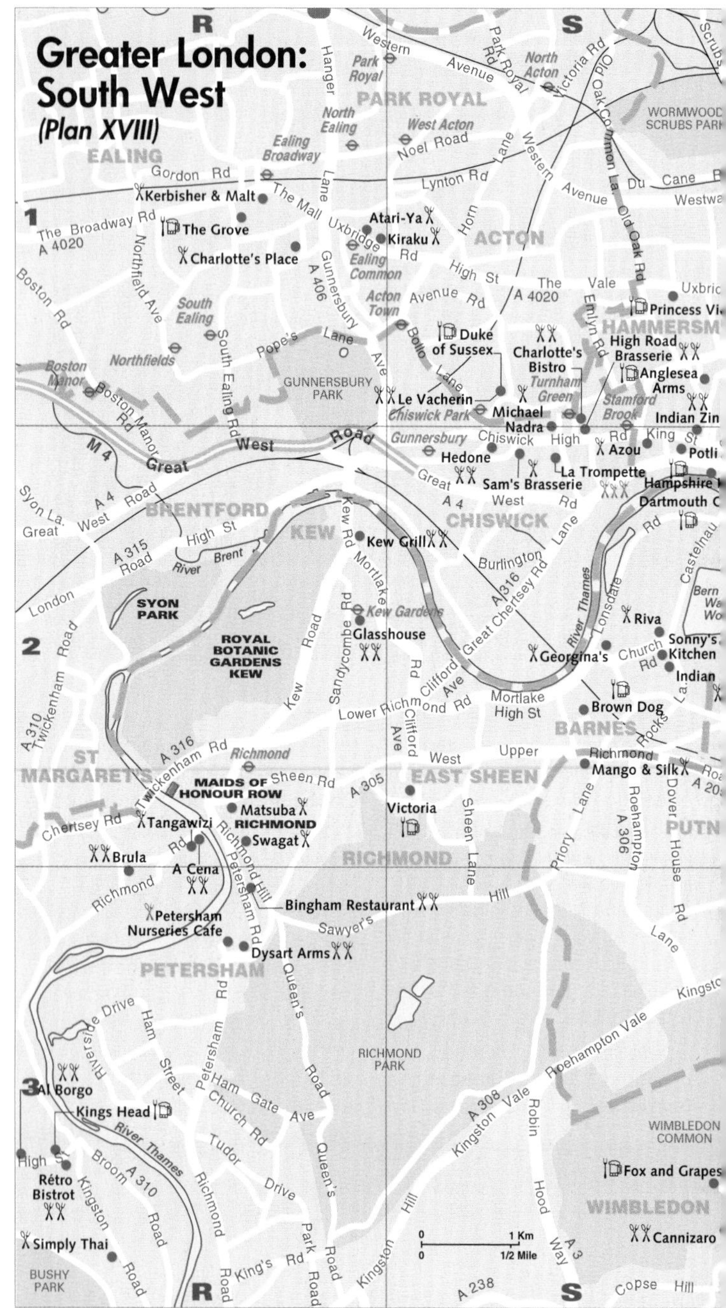
Greater London: South West
(Plan XVIII)
R
S
1
2
3
EALING
PARK ROYAL
ACTON
HAMMERSMITH
CHISWICK
BRENTFORD
KEW
BARNES
EAST SHEEN
RICHMOND
ST MARGARET'S
PETERSHAM
PUTNEY
WIMBLEDON
WORMWOOD SCRUBS PARK
GUNNERSBURY PARK
SYON PARK
ROYAL BOTANIC GARDENS KEW
MAIDS OF HONOUR ROW
RICHMOND PARK
WIMBLEDON COMMON
BUSHY PARK
Park Royal
North Acton
North Ealing
West Acton
Ealing Broadway
Ealing Common
Acton Town
South Ealing
Northfields
Boston Manor
Turnham Green
Stamford Brook
Chiswick Park
Gunnersbury
Kew Gardens
Richmond
Kerbisher & Malt
The Grove
Charlotte's Place
Atari-Ya
Kiraku
Princess Victoria
Duke of Sussex
Charlotte's Bistro
High Road Brasserie
Anglesea Arms
Le Vacherin
Michael Nadra
Indian Zing
Hedone
Azou
Potli
Sam's Brasserie
La Trompette
Hampshire Hog
Dartmouth Castle
Kew Grill
Glasshouse
Riva
Sonny's Kitchen
Indian
Georgina's
Brown Dog
Mango & Silk
Matsuba
Tangawizi
Swagat
Victoria
Brula
A Cena
Petersham Nurseries Cafe
Bingham Restaurant
Dysart Arms
Al Borgo
Kings Head
Rétro Bistrot
Simply Thai
Fox and Grapes
Cannizaro
Western Avenue
Hanger Lane
Gordon Rd
The Mall
Uxbridge Rd
Noel Road
Lynton Rd
Horn Lane
High St
The Vale
Old Oak Common La
Victoria Rd
Du Cane Rd
The Broadway Rd
A 4020
Northfield Ave
Boston Rd
Gunnersbury Avenue
A 406
Pope's Lane
Bollo Lane
Emlyn Rd
Chiswick High Rd
King St
Great West Road
M 4
A 4
A 315
London Road
High St
River Brent
Syon La.
Kew Rd
Mortlake Road
Burlington Lane
A 316
Great Chertsey Rd
River Thames
Lonsdale Rd
Castelnau
Church Rd
Rocks La.
Sandycombe Rd
Clifford Ave
Lower Richmond Rd
Mortlake High St
Upper Richmond Road West
A 305
Twickenham Road
A 310
Sheen Rd
Chertsey Rd
Richmond Hill
Richmond Rd
Petersham Rd
Sheen Lane
Priory Lane
Roehampton Lane
A 306
Dover House Rd
Sawyer's Hill
Queen's Road
Riverside Drive
Ham Street
Ham Gate Ave
Church Rd
Tudor Drive
Broom Road
Kingston Road
King's Rd
Park Road
Roehampton Vale
Kingston Vale
A 308
Robin Hood Way
A 3
Kingston Hill
A 238
Copse Hill
Kingston Rd
0 1 Km
0 1/2 Mile

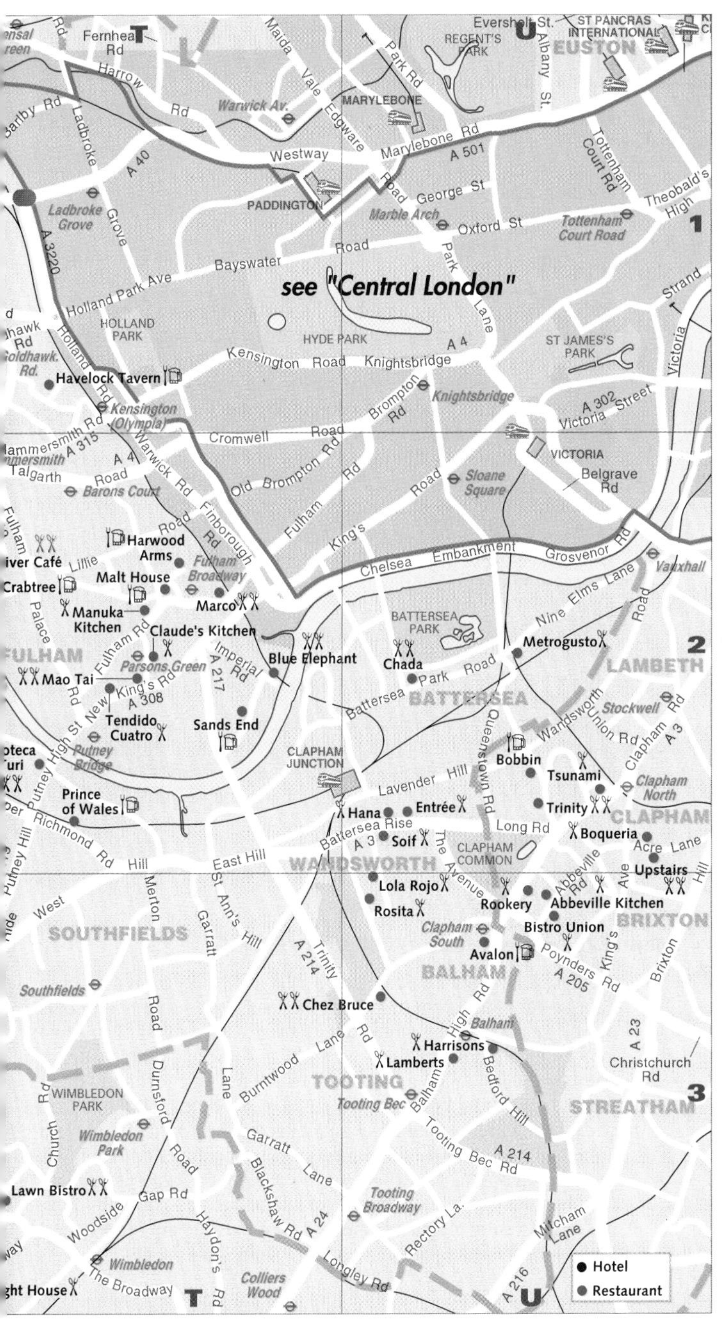
see "Central London"
Havelock Tavern
Harwood Arms
Malt House
Crabtree
Manuka Kitchen
Marco
Claude's Kitchen
Mao Tai
Tendido Cuatro
Sands End
Blue Elephant
Chada
Metrogusto
Prince of Wales
Bobbin
Tsunami
Trinity
Hana
Entrée
Soif
Boqueria
Upstairs
Lola Rojo
Rosita
Rookery
Abbeville Kitchen
Bistro Union
Avalon
Chez Bruce
Harrisons
Lamberts
Lawn Bistro
FULHAM
BATTERSEA
WANDSWORTH
CLAPHAM
LAMBETH
BRIXTON
BALHAM
TOOTING
STREATHAM
SOUTHFIELDS
HOLLAND PARK
HYDE PARK
ST JAMES'S PARK
REGENT'S PARK
BATTERSEA PARK
CLAPHAM COMMON
PADDINGTON
MARYLEBONE
VICTORIA
EUSTON
ST PANCRAS INTERNATIONAL
CLAPHAM JUNCTION
WIMBLEDON PARK
1
2
3
Hotel
Restaurant

Duke of Sussex

Mediterranean

S1

Acton Green

75 South Par ✉ W4 5LF

✆ (020) 8742 8801

www.realpubs.co.uk

⊖ Chiswick Park

Carte £18/33

Perhaps it's part of the plan but the Duke of Sussex seems like a typical London pub, even from the front bar, but step through into the dining room and you'll be in what was once a variety theatre from the time when this was a classic gin palace, complete with proscenium arch, glass ceiling and chandeliers. If that wasn't unusual enough, you could then find yourself eating cured meats or fabada, as the menu has a strong Spanish influence. Traditionalists can still get their steak pies and treacle tart but it's worth being more adventurous and trying the sardines, the paella and the crema Catalana. This is a fun, enthusiastically run and bustling pub and the kitchen's enthusiasm is palpable. On Mondays it's BYO; Sunday is quiz night.

Le Vacherin

French

S1

Acton Green

76-77 South Par ✉ W4 5LF

✆ (020) 8742 2121

www.levacherin.com

⊖ Chiswick Park

Closed Monday lunch

Menu £23 (weekday lunch)/28 – Carte £30/50

Le Vacherin calls itself a bistro but, with its brown leather banquette seating, mirrors and belle époque prints, it feels more like a brasserie, and quite a smart one at that. The most important element of the operation is the appealing menu of French classics which rarely changes, largely because they don't need to but also because the regulars wouldn't allow it. The checklist includes oeufs en cocotte, escargots, confit of duck and crème brûlée. Beef is something of a speciality, whether that's the côte de boeuf, the rib-eye or the chateaubriand. Portions are sensible, flavours distinct and ingredients good. The only thing missing in terms of authenticity are some insouciant French staff and a little Piaf playing in the background.

Avalon

British traditional U3

Balham

16 Balham Hill ✉ SW12 9EB

✆ (020) 8675 8613

www.theavalonlondon.com

⊖ Clapham South

Closed 25-26 December – booking advisable

Menu £23 (dinner) – Carte £22/34

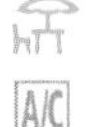

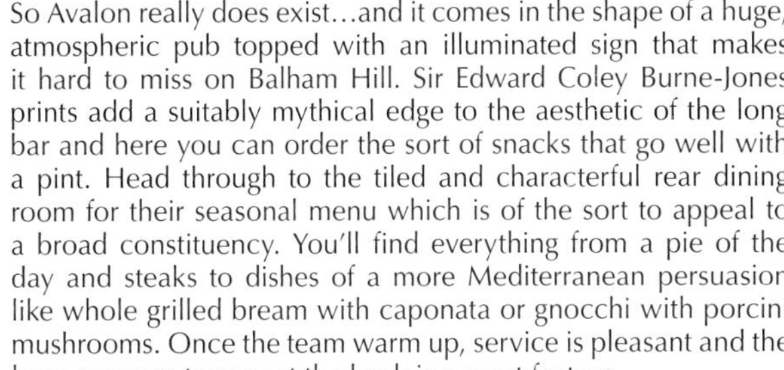

So Avalon really does exist...and it comes in the shape of a huge, atmospheric pub topped with an illuminated sign that makes it hard to miss on Balham Hill. Sir Edward Coley Burne-Jones prints add a suitably mythical edge to the aesthetic of the long bar and here you can order the sort of snacks that go well with a pint. Head through to the tiled and characterful rear dining room for their seasonal menu which is of the sort to appeal to a broad constituency. You'll find everything from a pie of the day and steaks to dishes of a more Mediterranean persuasion like whole grilled bream with caponata or gnocchi with porcini mushrooms. Once the team warm up, service is pleasant and the large summer terrace at the back is a great feature.

Harrison's

modern U3

Balham

15-19 Bedford Hill ✉ SW12 9EX

✆ (020) 8675 6900

www.harrisonsbalham.co.uk

⊖ Balham

Closed 24-28 December

Menu £14/26 – Carte £24/38

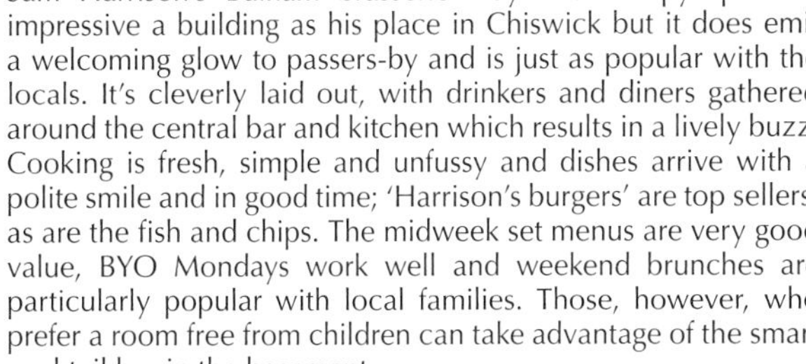

Sam Harrison's Balham brasserie may not occupy quite as impressive a building as his place in Chiswick but it does emit a welcoming glow to passers-by and is just as popular with the locals. It's cleverly laid out, with drinkers and diners gathered around the central bar and kitchen which results in a lively buzz. Cooking is fresh, simple and unfussy and dishes arrive with a polite smile and in good time; 'Harrison's burgers' are top sellers, as are the fish and chips. The midweek set menus are very good value, BYO Mondays work well and weekend brunches are particularly popular with local families. Those, however, who prefer a room free from children can take advantage of the smart cocktail bar in the basement.

Lamberts

British traditional U3

Balham

2 Station Par ✉ SW12 9AZ
(020) 8675 2233
www.lambertsrestaurant.com
⊖ Balham
Closed 24-26 December, 1-2 January, Sunday dinner and Monday

Menu £18/24 – Carte £29/38

Mr Lambert and his eponymous restaurant have succeeded by offering the locals exactly what they want: relaxed surroundings, hospitable service and tasty, seasonal food. The menu is updated each month and small suppliers have been sought out. The cooking is quite British in style and has a satisfying wholesomeness to it; Sunday's ribs of Galloway beef or legs of Salt Marsh lamb are hugely popular. Equal thought and passion have gone into the commendably priced wine list, which includes some favourites offered in 300ml decanters. Other nice touches include filtered water delivered gratis and velvety truffles brought with the coffee. The owner's enthusiasm has rubbed off on his team, for whom nothing is too much trouble.

Brown Dog

British modern S2

Barnes

28 Cross St ✉ SW13 0AP
(020) 8392 2200
www.thebrowndog.co.uk
Closed 25 December

Carte £23/36

Thankfully, changes of ownership don't appear to mean much here – perhaps you really can't teach an old dog new tricks – because The Brown Dog remains a terrific neighbourhood pub and the locals clearly love it just the way it is. Mind you, this pretty Victorian pub is so well hidden in the maze of residential streets that it's a wonder any new customers ever find it anyway. The look fuses the traditional with the modern and service is bubbly and enthusiastic. Jugs of iced water arrive without prompting and the cleverly concise menu changes regularly. A lightly spiced crab salad or pint of prawns could be followed by a succulent rump of lamb, while puddings like sticky toffee date pudding or gooseberry cheesecake are also commendably priced.

Georgina's

British modern

S2

Barnes

56 Barnes High St ✉ SW13 9LF

✆ (020) 8166 5559

www.georginasrestaurants.com

Closed Sunday dinner

Carte £17/29

A/C

Dubbed 'Superwoman' by the tabloids for juggling motherhood with a successful City career, Nicola Horlick has now turned her hand to the restaurant business by opening this bright, modern eatery which appears to be a perfect fit for Barnes. It certainly ticks all the on-trend boxes, from the clean white furnishings to the counter of artisan breads, salads and pastas – it resembles more of a smart café during the day and an informal restaurant by night. The cooking is simple, unadorned, easy to eat and comes with occasional Middle Eastern hints. They also do a weekend brunch and a take home service for the salads, cakes and breads. Service can be a little too serious at times but this is an undeniably pleasant spot.

Indian Zilla

Indian

S2

Barnes

2-3 Rocks Ln. ✉ SW13 0DB

✆ (020) 8878 3989

www.indianzilla.co.uk

(dinner only and lunch Saturday-Sunday)

Menu £15 (lunch) – Carte £12/15

A/C

Judging by the crowds, Barnes' locals are clearly delighted that their district was chosen as the third location for this bourgeoning little group, following on from the success of Indian Zing and Indian Zest. The bright restaurant has a lovely buzz to it and the young, eager-to-please service team are very attentive. The new-wave Indian cooking is surprisingly light yet full of flavour, with many of the dishes using organic ingredients. Whilst a few old favourites are offered, it is the more delicate options that really stand out, such as lobster Balchao and specialities from the owner's home province of Maharashtra, like vegetable Bhanavla. The breads are super as is the lemon and ginger rice, and be sure to end with the Tandoori figs.

Riva

Italian

Barnes

169 Church Rd. ✉ SW13 9HR

✆ (020) 8748 0434

Closed 3 weeks August, Christmas-New Year, Saturday lunch and bank holidays

Carte £28/54

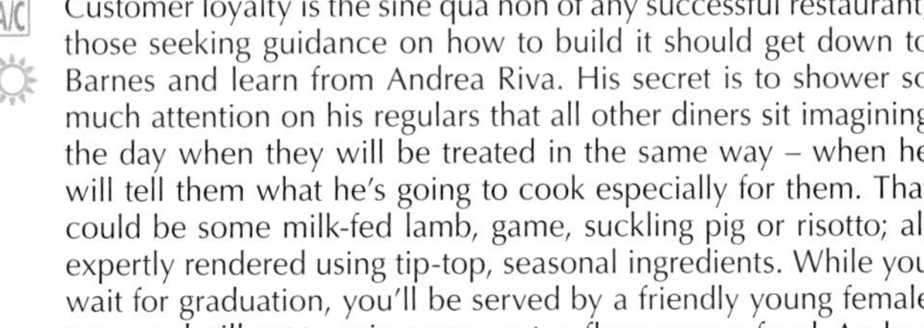

A/C

Customer loyalty is the sine qua non of any successful restaurant; those seeking guidance on how to build it should get down to Barnes and learn from Andrea Riva. His secret is to shower so much attention on his regulars that all other diners sit imagining the day when they will be treated in the same way – when he will tell them what he's going to cook especially for them. That could be some milk-fed lamb, game, suckling pig or risotto; all expertly rendered using tip-top, seasonal ingredients. While you wait for graduation, you'll be served by a friendly young female team and still get to enjoy some gutsy, flavoursome food. Andrea is also a keen wine collector so if you can talk oenology it could improve your chances of joining the club.

Sonny's Kitchen

modern

Barnes

94 Church Rd ✉ SW13 0DQ

✆ (020) 8748 0393

www.sonnyskitchen.co.uk

Menu £17/25 – Carte £26/43

A/C

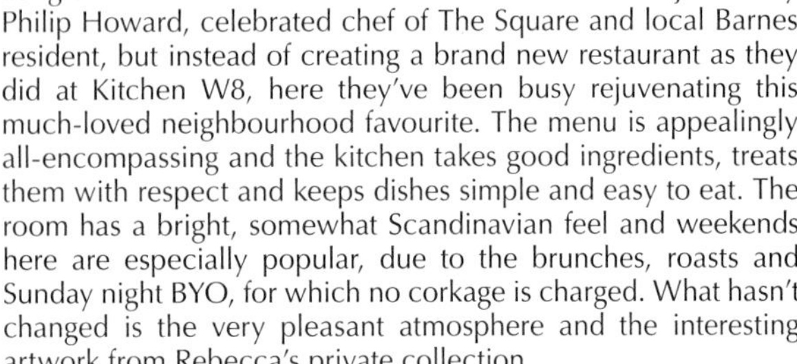

Long-time owner Rebecca Mascarenhas has been joined by Philip Howard, celebrated chef of The Square and local Barnes resident, but instead of creating a brand new restaurant as they did at Kitchen W8, here they've been busy rejuvenating this much-loved neighbourhood favourite. The menu is appealingly all-encompassing and the kitchen takes good ingredients, treats them with respect and keeps dishes simple and easy to eat. The room has a bright, somewhat Scandinavian feel and weekends here are especially popular, due to the brunches, roasts and Sunday night BYO, for which no corkage is charged. What hasn't changed is the very pleasant atmosphere and the interesting artwork from Rebecca's private collection.

Chada

Thai

Battersea

U2

208-210 Battersea Park Rd. ✉ SW11 4ND

✆ (020) 7622 2209

www.chadathai.com

Closed Sunday and bank holidays – (dinner only)

Carte £22/34

A/C Chada, whose positively resplendent façade marks it out on Battersea Park Road, is still going strong after 20 years, although it doesn't face huge competition. A striking carved Buddha dominates the simply dressed room but check out the owner's gilded headdress, displayed in a cabinet, which she uses for festivals. This may never be the busiest restaurant around but the welcome is always warm, the service polite and endearing and the Thai cooking satisfying and keenly priced. The menu is still a very long affair but it's easy to navigate through and the seafood selection is an undoubted highlight. Several dishes can be made with a choice of chicken, duck, prawn or vegetables; portions are generous and presentation is appealing.

Entrée

modern

Battersea

U2

2 Battersea Rise ✉ SW11 1ED

✆ (020) 7223 5147

www.entreebattersea.co.uk

Closed 24-28 December – (dinner only and lunch Saturday-Sunday)

Menu £19 (lunch) – Carte £26/32

The name doesn't quite fit as it implies a devotion to all things French and a degree of pretentiousness that is thankfully absent. In reality they have gone more for a casual bistro look which, along with an intimate basement bar and weekend pianist, appears to have hit the right note with the locals. The style of food is a little harder to categorise: the attractively priced menu offers a selection of French classics together with dishes of a more modern European persuasion, as well as other choices that could be considered as being more from the '80s. It is this third section which actually provides some of the highlights, such as the scallop and crab lasagne. Haunch of venison and the ubiquitous pork belly are also popular choices.

Hana

Korean

Battersea

60 Battersea Rise ✉ SW11 1EG
✆ (020) 7228 2496
www.hanakorean.co.uk
Closed 24-25 December

U2

Carte £18/27 

Most of the decent local restaurants are up at the Common end, so it's nice to see a few places opening further down the hill. The young owners of this sweet, warmly run little Korean restaurant are also benefitting from the growing popularity of Korean food in the capital. The cooking style may have been slightly westernised but the dishes still have plenty of vibrancy and freshness, and the aromas fill the air. Yang Yeum chicken and the Pa Jeon seafood pancake are popular starters; the bibimbap mixed rice dishes burst with flavour; they have their own take on the classic Bossam dish; and seafood cooked on the barbeque is particularly good. You can also try Korean teas, beers, wine and soju.

Lola Rojo

Spanish

Battersea

78 Northcote Rd ✉ SW11 6QL
✆ (020) 7350 2262
www.lolarojo.net
Closed 25-26 December and lunch 1 January – booking essential

U3 

Carte £12/26 

Northcote Road hosts a plethora of restaurants but few are as fun as this lively Spanish eatery. There's no denying the layout is a little cramped but the all-white look, dotted with splashes of red, makes it feel fresh. The owner-chef comes from Valencia so paella is a sure thing but other Catalan specialities are worth seeking out, such as the tomato bread, the creamy spinach with pine nuts, various salt-cod and shellfish dishes and, to finish, crema Catalana. Despite the volume of customers the kitchen delivers dishes promptly and consistently while the serving team just about keep up; 3 or 4 tapas per person should do it and there's an affordable wine list to lift the mood even more. It's little wonder the locals can't get enough.

Metrogusto

Italian

U2

Battersea

153 Battersea Park Rd. ✉ SW8 4BX
✆ (020) 7720 0204
www.metrogusto.co.uk
Closed 4-17 August, 25-26 December, Easter and Sunday dinner

Menu £12 (weekday lunch) – Carte £19/31

Ambro Ianeselli is one of London's most affable restaurateurs and his move from Islington back to his original Battersea base resulted in moans in the north and cheers in the south. This was once a pub and he's kept it uncluttered, although Metrogusto followers will recognise some of his modern art collection. They will also notice he's gone back to basics: the menu starts with 'morsels' such as delicious sweet and sour Sicilian aubergines, which can be followed by goat's cheese ravioli with a great walnut sauce or a generous helping of pappardelle with veal ragout and a decent panna cotta to finish. The food is simple and satisfying, matched with a fair range of wines from his homeland and his never-ending hospitality.

Rosita

Mediterranean

U2

Battersea

124 Northcote Rd ✉ SW11 6QU
✆ (020) 7998 9093
www.rositasherry.net
Closed 25-26 December and lunch 1 January – (dinner only and lunch Friday-Sunday)

Menu £15 (lunch) – Carte £15/26

From the same team as Lola Roja down the road comes this fun sherry and tapas bar, which is named after the owner's aunt. Brightly painted ceramic tiles and brass lanterns lend a subtle Moorish look to the room and cheery service adds to the buzzy atmosphere. Plate sizes vary from the diminutive to the generous – the latter being the more flavoursome and expensive dishes involving meats and seafood cooked by the Josper grill. The best action is to ask for advice as the staff are great at guiding you through ordering – and they are also keen to know you're enjoying yourself. The other aim of the place is to showcase the versatility of sherry: there's plenty of choice by the glass as well as suggested pairings with certain dishes.

Soif

French

U2 

Battersea

27 Battersea Rise ✉ SW11 1HG
✆ (020) 7233 1112
www.soif.co
Closed Christmas and New Year, bank holidays, Sunday dinner and Monday lunch – booking essential at dinner

Carte £23/37 

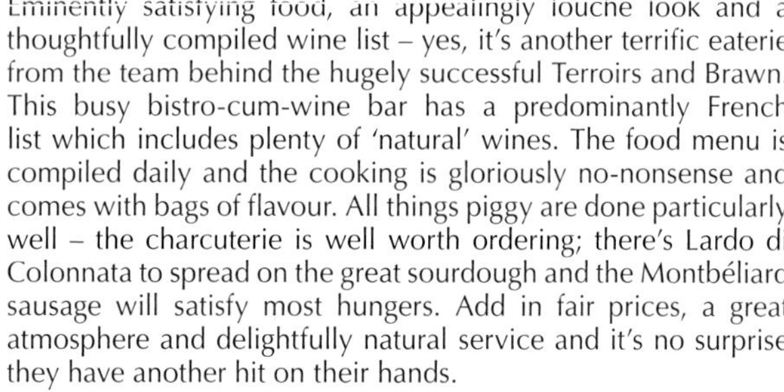

Eminently satisfying food, an appealingly louche look and a thoughtfully compiled wine list – yes, it's another terrific eaterie from the team behind the hugely successful Terroirs and Brawn. This busy bistro-cum-wine bar has a predominantly French list which includes plenty of 'natural' wines. The food menu is compiled daily and the cooking is gloriously no-nonsense and comes with bags of flavour. All things piggy are done particularly well – the charcuterie is well worth ordering; there's Lardo di Colonnata to spread on the great sourdough and the Montbéliard sausage will satisfy most hungers. Add in fair prices, a great atmosphere and delightfully natural service and it's no surprise they have another hit on their hands.

Boqueria

Spanish

U2 

Brixton

192 Acre Ln. ✉ SW2 5UL
✆ (020) 7733 4408
www.boqueriatapas.com
⊖ Clapham North
(dinner only and lunch Saturday-Sunday)

Carte £10/20 

Named after – and inspired by – Barcelona's famous food market, this contemporary tapas bar is a welcome addition to the neighbourhood and has quickly established a local fan-base. The menu doubles as a place mat and is a mix of recognisable classics and more adventurous offerings; it is also supplemented by specials on the blackboard. As everyone involved appears to hail from Andalucía, it makes sense to kick off with a glass of sherry. The Ibérico hams are in excellent order, the lamb medallions are full of flavour and be sure to save room for a particularly good Crema Catalana. It's worth sitting at the counter as the main dining area at the back lacks a little personality. Their café next door serves coffee and churros.

Upstairs

modern

U2

Brixton

89b Acre Ln. ✉ SW2 5TN

✆ (020) 7733 8855 – **www**.upstairslondon.com

⊖ Clapham North

Closed 22 December-7 January, 13-22 April, 17August-2 September, Sunday and Monday – (dinner only)

Menu £29/41

XX

A restaurant where one has to ring the doorbell to gain entry not only makes it the ideal choice if dining with someone one shouldn't be, but also heightens expectations. Upstairs is split over two floors and the French owner runs the place enthusiastically: service is unapologetically Gallic and there's as much kissing as there is shrugging. He may have saved on the décor but he spent lavishly on the table settings, with fine glassware and cutlery. The set menu of three choices per course changes fortnightly and the chef is keen to showcase his skills. There are certainly some unique touches, although they are sometimes marred by a tendency to over-complicate. That being said, this is a sweet operation doing something a little different.

Charlotte's Bistro

modern

Chiswick

6 Turnham Green Terr ✉ W4 1QP

✆ (020) 8742 3590

www.charlottes.co.uk

⊖ Turnham Green

Booking advisable

Menu £16/24

Unlike some desirable London neighbourhoods, Chiswick has always had plenty of restaurants, so locals never feel the need to venture too far from home for dinner. This little sister to nearby Ealing's Charlotte's Place provides them with another pleasantly unpretentious option. A large bar takes up most of the front section and then it's a few steps up to the bright dining room with a glass roof. The menu changes regularly and has a European accent, with such dishes as crab and celeriac tian, cod brandade, pan-fried halloumi, rolled leg of lamb and fishcakes. There's also a nice little cheese menu. Wines are listed by character and include bottles from some small producers. Service and prices are equally friendly.

Hedone ✿

modern

S2

Chiswick

301-303 Chiswick High Rd ✉ W4 4HH

✆ (020) 8747 0377 – **www**.hedonerestaurant.com

⊖ Chiswick Park

Closed 2 weeks August, Christmas-New Year, Sunday and Monday – (dinner only and lunch Thursday-Saturday)

Menu £35/55

Hedone

Swedish chef-owner Mikael Jonsson, an enthusiastic food blogger and former lawyer, put his money where his mouth is and his reputation on the line by opening his own restaurant. It didn't take long for Hedone, which is Greek for 'pleasure', to prove that gamble had paid off. The refreshingly unfussy food, from a small and daily changing menu, relies primarily on the superlative quality of the ingredients and, by cooking them carefully and sympathetically, Mikael ensures that their natural flavours are allowed to shine. This is food that is exceptionally easy to eat and, while you can choose four or five courses from the main menu, taking the 7 course Tasting Menu is a far from daunting prospect. His passion is palpable and is evident in every aspect of the restaurant, especially in the enthusiasm of his charming service team. The kitchen forms part of the room by being very open plan, with the counter proving particularly popular with various bands of foodies; others should ask for the seats along the wall where the back-rest cushions hang from poles.

First Course

- Slow-cooked duck's egg, morels, green peas and bell pepper.
- Scallops with watercress and Jerusalem artichokes.

Main Course

- Roasted squab and beetroot five ways.
- Turbot, baby artichokes, piattoni beans and confit Marinda tomatoes.

Dessert

- Apple millefeuille with caramel ice cream.
- Floating islands with beetroot and rhubarb.

High Road Brasserie

French

S2

Chiswick

High Road House Hotel,
162 Chiswick High Rd. ✉ W4 1PR
(020) 8742 7474 – **www**.highroadhouse.co.uk
⊖ Turnham Green
Booking essential

Carte £20/36

It's usually so busy you'll have trouble getting in the door – quite literally sometimes, as the entrance is often crowded with evening drinkers or lunchtime pushchairs. This modern take on the brasserie certainly has the look, with its mirrors, panelling and art deco lighting; turn right for the more comfy seating. Staff are used to being busy and get the job done, although without much time for pleasantries. What is surprising is that, despite the volume of customers, the kitchen is able to deliver a good standard of accurately cooked classics including steak frites, duck confit, grilled lobster or whole sea bass, along with salads and sandwiches. The bill can rise quickly as sides are required, but there's a good value daytime menu.

Michael Nadra

modern

S1/2

Chiswick

6-8 Elliott Rd. ✉ W4 1PE
(020) 8742 0766
www.restaurant-michaelnadra.co.uk
⊖ Turnham Green
Closed 24-26 December, 1 January and Sunday dinner

Menu £20/49

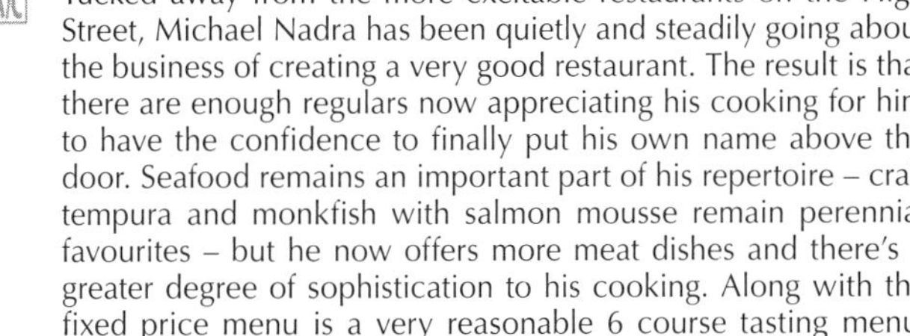

Tucked away from the more excitable restaurants on the High Street, Michael Nadra has been quietly and steadily going about the business of creating a very good restaurant. The result is that there are enough regulars now appreciating his cooking for him to have the confidence to finally put his own name above the door. Seafood remains an important part of his repertoire – crab tempura and monkfish with salmon mousse remain perennial favourites – but he now offers more meat dishes and there's a greater degree of sophistication to his cooking. Along with the fixed price menu is a very reasonable 6 course tasting menu, with suggested wine pairings. The restaurant has an intimate, local feel which is helped along by friendly staff.

Sam's Brasserie

Mediterranean

S2

Chiswick

11 Barley Mow Passage ✉ W4 4PH

✆ (020) 8987 0555

www.samsbrasserie.co.uk

⊖ Turnham Green

Closed 24-26 December

Menu £17 (weekdays) – Carte £20/38

The building was once a Sanderson wallpaper mill and the industrial feel works well in this bustling brasserie environment. An added helping of hipness comes courtesy of the artwork from local resident, and occasional diner here, Sir Peter Blake. Look out too for the regular Soul and Jazz evenings. Dining is on two levels; the mezzanine is the quieter one, while the larger room looks into the kitchen and has plenty of bustle. The modern brasserie food is prepared with more care and expertise that one expects when one considers the size of the operation and, with a wine list offering over half its bottles for under £30, it's no surprise that the place gets busy. Service is efficient but could be a little more communicative.

Abbeville Kitchen

Mediterranean

U3

Clapham Common

47 Abbeville Rd ✉ SW4 9JX

✆ (020) 8772 1110

www.abbevillekitchen.co.uk

⊖ Clapham Common

Closed Monday lunch – bookings advisable at dinner

Carte £21/27

The owner has a small boulangerie on this road where his customers would buy their baguettes and bemoan the lack of a decent local restaurant. Moved by their plight, he subsequently found an empty shop, recruited a chef – and his bistro was born. The narrow room has a simple yet homely feel, with the kitchen visible at the far end. The food is gutsy and wholesome and the daily changing menu offers the option of ordering small tasting plates or a more traditional three-courser. The choice is varied – it's not often one sees empanadas and braised goat on the same menu – and the prices are fair. The charcuterie boards stand out, as do those dishes involving slow cooking such as the shoulder of lamb for two. The bread is pretty good too.

La Trompette ✿

British modern

S2

Plan XVIII ▸ South-West

Chiswick

5-7 Devonshire Rd ✉ W4 2EU
✆ (020) 8747 1836
www.latrompette.co.uk
⊖ Turnham Green
Closed 24-26 December – booking essential

Menu £28 (lunch and early dinner), £33/45

La Trompette

One of the reasons for the success of La Trompette is that it has always looked after its customers – when the shop next door was bought and the restaurant expanded, the owners didn't add more tables, they merely used the extra room to add more space between the existing ones. The very pleasant service team also ensure that customers keep returning – they manage the feat of making service seem effortless and the diners do their bit by creating a warm, congenial atmosphere. These days there is a greater distinction between the lunch and dinner menus. Lunch is all about great value; dishes are quite simple but just as skilfully prepared and the kitchen uses lesser known cuts and fewer luxury ingredients. At dinner the mackerel is replaced by turbot and the cooking is a tad more ambitious, but it's never over-elaborate. Another reason for La Trompette's continued success is that, despite the very accomplished cooking, it never gives the impression that it would rather be in Mayfair – it suits Chiswick and the locals clearly like having it.

First Course

- Lasagne of braised rabbit and ceps with broad beans and lemon thyme.
- Parfait and rillette of duck with endive and pear, toasted sour dough.

Main Course

- Skate wing with smoked anchovy and shrimp beurre noisette.
- Grilled Dorset lamb with asparagus, herb gnocchetti and garlic cream.

Dessert

- Hot chocolate fondant with vanilla ice cream.
- Burnt vanilla cream with green apples, pears, and yoghurt sorbet.

Bistro Union

British modern

U3

Clapham Common

40 Abbeville Rd ✉ SW4 9NG

✆ (020) 7042 6400

www.bistrounion.co.uk

⊖ Clapham Common

Closed Sunday dinner – booking advisable

Carte £20/29

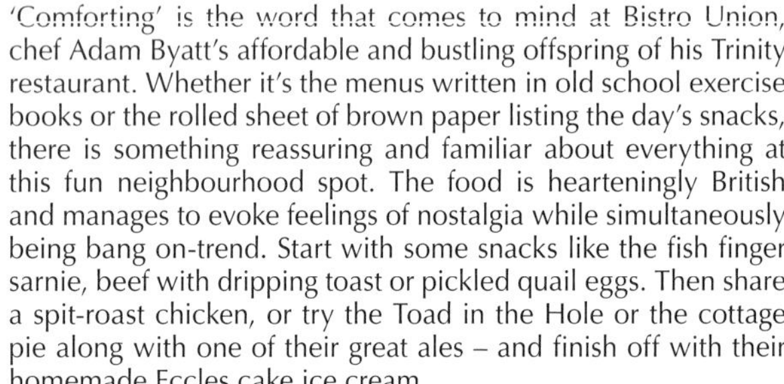

'Comforting' is the word that comes to mind at Bistro Union, chef Adam Byatt's affordable and bustling offspring of his Trinity restaurant. Whether it's the menus written in old school exercise books or the rolled sheet of brown paper listing the day's snacks, there is something reassuring and familiar about everything at this fun neighbourhood spot. The food is hearteningly British and manages to evoke feelings of nostalgia while simultaneously being bang on-trend. Start with some snacks like the fish finger sarnie, beef with dripping toast or pickled quail eggs. Then share a spit-roast chicken, or try the Toad in the Hole or the cottage pie along with one of their great ales – and finish off with their homemade Eccles cake ice cream.

Rookery

British traditional

U3

Clapham Common

69 Clapham Common South Side ✉ SW4 9DA

✆ (020) 8673 9162

www.therookeryclapham.co.uk

⊖ Clapham Common

Closed 25-26 December and Monday lunch

Carte £20/33

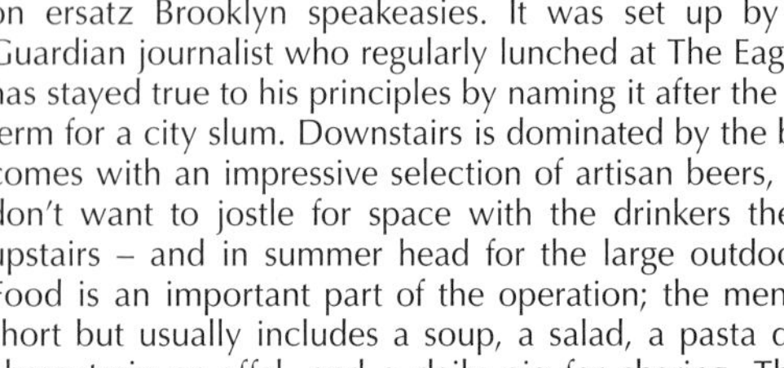

The on-trend Rookery shows that Soho doesn't have a monopoly on ersatz Brooklyn speakeasies. It was set up by a former Guardian journalist who regularly lunched at The Eagle, and he has stayed true to his principles by naming it after the colloquial term for a city slum. Downstairs is dominated by the bar, which comes with an impressive selection of artisan beers, but if you don't want to jostle for space with the drinkers then try the upstairs – and in summer head for the large outdoor terrace. Food is an important part of the operation; the menu may be short but usually includes a soup, a salad, a pasta dish, some charcuterie or offal, and a daily pie for sharing. The kitchen doesn't muck around and delivers some punchy flavours.

Trinity

innovative

Clapham Common

U2

4 The Polygon ✉ SW4 0JG
✆ (020) 7622 1199
www.trinityrestaurant.co.uk
⊖ Clapham Common
Closed 22-29 December, Monday lunch and Sunday dinner

Menu £27 (weekday lunch) – Carte £32/54

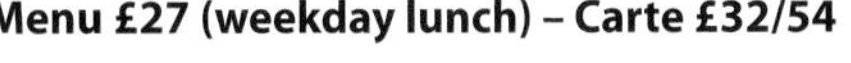

A/C

Trinity is smarter and a little more formal than your average neighbourhood restaurant and residents of Clapham Old Town have clearly taken to it, especially as it means they don't have to schlep up to the West End for a 'proper' night out. The cooking is suitably sophisticated, with the kitchen adding some innovative combinations to what is a fairly classical base. Offal dishes are often the highlight and the pig's trotter on toasted sourdough has become a signature dish. The lunch menu is simpler in style and content but is priced very appealingly. To underline its neighbourhood credentials, the restaurant also offers cookery classes. In summer, ask for a table by the windows, which open up to add a little continental colour.

Tsunami

Japanese

Clapham Common

U2

Unit 3, 5-7 Voltaire Rd ✉ SW4 6DQ
✆ (020) 7978 1610
www.tsunamirestaurant.co.uk
⊖ Clapham North
Closed 24-26 December – (dinner only and lunch Saturday-Sunday)

Carte £16/48

As fun, noisy and as lively as ever, particularly at weekends when it stays open until 2am, Tsunami continues to pull in plenty of Clapham locals, many of whom make the effort to scrub up nicely for this good looking Japanese restaurant with its popular club-like bar. The menu's focus is on modern fusion food but there is also an extensive selection of nigiri, sashimi and sushi rolls. Sharing is actively encouraged which is wise as some of the dishes are really quite substantial. Tempura is suitably light and allows the ingredient to shine, while steamed fish dishes such as the sea bass are often the highlight. Desserts are light and refreshing and presentation is appealing. There is another branch in Charlotte Street.

Atari-ya

Japanese

Ealing

R1

1 Station Par, Uxbridge Rd ✉ W5 3LD
✆ (020) 8202 2789
www.atariya.co.uk
⊖ Ealing Common
Closed bank holiday Mondays

Carte £12/26

Atari-ya are importers and suppliers of fish and assorted Japanese ingredients and are therefore well-placed to also run a few small shops and sushi bars around the capital. Their prices make their sushi bars very accessible and ideal for anyone yet to discover the joy of sushi as well as those wanting a quick fix. Rolls are available but go for nigiri; pieces can be ordered individually although the sets provide a balanced selection, from lighter offerings such as sea bream and scallop to stronger choices like salmon roe and the rich, filling eel; to finish order tamago (egg). Sashimi is also on offer, again individually or as chirashi (over rice). The fish is served at a temperature which allows one to fully appreciate its texture and flavour.

Charlotte's Place

modern

Ealing

16 St Matthew's Rd ✉ W5 3JT
✆ (020) 8567 7541
www.charlottes.co.uk
⊖ Ealing Common
Closed 26 December and 1 January

Menu £20/30

It's been a sweet shop, a transport café and a private club but really found its niche as an honest and warmly run local restaurant. The ground floor offers views over the Common so is more popular at lunch; downstairs is ideal for couples who only have eyes for each other. The à la carte offers ample choice and the cooking is largely British, with smoked fish, traditional Sunday lunches and homely puddings done well; there are also one or two Mediterranean influences and the beef onglet enjoys a constant presence. There is a small cover charge but it does cover bread and unlimited amounts of filtered water rather than being an accountant's wheeze for squeezing more money out of the customers.

The Grove

modern

Ealing

R1

The Green ✉ W5 5QX
(020) 8567 2439
www.thegrovew5.co.uk
⊖ Ealing Broadway

Menu £23/33

It's hard to avoid this beast of a place in central Ealing but then, why would you? It may be brewery owned and have undergone a typical London gastropub makeover, but it'll hit the spot – whether you're out with friends or after a candle-lit dinner. There's a huge front terrace dominated by drinkers but inside it's split into half-bar, half-restaurant; you can eat anywhere but the restaurant at the back is the quieter choice. The menus change monthly – lunch is pretty standard issue, but at dinner the skilful kitchen celebrates its classical roots. The easy-to-eat dishes add a distinctive French accent to the largely British ingredients; desserts are mostly crowd-pleasing classics and are equally satisfying.

Kerbisher & Malt

fish and seafood

Ealing

R1

53 New Broadway ✉ W5 5AH
(020) 8840 4418
www.kerbisher.co.uk
⊖ Ealing Broadway

Carte £11/21

There may have been a revolution in British cooking over the last two decades, but for many people, especially tourists, fish and chips will always be our national dish. Restaurants have been doing decent versions for years but Kerbisher & Malt represents a new wave of ethical fish and chip shops that are raising this classic dish to new heights. The fish here is fresh, sustainably sourced and cooked to order in rapeseed oil (which is then turned into biofuel); chips are made from British spuds and are fried separately; and all packaging is biodegradable. Choose your fish and a side order of thick 'Yorkshire caviar' or pickled onion rings, along with a pot of great tartare sauce. There's another branch in Hammersmith.

Kiraku

Japanese

R1

Ealing

8 Station Par, Uxbridge Rd. ✉ W5 3LD

☎ (020) 8992 2848 – **www**.kiraku.co.uk

⊖ Ealing Common

Closed Christmas-New Year, 10 days August, Monday and Tuesday following bank holidays

Carte £15/39

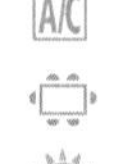

Ayumi and Erica became so frustrated with the lack of a decent local Japanese restaurant that they decided to open one themselves; and now it is not just the bourgeoning Japanese community who flock to this cute little place. It's modestly styled and enthusiastically lit, but service is very charming. Look out for the blackboard menu and its daily changing dishes. Zensai, or starters, include the popular Agedashi dofu; these can then be followed by assorted skewers, noodles and rice dishes. Fish is purchased daily and their sushi now displays a more modern touch; Bara Chirashi is the house speciality. Be sure to end with matcha ice cream or green tea sponge cake. The restaurant's name means 'relax and enjoy' and it's hard not to.

Mango & Silk

Indian

S2

East Sheen

199 Upper Richmond Rd. West ✉ SW14 8 QT

☎ (020) 8876 6220

www.mangoandsilk.com

Closed 25-27 December and Sunday – (dinner only and buffet lunch Sunday)

Carte £16/24

A/C

Mango and Silk was opened by the late Udit Sarkhel who did so much to change the image of Indian restaurants in the UK. His culinary philosophy lives on in the cooking from the young North Indian chef, who ensures that the spicing of the dishes remains sufficiently pronounced but subtle enough to add to the flavour of the ingredients, instead of dominating them. The kitchen also uses very little fat and oil which adds to their fresh, healthy taste. The daily changing specials board is where you'll find the more interesting seasonal dishes like tandoori squid; the house favourite is Saag Gosht, a Punjabi dish which uses tender pieces of lamb; and the kulfi is rich and creamy – a world away from what's offered in many Indian restaurants.

Victoria

British modern

East Sheen

S2

10 West Temple Sheen ✉ SW14 7RT
✆ (020) 8876 4238
www.thevictoria.net

Menu £13 (weekdays) – Carte £23/40

Many pubs claim to be genuine locals – The Victoria is the real deal: it sponsors local clubs and the chef is patron of the local food festival; he also holds cookery workshops at the school next door. This is a beautifully decorated pub, with a restored bar with a wood burning stove and plenty of nooks and crannies; a few steps down and you're in the more formal conservatory overlooking the terrace. The cooking is modern British with the odd international note. Warm homemade bread could be followed by Scotch egg with roast beetroot, cod with a white bean stew and, to finish, blood oranges with rhubarb sorbet. Produce is local where possible: veg is from Surrey and honey from Richmond. Service is engaging and there are bedrooms available.

Blue Elephant

Thai

Fulham

T2

The Boulevard, Imperial Wharf ✉ SW6 2UB
✆ (020) 7751 3111
www.blueelephant.com
Closed 25-26 December and 1 January – booking advisable

Menu £18/55 – Carte £27/54

The Blue Elephant was a Fulham Road landmark for so long that everyone was taken by surprise when it packed its trunk and relocated. Fortunately for its followers, it didn't wander too far and these swankier premises within the large development that is Imperial Wharf have given it a new lease of life. Spread over two floors, the decoration is as exotic as one expects – except that instead of the koi ponds you have the Thames outside, along with two terrific terraces; even the golden dragon made the journey from the old address but can now be found in a different guise at the bar. The appealing menu traverses Thailand and in amongst the classic dishes are a few more contemporary offerings; the curries here are always worth ordering.

Claude's Kitchen

modern

T2

Fulham

51 Parsons Green Ln ✉ SW6 4JA

✆ (020) 7371 8517 – **www**.amusebouchelondon.com

⊖ Parsons Green.

Closed Sunday and Monday – booking essential – (dinner only and lunch Saturday-Sunday)

Carte £23/32

The eponymous Claude has created two little operations within one converted Victorian pub. On the ground floor is 'Amuse Bouche', a champagne bar where the bubbles are sold at competitive prices, along with assorted boards of cheese or cured meats. Upstairs is a small and intimate dining room where you'll find a concise but nicely balanced à la carte menu which changes every Tuesday. Indeed, if you actually come on a Tuesday (or 'guinea pig night' as it is known), you get to enjoy three courses at a considerably reduced price. Everything is homemade here, including the terrific bread, and the food is colourful and fresh, although Claude does have the occasional urge to drop in one or two challenging flavour combinations.

Malt House

British modern

T2

Fulham

17 Vanston Pl ✉ SW6 1AY

✆ (020) 7084 6888

www.malthousefulham.co.uk

⊖ Fulham Broadway

Closed 25 December

Menu £20 (weekday lunch) – Carte £26/54

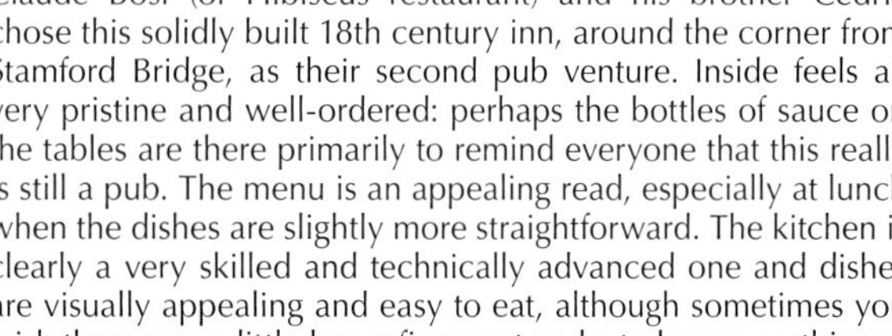

Following the success of the Fox and Grapes in Wimbledon, Claude Bosi (of Hibiscus restaurant) and his brother Cedric chose this solidly built 18th century inn, around the corner from Stamford Bridge, as their second pub venture. Inside feels all very pristine and well-ordered: perhaps the bottles of sauce on the tables are there primarily to remind everyone that this really is still a pub. The menu is an appealing read, especially at lunch when the dishes are slightly more straightforward. The kitchen is clearly a very skilled and technically advanced one and dishes are visually appealing and easy to eat, although sometimes you wish there was a little less refinement and a tad more earthiness. There are six elegant bedrooms upstairs.

Harwood Arms ✿

British modern

Fulham

Walham Grove ✉ SW6 1QP
✆ (020) 7386 1847
www.harwoodarms.com
⊖ Fulham Broadway
Closed 24-27 December, 1 January and Monday lunch – booking essential

T2

Menu £20 (weekday lunch) – Carte £35/43

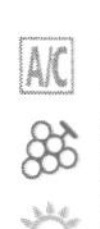

Michelin

Its reputation may have spread around London like wildfire but what many visitors find most reassuring is how unaffected the Harwood Arms has remained. This is still a proper local pub, just one that happens to serve really good food; Tuesday is quiz night and it's packed when Chelsea are playing at home. The reason for its success is largely down to the shared passion of the three owners. Accordingly, it comes as no surprise that, despite a recent change in the kitchen, there has been no discernible deviation in the standard of the food. The cooking remains very seasonal and properly British; faggots, nettle soup, beef cheeks and Hampshire lamb all make regular appearances. There is obvious skill in the cooking but none of the dishes ever seem out of place in this relaxed environment – it's cooking that's all about carefully matched ingredients and great flavours, and not about technique and ego. The wine list has clearly been complied by someone who knows their food and the bar snacks are pretty good too.

First Course

- Crisp pheasant eggs with wild garlic, parsley and ham hock.
- Braised shoulder and roasted leg of rabbit with celery.

Main Course

- Roast Berkshire wood pigeon with Yorkshire rhubarb, beetroot and chicory.
- T-bone of fallow deer with greens and mushroom ketchup.

Dessert

- Bramley apple and cinnamon ice cream with salted caramel.
- Blackberry trifle with sherry sponge and brandy snap.

Ⓝ Manuka Kitchen

modern

Fulham

510 Fulham Rd ✉ SW6 5NJ
✆ (020) 7736 7588
www.manukakitchen.co.uk
⊖ Fulham Broadway
Closed 16-30 August, 25-26 December, Sunday dinner and Monday

Carte £20/28

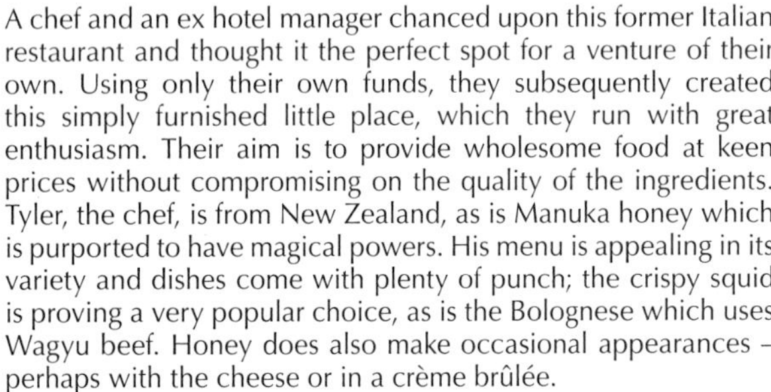

A chef and an ex hotel manager chanced upon this former Italian restaurant and thought it the perfect spot for a venture of their own. Using only their own funds, they subsequently created this simply furnished little place, which they run with great enthusiasm. Their aim is to provide wholesome food at keen prices without compromising on the quality of the ingredients. Tyler, the chef, is from New Zealand, as is Manuka honey which is purported to have magical powers. His menu is appealing in its variety and dishes come with plenty of punch; the crispy squid is proving a very popular choice, as is the Bolognese which uses Wagyu beef. Honey does also make occasional appearances – perhaps with the cheese or in a crème brûlée.

Mao Tai

Chinese

Fulham

58 New Kings Rd, Parsons Grn ✉ SW6 4LS
✆ (020) 7731 2520
www.maotai.co.uk
⊖ Parsons Green
Closed 25-26 December – (dinner only)

Carte £24/63

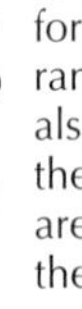

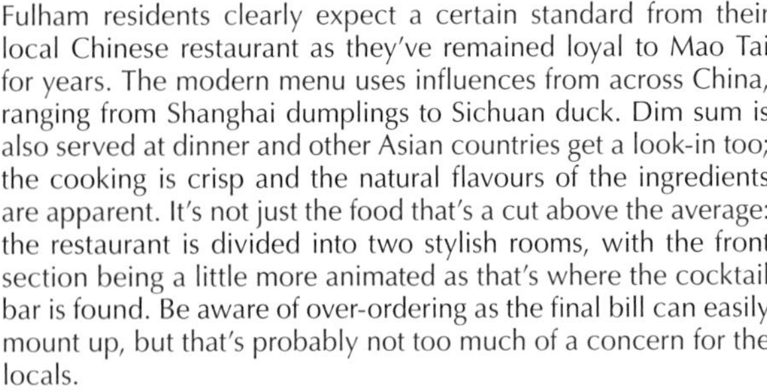

Fulham residents clearly expect a certain standard from their local Chinese restaurant as they've remained loyal to Mao Tai for years. The modern menu uses influences from across China, ranging from Shanghai dumplings to Sichuan duck. Dim sum is also served at dinner and other Asian countries get a look-in too; the cooking is crisp and the natural flavours of the ingredients are apparent. It's not just the food that's a cut above the average: the restaurant is divided into two stylish rooms, with the front section being a little more animated as that's where the cocktail bar is found. Be aware of over-ordering as the final bill can easily mount up, but that's probably not too much of a concern for the locals.

Sands End

British modern

Fulham

135-137 Stephendale Rd ✉ SW6 2PR
✆ (020) 7731 7823
www.thesandsend.co.uk
⊖ Fulham Broadway
Closed 25 December – booking advisable

T2

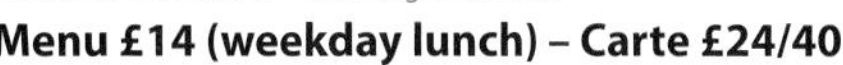

Menu £14 (weekday lunch) – Carte £24/40

Sands End is probably not the best known part of London, or indeed Fulham, but no doubt its residents prefer it that way so they can keep their eponymous pub to themselves. It's a cosy, warm and welcoming one, with a central bar offering some nifty homemade snacks, but try resisting because the main menu – which changes every few days – is pretty appealing itself. There's a distinct British bias which amounts to more than merely name-checking the birthplace of the ingredients. Winter dishes like braised lamb neck or roast partridge with Savoy cabbage are particularly pleasing and West Mersea oysters a good way of starting things off. There's a well-chosen and equally equitably priced wine list that sticks mostly to the Old World.

Tendido Cuatro

Spanish

Fulham

108-110 New Kings Rd ✉ SW6 4LY
✆ (020) 7371 5147
www.cambiodetercio.co.uk
⊖ Parsons Green
Closed 2 weeks Christmas and lunch Sunday-Monday

T2

Carte £24/50

Any resemblance to their other restaurants in Old Brompton Road is entirely intentional: here too the front panels burst open in summer to reveal a warm interior where vivid colours are used with wild abandon. The main difference is that, along with tapas, the speciality is the Valencian classic, paella. Using bomba rice, the choice varies from seafood to quail and chorizo; cuttlefish ink to vegetarian. They are designed for two but that assumes a more than eager appetite, especially if you've had a couple of small dishes as a run-up. The tapas is nicely varied, from refreshing baby anchovies to crisp pigs ears. Service is spirited and the room comes alive later in the evening as the locals return from work and wander over.

Anglesea Arms

British traditional S1

Hammersmith

35 Wingate Rd ✉ W6 0UR
✆ (020) 8749 1291
www.anglesea-arms.com
⊖ Ravenscourt Park
Closed 25-26 December – bookings not accepted

Carte £24/40

While the menu here changes daily and is largely governed by what its suppliers bring, some aspects remain constant: there's always pig's head terrine, prawns, a tart and a seasonal salad. Fish and game are handled well and dishes are pleasingly robust – try the delicious Orb of Joy: braised onion which comes with roast partridge. The treacle tart has a cult following but the ice creams and sorbets are delicious too. The pub has a cluttered, very lived-in look and gets properly crowded but has a refreshing honesty, with staff providing thoughtful advice. Look for its windows etched with the inviting words 'Pies and Hams' and 'Stout and Oysters'. Above the door is 'Mon Mam Cymru', Mother of Wales, as the Isle of Anglesey is known.

Azou

North-African S2

Hammersmith

375 King St. ✉ W6 9NJ
✆ (020) 8563 7266
www.azou.co.uk
⊖ Stamford Brook
Closed 1 January, 25 December – booking essential – (dinner only)

Carte £20/38

You'll probably walk past the first time and not notice this unassuming little place but, once visited, you won't walk past again. Inside is all silks, lanterns and rugs but it is also very personally run; the owner will often pop out from his kitchen to offer guidance – and his advice is well worth listening to. The cooking skips across North African countries – order some Algerian olives while you choose from the wide choice of main courses. Understandably, most of the regulars come here for a tajine, especially the Constantine with its tender lamb and triple-steamed couscous. Highlights to start include the terrific baba ganoush with homemade bread and fresh briouat. It's the perfect food to share as the dishes come in large portions.

Crabtree

modern

T2 

Hammersmith

4 Rainville Rd ✉ W6 9HA
✆ (020) 7385 3929
www.thecrabtreeW6.co.uk
⊖ Barons Court

Carte £24/35

On a sunny day few things in life beat being by the river in a London pub and The Crabtree certainly makes the most of its location. Its beer garden, with its barbeque-style menu, can seat over 80, while the dining room boasts its own terrace overlooking the river – and if you haven't yet booked for lunch on Boat Race day then you're probably already too late. A variety of ploys are used to fill the equally large interior of this Victorian beauty, from BYO Mondays to quiz nights on Tuesdays. For lunch the selection varies from ciabatta sarnies to shepherd's pie; the evening menu is more adventurous. The kitchen does things properly – parfaits and terrines are highlights and fish is perfectly timed – but vegetarians are also looked after.

Dartmouth Castle

Mediterranean

S1

Hammersmith

26 Glenthorne Rd ✉ W6 0LS
✆ (020) 8748 3614
www.thedartmouthcastle.co.uk
⊖ Hammersmith
Closed 23 December-2 January and Saturday lunch

Carte £20/33

Plenty of locals pop into this Victorian pub just for a drink so you may find one of them has nabbed your table. It's worth biding your time though, as it's better than decamping to the upstairs room as the atmosphere up there isn't a patch on the bustling ground floor with its worn-in look and etched mirrors. Simply hand over your credit card and order at the bar to enjoy dishes from the well-priced and quite lengthy Mediterranean-influenced menu which is the same lunch and dinner. The antipasti platter for two is a winner and pasta dishes appear to come in two sizes – big or even bigger. The blackboard wine list is also a cut above your average pub list and uses the reliable Italian orientated merchant Liberty.

Hampshire Hog

British modern S2

Hammersmith

227 King St ✉ W6 9JT
(020) 8748 3391
www.thehampshirehog.com
⊖ Ravenscourt Park
Closed 24-25 December and Sunday dinner

Menu £15/18 – Carte £23/42

For many years the owners ran The Engineer, a much loved pub in Primrose Hill, before their lease ran out. They subsequently moved west, took over what was the Ruby Grand, did it up and gave it back its original name. The Hampshire Hog is a big old place and calls itself a 'pub and pantry' – the pantry is open for breakfast, tea and cakes and doubles as a private party room; the bright bar serves cocktails and snacks like Scotch quail eggs and pork boards; and the large dining room focuses on freshness and seasonality. So, in spring, that means asparagus or broad bean risotto; a choice of daily salads and popular main courses like marinated leg of lamb. Like The Engineer, The 'Hog' comes with a terrific terrace and garden.

Havelock Tavern

Mediterranean T1

Hammersmith

57 Masbro Rd, Brook Grn ✉ W14 0LS
(020) 7603 5374
www.havelocktavern.com
⊖ Kensington Olympia
Closed 25-26 December – bookings not accepted

Carte £19/29 s

The word 'gastropub' was first coined in the early '90s to describe pubs that offered great food while remaining true to their roots – and was never about pubs masquerading as restaurants. The warm and friendly Havelock Tavern was at the vanguard of this movement and little about its lived-in look has changed here over the years, which is probably why it's as busy as ever. Put your name down for a table at the bar, order a drink and then place your order from the blackboard menu which changes with each service and reflects the seasons. The food is comforting and prices fair while the freshness is underlined by the fact that dishes often run out; there could be a grilled mackerel or goujons of coley alongside a tagine or roast pork belly.

Indian Zing

Indian

S1/2

Hammersmith

236 King St. ✉ W6 0RF

✆ (020) 8748 5959

www.indianzing.co.uk

⊖ Ravenscourt Park

Menu £12/15 – Carte £20/36

Despite opening a couple more restaurants, none of the zing appears to have gone out of this keenly run Indian neighbourhood favourite. Chef-owner Manoj Vasaikar flits between them and remains committed to seeing his customers satisfied, so much so that he has been known to send out an extra dish on the house if he feels an order is not sufficiently balanced. While he is from Bombay, his cooking seeks inspiration from all over India; from sweet fish dishes to drier North Indian dishes or spicier Madras specialities. Effort is also made to match wines with the food and the list even offers a couple of choices from India. The restaurant is colourfully decorated while the serving team are keen if a little disorganised at times.

Potli

Indian

S2

Hammersmith

319-321 King St ✉ W6 9NH

✆ (020) 8741 4328

www.potli.co.uk

⊖ Ravenscourt Park

Menu £12/30 – Carte £18/25

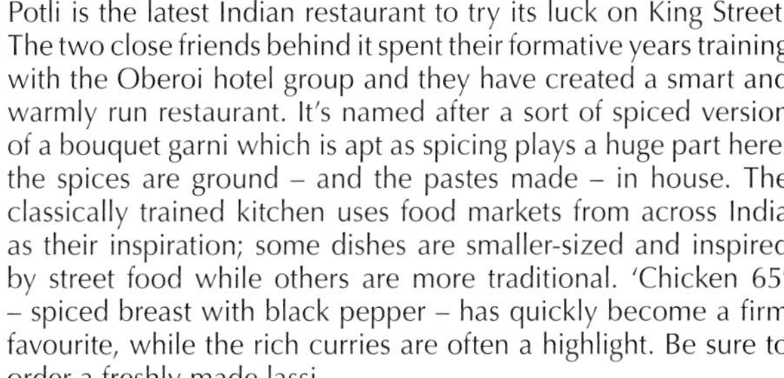

Potli is the latest Indian restaurant to try its luck on King Street. The two close friends behind it spent their formative years training with the Oberoi hotel group and they have created a smart and warmly run restaurant. It's named after a sort of spiced version of a bouquet garni which is apt as spicing plays a huge part here: the spices are ground – and the pastes made – in house. The classically trained kitchen uses food markets from across India as their inspiration; some dishes are smaller-sized and inspired by street food while others are more traditional. 'Chicken 65' – spiced breast with black pepper – has quickly become a firm favourite, while the rich curries are often a highlight. Be sure to order a freshly made lassi.

River Café ✿

Italian

T2

Hammersmith

Thames Wharf, Rainville Rd ✉ W6 9HA
✆ (020) 7386 4200 – **www**.rivercafe.co.uk
⊖ Barons Court
Closed 24 December-1 January, Sunday dinner and bank holidays – booking essential

Carte £51/75

River Cafe

They should run a shuttle service from local catering colleges to the River Café so that the students can learn the secret of good cooking: good ingredients. There's a vigour and honesty to the kitchen and, with the chefs all on view as they go about their work, there seems to be more of a relationship here between cook and customer than is found in most restaurants. The big wood-fired oven really catches the eye and the restaurant seems to attract a wonderfully mixed bunch of customers, united in their appreciation of what makes a restaurant tick. That includes charming service: on looks alone, the team can rival those in glossier and glitzier restaurants but they break ranks here by actually smiling and caring about their customers. The menu is still written twice a day and head chef Sian Wyn Owen brings an added sparkle to the cooking. Things taste just the way you want them to taste. Ordering a pasta dish ought to be made compulsory and the Chocolate Nemesis dessert should be a recognised treatment for depression.

First Course

- Wood roasted langoustines, chilli and oregano.
- Chargrilled squid with red chilli and rocket.

Main Course

- Roast turbot with an anchovy and rosemary sauce and broad beans.
- Veal sweetbreads with capers, sage, lemon and Castelluccio lentils.

Dessert

- Panna cotta with Champagne rhubarb.
- Plum and almond tart.

The Glasshouse ✿

modern

R2

Kew

14 Station Par. ✉ TW9 3PZ
✆ (020) 8940 6777
www.glasshouserestaurant.co.uk
⊖ Kew Gardens
Closed 24-26 December and 1 January

Menu £28 (weekday lunch), £43/43

The Glasshouse

There are some restaurants where the style of food matches the setting perfectly and The Glasshouse is one such example. Despite opening on the eve of the new millennium, the bright and open interior still feels fresh and contemporary. Meanwhile, the seasonally informed cooking is as crisp and vibrant as ever. A seamless change of head chef has seen no drop in the general standard and the flavours are allowed to shine on each dish. The menu is a lesson in balance and the cooking is predominantly modern European but the kitchen is not averse to slipping in a few tastes of the East. Offal remains something of a highlight and wines are shrewdly recommended and graciously served. The service team are imbued with an unflappable confidence which, in turn, relaxes the room, although most of the customers appear to already have the imperturbable demeanour of those who know their food and recognise a decent restaurant when they see one. Reservations for weekends, when lunches are largely family affairs, need to be made about a month in advance.

First Course

- Mackerel tartare with beetroot, quail eggs, crème fraîche and mustard cress.
- Rabbit tortellini with serrano ham, carrots and baby artichokes.

Main Course

- Breast of guinea fowl with curry leaf potato gratin, black lentil sauce and coriander.
- Calf's liver with endive, anchovy and Madeira sauce.

Dessert

- Valrhona chocolate Jaffa tube with chocolate brownie and burnt orange ice cream.
- Pistachio and polenta cake with custard and cassis ice cream.

Kew Grill

meats and grills

R2

Kew

10b Kew Grn. ✉ TW9 3BH

✆ (020) 8948 4433

www.awtrestaurants.com/kewgrill

⊖ Kew Gardens

Closed 25 December-4 January – booking essential

Menu £14 (weekday lunch) – Carte £25/70

A/C

Busy, relaxed and fun are the hallmarks of this neighbourhood joint which specialises in meats. Top quality steaks come with a choice of a sauce or butter; there are daily specials like shepherd's pie or duck confit and even a section dedicated to pork. There are seasonal dishes like haunch of venison but fish-eaters and Veggies are also catered for and children aren't forgotten either. The cooking is heart-warming and unfussy, the aged beef really is excellent and the nursery puds will finish you off. The concise wine list offers a good selection by the carafe. It's all done in quite a narrow room with something of a country feel; the friendly staff help the atmosphere along nicely.

Enoteca Turi

Italian

T2

Putney

28 Putney High St ✉ SW15 1SQ

✆ (020) 8785 4449 – **www.**enotecaturi.com

⊖ Putney Bridge

Closed 25-26 December, 1 January, Sunday and lunch bank holiday Mondays

Menu £18/33 – Carte £27/46

He may originally be from Puglia, but Giuseppe Turi has been Putney's favourite Italian restaurateur for over 20 years. In that time hardly a day has gone by without his restaurant bursting with chat and buzz – this is a local institution. He began life in London as a sommelier in the city's grandest hotels and so the grape plays an important role here: the menu matches wines with the dishes, the list has over 300 bins, he hosts regular food and wine evenings and the cellar hosts larger parties. The cooking is undertaken with a clear passion and the flavours pack a punch, which points to more northerly influences; dishes are satisfying and authentic. The restaurant is divided into three - the roomier front section is the best place to sit.

Prince of Wales

British modern

T2

Putney

138 Upper Richmond Rd ✉ SW15 2SP

✆ (020) 8788 1552

www.princeofwalesputney.co.uk

⊖ East Putney.

Closed 23 December-1 January and Monday lunch except bank holidays

Carte £24/42

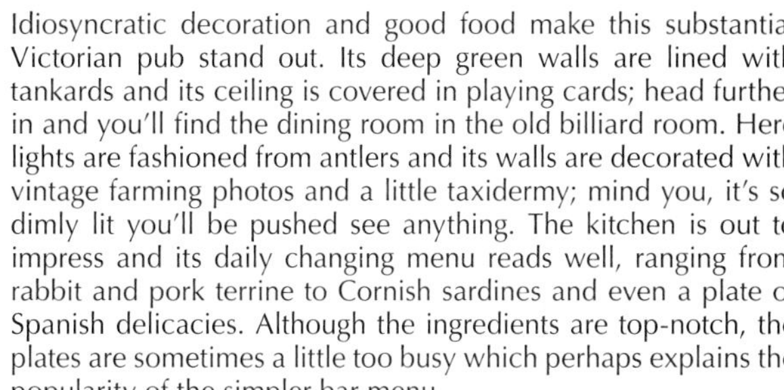

Idiosyncratic decoration and good food make this substantial Victorian pub stand out. Its deep green walls are lined with tankards and its ceiling is covered in playing cards; head further in and you'll find the dining room in the old billiard room. Here lights are fashioned from antlers and its walls are decorated with vintage farming photos and a little taxidermy; mind you, it's so dimly lit you'll be pushed see anything. The kitchen is out to impress and its daily changing menu reads well, ranging from rabbit and pork terrine to Cornish sardines and even a plate of Spanish delicacies. Although the ingredients are top-notch, the plates are sometimes a little too busy which perhaps explains the popularity of the simpler bar menu.

Bingham Restaurant

modern

R3

Richmond

Bingham Hotel,

61-63 Petersham Rd. ✉ TW1O 6UT

✆ (020) 8940 0902 – **www**.thebingham.co.uk

⊖ Richmond

Closed Sunday dinner

Menu £25/65

The Bingham always feels part of the local community and has lots of supporters in the neighbourhood who use it for a variety of different occasions. Perhaps its location, within a relatively unremarkable looking building, does it a favour as the restaurant has something of a 'hidden jewel' feel about it and the décor is surprisingly swish and comfortable. Come on a warm summer's day and you could find yourself having lunch on the balcony terrace, looking out over a garden and the Thames – and you don't get that everywhere. The cooking is contemporary and displays some original touches, however, dishes don't always deliver the flavours promised by the impressive presentation.

N Dysart Arms

modern

Richmond

R3

135 Petersham Rd ✉ TW10 7AA
✆ (020) 8940 8005
www.thedysartarms.co.uk
Closed 25 December and Sunday dinner – booking advisable

Menu £20 (weekdays) – Carte £33/48

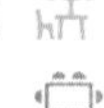

Overlooking Richmond Park and built in the early 1900s as part of the Arts and Crafts movement, the Dysart Arms is named after the family who once lived in Ham House. The owners decided to run it as a restaurant rather than a pub and have created a bright and fresh space that successfully blends its period features with more contemporary design elements. Service comes with a formality that seems somewhat at odds with this environment yet the formula clearly pleases the locals. The menu is also a blend of styles – the young chef uses top-notch ingredients and his cooking comes with a classical base to which he adds subtle Asian tones to create quite refined, delicately flavoured dishes. Look out for the occasional musical recital evening.

Matsuba

Japanese

Richmond

R2

10 Red Lion St ✉ TW9 1RW
✆ (020) 8605 3513
⊖ Richmond
Closed 25-26 December, 1 January and Sunday

Carte £21/39

Matsuba is a small, family-run place that is so understated it's easy to miss – look out for the softly lit sign above the narrow façade. The interior is equally compact and low-key, with just a dozen or so tables along with a small counter at the back with room for four more. In fact the biggest thing in the room is the menu, which offers a comprehensive tour through most recognisable points in Japanese cooking. The owners are Korean so you can also expect to see bulgogi, the Korean barbecue dish of marinated meat that comes on a sizzling plate. All the food is fresh and the ingredients are good; lunch sees some very good value set menus. The service is well-meaning and it's hard not to come away thinking kind thoughts.

Petersham Nurseries Café

modern R3

Richmond

Church Ln (off Petersham Rd) ✉ TW10 7AG
☎ (020) 8940 5230
www.petershamnurseries.com
Closed 25-26 December and Monday – booking advisable – (lunch only)

Carte £37/52

On a summer's day there can be few more delightful spots for lunch than the Café at Petersham Nurseries. Buy into the whole Sunday-supplement charm of the place and you'll find that, whether you're on the terrace or inside the greenhouse with its wobbly tables and soil floor, the hustle and hassle of modern life seem a world away. The cooking is a perfect match for this rural retreat: it uses the freshest of seasonal produce in unfussy and flavoursome dishes. Nothing – apart from the daily sorbet – is frozen here and fridges are nigh on empty at the end of each day. Many herbs and leaves come from their own gardens and dishes, like shoulder of lamb with cime di rapa and anchovies, come with a subtle Italian accent.

Swagat

Indian R2

Richmond

86 Hill Rise ✉ TW10 6UB
☎ (0208) 9407 557 – **www**.swagatindiancuisine.co.uk
⊖ Richmond
Closed 25-26 December, 1 January and Sunday – booking essential – (dinner only)

Menu £30/35 – Carte £16/29

A/C

This likeable little Indian restaurant is run by two friends; they met while training with Oberoi hotels in India before coming to London to work in the capital's best Indian restaurants. One organises the warm, well-meaning service while the other partner ensures his kitchen delivers the authentic and satisfying dishes, some of which come with North Indian influences. Dishes display a pleasing degree of lightness and subtlety so the first taste is always that of the prime ingredient rather than the spice; there's a health dividend to some of the dishes, such as sea bass with chilli with ginger; and vegetarians have plenty of choice. Add in complimentary poppadoms and chutneys and you can see why it's a hit with the locals.

Princess Victoria

British traditional S1

Shepherd's Bush

217 Uxbridge Rd ✉ W12 9DH

✆ (020) 8749 5886

www.princessvictoria.co.uk

⊖ Shepherd's Bush.

Closed 24-28 December

Carte £23/36

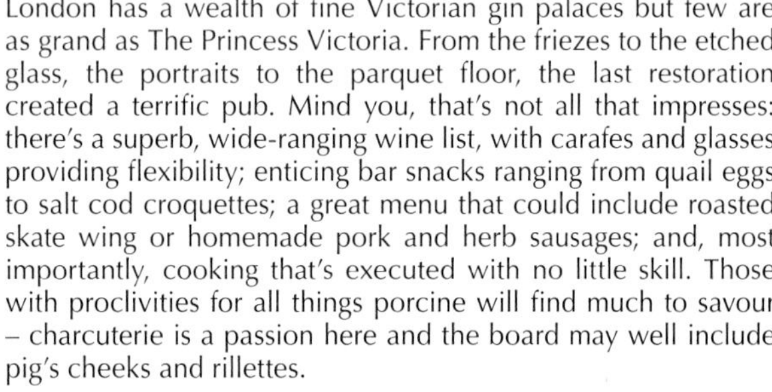

London has a wealth of fine Victorian gin palaces but few are as grand as The Princess Victoria. From the friezes to the etched glass, the portraits to the parquet floor, the last restoration created a terrific pub. Mind you, that's not all that impresses: there's a superb, wide-ranging wine list, with carafes and glasses providing flexibility; enticing bar snacks ranging from quail eggs to salt cod croquettes; a great menu that could include roasted skate wing or homemade pork and herb sausages; and, most importantly, cooking that's executed with no little skill. Those with proclivities for all things porcine will find much to savour – charcuterie is a passion here and the board may well include pig's cheeks and rillettes.

Al Borgo

Italian R3

Teddington

3 Church Rd. ✉ TW11 8PF

✆ (020) 8943 4456

www.alborgo.co.uk

Closed Sunday and bank holidays

Menu £17 (weekdays) – Carte £25/49

Aside from being home to Ted, love rival to Ernie the Fastest Milkman in the West, Teddington has rarely featured in the national consciousness – but a few more restaurants like Al Borgo may start to change people's perceptions. This refreshingly unpretentious Italian eatery, owned and keenly run by Brescia born Marco and his partner Nikola, exudes warmth and bonhomie in the way that only a true neighbourhood restaurant can. The menu cleverly appeals to both traditionalists and those a little more adventurous. The focaccia is homemade, as is the pasta; try the tagliolini with scallops or the pumpkin tortelli with sage. Special seasonal offerings such as a black truffle menu prove popular and there's a great value lunch menu too.

King's Head

modern

R3

Teddington

123 High St ✉ TW11 8HG
✆ (020) 3166 2900
www.whitebrasserie.com
⊖ Teddington (Rail)
Closed 25 December

Menu £14/17 – Carte £18/34

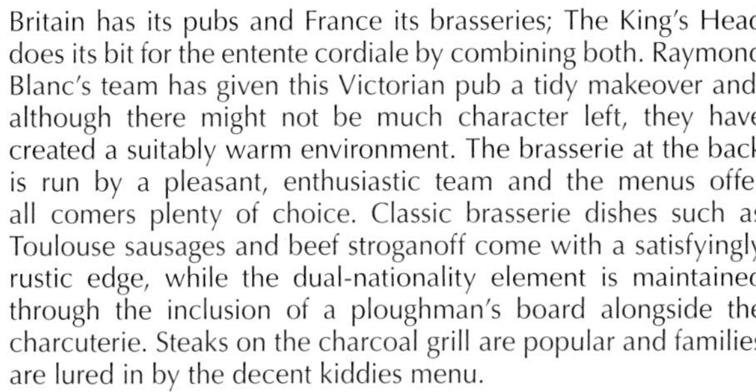

Britain has its pubs and France its brasseries; The King's Head does its bit for the entente cordiale by combining both. Raymond Blanc's team has given this Victorian pub a tidy makeover and, although there might not be much character left, they have created a suitably warm environment. The brasserie at the back is run by a pleasant, enthusiastic team and the menus offer all comers plenty of choice. Classic brasserie dishes such as Toulouse sausages and beef stroganoff come with a satisfyingly rustic edge, while the dual-nationality element is maintained through the inclusion of a ploughman's board alongside the charcuterie. Steaks on the charcoal grill are popular and families are lured in by the decent kiddies menu.

Rétro Bistrot

French

R3

Teddington

114-116 High St ✉ TW11 8JB
✆ (0208) 9772 239
www.retrobistrot.co.uk
Closed first 2 weeks August, first 10 days January, Sunday dinner and Monday

Menu £15/23 – Carte £26/48

There's substance as well as style to this classic French bistrot. The kitchen brigade were once teammates at the much missed Monsieur Max, so they know their way around a French menu. Moules marinière, coq au vin, foie de veau and crème brûlée – all the classics of bourgeois cuisine are here and all are prepared with innate skill and understanding. Lunch and early evening menus are a steal, and the service team display equal commitment to the cause as cheeks are kissed and cries of "bon appétit" ring out. The mix of fabrics, exposed brick walls, simple tables and art for sale creates a very genial environment. The best seats are in the room at the back with the partially open kitchen, which adds aroma and a little more noise.

Simply Thai

Thai

Teddington

R3

196 Kingston Rd. ✉ TW11 9JD
✆ (020) 8943 9747
www.simplythai-restaurant.co.uk
Closed 25-26 December and Sunday – (dinner only)

Menu £19/25 – Carte £21/29

A/C The delightful owner, Patria Weerapan, made her television debut on Gordon Ramsay's 'The F Word'. Her restaurant wasn't exactly quiet beforehand, but now her long term future here seems assured. Decoratively it's as modest inside as the unassuming façade suggests but everyone comes here for the food and forgives the occasional delay. She cooks everything fresh, from a bewilderingly large menu; dishes themselves are quite small so order one dish more than you think you need, which shouldn't be too difficult as the prices are far from high. Along with the new creations that are often being added to the menu are the favourites like spicy sweet pork, fishcakes, a refreshing trout salad and crisp deep-fried soft shell crab.

A Cena

Italian

Twickenham

R2

418 Richmond Rd. ✉ TW1 2EB
✆ (020) 8288 0108
www.acena.co.uk
⊖ Richmond

Closed Sunday dinner, Monday lunch and bank holidays

Carte £26/39

A/C A Cena is a little unusual for an Italian restaurant insofar as the owners and the chef are all Brits, but their passion for all things Italian is palpable. More relevantly, they have wholeheartedly embraced the Italian ethos of using fresh produce, cooked carefully, in simply presented dishes. The menu, written in both languages, is constantly evolving. Not all dishes exude the appropriate zing but pasta dishes are usually a highlight. The place looks a little deceptive from the outside as it's not as small as it appears: avoid the tables at the front and head for the more open-plan rear area from where you can see what's going on. The restaurant's local popularity had led to the opening of a nearby foodstore and bakery.

Brula

French

Twickenham

R3

43 Crown Rd., St Margarets ✉ TW1 3EJ
✆ (020) 8892 0602
www.brula.co.uk
Closed 26 December, Sunday dinner and Monday – booking essential

Menu £19/28 – Carte £28/43

Brula is already well past its tenth birthday and this relative longevity can be put down to a combination of reliable cooking, sensible prices and personable service. This pretty Victorian building has been both a pub and a butcher's shop in the past but now thoroughly suits its role as an authentic looking bistro. France remains at the heart of the cooking but over the past couple of years influences from Spain and Italy have started to appear on the menu, which is priced per dish rather than per course as it once was. Cooking is also more exact in its execution. The cheeses and the thoughtfully arranged wine list remain exclusively French. The friendly and helpful service also extends to those using one of the private rooms.

Tangawizi

Indian

Twickenham

R2

406 Richmond Rd., Richmond Bridge ✉ TW1 2EB
✆ (020) 8891 3737
www.tangawizi.co.uk
⊖ Richmond
Closed 25-26 December and 1 January – (dinner only)

Carte £15/32

Rich in colour and vitality, Tangawizi - meaning 'ginger' in Swahili – is another in the new breed of Indian restaurants. That means thoughtful design with clever use of silks and saris, attentive and elegant staff but, above all, cooking that is original, fresh and carefully prepared. North India provides much of the influence and although the à la carte menu offers plenty of 'safe' options, there are gems such as the roasted then stir-fried 'liptey' chicken. Diners should, however, head for the 'specials' section where the ambition of the kitchen is more evident. Lamb is another house speciality and is marinated to ensure it arrives extremely tender. For cooking this good, the prices are more than fair.

Chez Bruce ✿

French

U3

Wandsworth

2 Bellevue Rd ✉ SW17 7EG

✆ (020) 8672 0114

www.chezbruce.co.uk

⊖ Tooting Bec

Closed 24-26 December and 1 January – booking essential

Menu £28/45

Chez Bruce

Not only did Chez Bruce weather the choppy waters of recession better than most but it finally expanded into the old deli next door. What this meant for its merry band of dependable followers was nothing more than 'business as usual', as Chez Bruce has had a successful formula for years. That means flavoursome and uncomplicated food, sprightly service, sensible prices and an easy-going atmosphere. Matthew Christmas is the head man in the kitchen, having worked closely with Bruce Poole for over 10 years. His cooking provides an object lesson in the importance of flavours and balance: dishes are never too crowded and natural flavours are to the fore. The base is largely classical French but comes with Mediterranean tones, so expect words like parfait, pastilla, brandade and confit. The menu offers an even-handed selection, with a choice of around seven dishes per course. Cheese is always worth exploring and coffee comes with shortbread at lunch and terrific palmiers at dinner.

First Course

- Foie gras and chicken liver parfait with toasted brioche, walnuts and pear.
- Chilled cucumber soup with mackerel rillettes and horseradish.

Main Course

- Cod with olive oil mash, provençale tomato and gremolata.
- Shetland salmon with grilled asparagus and potted shrimp butter.

Dessert

- Hot chocolate and almond pudding with praline parfait.
- Raspberry clafoutis with toasted almond and amaretto ice cream.

Cannizaro House

modern

S3

Wimbledon

Cannizaro House Hotel,
West Side, Wimbledon Common ✉ SW19 4UE
✆ (020) 8879 1464 – **www**.cannizarohouse.com
⊖ Wimbledon

Menu £29 – Carte £32/48

A/C

London can offer the curious diner a vast number of dining options and, with Cannizaro House, that now includes a part-Georgian mansion in 34 acres of parkland. There is a choice to be made once you're here: you can sit in the elegant and classically dressed main room or the more intimate, glass fronted Loggia overlooking the Italian sunken garden. The daily changing set menu offers a range of carefully prepared and quite simple modern British dishes. The à la carte deals with more elaborate, but never overcomplicated, constructions; flavours and textures work well together and presentation is appealing. A preponderance of business types can sometimes lend too much of a corporate feel to proceedings but staff keep things light and relaxed.

Fox and Grapes 

British modern

S3

Wimbledon

9 Camp Rd ✉ SW19 4UN
✆ (020) 8619 1300
www.foxandgrapeswimbledon.co.uk
⊖ Wimbledon.

Closed 25 December – booking advisable

Carte £25/36

A/C

Claude Bosi first made his mark in Ludlow where, along with his Hibiscus restaurant, he also had a pub. When he moved to London the plan was to open a pub again once his restaurant was established and this he duly did in 2011. Cedric, his brother, runs the show and one look at the menu confirms their credentials as honorary Brits: this is proper pub food. Their prawn cocktail is hugely popular, as is the Cumberland sausage with mash, the ale battered hake and Angus sirloin. Scotch egg is made with wild boar, and junket makes an appearance, which makes you forgive their sneaking in the odd Gallic touch like snails and some of the over-formality. Thankfully, the pub's bigger than it looks as it's very popular. It also has three cosy bedrooms.

Lawn Bistro

modern

Wimbledon

T3

67 High St. ✉ SW19 5EE
✆ (020) 8947 8278
www.thelawnbistro.co.uk
⊖ Wimbledon
Closed 25-26 December, 1 January and Sunday dinner

Menu £15/38

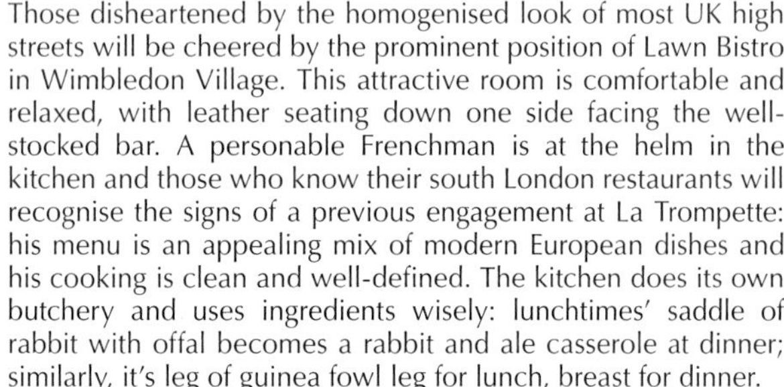

Those disheartened by the homogenised look of most UK high streets will be cheered by the prominent position of Lawn Bistro in Wimbledon Village. This attractive room is comfortable and relaxed, with leather seating down one side facing the well-stocked bar. A personable Frenchman is at the helm in the kitchen and those who know their south London restaurants will recognise the signs of a previous engagement at La Trompette: his menu is an appealing mix of modern European dishes and his cooking is clean and well-defined. The kitchen does its own butchery and uses ingredients wisely: lunchtimes' saddle of rabbit with offal becomes a rabbit and ale casserole at dinner; similarly, it's leg of guinea fowl leg for lunch, breast for dinner.

Light House

Mediterranean

Wimbledon

T3

75-77 Ridgway ✉ SW19 4ST
✆ (020) 8944 6338
www.lighthousewimbledon.com
⊖ Wimbledon
Closed 25-26 December, 1 January and Sunday dinner

Menu £14/24 – Carte £24/42

The façade may have been smartened up but one's first impression is of being in a branded operation. Fortunately, that notion is quickly dispelled by the quality of the food. While they still have the odd Thai dish, it is in Italy where the majority of the menu and the kitchen's strength lie, with a roll call of favourites that include tagliatelle, gnocchi, saltimbocca and panna cotta. The food is wholesome and confident, with plenty of bold flavours and prices at lunch and early evening are attractive, which ensures that it is often very busy. The result is that the young team can sometimes struggle to keep up, but they remain admirably calm and cheery. As this was once a shop selling lights and fittings, it is fittingly well lit.

7117
District line
0 5 7

Thierry Burot/Fotolia.com

Where to **stay**

▶ *These 50 recommended hotels are extracted from the Great Britain & Ireland 2014 guide, where you'll find a larger choice of hotels selected by our team of inspectors.*

Ampersand

10 Harrington Rd
SW7 3ER
(020) 7589 5895
www.ampersandhotel.com
South Kensington.

E6

111 rm – †£150/216 ††£150/360, £10 – 5 suites

The Ampersand

The Ampersand hotel is an elegant, converted Victorian hotel surrounded by some of the world's greatest museums in the heart of London's cultural centre. Its bedroom decoration is inspired by five themes which inform these museums: botany, music, geometry, ornithology and astronomy. This undoubtedly adds some personality to the bedrooms, which come in all sorts of different categories: some have balconies, others free-standing baths. All are thoughtfully lit and although they are far from being the largest rooms around, they do all have smart bathrooms and a good number of extras. Snacks, coffee, tea and cakes are served in the brightly decorated Drawing Rooms, while Apero is the intimate restaurant in the basement offering a Mediterranean-influenced menu. Traditionalists may need time getting used to seeing staff wearing jeans but they'll also find that this is a professionally run, smart and comfortable hotel in a terrific location.

Andaz Liverpool Street

40 Liverpool St.
✉ EC2M 7QN
✆ (020) 7961 1234
www.andaz.com
⊖ Liverpool Street

M2

267 rm – †£126/402 ††£162/438, ☕ £24 – 3 suites

🍴 **1901** *(See restaurant listing)*

Andaz Liverpool Street

The philosophy behind Hyatt's Andaz brand is to create luxury hotels with a less structured, less formal feel. On a practical level, this means that there is literally no barrier between arriving guest and receptionist, nor between cocktail-drinker and barman – it's all central islands and general mingling. This does create a more relaxed environment – being served a drink while someone checks you in on their iPad does come as a nice change – but you do subsequently find yourself trying to work out who are the guests and who are the staff. The bedrooms are modern and slick; those in the older Victorian part of the hotel are the best, with high ceilings and quite a masculine feel. The hotel is a labyrinth of corridors, floors and different areas which means there is also a plethora of dining options available to discourage you from ever leaving: there's the ersatz pub called George, the grandiose 1901, the rather sweet little Japanese Miyako restaurant and a big brasserie that specialises in the grilling of red meats.

Arch

50 Great Cumberland Pl
✉ W1H 7FD
✆ (020) 7724 4700
www.thearchlondon.com
⊖ Marble Arch

F2

80 rm – †£246/360 ††£246/360, ☕ £22 – 2 suites

The Arch

If God is in the detail, then The Arch shows touches of the divine. Fashioned out of a row of seven terraced houses and a couple of mews cottages, the hotel has been thoughtfully put together by people who have clearly stayed in a lot of places and who know what it takes to make them comfortable. For starters, the bedrooms offer an impressive list of extras such as HD TVs and internet radios; beds have oversized duvets so there's no nocturnal wrestling required to secure one's half; there are complimentary soft drinks and coffee; and some of the larger rooms not only have a TV in the bathroom but also have a pillow in the tub to make the watching of it more comfortable. The public areas are relatively compact but are smartly designed. The restaurant, which doubles as a champagne bar and is named after the dialling code from the '50s, has an easy-going menu, with a kitchen that makes good use of its wood fired oven. The Martini bar has discreet call buttons to summon service and interesting pieces of art are scattered liberally around the hotel.

Aster House

3 Sumner Pl.
✉ SW7 3EE
✆ (020) 7581 5888
www.asterhouse.com
⊖ South Kensington

E6

13 rm ☕ – †£120/180 ††£240/360

Michelin

If you made a mathematical calculation to find the best location for a tourist in London, then chances are the X would mark a spot somewhere near Aster House on Sumner Place. You've got all the best museums within strolling distance; Hyde Park mere minutes away; all the famous shops and, above all, you're staying in a charming Victorian house in a typical Kensington street where people actually live rather than in a faceless hotel district. Mr and Mrs Tan keep the house commendably shipshape and are enthusiastic hosts. The bedrooms at the front of the house benefit from larger windows while those at the back are quieter and overlook the garden, but all boast fairly high ceilings and room to breathe. Wi-fi is available without charge in all the rooms, while L'Orangerie, a first floor conservatory looking down over Sumner Place, doubles as the breakfast room and guests' sitting room. Prices are also kept within the parameters of decency so bookings need to be made plenty of time in advance.

Berkeley

Wilton Pl
✉ SW1X 7RL
✆ (020) 7235 6000
www.the-berkeley.co.uk
⊖ Knightsbridge

G4

184 rm – ♦£310/660 ♦♦£378/900, ☕ £32 – 26 suites
Marcus Wareing at The Berkeley and Koffmann's
(See restaurant listing)

The Berkeley

You'd have thought that having Marcus Wareing's luxury restaurant on one side of the hotel would be enough, but the hotel then coaxed Pierre Koffmann out of retirement and his restaurant now provides the bookend on the other side. In the middle you have the Blue Bar which is as cool as the name suggests and, on the other side of the lobby, the Caramel Room whose target audience is obvious when you consider that tea is called "Prêt-à-Portea" and the biscuits look like mini handbags. The most unique area of the hotel must be the 7th floor, with its rooftop pool, treatment rooms and personal training services to satisfy the most slavishly health-conscious traveller. By using a number of different designers, bedrooms have been given both personality and a sense of individualism; the most recent have softer, calmer colours and a lighter, more contemporary feel while the classic rooms feel richer, thanks to their deeper, more intense colours. All the rooms are immaculately kept and several of the suites have their own balcony.

Blakes

33 Rowland Gdns
✉ SW7 3PF
✆ (020) 7370 6701
www.blakeshotels.com
⊖ Gloucester Road

D6

47 rm ☕ – 🛉£215/300 🛉🛉£263/359 – 8 suites

Blakes

Following a couple of years of uncertainty, Blakes is now back in private hands and the young owner is busy investing considerable funds in its upgrade and upkeep. Created by Anouska Hempel in the early '80s, this was one of London's original 'boutique' hotels. It was exuberantly decorated then and remains so now; it also represents the perfect antidote to the plethora of generic corporate hotels that seemingly pop up overnight. The lavish decoration, the dramatic four-poster beds and the rich fabrics remind you that staying in a hotel can be a thrilling, erotic and sensual experience – this isn't the sort of hotel for those who get excited by the sight of a trouser-press and a miniature kettle. That being said, the mod cons are all here, but they're camouflaged and concealed. Downstairs is a slick and stylish affair, from the dark and mysterious Chinese Room and bar, to the intimate restaurant with its ambitious Asian-influenced menu – and there is a charming courtyard at the back, perfect for hiding out.

Brown's

Albemarle St
✉ W1S 4BP
✆ (020) 7493 6020
www.roccofortehotels.com
⊖ Green Park

H3

117 rm – 👤£426/1,116 👥£426/1,116, ☕ £25 – 12 suites
🍴 **Hix Mayfair** *(See restaurant listing)*

Brown's

Opened in 1837 by James Brown, Lord Byron's butler, Brown's has a long and distinguished history and has been the favoured hotel of many a visiting dignitary: it was here that Alexander Graham Bell first demonstrated his telephone and The Kipling Suite is just one named after a former guest. It reopened in 2005 after a full face-lift, with Olga Polizzi personally overseeing the design and her blending of the traditional with the modern works well. The bedrooms have personality and reflect the character of the hotel, albeit with all of today's required gadgetry. One thing that has remained constant is the popularity of the afternoon teas – the selling point, apart from the pianist, is that the waiter replenishes all stands and pots without extra charge. The wood-panelled restaurant took slightly longer to bed in and now goes by the name of Hix at The Albemarle; the menu features British comfort food. The Donovan Bar is probably the hotel's best feature and celebrates the distinguished work of British photographer Terence Donovan.

Bulgari

171 Knightsbridge
✉ SW7 1DW
✆ (020) 7151 1010
www.bulgarihotels.com/london
⊖ Knightsbridge

F4

85 rm – †£528/828 ††£588/948, ☕ £32 – 7 suites

Bulgari

Having wowed them in Milan, Bulgari waited until they'd found the perfect location before creating this London jewel. This is a hotel that shouts style, with silver its underlying theme in homage to the brand's silversmith origins. Actually, it is so cool, so impeccably tailored, it wouldn't possibly be caught shouting anything. The dark lobby, with its camouflaged staff, sets the tone of restrained elegance and leads into the sleek bar. From there it is down a sweeping staircase to the restaurant, where the influences run from Nice to Tuscany, with a few other classics thrown in. The hotel is on 15 floors but six of those are underground and used for a state-of-the-art spa, a ballroom and a terrific cinema. The bedrooms are stunning and all about sensual curves, polished mahogany, silks and black marble; the bathrooms are worth the price of admission alone and there are some delightful touches, such as minibars hidden within upright trunks. Unlike other fashion-led hotels, there is real substance behind the style here and an emphasis on comfort.

The Capital

22-24 Basil St.
✉ SW3 1AT
✆ (020) 7589 5171
www.capitalhotel.co.uk
⊖ Knightsbridge

F5 

49 rm – †£240/350 ††£290/500, ☕ £20 – 1 suite
Outlaw's at The Capital *(See restaurant listing)*

The Capital

The Capital is one of London's most enduringly discreet and comfortable hotels and is thoroughly British in its feel. It is owned by David Levin, who opened it in 1971, and it is this continuity which has lead directly to there only being five head chefs in over 40 years. The restaurant is as elegant as ever, with a menu filled with classic British seafood and an extensive wine list that includes selections from the Levins' own winery in the Loire. Bedrooms remain classically chic and the contemporary embellishments are restrained and in keeping with the general atmosphere. Each floor is slightly different and uses designs from the likes of Mulberry, Ralph Lauren and Nina Campbell. What has always raised The Capital to greater heights than similarly styled hotels has been the depth and detail of the service. No one can walk through the small lobby without being greeted and the concierge is old-school in the best sense of the word and can arrange anything for anyone.

Charlotte Street

15 Charlotte St
W1T 1RJ
(020) 7806 2000
www.charlottestreethotel.co.uk
Goodge Street

52 rm – £300 £300, £18 – 4 suites

Firmdale

Expect the lobby and bar to be full of men with man-bags and horn-rimmed specs, for Charlotte Street is the hotel of choice for those in the advertising industry. But even if you've never pitched, promoted or placed a product and are just after a stylish, contemporary hotel in a street thronged with bars and restaurants then get on the mailing list here. Oscar is the busy bar and restaurant that spills out onto the street in summer; its sunny contemporary European menu and vivid mural brighten it in winter. Film Club is on Sunday evening: dinner followed by a film in the downstairs screening room. Those after some quiet can nab one of the sofas in the Drawing room or Library. The bedrooms are, as with all hotels in the Firmdale group, exceptionally well looked after. Every year, three or four are fully refurbished and one thing you'll never see is a bit of dodgy grouting or a scuff mark. They are all decorated in an English style but there is nothing chintzy or twee about them. Bathrooms are equally immaculate and the baths face little flat screen TVs.

Claridge's

Brook St
✉ W1K 4HR
✆ (020) 7629 8860
www.claridges.co.uk
⊖ Bond Street

G3

203 rm – †£480/780 ††£540/900, ☕ £32 – 67 suites

Claridge's

Stand in the lobby looking bewildered and, before you know it, a liveried member of staff will appear promptly before you to enquire after your wellbeing; Claridge's may have a long and very illustrious history but it recognises that reputations are forged because of service rather than longevity. That being said, no modern, purpose-built hotel could afford the extravagance of having such wide corridors or such ornate decoration. The hotel's most striking g feature is its art deco detailing, which is kept suitably fresh and buffed. Despite its long and glittery past, Claridge's has never been in danger of being a museum piece; the David Collins designed bar attracts a more youthful crowd these days and The Foyer, with its eye-catching light sculpture, proves that afternoon tea need not be a stuffy or quaint affair. Gordon Ramsay's restaurant has now closed and, as we go to print, its replacement has yet to be revealed. Further bedrooms and other guest facilities are due to be added over the next few years and the challenge will be to make these changes as seamless as possible.

Connaught

Carlos Pl.
✉ W1K 2AL
✆ (020) 7499 7070
www.the-connaught.co.uk
⊖ Bond Street

G3

121 rm – †£300/840 ††£360/840, ☕ £30 – 26 suites
Hélène Darroze at The Connaught *(See restaurant listing)*

The Connaught

The restored, refurbished and rejuvenated Connaught still retains a sense of effortless serenity and exclusivity – but has now been discovered by a new generation. These sprightlier guests should take the stairs up to their room, that way they'll see the largest mahogany staircase in the country. The bedrooms are now more contemporary in style; they have wooden floors, leather worked into the soft furnishings and come with larger marble bathrooms; some overlook a small oriental garden, others peer down on mews houses. All rooms have full butler service, use linen specially woven in Milan and toiletries from Daylesford. The Coburg Bar honours the hotel's original name and its seats are so deep it's a wonder anyone ever leaves. In contrast, the Connaught Bar attracts a more youthful clientele. Hélène Darroze oversees the restaurant with her refined French cooking and Espelette is an all-day venue just off the lobby that offers a weekly changing list of classic French and British dishes. If you need anything, just ask one of the hotel's 300 members of staff.

Covent Garden

10 Monmouth St.
✉ WC2H 9HB
✆ (020) 7806 1000
www.firmdalehotels.com
⊖ Covent Garden

I3

58 rm – †£315 ††£315, ☕ £18 – 1 suite
Brasserie Max *(See restaurant listing)*

Firmdale

The Covent Garden Hotel has always been hugely popular with those of a theatrical bent, whether cast or audience member, not least because of its central location, a mere saunter away from the majority of playhouses and productions. The hotel was once a French hospital – the words 'Nouvel hopital et dispensaire francais' are still etched into the brickwork – but the style is essentially British. Mannequins, soft fabrics and antique furniture are juxtaposed with crisp lines and contemporary colours to create a very stylish and comfortable environment. The first floor residents-only wood-panelled sitting room is a delight and so is occasionally used by a visiting grandee for a backdrop to an interview; the presence of an honesty bar adds further to the appeal. The Screening Room holds weekend dinner-and-a-film nights, while Brasserie Max feels much more like a proper restaurant than a mere addendum; its menu is appealingly accessible and afternoon tea is a popular event.

Dorchester

Park Ln.
W1K 1QA
(020) 7629 8888
www.thedorchester.com
Hyde Park Corner

G4

250 rm – £510/894 £510/894, £26 – 50 suites
Alain Ducasse at The Dorchester and China Tang and The Grill *(See restaurant listing)*

The Dorchester

The Dorchester has been a byword for luxury and elegance since it opened in the 1930s and constant reinvestment over the decades has ensured that this grandest of hotels has remained one of London's finest. For many, The Promenade is the first port of call: afternoon tea in its gilded surroundings is as popular as ever, so much so that there's now a mezzanine level above the lobby. If you're coming here to dine you have the choice of three restaurants: The Grill, with its exuberant tartan decoration, is for all things British; the luxuriously adorned Alain Ducasse restaurant, with its exceptional cuisine, waves Le Tricolore, while downstairs China Tang celebrates the communal cuisine of China. The bedrooms are constantly being upgraded and each floor has its own colour scheme. There's an elegance to all the rooms, whether they're traditional decorated or in a more contemporary style; Park-facing bedrooms must be some of the most sought after real estate in the capital. But comfort is nothing without service – and standards here remain impeccable.

Dukes

35 St James's Pl.
✉ SW1A 1NY
✆ (020) 7491 4840
www.dukeshotel.com
⊖ Green Park

H4

90 rm – †£234/454 ††£276/496, ☕ £24 – 6 suites

Dukes

Every hotel needs a little reinvention now and again and Dukes has been steadily changing its image over the last few years. It has enjoyed a constant presence in St James's for over a century and traditionally had a clubby, very British feel but this has given way to a brighter, fresher look which seems to suit it equally well. What hasn't been lost is the discreet atmosphere which is largely down to the very central, yet surprisingly quiet, location. The basement restaurant, which looks out at street level thanks to the vagaries of local topography, now offers an ambitious, modern menu with dishes that are original in look and elaborate in construction. The comfortable sitting rooms still do a brisk trade in afternoon tea but there is now also an outside cigar lounge. The bar is something of a London landmark (and was reputedly one of Ian Fleming's old haunts). Bedrooms are devoid of chintz and come in warm, calming colours; they have smart marble bathrooms and are decently proportioned.

Egerton House

17-19 Egerton Terr
✉ SW3 2BX
✆ (020) 7589 2412
www.egertonhousehotel.com
⊖ South Kensington

F5

28 rm – 🚹£276/516 🚹🚹£276/516, ☕ £29

Egerton House

In challenging economic times hotels can either panic and cut staff and slash rates – a course of action which usually ends in ruin – or they can hold their nerve and provide greater value for their guests. Anyone wondering what more a hotel can do should get along to Egerton House. This is a townhouse whose decorative style is at the lavish end of the scale; the fabrics are of the highest order and the colours neatly coordinated. The ground floor Victoria and Albert Suite comes with its own little decked terrace and a row of filled decanters for company. All the rooms are slightly different; the marble bathrooms are very neat and the hotel has made the best use of limited space – ask for one of the quieter rooms at the back overlooking the little garden. What really makes this little place stand out, though, is the service and the eager attitude of the staff. Lots of hotels spout tosh about being 'a home from home' but here they do make a genuine effort to make their guests feel part of things by, for example, arranging complimentary admission to events at the V&A.

Four Seasons

Hamilton Pl, Park Ln
✉ W1J 7DR
✆ (020) 7499 0888
www.fourseasons.com/london/
⊖ Hyde Park Corner

G4

193 rm – †£800/980 ††£800/980, ☕ £32 – 33 suites
Amaranto *(See restaurant listing)*

Four Seasons

These days competition is pretty fierce at the luxury end of the hotel market so, to stay ahead of the game, contenders need to do more than just tinker with the cosmetics. The Four Seasons, which was the group's first hotel outside the US, closed for a couple of years and in that time was stripped right back, before being put together again. The result is that Park Lane now has a hotel that's really raised the bar in the comfort stakes. The bedrooms, trimmed with plenty of walnut, sycamore, marble and shiny steel, are particularly striking and come with all the latest wizardry like self-regulating ambient heating. They also occupy impressive square footage, as do the suites, the number of which has been greatly increased. Dining is a flexible feast – Amaranto is divided into a three areas: a bar, restaurant and lounge and you can eat what you want, where you want it, and that includes on the secluded outdoor terrace. The stunning top-floor spa, with its fantastic views, caps off this hotel's dazzling renaissance.

45 Park Lane

45 Park Ln
W1K 1PN
(020) 7493 4545
www.45parklane.com
Hyde Park Corner

G4

36 rm – †£395/695 ††£495/945, £30 – 10 suites

Cut *(See restaurant listing)*

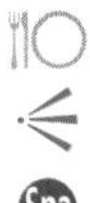

45 Park Lane

It was the original site of the Playboy Club and has also been a car showroom but now 45 Park Lane has been reborn as The Dorchester's little sister and, lit up at night, her art deco façade makes her look rather cute. The style is certainly different from her famous sibling but the quality and depth of service come from the same top drawer. On each floor you'll find the work of a different contemporary British artist as well as a couple of hosts to take care of everything from unpacking your bags to booking you a restaurant. The bedrooms, which all have views over Hyde Park, are wonderfully sensual, with velvet walls, leather-wrapped doors and warm, heavy fabrics and the marble bathrooms are beautiful. Suites take up great positions on the corners of the building and have the best views, while the penthouse occupies the entire top floor. The red leather makes the cocktail bar on the mezzanine level a very sexy spot, while on the ground floor sits Wolfgang Puck's glamorous restaurant Cut which specialises in steaks.

The Gore

190 Queen's Gate
✉ SW7 5EX
✆ (0207) 7584 6601
www.gorehotel.com
⊖ Gloucester Road

D5 

50 rm – †£160/250 ††£180/280, ☕ £15

The Gore

Being the nearest hotel to the Royal Albert Hall makes The Gore a popular choice for performers as well as attendees and the bright, casual bistro is always busier early and late in the evening than it ever is at 8pm. The hotel clearly stands out at the top of Queen's Gate with its fluttering Union flag and gleaming brass plaque and who needs a fitness room when you've got Kensington gardens just yards away. If you were in any doubt that this is the part of London most closely associated with Queen Victoria, then just step through the door because the walls are covered with pictures and paintings relating to her reign. But, despite the plethora of antiques and all that Victoriana, this is a hip little hotel with a large element of fun attached. Rooms like Miss Fanny and Miss Ada are as camp as they sound; the Tudor Room has a secret bathroom and minstrel's gallery, and many of the bathrooms give meaning to the expression 'sitting on the throne'. Bend down in the rooms and you might find a card saying "Look, we've cleaned here too".

Goring

15 Beeston Pl
SW1W 0JW
(020) 7396 9000
www.thegoring.com
Victoria

H5 

69 rm – †£290/595 ††£290/950, £30 – 8 suites 

Dining Room *(See restaurant listing)*

The Goring

Not only has The Goring celebrated its centenary, but it is still owned by the family who built it. Jeremy Goring, the great-grandson of the founder, is now at the helm and this lineage is clearly welcomed by the staff – many of whom have been working at the hotel for years – as well as being appreciated by regular guests, who benefit from the excellent service. The hotel still has a pervading sense of Britishness, which designers like Nina Campbell fully respected when they were asked to update its look. There has been a clever introduction of new technology, from the TVs that rise from the desk to the touch panels that control everything but, reassuringly for those less familiar or enamoured with the modern world, one can still get a proper key with which to open one's bedroom door. The ground floor restaurant is a bright, discreet and comfortable affair and its menu celebrates Britain's own culinary heritage; the bar is colonial in its feel and the veranda overlooks the hotel's surprisingly large back garden.

Halkin

5 Halkin St
✉ SW1X 7DJ
✆ (020) 7333 1000
www.comohotels.com/thehalkin
⊖ Hyde Park Corner

G5

41 rm – †£324/564 ††£504/804, ☕ £28 – 6 suites
🍴 **Ametsa with Arzak Instruction** *(See restaurant listing)*

Halkin

These days every hotel thinks it's 'boutique' or likes to call itself a 'townhouse'. The Halkin can claim to be both, and was one of the originals, to boot. It's also still looking pretty sharp considering it opened over 20 years ago. It's certainly more discreet than its sibling, The Metropolitan, which attracts a livelier and feistier crowd. The hotel's bedrooms are neatly set out and cleverly thought through. The touch pad operation makes everything seem so effortless but the technology never reaches baffling proportions. All rooms have silk covered walls and marble bathrooms, along with lots of natural minerals. Staff are in abundance and many appear to stay for a long time, which improves standards of service and pleases the regulars; they also all wear Armani, so no pressure there, then. The public areas are limited to two separate operations on the ground floor: a neat, perfectly formed bar at the front and, behind it, a Spanish restaurant called Ametsa from the celebrated Arzak family.

Hart House

51 Gloucester Pl
W1U 8JF
(020) 7935 2288
www.harthouse.co.uk
Marble Arch

F2

15 rm – £98/145 £145/195

Michelin

Hart House has been in the same family for nearly 40 years and while the owner may not spend as much time in the hotel as he used to, he's got enough friendly staff running the place in his absence. Equally importantly, he's also still writing the occasional cheque, as the recent introduction of new LCD TVs would testify. The hotel wouldn't win any design awards but what you get, for a fair price, is clean and tidy accommodation in a late Georgian terrace house that's in a useful central location: it's just a short walk from Oxford Street and Hyde Park and less than a ten minute cab ride from Paddington for those who've taken the Heathrow Express. Gloucester Place may be a fairly busy thoroughfare but the bedrooms on the front have sufficient double glazing; there are family rooms available as well as rooms on the ground floor. Ceilings get lower the higher you climb, reflecting the time when the house's staff had their quarters at the top of the house. The only public area is the small, basement breakfast room but the hotel still manages to have a sociable, international atmosphere.

Haymarket

1 Suffolk Pl.
✉ SW1Y 4HX
✆ (020) 7470 4000
www.haymarkethotel.com
⊖ Piccadilly Circus

I4

50 rm – †£320 ††£320, ☕ £20 – 3 suites

🍴 **Brumus** *(See restaurant listing)*

Firmdale

It's hard to believe that The Haymarket hotel opened back in 2007 – you would think it no more than a few months ago, which is testament to its housekeeping department. The hotel is a stylish, hip place, fashioned out of a grand John Nash Regency building that had been a gentleman's club and office before being gutted by a fire. Art and an eclectic collection of furniture now run through it; the lobby, conservatory and library are immaculately decorated and set the tone. No two rooms are the same but all come with dressed mannequins – the motif of the Kemp's hotels – and custom-made furniture. Those on the front could be used to advertise double-glazing but for extra quiet, ask to overlook the inner decked courtyard. The location couldn't be better: theatre-land is literally just outside – indeed, the hotel adjoins the Haymarket Theatre – and all that London offers is a short stroll away. If that isn't enough, there's a very swish swimming pool downstairs, just for residents. Brumus is the spacious restaurant serving easy, Italian food.

Hazlitt's

6 Frith St
✉ W1D 3JA
✆ (020) 7434 1771
www.hazlittshotel.com
⊖ Tottenham Court Road

I3

30 rm – †£198/222 ††£215/288, ☕ £12

Hazlitt's

Along with its central Soho location, one of the best features of Hazlitt's has always been its intimate and chummy atmosphere, which even the addition of eight rooms in 2009 failed to disrupt. The building dates from 1718 and was named after the essayist and critic William Hazlitt, whose home it was. Appropriately, it still attracts plenty of writers today, but while there is much character to be found in all the bedrooms - from the wood panelling and busts to the antique beds and Victorian fixtures - you do also get free wi-fi. Duke of Monmouth is the most striking of the newer rooms: it's spread over two floors and has its own terrace with a retractable roof. Madam Dafloz, named after another of Soho's former roguish residents, is also appealing, with a sultry, indulgent feel. The Library, with its 24/7 honesty bar, is the hotel's only communal area and was slightly enlarged when the newer rooms were added. This is also one of the few hotels where breakfast in bed really is the only option – and who is going to object to that?

K + K George

1-15 Templeton Pl
✉ SW5 9NB
(020) 7598 8700
www.kkhotels.com
⊖ Earl's Court

C6

154 rm – £150/300 £180/350

K&K Hotels

Providing a model lesson on the importance of keeping on top of your product, The K+K hotel spent time during the recent economic turndown refurbishing all its bedrooms; they now boast fast internet, 320 thread count linen, American cherry wood panelling, flat screen TVs, full minibars, and under-floor heating in the bathroom; and the hotel is reaping the rewards. It occupies seven houses of a stucco fronted terrace; its interior in contrast to the period façade, is colourful and contemporary and fresh flowers and bowls of fruit are scattered around the lobby. The unexpectedly large rear garden, for which most hotels would give their eye teeth, has won local horticultural prizes and hosts breakfast on warm summer days. A simple menu is served in the bar but most guests take advantage of the central location and go out to eat. The hotel may be part of an international chain but there are plenty of staff on hand to add a personal touch and it also manages to feel part of the local community.

Knightsbridge

10 Beaufort Gdns
✉ SW3 1PT
✆ (020) 7584 6300
www.knightsbridgehotel.com
⊖ Knightsbridge

F5 

44 rm – †£235 ††£290/475, ☕ £19

Firmdale

Firmdale Hotels all seem so quintessentially British that it'll be interesting to see what New Yorkers make of them now they have one of their own. The Knightsbridge, converted from a row of Victorian terrace houses in an attractive square, is another typical example of what they do so well: it proves style and comfort are not mutually exclusive and that a hotel can be fashionable without being fuzzy. The work of British artists, such as Carol Sinclair's slate stack and Peter Clark's dog collages sets the tone and the bedrooms are constantly being refreshed and rearranged. Those facing the square on the first floor benefit from floor to ceiling windows, while the Knightsbridge Suite stretches from the front to the back of the building. All rooms are so impeccably tidy and colour coordinated it'll make you question your own dress sense. The Library Room differs from many similarly named hotel sitting rooms by actually containing books, along with an honesty bar which holds everything from fruit and snacks to champagne and ice cream.

Lanesborough

Hyde Park Corner
✉ SW1X 7TA
✆ (020) 7259 5599
www.lanesborough.com
⊖ Hyde Park Corner

G4

83 rm – †£495/570 ††£665/775, ☕ £35 – 10 suites
Apsleys *(See restaurant listing)*

The Lanesborough

Many of London's luxury hotels boast long and illustrious histories and have names that are recognised the world over. Having opened relatively recently in 1991, The Lanesborough still feels like something of a newcomer, but there is no doubt that it deserves its place among the top tier of London hotels. Constructed in 1733 as Viscount Lanesborough's country house, the building was perhaps better known as a hospital before it was converted into a hotel. The series of drawing rooms are smartly kitted out; the clubby library bar offers a vast selection of whiskies and cognacs and the Garden Room provides a hugely popular sanctuary for cigar smokers. Apsleys is their lavishly dressed Italian restaurant with superlative cooking. Bedrooms come in a rich and decorative Regency style and boast a host of extras, including laptops. There's a butler on each floor, on call 24 hours a day, and rooms are tripled-glazed. Ask for a room facing Hyde Park – you may not hear anything of the outside world but you can enjoy some pretty terrific views.

Langham

1c Portland Pl., Regent St.
W1B 1JA
(020) 7636 1000
www.langhamhotels.com
Oxford Circus

H2

380 rm – †£288/852 ††£288/852, ☕ £30 – 25 suites
Roux at The Landau *(See restaurant listing)*

Langham

The Langham was one of Europe's first purpose-built Grand hotels when it opened in 1865. Since then it has been owned by all sorts, including at one stage the BBC – they used it as their library and was where 'The Goon Show' was recorded. In 2009 it emerged from an extensive refurbishment programme that didn't provide much change from £80 million and it is now competing with the big boys once again. Pride of place must be the Palm Court, a twinkling ersatz art deco space, which serves light meals and afternoon teas. The Artesian bar is a stylish affair and does interesting things with gin; there's a small courtyard terrace named in honour of a BBC radio gardener and the striking restaurant is under the aegis of the Roux organisation. The bedrooms have personality and, for a change, the furniture is free-standing rather than fitted; the boldly decorated Club rooms are particularly distinctive. The health and fitness club is impressively kitted out and includes a swimming pool in what was once a bank vault.

The Levin

28 Basil St.
✉ SW3 1AS
✆ (020) 7589 6286
www.thelevinhotel.co.uk
⊖ Knightsbridge

F5

12 rm ☕ – 🚹£250/600 🚹🚹£275/650

The Levin

Its bigger sister, The Capital, is a few strides down the road and may be better known, but The Levin still does the (Levin) family proud. Here you'll find a different decorative style but still the same level of care and enthusiasm in the service. The eye-catching fibre optic chandelier dominates the staircase, while the collection of Penguin paperbacks reminds you that this is a fundamentally British hotel. All 12 bedrooms are light and fresh-feeling; there are subtle nods in the direction of art deco in the styling but these are combined with a cleverly contemporary look which blends in well with the building. The best room is the top floor open-plan suite. Mini-bars are stocked exclusively with champagne - along with some helpful hints on how to prepare an assortment of champagne cocktails. In the basement you'll find Le Metro which provides an appealing, all-day menu with everything from quiche and salads to shepherd's pie and sausage and mash, along with selections from the family estate in the Loire.

Mandarin Oriental Hyde Park

66 Knightsbridge
✉ SW1X 7LA
✆ (020) 7235 2000
www.mandarinoriental.com/london
⊖ Knightsbridge

F4

194 rm – †£354/882 ††£354/882, ☕ £32 – 25 suites
Bar Boulud and Dinner by Heston Blumenthal
(See restaurant listing)

Mandarin Oriental Hyde Park

When the bewilderingly expensive new apartments next door went on sale things could finally quieten down in this part of town for a while. That said, during their construction there was also plenty of work being done on the hotel too. Bar Boulud, celebrated New York based chef Daniel Boulud's first European venture, occupies what was previously the hotel's housekeeping storeroom and proved a hit from day one. But that was nothing compared to the frenzy caused by Heston Blumenthal's enigmatically named restaurant with its thrilling menu of rediscovered and re-imagined British dishes. Meanwhile, the hotel continues to constantly upgrade and redecorate its bedrooms which all offer every imaginable luxury and extra. They are decorated in a classic English country house style and come in either beige and blue or red and gold – although the TVs do seem to be incongruously large. If evidence were still needed that the hotel is keen to remain one of the most luxurious in the capital, it comes in the fact that it recently spent a mere £1 million just on doing up its Royal Suite.

Mayflower

26-28 Trebovir Rd.
✉ SW5 9NJ
✆ (020) 7370 0991
www.mayflowerhotel.co.uk
⊖ Earl's Court

C6

48 rm – £99/199 £129/250

Mayflower

The Mayflower shares the same ownership as Twenty Nevern Square just around the corner and it too offers good value accommodation. It is also twice the size so the chances of actually getting a room are somewhat greater. Some of those rooms can be a little tight on space but this is also reflected in the room rates. Rooms 11, 17 and 18 are the best in the house and the general decoration is a blend of the contemporary with some Asian influence; some of the rooms have jet showers and others balconies. But what makes the hotel stand out is that the owner is nearly always on the property and his enthusiasm has been passed to his staff. This may not be a glitzy West End hotel but they really do make an effort to get to know their guests and help in anyway they can. There is no restaurant, but then it doesn't need one: there are plenty of places in which to eat that are no more than a vigorous stroll away. A plentiful breakfast is provided and, on summer days, can even be taken on the small terrace.

Metropolitan

Old Park Ln
✉ W1K 1LB
✆ (020) 7447 1000
www.metropolitan.como.bz
⊖ Hyde Park Corner

G4

147 rm – †£409 ††£439, ☕ £22 – 3 suites
🍴 **Nobu** *(See restaurant listing)*

Metropolitan

The Metropolitan is inextricably linked to its über-cool hang-out, The Met Bar. If you've never managed to blag your way past the doorman at night you can now secure entry by grabbing yourself some 'Afternoon Delight': a healthy version of afternoon tea with low-fat cakes and breadless sandwiches. The Metropolitan Hotel is well over a decade old now; in design terms, there may be more contemporary competitors around but it continues to hold its own in the fashion stakes by letting its guests create their own atmosphere. The bedrooms are neutral in colour and gadgets are discreetly integrated; all get regular licks of paint or, following an overnight stay from the occasional wannabe rock star, a full redecoration. Plenty of rooms overlook the park but the more interesting views are those facing east over the rooftops. The spa promises plenty of holistic treatments while London's original Nobu on the first floor ensures a further sprinkling of stardust. Even better, the staff now provide good service instead of just standing at an angle, looking cool.

The Milestone

1-2 Kensington Ct
W8 5DL
(020) 7917 1000
www.milestonehotel.com
High Street Kensington

D4

56 rm – †£342/450 ††£402/630, ☕ £25 – 6 suites

The Milestone

The Milestone proves that it is the service, not the space, which makes a hotel. With 100 members of staff for 57 bedrooms, it's odds-on you'll be well looked after; the hotel prides itself on keeping records of the whims and preferences of their regulars. Plenty of thought has gone into the design and decoration of the bedrooms which are undergoing a refurbishment. It's in the detail where you notice the extra effort: there's a little gift with the turn-down service and the bathrobes are seasonally adjusted so one gets a lighter robe in summer. The suites display greater levels of whimsy than the standard rooms – just check out the art deco inspired Mistinguett Suite, named in honour of the celebrated music hall entertainer, while Johnny Weissmuller would feel more at home in The Safari Suite. The sitting room is a comfy place, with a jaunty looking Noel Coward hanging above the fireplace. The Jockey bar is so named as this was where the horses were stabled in the days when this Victorian building was a private house. The dining room is an intimate, wood-panelled affair.

Number Sixteen

16 Sumner Pl.
✉ SW7 3EG
✆ (020) 7589 5232
www.numbersixteenhotel.co.uk
⊖ South Kensington

E6

41 rm – †£180 ††£235, ☕ £19

Firmdale

Number Sixteen opened back in 2001 and was the first one in Tim and Kit Kemp's Firmdale Group of hotels not to have its own restaurant. This actually suits it because it feels more like a private house than the others and, with repeat business standing at around 55%, they've clearly got it right. Attention to detail underpins the operation, whether in the individual styling of the bedrooms or the twice-daily housekeeping service. Breakfast is in the conservatory overlooking the little garden – don't miss the smoothie of the day – and is served until midday: welcome acknowledgement that not every guest has an early morning meeting. Firmdale also operates its own laundry service which explains how the bed linen retains such crispness. Rooms 2 and 7 have their own private patio terrace and all the first floor rooms benefit from large windows and balconies. The drawing room, with its plump sofa cushions and pretty butterfly theme, is a very charming spot and there's the added bonus of a nearby honesty bar.

One Aldwych

1 Aldwych
✉ WC2B 4RH
(020) 7300 1000
www.onealdwych.com
⊖ Temple

J3

105 rm – ♀£260/435 ♀♀£260/435, ☕ £26 – 12 suites
Axis *(See restaurant listing)*

One Aldwych

Things have gone all green down at One Aldwych. The hotel is hoping to take a lead within the hospitality industry on matters environmental (without, of course, neglecting its duties as a luxury hotel) and has appointed a 'green team' to oversee and coordinate procedures. The swimming pool is chemical and chlorine free; bath products are organic; and the chocolate on your pillow has been replaced by a book called 'Change the World'. As far as guests are concerned though, it's business as usual, which means extremely comfortable bedrooms and plenty of polished staff. Fruit and flowers are changed daily in the rooms, which are awash with Bang & Olufsen toys and also come with Frette linen; deluxe rooms and corner suites are particularly desirable. There's a choice of restaurant: the first floor Indigo offers a light, easy menu while Axis boasts more personality and greater ambition in its cooking. The lobby of the hotel is perhaps its most well-known feature; not only does it double as a bar surprisingly successfully but it also changes its look according to the seasons.

The Pelham

15 Cromwell Pl
SW7 2LA
(020) 7589 8288
www.thepelhamhotel.co.uk
South Kensington

E6

52 rm – †£180/335 ††£260/480, £18 – 1 suite

The Pelham

It may no longer be part of the Firmdale group – it is owned by the people who have The Gore in Queensgate – but The Pelham retains that stylish look which comes from juxtaposing the feel of a classic English country house with the contemporary look of a city townhouse. Originally three houses, the hotel has a pleasing lack of conformity in its layout. Bold pastel colours, fine fabrics and a housekeeping department that could satisfy Howard Hughes combine to create bedrooms that are pristine, warm and comfortable. Spend too long in the panelled sitting room or library, with all those cushions, an honesty bar and a fridge full of ice cream and the world outside will seem positively frenzied. Downstairs you'll find Bistro Fifteen, a relaxed all-day affair which becomes a cosy and romantic dinner spot. Its menu is mostly centred on Europe with an extra Gallic element – a nod to the high number of French émigrés in the neighbourhood. There's a genuine helpfulness and an eagerness to please amongst the staff.

Ritz

150 Piccadilly
✉ W1J 9BR
✆ (020) 7493 8181
www.theritzlondon.com
⊖ Green Park

H4

133 rm – †£315/780 ††£360/925, ☕ £35 – 45 suites
Ritz Restaurant *(See restaurant listing)*

The Ritz

Henry James considered that, "There are few hours in life more agreeable than the hour dedicated to the ceremony known as afternoon tea". Such is the popularity of Tea at the Ritz, which is served daily in the grand surroundings of the Palm Court, that the ceremony begins at 11.30 am – an hour before lunch is served in their restaurant – and doesn't cease until 7.30pm. Meanwhile, the rest of the hotel, built in 1906 in the style of a French chateau, remains in fine form thanks to constant re-investment by its owners, the Barclay Brothers. The William Kent Room must be the most ornate private dining room in London and the bedrooms are all immaculately kept. The Royal and Prince of Wales Suites both have enormous square footage and are often booked for long stays by those for whom the credit crunch is no more than a mild irritant. The Ritz Restaurant, with its dinner dances, lavish surroundings and brigades of staff, evokes images of a more formal but more glamorous age and the art deco Rivoli bar remains a veritable jewel.

The Rockwell

181-183 Cromwell Rd.
✉ SW5 0SF
✆ (020) 7244 2000
www.therockwell.com
⊖ Earl's Court

C5/6

40 rm ☕ - †£110/130 ††£140/190

The Rockwell

The Rockwell is steadily establishing itself on the London hotel scene and is building up quite a loyal client base. They certainly get a lot of things right: the reception is manned 24/7 and staff are imbued with sufficient self-confidence to make eye-contact with their guests and offer help when needed; the housekeeping department also do an evening service of all the rooms. The lobby is a comfortable space, with its fireplace and generous scattering of newspapers. The hotel is made up of two Victorian houses; the best two rooms are the split level 104 and 105 and those on the lower ground floor have their own private patios. All rooms have showers rather than baths, and come with top-brand toiletries, mini bars and free internet – you can even borrow a laptop. Meals are relaxed affairs with plenty of favourites and decent cocktails. Freshly baked croissants and homemade breads are a feature of breakfast; sometimes served on the south-facing garden terrace which is the hotel's most appealing feature.

The Rookery

L2

12 Peters Ln, Cowcross St
EC1M 6DS
(020) 7336 0931
www.rookeryhotel.com
Barbican
Closed 24-26 December

33 rm – †£245/285 ††£245/285, £12

A/C

The Rookery

The mere fact that the original opening of the hotel was delayed because the owner couldn't find quite the right chimney pots tells you that authenticity is high on the agenda here. Named after the colloquial term for the local area from a time when it had an unruly reputation, the hotel is made up of a series of Georgian houses whose former residents are honoured in the naming of the bedrooms. Its decoration remains true to these Georgian roots, not only in the antique furniture and period features but also in the colours used; all the bedrooms have either half-testers or four-poster beds and bathrooms have roll-top baths. Rook's Nest, the largest room, is often used for fashion shoots. However, with the addition of flat screen TVs and wireless internet access, there is no danger of the hotel becoming a twee museum piece. Breakfast is served in the bedrooms and there is just one small sitting room which leads out onto a little terrace - its mural of the owner herding some cows goes some way towards blocking out the surrounding sights of the 21C.

St James's Hotel and Club

7-8 Park Pl.
SW1A 1LS
(020) 7316 1600
www.stjameshotelandclub.com
Green Park

H4

55 rm – †£260/3,000 ††£260/3,000, £16 – 10 suites
Seven Park Place *(See restaurant listing)*

A/C

St James's Hotel & Club

Dating from 1892, this building was a private club for many years and the hotel manages to retain something of that clubby spirit. It certainly feels as though it is run for the benefit of its guests rather than a balance sheet, and staff make genuine efforts to get to know the guests and their individual peculiarities. While the public areas are quite compact, the interior has been sympathetically modernised and features over 300 pieces of art, most of which are German works from the 1930s and '40s. Bedrooms are well-equipped and have smart, marble bathrooms; a few have small terraces and the Presidential Suite comes with an enormous one that can host up to 60 people. The restaurant is intimate and the cooking and service are undertaken with considerable expertise. The hotel's other great bonus is its location: this is the centre of central London but Park Place is also a cul-de-sac so it's quiet to boot. There's also a cut-through to Green Park where you'll find a pile of towels and water, placed there by the hotel for those who insist on running round it.

St Martins Lane

45 St Martin's Ln
✉ WC2N 3HX
✆ (020) 7300 5500
www.stmartinslane.com
⊖ Charing Cross

13

206 rm – †£262/360 ††£288/384, ☕ £25 – 2 suites
Asia de Cuba *(See restaurant listing)*

St Martin's Lane

If you're uncomfortable with the idea of hotel staff calling you by your first name or have never considered working out in a gym wearing a pair of stilettos then St Martins Lane is probably not the hotel for you; nor you the right guest for them. Philippe Starck's design of the modern juxtaposed with the baroque creates an eye-catching lobby. The bedrooms are decorated in a blizzard of white, although you can change the lighting according to your mood. The views get better the higher you go but all have floor to ceiling windows. Thanks to the paparazzi, readers of the more excitable magazines will be familiar with Bungalow 8: Anne Sacco's London outpost of her hip New York club is a favoured hang-out for the already-famous, the would-be-famous and the related-to-someone-famous-famous. Asia de Cuba is Scarface meets Dr No: fiery Floridian Cuban mixed with teasing influence from across Asia – dishes are designed for sharing. The Light Bar is sufficiently hip and the Gymbox is a branded gym with a nightclub vibe – what else?

Sanderson

50 Berners St
W1T 3NG
(020) 7300 1400
www.morganshotelgroup.com
Oxford Circus

H2

150 rm – ♦£276/960 ♦♦£288/960, £25

Suka *(See restaurant listing)*

A/C

Sanderson

When the doorman greets you with a "how ya doing?" you know this is not a hotel that stands on ceremony. The staff do now smile here, something that was all too rare in the early days when they were mostly recruited from model agencies and had a somewhat disdainful attitude towards the whole concept of service. The Sanderson has always worn its exclusivity with confidence but now there's some substance to it. The Philippe Starck designed bedrooms still impress, with their celestial whiteness, sleigh beds in the middle of the room and idiosyncrasies such as the framed print hung on the ceiling – its actually the same print in all the rooms, is called 'Pathway to Heaven' and is designed to encourage heavenly thoughts before sleep. Some bedrooms have their own treadmills while others boast small terraces; the top two suites have their own lifts. On the ground floor the Purple Bar has over 75 different vodkas, miniature chairs and a selective door policy; the Long Bar is more accessible and leads into Suka, their modern Malaysian restaurant.

Savoy

Strand
✉ WC2R 0EU
✆ (020) 7836 4343
www.fairmont.com/savoy
⊖ Charing Cross

G5

268 rm – †£420 ††£420, ☕ £30 – 30 suites
110 **Savoy Grill** *(See restaurant listing)*

The Savoy

The Savoy is one of the grande dames of the London hotel scene. The comprehensive restoration took nearly three years but the best news for the hotel's legions of regulars was that many of the familiar Edwardian and art deco features were retained. The lobby still offers a welcoming air and adds to the sense of expectation, with plenty of staff on hand to offer help or directions. Afternoon tea is served in the Thames Foyer, which remains at the heart of the operation – although it now has a steel gazebo beneath a glass dome. There is a choice of two bars: the world famous American Bar and the Beaufort Bar which occupies the space from which the BBC once broadcast. However, the hotel were clearly not happy with everything because in 2013 they replaced the legendary River restaurant with Kaspar's, a more informal seafood bar and grill – tables here are easier to secure than those in the famous Savoy Grill. They did get it right first time with the bedrooms though: they remain true to the hotel's origins and are split between Edwardian and art deco styles.

Soho

4 Richmond Mews
✉ W1D 3DH
✆ (020) 7559 3000
www.sohohotel.com
⊖ Tottenham Court Road

I3 

91 rm – †£355 ††£355, ☕ £20 – 5 suites
Ⅱ○ **Refuel** *(See restaurant listing)*

A/C

Firmdale

It's almost as if they wanted to keep it secret. The hotel is on a relatively quiet mews – not something one readily associates with Soho – and, even as you approach, it gives little away. But inside one soon realises that, if it was a secret, it wasn't very well kept as it's always buzzing with people. Their guests' every dietary whim or food mood should find fulfilment in 'Refuel', the restaurant with its own bar as a backdrop. Whether your diet is gluten-free, vegetarian, vegan, carnivorous or organic you'll discover something worth ordering and, if you're off out, you'll find the early dinner menu a steal. It's also worth checking out the Film Club for a meal and a movie in the screening room. Upstairs and the bedrooms are almost celestial in their cleanliness. From jazzy orange to bright lime green, from crimsons to bold stripes, the rooms are vibrant in style and immaculate in layout; those on the top floor have balconies and terraces. Add infectiously enthusiastic service and it's little wonder the hotel has so many returning guests. And to think this was once an NCP car park.

South Place

3 South Pl
✉ EC2M 2AF
(020) 3503 0000
www.southplacehotel.com
⊖ Moorgate

M2

80 rm – ♀£170/380 ♀♀£210/420, ☕ £20 – 1 suite
Angler *(See restaurant listing)*

South Place / Finsbury

Restaurant group D&D's first venture into the hotel business is a very stylish looking affair, and for that credit goes to their erstwhile boss, in the shape of Conrad & Partners, who designed the interior. The bedrooms are a treat for those with an eye for aesthetics and a great advert for how design can enhance one's mood. They are understated, uncluttered and cool yet no detail has been forgotten, from blackout blinds to all manner of high-tech gizmos; contemporary artwork lines the walls and the bathrooms are a great balance between form and function. On the food front you have a choice of two restaurants: 3 South Place is a bustling bar and grill on the ground floor, with a good range of modern brasserie dishes and food-inspired pop art on the walls; Angler, a more formal seafood restaurant is on the top floor. The hotel is actually fashioned out of two former offices but you wouldn't know it from the exterior – the atmosphere is relaxed yet animated, helped along by service that is discreet and professional. D&D's first attempt appears to have hit the bullseye.

Stafford

16-18 St James's Pl.
✉ SW1A 1NJ
✆ (020) 7493 0111
www.kempinski.com/london
⊖ Green Park

H4

213 rm ☕ – †£403/565 ††£428/590 – 8 suites

Stafford

The Stafford has, for a few years, been a mix of the new and the more traditional. Recently, the owners have been busy injecting considerable amounts of money into its refurbishment; something which no doubt terrifies many of its loyal and longstanding guests who appear to like things just the way they are. Thanks to some judicious lighting, the lobby and lounge appear brighter and more inviting. The dining room now opens out more into the drawing room and has changed its name to the Lyttleton, after a family who once lived here, but it has wisely kept its traditional British menu. The relatively recently created suites in the Mews House, a converted office block in the rear courtyard of the hotel, are the most impressive of all the bedrooms. What will never change at The Stafford is the celebrated American Bar, which is festooned with an impressive collection of assorted ties, helmets and pictures and is one of the best in London for those who like their bars with chairs and without music.

Twenty Nevern Square

20 Nevern Sq.
✉ SW5 9PD
✆ (020) 7565 9555
www.twentynevernsquare.co.uk
⊖ Earl's Court

C6

20 rm – †£80/160 ††£100/330

Michelin

It's wise to book well in advance here, as this small but friendly hotel – with its quiet location in a typical Victorian Square – represents decent value for money and gets booked up pretty quickly. The two best rooms are the Pasha and the Ottoman Suites and both have their own terraces, but all rooms are well looked after and given regular refits. Ten of the rooms overlook the gardens opposite; those at the front of the house tend to be larger, while those on the top floor are better suited to individual travellers. Hand-carved Indonesian furniture is found throughout which, together with the elaborately draped curtains, adds a hint of exoticism. You'll find gratis tea, coffee, water and a pile of daily newspapers laid on in the pleasant lounge. Continental breakfast comes included in the room rate; it can be taken in one's bedroom or in the bright conservatory. The hotel's other great selling point is the genuine sense of neighbourhood one feels. Its sister hotel, the Mayflower, is around the corner.

The Wellesley

11 Knightsbridge
✉ SW1X 7LY
✆ (020) 7235 3535
www.thewellesley.co.uk
⊖ Hyde Park Corner

G4

36 rm – †£420/850 ††£420/850, ☕ £25 – 15 suites

The Wellesley/ Belgravia

It may once have been one of the entrances to Hyde Park Corner tube, but for nearly three decades this site was occupied by the legendary Pizza on the Park, which was celebrated by its fans less for the pizzas and more for being a great venue for live jazz. It was subsequently gutted and rebuilt and emerged as the very end of 2012 as this very stylish, intimate boutique named after the Sir Arthur Wellesley, the first duke of Wellington. The owners were not blind to the building's past: not only were some of the decorative features inspired by the jazz age but live music is also performed in the Jazz Lounge. The discreet restaurant serves modern Italian food and, in perhaps another nod towards the appetite of your typical jazz fan, the hotel has a great cigar lounge and a bar with a superb selection of whiskies and cognacs. The smart, elegant bedrooms have been beautifully finished and come with every conceivable facility, including a full butler service; those in most demand are the ones facing the park.

Westbury

Bond St
✉ W1S 2YF
✆ (020) 7629 7755
www.westburymayfair.com
⊖ Bond Street

H3

246 rm – ♦£270/499 ♦♦£270/499, ☕ £26 – 13 suites
🍴 **Alyn Williams at The Westbury** *(See restaurant listing)*

Westbury

The Westbury opened in the 1950s and caused quite a commotion with its New York sensibilities. Over recent years, considerable funds have been spent restoring it to its former glory with the result that this is now one of Mayfair's more comfortable hotels. It is traditional without being staid and discreet without appearing previous; the staff are suitably enthusiastic and clearly proud of their hotel. There is no doubt that its location is also a huge draw: there are enough exclusive designer brands just outside the front door to satisfy even the most committed disciple of Edina and Patsy. The bedrooms are sleek and comfy and each floor is decorated with photos from the corresponding decade (so 1960s style icons adorn the 6th floor). The suites are particularly smart, especially those with art deco styling. The iconic Polo bar is elegantly dressed in Gucci and Fendi and its celebrated cocktail list ensures it's busy at night. Along with a sushi bar the hotel now offers sublime dining courtesy of chef Alyn Williams' creative and elaborate cuisine.

Zetter

St John's Sq., 86-88 Clerkenwell Rd.
✉ EC1M 5RJ
✆ (020) 7324 4444
www.thezetter.com
⊖ Farringdon

K1

72 rm – †£162/234 ††£162/450, ☕ £10
Bistrot Bruno Loubet *(See restaurant listing)*

The Zetter

It doesn't matter how good looking and coolly dressed you are – if you never crack a smile no one will want to know you. What makes the Zetter more than just another hip hotel lies in the friendliness of its staff: instead of checking their pose or practising their pout they'll actually greet you with a warm smile and this is one of the reasons why guests keep returning. The main part of the hotel is within a converted Victorian warehouse, although the Bistrot on the ground floor adds a little continental element. Not only does the hotel have impressive eco-credentials – it bottles the water from its well – it also comes with some nice touches, like affordable vending machines on each floor; you can even borrow a folding bike from reception, complete with helmet and map. The rooms in this part of the hotel are understated and come with a cool retro edge; the more idiosyncratic Townhouse across the room acts as an overflow with more colourfully decorated rooms and a cocktail bar that has become a destination in its own right.

The Michelin Adventure

It all started with rubber balls! This was the product made by a small company based in Clermont-Ferrand that André and Edouard Michelin inherited, back in 1880. The brothers quickly saw the potential for a new means of transport and their first success was the invention of detachable pneumatic tyres for bicycles. However, the automobile was to provide the greatest scope for their creative talents. Throughout the 20th century, Michelin never ceased developing and creating ever more reliable and high-performance tyres, not only for vehicles ranging from trucks to F1 but also for underground transit systems and aeroplanes.

From early on, Michelin provided its customers with tools and services to facilitate mobility and make travelling a more pleasurable and more frequent experience. As early as 1900, the Michelin Guide supplied motorists with a host of useful information related to vehicle maintenance, accommodation and restaurants, and was to become a benchmark for good food. At the same time, the Travel Information Bureau offered travellers personalised tips and itineraries.

The publication of the first collection of roadmaps, in 1910, was an instant hit! In 1926, the first regional guide to France was published, devoted to the principal sites of Brittany, and before long each region of France had its own Green Guide. The collection was later extended to more far-flung destinations, including New York in 1968 and Taiwan in 2011.

In the 21st century, with the growth of digital technology, the challenge for Michelin maps and guides is to continue to develop alongside the company's tyre activities. Now, as before, Michelin is committed to improving the mobility of travellers.

MICHELIN TODAY

WORLD NUMBER ONE TYRE MANUFACTURER

- 69 production sites in 18 countries
- 115,000 employees from all cultures and on every continent
- 6,000 people employed in research and development

Moving for a world

Moving forward means developing tyres with better road grip and shorter braking distances, whatever the state of the road.

CORRECT TYRE PRESSURE

RIGHT PRESSURE

- Safety
- Longevity
- Optimum fuel consumption

-0,5 bar

- Durability reduced by 20% (- 8,000 km)

-1 bar

- Risk of blowouts
- Increased fuel consumption
- Longer braking distances on wet surfaces

forward together
where mobility is safer

It also involves helping motorists take care of their safety and their tyres. To do so, Michelin organises "Fill Up With Air" campaigns all over the world to remind us that correct tyre pressure is vital.

WEAR

DETECTING TYRE WEAR

MICHELIN tyres are equipped with tread wear indicators, which are small blocks of rubber molded into the base of the main grooves at a height of 1.6 mm. When tread depth is the same level as indicators, the tyres are worn and need replacing.

Tyres are the only point of contact between vehicle and the road, a worn tyre can be dangerous on wet surfaces.

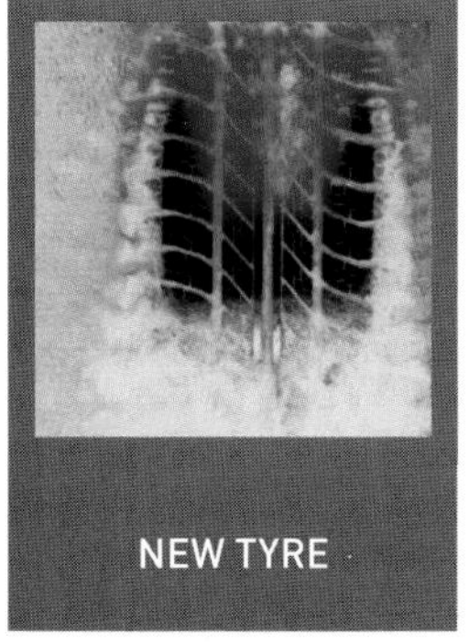

NEW TYRE

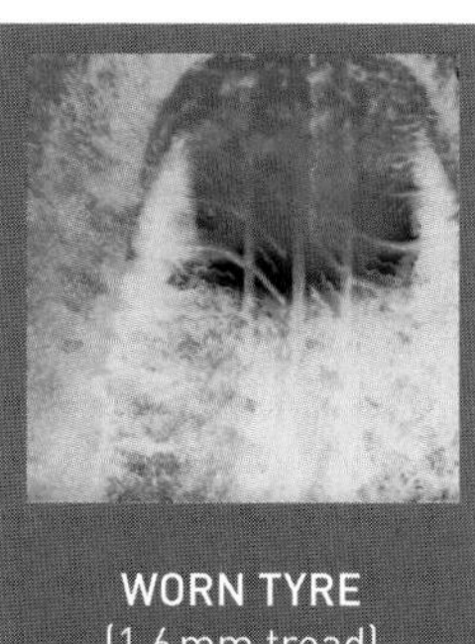

WORN TYRE
(1,6 mm tread)

The photo shows the actual contact zone on wet surfaces.

Moving forward means sustainable mobility

INNOVATION AND THE ENVIRONMENT

By 2050, Michelin aims to cut the quantity of raw materials used in its tyre manufacturing process by half and to have developed renewable energy in its facilities. The design of MICHELIN tyres has already saved billions of litres of fuel and, by extension, billions of tonnes of CO2.

Similarly, Michelin prints its maps and guides on paper produced from sustainably managed forests and is diversifying its publishing media by offering digital solutions to make travelling easier, more fuel efficient and more enjoyable!

The group's whole-hearted commitment to eco-design on a daily basis is demonstrated by ISO 14001 certification.

Like you, Michelin is committed to preserving our planet.

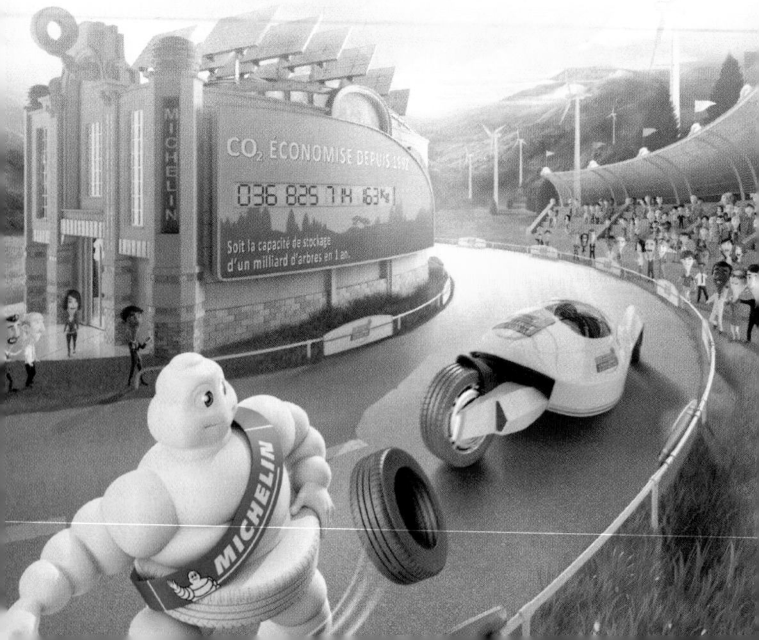

Chat with Bibendum

Go to www.michelin.com/corporate/EN/home
Find out more about Michelin's history and the latest news.

QUIZ

Michelin develops tyres for all types of vehicles. See if you can match the right tyre with the right vehicle…

Solution : A-6 / B-4 / C-2 / D-1 / E-3 / F-7 / G-5

Index & Maps

▸ Alphabetical list of restaurants 486

▸ Index of Maps 494

▸ Map of London Underground 495

Alphabetical list of restaurants

A

Restaurant	Category	Page
Abbeville Kitchen	X	396
L'Absinthe	X	332
A Cena	XX	420
Admiral Codrington	🍺	266
Alain Ducasse at The Dorchester	XXXXX ✿✿✿	40
Albion	🍺	349
Al Borgo	XX	418
Al Duca	XX	41
Alloro	XX	41
Almeida	XX	349
Alyn Williams at The Westbury	XXXX ✿	42
Amaranto	XXX	43
Amaya	XXX ✿	136
Ametsa with Arzak Instruction	XXX ✿	137
Anchor and Hope	🍺 ☺	216
Angel and Crown	🍺	119
Angelus	XX	202
Angler	XX ✿	217
Anglesea Arms	🍺	408
L' Anima	XXX	353
Antico	X	216
Apsleys	XXXX ✿	138
Aqua Kyoto	XX	43
Aqua Nueva	XXX	44
Arbutus	X ✿	45
Archipelago	XX	158
Asadal	XX	185
Asia de Cuba	XX	119
Assaggi	X	202
Atari-ya	X	400
L'Atelier de Joël Robuchon	XX ✿	120
Au Lac	X	347
Aurelia	XX	44
Automat	X	46
L'Autre Pied	XX ✿	159
Avalon	🍺	385
L'Aventure	XX	158
Avenue	XX	46
A. Wong	X ☺	139
Axis	XXX	121
Azou	X ☺	408

B

Restaurant	Category	Page
Babur	XX	373
Babylon	XX	299
Baku	XXX	266
Balcon	XX	47
Balthazar	XX	121
Baltic	XX	218
Bangkok	X	267
Baozi Inn	X	47
Barbecoa	XX	218
Bar Boulud	XX	267
Barnsbury	🍺	350
Barrafina	X ☺	48
Barrica	X ☺	185
Barshu	X	48
Ba Shan	X	49
Beagle	X	347
Beard to Tail	X	353
Bedford and Strand	X	122
Beijing Dumpling	X	49
Belvedere	XXX	299
Benares	XXX ✿	50
Bentley's (Grill)	XXX	51
Bentley's (Oyster Bar)	X	51
Bibendum	XXX	268
Bibigo	X	53
Bingham Restaurant	XX	415
Bird of Smithfield	X	219
Bistro Aix	X	326

Bistrot Bruno Loubet 219
Bistrotheque 364
Bistro Union 398
Bleeding Heart 186
Bluebird 268
Blue Elephant 403
Blueprint Café 220
Bob Bob Ricard 52
Bocca di Lupo 52
Boisdale of Belgravia 139
Boisdale of Bishopsgate 220
Boisdale of Canary Wharf 367
Bo London 54
Bombay Brasserie 269
Bonds 221
Bone Daddies 53
Bonnie Gull 160
Boqueria 392
The Botanist 269
Le Boudin Blanc 55
Boundary 354
Bradley's 334
Brasserie Chavot 56
Brasserie Max 186
Brasserie Zédel 55
Brawn 364
Bread Street Kitchen 221
Briciole 161
Brown Dog 386
Brula 421
Brumus 57
Brunello 300
Builders Arms 270
Bull and Last 327
Bumpkin (North Kensington) 300
Bumpkin (South Kensington) 270
Burger and Lobster (Mayfair) 58
Burger and Lobster (Soho) 57
Butlers Wharf Chop House 222

C

Cadogan Arms 271
Le Café Anglais 203
Cafe at Sotheby's 58
Cafe Spice Namaste 378
Caffé Caldesi 161
Cambio de Tercio 271
Cannizaro House 423
Canonbury Kitchen 343
Cantina Del Ponte 222
Canton Arms 377
Capote y Toros 272
Le Caprice 59
Caravan (Finsbury) 223
Caravan (King's Cross St Pancras) 329
Casa Malevo 203
Cassis 272
Cat and Mutton 344
Cây Tre 59
Cecconi's 60
Cellar Gascon 223
Le Cercle 273
Ceviche 60
Chabrot (City of London) 224
Chabrot (Hyde Park and Knightsbridge) 273
Chada 389
Chakra 301
The Chancery 224
Chapters 365
Charlotte's Bistro 393
Charlotte's Place 400
Chelsea Ram 274
Chez Bruce 422
Chicken Shop 329
China Tang 61
Chiswell Street Dining Rooms 225
Chutney Mary 274
Cibo 301
Cicada 225
Cigala 187
Cigalon 226
The Cinnamon Club 140

Restaurant	Category	Page
Cinnamon Kitchen	XX	226
Cinnamon Soho	X	61
Clarke's	XX	302
Claude's Kitchen	X	404
Clerkenwell Kitchen	X	227
Clissold Arms	🍺	327
Clos Maggiore	XX	122
Clove Club	X	354
Club Gascon	XX ✿	228
Colbert	XX	275
Colchis	XX	204
Le Colombier	XX	275
Comptoir Gascon	X ☺	227
Copita	X ☺	62
Corner Room	X ☺	365
Corrigan's Mayfair	XXX	62
Cotidie	XX	162
Coya	XX	63
Crabtree	🍺	409
Crooked Well	🍺	229
Cut	XXX	63
D		
Dabbous	X ✿	188
Daphne's	XX	276
Dartmouth Castle	🍺	409
Dean Street Townhouse Restaurant	XX	64
Dehesa	X	64
Delaunay	XXX	123
Del Mercato	XX ☺	229
Le Deuxième	XX	123
Les Deux Salons	XX	124
Dining Room	XXX	141
Dinings	X	162
Dinner by Heston Blumenthal	XX ✿✿	277
Dishoom	X	124
Dock Kitchen	X	302
Dockmaster's House	XXX	367
Donostia	X	163
Drapers Arms	🍺 ☺	350
Duck and Waffle	XX	230
Ducksoup	X	65
Duke of Sussex	🍺	384
Dysart Arms	XX	416
E		
E and O	XX	303
The Ebury Restaurant and Wine Bar	XX	141
Edera	XX	303
Eight over Eight	XX	276
Electric Diner	X	304
Eleven Park Walk	XXX	278
Elliot's	X ☺	230
El Pirata De Tapas	X	206
Empress	🍺 ☺	345
Enoteca Turi	XX	414
Entrée	X	389
Eriki	XX	335
L'Etranger	XX	278
Eyre Brothers	XX	355
F		
Fellow	🍺	
Fifteen London	X	348
Fifth Floor at Harvey Nichols	XXX	279
Fino	XX	187
Fish Market	X	231
Five Fields	XXX	279
500	X ☺	322
Floridita	XX	65
Fox and Grapes	🍺 ☺	423
Foxtrot Oscar	X	280
Franco's	XX	66
G		
Gail's Kitchen	X ☺	189
Galvin at Windows	XXX ✿	68
Galvin Bistrot de Luxe	XX	163
Galvin Café a Vin	X ☺	374
Galvin Demoiselle	X	280
Galvin La Chapelle	XXX ✿	375
Garnier	XX	281
Garrison	🍺	231
Gauthier - Soho	XXX	66

Le Gavroche	XXXX ✿✿	67
Geales	X	281
Georgina's	X	387
Giaconda Dining Rooms	X	189
Gilbert Scott	XX	330
The Glasshouse	XX ✿	413
Good Earth	XX	282
Goodman	XX	69
Goodman Canary Wharf	XX	368
Goodman City	XX	232
Gordon Ramsay	XXXX ✿✿✿	283
Grain Store	X ☺	331
Grand Imperial	XXX	142
Granger and Co	X	304
Grazing Goat	🍺	164
Great British	X	69
Great Queen Street	X ☺	190
Greenhouse	XXX ✿✿	70
Green Man and French Horn	X ☺	125
The Grill	XXX	71
The Grove	🍺	401
Gun	🍺	368

H

Hakkasan Hanway Place	XX ✿	191
Hakkasan Mayfair	XX ✿	72
Hampshire Hog	🍺	410
Hana	X	390
Haozhan	XX	71
Harrison's	X	385
Harwood Arms	🍺 ✿	405
Havelock Tavern	🍺	410
Hawksmoor (City of London)	X	232
Hawksmoor (Mayfair)	XX	73
Hawksmoor (Spitalfields)	X	374
Hawksmoor (Strand and Covent Garden)	X	125
Hedone	XX ✿	394
Hélène Darroze at The Connaught	XXXX ✿✿	74
Henry Root	X	282
Hereford Road	X ☺	204
Hibiscus	XXX ✿✿	75
High Road Brasserie	X	395
High Timber	XX	233
Hispania	X	233
HIX (Soho)	X	73
Hix Mayfair	XXX	76
Hix Oyster and Chop House	X	234
HKK	XX ✿	356
Honey and Co	X ☺	190
House	🍺	343
Hush	XX	76

I

Iberica Canary Wharf	XX	369
Iberica Marylebone	XX	164
Il Baretto	X	160
Il Convivio	XX	140
il trillo	XX	284
Imli Street	X	77
Imperial China	XXX	77
Indian Zilla	XX	387
Indian Zing	XX	411
Inside	XX	371
The Ivy	XXX	126

J

Joe's	XX	284
John Salt	🍺	351
José	X ☺	234
J. Sheekey	XX	126
J. Sheekey Oyster Bar	X	127
Jugged Hare	🍺	235

K

Kai	XXX ✿	78
Kateh	X ☺	205
Kennington Tandoori	XX	372
Kensington Place	X	305
Kenza	XX	235
Kerbisher and Malt	X	401

Restaurant	Category	Page
Kew Grill	XX	414
Kiku	XX	79
King's Head	🍺	419
Kiraku	X	402
Kitchen Table at Bubbledogs	XX	192
Kitchen W8	XX ✿	306
Koffmann's	XXX	142
Kopapa	X	192
Koya	X ☺	79

L

Restaurant	Category	Page
Lady Ottoline	🍺	193
Lamberts	X	386
Lardo	X	345
Latium	XXX	165
Launceston Place	XXX ✿	307
Lawn Bistro	XX	424
Ledbury	XXX ✿✿	308
Levant	XX	165
Light House	X	424
Lima	X ✿	166
Little Social	X	80
Lobster Pot	X	372
Locanda Locatelli	XXX ✿	167
Lola Rojo	X	390
Lots Road Pub and Dining Room	🍺	285
Luc's Brasserie	XX	236
Lutyens	XXX	236

M

Restaurant	Category	Page
Made in Camden	X ☺	324
Magdalen	XX	237
Malabar	XX	305
Malt House	🍺	404
Manchurian Legends	X	80
Mango and Silk	X ☺	402
Manicomio (Chelsea)	XX	285
Manicomio (City of London)	XX	237
Manuka Kitchen	X	406
Mao Tai	XX	406
Marco	XX	286
Marcus Wareing at The Berkeley	XXXX ✿✿	143
Market	X ☺	325
Market Cafe	X	346
MASH	XX	81
Massimo	XX	144
Master and Servant	X	348
Matsuba	X	416
Matsuri	XX	81
Maze	XX ✿	82
Maze Grill	XX	83
Mazi	X	309
Medcalf	X ☺	238
Medlar	XX ✿	287
Mele e Pere	X	83
The Mercer	XX	238
Metrogusto	X	391
Mews of Mayfair	XX	84
Michael Nadra	XX	395
Michael Nadra Primrose Hill	XX	333
Min Jiang	XXX	309
Mint Leaf	XX	84
Mint Leaf Lounge	XX	239
Mishkin's	X	127
The Modern Pantry	X	239
Momo	XX	85
Mon Plaisir	XX	193
Morgan Arms	🍺	342
Morgan M	XX	240
Morito	X ☺	240
Moro	X	241
Moti Mahal	XX	194
Mr Chow	XX	286
Murano	XXX ✿	86

N

Restaurant	Category	Page
Naamyaa Café	X	241
Narrow	🍺	373
The National Dining Rooms	X	85
Newman Street Tavern	🍺	168
New St Grill	XX	242
1901	XXX	242
Nipa	XX	205

Restaurant	Category	Page
Nobu	XX ✿	87
Nobu Berkeley St	XX ✿	88
Nopi	X	89
Northall	XXX	144

O

Restaurant	Category	Page
Oblix	XX	243
Odette's	XX	333
Olivo	X	145
Olivocarne	X	145
Olivomare	X	146
One Blenheim Terrace	XX	168
One Leicester Street	XX ✿	90
One-O-One	XXX	288
Only Running Footman	🍺	89
Opera Tavern	X ☺	128
The Orange	🍺	146
Orrery	XXX	169
Osteria Dell' Angolo	XX	147
Ottolenghi	X	351
Outlaw's at The Capital	XX ✿	289
Oxo Tower	XXX	243
Oxo Tower Brasserie	X	244
Ozer	XX	169

P

Restaurant	Category	Page
Painted Heron	XX	288
Palmerston	🍺	370
Pantechnicon	🍺	147
Paradise by way of Kensal Green	🍺	328
Paramount	X	194
Paternoster Chop House	X	244
Pearl Liang	XX	206
Peasant	🍺	245
Petersham Nurseries Café	X	417
La Petite Maison	XX	91
Pétrus	XXX ✿	148
Phoenix	🍺	290
Phoenix Palace	XX	170
Picture	X ☺	170
Pied à Terre	XXX ✿	195
Pig's Ear	🍺	290
Pig and Butcher	🍺	352
Pitt Cue Co.	X	91
Pizarro	X	245
Plateau	XX	369
Plum + Spilt Milk	XX	331
Plum Valley	XX	92
Poissonnerie	XX	291
Pollen Street Social	XX ✿	93
Polpo Covent Garden	X ☺	128
Polpo Smithfield	X ☺	246
Polpo Soho	X ☺	92
Le Pont de la Tour	XXX	246
Portman	🍺	171
Portobello House	🍺	310
Portrait	X	94
Potli	XX	411
Prince Alfred and Formosa Dining Room	🍺	207
Prince Arthur	🍺	346
Prince of Wales	🍺	415
Princess of Shoreditch	🍺 ☺	355
Princess Victoria	🍺	418
Provender	X ☺	358
The Providores	XX	171

Q

Restaurant	Category	Page
Quaglino's	XX	94
Quality Chop House	X	247
Quilon	XXX ✿	149
Quo Vadis	XXX	95

R

Restaurant	Category	Page
Racine	XX	291
Rasoi	XX ✿	292
Red Fort	XXX	95
Redhook	XX	247
Refuel	XX	96
Restaurant at St Paul's Cathedral	X	248
Rétro Bistrot	XX	419
Retsina	X	323
Rib Room	XXX	293
Riding House Café	X	172
Ritz Restaurant	XXXXX	96

Restaurant		Page
Riva	X	388
River Café	XX ✿	412
Rivington Grill (Greenwich)	X	371
Rivington Grill (Shoreditch)	X	357
Roast	XX	248
Roka	XX	196
Roka Canary Wharf	XX	370
Rookery	X	398
Roots at N1	XX	342
Rosa's	X	97
Rosita	X	391
Roti Chai	X	172
Roux at Parliament Square	XXX	150
Roux at the Landau	XXX	173
Royal China	XX	173
Rules	XX	129

S

Restaurant		Page
St John	X ✿	249
St John Bread and Wine	X ☺	376
St John's Tavern	🍺	322
Sake No Hana	XX	97
Salt Yard	X ☺	196
Salusbury	🍺	334
Sam's Brasserie	X	396
Sands End	🍺	407
Santini	XXX	150
Sartoria	XXX	98
Sauterelle	XXX	250
Savoy Grill	XXXX	129
Scott's	XXX	98
Seven Park Place	XXX ✿	99
Seventeen	XX	310
1701	XX	250
Shayona	X	326
The Shed	X	311
Shoryu	X	100
Shrimpy's	X	332
Simply Thai	X ☺	420
Singapore Garden	XX	335
Sketch (The Lecture Room and Library)	XXXX ✿✿	101
Sketch (The Gallery)	XX	100
Skylon	XXX	251
Smith's of Wapping	XX	377
Social Eating House	X ✿	102
Soif	X ☺	392
Sonny's Kitchen	XX	388
Spice Market	XX	103
Spuntino	X	103
Square	XXXX ✿✿	104
Story	XX ✿	252
Suda	X	130
Suka	XX	174
Sumosan	XX	105
Sushisamba	XX	251
Sushi-Say	X ☺	336
Swagat	X	417

T

Restaurant		Page
Tamarind	XXX ✿	106
Tandis	X	323
Tangawizi	X	421
Tapas Brindisa (London Bridge)	X	253
Tapas Brindisa (Soho)	X	105
Tate Modern (Restaurant)	X	253
10 Cases	X	130
Tendido Cero	X	293
Tendido Cuatro	X	407
10 Greek Street	X	107
Terroirs	X ☺	131
Texture	XX ✿	175
Theo Randall	XXX	107
34	XXX	108
Thomas Cubitt	🍺	151
Tinello	XX	151
Tom Aikens	XXX ✿	294
Tom's Kitchen	X	295
Tonkotsu	X	108
Tramshed	X	357
Trinity	XX	399
Trishna	X ✿	176
Les Trois Garcons	XX	376
La Trompette	XXX ✿	397
Trullo	X ☺	344

Tsunami (Bloomsbury) X 197
Tsunami (Clapham) X 399
28°-50° Marylebone X 174
28°-50° Fetter Lane X 254

U

Umu XX ✿ 109
Upstairs XX 393

V

Le Vacherin XX 384
Vanilla Black XX 254
Vasco and Piero's Pavilion XX 110
Veeraswamy XX 110
Verru XX 177
Viajante XX ✿ 366
Victoria 🍺 403
Viet Grill X 358
Village East X 255
Vinoteca (Clerkenwell) X 255
Vinoteca (Regent's Park and Marylebone) X 177
Vinoteca (Soho) X 111
Vivat Bacchus X 256
Vivat Bacchus London Bridge X 256

W

The Wallace X 178
Wapping Food X 378
Waterway 🍺 207
Well 🍺 257
Wells 🍺 328
Whitechapel Gallery Dining Room X 379
The White Swan XX 257
Wild Honey XX ✿ 112
Winter Garden XX 178
The Wolseley XXX 111
Wright Brothers X 258
Wright Brothers Soho X 113

X

XO XX 324

Y

Yalla Yalla X 179
Yashin XX 311
Yauatcha XX ✿ 114
Yipin China X 352
York and Albany 🍺 325

Z

Zafferano XXX 152
Zaika XX 312
Zayna XX 179
Zoilo X 180
Zucca X 😋 258
Zuma XX 295

Index of maps

Central London

Plan I 34

- ▶ Mayfair • Soho • St James's — Plan II 38
- ▶ Strand • Covent Garden — Plan III 118
- ▶ Belgravia • Victoria — Plan IV 134
- ▶ Regent's Park • Marylebone — Plan V 156
- ▶ Bloomsbury — Plan VI 184
- ▶ Bayswater • Maida Vale — Plan VII 200
- ▶ City of London — Plan VIII 210
- ▶ Clerkenwell • Finsbury — Plan IX 212
- ▶ Southwark — Plan X 214
- ▶ Chelsea • Earl's Court • South Kensington — Plan XI 262
- ▶ Hyde Park • Knightsbridge — Plan XII 264
- ▶ Kensington • North Kensington • Notting Hill — Plan XIII 298

Greater London

Plan XIV 316

- ▶ North-West — Plan XV 320
- ▶ North-East — Plan XVI 340
- ▶ South-East — Plan XVII 362
- ▶ South-West — Plan XVIII 382

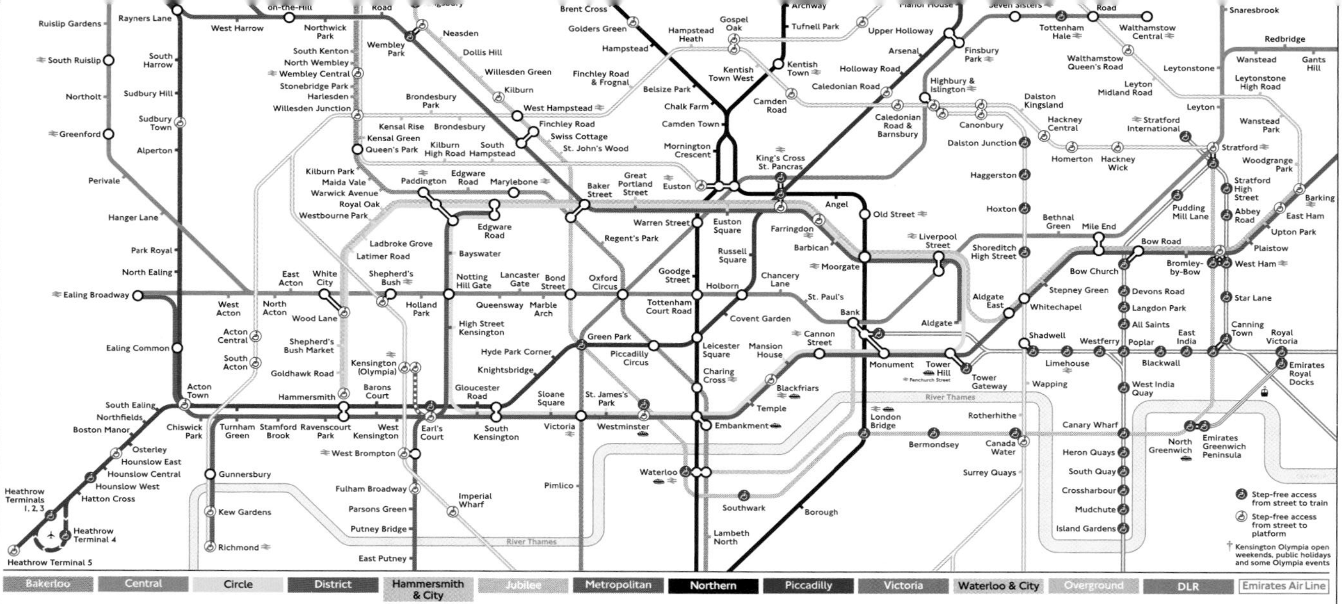

Ruislip Gardens
South Ruislip
Northolt
Greenford
Perivale
Hanger Lane
Park Royal
North Ealing
Ealing Broadway
Ealing Common
Rayners Lane
South Harrow
Sudbury Hill
Sudbury Town
Alperton
West Harrow
Northwick Park
South Kenton
North Wembley
Wembley Central
Stonebridge Park
Harlesden
Willesden Junction
Wembley Park
Neasden
Dollis Hill
Willesden Green
Kilburn
West Hampstead
Finchley Road
Swiss Cottage
St. John's Wood
Brondesbury Park
Kensal Rise
Brondesbury
Kensal Green
Queen's Park
Kilburn High Road
South Hampstead
Kilburn Park
Maida Vale
Warwick Avenue
Royal Oak
Westbourne Park
Paddington
Edgware Road
Marylebone
Baker Street
Great Portland Street
Euston
Brent Cross
Golders Green
Hampstead
Hampstead Heath
Gospel Oak
Finchley Road & Frognal
Belsize Park
Chalk Farm
Camden Town
Mornington Crescent
Kentish Town West
Kentish Town
Camden Road
Archway
Tufnell Park
Upper Holloway
Holloway Road
Caledonian Road
Caledonian Road & Barnsbury
Arsenal
Finsbury Park
Highbury & Islington
Canonbury
Dalston Kingsland
Dalston Junction
Haggerston
Hoxton
Shoreditch High Street
Hackney Central
Homerton
Hackney Wick
Tottenham Hale
Walthamstow Central
Walthamstow Queen's Road
Leyton Midland Road
Leytonstone
Leyton
Stratford International
Stratford
Snaresbrook
Redbridge
Wanstead
Gants Hill
Leytonstone High Road
Wanstead Park
Woodgrange Park
Stratford High Street
Abbey Road
Barking
East Ham
Upton Park
Plaistow
West Ham
Pudding Mill Lane
Bethnal Green
Mile End
Bow Road
Bow Church
Bromley-by-Bow
Star Lane
Devons Road
Langdon Park
All Saints
Canning Town
Royal Victoria
Emirates Royal Docks
East Acton
White City
Shepherd's Bush
West Acton
North Acton
Wood Lane
Acton Central
South Acton
Shepherd's Bush Market
Goldhawk Road
Hammersmith
Kensington (Olympia)
Barons Court
Ladbroke Grove
Latimer Road
Holland Park
Notting Hill Gate
Bayswater
Queensway
High Street Kensington
Lancaster Gate
Bond Street
Marble Arch
Oxford Circus
Hyde Park Corner
Knightsbridge
Gloucester Road
Green Park
Piccadilly Circus
Sloane Square
Regent's Park
Warren Street
Euston Square
Goodge Street
Tottenham Court Road
Russell Square
Holborn
King's Cross St. Pancras
Angel
Old Street
Farringdon
Barbican
Moorgate
Liverpool Street
Chancery Lane
St. Paul's
Covent Garden
Leicester Square
Charing Cross
Bank
Aldgate
Aldgate East
Whitechapel
Stepney Green
Cannon Street
Mansion House
Blackfriars
Temple
Monument
Tower Hill
Fenchurch Street
Tower Gateway
Shadwell
Limehouse
Wapping
Westferry
Poplar
East India
Blackwall
West India Quay
Acton Town
South Ealing
Northfields
Boston Manor
Osterley
Hounslow East
Hounslow Central
Hounslow West
Hatton Cross
Heathrow Terminals 1, 2, 3
Heathrow Terminal 4
Heathrow Terminal 5
Chiswick Park
Turnham Green
Stamford Brook
Ravenscourt Park
West Kensington
Earl's Court
South Kensington
Victoria
St. James's Park
Westminster
Embankment
Gunnersbury
Kew Gardens
Richmond
West Brompton
Fulham Broadway
Parsons Green
Putney Bridge
East Putney
Imperial Wharf
Pimlico
Waterloo
Southwark
Lambeth North
Borough
London Bridge
Bermondsey
Rotherhithe
Canada Water
Surrey Quays
River Thames
Canary Wharf
Heron Quays
South Quay
Crossharbour
Mudchute
Island Gardens
North Greenwich
Emirates Greenwich Peninsula
River Thames

Step-free access from street to train
Step-free access from street to platform
† Kensington Olympia open weekends, public holidays and some Olympia events

Bakerloo	Central	Circle	District	Hammersmith & City	Jubilee	Metropolitan	Northern	Piccadilly	Victoria	Waterloo & City	Overground	DLR	Emirates Air Line

MAYOR OF LONDON

tfl.gov.uk

24 hour travel information 0843 222 1234*

tfl.gov.uk/socialmedia

Transport for London

*You pay no more than 5p per minute if calling from a BT landline. There may be a connection charge. Charges from mobiles or other landline providers may vary.

 Reg. user No. 13/2497/P Version C 05.2013

Improvement works may affect your journey, please check before you travel Correct at time of going to print

Cover photography: Wild Honey

Michelin Travel Partner

Société par actions simplifiées au capital de 11 629 590 EUR
27 Cours de l'Ile Seguin - 92100 Boulogne Billancourt (France)
R.C.S. Nanterre 433 677 721

Dépôt légal Juillet 2013

Printed in Italy - Août 2013
Printed on paper from sustainably managed forests

Compogravure : Nord Compo à Villeneuve d'Ascq (France)
Impression et Finition : La Tipografica Varese (Italie)